사관학교

기출문제 정복하기

영어

Preface

사관학교는 문무를 겸비한 지도자를 양성하는 국비 교육 기관입니다. 흔히 장교 양성 교육기관으로만 오해하기 쉽지만, 실제로 사관학교는 학사학위를 수여하는 특수 목적 대학입니다. 선진국형 교육 시스템과 최신 설비의 교육시설을 갖추고 있는 최고의 교육기관으로 세계화에 발 맞춰 정보화 시대에 부합하는 교과과정을 편성하고, 인성을 중시하는 교육으로 많은 학생들에게 인기를 얻고 있기도 합니다.

첨단과학기술과 무기체계의 발전에 따라 현대전에서 군인의 역할과 위상이 높아지고 있는 가운데, 올바른 품성과 탁월한 역량을 구비하고 국가와 군에 헌신하며 장차 우리 군을 선도할 군인을 양성하는 것은 가장 중요한 과제이기도 합니다. 이러한 역할을 사관학교가 해나가고 있는 것입니다.

본서는 큰 뜻을 가지고 사관학교에 진학하고자 하는 수험생들에게 도움을 주고자, 총 10개년의 기출문제를 수록하였습니다. 2011학년도부터 2020학년도까지의 기출문제를 통해 사관학교의 출제 경향을 살펴볼 수 있도록 하였습니다. 해를 거듭할수록 문제가 더욱 어렵고 까다로워지고 있습니다. 자세한 해설집을 통해서 자신의 실력을 점검해볼 수 있는 기회가 될 것입니다.

신념을 가지고 도전하는 사람은 반드시 꿈을 이룰 수 있습니다.
서원각이 수험생 여러분의 꿈을 응원합니다.

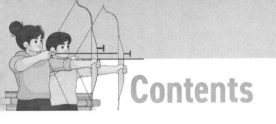

Contents

01 사관학교 기출문제

02 사관학교 정답 및 해설

정답 및 해설

상세하고 꼼꼼한 해설을 함께 수록하여 학습
효율을 확실하게 높였습니다.

기출문제

2011학년도부터 2020학년도까지 10개년의 사관
학교 기출문제를 수록하여 실전에 완벽하게 대비
할 수 있습니다.

01 육군사관학교

1. 모집인원 : 330명(여자 40명 포함)

남자 문과 50%, 이과 50%

여자 문과 60%, 이과 40%

2. 입학 자격

① 만 17세 이상 21세 미만의 미혼일 것 : 2000년 3월 2일부터 2004년 3월 1일 사이(만 17세 이상~21세 미만)에 출생한 미혼 남녀

② 「군인사법」 제10조 제2항에 따른 다음 결격사유에 어느 하나에도 해당하지 아니할 것

㉠ 대한민국의 국적을 가지지 아니한 사람 또는 대한민국 국적과 외국 국적을 함께 가지고 있는 사람

　※ 복수국적자가 입학을 희망하는 경우는 가입학 등록일 전까지 해당 외국에 국적 포기 신청을 마치고 관련 증빙서류를 제출하여야 함. 이후, 화랑기초훈련 수료일 전까지 해당 외국에서 발급한 「국적포기(상실) 증명서」를 제출하여야 하며, 최종 「외국국적 포기확인서」를 2021년 6월 30일까지 제출하여야 하며, 제출하지 않을 경우 입학이 취소될 수 있음.

㉡ 피성년후견인 또는 피한정후견인

㉢ 파산선고를 받은 사람으로서 복권되지 아니한 사람

㉣ 금고 이상의 형을 선고받고 그 집행이 종료되거나 집행을 받지 아니하기로 확정된 후 5년이 지나지 아니한 사람

㉤ 금고 이상의 형의 집행유예를 선고받고 그 유예기간 중에 있거나 그 유예기간이 종료된 날부터 2년이 지나지 아니한 사람

㉥ 자격정지 이상의 형의 선고유예를 받고 그 유예기간 중에 있는 사람

㉦ 공무원 재직기간 중 직무와 관련하여 「형법」 제355조 또는 제356조에 규정된 죄를 범한 사람으로서 100만원 이상의 벌금형을 선고받고 그 형이 확정된 후 3년이 지나지 아니한 사람

㉧ 「성폭력범죄의 처벌 등에 관한 특례법」 제2조에 따른 성폭력범죄로 100만 원 이상의 벌금형을 선고받고 그 형이 확정된 후 3년이 지나지 아니한 사람

㉨ 미성년자에 대한 다음 각 목의 어느 하나에 해당하는 죄를 저질러 파면 해임되거나 형 또는 치료감호를 선고받아 그 형 또는 치료감호가 확정된 사람(집행유예를 선고받은 후 그 집행유예기간이 경과한 사람을 포함한다)

　가) 「성폭력범죄의 처벌 등에 관한 특례법」 제2조에 따른 성폭력범죄
　나) 「아동 청소년의 성보호에 관한 법률」 제2조 제2호에 따른 아동 청소년 대상 성범죄

㉩ 탄핵이나 징계에 의하여 파면되거나 해임처분을 받은 날부터 5년이 지나지 아니한 사람

㉪ 법원의 판결 또는 다른 법률에 따라 자격이 정지되거나 상실된 사람

---

③ 「고등교육법」 제33조 제1항에 따른 학력이 있을 것 : 고등학교를 졸업한 사람이나 법령에 따라 이와 같은 수준 이상의 학력이 있다고 인정된 사람

※ 고등학교 졸업학력 검정고시 응시자는 2018년 9월 1일 이전 합격자에 한해 응시자격이 있음

④ 학칙으로 정하는 신체기준에 맞을 것 : 육군사관생도 선발시험에서 시행하는 신체검사, 체력검정 등의 기준에 합격한 사람

3. 전형 유형

구분		정원	선발방법	배점							비고
				계	1차시험	2차시험			내신	수능	
						신체	면접	체력			
일반전형	우선선발	고교학교장추천	30%	• 고교학교장 추천 공문 제출(학교당 재교생 3명, 졸업생 2명) • 고교교사 추천서 제출 • 배점기준에 따라 총점 득점 순으로 성별/계열별로 구분하여 우선선발	1000	합불	합불	640	160	200	–	선발되지 않은 인원은 적성 우수선발 대상이 됨
		적성우수	30%	• 고교교사 추천서 제출 • 배점기준에 따라 총점 득점 순으로 성별/계열별로 구분하여 우선선발	1000	300	합불	500	100	100	–	선발되지 않은 인원 중 2차 시험 합격자는 종합선발 대상이 됨
	종합선발		35%내외	• 고교교사 추천서 제출 • 종합선발 최종 성적의 득점 순으로 성별/계열별로 구분하여 선발	1000	50	합불	200	50	100	600	수능포함
특별전형	고른기회	독립유공자 손자녀 및 국가유공자 자녀	5%내외	• 고교교사 추천서 제출 • 선발심의 대상자 중 전형 내 최종 성적 득점 순으로 선발	1000	300	합불	500	100	100		• 선발되지 않은 인원은 적성 우수 선발 대상이 됨 • 적성 우수에 선발되지 않은 인원 중 2차 시험 합격자는 종합선발 대상이 됨
		농어촌학생		• 고교교사 추천서 제출 • 선발심의 대상자 중 전형 내 최종 성적 득점 순으로 선발								
		기초생활수급자 및 차상위계층		• 고교교사 추천서 제출 • 선발심의 대상자 중 전형 내 최종 성적 득점 순으로 선발								
	재외국민자녀		5명이내	• 외국어 : 7개국 언어로 제한(영어, 독일어, 프랑스어, 스페인어, 중국어, 러시아어, 일본어) • 선발심의 대상자 중 전형 내 최종 성적 득점 순으로 선발	600	합불	합불	500	100	–	–	(단, 재외국민 자녀의 경우 남 5배수, 여 8배수 이내 인원에게만 기회부여)

4. 1차시험

① 일자 : 매년 7월 말

② 장소 : 전국 9개 지역 15개 고사장

③ 시험 과목 및 범위

    ㉠ 시험 과목 : 국어, 영어, 수학(대학수학능력시험과 유사한 형식)

    ㉡ 출제 범위 : 대학수학능력시험과 동일(영어 듣기 제외)

영역		과목
국어		화법과 작문, 문학, 독서, 언어
영어		영어Ⅰ, 영어Ⅱ
수학	가형	수학Ⅰ, 수학Ⅱ, 확률과 통계
	나형	미적분, 확률과 통계, 수학Ⅰ

④ 계열별 반영 과목

    ㉠ 문과 : 국어, 영어, 수학 나형

    ㉡ 이과 : 국어, 영어, 수학 가형

⑤ 합격자 선발 : 아래 수식에 의한 1차시험 성적순으로 남자는 전체 모집정원의 5배수, 여자는 8배수 이내의 지원자를 1차시험 합격자로 선발(계열별, 성별 구분 선발)

$$\text{1차시험 성적(50점 만점 기준)} = \frac{1}{3}\sum_{i=1}^{3}\left(\frac{\text{과목 개인 취득 표준점수}}{\text{과목별 최고 표준점수}} \times 50\text{점}\right)$$

5. 2차시험

① 일자 : 매년 8월 말~9월

② 시험 분야 : 신체검사, 체력검정, 면접시험

구분	1일차	2일차	
오전	등록, 2차시험 OT, 면접시험 준비	신체검사(A조)	면접시험(B조)
오후	면접시험 준비, 체력검정	면접시험(A조)	신체검사(B조)
야간	신체검사 OT	–	–

※ 조별 1박 2일(교내숙박)

㉠ 신체검사

- 신체등위(신장/체중) 및 장교 선발 및 입영기준 신체검사로 구분
- 신체등위(신장/체중) 3급인 경우 2차 시험 최종심의위원회에서 합·불 결정
- 신체등위 4급 이하인 경우 불합격
- 장교 선발 및 입영기준 신체검사 기준표에서 하나라도 4급 이하인 경우 불합격

㉡ 체력검정

- 평가 종목 : 오래달리기(남자 1.5km / 여자 1.2km), 윗몸일으키기(2분), 팔굽혀펴기(2분)
- 불합격 기준
- 오래달리기에만 불합격 기준 적용 : 남자 7분 39초 이상, 여자 7분 29초 이상은 불합격
- 2종목 이상 16급(보류) 획득 시 2차 시험 최종심의위원회에서 합불 결정
- 우선선발 지원자의 체력검정 과락 기준 : 오래달리기 종목 기준 별도 적용

㉢ 면접 : 집단토론, 구술면접, 학교생활, 자기소개, 외적자세, 심리검사, 종합판정 등 총 7개 분야 면접 실시

㉣ 한국사능력검정시험 가산점 : 우선선발 및 특별전형 합격자 선발 시에만 적용

가. 등급별 가산점

1) 舊 급수체계 (46회 시험('20. 2. 8. 시행)까지 적용)

등급	고급		중급		초급	
	1급	2급	3급	4급	5급	6급
가산점	3점	2.6점	2점	1.6점	1점	0.6점

2) 新 급수체계 (47회 시험('20. 5. 23. 시행)부터 적용)

등급	고급		중급		초급	
	1급	2급	3급	4급	5급	6급
가산점	3점	2.6점	2.2점	1.5점	1.1점	0.7점

나. 성적 유효기간 : 2021년 3월 1일 기준, 3년 이내 검정시험 성적

※ 舊급수체계 인정 시험 회차 : 한국사능력검정시험 39회 ~ 46회

※ 新급수체계 인정 시험 회차 : 한국사능력검정시험 47회

02 해군사관학교

1. 모집인원 : 170명

① 남자 : 150명(문과 45%, 이과 55%)

② 여자 : 20명(문과 60%, 이과 40%)

2. 수업연한 : 4년

3. 입학자격

2000년 3월 2일부터 2004년 3월 1일 사이에 출생한 대한민국 국적을 가진 미혼 남·여로서, 다음 조건을 모두 갖추어야 함

① 고등학교 졸업자와 2021년 2월 졸업예정자 또는 교육부 장관이 이와 동등 이상의 학력이 있다고 인정한 자('20. 9. 1일 이전 검정고시 합격자)

② 외국에서 12년 이상의 학교 교육과정을 이수하였거나, 정규 고교 교육과정을 이수한 자

③ 군 인사법 제10조 1항의 임용자격이 있는 자

④ 군 인사법 제10조 2항에 의한 결격 사유에 해당되지 않는 자

※ 단, 복수 국적자는 지원 가능하나, 가입교 등록일 전까지 외국국적을 포기하여야만 입학 가능

4. 전형종류

① 고교학교장추천 전형

㉠ 대상 : 해당 고교학교장 추천을 받은 자(학교장 추천인원은 2명 이내)

㉡ 선발인원 : 모집인원의 20% 이내

㉢ 선발절차

· 1차시험 성적 : 과목별 환산식[(과목 개인취득 표준점수 ÷ 과목 최고 표준점수) × 100점]에 의한 3과목 점수의 합계 × $\frac{200}{300}$

· 비교과영역 평가 : 학교장 추천서, 학교생활기록부, 자기소개서

· 1차시험 합격자 발표, 2차시험 등록

· 2차시험 : 신체검사(합·불), 체력검정, 면접, 잠재역량평가

· 학교생활기록부 성적 반영

· 우선선발 : 1/2차 시험, 학생부 성적 등을 종합하여 최종합격자 선발

※ 고교학교장추천 전형 지원자 중 2차시험까지 합격하였으나, 해당 전형으로 미선발된 자는 일반우선 전형으로 전환되며, 일반우선 전형에서도 미선발된 자는 종합선발 대상자로 전환

㉣ 선발배점

구분	총점	1차시험	학생부	면접	잠재역량평가 (비교과, 심층면접 등)	체력검정	한국사 가산점	체력 가산점
점수	1,000	200	100	400	200	100	(5)	(3)

② 일반우선 전형

  ㉠ 선발인원 : 모집인원 55~60% 내외

  ㉡ 선발절차

  • 1차시험 성적 : 과목별 환산식[(과목 개인취득 표준점수 ÷ 과목 최고 표준점수) × 100점]에 의한 3과목 점수
    의 합계 × $\dfrac{400}{300}$

  • 1차시험 합격자 발표, 2차시험 등록

  • 자기소개서 입력(1차시험합격자 필수사항)

  • 2차시험 : 신체검사(합 · 불), 체력검정, 면접

  • 학교생활기록부 성적 반영

  • 우선선발 : 1/2차 시험, 학생부 성적을 종합하여 최종합격자 선발

    ※ 2차시험 합격자 중 우선선발되지 않은 사람은 종합선발 대상자로 전환

  ㉢ 선발배점

구분	총점	1차시험	학생부	면접	체력검정	한국사 가산점	체력 가산점
점수	1,000	400	100	400	100	(5)	(3)

③ 독립 · 국가유공자 전형

  ㉠ 대상 : 독립유공자 (외)손자녀 및 국가유공자 자녀

  ㉡ 선발인원 : 2명 이내

  ㉢ 선발절차 : 일반우선 전형과 동일

  ㉣ 선발배점 : 일반우선 전형과 동일

④ 고른기회 전형

  ㉠ 대상

  ㉡ 선발인원 : 4명 이내

  ㉢ 선발절차 : 일반우선 전형과 동일

  ㉣ 선발배점 : 일반우선 전형과 동일

⑤ 재외국민자녀 전형

　㉠ 대상

　㉡ 선발인원 : 2명 이내

　㉢ 선발절차 : 일반우선 전형과 동일

　㉣ 선발배점

구분	총점	1차시험	학생부 또는 비교내신	면접	체력검정	한국사 가산점	체력 가산점
점수	1,000	400	100	400	100	(5)	(3)

⑥ 종합선발 전형

　㉠ 선발인원 : 모집정원 20% 내외

　㉡ 선발절차

　　• 총점 순으로 성별 및 계열별 선발비율에 따라 선발

　　• 대학수학능력시험 반영 방법

　　　※ 국어, 수학 : (지원자의 해당 과목 표준점수÷해당 과목 전국 최고 표준점수)×200

　　　※ 영어 : 등급별 점수 반영

등급	1	2	3	4	5	6	7	8	9
점수	200	180	160	130	100	80	60	40	20

　　　※ 탐구영역 : (지원자의 해당 과목 표준점수÷해당 과목 전국 최고 표준점수)×50

　　　※ 한국사 배점 : 등급별 점수 반영

등급	1	2	3	4	5	6	7	8	9
점수	50	45	40	35	30	25	20	15	10

　　　※ 총점 환산 : 국어, 영어, 수학, 탐구영역, 한국사 전 과목 취득점수의 합계×500/750

　㉢ 선발배점

구분	총점	수능시험	학생부	면접	체력검정	체력 가산점
점수	1,000	500	100	300	100	(3)

5. 1차시험

① 일시 : 매년 7월 말

② 장소 : 전국 12개 중·고교

③ 출제형식 및 범위

　ㄱ 출제형식 : 대학수학능력시험과 유사

　ㄴ 출제범위 : 대학수학능력시험과 동일(국어 및 영어 듣기 제외)

과목		문항수	비고
국어(공통)		45문항(객관식)	5지선다형
영어(공통)		45문항(객관식)	
수학	가형(이과)	30문항 (객관식 70%, 주관식 30%)	1~21번 5지선다형
	나형(문과)		22~30번 단답형

6. 2차시험

① 일정 : 매년 8월 말~9월(기간 중 개인별 2박3일)

② 시험 종목 및 방법

구분		주요 내용
공통	신체검사	• 신체검사 기준에 따라 합격·불합격 판정
	체력검정	• 3개 종목 : 윗몸일으키기, 팔굽혀펴기, 1500m(남)·1200m(여)
	면접	• 5개 영역에 대해 심층면접 실시 ※ 국가관·역사관·안보관, 군인기본자세, 주제토론, 적응력, 종합평가
	AI 면접	• 2차시험 응시 전 별도 기간에 AI 면접 ※ 응시기간 등 세부사항은 1차시험 합격자 대상 별도 공지 예정 ※ AI 면접은 반드시 실시하여야 하며, 면접 결과는 선발과정에 참고자료로 활용됨

03 공군사관학교

1. 모집인원 : 215명(여자 22명 포함)

　① 남·여 비율 : 남자 90%, 여자 10% 내외

　② 계열별 비율

　　• 남자 : 인문계열 45%, 자연계열 55% 내외

　　• 여자 : 인문계열 50%, 자연계열 50% 내외

2. 모집전형

구분		내용
일반전형		
특별전형	• 재외국민자녀전형 • 독립유공자 (외)손자녀·국자유공자 자녀전형 • 고른기회전형(농·어촌 학생, 기초생활수급자·차상위계층 학생)	공중근무자 신체검사 기준 충족자 선발
종합선발(정원의 20% 내외) ※ 우선선발 비선발자 대상 '수능' 성적 포함 선발		

3. 지원자격

　① 대한민국 국적을 가진 미혼 남·여

　② 2000년 3월 2일부터 2004년 3월 1일까지 출생한 자

　③ 고등학교 졸업자, 2021년 2월 졸업예정자 또는 교육부장관이 이와 동등한 학력이 있다고 인정한 자

　④ 군인사법 제10조 2항의 결격사유에 해당되지 않는 자

4. 1차시험

　① 시험일자 : 매년 7월 말

　② 시험장소 : 전국 16개 시험장

　③ 선발인원 : 남자(인문 4배수, 자연 4배수), 여자(인문 6배수, 자연 6배수)

　④ 시험과목 및 배점(표준점수 반영)

구분	시험과목	시험시간(소요시간)	배점	비고
수험생 입실 09:20~09:30				※ 09:20까지 시험장 도착, 교실 확인
1교시	국어	09:50~10:00(10분)	200	시험지 배부 : 인문/자연 '공통'
		10:00~11:20(80분)		45문항
휴식 11:20~11:40(20분)				
2교시	영어	11:40~11:50(10분)	200	시험지 배부 : 인문/자연 '공통'
		11:50~13:00(70분)		45문항(듣기 제외)
중식 13:00~14:20(80분)				

3교시	수학	14 : 20~14 : 30(10분)	200	시험지 배부 : 인문 '나'형/자연 '가'형
		14 : 30~16 : 10(100분)		30문항

※ 출제범위는 해당년도 대학수학능력시험과 동일(출제형식 유사)

※ 과목별 '원점수 60점 미만이면서 표준점수 하위 40% 미만'인 자는 불합격

5. **2차시험**

① **신체검사** : 신체검사 당일 합격 · 불합격 판정

ⓐ 공중근무자 신체검사 기준 적용

ⓑ 공중근무자 신체검사 시력 및 굴절 기준 미충족자 중 공군사관학교 신체검사를 통해 PRK/LASIK 수술 적합 자는 합격 가능(단, 신체검사 이전에 굴절교정술을 받은 경우 불합격)

② **체력검정** : 합격/불합격, 150점

ⓐ 3개 종목 : 오래달리기(남자 1,500m/ 여자 1,200m, 65점), 팔굽혀펴기(40점), 윗몸일으키기(45점)

ⓑ 불합격 기준

• 오래달리기 불합격 기준 해당자

• 3개 종목 중 15등급이 2개 종목 이상인 자

• 총점이 150점 만점에 80점 미만인 자

ⓒ 합격자는 취득점수를 최종선발 종합성적에 반영

③ **역사 · 안보관 논술** : 30점

ⓐ 논제 형식 및 문항 : 우리나라 역사와 국가안보 관련 지문을 읽고, 그에 대한 수험생의 견해 논술(1문제, 30분 이내로 평가)

ⓑ 취득점수는 최종선발 종합성적에 반영

④ **면접** : 300점

ⓐ 평가항목 : 품성, 가치관, 책임감, 국가 · 안보관, 학교생활, 자기소개, 가정 · 성장환경, 지원동기, 용모 · 태도 등 9개 항목 및 심리 / 인성검사

ⓑ 적격자는 취득점수를 최종선발 종합성적에 반영

6. **최종선발**

① **선발기준** : 2차시험 합격자 중 모집단위별(성/계열) 종합성적 서열 순으로 선발

② **종합성적**(1,000점)

구분	1차시험	2차시험			학생부	한능검 가산점	합계
		역사 · 안보관 논술	체력검정	면접			
점수	400점	30점	150점	300점	100점	20점	1,000점

※ 한국사능력검정시험 가산점 부여방법 : 중급 이상 취득점수 × 0.1(고급 성적도 중급 성적과 동일하게 반영) + 10

04 국군간호사관학교

1. 모집인원 : 90명(남자 10% 내외, 여자 90% 내외)

2. 교육기간 : 4년

3. 지원자격

① 2000년 3월 2일부터 2004년 3월 1일 사이에 출생한 대한민국 국적을 가진 미혼 남·여로서 신체 건강하고 사관생도로서 적합한 가치관을 가진 사람

② 고등학교 졸업자 또는 2021년 2월 졸업예정자와 이와 동등 이상의 학력이 있다고 교육부 장관이 인정한 사람

③ 군인사법 제10조 제2항에 의한 결격사유에 해당되지 않는 사람(복수국적자는 기초군사훈련 등록일까지 출입국관리사무소 발급 외국국적포기 확인서 제출 필요)

④ 국군간호사관학교 학칙으로 정하는 신체기준에 적합한 사람

⑤ 현역 복무 부적합 등 불명예 전역한 사람과 본교 또는 각 군 사관학교 및 후보생과정에서 퇴교된 사람(신병으로 인한 퇴교는 제외)은 지원할 수 없음

4. 전형별 모집인원

구분		비율	성별	계열			비고
				계	인문	자연	
총 모집인원				90	36	54	
일반전형	우선선발	50% 이내	남/여	42	17	25	
	종합선발	50% 이내	남/여	42	16	26	
특별전형	독립유공자 손자녀 및 국가유공자 자녀 전형			2	1	1	종합성적 서열이 종합선발 정원의 2배수 이내 선발
	고른 기회 전형			2	1	1	
	재외국민 자녀 전형			2	1	1	종합성적 서열이 우선선발 정원의 2배수 이내 선발

5. 1차시험

① 일자 : 매년 7월 말

② 장소 : 전국 8개 시험장

③ 1차 선발인원 : 모집정원 기준 남자 인문 4배수, 자연 8배수 / 여자 4배수(총점 순)

④ 시험과목 및 배점(표준점수 반영)

구분	시험과목	시험시간(소요시간)	배점	내용
• 수험생 입실 09 : 00~09 : 20 • 주의사항 및 답안지 작성요령 교육 09 : 30~09 : 50				• 09 : 00까지 도착, 시험장 확인 • 09 : 50 이후는 시험교실 입장불가
1교시	국어(45)	09 : 50~10 : 00(10분)	100	시험지 배부 : 인문/자연 '공통'
		10 : 00~11 : 20(80분)		시험
휴식 11 : 20~11 : 40(20분)				
2교시	영어(45)	11 : 40~11 : 50(10분)	100	시험지 배부 : 인문/자연 '공통'
		11 : 50~13 : 00(70분)		시험, 듣기 제외
중식 13 : 00~14 : 20(80분)				3교시 시작 10분 전 입장완료
3교시	수학(30)	14 : 20~14 : 30(10분)	100	시험지 배부 : 인문 '나'형/자연 '가'형
		14 : 30~16 : 10(100분)		시험

※ 원서접수 시 지원계열과 대학수학능력시험 응시계열, 고교재학 이수계열은 일치해야 함

6. 2차시험

① 일자 : 매년 9월 중

② 일자별 시험내용 및 배점

구분		내용	배점	
			우선/특별	종합선발
1일차		등록, 신체검사 문진, 다면적 인성검사(MMPI), 역사관 약술(면접 시 활용)	–	–
2일차	신체검사	신체검사 당일 합격 · 불합격 판정	–	–
	체력검정	• 3개종목 : 오래달리기, 윗몸일으키기, 팔굽혀펴기 • 체력검정 결과 종합 합격 · 불합격 판장, 취득점수 최종선발에 반영	50	50
3일차	면접	• 내적영역, 대인영역, 외적 영역 · 역사관 · 안보관 등 • 면접 분과에서 한 분과라도 40% 미만 득점하면 불합격 처리됨	200	150

PART 01

기출문제 정복하기

▶ 해설은 p. 2에 있습니다.

01 Where is the following dialogue taking place?

> Tom : Did you remember to pack the water?
> Jane : Of course. It's two hours to the summit, so I'm sure we'll get thirsty. I even packed us lunch.
> Tom : We can eat it at the top. I heard the views are wonderful. Will it be a steep climb?
> Jane : I think only at the very end. Most of it's gradual. It'll be some good exercise.
> Tom : We should keep our eyes on the trees. They say there are some interesting birds in this area.
> Jane : Did you bring the binoculars your sister got you for your birthday?
> Tom : Yes, I have them. Look, there's the trail marker.

① at the office   ② at the zoo

③ at the beach   ④ at the gym

⑤ at the mountain

02 Based on the dialogue, which of the following items on the itinerary must be changed?

> Sue : There's so much to see in New York City. Are you finished with our itinerary?
> Joe : Yes, but let me double check. Did you make the dinner reservation for us at Periguino's?
> Sue : That's on Monday at 8 p.m.
> Joe : How about the museums? Which days are they open?
> Sue : The City History Museum, the Art Museum, and the Longfellow Gallery are open Tuesday through Sunday. The Natural History Museum and the Film Museum are open Monday through Friday.

Joe : We should see the Statue of Liberty right when it opens on Tuesday morning, before there's a long line.

Sue : And when can we see a Broadway musical?

Joe : I ordered tickets for a Tuesday night performance.

Sue : I'm so excited about this trip!

① • Art Museum
　 • Mon. 9 a.m.

② • Dinner at Periguino's
　 • Mon. 8 p.m.

③ • Statue of Liberty
　 • Tues. 9 a.m.

④ • Broadway performance
　 • Tues. 8 p.m.

⑤ • City History Museum
　 • Wed. 10 a.m.

※ Based on the dialogue, which of the following is true? [03~04]

03
[3점]

Woman : Can you tell me when the next available flight to London is?

Man : There's a flight on Wednesday at 6 p.m., ma'am.

Woman : I need to attend a conference in London on Wednesday morning. Can you double check if you have any flights leaving on Tuesday?

Man : Sorry, but all the flights to London are fully booked. We can place your name on standby if you'd like.

Woman : I can't take a chance on missing this conference. Can you route me to London through another city?

Man : Let me check for you, ma'am. It looks like there's a flight to Paris, with a connecting flight to London. It departs at 10 a.m., arriving in Paris at noon on Tuesday, with a two – hour layover before the London flight. Would you like to book this ticket?

Woman : Yes, I would. Thank you.

① The woman would like the 6 p.m. flight on Wednesday.

② The woman doesn't think the conference in London is important.

③ The woman only wants a direct flight to London.

④ The woman will take the Paris to London flight at 2 p.m. on Tuesday.

⑤ The woman must wait for four hours in Paris.

04

2점

Doctor : What seems to be the problem?

Patient : I was up the whole night, sick and vomiting. My stomach still feels nauseous and I'm feverish.

Doctor : When did the symptoms begin?

Patient : Around 10 p.m., two hours after my wife and I ate dinner at a restaurant on Main Street.

Doctor : Was your wife sick, too?

Patient : No, she's fine.

Doctor : What did you eat there?

Patient : We both had a green salad and vegetable soup, but we had different orders for our main dish. I had the fish and she had the chicken.

Doctor : It sounds like a case of food poisoning. I'll prescribe something to help soothe your stomach and bring the fever down. Meanwhile, drink plenty of water and get lots of rest. If your symptoms persist after three days, call us and we'll bring you in for another appointment.

① The patient and his wife finished dinner at 6 p.m.

② The patient's wife is ill with food poisoning, too.

③ The fish probably caused the food poisoning.

④ It is not good for the patient to drink water for his sickness.

⑤ The patient has to make a new appointment with the doctor tomorrow.

05 Which is the best sequence of answers for the blanks?

2점

> Woman : Are you lost? Do you need some help?
>
> Man : I'm looking for the central post office, _____.
>
> Woman : I think I know what the problem is. The central post office was relocated to another building two months ago, _____.
>
> Man : Is the new location very far from here?
>
> Woman : No, not really. It's about a fifteen-minute walk.
>
> Man : Can you tell me which way to go?
>
> Woman : Sure. First, you follow this street until the third intersection, _____. You'll go up a little hill. At the top, there's a park. The new central post office building is along the south corner of the park.
>
> Man : Thank you very much.

ⓐ and they haven't updated the city maps
ⓑ and then make a left at the light
ⓒ on your right next to the police station
ⓓ but my map is a little confusing
ⓔ but he'll need a taxi to go there

① ⓐ − ⓔ − ⓓ   ② ⓓ − ⓐ − ⓑ
③ ⓓ − ⓒ − ⓔ   ④ ⓔ − ⓒ − ⓑ
⑤ ⓔ − ⓑ − ⓒ

06 Which of the following is the best choice for the blank?

> Kijoo : This English class is so difficult. I don't think our professor understands the tough life we have at the academy.
>
> Minji : Maybe you need to pay more attention. I've seen you nod off a couple of times during class.
>
> Kijoo : But it's the first class on Monday morning. Sometimes I'm just so tired from the weekend.
>
> Minji : So you're tired from all the weekend studying you're doing?
>
> Kijoo : Uh… not exactly. Sometimes I play computer games during my free time on Sundays. I've been playing computer games since I started high school.
>
> Minji : I think you need to stop complaining about the class and manage your time more wisely. There's nothing wrong with using free time to relax, but only after your studies are in order. And then get some rest.
>
> Kijoo : That's good advice.   .

① You'll have to study harder for the next exam.

② We both like to stay up late on Saturdays and Sundays.

③ I'll study and then make sure I go to sleep early this Sunday.

④ I always get the highest score on my favorite computer games.

⑤ This math class would be better if it were on Tuesday afternoon.

07 밑줄 친 They[they]가 가리키는 대상이 나머지 넷과 다른 것은?

> Aborigines are the native peoples in Australia. Throughout their history, ①they have used art to reflect their religious beliefs. ②They believe that their culture and environment are the result of the jugurrba or the Dreaming. During the Dreaming, spirit beings took the forms of men and animals and created the land and animals. Wherever the spirits created and whatever they touched, ③they supposedly left behind some of their essence. The Aborigines believe that the spirits' essence caused life to spring up. ④They still call on the spirits of animals and places to ensure such things as good weather or a successful hunt. Since the 1960s, the art world has become interested in Aboriginal bark painting. This interest has generated a big market for the Aborigines, and ⑤they are producing more art to sell than ever before.

08

Punctuation comes from the Latin word punctus, meaning "point." When punctuation began, it was mainly to help people read aloud. Until a few hundred years ago, not many people were taught to read, so there was a lot more reading aloud by the few people who could. To help those reading aloud in the ancient world, signs known as "points" were added to pages of writing. ①These points told readers when to pause or take a breath, and what to emphasize. ②Likewise, the comma, the punctuation mark which usually causes writers the most trouble, is hard to master. ③In Europe, from the early centuries A.D., these points were widely used, although not everybody used the same points for the same thing. ④However, when the printing press was invented in the 15th century, printers wanted firmer guidelines about what to put where, so that everyone was doing the same thing. ⑤Since then, all sorts of punctuation rules have been discovered, invented and even argued about.

09

As the range of benefits has grown in almost all companies, so has concern about containing their cost. ①Many companies are experimenting with cost-cutting plans under which they can still attract and retain valuable employees. ②One approach is the cafeteria benefit plan, where a certain dollar amount of benefits per employee is set aside so that each employee can choose from a variety of alternatives. ③A recent variation on cafeteria plans permits employees to choose whether their portion of benefits comes from their salaries before or after taxes are computed. ④Most companies are required by law to allow a seven-day leave when an immediate family member passes away. ⑤For most individuals, the right choice results in real tax savings because benefits themselves are not taxed.

※ 다음 글의 밑줄 친 부분 중, 어법상 틀린 것을 고르시오. [10~11]

10
[3점]

Occasions that celebrate special events or that mark the beginning or end of a process often ①call for an after-dinner speech. Political rallies, award banquets, the kickoff of a fund-raising campaign, or the end of the school year may provide the setting for such a speech. ②In keeping with the nature of the occasion, after-dinner speeches should not be too difficult to digest. Speakers ③making these presentations usually do not introduce radical ideas that require listeners to rethink their values or that ask for dramatic changes in belief or behavior. ④None are such occasions the time for anger or negativity. ⑤They are a time for people to savor who they are, what they have done, or what they wish to do.

11
[2점]

Alexander the Great ①was never defeated in battle, and his tactic, called the phalanx formation, is still being studied today. The phalanx, whose name is derived from *phalangos*, the Greek word for finger, was a formation based on a full frontal assault against the enemy while ②preventing the enemy from penetrating the ranks of the attackers. It ③consisted of a tightly linked blockade of soldiers that stationed itself in a rectangular offensive posture. Each soldier stood shoulder to shoulder with the next, with weapons such as long spears or pikes ④point forward toward the enemy. The phalanx would advance as a unit of collective force, creating a formidable tactical system nearly impossible to penetrate and ⑤mowing down the enemy with a forward-moving wall of men and weapons.

※ (A), (B), (C)의 각 네모 안에서 어법에 맞는 표현으로 가장 적절한 것을 고르시오. [12~13]

12

Studies have found three different types of kindness. First of all, there is natural kindness, based on our ability to identify with others and sense (A) | what / which | they are feeling. This kindness shows up at a very early age. A grade school child who says that a caged gorilla looks sad or who gets upset when another child is bullied (B) | shows / showing | this natural kindness. The second type of kindness is rule-guided. Rule-guided people have learned, "It's wrong to do that." For example, rule-guided children do not hit others because they have been taught hitting (C) | wrong / is | wrong . The last type of kindness is imitative. We imitate the behavior of people we admire. For instance, imitative children who admire their parents will avoid behavior of which their parents disapprove.

	(A)	(B)	(C)
①	what	shows	is wrong
②	what	showing	is wrong
③	which	shows	wrong
④	which	shows	is wrong
⑤	which	showing	wrong

13

My wife fell in love with an antique bowl at an auction, and her sister offered to help her get it. When the bidding began, we were (A) | seating / seated | in different parts of the room, with me waiting for them in the last row. The price of the bowl began to skyrocket, (B) | when / where | I realized the problem. My wife and sister-in-law were bidding against each other. I quickly motioned to them (C) | to stop / stopping |, but it was too late. The auctioneer's hammer came down. "Sold," he said, "to the gentleman in the back."

	(A)	(B)	(C)
①	seating	when	to stop
②	seating	when	stopping
③	seated	when	to stop
④	seated	where	to stop
⑤	seated	where	stopping

14 다음 글을 쓴 목적으로 가장 적절한 것은?

2점

> As I mentioned at our last meeting, I would like you to conduct a one-month feasibility study on our proposal to extend our operations to include the Pacific Rim markets. If the results are positive, your report will go before the board of directors as we attempt to secure financing for this expansion. Since we are working under the current budget, your travel allowance will be tight. But I know you will make careful choices. I have included a copy of Neumann's Report on this matter. It is a bit out of date, but may still prove useful as a model. I look forward to weekly reports and, of course, to your final report, which is due no later than July 14th.

① to authorize a research project

② to ask for personal advice

③ to announce a special meeting

④ to make a formal invitation

⑤ to appreciate a financial donation

※ 다음 글을 읽고, 빈칸에 가장 적절한 것을 고르시오. [15~20]

15

2점

> I don't believe in humiliating children in front of their peers. I was embarrassed when my mother told me in front of my friends, "Don't behave that way!" or "Don't gossip!" Regarding this, I've learned so much from other moms that has helped me raise my daughter, Jane. When she was little, we were on a playdate with her friend, Mary. When Mary did something wrong, her mother said, "Will you excuse us for a second?" Later I asked, "What happened?" She said, "I didn't like something that Mary had done, but I didn't want to humiliate her in front of Jane." I thought that it was so considerate to _____.

① be tenderhearted toward strangers

② thank other moms for their support

③ tolerate my daughter's wrongdoing

④ be respectful of the little girl's feelings

⑤ compliment children in front of their friends

16

3점

The effect of technology on an organization's structure has been a topic of debate since the 1950s. Theory and research in this area can be roughly separated into two groups. One group, sometimes referred to as technological determinists, views technology as the primary determinant of an organization's structure. This group holds that different structures are required for different technologies, and that the former are strictly reliant on the latter. This notion is frequently referred to as the technological imperative. The second group views organizations as open systems, and argues that _____ . It thus maintains that technology can both influence the organization and be influenced by the organization.

① technology and structure are interdependent

② structure is heavily dependent on technology

③ obtaining new technologies is very expensive

④ any organization can function without technology

⑤ technology should be shared by many organizations

17

2점

In recent years, nonprofit agencies involved in disaster relief have increasingly come under fire, facing growing accusations that the relief is failing to reach victims due to mismanagement by agencies and corruption in recipient nations. Stung by the criticism, aid agencies have been galvanized into action. In a move that may seem unusual, they are replacing traditional forms of aid with _____ . Until now, most people have taken it for granted that aid should be composed of what victims of a disaster actually need, such as food and blankets. However, a system that provides actual money in the form of debit cards offers advantages because it is cheaper to administer and eliminates transportation costs. It also stimulates local economies, offering a boost to farmers and small businesses, whereas food donations can have the effect of reducing local sales.

① cash   ② grain

③ clothing   ④ medicine

⑤ employment

18

2점

Primitive peoples' lives are commonly thought to be harsh – their existence dominated by the incessant quest for food. In fact, some primitives do little work. By contemporary standards, we would have to judge them very lazy. If the Kapauka of Papua work one day, they do no labor on the next. Kung Bushmen put in only two and a half days per week and six hours per day. In the Sandwich Islands of Hawaii, native inhabitants only work for four hours per day. The key to understanding why they do not increase their work effort to get more things as we do is that _____. In the race between wanting and having, they have kept their wants low — and in this way, ensure their own kind of satisfaction. They are materially poor by contemporary standards, but in at least one aspect — time — we have to count them as richer.

① they have limited desires

② they live in great material wealth

③ their productivity is relatively low

④ they don't have a concept of time

⑤ they exchange goods with each other

19

2점

As for your use of language, remember that two great masters, William Shakespeare and James Joyce, wrote sentences which seemed almost childlike when their subject matter was most profound. "To be or not to be?" asks Shakespeare's Hamlet. The longest word has only three letters. Joyce, when he was frisky, could put together a sentence as intricate and as glittering as a necklace for Cleopatra, but my favorite sentence in his short story Eveline is this one: "She was tired." At that point in the story, no other words break the heart of a reader as those three words do. _____ is not only admirable, but perhaps even sacred. Your rule might be this : If a sentence, no matter how excellent, does not illuminate your subject matter in some clever and efficient way, scratch it out.

① Writing a drama   ② Reading classical works

③ Accuracy of gramma   ④ Understanding of characters

⑤ Simplicity of language

20

2점

Sports are about competition. The goal of every athlete, or every team, is to win. Unfortunately, two factors have been pushing today's sports in an unhealthy direction. One is the obsession with winning at any cost. The other is money. These two factors put extreme pressure on both players and coaches to focus only on winning. This has resulted in a problem that is spreading and becoming more serious. That problem is cheating. Of course, there are rules in all sports to penalize cheating. Yet some coaches and players have come up with ingenious ways to bend the rules. Getting an unfair competitive edge is seen as a "strategy" rather than cheating. Illegal acts are now even _____. Some coaches encourage players to cheat, while others simply look the other way when they know their players commit illegal acts during games.

① providing no real advantages
② reducing the actual time of a game
③ being ruled out as unfair acts
④ being accepted as part of the game
⑤ making coaches and players lose more

21 다음 글의 밑줄 친 부분 중, 문맥상 낱말의 쓰임이 적절하지 않은 것은?

3점

Authors use figures of speech to paint vivid pictures in the reader's mind or to achieve some other ①specific effect such as emphasis or humor. One example of this is hyperbole. It is a figure of speech in which the author makes an obvious ②exaggeration for emphasis. The reader must realize that the words do not ③literately mean what they say. In other words, the reader must ④interpret the author's intended meaning. An example of hyperbole is, "I'm so exhausted that I could sleep for a week." The overstatement is "I could sleep for a week." The point the author wants to ⑤convey is that he or she is extremely tired.

22

2점

Naomi Sims arrived in New York City to attend the Fashion Institute of Technology in 1966 and decided to try modeling to support herself. After most agencies turned her down, (A) proclaiming / praising her skin color as too dark, she forged ahead on her own, landing a photo spread with the New York Times by contracting a photographer directly. Her (B) appearance / apparel on the cover of Ladies' Home Journal in 1968 broke the color barrier of mainstream women's magazines, and she went on to grace the covers of Cosmopolitan, Essence and Life. She opened the runway door for others, including another supermodel Naomi — Naomi Campbell. And she made it possible for girls of all color to (C) disgrace / embrace their own inner beauty.

	(A)	(B)	(C)
①	proclaiming	appearance	disgrace
②	proclaiming	appearance	embrace
③	proclaiming	apparel	disgrace
④	praising	appearance	embrace
⑤	praising	apparel	disgrace

23

2점

Throughout recorded history, the origin of the universe has been a topic of ongoing (A) controversy / contradiction . In particular, debate has centered around how the universe began. One school of thought, especially held by Jewish, Christian, and Islamic religions, is that the universe was created. Thus, there was a time when there was no universe, and equally, there will be a time when there will be an end to the universe. On the other hand, some people, like Greek philosopher Aristotle, did not believe that the universe had a beginning. He theorized that the universe had existed and would exist forever and that it was (B) eternal / internal and perfect. One thing that these two schools of thought originally had in common was that no matter what the origin or the ending of the universe, the universe itself was (C) static / statistical . Since the 19th century, however, evidence has begun to challenge the idea of a motionless, unchanging universe.

	(A)	(B)	(C)
①	controversy	eternal	static
②	controversy	internal	static
③	contradiction	eternal	static
④	contradiction	eternal	statistical
⑤	contradiction	internal	statistical

※ 다음 글의 제목으로 가장 적절한 것을 고르시오. [24~25]

24
[3점]

According to a new study, during most armed conflicts on the globe since the 1970s, mortality rates have actually declined. That's not to say that war, in and of itself, leads to longer life spans. Instead, a major reason for the drop is that conflict has motivated international humanitarian groups to strengthen their efforts in poor countries, and they've learned to work public health miracles in a short amount of time. In the Democratic Republic of the Congo, for instance, just 20 percent of children were vaccinated for measles in 1997, at the start of a decade-long civil war. But by 2007 that figure was 80 percent. The history of other health initiatives, from treating malnutrition to distributing bed nets, tells a similar story.

① A Cry for Freedom in Africa
② Modern Warfare's Silver Lining
③ Young Warriors of Modern Warfare
④ The Dark Side of African Civil Wars
⑤ Deadly Epidemics Spreading Like Wildfire

25

2점

A guided missile, once programmed onto its target, will move unerringly toward the target, no matter where the target moves. A sophisticated weapon, such as a Cruise or an Exocet Missile, will lock onto the target and continually adjust course and direction until it hits what it was aimed at. No evasive action will allow the target to escape destruction. You are like a guided missile as well. To achieve greatly and create your future, you must launch toward your target. Once you begin moving forward with a clear idea of what you want, you will receive continuous feedback that will enable you to adjust your course. This feedback, in the form of difficulties and obstacles, will allow you to make course corrections as you move ahead. These course corrections will eventually bring you to your target, but you must keep moving.

① Speed Provides the Best Escape
② Feedback Is an Unhelpful Distraction
③ Don't Make the Same Mistake Again
④ Setting Your Goal Takes Much Time
⑤ Determination and Flexibility Lead to the Goal

※ 다음 글의 요지로 가장 적절한 것을 고르시오. [26~27]

26

2점

The initial reaction by managers in many successful organizations to a downturn is "weathering the storm," which means doing as little as possible and waiting for the situation to pass. Minor actions that address the symptoms of a downturn by increasing cash flow are the norm—deferring maintenance, reducing spending on new-product development, decreasing capital spending to modernize plants and equipment, halting new hiring, and reducing R&D funding, for example. Little attention is paid to diagnosing the causes of declining profitability or decreasing cash flow. This response creates a problem if a downturn is not temporary. Managers have wasted valuable time and resources that could have been used to turn around an organization's operations. And if the response of "curing" the symptoms seems initially successful, the motivation to understand environmental changes is reduced, usually resulting in a major crisis a short time later.

① 경기 침체기에는 업무에 대한 권한을 분산시켜야 한다.
② 경기 침체가 장기화될 때에는 인력 채용을 중단해야 한다.
③ 경기 침체에 대비하여 기업은 충분한 현금을 비축해야 한다.
④ 경기 침체에 대한 단기적 대책보다는 원인 분석이 중요하다.
⑤ 경기 침체기에는 과감한 실비확장 및 연구개발 투자가 필요하다.

27

2점

When I was in competitive Taekwondo some years ago, I learned an important technique from one of the top masters in the world. He taught me that if I advance toward my opponent in a Taekwondo match, even half an inch at a time, my opponent would move backward to keep the relative distance the same between us. While I was approaching the opponent, 100 percent of my energy and attention was focused on him. But when the opponent was backing up, nearly half his energy was taken up by thinking about what was behind him and the edge of the mat. Thanks to this strategy, I was able to compete successfully against better opponents and win prizes in several national championship matches. It helped me have full confidence and made all the difference.

① Always be prepared for unexpected reverses.

② Opportunities are sometimes hard to identify.

③ Moving forward will give you a critical edge.

④ The best players are the most cautious players.

⑤ You can make a strategic retreat to advance farther.

28 다음 글이 시사하고 있는 바로 가장 적절한 것은?

2점

When our first daughter, Laura, needed comforting during infancy, my wife and I would usually use one of two phrases. When Laura was crying and we didn't know why, first we tried all the obvious solutions like feeding her or taking care of hygiene issues. When she was still distressed, we would hold her and repeat over and over in our most empathic tones — "Honey, honey, honey," or "I know, I know" — nodding our heads as if we really did know. We generally didn't know, but it seemed reassuring to say we did. After a while, Laura internalized this. By the time she was approaching her first birthday, she would sometimes wake up in the morning and begin to cry ; but instead of just making crying sounds like other babies, she would cry words to herself over and over, "Honey, honey, honey... I know, I know." Laura would cry them to herself with great compassion, nodding her little head just as she had seen us do.

① Little troubles are great to little people.

② You have to take the good with the bad.

③ Without health, no one can be truly happy.

④ As the old cock crows, the young cock learns.

⑤ You never miss the water till the well runs dry.

3점

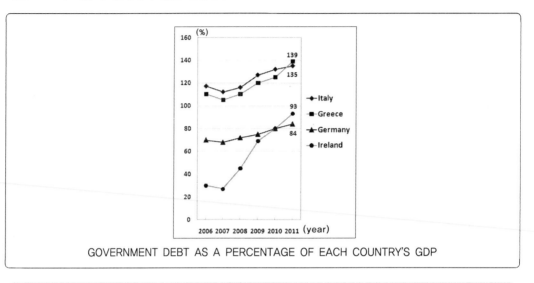

GOVERNMENT DEBT AS A PERCENTAGE OF EACH COUNTRY'S GDP

This chart shows the percentage of each country's annual government debt per GDP. ① As this chart demonstrates, there was a slight dip between 2006 and 2007 in all four countries. ② However, each country experienced an overall increase after 2007. ③ The most dramatic projected increase from 2007 to 2011 will occur in Ireland, with the percentage of government debt per GDP more than tripling. ④ In 2011, Germany's government debt per GDP is expected to be the lowest of the four countries. ⑤ Italy and Greece follow a very similar course, with Italy projected to have a slightly higher percentage of government debt than Greece in 2011.

30

2점

Patients and their doctors tend to overlook the impact of joy on health. Why is this so? Perhaps because there is no number to measure such a factor. Instead, we focus on "hard" values for cholesterol, blood pressure, weight, etc. Those are all important — but so are relationships, personal fulfillment, and optimism. There are plenty of medical studies that link optimism, happiness, and joy with good health. Research also shows that good marriages predict good health, whereas marital stress predicts the reverse. So I guess I do have a secret shortcut to health. Her name is Rita, and we have been married for 43 years.

① the difficulty of measuring invisible joy
② the importance of sharing ideas about work
③ the need for controlling your blood pressure
④ the relationship between marriage and stress
⑤ the effects of a happy life on physical health

31

3점

Organizational successes and failures are often attributed to effective or ineffective leadership, although followers may have been the true reason behind the outcome. When examining the question of what distinguishes high-performance teams and organizations from average ones, most scholars and practitioners agree that high-performance organizations have good leaders and good followers. Competent, confident, and motivated followers are key to the successful performance of any leader's work group or team. Increasingly, many people are replacing old negative conceptions of followers with positive conceptions. Rather than the conforming and passive role in which followers have been cast, effective followers are described as courageous, responsible, and active.

① motivating followers with financial support
② examining the reasons for failures in leadership
③ encouraging conformity and passive followership
④ combining traditional and contemporary followership
⑤ achieving organizational success by effective followership

32

[2점]

A severe storm brought down trees and fences all over our neighborhood. While I was checking our front yard, I heard the squeal of brakes and a thud. To my horror, I saw a small fox terrier lying in the middle of the road. The traffic was dense, and no driver had stopped.

(A) One car finally stopped and the driver gently carried the fox terrier to the sidewalk, with the German shepherd attentively watching the proceedings. I gave him some water and food, and then called the police.

(B) Suddenly, a German shepherd appeared from nowhere, dodging the cars on the busy road, and stopped to stand guard over the smaller, wounded dog. With his head erect, unbowed and courageous as cars screeched all around him, the dog protected what I later found out was his companion.

(C) Fortunately, this splendid dog and his companion were reunited with their worried master the next day. It turned out their fence had fallen during the storm and the two dogs had escaped together.

① (A) − (C) − (B)　　　　　② (B) − (A) − (C)

③ (B) − (C) − (A)　　　　　④ (C) − (A) − (B)

⑤ (C) − (B) − (A)

33

[2점]

The purpose of art during the Middle Ages was to teach religion. Since many people living in medieval times could neither read nor write, paintings and sculptures served as vehicles through which religious leaders could promote spirituality and devotion to God.

(A) The Renaissance artists, however, viewed art as a means for personal and aesthetic expression and were most interested in secular themes. They wanted to portray the world as it was.

(B) Consequently, medieval artists were not so concerned with creating lifelike figures and forms. For them, propagating religious morals and meaning was more important.

(C) Their intent was not only to achieve accurate appearances and proportions in reality, but also to celebrate nature and humanity. Therefore, they often endowed their subjects with beauty and dignity.

① (A) − (C) − (B)

② (B) − (A) − (C)

③ (B) − (C) − (A)

④ (C) − (A) − (B)

⑤ (C) − (B) − (A)

34 Tudor period에 관한 다음 글의 내용과 일치하지 않는 것은?

2점

While the Tudor period was the time of Shakespeare and heroic explorers, it wasn't all great feasts and beautiful music. For most, living in Tudor England was hard, to say the least. Social classes were important in Tudor England, where there were four main classes. Nobility made up the smallest and richest class. Just below them was the gentry, including knights and wealthy landowners who lived in mansions with tons of servants. In the next class were the professionals, such as merchants and lawyers. The largest and lowest class included farmhands, servants, and the impoverished. Most people lived in the countryside. There were no sewers. The lack of sanitation led to many outbreaks of plague, and the lack of medical knowledge meant that many people faced illness and death. Be very happy you didn't live in Tudor England, where taking a bath was a rarity.

① 탐험가들이 영웅적인 역할을 한 시대였다.

② 사회 계층이 네 단계로 구성되어 있었다.

③ 법률가들은 최상위 계층에 속해 있었다.

④ 위생시설이 부족하여 질병이 만연하였다.

⑤ 목욕을 하는 것은 매우 희귀한 일이었다.

35 virtual advertisement에 관한 다음 글의 내용과 일치하지 않는 것은?

2점

The technology for creating virtual advertisement has been around since 1955. Originally, this type of advertising was used in sports broadcasts. The virtual advertisements were placed where real advertisements would be a distraction for players. For example, at a baseball game, the wall behind the batter and the umpire is called the backstop. Using computer technology, pictures of products and slogans can be projected on this wall and then broadcast during the game. Viewers of the game at home would see huge red-and-white advertisements for Coca-Cola plastered all across the backstop, but the pitcher in the stadium only sees the blank backstop. Advertisements can also be drawn by computers in the grass covering center field at a soccer game or displayed on the side of a virtual blimp above the stadium.

* blimp : 소형 비행선

① 스포츠 중계에 처음으로 사용되었다.
② 선수들의 집중력을 떨어뜨릴 수 있다.
③ 컴퓨터 기술을 사용하여 만들어진다.
④ 경기와 광고를 동시에 시청할 수 있게 한다.
⑤ 가상의 비행선에 광고가 보이도록 할 수 있다.

36 글의 흐름으로 보아, 주어진 문장이 들어가기에 가장 적절한 곳은?

2점

They deprived Dickey of his breakfast so that food could be used as a reward, and he received a bit of food each time he picked up eyeglasses.

"Shaping" is a way to teach a new behavior by encouraging a series of "small bits of the whole" behavior. This approach, for instance, was used to teach a disturbed little boy named Dickey to wear eyeglasses after cataract surgery. (①) His physician feared that without glasses, his vision would deteriorate permanently. (②) At the mere mention of eyeglasses, however, Dickey threw terrible temper tantrums. (③) So researchers began to use shaping to ease him into the idea of wearing his glasses. (④) Later in the procedure, he had to put glasses on in order to receive another reward. (⑤) Within eighteen days, Dickey had learned through gradual steps to wear his glasses for twelve hours a day.

* cataract surgery : 백내장 수술

37 다음 글의 내용을 한 문장으로 요약하고자 한다. 빈칸 (A)와 (B)에 들어갈 말로 가장 적절한 것은?

2점

If you daydream about something during a lecture, little or nothing about the lecture will reach your brain. You may take notes and make an effort to remain alert, but you are likely to find your mind wandering. Have you ever driven down a highway with your gas needle nearing "empty"? Chances are you become preoccupied with the location of a gas station. Another day when your fuel tank was full but your stomach was empty, the gas stations might have been overlooked, but every diner and restaurant would have caught your eye. If you are hungry or thirsty right now, you might have a problem keeping your mind focused on reading this paragraph rather than on the refrigerator. You simply cannot concentrate on every stimulus around you, so only certain ones are selected.

⇩

Perception is strongly influenced by ___(A)___ , which is usually focused on ___(B)___ things.

	(A)	(B)		(A)	(B)
①	attention	simple	②	attention	needed
③	intellect	simple	④	personality	needed
⑤	personality	rare			

※ 다음 글을 읽고, 물음에 답하시오. [38~39]

Jimin had worried about taking public speaking class for some time. She didn't see herself as a public speaker and wasn't sure she could carry it off. But the time came when she simply couldn't put off taking the course any longer. At her first class, she saw about twenty other stone-faced students who looked as uncomfortable as she felt. Her teacher later confessed that ⓐ she felt discouraged when she saw her sullen students. Jimin thought about dropping the class, but realized it was not an option. So she decided to try to stick it out.

Jimin's first assignment was to present a self-introduction speech. As ⓑ she worked on this, she came to think about her favorite subject, and it dawned on her why she found marine biology so fascinating. When she spoke, she forgot much of her nervousness in her excitement over the subject. While her speech was certainly not perfect, she did some things quite well. ⓒ She helped others get to know her, and she generated respect for the informative and persuasive speeches she later made in class on the fate of the oceans. She was pleased when her classmates discussed the positive things she had done.

As ⓓ she listened to her classmates, Jimin found that she was beginning to enjoy the class. Some of the speeches were very interesting, and ⓔ she participated in the discussions on what worked well in the speeches and what could be improved. The "great stone faces" began to chip away and reveal the real human beings they had masked.

38 Jimin에 대한 설명 중 위 글의 내용과 일치하는 것은?

[2점]

① 'Public Speaking' 수업을 듣기 전에는 연설에 자신이 있었다.

② 'Public Speaking' 수업의 첫 과제로 가족 소개를 해야 했다.

③ 첫 발표 준비를 하면서 해양 생물학에 대한 관심을 잃게 되었다.

④ 첫 발표를 하는 동안 발표에 대한 긴장감과 두려움이 더욱 늘어났다.

⑤ 다른 학생들의 발표를 들으며 'Public Speaking' 수업에 흥미를 갖게 되었다.

39 ⓐ~ⓔ 중 가리키는 대상이 나머지 넷과 다른 것은?

[2점]

① ⓐ ② ⓑ

③ ⓒ ④ ⓓ

⑤ ⓔ

※ 다음 글을 읽고, 물음에 답하시오. [40~41]

(A)

It is emphasized that rationality and calculation underlie economic behavior. If so, why do so many prices end in .99? Do consumers really think that $18.99 is only $18? A more likely explanation is that these prices are designed not to exploit incompetence but to _____.

(B)

However, the more awkward the pricing, the more unlikely it is that a thieving cashier could pull off the trick. The customer would want change, and it is unlikely that a cashier would reach into his or her pocket for this change. The cashier needs to ring the item through the cash register for the correct change.

(C)

In such cases, it would be simple for the cashier to bag the item without ringing it through the cash register, and to pocket the cash. The book would appear to have been stolen by the customer. This is a far more attractive proposition than trying to sell a stolen copy of the book, and the risk of getting caught is probably lower. Rational shoplifters might then want to get jobs in shops.

(D)

A typical shop will experience a certain amount of shoplifting. Nobody is better placed to benefit from shoplifting than the cashiers. If books — or any products — were roundly priced at $10, $15, or $20, then customers would frequently offer the correct amount.

40 위 글 (A)에 이어질 내용을 순서에 맞게 배열한 것으로 가장 적절한 것은?

[2점]

① (B) − (D) − (C)
② (C) − (B) − (D)
③ (C) − (D) − (B)
④ (D) − (B) − (C)
⑤ (D) − (C) − (B)

41 위 글 (A)의 빈칸에 들어갈 말로 가장 적절한 것은?

[3점]

① include tax
② promote sales
③ fight dishonesty
④ keep the change
⑤ create more jobs

※ 다음 글을 읽고, 물음에 답하시오. [42~43]

Many scientific studies on dolphins have shown that they seem to be able to think, understand, and learn things quickly. Then, are they smart like humans, or more like cats or dogs? Dolphins use their brains differently than people do. However, scientists say dolphin intelligence and human intelligence are alike in some way. How?

Like humans, every dolphin has its own "name." The name is a special whistle. Each dolphin chooses this specific whistle for itself, usually around its first birthday. Actually scientists think dolphins, like people, "talk" to each other about a lot of things, such as their age, their feelings, or finding food. In addition, like humans, dolphins use a system of sounds and body language to communicate. Nevertheless, understanding their conversations is not easy for humans. No one "speaks dolphin" yet, but some scientists are trying to learn.

Dolphins are also social animals. They live in groups called pods, and they often join others from different pods to play games and have fun — just like people. In fact, playing together is something only intelligent animals do.

Dolphins and humans are similar in another way : both make plans to get something they want. In the seas of southern Brazil, for example, dolphins use an interesting strategy to get food. When fish are near a boat, dolphins signal to the fishermen to put their nets in the water. Using this method, the men can catch a lot of fish. What is the advantage for the dolphins? Why do they assist the men? The fishermen share some of their fish with the dolphins.

42 위 글의 요지로 가장 적절한 것은?

① Dolphins are humans' favorite animal.

② Dolphins tend to live solitary lives.

③ Dolphins are proven to be very intelligent.

④ Dolphins live in many different climates.

⑤ Dolphins have a unique way of catching fish.

43 위 글의 내용과 일치하는 것은?

① A dolphin gets its name from its mother.

② Dolphins use language to talk about many things.

③ Dolphins whistle, but they don't use body language.

④ Dolphin conversation is easy for humans to understand.

⑤ Dolphins help fishermen catch fish to protect their pods.

※ 다음 글을 읽고, 물음에 답하시오. [44~45]

A social psychologist, Philip Zimbardo, set out to test a theory. He arranged to have an automobile abandoned in two different locations: New York City and Palo Alto, a medium-sized suburban community in California. The cars' license plates were removed and their hoods were raised to signal that they were abandoned. Then each car was secretly watched for sixty-four hours.

The person assigned to watch the New York City car did not have long to wait. Within ten minutes, the car received its first auto strippers — a father, mother, and eight-year-old son. The mother appeared to be a lookout, while the son aided the father in searching the trunk, glove compartment, and engine. He then handed his father the tools necessary to remove the battery and radiator. The total time of destructive contact was seven minutes.

This, however, was only the first contact. By the end of the sixty-four hours, the car had been vandalized twenty-four times, often by well-dressed, seemingly middle-class adults. What remained when the experiment was over was a useless hunk of metal. In contrast, the Palo Alto car was approached only once. When it started to rain, a passerby stopped to lower the hood. According to Zimbardo, the crucial factor in the different fates of the two cars was _____.

In a large city, where the chances of being recognized outside of one's own neighborhood are extremely slim, even upstanding citizens can afford a temporary turn at thievery or vandalism. In a smaller community, on the other hand, the higher probability of being recognized and caught keeps people honest.

44 위 글의 빈 칸에 들어갈 말로 가장 적절한 것은?

3점

① anonymity
② curiosity
③ disobedience
④ greediness
⑤ overconfidence

45 위 글의 내용과 일치하는 것은?

2점

① Philip Zimbardo's experiment in New York City ended in only ten minutes.

② In New York City, a family of auto strippers drove the abandoned car somewhere else.

③ In New York City, a boy in a family of auto strippers watched to see if anyone was coming.

④ In Palo Alto, a pedestrian closed the hood of the abandoned car when it rained.

⑤ Citizens in a small city were proven to commit crimes regardless of their social status.

▶ 해설은 p. 20에 있습니다.

01 What does Julie recommend for Frank's illness?

2점

> Julie : You look terrible. What's the matter?
> Frank : I have a runny nose, hacking cough, and the worst headache. I think I should go to the hospital.
> Julie : Have you taken any medicine?
> Frank : No, I haven't yet. I think I'll just go see Dr. Smith.
> Julie : You just have a cold. There's no need to go to a doctor. You should just lie down and take it easy for a while and I'll make you some tea. You'll feel better in no time.

① that he visit Dr. Smith   ② that he get some rest

③ that he get an injection   ④ that he go to the hospital

⑤ that he take some medicine

02 Which is the best sequence of answers for the blanks?

2점

> Gary : I really like this apartment. ＿＿＿＿＿＿＿ It looks a little pricy.
> Landlord : it's really not that much. It's just $950 a month.
> Gary : ＿＿＿＿＿＿＿ I don't have my own vehicle.
> Landlord : There is a bus stop just two blocks away. It's very convenient.
> Gary : ＿＿＿＿＿＿＿ I really hope that they are quiet.
> Landlord : Most of them are senior citizens and are in bed early. You don't have to worry about that.
> Gary : Well, I think I'll take it. ＿＿＿＿＿＿＿
> Landlord : Just give me a few days to clean it up and then it's all yours.

ⓐ How about the neighbors?   ⓑ How much is the rent?

ⓒ What about public transportation?   ⓓ Are pets allowed?

ⓔ When cal I move in?

① ⓐ － ⓑ － ⓒ － ⓔ
② ⓑ － ⓒ － ⓔ － ⓓ
③ ⓑ － ⓒ － ⓐ － ⓔ
④ ⓒ － ⓐ － ⓔ － ⓑ
⑤ ⓒ － ⓓ － ⓑ － ⓐ

03 What are Tom and Jane about to do?

> Tom : Are you ready yet, honey?
>
> Jane : I've just got to grab the present. Do you think they will like it? Maybe I should exchange it for something else.
>
> Tom : No, they'll love it. And we don't have time. We're supposed to be there in thirty minutes and traffic at this time is horrible. Hurry up!
>
> Jane : Relax. If we're a little late, no one will mind. My parents have an anniversary every year.
>
> Tom : I know, but being married for forty years is a big deal. And your brother would be really upset. He went to a lot of effort to plan this party.

① go to exchange a gift
② go to Tom's brother's birthday party
③ go to Tom's brother－in－law's birthday party
④ go to Jane's parents' wedding anniversary party
⑤ go to Tom and Jane's wedding anniversary party

04 Based on the dialogue, which of the following is FALSE?

Sarah : Can you believe that we're going to be parents in just two months?

Mike : I'm bouncing off the walls with excitement. I can't wait to have our own little Einstein running around.

Sarah : First of all, do you really think that our child will be a genius? Second of all, what if it's a girl?

Mike : Of course honey, with me as his father, our baby will surely be the smartest kid around! But it will be a boy, I just fell it! And with you as his mother, he'll be one of the best—looking kids around, too.

Sarah : You're wrong about one thing, as I really hope to be buying pink baby clothes for her. But with me as her mother, she will be a beautiful baby.

① Mike and Sarah are going to have a baby in two months.

② Mike thinks that their baby will be very smart.

③ Mike and Sarah agree on the baby's gender.

④ Mike is looking forward to being a father.

⑤ Sarah wants to have a daughter.

05 Which of the following is the best choice for the blank?

Dave : My wife says I need to lose some weight, but I think I'm in pretty good shape. What do you think?

Brett : I think you could stand to lose a few pounds. You're not getting any younger, you know. Plus, didn't your father have diabetes? If so, there is a high chance that you could develop the disease as well if you are not careful.

Dave : That's true. When he got really heavy, his diabetes caused all kinds of serious health problems. He was in and out of the hospital for years.

Brett : There you go. Maybe you should listen to your wife. She's a smart woman.

Dave : _____

① You've got a good point. Let's order a pizza.

② You're right. I'll go work out right now.

③ No, she has always been in good shape.

④ I was an athlete when I was young, too.

⑤ I don't think I should eat like that.

06 Where is the following dialogue taking place?

2점

> Joe : So what seems to the problem?
> Bob : Well, it's been making a strange noise for past couple of months.
> Joe : A couple of months! Why didn't you bring it in sooner? Whatever the problem is, it may have caused some serious damage.
> Bob : I just don't have time to worry about proper maintenance. I'm always on the road.
> Joe : That's exactly why taking good care of it should be a big priority. When was the last time you had it in for a tune-up and oil change?
> Bob : Well, since I bought it three years ago, never.
> Joe : OH MY GOODNESS!

① the police station

② the dentist's office

③ the hardware store

④ the auto repair shop

⑤ the computer repair shop

07 밑줄 친 It[it]가 가리키는 대상이 나머지 넷과 다른 것은?

2점

Hail is one of the cruelest weapons in Nature's armory and one of the most incalculable. ①It can destroy one farmer's prospects of a harvest in a matter of seconds. Yet it can leave his neighbor's untouched. ②It can destroy a flock of sheep in one field, while the sun continues to shine in the next. To the meteorologist, its behavior is even more cunning than that of a thunderstorm. Difficult as it undoubtedly is for him to forecast the onset of a thunderstorm, he knows pretty well what its course and duration will be once ③it has started. However, all he can do with hail is measure the size of the stones once they have hit the ground—and they have a habit of melting as soon as he gets his hands on them. He is not even too sure about the way in which ④it forms—and until he knows this, of course, he isn't likely to stumble upon any very reliable method of prediciting when or where ⑤it may strike.

※ 다음 글에서 전체 흐름과 관계 없는 문장을 고르시오. [08~09]

08

3점

The disturbing reality is that the Internet is replete with out-of-date, conflicting, and inaccurate information. ①Rumor mills abound, and even trustworthy sites are often slow at updating facts and figures, leaving both the information givers and users exasperated. ②A greater injustice in the eyes of some people are the old or unflattering photographs that make it into the Internet's search engines. ③It is difficult, if not impossible, to get such things removed or to chase down a trail of negative or false information once it's been able to fester on the Web. ④The Internet minimizes the differences people face when they look for certain information, whether they are rich or poor, whether they have access to a terrific library or none at all. ⑤Just ask your friends who have photos from their fat, unpopular school days still floating around the Web.

Overall, the do−it−yourself (D−I−Y) market for home improvement in the United States is estimated to run about $200 billion annually. ①The comparable estimate for Japan, where houses are much smaller and more sparsely furnished, exceeds $30 billion and in Germany, D−I−Y companies ring up $33 billion. ②These are surprisingly large numbers compared with those of the previous years. ③In 2008, this market was spurred by a rapidly growing audience for home−improvement programs on television. ④D−I−Y products are apt to cause a lot of health problems among infants due to the toxic chemicals introduced into the home. ⑤In Britain, shows such as *Changing Rooms* and *Ground Force*, which offer hands−on, how−to advice to D−I−Yers, were among the most watched on the BBC.

10 다음 글을 쓴 목적으로 가장 적절한 것은?

2점

Working in a large company such as this can be oddly isolating. If we were out in the field, like some of our fortunate colleagues, we would be active, meeting new people and moving around. However, for us office workers, we tend to just park our cars in the underground parkade, take an elevator to our floor and head to our little corners where we work the day away. The cafeteria may be a gathering place, but people tend to sit with those who work in the same office or on the same floor. I think a gym would provide an informal place which would bring together company personnel of all different departments and offices, of all different ages and backgrounds. If this idea were to be entertained, a suitable place to put it might be in the back room in the basement that is currently used for storage, or even in the 10th floor lounge which is rarely used. I believe such an investment would definitely be worth it, if not only for our health, also to help build company unity.

① 사무실 배정을 위한 아이디어를 모집하려고
② 직원들을 위한 체력단련장 신설을 제안하려고
③ 사무실 근무 직원의 하루 일과를 소개하려고
④ 사무실 칸막이 공사에 대한 반대의견을 밝히려고
⑤ 사내 친목 도모를 위한 점심 모임 참여를 독려하려고

11
3점

We know from eveyday experience that we can make useful guesses which usually turn out to be roughly ①accurate, even if we cannot definitively predict the future. If there ②were no patterns in the past that continued into the future, the existence of humans and other animals on earth would be impossible. It is on the basis of what we have established about human motivation and what we have seen in the pattern of past events ③that we make endless decisions, big and small. There are no absolute laws, but there are probabilities and tendencies. For cxample, you and I expect to hear the fish─and─chip van ④ring its bell on a Wednesday evening─and it almost comes. You wouldn't undertake the smallest action, from eating a meal to playing a game or riding a bicycle, if this predictability based on past patterns recurring could not be ⑤relied.

12
2점

'In foruteen hunderd and ninety─two, Columbus ①sailed the ocean blue.' Every American schoolkid knows this rhyme, and American history books refer to Christopher Columbus more than any other historical ②figure. In them, he is portrayed as the original great American hero. He is even one of only two people the United States honors ③him by name with a national holiday. Even though every history textbook includes his name and every schoolchild remembers the year 1492, these textbooks leave out ④virtually all the unfavorable facts that are important to know about Columbus and the European exploration of the Americas. Meanwhile, they make up all kinds of favorable details to create a better story and ⑤humanize Columbus so that readers will identify with him.

13

Since scientists now have evidence to prove that the moon is not made of 'green cheese' as the old myth suggests, attention has turned from the composition of the lunar body to theories of its origin. One of the early theories proposes that the moon formed at the same time as the Earth from the same elements. However, samples (A) collected / collecting from the moon's surface by lunar probes show that moon rocks do not contain iron, an element common in Earth samples. The model (B) currently / current in favor suggests that the moon was formed when a large planetary body struck Earth's surface and broke off a chunk, which spun into orbit. This theory explains the missing iron by theorizing that the iron in the Earth had drifted into its core, leaving an iron—free outer layer (C) from which / which the moon was formed.

	(A)	(B)	(C)
①	collected	currently	from which
②	collecting	current	which
③	collected	current	from which
④	collecting	current	from which
⑤	collected	currently	which

14

The security camera is one of the greatest inventions in the field of security. It is 'the eye in the sky' and 'the eyes in the back of your head.' Security cameras are widely used, almost everywhere, in places such as shops, libraries, schools, banks and even on public streets. Some claim that they are an invasion of privacy. However, there are clear advantages of (A) employing / employment such cameras. They have been proven to help catch criminals and prevent crime more effectively than any other method available. The only problematic issue is to have (B) qualified / qualifying people watching the monitors. A single security guard sitting in a room with 50 monitors is not effective. What is effective is a few tranined and motivated plainclothes grards patrolling inside and outside the property monitoring every corner. They should be working hand—in—hand with (C) whosever / whoever is watching the monitors.

	(A)	(B)	(C)
①	employing	qualified	whosever
②	employing	qualified	whoever
③	employing	qualifying	whoever
④	employment	qualified	whosever
⑤	employment	qualifying	whosever

※ 다음 글을 읽고, 빈칸에 가장 적절한 것을 고르시오. [15~19]

15

[2점]

When you write your university admission essay on your personal achievements, don't fall into the trap of _____ your experiences or the lessons you've learned. Instead, think critically about your topic even if it seems mundane to you, and try to understand and clearly express why that experience was valuable for you. Try to avoid too long—winded sentences that are not based on facts. The more you try to puff yourself up, the less honest you look in admission officers' eyes. Stick with 'factual writing,' and you can create a more impressive, memorable essay without embellishing your experiences.

① exaggerating ② personalizing

③ reorganizing ④ underestimating

⑤ simplifying

16

One tremendous advantage of directing musicians and actors in a music video instead of a feature film is that you _____. You can shout at the subjects while the camera rolls just as a fashion photographer is constantly repositioning models. In front of a rolling camera, most people feel so on—the—spot that they'll do whatever you say if you bark orders at them. This works especially well while shooting. if the guitar player puts on a silly grin in the middle of a scene, you don't need to yell 'cut' and start all over again. Just yell at the guy, loudly enough so that you're audible over the music. His music will be placed into the video after you have finished your job, so you only have to create images to accompany the previously recorded music.

① keep silent while directing

② record only the video, not the audio

③ mix different art genres

④ get to listen to live music

⑤ hire any artist you want

17

In 1987, a mining company stripped the vegetation from twelve acres of extremely steep land at a creek head in rural Montana. A flash flood proceeded to send masses of mining debris tumbling into the swollen river. Though no lives were lost, the flood destroyed all the homes in the valley. When the valley residents sued the mining company, they won a verdict for a substantial compensation package. However, the company appealed the lower court's decision to a more business—sympathetic state court. To the residents' dismay, the original ruling was overturned. The state judge proclaimed that the masses of soil, uprooted trees, and slabs of rock had originally been harmless upon sliding down the slope. It was only when they were set in motion by the force of the water that they became hazardous. Thus, the court declared that _____.

① the original judgment be upheld

② the deaths be covered by insurance

③ such floods be predicted in the future

④ stricter mining guidelines be enforced

⑤ the mining company not be held responsible

18

3점

Sponsorship of big events is a serious business. But what can you do if you aren't an official sponsor, but you'd still like to benefit from the publicity surrounding the event? Simple! Just do a bit of ambush marketing! Ambush marketing involves _____. Imagine that Beer Company A is sponsoring a massive sports event. In return for vast amounts of money, it has permission to affiliate itself with the event. Beer Company B also wants to be associated with the event, but doesn't want to pay for it. In order to get any publicity, Beer Company B does something spectacular in the middle of the event to draw the eyes of TV cameras and spectators —they ambush the event. A recent example of ambush marketing occurred during a World Cup match. A Dutch beer company organized 36 young, attractive women in mini−skirts, wearing shirts with the company's logo, to storm the stands in the middle of a game. Predictably, the cameras turned towards them, beaming their image around the world and providing the company with an invaluable, yet inexpensive, marketing opportunity.

① offering a huge discount for a product

② damaging the image of rival companies

③ increasing the advertising budget for a product

④ getting official permission to co−sponsor an event

⑤ grabbing attention for a product during a big event

19

2점

A clever chimp at a Swedish zoo proves that nonhuman primates can _____. For the past several years, Santino, a male chimp, has put on a show of dominance every day at around 11 A.M. by yelling and running around, which is typical of male chimps. However, he would also prepare another spectacle for zoo visitors. Almost every day, workers found that earlier in the morning he would calmly fish rocks out of the moat around his habitat and then chip away at the concrete on his inland to form small disks. Santino would pile them all up and wait, up to several hours, for visitors to come near. When they approached, he would begin to launch his carefully arranged stockpile at them.

① share with others ② plan for the future

③ show appreciation ④ control their temper

⑤ gather food for their mates

20

다음 글의 빈칸 (A), (B)에 들어갈 말로 가장 적절한 것은? [2점]

_____(A)_____ is one of the most commonly used techniques in chemistry. All you have to do is heat the liquid till it boils and draw the gas off it. The gas coming off it is sent into a container where it cools back into a liquid. Since different chemicals turn to gas at different temperatures, different chemicals will boil off one by one as the mixture that includes a variety of chemicals heats up. So, some will pass into the container and some will be left at the bottom of the boiling container as a revolting sludge. Simply put, the technique is meant to _____(B)_____ which a liquid contains.

	(A)	(B)
①	Compounding	mix the various elements
②	Alloying	combine two different metals
③	Purifying	draw water from the sludge
④	Sterilization	burn off the bacteria
⑤	Distillation	separate out the chemicals

21

다음 글의 밑줄 친 부분 중, 문맥상 낱말의 쓰임이 적절하지 않은 것은? [2점]

Thousands of small businesses around the world actually originate when some hobbyists begin to sell what they have ①previously made only for themselves or for friends and neighbors. For example, ②inspired by his Aunt Della, Wally Mos began baking as a hobby, handing out cookies to friends and family. He says, "It ③reached a point where people wouldn't say 'hello' when they saw me. They'd say, 'Where are my cookies?' Everybody told me I should go into the cookie business." He adds, "But I didn't take it ④seriously at the time." When he finally did take the idea of a business seriously, Wally Mos ⑤abandoned Famous Amos Chocolate Chip Cookies, now one of the best−known brands in the United States and a pioneering force in the gourmet−cookie business.

22 다음 글이 시사하고 있는 바로 가장 적절한 것은?

2점

What is a classroom like when the teacher always tries to be nice? We're talking about the teacher who values being friends with students over teaching them and demonstrating leadership. It feels really good in the beginning. The kids are excited about this 'closer' relationship that they ger to have with an adult. A few weeks into the semester, though, they begin to have doubts about it all. It feels like no one is in charge. Pretty soon there is chaos. Children need and desire structure and discipline. Assignments should be clear, and rules should be enforced. Children don't know how to ask for them directly. In weak systems, they can be seduced by the lack of structure and discipline, get used to it, and even intoxicated by it. The ultimate dilemma for teachers and children, when it comes to this issue, is that they both care about each other, and yet they both need structure and rules. Surely it isn't the children's job to provide them.

① 학생 스스로 규칙을 정하게 해야 한다.
② 학생-교사 간 신뢰구축이 교육의 기본이다.
③ 교사는 학생들의 감정을 이해해야 한다.
④ 교사는 체계와 규율을 강조할 필요가 있다.
⑤ 교사는 학생을 통제하기보다는 모범을 보여야 한다.

23
2점

TIME magazine is read weekly by millions of people around the world and is recognized by millions more. Its up—to—date, informative articles (A) attract / contract readers with issues of international interest, as well as with topics of specific concern to Americans and to those interested in life in the United States. Just as TIME, the original publication, offers a unique view of the United States and its people, TIME : Reaching for Tomorrow, its special edition, presents a distinctive reading opportunity for students of English. Those already familiar with TIME will be pleased to see that this is an all—new volume (B) comprising / compromising forty —three recently published articles. The articles have been selected to present a broad overview of aspects of life in the United States—both the positive and the negative, the permanent and the transitory. Each article appears in its original form without simplification. Photographs, illustrations, charts, and other graphics (C) acclaim / accompany the articles.

	(A)	(B)	(C)
①	attract	comprising	acclaim
②	attract	compromising	accompany
③	attract	comprising	accompany
④	contract	compromising	acclaim
⑤	contract	comprising	acclaim

24
3점

Pirates have plagued seafarers for millenniums. In the 16th and 17th centuries, piracy enjoyed its golden age, when outlaws like Blackbeard roamed the sun—splashed islands, plundering gold and silver. However, piracy declined in subsequent centuries, thanks to increasingly (A) ignorant / vigilant militaries and the development of the steam engine. But amid a drop in naval patrols and a boom in international trade following the end of the cold war, piracy has (B) dwindled / flourished , particularly in narrow choke points such as Asia's Strait of Malacca and the Gulf of Aden, which links the Red and Arabian seas. Equipped with fast boats, fearsome weaponry, and high—tech communications gear, pirates carried off 263 reported heists in 2007m 28% of which occurred in the lawless waters off Somalia. With its vast coastline and crippled government, it is the country which is most (C) infested / unacquainted with pirates. Ships are now warned to stay 200 nautical miles offshore.

* heist : 강도, 도둑

	(A)	(B)	(C)
①	ignorant	dwindled	infested
②	ignorant	dwindled	unacquainted
③	vigilant	flourished	infested
④	vigilant	dwindled	infested
⑤	vigilant	flourished	unacquainted

✦ 다음 글의 제목으로 가장 적절한 것을 고르시오. [25~26]

25
2점

One way to nourish positive emotions is to take a moment to, well, appreciate the moment. Just give yourself two or three short activities that offer you a chance to appreciate your day. In the morning, for instance, instead of trying to do ten things at once, take your cup of coffee to the window and slowly sip it while watching your child play in the backyard. Take a look around and savor the moment. Will it change your life? Probably not, but you'll probably feel at ease. An even simpler way to do this is to just take 10 seconds out of every hour to look at what you are doing from a higher place. Take a moment to appreciate what a wonderful life you have, and try to share that joy with someone who will rejoice in it with you. These are just a couple of ways to grab onto the good stuff in life.

① Find Your Happy Moment
② Organize Your Days
③ Don't Be Too Emotional
④ Settle Down and Have a Family
⑤ Take Care of Your Health

26

2점

When I was seventeen, I spent my life savings on a 1969 Chevy Camaro, the coolest—looking car I had ever seen. A few months later, it was stolen from a mall parking lot. The police found it, stripped and lying in the street without any wheels and badly in need of a paint job. With the insurance money, the car was restored and became quite valuable. But then it looked too nice, and with the prior theft, I was paranoid about leaving it anywhere. It Was no longer basic transportation but rather an expensive headache. I sold it for a pretty good price, put the money in a couple of certificates of deposit at the bank, and then lived off that money when I was in graduate school some years later. Today, you won't find me driving anything but a small ordinary domestic car.

① Sometimes Less Is Better

② Your Car Tells Who You Are

③ Downsize Your Life, Save the Planet

④ Who's the Enemy of Economy?

⑤ Public Transportation : Solution to Car Headaches

※ 다음 글의 주제로 가장 적절한 것을 고르시오. [27~28]

27

2점

In South Korea, an estimated 6.5 million residents serve as volunteers. They provide relief after typhoon flooding, take care of senior citizens in need of care, work at orphanages spending time with the kids, and even teach refugees from North Korea how to adapt to life in the South. In Italy, volunteers help care for cancer patients and work in hospices. And when unprecedented floods struck Germany in 2002, tens of thousands of volunteers traveled cross—country to battle the rising waters. Volunteers are a vital part of each nation's economy, social atmosphere, and overall well—being. Not only do they provide vital services and relieve a huge burden from the public sector, but also create an environment of community and cooperation.

① the downside of volunteer work

② the difficulty in organizing volunteer work

③ the importance of volunteer work

④ how to become a competent volunteer

⑤ types of international volunteer organizations

28

Early settlements in the Fertile Crescent, between nine and ten thousand years ago, created a completely new environment for many of the wild animal species in the area that were sufficiently adaptable and inquisitive. Trash heaps on the outskirts of these settlements proved a big attraction for cats, which found a great source of food not only in the garbage itself, but also in the mice lured in by the enticing aroma. While mice, due to their propensity to carry disease and crawl into every corner of the home, may not have endeared themselves to humans, cats received a much warmer welcome. Considering the inherent 'cuteness' of kittens, and the practical services they provided in helping to rid the area of local vermin such as the disease—carrying rodents or detested snakes, cats were encouraged to 'stick around.' With this adaptability and bold nature, along with the harmonious relationship they developed with their new 'neighbors,' cats have forever since been welcomed at the human hearth.

① hardships faced by early settlers

② factors that led to cats' domestication

③ evolutionary forces upon the size of cats

④ how cats developed their hunting skills

⑤ how cats and mice became mortal enemies

29 다음 도표의 내용과 일치하지 않는 문장은?

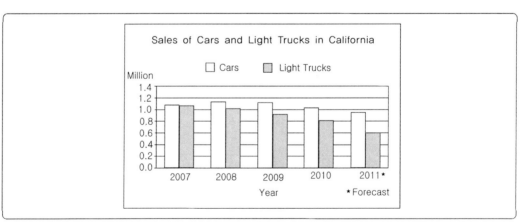

The above chart compares the number of cars with that of light trucks sold in the state of California from 2007 to 2010, and projects their sales for 2011. ①In 2007, sales of both kinds of vehicles were nearly identical, hovering just above the 1 million mark. ②In 2008, sales of cars slightly increased, followed by a steady drop in subsequent years. ③Sales of light trucks were consistently on the downtrend from 2007 to 2010. ④It is even predicted that light truck sales should take a big hit in 2011 falling to 0.6 million from 0.8 million in 2010. ⑤According to the chart, overall vehicle sales in 2011 will be down, plus the gap between sales of cars and light trucks will continue to shrink, with cars grabbing a much larger percentage of the market.

※ 다음 글의 요지로 가장 적절한 것을 고르시오. [30~31]

30
2점

Nearly all television animation these days is done overseas. This means that the scripts have to be translated into Japanese, Korean, French, German, and so on for non—English—speaking animation—production houses. This can create some quite funny problems, particularly when it comes to the use of idioms. A friend of mine likes to tell the story of a *G.I. Joe* script he wrote in which his characters were in a desert location having an argument. He used the idiom 'X decides to stick his oar in the water,' meaning character X decides to give his opinion. When the animation came back, his characters suddenly went from standing in the desert to sitting in a rowboat with oars in water that suddenly appears out of nowhere. It has become necessary to avoid using idioms in animation scripts because they usually go overseas for production. They are sometimes too obscurely language—specific and might mean nothing to an overseas animator.

① 만화영화는 문화의 전파에 중요한 역할을 한다.
② 만화영화 등장인물들의 국적이 다양해지고 있다.
③ 만화영화 대본은 주인공의 성격을 감안해서 제작된다.
④ 국가 이미지를 위해 만화영화 대본에 속어를 사용하지 않는다.
⑤ 만화영화 대본에 관용어를 사용하면 제작에 지장을 초래할 수 있다.

The conventional definition of an ESL(English as a Second Language) country is one in which English is not a native language but where it is used widely as a medium of communication in domains such as education and government. This is so in countries like Nigeria and Singapore. The term ESL is also standard in the USA to describe programs teaching English to people whose first language is not English. In an EFL(English as a Foreign Language) country, English is not the language of instruction or government, but it is learned at school, as is the case in France or Japan, for communicating with speakers of the language, or for reading texts in the language. There are quite different teaching needs and strategies in ESL and EFL situations because of the differing degree of exposure to the language outside school, and the different roles for English both within the education system and in the wider community.

① In ESL and EFL countries, the purposes of English teaching are different.

② In ESL and EFL countries, the English education environment is identical.

③ In ESL and EFL countries, the extent to which English is used is similar.

④ English is used as a medium of communication in EFL countries.

⑤ France and Japan are examples of ESL countries.

※ 주어진 글 다음에 이어질 글의 순서로 가장 적절한 것을 고르시오. [32~33]

32
3점

The use of photography to reduce the size of messages to be transmitted was pioneered by the French during the Franco–Prussian War.

(A) For it to work, however, the messages would have to be small and lightweight. The solution was to produce photographic copies of the original messages. These would be printed on paper roughly 1.5 inches square and rolled into a tube which was strapped to the pigeon. During the eight months of the siege, nearly 60 messages got past the watchful eyes, and guns, of the Prussians.

(B) It was during that war that the city of Paris was completely surrounded and cut off from all outside communications. The Prussians who had laid siege to the city had cut all telegraph lines and weren't about to let the mail go through. In such a circumstance, it was impossible for Parisians to communicate with the outside world.

(C) Parisians had tried a number of means to pass communications past the Prussians, including floating watertight balls containing official letters down the Seine River and sending messages aloft in balloons, but none of them proved effective. At that time, one of the pigeon–racing clubs suggested strapping messages to the tail feathers of their birds.

① (A)–(C)–(B)

② (B)–(A)–(C)

③ (B)–(C)–(A)

④ (C)–(A)–(B)

⑤ (C)–(B)–(A)

33
2점

Home schooling is becoming more and more desirable because children do not have the burden of traveling to school and becoming exposed to other children's sickness and everything else that goes with being in a crowded room.

(A) However, in many studies, it has been shown that students benefit more in a classroom setting since the interaction and dialogue with other students creates a stimulating learning environment.

(B) There is also individual attention that the parent or tutor can give the student, creating a better and more efficient learning environment. As social standards become more and more flexible, home schooling may in fact be the norm of the future.

(C) In addition, the more students that are in a class, the more diversity of the group and the more varied the feedback. With a good teacher, a classroom can be very beneficial for the student's cognitive development.

① (A)−(C)−(B)　　　　　　② (B)　(A)−(C)

③ (B)−(C)−(A)　　　　　　④ (C)−(A)−(B)

⑤ (C)−(B)−(A)

34 cardamom에 관한 다음 글의 내용과 일치하지 않는 것은?

2점

Cardamom is the world's third most expensive spice after saffron and vanilla. It's the seed of a plant in the ginger family that is indigenous to the mountains of southwest India and was grown only there until 1900. German immigrants then brought it to Guatemala, which is now the largest producer. Cardamom seeds are borne in clusters of fibrous capsules that ripen at different times, so the capsules must be picked by hand one by one. They should be harvested slightly before full ripeness when the capsule splits. Cardamom is mentioned alongside cinnamon in the Old Testament, but it didn't reach Europe until the Middle Ages. Today, Nordic countries consume 10% of its world trade, mainly in baked goods, while Arab countries take 80% for their cardamom coffee. This coffee is made by boiling freshly roasted ground coffee with green cardamom pods.

* cinnamon : 계피

① 1900년까지 인도 남서부에서만 재배되었다.

② 현재는 과테말라가 최대 생산지이다.

③ 캡슐이 갈라지기 전에 수확해야 한다.

④ 중세 이후에 유럽에 전파되었다.

⑤ 아랍권에서 커피 대신 차로 끓여 마신다.

35 다음 글의 내용과 일치하지 않는 것은?

2점

Mayor Daley and other white political and religious leaders in Chicago accused Dr. Martin Luther King of causing trouble. They demanded that he call off plans for another march. Dr. King, however, told them that if they wanted him to stop marching, they would have to make justice a reality. So Daley called Dr. King to a meeting with the local labor and business leaders. They agreed that Chicago's Commission on Human Rights would make real estate agents post the city's open-housing policy, which would allow all races access to previously restricted housing—and the city would enforce it. Also, banks of Chicago agreed to lend money to qualified families regardless of ethnic background. Dr. King proved that nonviolent protest worked in the North.

① 시카고의 백인 정치 지도자들은 Martin Luther King을 비난했다.
② 행진 중단 요구에 대해 Martin Luther King은 정의실현을 요구했다.
③ Martin Luther King은 현지 지도자들과의 모임에 Daley 시장을 불렀다.
④ 시카고의 은행들은 인종차별 없는 대출을 해 주기로 동의했다.
⑤ Martin Luther King은 북부에서 비폭력 저항이 통했다는 것을 증명했다.

36 글의 흐름으로 보아, 주어진 문장이 들어가기에 가장 적절한 곳은?

3점

It claims that readers fit the text into knowledge (cultural, syntactic, linguistic, historical) they already possess, then check back when new or unexpected information appears.

There are three main models of how reading occurs. (①) Bottom-up theory argues that the reader constructs the text from the smallest units (letters to words to phrases to sentences, etc.) and that the process of constructing the text from those small units becomes so automatic that readers are not aware of how it operates. (②) Top-down theory argues that readers bring a great deal of knowledge, expectations, assumptions, and questions to the text and, given a basic understanding of the vocabulary, they continue to read as long as the text confirms their expectations. (③) The interactive school of theorists—which most researchers currently endorse—argues that both top-down and bottom-up processes are occurring, either alternately or simultaneously. (④) These theorists describe a process that moves both bottom-up and top-down, depending on the type of text as well as on the reader's background knowledge, language proficiency level, motivation, strategy use, and culturally shaped beliefs about the reading. (⑤) Bottom-up and top-down processes occur interactively when readers construct meanings from texts.

37 다음 글의 내용을 한 문장으로 요약하고자 한다. 빈칸 (A)와 (B)에 들어갈 말로 가장 적절한 것은?

2점

At a shopping mall, the slowest-selling batteries were for use in hearing aids, so the conventional wisdom dictated they should be stocked at the bottom of the shelves with the other unattractive items. However, it is of course old people who buy them, the shoppers least able to stoop. The batteries were subsequently moved higher on the shelves, which resulted in four times more batteries being sold. There are some products whose prime purchasers are the elderly. What if they are stocked with extra care, no higher than waist level, and no lower, either? In most supermarkets, products stocked too low or too high are virtually off-limits to old shoppers. Making life easy on older shoppers engenders warm feelings among a group that is often badly served by retailers. In addition, in doing so, word will spread. The man who comes in for hearing-aid batteries will probably bring his friend who needs to buy a telephone or a computer.

⇩

When you change the   (A)   of products at a store, you can expect   (B)   from old people.

	(A)	(B)
①	arrangement	increased sales
②	sizes	impulsive purchase
③	arrangement	physical exercise
④	packaging	marketing advice
⑤	packaging	decreased complaints

Let me explain my aversion to noise. If you cut up a large diamond into little bits, it will entirely lose the value it had as a whole; and an army divided up into small bodies of soldiers loses all its strength. So a great intellect sinks to the level of an ordinary one as soon as it is interrupted and disturbed, its attention distracted and drawn from the matter in hand; for its superiority depends upon its power of _____, in the same way as a concave mirror collects into one point all the rays of light that strike upon it.

Noisy interruption is a hindrance. That is why distinguished minds have always shown such an extreme dislike to disturbance in any form, as something that breaks in upon and distracts their thoughts. Above all, they have been averse to that violent interruption that comes from noise. Ordinary people are not much bothered by anything of the sort. The most sensible and intelligent of all nations in Europe lays down the rule, 'Never Interrupt!' as the eleventh commandment. Noise is the most impertinent of all forms of interruption. It is not only an interruption, but also a disruption of thought. Of course, where there is nothing to interrupt, noise will not be so particularly painful. Occasionally, it happens that some slight but constant noise continues to bother and distract me for a time before I become distinctly conscious of it. All I feel is a steady increase in the labor of thinking—just as though I were trying to walk with a weight on my foot. At last I find out what it is.

* concave mirror : 오목 거울

38 위 글의 빈칸에 들어갈 말로 가장 적절한 것은?

 ① curiosity ② creativity

③ imagination ④ concentration

⑤ memorization

39 위 글의 요지로 가장 적절한 것은?

① Noise distracts the intellectual.

② Noise tolerance varies greatly across cultures.

③ Indiscernible environmental noise affects health.

④ Proper levels of noise enhance the thinking process.

⑤ The more absorbing the work, the easier it is to block out noise.

The United States was in the midst of an economic depression brought on by the monetary policies adopted by the previous administration in Washington, D.C. It needed stability and a strong leader to put an end to inflation and bring the jobs back. With those issues in mind, the country elected Stephen Grover Cleveland as the twenty—fourth president of the United States. (a) He was to deliver a major address to Congress in August of that year.

But there was a problem. Cleveland had become aware of a rough spot on the roof of his mouth. He didn't think too much of it, but (b) he didn't want to ignore it either. He asked a doctor to take a look. (c) He discovered an injury, nearly the size of a quarter, and said that the president had cancer which required immediate surgery. It wasn't quite that simple. The August address to Congress had been set and announced; it could not be postponed without the probability of serious damage to the cause. Further, the country needed to know that it was in the hands of a healthy man.

During a vacation trip to New York, the president underwent the surgical procedure in secret. The surgeons removed two teeth, most of his upper left jaw, and about half of the roof of his mouth. The tumor had grown to nearly the size of a golf ball. Once it had been removed, the hole was packed with gauze. Since the surgery was successful and produced no external scars, (d) he showed no visible effects of the operation. There was no swelling, bruising, or scarring. His face looked no different, and his speech returned without incident. (e) He was able to keep his appointment before Congress and the public never knew.

It wasn't until 1917, nearly 25 years after the fact and 10 years after Cleveland's death, that the secret was made known through an article in the *Saturday Evening Post* that had been authored by the chief surgeon with the family's permission.

40 위 글 (a)~(e) 중 가리키는 대상이 나머지 넷과 다른 것은?

2점

① (a) ② (b)

③ (c) ④ (d)

⑤ (e)

41 위 글의 내용과 일치하지 않는 것은?

[3점]

① The address was made without delay.

② The surgery was conducted during a vacation.

③ The operation was not known to the public during Cleveland's lifetime.

④ Cleveland's family has prohibited the story from being published to the present day.

⑤ Cleveland was considered the leader to solve the economic problems of the time.

※ 다음 글을 읽고, 물음에 답하시오. [42~43]

(A)

Somewhere along the way we encounter special people who change us in powerful, positive, and sometimes unexpected ways. One such person I was blessed to have in my life was a flight instructor I met. I was just a teenager when I started taking lessons. About the time I was finishing my training, he told me that I had met all of the requirements, and could certainly go get my license and wing happily off.

(B)

I had just five minutes to work with. Looking back, I realize that I probably went into a kind of 'internal autopilot.' All my training and preparation kicked in. During those additional training exercises, I had simulated emergency dead-stick landings dozens and dozens of times, some during the day, some in the black of night. And in that cockpit I felt very alone, but I calmed myself with the fact that _____. My emergency just meant that all those practice drills were for a purpose. It was now 'showtime.' It was a 'good' landing because I did walk away and now I type this story.

(C)

I realized the significance of that exchange, because he had just spoken more words than I had ever heard him say at once. Fast-forward four years and several hundred hours of flying later. I took off in a high-performance single-engine airplane just before midnight and on the heels of a strong winter storm. I was cruising 10,000 feet when all of a sudden the engine just quit. The sky was pitch black without even the tiniest sliver of moon, and there were two feet of fresh snow blanketing the ground so that everything below me looked one-dimensional.

He then paused and said something that really got my attention. "Mike," he said, "you've got the basics, you know how to get her up and down and around the patch, and frankly you aren't half bad. But chances are that somewhere along the way this plane will carry you into a crisis. When you are airborne, all you've got is yourself. If you aren't prepared for it ahead of time, you can die. Know that it may come and if it does, you'll be one of two types of pilots : one who was ready and survives to tell the story, or one who wasn't and doesn't."

42 위 글 (A)에 이어질 내용을 순서에 맞게 배열한 것으로 가장 적절한 것은?

3점

① (B) - (D) - (C)

② (C) - (B) - (D)

③ (C) - (D) - (B)

④ (D) - (B) - (C)

⑤ (D) - (C) - (B)

43 위 글 (B)의 빈칸에 들어갈 말로 가장 적절한 것은?

2점

① I was completely prepared for this exact situation

② I was totally alone and nobody could disturb me

③ my license had not been valid for a long time

④ I had crash-landed an airplane in real life before

⑤ the plane had to arrive at its destination as planned

※ 다음 글을 읽고, 물음에 답하시오. [44~45]

Real transformation is possible in the public sector as William J. Bratton showed when he took command of the New York Police Department (NYPD) in 1994. Its function, he declared, was no longer just to catch criminals but to focus on the future and prevent crime as well.

Until Bratton arrived, the NYPD had measured its performance in comparison with other police departments on the basis of FBI data supplied only once every six months. But Bratton forced unwilling, overworked and sometimes angry police captains to prepare weekly reports for his new database showing which particular types of crime were increasing or diminishing in their districts. Then they were asked—once a week—to explain what they were doing about it. The better, faster feedback from the field quickly improved performance.

His most publicized innovation was implementation of the 'broken window' policy, which directed police to crack down even on minor crimes like breaking windows, scrawling graffiti or bothering motorists. In the long run, it turned out that it contributed to reducing more serious crimes.

With innovations at all these levels, Bratton is widely credited with reducing homicides in New York by 44 percent and 'serious crime' by 25 percent in the twenty—seven months of his tenure there. He transformed the department, and is well on his way to doing the same for the Los Angeles police.

44 위 글의 Bratton에 대한 내용과 일치하지 않는 것은?

① 1994년에 뉴욕시의 경찰에 지휘하게 되었다.

② 범죄유형별 증감상황을 매주 보고하게 했다.

③ 더 빠른 현장 피드백을 통해 경찰 업무수행을 향상시켰다.

④ 유리창을 깨는 것과 같은 경범죄를 단속하도록 지시했다.

⑤ 27개월의 재임기간 중 자살과 중범죄가 각각 44%와 25% 감소했다.

45 위 글의 제목으로 가장 적절한 것은?

① How Did a New Chief Change the NYPD?

② Is Los Angeles Safe from Serious Crimes?

③ What Is the 'Broken Window' Policy?

④ How to Prevent Minor Crimes in New York

⑤ A Long Way to a Homicide—free New York

▶ 해설은 p. 35에 있습니다.

01 What is the relationship between Thomas and Sarah?

2점

> Sarah : Oh, how cute! I love that picture of Thomas when he was a baby.
>
> Carolyn : Yes, that was a fun day. I think it was his third birthday celebration. We had our family and many friends over that day.
>
> Sarah : I wish I could have been there. It seems as if I have known him my whole life.
>
> Carolyn : You have known each other for the best part of your lives. I can't really think of a time other than his childhood when you weren't around.
>
> Sarah : Yes, I have known Thomas since middle school. Well, now we have our entire lives to spend together, in sickness and in health.

① father − daughter   ② uncle − niece

③ manager − employee   ④ husband − wife

⑤ brother − sister

02 Choose the sentence that best describes the situation.

2점

> Paul : Hey John, what's on your mind? You look a little worried.
>
> John : I can't think of anything to get my sweetheart for Christmas. She is really hard to buy for, and I have no idea what she would like this year.
>
> Paul : What does she like? Does she have any hobbies or interests? What does she like to do in her spare time?
>
> John : She really likes to read, hang out with her friends, and go shopping, of course.
>
> Paul : What about getting her a gift card to one of her favorite stores? That way she can get a gift from you, but can choose what she specifically wants.
>
> John : Sounds like a great idea, but I'm not so sure about that. A gift card seems so impersonal.
>
> Paul : You could be right about a gift card being impersonal. Well, you could always resort to jewelry.

① John decided to get his girlfriend some jewelry for Christmas.

② Paul is recommending that John take a short trip to a resort.

③ John is having difficulties deciding what to buy for his girlfriend.

④ Paul's girlfriend likes to read and hang out with her mother.

⑤ John is considering breaking up with his girlfriend this Christmas.

03 Where is the dialogue most likely taking place?

Susan : Oh no! I think I left my wallet at the ticketing counter when I checked my suitcase.

Scott : What? That would be terrible to lose. When did you notice it was missing?

Susan : Just a few moments ago. Hold on, I am still checking my purse. Nope, it isn't in here. What am I going to do? I don't want to be stranded here.

Scott : Quick! Let's ask him to turn around at this upcoming exit and go back to see if it has been found. I don't think he will mind. We might have to give him an extra tip for his troubles.

Susan : I really hope it is at the counter. That is where I last had it. I have been planning this trip for a long time.

① At the car wash　　　　② In a taxi

③ At the airport counter　　④ On the sidewalk

⑤ In a restaurant

04 Which of the following is true according to the dialogue?

2점

> Herbert : Hello, your sign says there is a sale going on, and discounts can be as much as 50%.
>
> Salesman : Welcome to our store! Yes, our biggest sale of the year started today. What exactly are you looking for?
>
> Herbert : Well, I need a new winter coat. I think I take a size 38 or 40.
>
> Salesman : Great! I have just the coat for you. The outer layer is made from 100% wool. The price is regularly $400.00, but now it is discounted to just $200.00.
>
> Herbert : Well, can I try it on? (He tries on the coat.) Wow, I really like this style! Unfortunately, it is still a bit too pricey for me. Is there any chance you could decrease the price even further?
>
> Salesman : I'm sorry, but my manager has already stated all prices are final. Next week the sales tax will be increasing from 5% to 7%. If you buy the coat today, you will pay $10.00 in tax. If you wait until next week, then you will have to pay $14.00 in tax.
>
> Herbert : What time are you open until tonight? Maybe I can bring my wife in and see what she thinks.

① Herbert is looking for a coat to buy for his wife.

② The external layer of the coat is made from 100% rayon.

③ Herbert would pay $4.00 less if he bought the coat next week.

④ The salesman said his manager wouldn't discount the coat any more.

⑤ Herbert will bring his wife back next week to look at the coat.

05 Which of the following is NOT true according to the dialogue?

2점

Peter : Do you know what the weather forecast is for this weekend?

Robert : Hmm, I'm not so sure, but I heard the weatherman might be calling for rain.

Peter : Really? I hope not. I have plans to go to the beach this weekend.

Robert : Well, I hope for your sake it won't rain then.

Peter : Yes, me too. I'm planning on meeting my best friend. This is our last chance to meet before we go to university. We have been best friends since elementary school.

Robert : Maybe you should have Plan B to fall back on. That way you won't be disappointed if the weather doesn't cooperate.

Peter : I think you are right. I will call my best friend now to see what he might choose as a second option instead of the beach.

Robert : Good idea. By the way, I hear there is a new movie coming out this weekend. It is supposed to be a blockbuster.

① Robert says the weatherman is calling for rain.

② Peter is planning on going to the beach.

③ Peter is going to meet his long-time best friend.

④ Robert recommends that Peter stick to the original plan.

⑤ Robert says a new blockbuster movie will come out soon.

06 Which is the best sequence of answers for the blanks?

2점

Krista : _____

Darren : What do you have in mind? Some place tropical? How about Europe? Where have you always wanted to travel?

Krista : I would go almost anywhere. Both of those suggestions sound really nice, but I don't know if my pocketbook can handle such expensive and distant places.

Darren : Well, there are always alternatives._____

Krista : Not really. What is it?

Darren : It is a new catch phrase. It means that you stay at home on your vacation and explore local places, attractions, and restaurants that you don't normally go to. It is easy on the pocketbook and you might be surprised at what is already in your own area.

Krista : That sounds like a lot of fun, actually. I think that I will start planning my staycation for now._____

ⓐ Have you ever heard about a "staycation"?

ⓑ I can't decide where I should go on vacation this summer.

ⓒ Then the next time I have time off, I can make plans to go to a tropical island I have always dreamed of.

① ⓐ − ⓑ − ⓒ   ② ⓐ − ⓒ − ⓑ

③ ⓑ − ⓐ − ⓒ   ④ ⓑ − ⓒ − ⓐ

⑤ ⓒ − ⓑ − ⓐ

07 밑줄 친 she가 가리키는 대상이 나머지 넷과 다른 것은?

According to Deborah Tannen, different cultures have different ways of showing politeness. For example, an American woman was sitting in a booth in a railroad station cafeteria. After a while, a British couple started to settle into the opposite seat in the same booth. They unloaded their luggage; he asked what ① she would like to eat and went off to get it; she slid into the booth facing the American. And throughout all this, ② she showed no sign of having noticed that someone was already sitting in the booth. When the British woman lit up a cigarette, the American had a concrete object for her anger. ③ She began to look around for another table to move to. Of course, there was none; that's why the British couple had sat in her booth in the first place. ④ She immediately crushed out her cigarette and apologized. This showed that ⑤ she had noticed that someone else was sitting in the booth, and that she was not inclined to disturb her.

※ 다음 글에서 전체 흐름과 관계없는 문장을 고르시오. [08~09]

08

Technology seems to be inevitably linked to all aspects of human life. Computers, in particular, have dramatically influenced the way we live, and as a natural consequence, have also had an impact on pedagogical applications. ① Most of the schools and institutions in which learning takes place now have access to computers and the Internet. ② Students do their assignments using a word processor and think of the Internet as a resource for obtaining information. ③ Teachers also depend on computers when developing materials and implementing their lessons. ④ The development of computers has experienced a significant growth recently with respect to their hardware and software. ⑤ Many countries around the world provide distance learning in which most of the instruction is delivered via computers.

09

3점

It is said that accounting is the language of business. Managers use accounts of operating income and losses to see whether they are doing well and should expand, or whether they are doing badly and should contract. ① Accounting is the basis of capital decisions for another reason : Outsiders' view of the financial condition of a firm is based on its accounts. ② It is then the basis for stock prices; it is also the basis on which lenders to the firm decide what interest rate they will charge, or even whether they will lend at all. ③ Given the controversial role of accounting, we need to develop a new theory to tell us what must have been the motivation for those decisions. ④ ccounts are the basis for much of the taxation of a firm as well. ⑤ They also play a role in determining when, or whether, a firm will be declared bankrupt.

10 다음 글의 요지로 가장 적절한 것은?

2점

A lot of people like to provide care for others. They look after old people and take care of young children — but they may or may not receive money for it. Be clear about it: If you ask for a fee, you don't devalue your work; in fact, you enhance its value. If you assist a helpless person without any payment, you may create an inequality; it could imply you are strong and the other person is weak. If you allow the person to pay a reasonable sum of money, the inequality is reduced. That's good for both sides. It's wise to recognize when to receive money for your help. I hope that you will never say "I don't accept money on principle." That way you don't have to offend people who are willing to pay for your help.

① 수고에 대한 대가를 거부할 필요는 없다.
② 수고에 대한 대가를 바라면 그 일의 가치가 떨어진다.
③ 수고에 대한 대가를 지불하면 평등한 관계를 유지할 수 없다.
④ 수고에 대한 대가를 요구하는 것은 상대방에게 불쾌감을 야기한다.
⑤ 수고에 대한 대가를 바라고 노인들과 아이들을 돌보아서는 안 된다.

11

[2점]

In the 18th century, Sebastian Chamfort wrote, "The most ① wasted day is one in which we have not laughed." How many days have you wasted ② recently? When was the last time you had a really good belly-laugh? The famous editor and writer, Norman Cousins, explained in his best-seller, Anatomy of an I llness, how laughter helped him ③ overcome the pain of his severe disease. "I made the joyous discovery ④ which ten minutes of genuine belly laughter had a numbing effect and would give me at least two hours of pain-free sleep." Part of the therapy ⑤ that he designed for himself included watching Marx Brothers' movies and reading humor books.

12

[3점]

In 1881, Pasteur began studying rabies, an agonizing and deadly disease ① spread by the bite of infected animals. Pasteur and his assistant spent long hours in the laboratory, and the determination ② paid off : Pasteur developed a vaccine that prevented the development of rabies in test animals. But on July 6, 1885, the scientists were called on ③ to administer the vaccine to a small boy who had been bitten by a rabid dog. Pasteur hesitated to provide the treatment, but as the boy faced a certain and painful death from rabies, Pasteur proceeded. ④ Followed several weeks of painful injections to the stomach, the boy did not get rabies. Pasteur's treatment was a success. The curative and preventive treatments for rabies we know today ⑤ are based on Pasteur's vaccination, which has allowed officials to control the spread of the disease.

* rabies: 광견병

13

In their native land, fire ants form discrete colonies with just one or a few queen ants at the center of each. This is how most ants live, but something very (A) strange / strangely happened to the fire ants soon after they reached America. They gave up founding colonies by the traditional method of sending off flights of virgin queens, and instead (B) began / beginning producing many small queens, which spread the colony rather in the way an amoeba spreads, by establishing extensions of the original body. Astonishingly, at the same time the ants ceased to defend colony boundaries against other fire ants. With territorial boundaries (C) erasing / erased, local populations now coalesce into a single sheet of coexisting ants spread across the inhabited landscape.

	(A)	(B)	(C)
①	strange	began	erasing
②	strangely	beginning	erasing
③	strange	beginning	erased
④	strangely	beginning	erased
⑤	strange	began	erased

14

I was born one of a set of triplets. In those days, triplets were dressed in the same way, (A) given / gave the same toys, enrolled in all the same activities, and so on. People even responded to us not as individuals, but as a set. No matter how good we three were in school, I quickly learned that whether I tried or not, we would always get C's. One of us may have earned an A and the (B) other / others F's, but the teachers always confused us, so it was safer to give all of us C's. Sometimes when I would sit on my father's lap, I knew he did not know which one I was. Can you imagine what this does to your identity? Nowadays, we know how important it is to recognize the individual, to recognize how different each of us is. These days, when multiple births have become routine, parents have learned not to dress and treat their kids (C) alike / like.

	(A)	(B)	(C)
①	given	other	alike
②	gave	others	like
③	given	others	like
④	gave	other	like
⑤	given	others	alike

※ 다음 글을 읽고, 빈칸에 가장 적절한 것을 고르시오. [15~19]

15

2점

In the old days, before cash registers became a staple in almost every store, merchants used to add up the bill by writing the price of each item on the outside of the bag. When customers phoned in orders, however, some merchants — whether by accident or by design — wrote the address or apartment number at the top of the bag and then added that number into the total as well. The introduction of this irrelevant information is a(n)_____ error. A publisher who accidently printed Hamlet's monologue as, "To be sure, or not to be believed, that is their question..." would be charged with a similar error.

① repetition   ② insertion

③ substitution   ④ transposition

⑤ omission

16

2점

When you were a child and your mother greeted you at the door with her arms foldedacross her chest, her foot tapping, her brow furrowed, and her lips in a straight line, you probably said to yourself: "Mom's angry." She didn't have to say a word. We sense when someone seems sullen, or nervous, or happy, or any other mood because that's how he or she looks. However, looks can be_____. Just as a small baby's frown may be mistaken for a smile, the same is true with adults. A nervous laugh is not a sign of amusement. Tears may flow from disappointment or happiness. Some people are more open about what they are thinking than others. They wear their hearts on their sleeves. But others are not as obvious — or not obvious all the time.

① convincing ② deceiving

③ positive ④ penetrating

⑤ straightforward

17

2점

Businesspeople make decisions with fundamental uncertainty about the future. In his book, Risk, Uncertainty and Probability, Frank Knight made a distinction between economists' concept of risk and the different sort of uncertainty in almost all business decisions. Risk, he said, refers to something that can be measured by mathematical probabilities. In contrast, uncertainty refers to something that cannot be measured because there are no objective standards to express probabilities. Theoretical economists have been struggling ever since to make sense of how people handle such true uncertainty. Jack Welch's phrase "straight from the gut" sums up their efforts: Decisions that matter for investment are _____. That intuition is a social process that follows the laws of psychology—and in particular, since group decisions are being made, social psychology.

① tested beforehand

② important steps forward

③ strategic and psychological

④ based on logical thinking

⑤ intuitive rather than analytical

18

2점

Contrary to popular perception, leaders are not people who are always certain of themselves and their direction. Rather, leaders are people who _____. What's more, they are not afraid to let others see them in this light. In fact, creating an environment in which learning and its natural by-product, mistakes, are okay can be a potent tool to unite a group and inspire creativity, risk-taking, and effort. Today, those who practice leadership must be open to learning about their colleagues and followers. That includes their differences in personality and work styles, their lifestyle as it affects their effort, and the interplay of such factors as age, race, religion, and gender. No one can be expected to grasp all the implications of such a wide range of differences, so leaders especially must show they are willing and able to learn.

① are open-minded learners   ② are unconditionally sacrificial
③ know what they are doing   ④ always maintain a strict attitude
⑤ take on important responsibilities

19

3점

Peoples in prehistoric times, children, and even animals with a certain degree of intelligence have demonstrated that one _____ to use artificially contrived symbols to represent objects, actions, quantities, or other aspects of reality. To both primitive and sophisticated peoples, an arrow indicates a particular direction, while a cairn marks a certain location. Holding two fingers up can mean two crayons, two tickets to the movies, or two sodas. Similarly, on an abacus, each bead represents whatever is being counted or calculated. More abstract symbols require a greater degree of sophistication and intelligence. Yet we recognized and made some primitive use of numerals long before we knew how to perform simple arithmetic. We familiarize ourselves with the basic symbols before we can begin to master the infinite range of possible meanings created by combining them.

* cairn: 돌무덤

① doesn't need to be literate
② should be familiar with mapping
③ doesn't need to deny reality
④ should look closely at the mental processes
⑤ should be able to perform simple arithmetic

2점

In the 17th century, the philosopher Benedict de Spinoza engaged in his own mid-life repacking. He began by considering the efforts involved in ① <u>pursuing</u> what most people esteemed as the highest good — riches, fame, and the pleasure of the senses. Spinoza ② <u>concluded</u> that, while these had their attractions, they could never provide him with the authentic happiness for which he was searching. He made a great discovery, which he phrased as follows: "Happiness or unhappiness is made wholly to depend on the ③ <u>quantity</u> of the object which we love." If we love transient attractions and values, our happiness will be ④ <u>fleeting</u> and transitory as well. On the other hand, if we seek to fix our love to longer-lasting values, our happiness likewise tends to ⑤ <u>persevere</u>.

21 다음 글의 빈칸 (A), (B)에 들어갈 말로 가장 적절한 것은?

3점

When my children were very young, I read them the book Winnie-the-Pooh by A. A. Milne. The story evokes a childlike view of nature as enchanted, animated by _____(A)_____ . Early in the book, Winnie-the-Pooh is walking into the forest and comes to a large oak tree. From the top of the tree, "there came a loud buzzing-noise." Winnie-the-Pooh sat down at the foot of the tree, put his head between his paws and began to think. First of all, he said to himself:"That buzzing-noise means something. You don't get a buzzing-noise like that, just buzzing and buzzing, without its meaning something. If there's a buzzing-noise, somebody's making a buzzing-noise, and the only reason for making a buzzing-noise that I know of is because you're a bee." Then he thought another long time, and said: "And the only reason for being a bee that I know of is making honey." And then he got up, and said: "And the only reason for making honey is so as I can eat it." So he began to _____(B)_____ .

	(A)	(B)
①	birth and growth	taste the honey
②	wonder and miracle	listen to a song
③	method and process	make honey
④	meaning and purpose	climb the tree
⑤	disorder and irregularity	dig the earth

22 다음 글에서 필자가 주장하는 바로 가장 적절한 것은?

2점

Recently, the case of a power blogger reveals the ugly side of online pundits. A total of 4,983 people staged a cyber protest against an online homemaking pundit, calling for an apology and compensation for the blogger's public deception. This incident brought light into the extent of the professional bloggers' powers and responsibilities. In a survey, online media, including blog posts, placed second in credibility ranking after TV broadcasters. This suggests that they are rapidly replacing the old media and their influence has grown among tech savvy people. These bloggers do not just entertain readers. They affect people's shopping patterns and create promotional effects. Online Today reported that these power bloggers could create 10 times more promotional effects than conventional media advertisements. Now, it's time the society came up with ways to wage responsibilities on bloggers' conducting businesses as much as any other online businessman. We should first think of ways to make them responsible for their articles and deeds.

① 영향력 있는 블로거들을 이용한 간접적인 정치 활동을 규제해야 한다.
② 블로거들의 상업 활동과 일반 사업자들의 활동을 엄격히 구별해야 한다.
③ 블로거들이 적절한 이익을 창출할 수 있는 제도적 기반을 마련해야한다.
④ 영향력 있는 블로거들의 상업적인 활동에 과도한 책임을 부과해서는 안 된다.
⑤ 블로거들이 온라인에서의 자신의 활동에 책임지게 하는 방안을 강구해야 한다.

※ (A), (B), (C)의 각 네모 안에서 문맥에 맞는 표현으로 가장 적절한 것을 고르시오. [23~24]

23

3점

The decline in death rates, which has meant an overall increase in the world population, (A) [brought under / brought about] the birth control movement. Scientific advances during the eighteenth and nineteenth centuries (B) [resulted from / resulted in] better food supplies, the control of diseases, and safer work environments for those living in developed countries. These improvements combined with progress in medicine to save and prolong human lives. During the 1800s, the birth rate, which in earlier times had been (C) [added to / offset by] the death rate, became a concern to many who worried that population growth would outstrip the planet's ability to provide adequate resources to sustain life.

	(A)	(B)	(C)
①	brought under	resulted from	added to
②	brought about	resulted in	added to
③	brought under	resulted in	offset by
④	brought about	resulted in	offset by
⑤	brought under	resulted from	offset by

24

Certain actions may (A) inquire / require our full conscious attention as we learn them, but eventually they become so routine and automatic that we can safely engage in other activities at the same time. For example, after mastering the essential skills, we can drive a car while talking or listening to music. But we actually attend to such skills very little while performing them. Only when something (B) disrupts / erupts the normal routine do we return the focus of our attention to the now automatic task. Also, the first thing most people do when they realize they've gotten lost is to turn off the car radio. It's as if the radio waves have (C) disclosed / distorted our ability to concentrate on the road. Our conscious attention is limited to one task at a time.

	(A)	(B)	(C)
①	inquire	disrupts	disclosed
②	inquire	erupts	distorted
③	require	disrupts	disclosed
④	require	erupts	distorted
⑤	require	disrupts	distorted

※ 다음 글의 제목으로 가장 적절한 것을 고르시오. [25~26]

25

3점

Whether we think someone has "good luck" or "bad luck," in the end all so-called luck comes down to probability. It's tempting to interpret the outcomes of probability in such a way that it seems something was "meant to happen," but the truth is that winning the lottery or taking a direct hit from a hurricane are statistically explainable events regardless of how pleasant or horrific they are to experience. This is tough to accept, particularly for the human brain that craves certainty. Knowing that probability underlies everything we do does not necessarily make the outcomes any easier to swallow, but there is satisfaction in accepting the truth as it is without a veneer of mystification.

① Make Peace with Probability
② Good Luck Is Always Pleasing
③ Hurricanes : Horrific Experiences
④ Randomness : Obstacles to Solving Problems
⑤ Differences Between Statistics and Probability

26

2점

Time passes at different rates depending on whether you are standing still or moving. Time runs differently if you take a trip on a spaceship or even a plane or subway. In 1975, the navy did an experiment using two identical clocks; they placed one on the ground and the other in a plane. For fifteen hours the plane flew while lasers were sent between two clocks comparing time. The result proved that the time was slower in the moving plane. Time is also dependent on perception. Imagine a man and a woman watching the exact same movie together, except she loves the film while he hates it. For her, the movie ends too soon. For him, it lasts forever. They both agree that the movie started at 7 P.M., and that the final credits rolled at 8:57 P.M. But they don't agree on the experience of that one hour and fifty-seven minutes. In a tangible way, one person's time is not another's.

① Time and Human Relations
② Time in the Observatory
③ Time in Virtual Reality
④ How to Control Time
⑤ Relativity of Time

※ 글의 흐름으로 보아, 주어진 문장이 들어가기에 가장 적절한 곳을 고르시오. [27~28]

27

2점

This means that water stays in the soil longer and that plants can survive during extended dry periods.

Compost is an organic substance which can be added to garden soil or dirt to improve its overall quality. It is beneficial in several ways. First, adding compost to garden soil makes plants healthier. (①) This is because compost contains nutrients which are extremely important and act as food for the plants. (②) In addition, soil with compost added to it retains water for a longer period of time. (③) Another benefit of compost is that it reduces the amount of garbage that a household needs to get rid of. (④) Twenty-four percent of household trash in the United States is made up of organic material which can be composted instead of being thrown away. (⑤) This includes such items as used coffee grounds, banana peels, and old newspapers. When these items are composted instead of being put in the trash, it benefits the entire community.

28

2점

Communications satellites carry TV programs and telephone messages around the world.

Hundreds of satellites circle the Earth in space. They are launched into space by rockets and may stay there for ten years or more. These satellites each have their own job to do such as looking at the Earth, or the weather, or out into space. Weather satellites help the forecasters tell us what the weather will be like. (①) Those satellites can see where the clouds are forming and which way they are going. They watch the winds and rain and measure how hot the air and the ground are. (②) These let us talk to people on the other side of the world and watch events while they are happening in faraway countries. (③) Earth-watching satellites look out for pollution. Oil slicks in the sea and dirty air over cities show up clearly in pictures from these satellites. (④) They can help farmers by watching how well crops are growing and by looking for pests and diseases. Satellite telescopes let astronomers look far out into the universe and discover what is out there. (⑤) They can also tell astronomers where there may be a black hole.

29 다음 글의 내용과 일치하지 않는 것은?

[2점]

Here's a strong incentive for everyone who is overweight: Losing weight can immediately reduce your risk of suffering a heart attack or stroke. It's the first thing to do if your blood cholesterol level is high. However, don't lose so much so fast that you just gain it back. Research suggests that if your weight fluctuates more than ten pounds, up or down, you can double your risk of dying from heart disease. If you are overweight, you're more likely to have heart disease, diabetes, and high blood pressure, all of which make a stroke more likely. Yet, how your weight is distributed seems to be even more important than what your weight is. People who are apple-shaped (body fat concentrated in their stomach area) have double the risk of stroke than those who are pear-shaped (body fat in their hips and thighs). However, regardless of one's body shape, researchers have discovered that being overweight carries more of a stroke risk for women than for men.

① 몸무게가 10파운드 이상 오르내리면 심장병으로 사망할 위험이 두 배로 커진다.
② 심장병, 당뇨병, 고혈압은 뇌졸중을 일으킬 가능성을 높인다.
③ 몸무게의 분포보다는 몸무게 자체가 훨씬 더 중요하다.
④ 사과모양의 체형을 가진 사람이 배모양의 체형을 가진 사람보다 뇌졸중 위험이 두 배 크다.
⑤ 체형에 관계없이 비만인 여자가 비만인 남자보다 뇌졸중 위험이 더 높다.

30 다음 글이 함축하는 바로 가장 적절한 것은?

[3점]

Human mobility tracking and modeling has great potential to improve the lives of people but could be used for more controversial purposes. These days, whether or not researchers, corporations, and governments are able to acquire and benefit from knowledge about our individual locations and movements is largely up to us. In a sense, we all choose to allow these parties to gather information about us. By opting to use the mobile technologies and apps that enable our locations and movements to be recorded, we are agreeing, either explicitly or implicitly, to allow others to benefit from our personal information. Once we have lost ownership of our location information, another party may, within the boundaries of the law, use or sell that information for profit without our permission. While for now we might take some comfort in knowing we can flip the switch to "off," the increasingly ubiquitous nature of mobile computing technologies implies they will soon become difficult to avoid.

① We may have to give up at least some of our privacy in order to benefit from mobile computing technologies.

② The future of mobile computing technologies will depend on how we as a society collectively assess their financial costs.

③ Human mobility tracking and modeling yields great benefits for mankind and influences all of our lives in positive ways.

④ At present, human mobility tracking and modeling doesn't provide any information about individual human locations and movements.

⑤ Direct government regulation of private-sector human mobility tracking could impede many efforts in this area that are being directed at genuinely altruistic ends.

※ 다음 글의 주제로 가장 적절한 것을 고르시오. [31~32]

31

2점

For many years, there were only two types of fillings available — amalgam (a compound of zinc, copper, tin, silver and mercury) and gold. However, advances in plastics technology have yielded some excellent alternatives to these old standbys. The best material for fillings is indisputably gold. However, it can cost as much as ten times more to fill a tooth with gold than with amalgam or a plastic composite. Gold fillings can last up to 20 years — much longer than the others. Although there have been inconclusive studies questioning the safety of amalgam fillings (because of their mercury content), most dentists still swear by them because of their relative durability, their ease of installation, and their low cost. The American Dental Association also remains committed to their position that the material is safe. Perhaps because of the amalgam controversy, plastic composite fillings are gaining popularity. They also confer the advantage of being tooth-colored, rendering them practically invisible. Ongoing research may improve their future durability and ease of installation.

① the stuff that fillings are made of

② the reason why fillings are invented

③ the comparison of the prices of fillings

④ the importance of the durability of fillings

⑤ the process of installing various types of fillings

32

Salaries should be directly related to both the level of job the employees have and how well they are performing their responsibilities. All job assignments can be performed at different levels of effectiveness, productivity, and quality, so it is only logical that each job should have a salary range associated with it. The employee that puts out large quantities of work at high quality levels should be paid more than the employee that just meets the minimum standards and frequently makes errors. The yearly performance evaluation provides an ideal way to relate the employees' salaries to their performance. By relating the individual's performance evaluation to the quality of output and then by relating performance level directly to salary, you have provided a financial incentive to the individual.

① adjustment of salary by performance level
② clarification of work description and standards
③ examples of employees' duties and responsibilities
④ methods of distinguishing performance from output
⑤ advantages of paying equal salary regardless of efforts

33 다음 글이 시사하는 바로 가장 적절한 것은?

Biologists often talk about the "ecology" of an organism: The tallest oak in the forest is the tallest not just because it grew from the hardiest acorn; it is the tallest also because no other trees blocked its sunlight, the soil around it was rich, no rabbit chewed through its bark, and no lumberjack cut it down before it matured. Figuratively speaking, we all could suppose that successful people come from hardy seeds. But do we know enough about the sunlight that warmed them, the soil in which they put down the roots, and the rabbits and lumberjacks they were lucky enough to avoid? The people who stand before kings may look like they did it all by themselves. But in fact, they are invariably beneficiary of hidden advantages and extraordinary opportunities and cultural legacies that allow them to learn and work hard and make sense of the world in ways others cannot.

① Success comes through disadvantages.

② Heroes are born in difficult circumstances.

③ Brilliance and insight are the keys to success.

④ Success is only associated with individual efforts.

⑤ Success stems from the accumulation of advantages.

34 다음 도표의 내용과 일치하지 않는 것은?

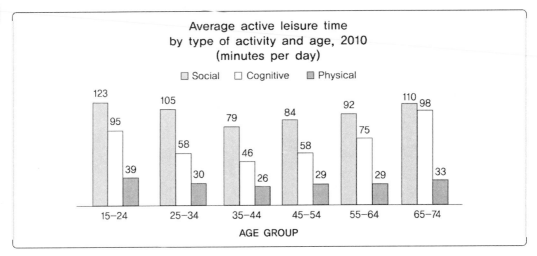

The graph above shows average active leisure time by type of activity and age. ① People aged 15-24 spent more time on active leisure activities than did those in the other age groups while the 35-44 age group spent the least amount of time on active leisure. ② The average amount of time spent per day on active leisure tended to decrease until age 45, then increased again after that point. ③ Those aged 15-24 spent much of their active leisure time on social activities, and they also spent more time on physical leisure activities than did those in the other age groups. ④ Those aged 65-74 spent 31 more minutes per day on cognitive leisure activities than did those between the ages of 35-44. ⑤ Time spent on cognitive leisure tended to increase after age 45 and increased most dramatically in the 65-74 age group.

※ 주어진 글 다음에 이어질 글의 순서로 가장 적절한 것을 고르시오. [35~36]

35

2점

Many adolescents will gradually shift from what Jean Piaget called concrete operational thinking to formal operations, which includes among others, the ability to truly hypothesize and the ability to empathize with others at a much deeper level.

(A) Parents who recognize this emerging autonomous question as a sign that their teenagers are healthy, normal and "right on schedule" will rejoice and feel relief, even if they find their adolescent's challenges exasperating at times.

(B) Part of this transformation is the crucial need to question and wonder, and especially to question many of the values and beliefs that we were given in childhood. In other words, not only is it normal, it is also essential for teenagers to ask things like "Can a truly good person feel hatred?"

(C) On the contrary, parents who don't understand that this is healthy and normal may find themselves anxious about it, which may cause them to try to control or even prevent this exciting milestone, resulting in unfortunate consequences.

① (A) — (B) — (C) 　　② (B) — (A) — (C)

③ (B) — (C) — (A) 　　④ (C) — (A) — (B)

⑤ (C) — (B) — (A)

36

3점

You might think that as there are more pedestrians or cyclists on a street, the more chances there are for them to be hit. You are right.

(A) In other words, as the number of pedestrians or cyclists increases, the fatality rates per capita begin to drop. The reason is not that pedestrians begin to act more safely when surrounded by more fellow pedestrians. In fact, the opposite is true.

(B) More pedestrians are injured or killed by cars in New York City than anywhere else in the United States. But Peter Jacobsen, a public-health consultant in California, found that these relationships are not linear.

(C) It is the behavior of drivers that changes. They are suddenly seeing pedestrians everywhere. The more they see, the slower they drive; and, in a neatly perpetuating cycle, the more slowly they drive, the more pedestrians they effactually see because those pedestrians stay within sight for a longer period.

① (A) − (C) − (B) 　　　② (B) − (A) − (C)

③ (B) − (C) − (A) 　　　④ (C) − (A) − (B)

⑤ (C) − (B) − (A)

37 다음 글의 내용을 한 문장으로 요약하고자 한다. 빈칸 (A)와 (B)에 들어갈 말로 가장 적절한 것은?

> Psychologists designed an interesting experiment. At the start of this experiment, they asked some of the participants to answer the following question: If a company bought 15 computers at $1,200 each, then, by your calculation, how much did the company pay in total? This was not a mathematical question; its goal was to prime the participants in a more calculating way. The other participants were asked a question that would prime their emotions. After answering the questions, the participants were given the information either about an African girl's sad story as an individual or about the general problem of food shortage in Africa. Then they were asked how much money they would donate to the given cause. The result showed that those who were primed to feel emotion gave much more money to the African girl than to help fight the general food shortage. And those who thought in a more calculating way became equal-opportunity misers by giving a similarly small amount to both causes.

> According to the experiment, the participants who were primed to feel emotion became more _____(A)_____ than those who thought in a more ____(B)____ way.

	(A)	(B)
①	doubtful	empathic
②	altruistic	calculating
③	sentimental	conservative
④	prudent	rational
⑤	conscientious	generous

※ 다음 글을 읽고 물음에 답하시오. [38~39]

Martin stood in front of the assembled crowd. He was about to give a talk to a sympathetic and anticipating audience of prospective clients who wanted to choose the most suitable architectural firm for a large construction project. Martin was one of the architectural firm's key designers, and he needed to convince his audience that they were in good hands with his firm and that he understood the job and the needs of the client better than anyone else they had invited to bid so far.

Yet, when he started to speak, thanking the audience for the opportunity to present to them and telling them that he was excited to share his firm's vision with them, ___. There was no sign of joy, nor was there even a hint of excitement or any other positive emotion on his face. His words were in sharp contrast to the emotions he felt and portrayed. Martin felt as if his facial muscles were frozen in place. Unable to force a smile during his introduction or even a neutral relaxed facial expression, he looked tense, uncomfortable, and anxious.

38 위 글의 Martin에 대한 내용과 일치하지 않는 것은?

[2점]
① 가장 적합한 건축회사를 선택하려는 청중 앞에 서 있었다.
② 한 건축회사의 핵심 디자이너중의 한 명이었다.
③ 자신이 고객의 요구를 가장 잘 안다고 설득할 필요가 있었다.
④ 발표할 기회를 준 것에 대해 청중에게 감사했다.
⑤ 긴장되고 불안했지만 청중에게 환한 미소를 지어 주었다.

39 위 글의 빈칸에 들어갈 말로 가장 적절한 것은?

[2점]
① his face betrayed him
② he felt greatly relieved
③ his eyes twinkled brightly
④ he had his fingers crossed
⑤ he held his head very high

※ 다음 글을 읽고 물음에 답하시오. [40~41]

Marine biologists are often frustrated by how hard it is to actually see what is going on in the ocean. Observing the complex behavior of large marine animals like seals, sea lions, and whales has always been a problem. As we know, (a) <u>they</u> move too fast, and too far, for a human diver, much less a stationary camera, to possibly record their behavior. Even if people could somehow keep up with them, (b) <u>they</u> would almost certainly be a disruptive presence, and the animals would be unlikely to behave normally. So, why not let the animals themselves take the pictures? This is the idea behind "Crittercam," a compact, streamlined, underwater video camera that can be attached to these animals. Our knowledge of these animals' behavior once came almost entirely from watching (c) <u>them</u> on land and at the surface. Crittercam lets us observe them underwater, where (d) <u>they</u> spend most of their time. This has given us new, and constantly growing, insight into what (e) <u>they</u> do underwater. Recently, for example, Crittercam recorded the first underwater views of humpback whales using curtains of bubbles to herd schools of herring into a tight ball before rocketing into the school to feed. It is giving us revealing new glimpses of life in the ocean.

40 밑줄 친 (a)~(e) 중에서, 가리키는 대상이 나머지 넷과 다른 것은?

 2점

① (a)　　　　　　　　② (b)

③ (c)　　　　　　　　④ (d)

⑤ (e)

41 "Crittercam"에 대한 설명으로 적절하지 않은 것은?

3점

① It is a compact, streamlined video camera which is operated underwater by a human diver.

② It reduces the risk of disrupting marine animals like seals, sea lions, and whales, so it can record their normal behavior underwater.

③ It provides us with new, and constantly increasing, insight into the lives of marine animals.

④ It can record the complex behavior of marine animals more easily than a stationary camera.

⑤ It was able to record the sight of humpback whales which drove schools of herring into a ball before eating.

※ 다음 글을 읽고 물음에 답하시오. [42~43]

(A)

The idea for Arbor Day started in Nebraska in the 1800s. This special day got its name from arbor, a word that means tree in several different languages. In those days, Nebraska, a state in the middle part of the US, had very few trees. People who moved to Nebraska from other states were unhappy because they liked to see trees and have them around their homes, parks, and fields.

(B)

Because Morton and his wife wanted to be an example for everyone, they began to plant large numbers of trees on their own land. Morton also wrote articles about trees for the newspaper where he worked. People became very interested in his ideas and began to realize how important trees were.

(C)

Soon after he started writing his articles, people in Nebraska began to plant trees. By the1870s Nebraska had more than one million trees. Morton was very proud to know that his ideas helped. He was also very proud in 1872 when people chose April 22, his birthday, to be Arbor Day in the US.

(D)

Among the people who moved to Nebraska were a man and his wife from the state of Michigan, a state in the northern part of the US. Mr. and Mrs. Sterling Morton loved the outdoors and appreciated the importance of trees. They saw that Nebraska needed to have trees for a better future.

42 위 글 (A)에 이어질 내용을 순서에 맞게 배열한 것으로 가장 적절한 것은?

2점

① (B) − (C) − (D)
② (B) − (D) − (C)
③ (C) − (B) − (D)
④ (C) − (D) − (B)
⑤ (D) − (B) − (C)

43 위 글의 Morton씨에 대한 내용으로 일치하지 않는 것은?

[2점]
① 모두에게 본보기가 되려고 공원에 많은 나무를 심었다.
② 자신이 일하는 신문사에 나무에 관한 글을 기고했다.
③ 그의 생각에 사람들이 흥미를 갖고 나무의 중요성을 인식하기 시작했다.
④ 자신의 생일이 미국의 식목일로 선정된 것을 자랑스럽게 여겼다.
⑤ 네브래스카의 더 나은 미래를 위해 나무가 필요하다고 생각했다.

◈ 다음 글을 읽고 물음에 답하시오. [44~45]

As the term drew to a close, Deborah Ball was overall pleased with the progress being made by her third-grade math class. But this afternoon, as the clock ticked toward the end of the day, she had a problem.

It started when Nancy, a small blond girl, noticed that the larger the number on top of a fraction, the bigger the piece you'll end up with. Ms. Ball asked the class to figure out if Nancy's conjecture was right. One student suggested 4/4 and 5/5. Ms. Ball could simply have told the class that these two fractions were the same. But instead, she had the students draw two rectangles in their notebooks, one divided into four parts and the other into five, and then shade in the numerators.

She was confident that everyone would soon realize that 5/5 did not have a bigger piece shaded in. But when she asked the students, she was astonished. Cassandra, a tall girl, said they were different numbers.

For Ms. Ball to figure out what to do at this moment clearly demanded some knowledge of math. But it demanded something more. In order to teach the students, it was not good enough that Ms. Ball understood math for herself. She thought about the hows and whys of correcting students, and about whether she should ask them to figure it out or tell them the correct answer. Finally, she decided to lean toward the position of John Dewey, who believed that students could only learn if teachers encouraged them to practice working things out.

She pulled out two envelopes, turned them into imaginary cookies, and cut one into four and one into five. She and the students talked about pieces and taped the pieces back together. At the end of the class, still the disagreement was not extinguished, but she could teach students to think mathematically and reason for themselves.

44 위 글의 제목으로 가장 적절한 것은?

2점 ① How to Use Drawings in Math

② Be a Professional Mathematician

③ Encourage Students to Learn by Doing

④ Over-learning Leads to Hate-for-learning

⑤ Reasons Why Students Feel Math Is Difficult

45 위 글의 Ms. Ball에 대한 내용과 일치하지 않는 것은?

2점 ① 3학년 학생들의 수학 실력이 향상된 것에 대체로 만족했다.

② 칠판에 사각형을 직접 그려 두개의 분수값이 같음을 설명했다.

③ 학생들이 스스로 문제를 해결하게 할지, 정답을 말해줄지 고민했다.

④ 존 듀이의 학습에 대한 견해를 따르기로 결정했다.

⑤ 분수를 이해시키기 위해 두 개의 봉투를 이용하였다.

04 | 2014학년도 영어영역

▶ 해설은 p. 48에 있습니다.

01 Based on the following dialogue, which one is NOT true?

[2점]

> Sarah : I know we made plans to go to the park today, but it's freezing. How about catching a movie?
>
> Megan : Great idea! I heard a new horror movie just came out last week.
>
> Sarah : I might throw up if I watch something too gruesome. You'd better go with somebody else.
>
> Megan : I'll call Jim later. He would like it. But for today, it's all up to you. What are you in the mood for?
>
> Sarah : My favorite actor just made a film about figure skating. Let's check it out.

① The weather is uncomfortably cold outside.

② Sarah and Megan will change their original plans for today.

③ Sarah can't stand scary movies.

④ Sarah is sick and feels like throwing up.

⑤ Jim would enjoy watching horror movies.

02 Which is the best sequence of answers for the blanks?

[2점]

Karen : I really appreciate the opportunity to interview with your company.

Interviewer : Thank you for coming. _____ First of all, what kind of experience do you have in advertising?

Karen : _____ I just completed a two-week internship producing TV commercials. But before that, I mostly worked in childcare and education.

Interviewer : Tell me more about that. Do you think your childcare background will be useful in an advertising career?

Karen : Absolutely! Young people are a valuable demographic for advertisers, so it is important to understand their thoughts and opinions.

Interviewer : _____ I have two children, and they are always asking me to buy the new electronics that they saw on TV.

ⓐ I couldn't agree more.

ⓑ Actually, I'm relatively new to this field.

ⓒ I have extensive qualifications.

ⓓ I'd like to start with some basic questions.

① ⓑ – ⓓ – ⓒ   ② ⓒ – ⓐ – ⓑ

③ ⓒ – ⓑ – ⓓ   ④ ⓓ – ⓑ – ⓐ

⑤ ⓓ – ⓒ – ⓐ

03 Where is the dialogue most likely taking place?

> Gina : How did you get involved with helping out here?
> Suzie : There are two answers, actually. First, my university encourages us to support local educational and cultural centers.
> Gina : What drew you here specifically?
> Suzie : That's the second answer! When he was my age, my great-grandfather was drafted to fight overseas. He already passed away, but I've poured over all of his old journals, and being involved here is another way to connect with his combat experiences. I felt like I stepped into his shoes when I set up the latest exhibition of wartime memorabilia here.
> Gina : It's a fitting tribute to the brave sacrifices of those in uniform. And I have to say, I'm blown away by how informative your tour has been. I'd love to return the favor some time by showing you around my gallery. Here's my card.

① at an art auction
② at a recreation center
③ in a military museum
④ in a student volunteer office
⑤ in a second-hand charity shop

04 Based on the following dialogue, which one is true?

> Roger : Can I see your notes? I still don't get what Professor Willis was trying to explain about artwork from the Romantic period.
> Molly : I was absent that day, remember? I had to catch up on that class afterward with Hannah in the study center, so I don't have any notes from that lecture.
> Roger : Oh no! The one thing I can't figure out is the one thing you missed out on, too.
> Molly : Don't freak out. Professor Willis always talks straight from the text, so if you just look over that chapter again then the test will be a breeze.
> Roger : Umm... I don't have the book, either. The price of the new edition was very exorbitant, so I figured I could just save a few bucks and rely on the lectures.

① Molly has perfect attendance.
② Molly has done additional makeup work outside of class.
③ Professor Willis often deviates from the book.
④ The class textbook is affordable for Roger.
⑤ Roger is thoroughly prepared for the exam.

05 Choose the best answer for the blank.

[3점]

> Professor : Hi, Pierre. Thanks for stopping by my office. What can I help you with today?
>
> Pierre : Well, I'm a little embarrassed to be here, but I'd like to discuss my grade. Frankly, I was pretty confused and disappointed with my final score in your history class. Is there any way for me to bring it up?
>
> Professor : In order to be fair to all students, my rules are inflexible. You did well on the exam, but you missed nearly half of the lectures. Attendance and participation are 30% of your grade. Also, you submitted your presentation report two weeks after the due date.
>
> Pierre : How about if I turn in an extra credit essay? I know the deadline was last week, but can't you give me some leeway?
>
> Professor : _____

① I don't mind. Punctuality isn't very important to me.

② Just this once, since you always showed up to class.

③ It's out of the question due to your dreadful exam score.

④ That won't be necessary. I'll make the changes right away.

⑤ You missed your chance. I'm afraid I never make exceptions.

06 Choose the sentence that best describes the situation.

[2점]

> Anthony : Hey, mister, watch where you're going!
>
> Bert : I'm terribly sorry. I didn't mean to bump into you.
>
> Anthony : Yeah, right! I bet you're one of those pickpockets I've heard so much about. Everybody back home warned me about people like you before I moved to New York.
>
> Bert : It really was an honest mistake.
>
> Anthony : Well, luckily for you, my wallet is still in my pocket. But if I ever see you around this neighborhood again, I'm going to call the cops.

① Anthony believes Bert is a thief.

② Anthony is being scolded by Bert.

③ Anthony is speaking with a police officer.

④ Anthony has recovered his missing wallet.

⑤ Anthony wants Bert's advice about living in New York.

07 밑줄 친 he[his]가 가리키는 대상이 나머지 넷과 다른 것은?

Regarded as perhaps the greatest composer of all time, Johann Sebastian Bach was known during his lifetime primarily as an outstanding organ player and technician. The youngest of eight children born to musical parents, ① he was destined to become a musician. While still young, he had mastered the organ and violin, and was also an excellent singer. At the age of ten, both of ② his parents died within a year of each other. His older brother, Johann Christoph, took in Johann Sebastian, and ③ he most likely continued his younger brother's musical training. At the age of fifteen, Bach secured ④ his first position in the choir of St. Michael's School in Luneburg. He traveled little, never leaving Germany once in his life, but held various positions during ⑤ his career in churches and in the service of the courts throughout the country.

※ 다음 글에서 전체 흐름과 관계없는 문장을 고르시오. [08~09]

08

The literature of an oppressed people reflects the conscience of man, and nowhere is this seen with more intense clarity than in the literature of African — Americans. ① An essential element of African-American literature is that the literature as a whole — not the work of occasional authors — is a movement against concrete wickedness. ② In African-American literature, accordingly, there is a grief rarely to be found elsewhere in American literature, and frequently a rage rarely to be found in other American letters. ③ Whenever an African-American author picks up a pen, his target is likely to be American racism, his subject the suffering of his people, and the core element his own grief and the grief of his people. ④ Some authors fall in line with the non-violent "love thy neighbor" approach of prominent African-American leader Martin Luther King, Jr. ⑤ Almost all of African-American literature carries the burden of protest.

09

[3점]

Layers of sediment are laid down over time, and build up to fill the valleys and seas until they form a sequence of rocks. ① The oldest rocks are always at the bottom, unless the beds of rock have been overturned, such as by folding or faulting. ② When there is too much molten lava under the earth or in a volcano, molten rock is forced through the layers of sediment. ③ These are known as igneous intrusions and they harden into volcanic dikes that cut through many layers of sedimentary rock. ④ Marble may begin as limestone and be changed by pressure from adjacent layers and heat from molten rock flow or a magma chamber. ⑤ Therefore, where an igneous intrusion cuts through a sequence of sedimentary rock, it is always more recent than the surrounding layers.

* igneous intrusion : 화성관입(火成貫入)

10 다음 글의 요지로 가장 적절한 것은?

[2점]

A French manufacturer of automotive accessories kept urging the German managing director of its subsidiary in Germany to advertise their product on German television. The German manager resisted for two reasons: he knew the target audience watched little television and the product was new in Germany. He suggested print ads instead. Finally, he gave in to the constant pressure from the Paris home office, but he decided to run a controlled test by advertising in four different media — television, radio, billboards, and print ads — simultaneously. The print ads were far and away the most effective. Why? Print ads permitted the company to describe in great detail the many features of the new product and to back up the description with the almost encyclopedic details that appealed to German consumers, who would otherwise have been skeptical because of its newness.

① 허위 광고에 대해서는 엄하게 처벌할 필요가 있다.
② 광고 제작에 첨단 기술을 적극 활용하는 것이 바람직하다.
③ 상품 광고는 방송 매체를 통해 이루어지는 것이 효과적이다.
④ 광고비용을 제한하여 상품의 가격을 낮추려는 노력이 필요하다.
⑤ 목표로 하는 소비자의 성향에 맞는 광고 전략을 세우는 것이 중요하다.

※ 다음 글의 밑줄 친 부분 중, 어법상 틀린 것을 고르시오. [11~12]

11

Satellite imaging has been used ① <u>to match</u> water temperature swirls drawn on a map of ocean currents made as long ago as 1539. The map was produced by a Swedish cartographer, Olaus Magnus. It had been thought that the rounded swirls, located between pictures of serpents and sea monsters, ② <u>was</u> there for purely artistic reasons. However, the size, shape, and location of the swirls matches changes in water temperature too ③ <u>closely</u> for this to be a coincidence. The map is likely to be an accurate representation of the ocean eddy current ④ <u>found</u> to the south and east of Iceland. It ⑤ <u>is believed</u> that the map-maker collected his information from German mariners of the Hanseatic League.

12

For decades, the Atlantic Ocean's ① <u>fabled</u> Bermuda Triangle has seized the human imagination with unexplained disappearances of ships, planes, and people. Some speculate that unknown and mysterious forces account for the disappearances, such as extraterrestrials ② <u>capture</u> humans for study, or the influence of the lost continent of Atlantis. Other explanations are more grounded in science, if not in evidence, such as disruptions in geomagnetic lines of flux. Environmental considerations could explain ③ <u>many</u>, if not most, of the disappearances. The majority of Atlantic tropical storms and hurricanes pass through the Bermuda Triangle, and in the days prior to improved weather forecasting, these dangerous storms claimed many ships. Also, the Gulf Stream can cause rapid, sometimes violent, changes in weather, ④ <u>while</u> the large number of islands in the Caribbean Sea creates many areas of shallow water that can be treacherous to ship navigation. The ocean has always been a mysterious place to humans, and when foul weather or poor navigation is involved, it can be a very ⑤ <u>deadly</u> place. This is true all over the world.

13

2점

Students' final career choice can be influenced by their interests and abilities. If students believe they have the skills (A) necessary / necessarily for success in a particular occupation, they are more likely to develop an interest in that occupation and to seek a career in it. The link between expectations of success and career choice (B) has / has been demonstrated in the laboratory with college students who were undecided about their choice of a major. Students in the experimental group took and passed (or were told they passed) a brief math test, thus increasing their expectations for success in math. Compared with students who did not take the test, more students in the experimental group (C) enrolling / enrolled in math or science courses for the following quarter or selected a math or science major.

	(A)	(B)	(C)
①	necessary	has	enrolling
②	necessary	has been	enrolling
③	necessary	has been	enrolled
④	necessarily	has	enrolled
⑤	necessarily	has been	enrolling

14

3점

"Early to bed, early to rise makes a man healthy, wealthy, and wise," quipped Benjamin Franklin. And indeed, research has repeatedly shown the far－reaching benefits of getting a good night's sleep. In long-term studies (A) compare / comparing adults who get ample sleep (around seven to eight hours a night) with those who are chronically under-rested (fewer than five hours of sleep per night), well-rested people typically outlive their sleep － deprived peers － perhaps by as much as ten years! However, the familiar advice to "get some rest" is often easier said than done. Healthy sleeping habits remain elusive for many employees, some of (B) them / whom work seemingly interminable night shifts or change their work schedules frequently. Truck drivers or airline employees are especially prone to such regular disruptions to their slumber. And even those who are out of the workforce can suffer from lack of sleep, too. For example, stay－at－home parents of a newborn might find it difficult to sleep soundly during their child's first year. Insomnia and other sleep disorders affect millions of people every year, but the good news is (C) that / whether safe and effective remedies are readily available.

	(A)	(B)	(C)
①	compare	them	that
②	compare	them	whether
③	comparing	them	that
④	comparing	whom	whether
⑤	comparing	whom	that

※ 다음 글을 빈칸에 들어갈 말로 가장 적절한 것을 고르시오. [15~18]

15

2점

Many of the white colonialists openly despised New Guineans as "primitive." Even the least able of New Guinea's white "masters," as they were still called in 1972, enjoyed a far higher standard of living than New Guineans. We all know that history has proceeded very differently for peoples from different parts of the globe. In the 13,000 years since the end of the last Ice Age, some parts of the world developed literate industrial societies with metal tools, other parts developed only nonliterate farming societies, and still others retained societies of hunter-gatherers with stone tools. Those historical _____ have cast long shadows on the modern world, because the literate societies with metal tools have conquered or exterminated the other societies. While those differences constitute the most basic fact of world history, the reasons for them remain uncertain and controversial.

① inequalities   ② resemblances

③ mistakes   ④ heroes

⑤ myths

16

In recent years there has been a boom in mountain walking among senior citizens. Unfortunately, because many of these senior citizens have taken up this hobby later in life, they lack the skills that are usually gained through years of experience. Instead, they rely on commercial group tours led by mountain guides to take them to the summits of their dreams. But, as increasing numbers of tragic incidents show, joining a tour does not guarantee their safety when things go wrong. Clearly, it is not realistic to try to prevent senior citizens from climbing mountains. Indeed, people go to the mountains to experience a sense of freedom in the wilds of nature, and to restrict hiking activity with rules and regulations would destroy the very spirit of the activity. More _____ and personal responsibility may be one way forward. If practiced safely, mountain walking is beneficial for physical and mental health. There are also considerable economic benefits associated with tourism in mountainous regions.

① education on mountain safety

② regulations on the outdoor activity

③ advertisements for mountain walkers

④ enforcement of mountain guide certificates

⑤ information about local economic advantages

17

As an alien, one of the things Ford Prefect had always found hardest to understand about human beings was their habit of continually stating and repeating the obvious, as in "It's a nice day," or "You're very tall," or "Oh dear, you seem to have fallen down a thirty-foot well, are you alright?" At first, Ford had formed a theory to account for this strange behavior. If human beings don't keep exercising their lips, he thought, their mouths probably seize up. After a few months' consideration and observation, he _____. If they don't keep on exercising their lips, he thought, their brains start working. After a while he abandoned this one as well as being obstructively cynical and decided he quite liked human beings after all.

① disowned this theory in favor of a new one

② continued to firmly support this strange theory

③ witnessed a certain event and understood people's habits

④ discovered that humans were smarter than he had imagined

⑤ realized that it was not worth comprehending human behavior

18

3점

When it comes to catching our attention, there are certain conditions which favor attention and others which hinder it. Other things being equal, the probabilities that any particular thing will catch our attention are in proportion to _____.
This may be illustrated in a specific case as follows: I had a card of convenient size and on it were four letters. This card was exposed to view for one twenty-fifth of a second, and in that time all the four letters were read by the observers. I then added four other letters and exposed the card one twenty-fifth of a second as before. The observers could read only four of the letters as in the previous trial but in this exposure there was no certainty that any particular letter would be read. I then added four more letters to the card and exposed the letters as in the previous trials. Specific letters were noticed randomly, and the observers were still able to recall only four of the twelve letters. That is to say, up to a certain point all could be seen. When the number of objects (i.e., letters) was doubled, the chances that any particular object would be seen were reduced to fifty percent. When the number of objects was increased threefold, the chances of any particular object's being seen were reduced to thirty-three percent.

① the quality of research design

② the importance it holds for us

③ the absence of competing attractions

④ the frequency of our encounter with it

⑤ the familiarity of the input information

19 다음 글의 밑줄 친 부분 중, 문맥상 낱말의 쓰임이 적절하지 않은 것은?

[3점]

It may be difficult for adults to learn not to ① interfere but rather to support a child's desire for freedom and autonomy. For example, if you watch a boy of three trying to tie his shoes, you may see him work with extraordinary motivation even though the loops aren't matched, and well over half the time as he tries for the final knot, he ends up with two ② separate laces, one in each hand. Then watch his parents as they watch their child attempt a task like this. Too often the parent will step in and take over, tie the shoes the "right way," and ③ nurture the child's growing attempt at self-mastery. The same goes for putting on boots, coats, and even playing with toys. It is also exceedingly easy to fall into the trap of almost always responding ④ negatively to a child at this age. Commonly, a parent might say no up to 200 times a day at this stage. Such nagging not only is aversive in the extreme, but also a constant ⑤ reminder to the child of his or her lack of self-control.

※ 다음 글의 빈칸 (A), (B)에 들어갈 말로 가장 적절한 것을 고르시오. [20~21]

20

[2점]

Alliances may be of short-term interests; they may be issue-based; they may also survive for longer periods if formed for strategic purposes or based on commonality of interests. Alliances are not permanent in character. As the states are independent and sovereign, they can make or break alliances whenever necessary. Alliances are actually arrangements made for _____(A)_____. They are mainly formed to prevent any state or a group of states from becoming sufficiently powerful in international politics, and thus play a significant role in maintaining balance of power. The temporary nature of alliances actually helps the balance of power system to remain operative. Most alliances are formed on the basis of converging interests, threats from common adversaries, or similar ideological orientations. When national interests converge in alliances, they tend to be a little more cohesive and organized. But generally, most alliances within the balance of power system are _____(B)_____ in nature because they are based on political calculations of participating nations.

	(A)	(B)		(A)	(B)
①	convenience	fragile	②	convenience	invincible
③	cooperation	robust	④	economy	brittle
⑤	economy	eternal			

21

2점

The Big Zipper at Penryhn Quarry, Bethesda, will carry riders at up to 100 mph over a distance of more than a mile. The first riders — mostly journalists — arrived yesterday, but due to poor weather and high winds the main attraction was out of action.   (A)   , they were able to make do with riding The Little Zipper — a smaller zip wire, but still almost half a kilometer in length, transporting riders at speeds of around 50 mph. It is hoped that The Big Zipper will be in service by March 29, when the attraction opens to the public. The company behind the attraction, Zip World, is owned by Sean Taylor — a former marine commando who runs the nearby Tree Top Adventure attraction.   (B)   riding the two zip wires, visitors to the site are also given a guided tour of the quarry in a former military vehicle.

	(A)	(B)		(A)	(B)
①	Likewise	As well as	②	Instead	As well as
③	Moreover	Contrary to	④	Instead	Contrary to
⑤	Likewise	On behalf of			

※ (A), (B), (C)의 각 네모 안에서 문맥에 맞는 표현으로 가장 적절한 것을 고르시오. [22~23]

22

2점

A zoned reserve is an extensive region of land that includes one or more areas undisturbed by humans. The lands surrounding zoned reserves are called buffer zones. While these continue to be used to support the human population, they are also protected from extensive alteration, in turn preventing artificial (A) intrusion into / intrusion from the undisturbed areas. The zoned reserve approach primarily seeks to develop a social and economic climate in the buffer zone that is (B) unsuitable for / compatible with the long-term viability of the protected area. For example, destructive practices that are disagreeable with ecological stability in the protected area, such as massive logging or large-scale single-crop agriculture, are (C) discouraged / encouraged in the buffer zone.

	(A)	(B)	(C)
①	intrusion into	unsuitable for	discouraged
②	intrusion into	compatible with	encouraged
③	intrusion into	compatible with	discouraged
④	intrusion from	unsuitable for	encouraged
⑤	intrusion from	unsuitable for	discouraged

23

3점

We live in the age of the triumph of form. In mathematics, physics, music, the arts, and the social sciences, human knowledge and its progress seem to have been reduced in startling and powerful ways to a matter of essential formal structures and their transformations. The magic of computers is the speedy (A) manipulation / subtraction of 1s and 0s. If they just get faster at it, we hear, they might replace us. Life in all its richness and complexity is said to be fundamentally explainable as combinations and recombinations of a finite genetic code. The axiomatic method (B) rules / wavers, not only in mathematics but also in economics, linguistics, and sometimes even music. The practical products of this triumph are now part of our daily life and culture. We eat genetically engineered corn. We announce births and send wedding congratulations and buy cars on the Internet. We buy groceries by having our credit cards (C) scattered / scanned. Our taxes are determined by formulas invented by demographers and economists. We clone sheep. Serialist composers choose their notes according to mathematical principles.

	(A)	(B)	(C)
①	manipulation	rules	scanned
②	manipulation	wavers	scanned
③	manipulation	rules	scattered
④	subtraction	rules	scanned
⑤	subtraction	wavers	scattered

※ 다음 글의 제목으로 가장 적절한 것을 고르시오. [24~25]

24

Many teens experience a very real fear of being rejected by their peers for attempting to take on daunting tasks and failing at them. This fear has caused many teens to quit striving for the things they want to achieve in life. Life is too short to worry about the possibility of failure. Teens must learn to overcome their anxiety of failure because many of life's lessons are learned from failing. The best advice to give to teenagers with this anxiety is that time will heal all wounds. Many years from now their peers may not even remember the thing that they attempted and failed. Some teens may want to do or achieve great things, but they have a hard time overcoming their fear of failure. In this case, a school guidance counselor, parent, or other trusted adult may be able to help them through this fear.

① Life's Hard-learned Lessons
② Memory of Unhealed Wounds
③ The Cause and Effect of Failure
④ Overcoming Teens' Fear of Failure
⑤ Adults or Their Peers: Who Can Teens Trust?

25

We constantly hear of damage done by computer viruses and other malicious programs, but even the best virus protection software cannot prevent a home personal computer from being stolen. Thus, computer security starts by protecting the facilities that house computers and computer data. This problem is especially acute in industry. Many a company can be wiped out if its computers or especially if its sensitive data are stolen or damaged. Damage can be intentional, inflicted by a criminal or a disgruntled employee; or accidental, caused by fire, power failure, or broken air conditioning. The solution is to physically protect this sensitive asset. A home should have an alarm system, and power to the computer should go through an uninterrupted power supply. A commercial entity should have a secure computer facility, with controlled access, heavy doors, card-operated locks, security cameras, and an automatic fire system.

① Benefits of Virus Protection Software
② Anti-theft Strategies for Safe Data Storage
③ Guidelines for Personal Information Protection
④ Preventive Measures Against Computer Viruses
⑤ Need for Physical Security of Computer Facilities

26

2점

When it did, Peirce immediately took a cab to the local district office and enlisted a detective to investigate.

In June 1879, the American philosopher and scientist Charles Sanders Peirce was on a steamship journey from Boston to New York when his gold watch was stolen from his stateroom. Peirce reported the theft and insisted that each member of the ship's crew line up on deck. (①) He interviewed them all but got nowhere, so after a short walk, he did something odd: he decided to guess who the perpetrator was, even though he had nothing to base his suspicions on. (②) Peirce confidently approached his suspect, but he called his bluff and denied the accusation. (③) With no evidence or logical reason to back his claim, there was nothing he could do—until the ship docked. (④) The detective found Peirce's watch at a pawnshop the next day, and Peirce asked the proprietor to describe the man who'd pawned it. (⑤) According to Peirce, the pawnbroker described the suspect "so graphically that no doubt was possible that it had been my suspect."

27

2점

That's one reason, for example, that people pay so much to be members of an exclusive as well as extravagant country club, even if they don't utilize the facilities.

Scientists call any group that people feel part of an "in-group," and any group that excludes them an "out-group." As opposed to the colloquial usage, the terms "in-group" and "out-group" in this technical sense refer not to the popularity of those in the groups but simply to the "us-them" distinction. (①) We all belong to many in-groups and as a result, our self-identification shifts from situation to situation. (②) At different times the same person might think of herself as a woman, an executive, or a mother, depending on which is relevant. (③) Both experimental and field studies have found, in fact, that people will make large financial sacrifices to help establish a feeling of belonging to an in-group they aspire to feel part of. (④) Once we think of ourselves as belonging to the country club or executive ranks, the views of others in the group seep into our thinking, and color the way we perceive the world. (⑤) Psychologists call those views "group norms," and seeing ourselves as a member of a group automatically marks everyone as either an "us" or a "them."

28 산사태 예방에 관한 다음 글의 내용과 일치하지 않는 것은?

Soil erosion is one of the most common reasons for landslides, and therefore preventing it can help you reduce the risk of landslides. The foremost thing to do is to divert the discharge water away from slopes by constructing gutters and using sandbags. If there is no possibility of diverting, you can contain its speed by building small dams. The velocity of water determines how much soil is eroded, and hence containing its speed is bound to be helpful. It is important to make sure that you divert or contain the water flow and not stop it altogether, as stopping it will result in pressure build-up over a period, which might give in at some point in time. Never redirect storm drains or street gutters down a slope, even if it seems to be an easy way out. Instead you can use flexible pipes and divert this water in a safe manner.

① 토양 침식을 막는 것이 산사태의 위험을 줄이는 데 도움이 된다.
② 도랑과 모래주머니를 이용하여 비탈로 내려가는 물길을 돌려야 한다.
③ 유속 조절용으로 만든 작은 둑이 물길을 완전히 막지 않도록 해야 한다.
④ 빗물 배수관을 이용하여 빗물이 비탈로 내려가도록 물길을 돌려야 한다.
⑤ 유연성이 있는 파이프를 이용하여 안전하게 물길을 돌릴 수 있다.

29 다음 글이 함축하는 바로 가장 적절한 것은?

Gal and Rucker recently conducted research where they used framing techniques to make people feel uncertain. For example, they told one group to remember a time when they were full of certainty, and the other group to remember a time when they were full of doubt. Then they asked the participants whether they were meat-eaters, vegetarians, vegans, etc., how important this was to them, and how confident they were in their opinions. People who were asked to remember times when they were uncertain were less confident of their eating choices. However, when asked to write up their beliefs to persuade someone else to eat the way they did, they would write more and stronger arguments than the group that were certain of their choice. The research was performed with different topics of preference (for example, desktop or laptop), and similar results were found.

① When people don't have a valid argument, they most likely start insulting others.

② People often become more confident in their beliefs when the majority of others disagree with them.

③ When people are less certain about their beliefs, then they tend to dig in and argue even harder.

④ As people get more information, they are able to look at the big picture, beyond their initial argument.

⑤ Opportunity, performance, and effectiveness jump to much higher levels when certainty outweighs uncertainty.

※ 다음 글의 주제로 가장 적절한 것을 고르시오. [30~31]

30

Even the most determined of parents can find it a challenge to encourage their child not to spend too long sitting in front of the television or computer. Furthermore, it can be very difficult to find alternative activities that children will find fun. Learning ballet can be an excellent solution as it provides many benefits for children. Any good dance school or dance academy will have well-managed lessons that are carried out in a safe and structured environment. These classes will challenge your child both physically and mentally, which will help focus their mind and maintain their interest. As their ability improves, so will their co-ordination, self-control, and discipline, which will in turn improve their self-confidence. Furthermore, it will provide a positive natural outlet for their abundance of energy. Learning ballet from an early age is particularly beneficial, as young children are far more receptive than adults. They find it easier to learn and also have far fewer inhibitions, so it's far less likely that they'll feel insecure or embarrassed about performing a particular move.

① reasons you should open dance academies

② benefits of ballet dancing for young children

③ alternative outdoor activities for young children

④ importance of children's self-control and discipline

⑤ danger of spending too much time with computers

31

3점

One of the key questions in cognitive psychology is how people represent knowledge about concepts such as 'football' or 'love.' Recently, some researchers have proposed that concepts are represented in human memory by the sensorimotor systems that underlie interaction with the outside world. These theories represent a recent development in cognitive science to view cognition no longer in terms of abstract information processing, but in terms of perception and action. In other words, cognition is grounded in embodied experiences. Studies show that sensory perception and motor actions support human understanding of words and object concepts. Moreover, even understanding of abstract and emotion concepts can be shown to rely on more concrete, embodied experiences. Finally, language itself can be shown to be grounded in sensorimotor processes. We can bring together theoretical arguments and empirical evidence from several key researchers in this field to support this framework.

① distortion of sensory perception in the environment

② human understanding of concrete, physical concepts

③ representation of concepts through sensorimotor systems

④ significance of abstract and emotion concepts in human life

⑤ relationship between abstract information and human knowledge

32 다음 글이 시사하는 바로 가장 적절한 것은?

2점

Since what you make of your life is up to you, you can either create a life filled with miraculous adventures or stay huddled and safe, never experiencing the joyful rush of journeying outside your world with boldness. A life devoid of adventure may be secure, but it is one that lacks texture and color. If you never venture forth, you can never expand and grow. Think about the adventures you have had in your lifetime. Those moments in which you took a leap of faith and expanded beyond your comfort zone are precious gifts, as they can remind you of the joy that is available to you when you embrace life with exuberance. These moments can be turning points in your personal history and inspire you to create new realities for yourself whenever you choose.

① Love little and love long.

② Nothing sought, nothing found.

③ Do as you would be done by.

④ Sit back and enjoy the ride.

⑤ One man sows and another man reaps.

33 다음 도표의 내용과 일치하지 않는 것은?

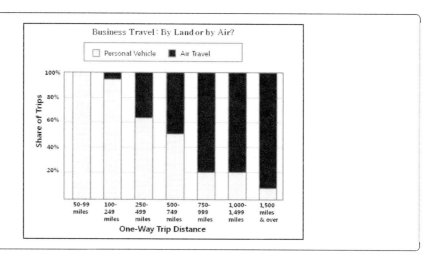

The graph above shows the share of the personal vehicle and air travel in long-distance business trips by miles traveled one-way. (This graph does not reflect other modes of transportation.) ① The decision to take a personal vehicle or fly to a destination changes with the distance of the trip; and the longer the distance, the greater the percentage of business trips traveled by air. ② For business trips of 100-249 miles, the personal vehicle is the dominant means of transportation, with only a few percent for the other type of transportation. ③ If a destination is between 250-499 miles away, over 60 percent of business trips are taken with a personal vehicle. ④ On the other hand, if the destination is 500-749 miles away, more than two-thirds of business trips are taken by air. ⑤ Between business trips of 750-999 miles and 1,000-1,499 miles, there is no apparent difference in the percentage of travelers who prefer to fly.

34

2점

On May 1, 1960, the Soviet Union shot down a United States U2 spy plane and seized the pilot together with illegal photographs of Soviet military installations. While the Soviet government feigned ignorance of their capture, the U.S. released a report that a weather research aircraft had gone missing.

(A) The summit collapsed within a day when the U.S. refused to do so. Soon after, the Cold War escalated with confrontation over the construction of the Berlin Wall and over the Cuban missile crisis.

(B) The heavily awaited meeting was designed to lighten Cold War tensions, but the spy plane incident overshadowed the entire event. Khrushchev of the Soviet Union refused to proceed with the summit unless Eisenhower issued an apology.

(C) This, of course, was proved to be embarrassingly false when the Soviets revealed the pilot's confession of his undercover mission, and the U.S. was forced to admit that it had authorized the flight. At that time the two countries were to participate in the Big Four summit, along with Great Britain and France.

① (A) – (C) – (B)
② (B) – (A) – (C)
③ (B) – (C) – (A)
④ (C) – (A) – (B)
⑤ (C) – (B) – (A)

35

One common motivational strategy is to first set lofty goals and then push yourself to achieve them. However, this strategy could potentially lead to disappointment instead if you try to meet unrealistic goals that are too far out of reach.

(A) Bob starved himself every day, determined to meet his goal, but when it came time to weigh himself, he had lost "only" three pounds. This is actually a remarkable accomplishment, yet he felt himself like he had failed because he didn't meet his declared objective.

(B) Feeling so inspired, Bob yelled out "Five pounds!" and then basked in the applause. Keep in mind that he hadn't lost any weight in the previous six months, but now he declared that in one short week he would knock off a big chunk.

(C) For instance, Bob heard someone speak about a new weight-loss program that really fired him up. At the end of the meeting, everyone was supposed to say out loud how much weight they would lose during the week.

① (A) – (C) – (B)   ② (B) – (A) – (C)

③ (B) – (C) – (A)   ④ (C) – (A) – (B)

⑤ (C) – (B) – (A)

36 다음 글에서 필자가 주장하는 바로 가장 적절한 것은?

The advances of modern medicine have done much to relieve suffering and advance human welfare, but modern medicine does not guarantee good health. Health is more than an absence of disease; it is a condition in which body and mind function efficiently and harmoniously as an integrated unit. Consequently, we must take an active part in achieving good health by assuming some responsibility for our own physical and emotional well-being. This means practicing such commonsense measures as eating properly, exercising moderately, and avoiding harmful excesses such as overeating, smoking, heavy drinking, or using drugs, which can disrupt physical or emotional well-being. Taking responsibility for one's health also requires using one's mind constructively, expressing emotions, and feeling good about oneself.

① 정신 건강을 위해 매사에 긍정적으로 생각하라.
② 응급 상황에 대비해 가까운 의료 기관을 파악하라.
③ 몸과 마음의 건강을 조화롭게 유지하도록 노력하라.
④ 질병 예방에 도움이 되는 기초 의학 지식을 갖춰라.
⑤ 건강 보조 약품을 과도하게 복용하지 않도록 주의하라.

37 다음 글의 내용을 한 문장으로 요약하고자 한다. 빈칸 (A)와 (B)에 들어갈 말로 가장 적절한 것은?

The explosion of creativity in the Renaissance was intimately tied to the recording and conveying of vast knowledge in drawings, graphs, and diagrams, as in the renowned diagrams of da Vinci and Galileo. Galileo revolutionized science by making his thought graphically visible while his contemporaries used only conventional mathematical and verbal approaches. Once geniuses obtain a certain minimal verbal facility, they seem to develop a skill in visual and spatial abilities that gives them the flexibility to display information in different ways. When Einstein had thought through a problem, he always found it necessary to formulate his subject in as many different ways as possible, including using diagrams. He had a very visual mind; he thought in terms of visual and spatial forms, rather than thinking along purely mathematical or verbal lines of reasoning. In fact, Einstein believed that words and numbers, as they are written or spoken, did not play a significant role in his thinking process.

By making their thoughts ___(A)___, geniuses are ___(B)___ their more conventional peers.

	(A)	(B)
①	visible	distinguished from
②	visible	related to
③	radical	indebted to
④	mathematical	aloof from
⑤	mathematical	inseparable from

※ 다음 글을 읽고, 물음에 답하시오. [38~39]

One day Joe Kohn, a sophomore, was reading the newspaper alone in a student lounge at MIT. Norbert Wiener, professor and renowned mathematician, entered the room and began to walk around. Presently he approached the somewhat intimidated Joe Kohn and said, "Young man! Do you play the game of chess?" Kohn allowed that he did, and Wiener exclaimed, "Then let us play a game of chess!" Kohn was scared to death, and sure that Wiener would make a fool of him. About fifteen moves into the game, Wiener moved his queen so that Kohn's pawn could take it. Kohn was _____. Surely Wiener was making a devilishly clever sacrifice and would then get a quick checkmate. Kohn spent twenty minutes feverishly peering at the board and trying to determine what Wiener was up to. Finally he said, "Professor Wiener, I'm stumped. Why are you sacrificing your queen?" Wiener's eyes grew wide and he said, "Oh my God. That's a mistake! Can I take that move back?" Of course Kohn let Wiener retract his move. It became rapidly clear that Wiener was actually quite an inept chess player, and he quickly lost.

* pawn : (체스의) 졸

38 위 글의 빈칸에 들어갈 말로 가장 적절한 것은?

① bored   ② relieved

③ overjoyed   ④ bewildered

⑤ enlightened

39 위 글의 Norbert Wiener에 관한 내용과 일치하지 않는 것은?

① 학생 라운지에 나타나 Kohn에게 체스를 두자고 제안했다.
② 자신의 퀸을 Kohn이 졸로 잡을 수 있는 위치에 놓았다.
③ 퀸을 희생시켜 게임을 빨리 끝내려는 의도를 가지고 있었다.
④ 자신이 실수한 수를 물러달라고 Kohn에게 요청했다.
⑤ 체스 실력이 형편없어서 금방 게임에서 패하고 말았다.

※ 다음 글을 읽고, 물음에 답하시오. [40~41]

Parents and teachers often report utter frustration with children who have attention deficit hyperactivity disorder (AD/HD), because they lie about obvious events. For example, a teacher may see a child take an object from another child's desk and put it in her desk. When (a) she questions her about it, the child denies that she took it and tends to blame someone else or shrug her shoulders. (b) She may also deny that she has homework, or that the teacher told her about a test. When the behavior persists, it is probably related to (c) her impulsiveness. In other words, the youngster will act on an idea that comes to mind without becoming conscious of it. For example, (d) she may see a nice pencil sharpener on another child's desk and say to herself, "I sure wish I had that pencil sharpener." The next thing she knows, it is in (e) her hand, and she never is aware of the process of taking it from the other child's desk! It is this same lack of conscious monitoring of behavior that causes children with AD/HD to blurt out embarrassing and outrageous statements or to be reported for having their hands all over other children. As a consequence of this disorder, children with AD/HD do a poor job of monitoring their behavior and, therefore, may be totally unaware of what they say or do in many instances.

40 위 글의 밑줄 친 (a)~(e) 중에서, 가리키는 대상이 나머지 넷과 다른 것은?

2점

① (a)　　　　　　　　　　② (b)

③ (c)　　　　　　　　　　④ (d)

⑤ (e)

41 위 글의 "children with AD/HD"에 관한 설명으로 적절하지 않은 것은?

3점

① They may not be conscious of their previous behavior.

② They are prone to unintentional and habitual dishonesty.

③ Their disorder is marked by insufficient behavior monitoring.

④ They sometimes bother other students around them.

⑤ They may act inappropriately due to a high level of frustration.

※ 다음 글을 읽고 물음에 답하시오. [42~43]

(A)

Before becoming a famous country comedian and star of "Hee Haw," Archie Campbell was homeless, coatless, and penniless on a bitterly cold night in Knoxville, Tennessee. After getting thrown out of the bus station where he had fallen asleep, Mr. Campbell started walking in an unsuccessful effort to keep warm.

(B)

Seeing an all-night restaurant, he went in and stood near a hot radiator. The owner, a Greek named Nick, asked him what he was doing. Mr. Campbell said that he lived nearby (a lie because he had no home), he had forgotten his coat (a lie because he had no coat), and he had dropped in to get warm (not a lie).

(C)

Mr. Campbell explained that he couldn't pay for the meal, but Nick said he didn't have to— he knew that Mr. Campbell was homeless because he lived in the apartment complex that Mr. Campbell had named. After becoming rich and famous, Mr. Campbell made sure to stop in at that restaurant whenever he was in Knoxville.

(D)

Nick asked where he lived, and Mr. Campbell answered with the name of the first apartment complex he could think of. Apparently satisfied, Nick invited him to sit in a booth and get warm. Mr. Campbell fell asleep in a booth, and when he woke up, Nick _____.

42 주어진 글 (A)에 이어질 내용을 순서에 맞게 배열한 것으로 가장 적절한 것은?

2점
① (B) – (D) – (C)
② (C) – (B) – (D)
③ (C) – (D) – (B)
④ (D) – (B) – (C)
⑤ (D) – (C) – (B)

43 위 글 (D)의 빈칸에 들어갈 말로 가장 적절한 것은?

① accused him of being homeless

② offered him work at the restaurant

③ invited him to appear on "Hee Haw"

④ presented a warm winter coat to him

⑤ set a huge, hot breakfast in front of him

※ 다음 글을 읽고, 물음에 답하시오. [44~45]

When he was a little boy his uncle called him "Sparky," after a comic-strip horse named Spark Plug. School was all but impossible for Sparky. In the eighth grade, he failed every subject including physical education. Throughout his youth, Sparky was awkward socially. It wasn't that the other students disliked him; it's just that no one really cared all that much. He never once asked a girl out in high school. He was too afraid of being turned down. Sparky was a loser. Everyone knew it. So he learned to live with it. He made up his mind early that if things were meant to work out, they would. Otherwise he would content himself with what appeared to be his inevitable mediocrity.

One thing was important to Sparky, however—drawing. He was proud of his artwork. No one else appreciated it. But that didn't seem to matter to him. In his senior year of high school, he submitted some cartoons to the school yearbook. The editors rejected the concept. Despite this brush-off, Sparky was convinced of his ability. He even decided to become an artist. So, after completing high school, Sparky wrote to Walt Disney Studios. They asked for samples of his artwork. Despite careful preparation, it too was rejected.

But Sparky still didn't give up. Instead, he decided to tell his own life's story in cartoons. The main character would be a little boy who symbolized the chronic underachiever. His cartoon character went on to become a cultural phenomenon of sorts. People readily identified with this lovable character. He reminded people of the painful and embarrassing moments from their own past, of their pain and their shared humanity. The character soon became famous worldwide. And Sparky, who you might know better as Charles Schultz, became a highly successful cartoonist. His cartoon strip reveals that life somehow finds a way for all of us, even the losers.

44 위 글의 제목으로 가장 적절한 것은?

2점
① Find the Best in Others and Success Is Yours
② Never Lose Hope and Never Ever Give Up
③ Do Not Jump In Before You Are Ready
④ Content Yourself with Small Success
⑤ Once Rejected, Forever Forgotten

45 위 글의 "Sparky"에 관한 내용과 일치하지 않는 것은?

2점
① 중학교 시절에 모든 과목에서 낙제한 적이 있었다.
② 사교성이 좋아서 학교 친구들에게 인기가 많았다.
③ 자신의 예술적 능력에 대해 자부심을 갖고 있었다.
④ Walt Disney Studios에 작품 샘플을 제출한 적이 있었다.
⑤ 세계적으로 유명한 만화 주인공을 창조했다.

▶ 해설은 p. 62에 있습니다.

01 Where is the following dialogue most likely taking place?

[2점]

> Captain Sim : And what can I do for you, young lady?
>
> Sonya : I'm not sure. I've been trying to figure out what I want to do with my life, and a friend recommended that I come here.
>
> Captain Sim : Wise decision. We have great career options to offer a bright young person such as yourself. What branch of service are you considering?
>
> Sonya : I have no idea really. I'd sure appreciate some advice.
>
> Captain Sim : Well, let me ask you to close your eyes and imagine yourself proudly wearing a uniform and serving your nation. Do you see yourself sailing the high seas, soaring into the vast skies, or traversing exotic foreign lands?
>
> Sonya : Well … I think flying sounds great.
>
> Captain Sim : Then, let me show you our Air Force brochures.

① at a military recruitment center

② in a soldiers' dining hall

③ in a cadet dormitory

④ in an air control tower

⑤ at a war memorial

02 Based on the following dialogue, which is NOT true?

2점

> Mr. Perez : I need to talk to you for a minute.
>
> Mrs. Perez : Sure, honey. What's up?
>
> Mr. Perez : I was offered a promotion today. It's a great opportunity and I'm excited, but it means being transferred to Sweden for a few years.
>
> Mrs. Perez : Wow! But ... I don't know. I'd have to resign from work. Plus, how can I get a new job there? I don't know the language.
>
> Mr. Perez : You don't have to worry about that, because the promotion comes with such a big pay raise that you wouldn't have to work.
>
> Mrs. Perez : Can we really leave our home and friends for so long? We really have to think about this.

① Mr. Perez will get a promotion if he accepts the transfer.

② Mrs. Perez is currently unemployed.

③ Mrs. Perez cannot speak Swedish.

④ Mr. Perez will make more money if he takes the job.

⑤ Mrs. Perez is hesitant to go to Sweden.

03 Which is the best sequence of sentences for the blanks?

2점

> Mrs. Won : Thanks so much for coming, finally! I've been calling for three days!
>
> Frank : _____ But due to the heat wave, it seems everyone in town needs their air conditioners serviced. I've been working twelve hours a day all week.
>
> Mrs. Won : I totally understand. However, my family and I have been baking in here.
>
> Frank : Well, then let's get this fixed and cool you guys off as fast as possible.
>
> _____
>
> Mrs. Won : When I turn it on, it just blows warm air.
>
> Frank : _____ It probably just needs its Freon gas refilled. If nothing is leaking, I can take care of that in no time.
>
> Mrs. Won : Great. But please hurry. I think I may be melting.

〈보기〉

a. What seems to be the problem?　　b. There's nothing I can do about that.
c. That should be a simple fix.　　　d. I do apologize.

① b – d – c　　　　　　　② c – a – b
③ c – b – d　　　　　　　④ d – a – c
⑤ d – b – a

04 What is the relationship between the woman and the man?

Woman : I'm calling because I'm in trouble and in need of your services.
Man : How can I help?
Woman : I got arrested because my boss reported me for stealing from his company. Now the police tell me I'll have to go to court.
Man : Tell me the whole story, and don't leave anything out.
Woman : I didn't do it exactly. It was a big misunderstanding. I just borrowed the money. I was going to pay it back.
Man : Now don't worry. I can take care of this. But if I am going to properly represent you in a court of law, we should meet and talk about this.

① client – attorney
② judge – accused
③ criminal – victim
④ police officer – suspect
⑤ employer – employee

05 Chose the best sentence for the blank.

Sam's Teacher : Thanks for coming in to school today. As I told you on the phone, I'm a little worried about Sam.

Sam's Dad : I was surprised to hear from you. Did he do something wrong?

Sam's Teacher : No, not at all. It's just that he seems distracted lately, unable to concentrate. At the beginning of the term, he was one of my best students. But recently he's been late with homework, his scores are dropping, and he seems distant from his classmates. Has something been going on at home?

Sam's Dad : That's so strange. I always thought he was good in school. I have no idea what the issue might be. In fact, family life has been great.

Sam's Teacher : _____

① If he does something like that again, he could be suspended.

② I hope he can continue his current level of school performance.

③ Sam has consistently improved as the semester has progressed.

④ Due to his disinterest in the class from the start, I've given up on him.

⑤ Please talk with him, because if he doesn't improve, he could fail the class.

06 Chose the sentence that best describes the situation.

Bobby : I'm bored, Grandpa. Can I play games on your smart-phone?

Grandpa : Those games are such a waste of time and energy. Why don't you go outside and play? It's a beautiful day.

Bobby : But there's nothing to do out there. When are Mom and Dad coming back from their trip?

Grandpa : There's a whole world to explore out there. When I was young, I played outside from sunrise to sunset, I always found ways to have fun without smart-phones or video games. We have one more week together, so we best find some ways to entertain ourselves.

Bobby : Would you come out and play with me?

Grandpa : I'd love to. Let's go.

① Grandpa is looking after Bobby.

② Bobby's parents are working late.

③ Bobby is playing a smart-phone game.

④ Bobby and Grandpa are on a trip together.

⑤ Grandpa doesn't want to play outside with Bobby.

07 밑줄 친 부분이 가리키는 대상이 나머지 넷과 다른 것은?

Memories can be easily fabricated so people become convinced of the reality of something that never happened. A famous example occurred to no less a personage than the Swiss psychologist Jean Piaget. Throughout ①his life, Piaget frequently spoke of a vivid memory of an incident from his early childhood. One day, while his nanny walked ②him in a pram down the street, a man leaped out from the bushes in an attempt to kidnap Piaget. The man struggled with the nanny, who successfully fought him off, but not before ③he inflicted scratches on her face. Piaget's memory of the frightening event was exquisitely detailed. ④He recalled the faces of the people at the scene, the uniform of the policeman, the scratches on his nanny's face, and the exact location of the assault. And yet, as Piaget and ⑤his family subsequently learned, the episode had never taken place. Years later, the nanny wrote to Piaget's parents and confessed to making up the whole story, including the scratches.

* pram : 유모차

※ 다음 글에서 전체 흐름과 관계없는 문장을 고르시오. [08~09]

08

2점

Muhammad Ali refused to fight in the usual way. Ali's style ran counter to the boxing wisdom of the time in almost every way, but this unconventional style was exactly what made him a legendary boxer. ① As children and young adults, we are taught to conform to certain codes of behavior and ways of doing things, learning that being different comes with a social price. ② But there is a greater price to pay for blindly conforming: we lose the power that comes from our individuality, from a way of doing things that is authentically our own. ③ Following social conventions forms the basic ground-work for building a safe and stable society. ④ the way to be truly unconventional is to imitate no one, to fight and operate according to your own rhythms. ⑤ If your peculiarity is authentic enough, it will bring you attention and respect — the kind the crowd always has for the unconventional and extraordinary.

09

2점

Developmental psychologists studying the impact of texting worry especially about young people because their interpersonal skills have not yet fully formed. ① Unlike kids, most adults were already stable social entities when they first got their hands on a text-capable mobile device. ② Besides, their ability to have a face-to-face conversation dramatically declines after extensive reliance on text messages. ③ However, this may not be the case with kids, according to Sherry Turkle, an interpersonal development researcher at MIT. ④ She believes kids are unlikely to develop face-to-face conversation skills if they overly rely on texting to communicate. ⑤ This may also prevent them from learning skills to think, reason, and self-reflect, as these skills are hard to acquire without sufficient experience in verbal communication.

10 다음 글의 요지로 가장 적절한 것은?

2점

Katrina was the first hurricane to hit the United states to the accompaniment of continuous (24/7) television coverage. In social science terms, television constructed the frame of meaning with which audiences and decision-makers came to understand Katrina. For some along the coast, personal experience with Katrina might have helped. If you were on Dauphin Island, Biloxi Bay, St. Louis, or in a bar on Bourbon Street, the storm was slightly different. However, for most of us, the reality of the storm came through television networks. Even for "victims" who lost electrical power, if it came back, the coffee pot and the television were the first appliances back on so that their own experiences would be understood and confirmed in the context of the information provided by the media.

* 24/7 : 24 hours a day / 7 days a week

① 재난에 대처하는 방법은 각 개인이 처한 상황에 따라 다르다.

② 텔레비전 보도가 자연재해의 경험에 대한 이해의 틀을 제공한다.

③ 부정적인 사건 · 사고에 치중하는 보도 관행은 바람직하지 못하다.

④ 자연재해 정보를 전문으로 다루는 텔레비전 네트워크가 필요하다.

⑤ 대중매체는 재난 복구와 이재민 구호 활동에서 핵심적인 역할을 한다.

※ 다음 글의 밑줄 친 부분 중, 어법상 틀린 것을 고르시오. [11~12]

11

2점

Your communication with others ① involves some kind of risk, since communication means presenting to others a statement of your self, your role, the situation, and the others that they may reject. The communication climate is an important part of your guessing how much risk is involved for you in a given situation. You behave on the basis of how safe you think you are. If you do not feel secure, you will ② likely use defensive strategies. Perhaps you have been in a classroom situation in which the teacher keeps ③ insisting that students participate by discussing issues openly, and then the teacher shoos down their comments or ridicules them when they do. It does not take you long ④ to figure out that publicly being cut down by sarcasm is not comfortable. You learn quickly that the climate is not safe. Your communication takes on defensive strategies ⑤ are designed to protect yourself.

12

3점

The quest of science has seen many triumphs and agonies. They usually went hand in hand and ① evidenced equally well the role of faith for science. The first major triumph was Copernicus' outline of the planetary order. He was far from proving definitely the heliocentric proposition. But he supplemented ② what he lacked in physical proofs with his faith in nature. From his belief ③ that nature was the handiwork of the Creator, he readily concluded that nature was simple. His system of the planets gave no better prediction of the motion of planets than did ④ Ptolemy's; the most attractive proof of Copernicus lay in the geometrical simplicity of the new ordering of the planets. It was a bold view, and he clung to it though people shock their heads in disbelief. But Galileo, whom people consider the father of the experimental method, ⑤ to praise Copernicus precisely for what he did: for staying with his belief.

※ (A), (B), (C)의 각 네모 안에서 어법에 맞는 표현으로 가장 적절한 것을 고르시오. [13~14]

13

3점

One of the biggest obstacles to (A) increase / increasing a hybrid car's range is the weight of the battery. More powerful batteries can power a car for a longer distance, but they also weigh more. A newly emerged concept of hybrid car, which can hold electricity in its doors, hood, and so on, is drawing attention as a potential breakthrough in dealing with this problem. Some researchers have already started experimenting with a prototype electric vehicle with an energy-storing trunk floor, whose extra energy storage could (B) reduce / be reduced the battery's weight by 15 percent. Ultimately, if this new technology reached the efficiency of the current lithium-ion battery, cars of this sort could store enough electricity to power (C) them / themselves for 80 miles in non-battery parts such as the roof or the doors.

	(A)		(B)		(C)
①	increase	······	reduce	······	them
②	increase	······	be reduced	······	themselves
③	increasing	······	reduce	······	them
④	increasing	······	reduce	······	themselves
⑤	increasing	······	be reduced	······	them

14

The following represents a classic study in perception. Twenty-three middle-level managers were asked to read a comprehensive case (A) | describing / described | the operational activities in a steel company. Six of the 23 executives worked in the area of sales, five in production, four in accounting, and eight in miscellaneous functions. After reading the case, each of these executives was then asked to identify the problem that a new company president should deal with first. Eighty-three percent of the sales executives rated sales most important, but only 29 percent of the others (B) | were / did |. Similarly, the production executives gave priority to the production area, and the accounting people focused on accounting problems. These findings led to the conclusion (C) | that / which | these participants interpreted the case's priorities in terms of the activities and goals of the functional areas to which the executives were attached.

	(A)		(B)		(C)
①	describing	……	were	……	that
②	describing	……	did	……	that
③	describing	……	did	……	which
④	described	……	did	……	which
⑤	described	……	were	……	that

15 다음 글의 밑줄 친 부분 중, 문맥상 낱말의 쓰임이 적절하지 않은 것은?

2점

Not much learning takes place unless you concentrate carefully on what you are learning. Concentration is basically thinking. Concentration can ① enhance your ability to do both mental and physical tasks. This is why many failures in school are due more to poor concentration than to ② low intelligence. Researchers note that one enemy of concentration is indecision: Indecision about when to study and which subject to study first is not only a great time-waster, but also a sure way to ③ eliminate a negative attitude toward studying. Personal problems also interfere with concentration. You will not make good use of your intelligence if you are ④ preoccupied with personal problems. After you have taken some ⑤ constructive action on your problem, you will then be in a better position to learn or perform well.

16
[3점]

The psychological effects of activities are not linear, but depend on their systematic relation to everything else we do. For instance, even though food is a source of pleasure, we cannot achieve happiness by eating around the clock. Meals raise our level of happiness, but only when we spend around five percent of our waking time eating; if we spent one hundred percent of the day eating, food would quickly cease to be rewarding. The same is true of most of the other good things in life: relaxation and television watching in small doses tend to improve the quality of daily life, but the effects are not _____; a point of diminishing returns is quickly reached.

① additive   ② reductive

③ temporary   ④ immediate

⑤ avoidable

17
[2점]

Over the course of the past century, National Geographic magazine has come to be one of the primary meas by which people in the United States receive information and images of the world outside their own borders. While National Geographic covers a range of topics — including the geographic and cultural wonders of the United States, wildlife and nature stories, and accounts of exploration of space, the oceans, and the polar ice caps — a good portion of its text and photographs is devoted to curious and exotic images of the peoples and cultures of the third world. National Geographic is located in a long tradition of travelogue as it sends its staff on expeditions to bring back stories and photos of faraway people and places. While its photographs and stories can be marveled at by readers in the privacy of their own homes, it draws people into contact with _____.

① their own traditions

② local economic issues

③ environmental movements

④ the realities of labor conditions

⑤ different cultures from their own

18

3점

Suppose five competing firms all manage to lower the production cost and selling price of a standard product that they all produce. One does it by cutting its workers' pay. One does it by working them longer hours. One does it by getting some of its materials at lower prices from a poorer country. One does it by replacing some of its workers with robots. One does it by inventing an improvement to some of its machinery that allows it to cut cork hours with no harm to anyone — no loss of output, profit, jobs, or pay. Ask which change was the most desirable, and scarcely will anybody name either of the first two. There may be votes for each of the other three, though perhaps on conditions. Were the foreign supplies produced by cruelly exploited labor, or with pollutant wastes? Could the workers displaced by robots depend on finding other jobs? Has the inventor of the improved machinery patented it, so that other firms and worker can't share its benefits? The respondents thus take _____ into account when considering the question.

① upcoming elections

② familiar social values

③ maximum productivity

④ national competitiveness

⑤ new technological advances

19 다음 글의 목적으로 가장 적절한 것은?

Dear Ms. Hart,

Upon completion of the screening of over one-hundred applicants, we are pleased to inform you that we sere extremely impressed with your resume, interview, and test results. Therefore, you have been chosen for one of the five job positions currently being filled here at the ACME Consulting Firm. Should you choose to accept, you would immediately enter a six month, unpaid, internship program. Upon successful completion, you would then become a regular employee at full salary, including all standard benefits. There may also be the opportunity to transfer to one of our many branches around the country, or stay at our main office here in town. Congratulations, Ms. Hart! Please inform us of your decision no later than the end of the month.

Sincerely,
Cheryl Smith
Human Resources, ACME Consulting Firm

① to encourage Ms. Hart to apply at the ACME Consulting Firm
② to congratulate Ms. Hart on the completion of her internship
③ to offer Ms. Hart a position at the ACME Consulting Firm
④ to inform Ms. Hart of her upcoming contract renewal
⑤ to notify Ms. Hart of her job application rejection

※ 다음 글의 빈칸 (A), (B)에 들어갈 말로 가장 적절한 것을 고르시오. [20~21]

20

Genes are pure information — information that can be encoded, recoded, and decoded, without any change of meaning. Pure information can be copied, and the accuracy of the copying can be (A). In fact, DNA characters are copied with an exactness that rivals anything modern engineers can do. They are copied down through the generations, with just enough occasional errors to introduce variety. Among this variety, those coded combinations that become more numerous in the world will obviously and automatically be the ones that, when decoded and obeyed inside bodies, make those bodies take active steps to preserve and propagate those same DNA messages. We — and that means all living things — are survival machines programmed to (B) the database that did the programming. Darwinism is now seen to be the survival of the survivors at the level of pure code.

* propagate : 유전시키다

	(A)		(B)
①	immense	......	remove
②	immense	......	reproduce
③	moderate	......	remove
④	insignificant	......	improve
⑤	insignificant	......	reproduce

21

A transition to an alternate energy cannot be motivated by a scarcity of fossil fuels. For decades, energy producers have continually identified new fossil fuel reserves and developed technologies to economically recover oil and gas from deposits previously deemed too difficult to access. (A), Japan recently announced that they were able to extract methane from undersea hydrate deposits, which appear to contain more than twice as much carbon as in all of Earth's fossil fuel combined. This means that humanity has burned just a small portion of our fossil fuels to date. Even though we have used such a small fraction of our fossil fuels, the planet has already experienced serious warming problems. If we continue to rely heavily on fossil fuels for our energy supply, climate-change related damage will become very severe long before there is any real pressure on our fossil fuel supply. (B), movement for an alternate energy must be driven by a concerted effort to keep the climate livable and healthy

	(A)		(B)
①	For example	······	Therefore
②	On the other hand	······	Nevertheless
③	For example	······	On the contrary
④	On the other hand	······	Therefore
⑤	In the same way	······	Nevertheless

※ (A), (B), (C)의 각 네모 안에서 문맥에 맞는 표현으로 가장 적절한 것을 고르시오. [22~23]

22

3점

The autotrophic nature of plants makes them very dependent upon light and there are only a few plant species that cannot photosynthesize. Therefore, it is crucial that plants can sense light and respond to it. Plants need to locate light sources and grow towards them. Then they need to ensure that their leaves are orientated in the correct way to (A) maximize / minimize light exposure to the photosynthetic organs. But there is further information than this that plants gain from sensing light. Plants live in a changing environment, with day and night changes, seasonal changes, weather changes, and habitat changes This means that plants need to be able to see their surroundings and then need to be very (B) flexible / rigid in their behavior to respond to these changes. Even photosynthesis has to be modified continually to cope with changing illumination. The sun should be brightest at midday, but few days are without clouds that can temporarily block out the sun. This leads to huge (C) constancy / variation in light intensity with which a plant needs to be able to deal.

* autotrophic : 자가(자급) 영양의

	(A)		(B)		(C)
①	maximize	·····	flexible	·····	variation
②	maximize	·····	flexible	·····	constancy
③	minimize	·····	rigid	·····	constancy
④	minimize	·····	flexible	·····	variation
⑤	minimize	·····	rigid	·····	variation

23

Once you have begun to use rewards to control people, you cannot easily go back. When behaviors become (A) irrelevant / instrumental to monetary rewards — in other words, when people behave to get rewards — those behaviors will last only so long as the rewards are forthcoming. In some cases that may be fine, but in most cases the activities we reward are ones that we would like to have (B) persist / cease long after the rewards have stopped. For example, if you offered rewards to your children for studying — a dollar for each "A" on their report cards — you would want the children to remain enthusiastic about studying after your reward system was (C) initiated / terminated. But it is pretty likely that if they study for the rewards, they will stop studying when there are no longer rewards.

	(A)	(B)	(C)
①	irrelevant	persist	terminated
②	irrelevant	cease	terminated
③	instrumental	cease	initiated
④	instrumental	persist	initiated
⑤	instrumental	persist	terminated

※ 다음 글의 제목으로 가장 적절한 것을 고르시오. [24~25]

24

We are accustomed to brushing our teeth every day. We know it to be a healthful ritual that preserves our teeth and gums and widens our smile. Its benefits are personal as well as social. But archaeologists working among the remains of eighteenth-century Annapolis — where a new class of people were eager for work — have suggested a new view of how and why we came to all this brushing and flossing and fussing. Mark Leone and his team of urban archaeologists found numerous toothbrushes under the streets of Annapolis. Eighteenth-century toothbrushes suggest a new emphasis on personal hygiene and the notion of the self-maintained individual. It's important: to have workers arrive on time and do a job, they have to develop discipline. So an industrial society emphasizes toothbrushes and a lot of other things like combs and clocks to help people make themselves orderly. Toothbrushes, it turns out, were instrumental in easing us into the Industrial Revolution.

① Annapolis: A Grand Archaeologist Attraction

② Appearance of "Toothbrush" in the English Language

③ Impact of the Toothbrush on the Dental Care Industry

④ Role of the Toothbrush in Developing an Industrial Workforce

⑤ Economic Changes Brought About by the Industrial Revolution

25

Researchers have noted a correlation between diet drink consumption and poor health for years. But many people simply believe that this undesirable correlation is due to the fact that people who are already unhealthy or heavy tend to drink diet soda in the first place. However, Susan Swithers of Purdue University claims that this superficial behavioral explanation does not address the health problems caused by unfounded faith in diet drinks. She points out that when the body responds normally to sugar, it releases the hormones needed to prepare itself for the increased intake of both calories and sugar. "What happens when you have diet soda is you sense the sweet taste — but calories and sugar don't show up," Swithers said. Accordingly, she warns that if this unnatural situation happens over time, people's brains and bodies may be trained no to release the protective hormones any longer, even when you actually intake real sugar.

① Preventing and Curing Soda Addiction

② Prevalence of Sugar Substitutes in Diet Drinks

③ Recent Consumer Preferences in the Soda Market

④ Disruptive Effect of Diet Drinks on Protective Hormones

⑤ How the Brain Copes with Excessive Sugar Consumption

※ 글의 흐름으로 보아, 주어진 문장이 들어가기에 가장 적절한 곳을 고르시오. [26~27]

26
[2점]

Even so, modern weather forecasting is one of the great achievements of modern meteorology and all of science.

Modern weather forecasting today fuses advanced computer modeling with collective human insight. Together, they save lives and protect property through increasingly accurate predictions, as in the "Storm of the Century" in March 1993 and Superstorm Sandy in October 2012. (①) Ensemble forecasting allows meteorologists to get many "second opinions" on which to base even better forecasts. (②) Limits exist on how good forecasts can become, however. (③) Imperfect data, imperfect knowledge of how the atmosphere works, limits on computing power, and even chaos theory cause inaccurate forecasts. (④) Our ability to forecast weather skillfully has improved at the rate of about one more day into the future every decade. (⑤) It will continue to improve during your lifetime, through new techniques such as ensemble forecasting.

* ensemble forecasting : 종합적 분석에 기반한 기상예보

27
[3점]

Rather, we are witnessing the rise of an increasingly homogenized popular culture underwritten by a Western "culture industry."

Does globalization make people around the world more alike or more different? This is the question most frequently raised in the subject of cultural globalization. (①) One group of people argue that the former may be unfortunately true. (②) They suggest that we are not moving towards a cultural rainbow that reflects the diversity of the world's existing cultures. (③) As evidence for their interpretation, these people point to Amazonian Indians wearing Nike training shoes, inhabitants of the Southern Sahara purchasing Yankees baseball caps, and Palestinian youths proudly displaying their Chicago Bulls sweatshirts in downtown Ramallah. (④) Referring to the spread of Anglo-American values and consumer goods as the "Americanization of the world," the proponents of this cultural homogenization theory argue that Western norms and lifestyles are overwhelming more vulnerable cultures. (⑤) Although there have been serious attempts by some countries to resist these forces of "cultural imperialism," the spread of American popular culture seems to be unstoppable.

28 Samuel Adams에 관한 다음 글의 내용과 일치하지 않는 것은?

As a young man, Samuel Adams (1722-1803) of colonial-era Boston developed a dream: the American colonies, he believed, should one day win complete independence from England and establish a government based on the writings of the English philosopher John Locke. According to Locke, a government should reflect the will of its citizens; a government that did not do so had lost its right to exist. Adams had inherited a brewery from his father, but he did not care about business. While the brewery went into bankruptcy, he spent his time writing articles on the ideas of Locke and the need for independence. He was an excellent writer, good enough to get his articles published. But few took his ideas seriously at that time: he seemed to be somewhat out of touch with the world. Adams began to sink into a depression, because his self-appointed mission seemed hopeless.

① 영국의 철학자 John Locke로부터 영향을 받았다.
② 아버지로부터 물려받은 사업을 돌보지 않았다.
③ Locke의 사상과 독립의 필요성에 관한 글을 썼다.
④ 자신의 글을 출판할 정도로 훌륭한 작가였다.
⑤ 그의 사상은 그 당시 많은 사람들의 공감을 얻었다.

29 다음 글의 함축하는 바로 가장 적절한 것은?

A recent study conducted by Mueller and Oppenheimer points to new evidence that people have better learning outcomes when they have taken handwritten notes, rather than typed ones. The researchers observed that the laptop note takers in their study generally produced long, word-for-word notes, while the handwriting note takers created relatively brief notes. Close attention was paid to the fact that the more copious, in-detail notes led to inferior retrieval of facts and concept comprehension, as revealed by the test scores. Those who were taking notes on the laptops did not have to choose what to type, as keyboarding is fast enough for word-for-word transcription. On the contrary, the longhand note takers had to process information more carefully to choose what to write down because their handwriting was not as fast. This initial selectivity is regarded as the reason for better long-term grasp of the lecture materials.

① Keyboard note-taking yields better factual content memorization.

② There is no evidence of the superiority of handwriting note-taking.

③ Handwriting note-taking is recommended for better academic performance.

④ Paper-and-pencil note-taking generally leads to more complete, detailed notes.

⑤ Word-for-word notes taken with laptops generally guarantee higher test scores.

※ 다음 글의 주제로 가장 적절한 것을 고르시오. [30~31]

30
[2점]

Social networks seem to be particularly important as they increase access of employees to individuals with varying areas and levels of expertise. Consequently, facilitating the development of network ties, particularly weak ties, will have a positive impact on creativity. It is also clear that within the workplace, both informational and emotional support from colleagues is related to higher levels of creativity. Therefore, organizations (or leaders) interested in generating creativity should encourage strong relationships among employees. Finally, the presence of creative colleagues may be necessary for leaders to realize the impact of their own efforts to enhance creativity. Individuals display the highest level of creativity in response to supervisor feedback when they are in the presence of creative coworkers. Clearly, fostering individual creativity requires a consideration not just of the individual, but of his or her social context.

① harmful effects of strong network ties on creativity

② need for social networks to support the underprivileged

③ importance of respecting individuality within the workplace

④ danger of placing too much emphasis on creative outcomes

⑤ value of supportive social networks for enhancing creativity

For a period of more than a thousand years, Rome was the hub of Western civilization. Eventually, however, the very life of the Empire was threatened by economic unrest and a series of rapid changes in government. Matters reached such a state that no person of importance dared to walk the streets of the capital without armed bodyguards, who were known as satellites. When the Empire fell, classical Latin ceased to be the language of commerce and science. but educated men brought back the ancient tongue ten centuries later and used it for most formal speech. Among the revived terms was satellite, which medieval rulers applied to their personal bodyguards. When Johannes Kepler heard about the strange bodies revolving about Jupiter, he thought of guards and courtiers encircling the king. So, in 1611 Kepler named them satellites; soon the term was applied to all heavenly bodies that revolve about primary masses.

① discovery of Jupiter's satellites

② rise and fall of the Roman Empire

③ revival of classical Latin for formal speech

④ Roman citizens' need for armed bodyguards

⑤ evolution of the meaning of the word satellite

32 다음 글이 시사하는 바로 가장 적절한 것은?

2점

The brilliance of warfare is that no amount of eloquence or talk can explain away a failure on the battlefield. A general has led his troops to defeat, lives have been wasted, and that is how history will judge him. You must strive to apply this ruthless standard in your daly life, judging people by the results of their actions, the deeds that can be seen and measured, and the steps they have taken to achieve their goals. What people say about themselves does not matter; people will say anything. Look at what they have done; deeds do not lie. You must also apply this logic to yourself. Stop bragging and set out to prove your worth by the fruits of your hard work. People will judge you by what you do, not what you say.

① Look before you leap.　　　　② Do as you would be done by.

③ Actions speak louder than words.　　④ The pen is mightier than the sword.

⑤ One swallow does not make a summer.

33 다음 도표의 내용과 일치하지 않는 것은?

2점

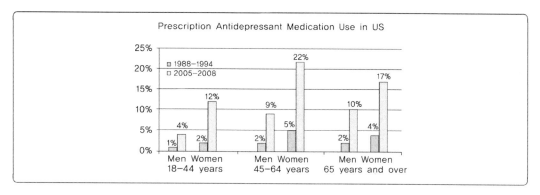

The above graph shows the percentage of Americans who answered yes to the question "Did you take prescription antidepressant medication in the past month?" by gender and age over two time periods, 1988−1994 and 2005−2008. ① There were general increases in the prescription antidepressant medication use across both genders and age groups between those two time frames. ② For men in the two older age categories, there were significant increases from 2% to 9% and 2% to 10%, respectively, yet men aged 18−44 showed a rather moderate increase from 1% to 4%. ③ In contrast, all three female groups showed more drastic increases of 10% in the 18−44 group, 17% in the 45−64 group, and 13% in the oldest group. ④ Men showed the greatest increase in the oldest group, while for women it was in the 45−64 year age range. ⑤ In the period 2005−2008, for those 45−64 years old, over twice as many males took prescription antidepressant medication as females.

34

2점

To be beautiful a thing must possess certain characteristics which awaken a feeling of appreciation in the normal person. It is true that the artistic judgment is not possessed equally by all, or at least it is not equally developed in all.

(A) The man without a musical education does not possess such knowledge, but he appreciates the harmony of tones when he hears it. The colorist knows how to produce pleasing effects with colors. He has acquired this knowledge which others do not possess, although they are able to apprcciate his work.

(B) There are, however, certain combinations of sounds which are universally called harmonies and others which are called discords. There are certain combinations of colors which are regarded as pleasing and others which are displeasing.

(C) There are likewise certain geometrical forms or space arrangements which are beautiful, and others which are displeasing. The musician knows what tones will harmonize and which ones will not.

① (A) – (C) – (B)　　　　② (B) – (A) – (C)

③ (B) – (C) – (A)　　　　④ (C) – (A) – (B)

⑤ (C) – (B) – (A)

35

2점

One day as John was riding to work on his bike, his cell-phone began to ring. As he reached for his phone to pull it from his pocket with his right hand, he hit the brake with his left hand. He lost control and went flying over the front of his bike.

(A) While John didn't feel much pain, his 돼 was hurt. He quickly pulled himself up and looked around to make sure no one had seen his embarrassing tumble. Lucky for John, there were no witnesses. He brushed the dirt off his face and got back on his way.

(B) After arriving at work, John became aware that he had severely scratched up his face and had a large cut across his cheek. He rushed to the hospital, where he was bandaged and received a few stitches. While not seriously injured, he still faced the shame of explaining the accident to his family.

(C) In that split second, his instinct was to protect his phone from damage at the cost of his own physical well-being. He held his arm up to keep his phone from hitting the pavement, instead using his face to break his fall.

① (A) – (C) – (B) ② (B) – (A) – (C)

③ (B) – (C) – (A) ④ (C) – (A) – (B)

⑤ (C) – (B) – (A)

36 다음 글에서 필자가 주장하는 바로 가장 적절한 것은?

2점

Fear will make you overestimate a problem and act too passively. Anger and impatience will draw you into rash actions that will cut off your options. Overconfidence, particularly as a result of success, will make you go too far. Love and affection will blind you to the treacherous actions of those apparently on your side. Even the subtlest gradations of these emotions can color the way you look at events. The only remedy is to be aware that the pull of emotion is inevitable, to notice it when it is happening, and to compensate for it. When you have success, be extra wary. When you are angry, take no action. Then you are fearful, know you are going to exaggerate the dangers you face. The more you can limit or compensate for your emotional responses, the closer you will come to seeing things as they are.

* treacherous : 배신하는

① 자신의 감정을 솔직하게 표현하라.
② 현실을 바로 보려면 감정에 휘둘리지 말라.
③ 원만한 문제 해결을 위해 이성에 호소하라.
④ 업무에 개인적인 감정을 개입시키지 말라.
⑤ 대화 시 상대방의 감정을 상하지 않게 하라.

37 다음 글의 내용을 한 문장으로 요약하고자 한다. 빈칸 (A)와 (B)에 들어갈 말로 가장 적절한 것은?

Dr. Zeray Alemseged made a remarkable contribution to the field of anthropology. Inspired by his experience of working in Ethiopia's National Museum, Alemseged went to the University of Paris for a Ph.D. program. After he returned to Ethiopia, he set his sight on an isolated region as an optimal place to look for new fossils. Other scientists had avoided this area, due to a centuries-old tribal conflict that made it too dangerous to work in, but he did not give up convincing both sides to allow him to work there. Alemseged and his team finally discovered the fossilized skeleton of a 3.3 million-year-old baby girl. It included the shoulder blades almost intact, which had never been found fossilized as they are paper-thin. Based on the shape of these blades, Alemseged and his colleagues pulished a study suggesting that Australopithecus afarensis was still a capable climber 3.3 million years ago, which means our ancestors gave up tree-climbing considerably later than many researchers had previously suggested.

* Australopithecus afarensis : 에티오피아 Afar 지역에서 화석이 발견된 오스트랄로피테쿠스

Thanks to his (A), Dr. Zeray Alemseged has contributed to a remarkable advancement in anthropology by finding evidence that human ancestors (B) their tree-climbing ability significantly later than other researchers had claimed.

	(A)	(B)
①	perseverance	abandoned
②	generosity	abandoned
③	perseverance	acquired
④	generosity	improved
⑤	creativity	acquired

※ 다음 글을 읽고, 물음에 답하시오. [38~39]

One of the most moving piano recitals I ever heard was by the late Rudolf Serkin, who delivered a luminous performance of the Beethoven Waldstein Sonata and the Schubert Wanderer Fantasy. During one of the virtuoso runs that make up the Schubert work, Serkin's fingers became audibly tangled. Despite the apparent mistake, Serkin wouldn't have this bother him, and went on playing. When he rose from the bench at the conclusion of the piece, he openly acknowledged his error by good-naturedly shaking his fist at the piano. In what could have been an embarrassing situation, Serkin was able to evoke laughter from the audience with his witty action. Needless to say, the audience were moved by the lovely performance as a whole. It was a more revealing, more beautiful version of this piece than many other "perfect" ones I have heart played by other musicians before or since. The lesson is obvious: Deliver a good performance overall, and you will be forgiven an error or two, even an obvious one. All the more, do not allow your mistakes to interrupt your performance. Just as Serkin's audience did not attend his recital for the purpose of catching him in a blunder, so it is highly unlikely that your audience will have gathered for the express purpose of seeing you make a mistake. And if you do err while performing, embrace the mistake and _____.

38 위 글의 빈칸에 들어갈 말로 가장 적절한 것은?

① take a brief time out

② get on with the show

③ shake your fist in anger

④ restart from the beginning

⑤ choose another piece to play

39 위 글의 Rudolf Serkin에 관한 내용과 일치하지 않는 것은?

① 연주회에서 Beethoven과 Schubert의 곡을 연주했다.

② 연주를 하다가 명백한 실수를 했다.

③ 연주를 중단하고 일어나서 청중에게 사과했다.

④ 재치 있는 행동으로 청중의 웃음을 자아냈다.

⑤ 아름다운 연주로 청중을 감동시켰다.

I'm always looking for communicators who create exciting ways to engage an audience. I've rarely seen anyone use more props than a young Italian entrepreneur and television host, Marco Montemagno.

Montemagno frequently speaks on the topic of Internet culture, showing Italians why the Internet should be embraced and not feared. He presents to groups as large as three thousand people in places such as Rome, Milan, and Venice. Since the majority of people in his audience are beginners in using the Web, (a) he uses language that everyone can understand (well, assuming you know Italian). His slides are very simple and visual; he often employs just photographs, animation, and video. But what truly differentiates Montemagno from the majority of presenters is (b) his unbelievable number of props and demonstrations.

In parts of his presentation, Montemagno will ask for his audience to join him onstage. For examply, (c) he asks a volunteer to fold a T-shirt on the stage. Like most people, the volunteer will take about twenty seconds to fold the shirt in a conventional way. When (d) he's done, the audience watch a popular YouTube video of someone demonstrating how to fold a shirt in five seconds. Montemagno then duplicates it as the audience cheer. (e) His point is that the Internet can instruct on a deep, intellectual level, but it can also make the most mundane tasks easier.

* prop : 소품

40 위 글의 밑줄 친 (a)~(e) 중에서, 가리키는 대상이 나머지 넷과 다른 것은?

① (a)　　　　　　　② (b)

③ (c)　　　　　　　④ (d)

⑤ (e)

41 위 글의 Marco Montemagno에 관한 내용과 일치하지 않는 것은?

① He engages in business and also hosts a TV program.

② He encourages his audience not to fear the Internet.

③ He makes presentations to very large groups in English.

④ He utilizes props and other visual materials in his presentations.

⑤ He incorporates the audience into his presentations.

※ 다음 글을 읽고, 물음에 답하시오. [42~43]

(A)

Haydn was delighted with London in most of its aspects, but there was one kind of pupil that he was perfectly willing to leave behind when he returned to his beloved Vienna. One day a nobleman visited him and, expressing his fondness for music, said he would like Haydn to give him a few lessons in composition at one pound per lesson.

(B)

Then Haydn suggested that the pupil rewrite the music to his own taste; but this he declined to do, though he persisted in his question about Haydn's composition choices. At last, Haydn lost all patience with this noble critic, and said, "I see that it is you who are so good as to give lessons to me. I do not want your lessons, for I feel that I do not deserve the honor of having such a master as yourself. I must say farewell," and showed the nobleman the door.

(C)

Haydn could offer no objection to this. They then set to work to examine the music. several places were found which, when asked why he did this and that, Haydn could only say he wrote it so to obtain a good effect. But the nobleman was not satisfied with such a reason and declared that unless the composer gave him a better reason for his innovations, they were good for nothing.

(D)

Haydn agreed and asked when they should begin. "At once, if you have no objection," said he, drawing from his pocket one of Haydn's quartets. "For the first lesson, let us examine this quartet and you tell me the reasons for some modulations and certain progressions that are contrary to all rules of composition."

* quartet : 4중주곡   ** modulation : 조음(조 바꾸기)

42 주어진 글 (A)에 이어질 내용을 순서에 맞게 배열한 것으로 가장 적절한 것은?

[3점]
① (B) – (D) – (C)
② (C) – (B) – (D)
③ (C) – (D) – (B)
④ (D) – (B) – (C)
⑤ (D) – (C) – (B)

43 위 글의 제목으로 가장 적절한 것은?

2점

① Money Buys Patience

② Pleasure of Examining Music

③ A Most Beautiful London Memory

④ Not a Good Pupil, But a Harsh Critic

⑤ Inspiration from a Challenging Question

※ 다음 글을 읽고, 물음에 답하시오. [44~45]

Despite the many eco-friendly movements to prevent global warming, Arctic ice is melting at previously unseen rates. The melting has let to coastal ice in parts of Canada and Alaska becoming quite (A). That ice easily breaks away in large chunks (a process known as calving) and melts in the open ocean.

There is also less sea ice in the Arctic Ocean because ice has floated into the Atlantic Ocean. A record low for Arctic sea ice was recorded on August 15, 2005, but the Arctic saw another milestone in the summer of 2007. In August, the Northwest Passage had almost no floating ice. It was the first time the Passage had been completely open to shipping since people started keeping records in 1972.

Arctic sea ice that was previously considered (B) is now rapidly disappearing. The disappearance of this ice must be noted seriously because it plays an important role in keeping temperatures down around the world. Whereas sea ice reflects eighty percent of sunlight back into the atmosphere, ocean water absorbs ninety percent. As melting ice exposes more ocean to direct sunlight, scientists expect water temperatures to rise even more, causing the melting ice to disappear at an ever-increasing rate.

44 위 글의 제목으로 가장 적절한 것은?

2점

① Developing a Plan to Battle Arctic Ice Melt

② Scientific Ways to Monitor Global Warming

③ Differing Effects of Sunlight on Land and Ocean

④ Vicious Circle of Global Warming and Arctic Ice Melt

⑤ Changes in Ocean Navigation Owing to Global Warming

45 위 글의 빈칸 (A)와 (B)에 들어갈 말로 가장 적절한 것은?

2점

	(A)		(B)
①	brittle	……	permanent
②	brittle	……	vulnerable
③	solid	……	defenseless
④	solid	……	permanent
⑤	soft	……	vulnerable

▶ 해설은 p. 79에 있습니다.

01 Based on the following dialogue, which one is NOT true?

2점

> Mr. Sanders : You'll never guess who I met when I picked up our daughter from her violin lesson today!
>
> Mrs. Sanders : Don't keep me in suspense. Who?
>
> Mr. Sanders : Our girl's first boyfriend. I can't believe she's already dating.
>
> Mrs. Sanders : Oh my goodness! Well, she is all grown up, isn't she? What did you think of him?
>
> Mr. Sanders : I'm a father! At first glance, of course I wasn't impressed. No one is good enough for our precious daughter.
>
> Mrs. Sanders : Come on! Objectively, tell me, what was he like?
>
> Mr. Sanders : Honestly, in talking with him for a minute, he seemed like a pretty decent guy. But I still want to know everything about him.

① The Sanders' daughter is learning violin.

② The Sanders' daughter is dating.

③ Mrs. Sanders says she doesn't like the guy.

④ Mrs. Sanders hasn't met the guy.

⑤ Mr. Sanders was originally skeptical about the guy.

02 Which is the best sequence of answers for the blanks?

2점

> Librarian : Hi there. What can I do for you?
>
> Tom : To be honest, this is my first time in a library and I need to find a book called "Bob's Big Barbecue," but I don't know who wrote it.
>
> Librarian : No problem. First of all, we'll just type the _____ of the book here in the computer, and it will give us a series of numbers. The first digit will tell us what _____ to look on, so it shows us we must take the stairs over there.
>
> Tom : What about the next numbers?
>
> Librarian : Those indicate what _____ to look on, so check the numbers on each bookcase until you find the correct range of numbers.
>
> Tom : Thanks so much for your help.

〈보 기〉

a. title   b. author
c. floor   d. shelf

① a — c — d   ② a — d — c
③ b — d — c   ④ d — a — c
⑤ d — c — a

03 Where is the dialogue most likely taking place?

2점

> Mr. Gupta : I'm glad you brought Mia in for treatment. The good news is that she will be okay, but the bad news is that her injury will require surgery.
>
> Susan : I was afraid of that. Since the accident, she has been limping badly, and that back paw just won't heal completely.
>
> Mr. Gupta : Yes, unfortunately, she has a broken bone in her back leg that will require an operation.
>
> Susan : But after that, she'll be fine?
>
> Mr. Gupta : Then she'll still have a few weeks of home recovery, during which she will have to wear a big plastic cone around her head to make sure she doesn't lick at her wound. But then she should be 100% recovered.
>
> Susan : Great! What a relief!

① Veterinary Clinic

② Dentist's Office

③ Pharmacy

④ Medical Supply Center

⑤ Hospital Information Desk

04 Based on the following dialogue, which one is true?

2점

> Steve : Wow, what a beautiful place! I could stay here forever. So where do you want to set up the tent?
>
> Dean : Are you sure you want to sleep out here? There was a reasonable hotel just down the road.
>
> Steve : Come on. What about over there near the water? The ground looks nice and flat.
>
> Dean : I don't know. It's right in the sun without any shade.
>
> Steve : So, what about back there a bit, under those trees?
>
> Dean : That's even worse, surrounded by bugs and closer to any wild animals stalking around in the dark.
>
> Steve : You're such a baby! Fine. I give up. But you're paying for the room.
>
> Dean : No problem. As long as we don't sleep outdoors.

① Dean wants to set up the tent near the water.

② Dean isn't fond of sleeping outdoors.

③ Steve and Dean are going to sleep in the tent.

④ Steve is afraid of wild animals.

⑤ Steve will pay for the accommodation.

05 Choose the best answer for the blank.

 3점

> Bank Manager : We've reviewed your small business loan application, but we are not entirely convinced of the potential of your plan.
>
> Loan Applicant : What are you talking about? It's fool-proof. Everyone loves ice cream, and there is not another ice cream store around for hundreds of miles.
>
> Bank Manager : The general desirability of your product is not really the problem.
>
> Loan Applicant : I don't understand. Is it my lack of experience? Because I promise you, I have learned everything there is to know about ice cream.
>
> Bank Manager : No, the real issue is location. You've chosen to open your business in a small village in Alaska where it is winter almost year-round. We just don't think an ice-cream shop is a viable business in such a place.
>
> —————

① It sounds like a great idea and we wish you luck.

② Please fill out these forms to begin your loan application.

③ We look forward to a long and healthy business relationship.

④ We're pleased to tell you that you've been approved for the loan.

⑤ We're sorry, but we will not be able to process your loan application.

06 Choose the sentence that best describes the situation.

2점

> Sam : This is Sam's Office Supplies, how can I help you?
>
> Donna : I'm calling because over a month ago I ordered 10 boxes of A4 printer paper, and at the time I was told delivery would only take one week.
>
> Sam : Absolutely, our orders are guaranteed to be delivered in one week or less, depending on your location. What seems to be the problem?
>
> Donna : The problem is, not only was the shipment two weeks late, but only half was delivered, and I'm still waiting for the rest.
>
> Sam : I'm terribly sorry. Our records show that all 10 boxes were delivered, but I will get to the bottom of the problem and get those remaining 5 boxes shipped out immediately.
>
> Donna : Thank you, and please make sure it doesn't happen again.

① Donna was completely satisfied with Sam's delivery service.

② Donna regrets that Sam has ignored her complaints for weeks.

③ The order was properly filled so there is nothing Sam can do.

④ Sam will try to solve the problem and make his customer happy.

⑤ Donna is planning to cancel her order with Sam's Office Supplies.

07 밑줄 친 부분이 가리키는 대상이 나머지 넷과 다른 것은?

2점

Misty May-Treanor and Kerri Walsh are great athletes, and they are great people. In the semifinals of the beach volleyball event at the 2008 Olympics in Beijing, ① they defeated a very good Brazilian team. Afterward, they shook hands with the members of the Brazilian team and said "thank you." ② They then shook hands with many, many volunteers who do such things as retrieve balls and rake the sand. In awe, journalist Mike Celizic wrote, "They literally chased down some of the volunteers from behind as they were leaving the court, not wanting ③ them to get away without knowing how much their efforts were appreciated." ④ They also waved to the fans and promised to come back after the mandatory drug testing. They did come back, posing for photographs and signing autographs for many, many fans. And yes, the fans really appreciated shaking hands with ⑤ them.

※ 다음 글에서 전체 흐름과 관계 없는 문장을 고르시오. [08~09]

08

2점

MSG is essentially a concentrated form of sodium, which is extracted from seaweed, beets, and grains. ① The Glutamate Association insists that MSG is perfectly safe. ② They argue that MSG is no different from the glutamate that is liberated by our bodies when we eat food protein, and that MSG added to food represents only a small fraction of the glutamate contained naturally in most foods. ③ For many of the same reasons, a number of chefs dislike MSG, believing that it deadens the taste of foods and is too often used to compensate for inferior products. ④ For example, most recipes call for half a teaspoon of MSG per pound of meat. ⑤ With these proportions, the MSG in a serving of chicken would constitute less than 10 percent of the glutamate already found in the chicken.

*glutamate 글루타민산염

09 Traditional advertisements are typically defined as persuasive, nonpersonal communications delivered to consumers via the mass media on behalf of identifiable sponsors, and humor is often a key tool employed. ① Because most consumers are exposed to a large number of advertisements on a daily basis, humorous advertisements may be the most frequent way that many come into contact with intentional humor. ② Advertisers use humor as a message tactic, with the intent of enhancing an advertisement's potential for achieving various strategic objectives. ③ Humor was used rather infrequently during the early years of modern advertising ; researchers, however, have confirmed that its use in contemporary advertising is prevalent, especially in the broadcast media. ④ It is widely accepted in the advertising industry that humor is quite ineffective and even counterproductive. ⑤ Although this is generally true for most industrialized, First World countries, humor is found somewhat more frequently in the advertising of Western countries and cultures than in Eastern ones.

10 다음 글의 요지로 가장 적절한 것은?

Most people have two potentially opposing needs: one is to be available to others for social contact ; the other is to have privacy. Some people need more privacy, others more social contact. If we think about the environment, whether at the level of public spaces or domestic spaces, we can see features which reflect these two needs. In western society the door is a ubiquitous architectural feature, and curtains are almost obligatory parts of our domestic props. The possibility of closing or opening doors and curtains is a device for signalling availability. Goffman has drawn attention to the prevalence of back (private) regions and front (public) regions both in domestic settings and in public settings. Back regions, which in houses include bedrooms, bathrooms and sometimes kitchens, are regions in which only intimates may penetrate without invitation. Front regions are open to the public.

① 현대사회는 사생활보다 사회생활을 중시한다.
② 사생활에 대한 인식과 중요성은 문화마다 다르다.
③ 사생활과 사회생활의 구분이 점차 희미해지고 있다.
④ 가정이 사회생활의 장이 되는 것은 바람직하지 않다.
⑤ 생활공간에는 사생활과 사회생활에 대한 필요가 반영된다.

11

[2점]

The triumph of antibiotics over disease-causing bacteria is one of modern medicine's greatest success ① stories. Since these drugs first became widely used in the World War II era, they have saved countless lives and ② blunted serious complications of many feared diseases and infections. After more than 50 years of widespread use, however, many antibiotics don't have the same effect that they once ③ were. Over time, some bacteria have developed ways to outwit the effects of antibiotics. Widespread use of antibiotics is thought to have spurred evolutionary changes in bacteria ④ that allow them to survive these powerful drugs. While antibiotic resistance benefits the microbes, it presents humans with two big problems: it makes it more ⑤ difficult to purge infections from the body ; and it heightens the risk of acquiring infections in a hospital.

12

[3점]

In a survey, when the response options are presented visually, it seems reasonable to assume that respondents typically start at the top of the list and ① work their way through the remaining options in order. Primacy effects would, therefore, seem to be the rule: Respondents will tend to prefer options at the beginning of the list over ② those at the end. However, the picture becomes somewhat murkier when the interviewer reads the response options to the respondent. Survey interviewers tend to read questions ③ quickly so that respondents will not generally have time to evaluate the first option before they must turn to the next. It is quite likely that respondents will begin by considering the final option, since that option is the one that will remain in working memory when the interviewer stops ④ to read. Consequently, we should expect recency effects — the tendency to choose options at the end of the list — when the question ⑤ is presented aloud to the respondent.

※ (A), (B), (C)의 각 네모 안에서 어법에 맞는 표현으로 가장 적절한 것을 고르시오. [13~14]

13

[2점]

"Hat-trick" was originally an English cricket term used to describe the tremendous feat of a bowler's taking three wickets on successive balls. The reward for this accomplishment at many cricket clubs (A) ⎡was / were⎤ a new hat. Other clubs honored their heroes by "passing the hat" among fans and giving the scorer the proceeds. The term spread to other sports (B) ⎡which / in which⎤ scoring is relatively infrequent — "hat-trick" is also used to describe the feat of scoring three goals in soccer. According to Belinda Lerner of the National Hockey League, the expression surfaced in hockey during the early 1900s: "There is some confusion about its actual meaning in hockey. Today, a 'true' hat-trick occurs when one player scores three successive goals without another goal (C) ⎡scoring / being scored⎤ by other players in the contest."

*take a wicket (크리켓 경기에서 투수가) 타자를 아웃시키다

	(A)	(B)	(C)
①	was	in which	being scored
②	was	which	scoring
③	was	in which	scoring
④	were	which	being scored
⑤	were	in which	scoring

14 Most of us choose the kinds of lives we lead. Although we may not be aware of it, each day we make choices that determine (A) ┃ what / whether ┃ we will be happy or unhappy, healthy or ill, creative or barren. We make the majority of these choices on an unconscious level, (B) ┃ guide / guided ┃ primarily by a sense of what has happened to us in the past and what might happen to us in the future. This apparently automatic process of decision making tends to hide the fact that we are making choices constantly. Over time, we lose the sense of making a choice at each new moment of life; as a result, we come to believe that a vague external force — destiny, fate, or luck — (C) ┃ influences / influencing ┃ how we live, what we accomplish, and sometimes, how we die.

	(A)	(B)	(C)
①	what	guide	influencing
②	what	guided	influences
③	whether	guided	influencing
④	whether	guide	influences
⑤	whether	guided	influences

※ 다음 글을 읽고, 빈칸에 들어갈 말로 가장 적절한 것을 고르시오. [15~18]

15 The melting pot view of society has some appeal, because it suggests that everyone can succeed if only they try hard enough. However, at some point we should realize that this type of equity usually means eliminating differences and variety. The melting pot ideal generally requires that an individual sacrifice his or her uniqueness to fit into an existing system. The only way to become successful, at least in a socially acceptable fashion (as opposed to becoming a famous gangster), requires developing ways to fit in while giving up on one's cultural background. We use the idea of the melting pot as a way to blend different ingredients, but we should recognize that the result of this melting pot is a homogeneous product wherein distinctive features are diluted. In short, the melting pot metaphor reflects a desire for _____.

① diversity
② challenge
③ sameness
④ originality
⑤ independence

16 Time adds an important and necessary dimension to our understanding of the world and our place in it — it seems almost impossible to conceive of what our world of experience might be like in the absence of time ; after all, events happen in time. This has resulted in physicists treating time, along with space, as a theoretical and an empirical primitive. The view that time constitutes, at some level, part of the physical fabric of the cosmos, and as such is physically real, accords with what I will term the common-place view of time. Most people believe in this view of time, a 'true' time, a time that actually exists in a physical sense ; on this account, time _____, as reflected in the physical laws which govern the environment we inhabit. While time may itself be "imperceptible," it is nonetheless real, manifesting tangible consequences. Without time's "passage" there could be no succession and thus no experience of duration.

① passes with its own driving force

② cannot be perceived physically

③ is not dealt with in the field of physics

④ is objectively embedded in the external world

⑤ is an imaginary construct of human experience

17 The problem that many of us face is that we have great dreams and ambitions. Caught up in the emotions of our dreams and the vastness of our desires, we find it very difficult to focus on the small, tedious steps usually necessary to attain them. We tend to think in terms of giant leaps toward our goals. But in the social world as in nature, anything of size and stability grows slowly. The piecemeal strategy is the perfect antidote to our natural impatience: it focuses us on something small and immediate, a first bite, then how and where a second bite can get us closer to our ultimate objective. It forces us to think in terms of a process, a sequence of connected steps and actions, no matter how small, which has immeasurable psychological benefits as well. Too often the magnitude of our desires overwhelms us ; _____ makes them seem realizable. There is nothing more therapeutic than action.

*antidote 해독제, 교정수단

① getting help from others

② taking that small first step

③ looking back into the past

④ sharing our desires with someone

⑤ sacrificing ourselves for a good cause

18 Anxiety, believe it or not, _____ . For you are born and raised with desires, preferences, and goals, and if you had no anxiety whatever, and were totally unconcerned about achieving your desires, you would tolerate all kinds of obnoxious things and would do nothing to ward them off or escape from them. Anxiety, basically, is a set of uncomfortable feelings and action tendencies that make you aware that unpleasant happenings — meaning things that go against your desires — are happening or are likely to happen and warn you that you'd better do something about them. Thus, if you are in danger of being attacked, and you desire to remain unhurt, you have a choice of several possible actions, such as running away, fighting off your attacker, calling the police, and so on. But you would probably do none of these things unless you were concerned, watchful, anxious, tense, cautious, vigilant, or panicked. You would perceive the danger of the attack, perhaps, but do nothing about it.

*obnoxious 불쾌한

① instills a sense of responsibility in you

② helps keep you alive and comfortable

③ makes you tolerate all kinds of insults

④ prevents you from pursuing your desires

⑤ inhibits clear thinking in stressful situations

19 다음 글에서 필자가 주장하는 바로 가장 적절한 것은?

[2점]

Right from the start, the main focus in AI research has always been with the issue of problem solving. Seen from this point of view, intelligence corresponds to the ability to solve complex problems, from the accurate autonomous movement of a robot arm to the understanding of a natural language sentence. The classical setting is that of a search in a space of solutions for the problem, where an intelligent agent looks for the best choices. One of the most common criticisms made of Artificial Intelligence methods of problem solving is their limited ability to deal with situations not predicted in the specification. The search space is normally strictly defined, however flexible, complex and adaptable the system seems to be. When facing a problem with no satisfactory solution in its search space, an AI system simply returns, at best, the least unsuccessful result that exists in that search space even when the solution is achievable via the simplest operation of changing perspective, relaxing a constraint or adding a new symbol. In other words, such systems are hardly capable of performing what we normally call creative behavior, a fundamental aspect of intelligence.

① 인공지능의 탐색 공간은 무한히 확장될 수 있다.
② 인공지능을 활용한 범죄에 대한 대책이 시급하다.
③ 도덕성 논란은 인공지능 기술 발전의 장애요인이다.
④ 인공지능 기술 개발 및 연구에 대한 투자가 부족하다.
⑤ 인공지능은 창의성 결여라는 한계를 극복하지 못하고 있다.

※ 다음 글의 빈칸 (A), (B)에 들어갈 말로 가장 적절한 것을 고르시오. [20~21]

20 What we call "mind" and what we call "body" are not two things, but rather aspects of one _____(A)_____ process, so that all our meaning, thought, and language emerge from the aesthetic dimensions of this embodied activity. Chief among those aesthetic dimensions are qualities, images, patterns of sensorimotor processes, and emotions. For at least the past three decades, scholars and researchers in many disciplines have piled up arguments and evidence for the embodiment of mind and meaning. However, the implications of their research have not entered public consciousness, and so the denial of mind/body dualism is still a highly provocative claim that most people find objectionable and even threatening. Coming to grips with your embodiment is one of the most profound philosophical tasks you will ever face. Acknowledging that every aspect of the human mind is _____(B)_____ specific forms of bodily engagement with an environment requires a far-reaching rethinking of who and what we are, in a way that is largely at odds with many of our inherited Western philosophical and religious traditions.

*sensorimotor 감각운동성의

	(A)	(B)
①	dividing	grounded in
②	organic	grounded in
③	organic	separated from
④	dividing	separated from
⑤	imaginary	unrelated to

21 In the early history of warfare, military leaders were faced with the following predicament : The success of any war effort depended on the ability to know as much about the other side — its intentions, its strengths and weaknesses — as possible. But the enemy would never willingly disclose this information. ___(A)___ , the enemy often came from an alien culture, with its peculiar ways of thinking and behaving. A general could not really know what was going on in the mind of the opposing general. From the outside the enemy represented something of an impenetrable mystery. And yet, lacking some understanding of the other side, a general would be operating in the dark. The only solution was to scrutinize the enemy for outward signs of what was going on within. ___(B)___ , a strategist might count the cooking fires in the enemy camp and the changes in that number over time; that would show the army's size.

*predicament 곤경 **scrutinize 면밀히 조사하다

(A)	(B)
① Instead	Otherwise
② Instead	However
③ In addition	However
④ In addition	For example
⑤ On the contrary	For example

※ (A), (B), (C)의 각 네모 안에서 문맥에 맞는 표현으로 가장 적절한 것을 고르시오. [22~23]

22 Stop-motion photography is used to fool the eye into seeing motion. A still photograph is made of an object, such as a clay model of a dinosaur. The object is moved (A) considerably / slightly and another photograph is taken. This delicate process is repeated thousands of times. When the photographs, or frames, are shown at the speed of a motion picture camera, 24 frames per second, the clay model appears to be (B) resting / moving . A major problem with stop-motion filming is that there are no "blurs." If you film a man running down the street, there will be a slight blur on each frame. Although not noticed by the audience, the blur helps make the running motion smooth and realistic. In stop-motion films, a running creature seems to have jerky movements. This problem has been solved with computer animation, which can be used to make frames (C) blurry / jerky to produce realistic movement.

	(A)	(B)	(C)
①	considerably	resting	blurry
②	considerably	moving	jerky
③	slightly	resting	blurry
④	slightly	resting	jerky
⑤	slightly	moving	blurry

23 Modern technology has provided us with countless time-saving devices. Cell phones with headsets (A) allow / forbid people to talk to friends or colleagues and battle rush hour at the same time. In a matter of seconds a computer can perform calculations that would take months if done by hand. Nonetheless, most of us complain about not having enough time. Surveys suggest that a majority of people subjectively feel that they have less and less time for themselves. Time has become a truly (B) common / precious commodity ; one national survey found that 51% of the adult respondents would rather have more time than more money. Part of the problem is that in our modern society, work follows people home. Thus, people find themselves bound to their jobs around the clock by the same nomadic tools — cell phones, tablets, wireless e-mail — that were heralded first as instruments of (C) constraint / liberation . To deal with this time crunch, more and more people are cutting back on their sleep as they attempt to juggle work, family, and household responsibilities.

	(A)	(B)	(C)
①	allow	precious	liberation
②	allow	precious	constraint
③	allow	common	liberation
④	forbid	common	constraint
⑤	forbid	precious	constraint

※ 다음 글의 제목으로 가장 적절한 것을 고르시오. [24~25]

24 According to explanatory critical theories of capitalism, crises occur when the inherent contradictions of capitalism lead to imbalances, i.e. the loss of the balances (e.g. between what is produced and what is consumed) which are necessary for the existing system to continue to function. Crises are not only inevitable but also necessary, for when imbalances develop, people have to impose some order on a situation of collapse and chaos. We can say that crises have a rationalizing function, the function of restoring rationality where it has been undermined. In Harvey's words, crises are "the irrational rationalisers of an always unstable capitalism." Crises have an objective or systemic aspect, but they also have a necessary and indeed crucial subjective aspect, which is agentive and strategic. In a crisis, people have to make decisions about how to act in response and to develop strategies for pursuing particular courses of action or policies which will hopefully restore balance and rationality.

① Destructive Nature of Crises

② Necessity of Crises in Capitalism

③ Avoiding Crises in a Capitalist System

④ Competition: Driving Force of Capitalism

⑤ Capitalism: Way Out of Crises and Chaos

25 "Children's playing is not sport and should be considered their most serious action," Montaigne, a sixteenth-century essayist, wrote. If we wish to understand our child, we need to understand his play. Freud, a founder of modern psychology, regarded play as the means through which a child expresses himself. He also noted how much and how well children express their thoughts and feelings through play. From a child's play we can gain understanding of how he sees and interprets the world — what he would like it to be, what his concerns and problems are. A child does not play spontaneously only to while away the time, although the adults observing him may think he does. Even when he engages in play partly to fill empty moments, what he chooses to play at is motivated by inner processes, desires, problems, anxieties.

① Harm Caused by Children's Violent Play

② Play: Expression of Children's Inner Self

③ Importance of Restricting Children's Play

④ How to Raise Physically Healthy Children

⑤ Children's Play: Means of Making Friends

※ 글의 흐름으로 보아, 주어진 문장이 들어가기에 가장 적절한 곳을 고르시오. [26~27]

26

And this will not ever go away — not now, not in the twenty-second century, not in a thousand years : All leaders die.

In looking at the charismatic leader model, we think the world is heading in exactly the opposite direction. Just look at the twenty-first century. Nearly the entire world has moved toward democracy. (①) The very essence of democracy is to avoid overdependence on any single leader and put the primary focus on the process. (②) Even Churchill — perhaps the single greatest leader of the last century — was secondary to the nation and its processes, kicked out of office at the end of World War II. (③) Hitler, Stalin, Mussolini — these were charismatic leaders who did not understand that they were fundamentally less important than the institutions they served. (④) And even if you don't buy the analogy between the shift to democracy and the evolution of corporations, the great charismatic leader model has one fundamental flaw. (⑤) To transcend this unchanging reality of human mortality, the focus must be first and foremost on building the characteristics of the organization, instead of being a great charismatic leader.

27

If there is disagreement or confusion at this stage, it is unlikely that the ensuing encounter will be fruitful.

In many interpersonal transactions, one encounter is influenced by decisions made and commitments undertaken in the previous meeting. (①) Again, it is important to establish that all parties are in agreement as to the main points arising from prior interactions and the implications of these for the present discussion. (②) This problem is formally overcome in many business settings, where minutes of meetings are taken. (③) The minutes from a previous meeting are reviewed, and agreed at the outset, before the main agenda items for the current meeting are discussed. (④) This procedure ensures that all participants are in agreement about what has gone before, and have therefore a common frame of reference for the forthcoming meeting. (⑤) In addition, agenda items are usually circulated prior to the meeting, and this in itself is a form of cognitive set, allowing individuals to prepare themselves for the main areas to be discussed.

※ 다음 글이 시사하는 바로 가장 적절한 것을 고르시오. [28~29]

28

When historians look at this period, they're going to conclude that we're in a different type of revolution: a revolution in war, like the invention of the atomic bomb. But it may be even bigger than that, because our unmanned systems don't just affect the "how" of war-fighting, but they affect the "who" of fighting at its most fundamental level. That is, every previous revolution in war, be it the machine gun or atomic bomb, was about a system that either shot faster, went further, or had a bigger boom. That's certainly the case with robotics, but they also change the experience of the warrior and even the very identity of the warrior. Another way of putting this is that mankind's 5,000-year-old monopoly on the fighting of war is breaking down in our very lifetime. It is likely that the effects of this may ripple outwards over time, substantially changing the very direction of human development, our society, our laws and our ethics, etc.

① Robotics is bringing about a revolution in warfare whose effects reach far into society.

② Unmanned systems are the only way to save human soldiers from the battlefield.

③ Robotics, which is developing rapidly, will eventually bring an end to warfare.

④ There will be little change in the way wars are fought.

⑤ Governments must make robotics investment a priority.

29 "What matters is not what people say or intend but the results of their actions." This is what Machiavelli called the "effective truth" — the real truth, in other words, what happens in fact, not in words or theories. You can apply the same barometer to your attempts at communication. If a man says or writes something that he considers revolutionary and that he hopes will change the world and improve mankind, but in the end hardly anyone is affected in any real way, then it is not revolutionary or progressive at all. Communication that does not advance its cause or produce a desired result is just self-indulgent talk, reflecting no more than people's love of their own voice. The effective truth of what they have written or said is that nothing has been changed. The ability to reach people and alter their opinions is a serious affair.

① It is important to remain consistent in applying your principles.
② The search for truth through actions has proven to be difficult.
③ People interpret others' words according to their own preconceptions.
④ Good speakers focus not only on their message but on their presentation.
⑤ Communication is effective only when it has the power to influence others.

※ 다음 글의 주제로 가장 적절한 것을 고르시오. [30~31]

30 Religion can exert strong influences over commerce. In medieval Europe, for example, the Christian Church was strongly opposed to money-lending at interest, and because Jews were not bound by these religious rules they took on the role of money-lenders. Until quite recently, banking institutions have not developed among Muslims because the Prophet prohibited acceptance of interest from borrowers. On the other side of the coin, literally, are the vast sums of money exchanged by religious pilgrims to holy sites. Pilgrimage plays a significant role in the economy of religious centres such as Mecca in Saudi Arabia, Lourdes in France, and Banaras in India. Religion can also strongly influence what type of employment a person has, particularly in Hindu society where caste prescribes certain duties and occupations by birthright rather than suitability.

*pilgrim (성지) 순례자

① how economic boom supports religion
② geographical features of religious centres
③ significant impact of religion on economy
④ pilgrimage as the heart of religious activity
⑤ why different religions exist in different regions

31 Perhaps the most important dimension of the way that we think about ourselves is that of evaluation, that is our level of self-esteem. The degree to which we globally approve of ourselves has an impact on how we behave, particularly with other people. To a certain degree our evaluations of ourselves are dependent on comparisons with other people. For example, in judging specific abilities our judgements can really only be relative: the question of how good a tennis player/musician/cook one is can only be meaningful with reference to a scale derived from other people's performances. There is ample evidence that we look for opportunities to compare ourselves with relevant others. By relevant we mean others who are likely to be sufficiently close to us in terms of some overall scale for the comparison to be meaningful. For example, the local tennis club provides a more meaningful set of comparisons about our tennis skills than international championships would.

① damaging effects of over-focusing on competition

② role of relevant comparison in self-evaluation

③ importance of having high self-esteem

④ development of a competitive spirit

⑤ sports as a measure of self-worth

32 러시아 문학에 관한 다음 글의 내용과 일치하지 않는 것은?

During the century that it has existed in adequate English translation, the Russian canon of novels and plays has acquired a reputation and a certain "tone." It is serious (that is, tragic or absurd, but rarely lighthearted and never trivial), somewhat preacherly, often politically oppositionist, and frequently cast in a mystifying genre with abrupt or bizarre beginnings and ends. The novels especially are too long, too full of metaphysical ideas, too manifestly eager that readers not just read the story for fun or pleasure but learn a moral lesson. These books are deep into good and evil even while they parody those pretensions. If there is comedy, there is a twist near the end that turns your blood to ice. Russian literary characters don't seek the usual money, career, success in society for its own sake, trophy wife or husband, house in the suburbs, but instead crave some other unattainable thing.

*canon 진짜 작품(목록)

① 소설과 희곡은 명성을 얻었다.

② 소설과 희곡은 다소 설교적인 색채를 띤다.

③ 소설은 도덕적 교훈을 배제하고 즐거움을 추구한다.

④ 희극의 끝부분에서는 뜻밖의 전개가 일어난다.

⑤ 문학작품의 등장인물은 얻기 어려운 것을 갈망한다.

33 다음 도표의 내용과 일치하지 않는 것은?

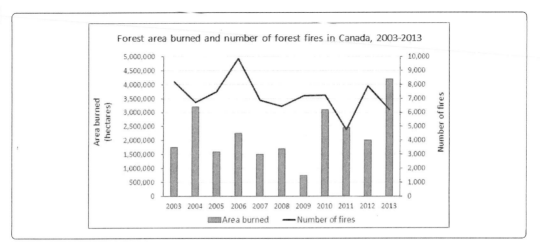

The graph above shows forest area burned and the number of forest fires in Canada between 2003 and 2013. ① The number of hectares burned in this period is shown to have three significant spikes of over 3 million in 2004 and in 2010, and more than 4 million in 2013. ② There was also a substantial drop in forest area burned in 2009 with much less than 1 million hectares. ③ In this period, the number of hectares burned was largest in 2013, which was over three times greater than in the previous year. ④ There were some significant fluctuations in the number of forest fires, such as in 2006 when there was a high of nearly 10,000 and a low of less than 5,000 in 2011. ⑤ Overall, there is no consistent correlation between forest area burned and the number of forest fires per year.

34

2점

Pesticides are an important component in pest management strategies for food production and public health. Despite their importance, these chemicals are often blamed for environmental pollution.

(A) In fact, few other chemicals commonly used by our society are more closely scrutinized. Moreover, insects can develop resistance with frequent applications of pesticides.

(B) Therefore, in order to use pesticides safely and effectively, not only must we know which pesticides to use in specific conditions, but we must also understand all biological, physiological, and environmental consequences.

(C) All of these issues have changed pest control from a simple task in the old days into the complex, publicly-sensitive operation of today. People who develop and supervise modern pest control methods must be highly trained in many areas of pesticide usage.

① (A) − (C) − (B)　　　　　② (B) − (A) − (C)

③ (B) − (C) − (A)　　　　　④ (C) − (A) − (B)

⑤ (C) − (B) − (A)

35

I was never a dog person. I'd even say I hated them. That was, until one day I found a pathetic ball of fur cowering under my car. It was a scared little dog. It looked as if she hadn't eaten or bathed in weeks.

(A) I had to go on a business trip the next day, but she was too weak to be left alone, so I asked a friend to watch her. When I got back I ran to pick her up, but apparently she had "escaped." I scoured the neighborhood through the night but came up empty.

(B) I made up posters with her description and my phone number, and put them up around the area. But nothing for over a week. Until finally, the phone rang. She was returned to me and we haven't been apart since. Needless to say, my feelings on dogs have drastically changed.

(C) She was so scared that I couldn't get her to come out, so I crawled under there and snatched her. And that's when it happened. She snuggled up to me. From that moment the bond was made ; she was mine, my responsibility, my best friend.

① (A) – (C) – (B)

② (B) – (A) – (C)

③ (B) – (C) – (A)

④ (C) – (A) – (B)

⑤ (C) – (B) – (A)

36 다음 글의 밑줄 친 부분 중, 문맥상 낱말의 쓰임이 적절하지 않은 것은?

[3점]

Physiological comfort is the sensation experienced in conditions relatively ① free of physiological stress. This comfort exists in certain ranges of temperature, incoming radiation, humidity, and wind speed deemed by a sophisticated instrument to be ② pleasant. The sophisticated instrument used to measure comfort is the human body. As long as the internal temperature of the body remains within a desirable range, the perception is one of comfort. Discomfort occurs when environmental conditions ③ exceed the range that supports this internal condition. As environmental temperatures rise, or as increased activity or fever raise internal temperatures, evaporative cooling (perspiration) on the surface of the skin increases to remove additional body heat. Increased air speed or decreased humidity can ④ reduce the stress that rising temperatures produce by increasing the benefit of evaporative cooling. Conversely, as ambient temperatures drop, provisions must be made to ⑤ accelerate the escape of body heat or to allow more solar radiation to be captured.

*ambient 주위의, 환경의

37 다음 글의 내용을 한 문장으로 요약하고자 한다. 빈칸 (A)와 (B)에 들어갈 말로 가장 적절한 것은?

[2점]

Many teenagers want to be like everyone in the school lunchroom. "We are not as unique as we would like to think," said Erica van de Waal, who conducted a study on monkey behavior. "We can find many of the roots of our behaviors in animals." Her study team gave 109 vervet monkeys, living in groups in the wild, food tinted pink or blue. One color for each group was tainted with aloe to give it a bad flavor, but only for the first few meals. Even after the flavor returned to normal the monkeys would not eat the color that they thought was bad. Then some blue-eating monkeys went to the pink-eating tribes and some pink-eating monkeys went to the blue-eating tribes. That is when the researchers saw peer pressure in action. The blue-food eaters that moved to an area full of pink-food eaters switched even though they had avoided pink food before. Pink eaters also changed when they moved to a blue-food area. They ate what everyone else ate.

The vervet monkeys' act of _____(A)_____ is thought to be a result of _____(B)_____ in a new group.

(A)   (B)

① switching food	social conformity
② switching food	food abundance
③ refusing to eat	power struggle
④ refusing to eat	food abundance
⑤ avoiding contact	social conformity

※ 다음 글을 읽고, 물음에 답하시오. [38~39]

Suppose you are having an argument with a friend and you "accidentally" knock off a shelf an irreplaceable statue belonging to that friend. The statue shatters beyond repair. You apologize, saying that you did not mean to do it. But is this really an accident? In Freud's view, many apparent accidents are in fact intentional actions stemming from unconscious impulses. Freud might argue that you were expressing an unconscious desire to hurt your friend when you broke his or her prized possession. Clients who claim to accidentally forget their regular therapy appointment might be displaying what Freud called resistance. Consciously, the clients believe they simply did not remember the appointment. Unconsciously, there has been a deliberate effort to _____ a therapist who may be close to uncovering threatening unconscious material. Similarly, reckless drivers might be setting themselves up for an accident to satisfy an unconscious desire for self−inflicted harm. To Freudian psychologists, many unfortunate events are accidents in the sense that people do not consciously intend them, but not in the sense that they are unintended.

38 위 글의 제목으로 가장 적절한 것은?

 2점

① How to Avoid Accidents

② Resistance to Undesirable Urges

③ Good Intention Matters More than Result

④ Unconscious Intention Hidden in Accidents

⑤ Unconscious Desire for Safety and Comfort

39 위 글의 빈칸에 들어갈 말로 가장 적절한 것은?

2점

① hinder   ② support

③ consult   ④ impress

⑤ motivate

※ 다음 글을 읽고, 물음에 답하시오. [40~41]

In later life, Arthur Rimbaud was an anarchist, businessman, arms dealer, financier, and explorer. But as a teenager, all (a) he wanted to be was a poet. In May 1871, the sixteen-year-old Rimbaud wrote two letters, one to Georges Izambard, (b) his former teacher, and one to Paul Demeny, a publisher he was keen to impress. Rimbaud waited around for Izambard every day, palely hanging around outside the school gates, eager to show the young professor his most recent verse. He also presented Demeny with copies of his work, accompanied by notes in which (c) he spoke about his poems and dropped heavy hints that he wanted to see them in print. In the letter to Demeny, Rimbaud outlined his vision for a new kind of poetry. "A Poet makes himself a visionary," Rimbaud lectured (d) him, "through a long, boundless, and systematized disorganization of all the senses." Only that, Rimbaud argued, could create a language that "will include everything: perfumes, sounds, colors, thought grappling with thought." (e) His poetic program involved upsetting conventional orders of perception, deranging habitual ways of seeing, hearing, smelling, touching, and tasting, and rearranging them in novel combinations. Fresh, vivid, and sometimes shocking images resulted when sense impression jostled sense impression, when thought grappled with thought.

*jostle 부딪치다

40 위 글의 밑줄 친 (a)~(e) 중에서, 가리키는 대상이 나머지 넷과 다른 것은?

2점

① (a)   ② (b)

③ (c)   ④ (d)

⑤ (e)

41 위 글의 "Arthur Rimbaud"에 관한 내용과 일치하지 않는 것은?

① He worked in fields unrelated to literature as an adult.

② He wanted to be a poet as a teenager.

③ He acquired his own unique vision for poetry from his teacher.

④ He hoped his poems would be published.

⑤ His poetic images were based on a conflict of senses or thoughts.

※ 다음 글을 읽고, 물음에 답하시오. [42~43]

Humans deliberately make and remake their social networks all the time. The primary example of this is homophily, the conscious or unconscious tendency to associate with people who resemble us (the word literally means "love of being alike"). Whether it's stamp collectors, coffee drinkers, or bungee jumpers, the truth is that we seek out those people who share our interests, histories, and dreams. As the saying goes, "_____"

But we also choose the structure of our networks in three important ways. First, we decide how many people we are connected to. Do you want one partner for a game of checkers or many partners for a game of hide-and-seek? Do you want to stay in touch with your crazy uncle? Second, we influence how densely interconnected our friends and family are. Should you seat the groom's college roommate next to your bridesmaid at the wedding? Should you throw a party so all your friends can meet each other? Should you introduce your business partners? And third, we control how central we are to the social network. Are you the life of the party, mingling with everyone at the center of the room, or do you stay on the sidelines?

Diversity in these choices yields an astonishing variety of structures for the whole network in which we come to be embedded. And it is diversity in these choices that places each of us in a unique location in our own social network. Of course, sometimes these structural features are not a matter of choice; we may live in places that are more or less conducive to friendship, or we may be born into large or small families. But even when these social-network structures are thrust upon us, they still rule our lives.

*conducive 도움이 되는

42 위 글의 주제로 가장 적절한 것은?

① how we shape our social networks

② how online social networks affect our life

③ tips for restoring damaged social networks

④ dangers of diversifying your social networks

⑤ necessity of social networks in finding a job

43 위 글의 빈칸에 들어갈 말로 가장 적절한 것은?

① Familiarity breeds contempt.　② Birds of a feather flock together.

③ Too many cooks spoil the broth.　④ Don't judge a book by its cover.

⑤ A rolling stone gathers no moss.

※ 다음 글을 읽고, 물음에 답하시오. [44~45]

(A)

When we were children, my brothers and I would get several presents from our parents for Christmas. Usually, our mother and father would give each of us one very expensive gift, as well as a few less costly items. This, however, was not the only gift-giving that happened in my house at Christmas time.

(B)

Since the papers were folded up, no one could tell whose name they were selecting. Also, no one would tell anyone else whose name they had chosen. In this way, our family members secretly bought something for one other person in the family. We really looked forward to Christmas Day, wondering from whom we would receive a gift.

(C)

We also had a unique tradition of our family. Every year, sometime in November, each person's name would be written on a small piece of paper, and the pieces of paper would be folded up and then placed into a hat. Next, one by one, we would each choose a piece of paper. The person whose name was on the paper was the family member that the person who chose it would buy a gift for.

(D)

Then one year something unexpected happened. On Christmas Day, when the time came to give out the "secret presents," my parents, my older brother, and I were all shocked to learn that each of us had purchased a gift for my younger brother, Joe. It was then that we realized that Joe had been the one to prepare the pieces of paper, and that _____!

44 주어진 글 (A)에 이어질 내용을 순서에 맞게 배열한 것으로 가장 적절한 것은?

 2점

① (B) − (D) − (C)

② (C) − (B) − (D)

③ (C) − (D) − (B)

④ (D) − (B) − (C)

⑤ (D) − (C) − (B)

45 위 글 (D)의 빈칸에 들어갈 말로 가장 적절한 것은?

2점

① he'd saved enough money to buy a present

② he'd written his own name on every one of them

③ he'd been proud of this unique tradition of our family

④ he'd properly finished what he had been expected to do

⑤ he'd wanted to give a gift to every member of our family

07 | 2017학년도 영어영역

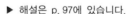

▶ 해설은 p. 97에 있습니다.

01 Based on the following dialogue, which one is NOT true?

2점

> Rachel : Hello, Dave. Welcome to the gym. Are you ready to start exercising?
> Dave : Good morning, Rachel. Actually, before we start, do you have any nutritional advice that might help me get in shape?
> Rachel : Okay. Did you drink plenty of fluids this morning?
> Dave : I sure did. You told me how important hydration is during your last lesson.
> Rachel : Great! Next up, are you eating a balanced diet? It should include grains, like bread or rice, healthy fats and oils, and plenty of fruits and vegetables.
> Dave : Oh, I love rice! Wow, I didn't realize that some fats are good for our bodies!
> Rachel : Of course! Healthy fats can be found in fish and are essential to a balanced diet. Also, rice is a great source of energy, but it contains many calories. Try replacing a little bit of rice with some fish in the future.

① Rachel is a gym instructor.

② Dave is well-hydrated.

③ A balanced diet should contain several types of food.

④ Some fats are important to a healthy diet.

⑤ Dave should eat more rice.

02 Which is the best sequence of answers for the blanks?

Ben : Hello, ma'am. You look lost. Could I help you?

Susan : Oh, yes. Thank you so much! This is my first time in New York City and I don't have a clue where I'm going.

Ben : It's my pleasure. Well, luckily for you, there's a great tourist site just around that corner. Have you visited the Empire State Building yet? _____

Susan : Not yet, but I certainly plan to! Where else should I visit?

Ben : If you love sports, then head up 5th Avenue toward the Yankees store on 36th Street. _____

Susan : Great! I also love reading. Could you recommend somewhere, please?

Ben : Actually, the New York Public Library is just past there, on 42nd Street. _____

Susan : Oh, I should hurry. Thank you so much for all of your advice!

〈보기〉

a. People buy baseball souvenirs there.

b. Just be aware that it closes at 6 p.m.

c. It was one of the first major skyscrapers.

d. It's a well-known hair salon.

① a − b − d

② b − c − d

③ c − a − b

④ c − b − a

⑤ d − c − a

03 Where is the dialogue most likely taking place?

Laura : Wow, it's beautiful out here! Oh, those look really fresh ; I'd love to get some for myself! Where did you find them?

Steven : Well, that depends. Are you talking about the strawberries or the apples?

Laura : How about both? Strawberries are definitely my favorite fruit, but I also enjoy baking apple pie. My grandmother's recipe is famous in my hometown.

Steven : Okay! Do you promise to share some pie with me if I help you pick some?

Laura : Sure thing. Where did you get them and how much were they, anyway?

Steven : Well, the strawberries cost $1 per kilogram and the plot is over there by the stream ; the apples cost $2 per kilogram and they can be found in the southern field. Let's go!

① in a florist's   ② in an orchard

③ in a greenhouse   ④ in a grocery store

⑤ in a fruit processing plant

04 Based on the following dialogue, which one is true?

[Telephone rings.]

Sam : Good morning. You've reached the customer service department of Big Electronics. This is Sam speaking. How may I help you?

Joe : Hi, I'm Joe Lee. I recently bought one of your cellphones and the screen is faulty.

Sam : I'm sorry, Sir. Can you tell me the date and location of the purchase, please?

Joe : Of course. I bought it two weeks ago, on the 3rd of July. The location was one of your LA stores, the large one on San Pedro Street.

Sam : Okay, Sir. Your phone is still within its warranty. You can choose to send your device to the manufacturer and receive a replacement. Or, one of our technicians can repair it for you if you'd prefer to visit a branch.

Joe : Well, I'd like it fixed quickly. I guess I can drop by the San Pedro store at 10 a.m.

Sam : I see, Sir. I'll call ahead and inform them that you'll be arriving in about an hour.

① Joe works at an electronics store.

② The phone won't turn on.

③ The phone's warranty has expired.

④ Joe prefers his phone to be replaced.

⑤ Joe wants to visit the store in the morning.

05 Choose the best answer for the blank.

> Emma : Hi, Tom. You're in advertising, right? I'd be grateful if you could offer me some expert marketing advice.
>
> Tom : Sure, Emma. I'd love to help! What kind of business is it?
>
> Emma : It's a take-out chicken place. I know my recipe is delicious, but there's just so much competition these days. Plus, TV advertising is very costly.
>
> Tom : Okay. Have you considered online marketing? It's a lot cheaper.
>
> Emma : Really? But I can't use computers very well. I don't even have a blog!
>
> Tom : It's okay. It's a simple strategy that's very effective. You can create a business page on social media sites and offer discounts to subscribers. It's a proven way for businesses to become well-known quickly.
>
> Emma : Wow! I really appreciate your advice. _____

① It sounds like a great idea! Could you help me set it up, please?

② However, I'm really worried about the high cost.

③ Okay. I'll give it a shot. My blog is linked to my business page.

④ I think I'd prefer to advertise on television, however. The prices are cheaper.

⑤ But I'm worried if this strategy is really effective. You made it sound too risky.

06 Choose the sentence that best describes the situation.

> Julia : Hi, Diana. Thanks for responding to my ad.
>
> Diana : Oh, no problem. I just hope that I'm making a good first impression!
>
> Julia : You certainly are. However, I just need to know a few things if we're to live together. First of all, can you cook and do you own any pets?
>
> Diana : Yes, I can. I try to live healthily. And I do have a cat, but she's quiet, well-trained and very affectionate.
>
> Julia : That sounds fine. I don't have any pets, but I prefer cats over dogs. Next, are you an organized person? I must admit that cleanliness is really important to me.
>
> Diana : Me too. I absolutely hate mess!

① Julia wants Diana's advice about raising a pet.

② Julia is searching for a roommate.

③ Julia and Diana are talking about their hobbies.

④ Diana is trying to make a new friend.

⑤ Diana is being interviewed for a job.

07 밑줄 친 부분이 가리키는 대상이 나머지 넷과 다른 것은?

2점

J. R. Kline liked to tell stories of other mathematicians. This one about Norbert Wiener was a favorite : One summer, the Klines and the Wieners had adjacent cottages on a lake in New Hampshire. Wiener was in the habit of swimming from ① his dock to a small island in the middle of the lake. On these swims, Kline would keep Wiener company by paddling a rowboat alongside, and they would carry on a conversation while Wiener was steadfastly progressing towards ② his goal. Wiener always tried to keep control of the conversation, even as ③ he was puffing and gasping towards the small land mass. On one such day, near the end of the swim, ④ he bleated out, "Kline, who are the five greatest living mathematicians?" Quietly, Kline replied, "That is an interesting question. Let's see." ⑤ He quickly ticked off four names (none of them "Wiener"). "Yes, yes, go on," spluttered Wiener. With delicate humor, Kline avoided mentioning the name of the fifth one.

※ 다음 글에서 전체 흐름과 관계 없는 문장을 고르시오. [08~09]

08

Scientific research clearly shows that a sustained high level of cortisol, triggered by chronic stress, has negative effects on long-term health. ① Among these effects is an increase in appetite and cravings for certain foods. ② Because one of the roles of cortisol is to encourage the body to refuel itself after responding to a stressor, an elevated cortisol level keeps your appetite high. ③ In addition, the type of fat that accumulates as a result of this stress-induced appetite will typically locate itself in the abdominal region to be ready for the next stress response. ④ Exercise increases cortisol levels, but this short-term increase is good for immune function, memory, and weight loss. ⑤ The major problem with abdominal fat is that this type of fat is also highly associated with the development of heart disease, diabetes, and cancer.

*cortisol 부신피질에서 생성되는 스테로이드 호르몬

One study evaluated the efficacy of a daily multivitamin to prevent cognitive decline among 5,947 elderly males. ① After 12 years of follow-up, there were no differences between the multivitamin and placebo groups in overall cognitive performance or verbal memory. ② The researchers concluded that the use of a multivitamin supplement in a well-nourished elderly population did not prevent cognitive decline. ③ This conclusion was further supported by a review of some other studies that evaluated supplementation with multivitamins, B vitamins, vitamins E, C and omega-3 fatty acids, in persons with mild cognitive impairment or mild to moderate dementia. ④ While all vitamins are required for optimal health and brain function, there are a few that stand out above the rest as being essential for a healthy brain. ⑤ None of the supplements improved cognitive function, indicating that multivitamin intake has no effect on the treatment of dementia.

*dementia 치매

10 다음 글이 시사하는 바로 가장 적절한 것은?

In an experiment, two groups of mice were conditioned to feel fear in a certain location, and later the researchers put them back in that location to see if the mice showed fear. Interestingly, the mice whose eating schedule was shifted to the normal sleeping time felt fear less often in the fearful situation than their normal-schedule peers, suggesting the odd eating and sleeping schedule affected the animals' memory of scary situations. "The misaligned mice showed severe deficits in their recall of the training that they received," Colwell said. His research team previously found that jet lag has similar effects on memory in both human and mouse studies. The researchers also measured the strengthening of neural connections—a measure of learning in the brain. Not surprisingly, they found that the mice that ate during normal sleeping periods learned less quickly than the mice that ate at normal mealtimes.

① 양질의 음식 섭취는 학습 능력을 강화시켜 준다.
② 음식 섭취를 늘리는 것은 학습 능력 향상에 도움이 되지 않는다.
③ 정상적인 수면 시간에 음식을 먹는 것은 인지 능력을 약화시킬 수 있다.
④ 시차증을 쉽게 극복하려면 정상적인 수면 시간에 잠을 자야 한다.
⑤ 규칙적인 식사 습관이 규칙적인 수면 습관으로 이어질 수 있다.

※ 다음 글의 밑줄 친 부분 중, 어법상 틀린 것을 고르시오. [11~12]

11

[2점]

Before jeans were pants, jean was a cotton cloth used for making sturdy work clothes. The textile was produced in Genoa, Italy, ① which French weavers called Genes, the origin of our word "jeans." The origin of blue jeans, though, ② is really the story of Levi Strauss, an American immigrant tailor. When he arrived in San Francisco during the gold rush in the 1850s, he sold canvas for tents and covered wagons. A clever observer, he realized that miners went through trousers ③ quickly, so Strauss stitched some of his canvas into pants. Though heavy and stiff, the pants held up so well ④ that Strauss was in demand as a tailor. In the 1860s, he replaced canvas with denim. And Strauss discovered that dying neutral-colored denim pants dark blue to minimize soil stains greatly ⑤ increasing their popularity.

12

[3점]

New experiences trigger change only if they cause us ① to question our beliefs. Remember, whenever we believe something, we no longer question it in any way. The moment we begin to honestly question our beliefs, we no longer feel absolutely certain about ② them. We are beginning to shake the reference legs of our cognitive tables, and as a result start to lose our feeling of absolute certainty. Have you ever doubted your ability to do something? How did you do it? You probably asked ③ yourself some poor questions like "What if it doesn't work out?" But questions can obviously be tremendously empowering if we use them to examine the validity of beliefs we may have just blindly accepted. In fact, many of our beliefs ④ supported by information we've received from others that we failed to question at the time. If we scrutinize them, we may find that ⑤ what we've unconsciously believed for years may be based on a false set of presuppositions.

13

2점

Communication in its broadest sense occurs both verbally (via language) and nonverbally. Despite the importance of nonverbal behaviors, however, we often take them for granted. Although we receive no formal training in (A) how / what to send or receive nonverbal messages and signals, by adulthood we have become so skilled at it that we do so unconsciously and automatically. Nonverbal behaviors are just as much a language as any other. Just as verbal languages differ from culture to culture, so (B) do / are nonverbal languages. Because we are aware of the differences between verbal languages, we do not hesitate to use dictionaries and other resources to help us understand different languages. But when it comes to nonverbal language, we often mistakenly assume that our systems of communicating nonverbally are all the same. (C) Understanding / Understand cultural differences in nonverbal behavior is a step in the process of truly appreciating cultural differences in communication.

	(A)	(B)	(C)
①	how	do	Understanding
②	how	are	Understanding
③	how	do	Understand
④	what	do	Understanding
⑤	what	are	Understand

14

In the developed world the widespread use of water-based toilets from the mid-nineteenth century meant that extensive, connected systems of sewage pipes (A) sending / sent the outflow into sewage processing plants were built in cities. These systems helped solve the cholera outbreaks that devastated so many urban populations in the growing industrial-commercial cities of the early nineteenth century, (B) where / which the untreated human waste was just dumped into the local rivers, contaminating the ground water and local water supplies. Although it took time to establish the link between outbreaks of disease and the faecal-contaminated water supplies, most cities in the developed world created extensive water supply systems from reservoirs and (C) build / built separate sewer systems to take the flow from the increasing numbers of toilets in buildings, which led to the development of sewage treatment systems to filter out the harmful material.

*faecal 배설물의

	(A)	(B)	(C)
①	sending	where	built
②	sending	where	build
③	sent	which	built
④	sent	which	build
⑤	sent	where	built

※ 다음 글을 읽고, 빈칸에 들어갈 말로 가장 적절한 것을 고르시오. [15~18]

15

The producers of manufactured foods have an advantage over farmers because they buy the farm output and have flexibility over what ingredients to use and where to source them. For example, the manufactured food requires a sweetener, but not necessarily sugar derived from the sugarcane plant. It requires oil, yet not necessarily oil from corn. It requires a starch, but that could be derived from a potato or wheat or a number of other grains. The production of potato chips provides a good example of this _____ effect: Producers can fry the chips in whatever oil is cheapest at the moment of production. This illustrates why farmers are often at a disadvantaged position within the agrofood system.

① integration
② substitution
③ conservation
④ simplification
⑤ overconsumption

16

2점

Theodore Berger has achieved successes with _____ by using implanted chips to replace damaged parts of the hippocampus in rats. Berger and his team at the University of Southern California have succeeded in recording and transforming into computer code memories that have been stored for an extended period of time in the hippocampus of these animals. They had the rats perform a memory task. Then, they downloaded and transformed the memory of that task into digital code. Afterwards, they removed the section of the rats' hippocampus that carried these memories and replaced that bit of the brain with a special computer chip, onto which they reloaded the artificially stored memories. They found that the rats' memories could be fully restored using this technique.

*hippocampus (뇌의) 해마상(狀) 융기

① long-term memory regeneration
② memory capacity increase
③ the selective distortion of memory
④ the deletion of traumatic memories
⑤ memory transfer speed enhancement

17

2점

There are at least two reasons why a subjective sense of "foreign-ness" may implicitly suggest the possibility of spreading disease. First, historically, contact with exotic peoples increased exposure to exotic germs, which tend to be especially contagious when introduced to the local population. Secondly, outsiders are often ignorant of local behavioral norms that serve as barriers to germ transmission (e.g., norms pertaining to hygiene, food-preparation) ; as a consequence, they may be more likely to violate these norms, thereby increasing the danger of germ transmission within the local population. Thus, in addition to other risks suggested by outgroup status, people perceived to be subjectively foreign are likely to be implicitly judged _____.

① to isolate a local population
② to pose the threat of infection
③ to transmit novel technologies
④ to harm a local economy
⑤ to meet local hygiene standards

18

3점

When Josephine Baker moved to Paris, in 1925, as part of an all-black revue, her exoticism made her an overnight sensation. But Baker sensed that the French's interest in her would quickly pass to someone else. To seduce them for good, she learned French and began to sing in it. She started dressing and acting as a stylish French lady, as if to say that she preferred the French way of life to the American. Countries are like people: they feel threatened by other customs. It is often quite seductive to a people to see an outsider adopting their ways. Benjamin Disraeli was born and lived all his life in England, but he was Jewish by birth, and had exotic features; the provincial English considered him an outsider. Yet he was more English in his manners and tastes than many an Englishman, and this was part of his charm, which he proved by becoming the leader of the Conservative Party. Should you be an outsider, turn it to your advantage in such a way as to show the group _____.

*revue 익살극 **exoticism 이국정서

① how deeply you prefer their tastes and customs to your own

② that you don't complain about how misunderstood you are

③ that you have distinct tastes, opinions, and experiences

④ how hard you try to do noble and charitable deeds

⑤ that you are willing to disclose your own identity

19 다음 글에서 필자가 주장하는 바로 가장 적절한 것은?

2점

Every member of the family is an individual, as well as a part of the whole family. As a parent, you have to balance your role as a caregiver with your needs as an individual. If you sacrifice all of your time and energy to your family without finding a way to socialize with adults, to feel intellectually stimulated, or to maintain a healthy body and mind, the whole family will suffer. Remember : You're modeling adulthood for your children — don't create a martyr model of parenthood. Being an empty, self — sacrificing shell of a person is hardly the role model you want them to see. Of course, it's tough, if not impossible, to satisfy all of these needs to the fullest every single day. Parenting usually involves some level of self-sacrifice, but you need to strive for a healthy balance that works for you and your family.

*martyr 순교자

① 부모와 자녀는 서로의 만족을 위해 함께 애써야 한다.
② 부모는 어른의 기준으로 자녀를 평가하지 말아야 한다.
③ 부모는 자녀 양육과 자신의 삶 사이에서 균형을 잡아야 한다.
④ 부모는 주위에서 자녀에게 좋은 역할 모델을 찾아 주어야 한다.
⑤ 부모는 자녀에게 권리에는 책임이 따른다는 것을 가르쳐야 한다.

※ 다음 글의 빈칸 (A), (B)에 들어갈 말로 가장 적절한 것을 고르시오. [20~21]

20

[2점]

The very systematicity that allows us to comprehend one aspect of a concept in terms of another (e.g., comprehending an aspect of arguing in terms of battle) will necessarily ___(A)___ other aspects of the concept. In allowing us to focus on one aspect of a concept (e.g., the battling aspects of arguing), a metaphorical concept can keep us from focusing on other aspects of the concept that are inconsistent with that metaphor. For example, in the midst of a heated argument, when we are intent on attacking our opponent's position and defending our own, we may lose sight of the cooperative aspects of arguing. Someone who is arguing with you can be viewed as giving you his or her time, a valuable commodity, in an effort to achieve mutual understanding. But when we are ___(B)___ the battle aspects, we often lose sight of the cooperative aspects.

	(A)	(B)
①	hide	indifferent to
②	reveal	engaged in
③	hide	preoccupied with
④	reveal	preoccupied with
⑤	affect	indifferent to

21
2점

Your body image doesn't develop overnight. Rather, it is something that develops slowly over time, and many things influence it. For example, years of playing sports and being involved in athletic activities can help build a positive body image by giving a person confidence in his or her body and its strengths and abilities.   (A)   , hearing one thoughtless or unkind comment about your body can have a long-lasting negative impact on your body image. Furthermore, body image continues to evolve and change throughout your whole life. Most people adjust their body images as they physically, mentally, and emotionally age and mature. You can have a negative body image at one time in your life and a positive body image at another time. Building a positive body image,   (B)   , is a never-ending process.

	(A)	(B)
①	On the other hand	therefore
②	On the other hand	for instance
③	In the same way	nevertheless
④	As a result	nevertheless
⑤	As a result	for instance

※ 다음 글의 밑줄 친 부분 중, 문맥상 낱말의 쓰임이 적절하지 않은 것을 고르시오. [22~23]

22
2점

In November 2007, a team of researchers from the National Institute of Mental Health and McGill University announced that they had ① uncovered the specific deficits of the ADHD brain. The disorder turns out to be largely a developmental problem ; often, the brains of children with ADHD develop at a significantly ② slower pace than normal. This lag was most obvious in the prefrontal cortex, which meant that these children literally lacked the mental muscles needed to resist tempting stimuli. The good news, however, is that the brain almost always ③ recovers from its slow start. By the end of adolescence, the frontal lobes in these children reached normal size. It's not a coincidence that their behavioral problems began to ④ emerge at about the same time. The children who had had the developmental lag were finally able to ⑤ counter their urges and compulsions. They could look at the tempting marshmallow and decide that it was better to wait.

*prefrontal cortex (뇌의) 전전두엽 피질 **frontal lobes 전두엽

23

3점

It has been said that the clothes make the man, and nowhere is this truer than in the military. A soldier's uniform ① <u>represents</u> everything from loyalty to title and rank. And as for camouflage, it can mean the difference between life and death—a point brought up by U.S. lawmakers as they prepared to pass a $106 billion emergency war-spending bill that will ② <u>fund</u>, among other things, some 70,000 new uniforms for troops in Afghanistan. Evidently, the country's muddy, mountainous terrain doesn't ③ <u>match</u> the "universal camouflage pattern" designed for dusty desert cities like Baghdad. The emergence of aerial and trench warfare during World War I gave rise to the strategy— and art — of camouflaged battle dress, resulting in a fruitful ④ <u>collaboration</u> among soldiers, artists and naturalists like Abbott Thayer, whose 1909 book *Concealing Coloration in the Animal Kingdom* became required reading for the U.S. Army's newly launched unit of camouflage designers. Now that troops had to avoid bombs and bullets from all directions, the traditional glorious uniform worn in an earlier era of warfare began to seem ⑤ <u>up-to-date</u>, if not downright dangerous.

*camouflage 위장 **trench 참호

※ 다음 글의 제목으로 가장 적절한 것을 고르시오. [24~25]

24

2점

When it comes to happiness, comparisons are rarely, if ever, helpful. Happiness is a subjective phenomenon; it is experienced differently by everyone and it means different things to different people. As the saying goes, one man's meat is another man's poison — our needs and desires vary, so what makes one person happy might not have the same impact on the next person. Although most of us realize the disparity between our individual requirements, it is easy to fall into the trap of looking over the fence, seeing what the neighbors have and thinking that we need that too. Simply put, this is unhelpful and almost certainly a direct path to unhappiness. Research strongly indicates that those who are happiest appreciate what they have and focus less on what they don't have. Long-term happiness studies clearly purport that, rather than judging themselves in relation to others, happy people simply clarify what's important to them and then focus on achieving and fulfilling their priorities.

*purport 주장하다

① Avoid the Trap of Self-satisfaction

② Subjectivity Comes from Objectivity

③ Happiness Is Tailored to Each Person

④ Assess Yourself Through the Eyes of Others

⑤ The More You Achieve, the Happier You Will Be

25
2점

Many people understand that eating too much salt, a major source of sodium, is a significant cause of cardiovascular diseases including a stroke or heart attack. However, fewer people know that too much sodium intake may also be harmful to bones. The amount of calcium that your body loses via urination increases with the amount of salt you eat. Triggered by low blood calcium levels, cells called osteoclasts break down bone to release calcium into the blood, potentially causing bone mass reduction. So, a diet high in sodium could have an additional unwanted effect — the bone — thinning disease known as osteoporosis. A 2009 study on elderly women, for example, showed that the loss of hip bone density over two years was related to the 24-hour urinary sodium excretion at the start of the study, and that the connection with bone loss was as strong as that for calcium intake. Other studies have shown that reducing sodium intake helps maintain calcium balance, suggesting that eating less salt could slow the calcium loss from your bones that occurs with aging.

*urination 배뇨(작용) **excretion 배출

① Significant Impact of Aging on Bone Thinning

② Relationship Between Losing Weight and Bone Weakness

③ Overlooked Causes of Abnormal Urinary Sodium Excretion

④ Bone Weakening : Another Threat of Excessive Sodium Intake

⑤ Calcium Balance : A Newly Discovered Shortcut to a Healthy Heart

※ 글의 흐름으로 보아, 주어진 문장이 들어가기에 가장 적절한 곳을 고르시오. [26~27]

26

That let him loosen the reins of command; with actors like Max von Sydow, he could just suggest what he had in mind and watch as the great actor brought his ideas to life.

Early in his career, the great Swedish film director Ingmar Bergman was often overwhelmed with frustration. (①) He had visions of the films he wanted to make, but the work of being a director was so demanding and the pressure so immense that he would scold his cast and crew, shouting orders and attacking them for not giving him what he wanted. (②) Some would stew with resentment at his dictatorial ways; others became obedient automatons. (③) With almost every new film, Bergman would have to start again with a new cast and crew, which only made things worse. (④) But eventually he put together a team of the finest camera operators, editors, art directors, and actors in Sweden, people who shared his high standards and whom he trusted. (⑤) Greater control could now come from letting go.

27
2점

Yet nations tend to restrict the import of certain goods for a variety of reasons.

There are a growing number of companies, large and small, that are doing business with firms in other countries. Some companies sell to firms in foreign countries; others buy goods around the world to import into their countries. (①) Whether they buy or sell products across national borders, these businesses are all contributing to the volume of international trade that is fueling the global economy. (②) Theoretically, international trade is every bit as logical and worthwhile as interstate trade between, say, California and Washington. (③) For example, in the early 2000s, the United States restricted the import of Mexican fresh tomatoes because they were undercutting the price levels of domestic fresh tomatoes. (④) Despite such restrictions, international trade has increased almost steadily since World War II. (⑤) Many of the industrialized nations have signed trade agreements intended to eliminate problems in international business and to help less-developed nations participate in world trade.

※ 다음 글의 요지로 가장 적절한 것을 고르시오. [28~29]

28
2점

Listening and reading critically — that is, reacting with systematic evaluation to what you have heard and read — requires a set of skills and attitudes. These skills and attitudes are built around a series of related critical questions. While we will learn them one by one, our goal is to be able to use them together to identify the best decision available. We could have expressed them as a list of things you should do, but a system of questions is more consistent with the spirit of curiosity, wonder, and intellectual adventure essential to critical thinking. Thinking carefully is always an unfinished project, a story looking for an ending that will never arrive. Critical questions provide a stimulus and direction for critical thinking; they move us forward toward a continual, ongoing search for better opinions, decisions, or judgments.

① 비판적인 질문은 비판적인 사고를 하는 데 필요하다.
② 어려서부터 비판적인 사고력을 길러 주는 것이 중요하다.
③ 상대방의 비판을 무조건 수용하는 것은 바람직하지 않다.
④ 작가가 독자의 비판적인 질문을 예상하며 글을 쓸 필요는 없다.
⑤ 호기심을 자극하는 질문은 학생의 수업 참여도를 높이는 데 효과적이다.

29
3점

Spatial cognition is a fundamental design requirement for every mobile species with a fixed territory or home base. And there is little doubt that it plays a central role in human thinking and reasoning. Indeed, the evidence for that centrality is all around us, in our language where spatial metaphors are used for many other domains and in the special role of place in memory. The idea that space is a fundamental intuition built into our nature goes back at least to Kant, and the idea that our perception of space is governed by cognitive universals informs much current cognitive science. But in some ways human spatial cognition is puzzling. First, it is unspectacular — we are not as a species, compared to bees or pigeons, bats or whales, particularly good at finding our way around. Second, human spatial cognition is obviously variable — hunters, sailors and taxi-drivers are in a different league from the ordinary city-dweller. This suggests that many aspects of effective spatial thinking depend on cultural factors, which in turn suggests limits to cognitive universals in this area.

① 언어와 공간의 개념은 인간의 삶에서 상호작용한다.
② 인간의 공간적 사고에는 인지적 보편성의 한계가 있다.
③ 인간의 공간적 사고는 시대와 문화를 초월하여 보편적이다.
④ 인간의 공간 인지 능력은 동물과 비교해서 뒤지지 않는다.
⑤ 인지과학은 공간 인지의 개념에 바탕을 두어야 한다.

※ 다음 글의 주제로 가장 적절한 것을 고르시오. [30~31]

30
[2점]

Inexperienced writers often make the mistake of thinking that they have a firmer grasp on their ideas than on their words. They frequently utter the complaint, "I know what I want to say ; I just can't find the words for it." This claim is almost always untrue, not because beginning writers are deliberate liars but because they confuse their intuitive sense that they have something to say with the false sense that they already know precisely what that something is. When a writer is stuck for words, the problem is rarely a problem only of words. Inexperienced writers may think they need larger vocabularies when what they really need are clearer ideas and intentions. Being stuck for words indicates that the thought one wants to convey is still vague, unformed, cloudy, and confused. Once you finally discover your concrete meaning, you will discover the proper words for expressing it at the same time.

① reasons why some writers are not truthful in their writings
② ways of training students how to develop ideas systematically
③ importance of a large vocabulary in making a piece of writing effective
④ beginning writers' mistake of confusing unclear ideas with a lack of words
⑤ difficulty of getting a clear idea without having enough words to express it

31

2점

The seemingly simple question of "what defines a sport?" has been the subject of argument and conversation for years, among professional and armchair athletes alike. There seems to be no doubt that vigorous and highly competitive activities such as baseball, football, and soccer are truly "sports," but when the subject of other activities such as darts, chess, and shuffleboard is brought up we find ourselves at the heart of a controversy. If say, billiards, is not a sport, then what exactly is it? Those who would dispute that it is a sport would respond that it is a simple leisure activity. They would go on to claim a true sport first and foremost requires some form of physical exertion. More to the point, if a player does not break a sweat, what he or she plays is not a sport. Beyond that, more important criteria would be the need for decent hand-eye coordination and the ever-present possibility of sustaining injury. Billiards only fits one of those specifications (hand-eye coordination), so according to the doubters, it is not a real sport.

① leisure activities embedded in sports

② popularity of highly competitive activities

③ dispute over the defining criteria for sports

④ influence of sports on humans' mental health

⑤ characteristics that define billiards as a sport

32 Andy Warhol에 관한 다음 글의 내용과 일치하지 않는 것은?

2점

In 1967, Andy Warhol was asked to lecture at various colleges. He hated to talk, particularly about his own art ; "The less something has to say," he felt, "the more perfect it is." But the money was good, so Warhol always found it hard to say no. His solution was simple : he asked an actor, Allen Midgette, to impersonate him. Midgette was dark-haired, tan, part Cherokee Indian. He did not resemble Warhol in the least. But Warhol and friends covered his face with powder, sprayed his brown hair silver, gave him dark glasses, and dressed him in Warhol's clothes. Since Midgette knew nothing about art, his answers to students' questions tended to be as short and enigmatic as Warhol's own. The impersonation worked. Warhol may have been an icon, but no one really knew him, and since he often wore dark glasses, even his face was unfamiliar in any detail.

*enigmatic 수수께끼 같은

① 자신의 예술에 대해 이야기하는 것을 싫어했다.
② 돈 때문에 강연 요청을 거절하기 힘들었다.
③ 자신을 전혀 닮지 않은 배우를 자신처럼 분장시켰다.
④ 예술에 조예가 깊은 사람을 골라 대신 강연하게 했다.
⑤ 짙은 색의 안경을 자주 썼기에 얼굴이 상세하게 알려지지 않았다.

33 다음 도표의 내용과 일치하지 않는 것은?

2점

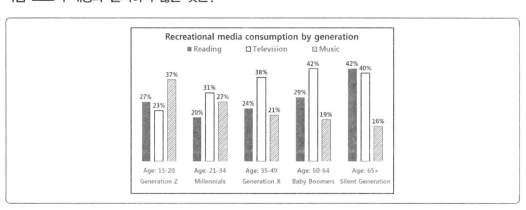

The graph above shows the generational participation percentages for three popular recreational media activities. ① Of the three leisure pursuits, music is the most popular spare-time activity among Generation Z, while reading is the most popular among the silent generation. ② The percentage of millennials who spend their spare time reading is visibly smaller than that of their counterparts from other generations. ③ Television is the most popular spare-time activity for all generations, except for Generation Z, less than a quarter of whom chose television as their favorite recreational activity. ④ Among Generation X, baby boomers, and the silent generation, music is less popular than reading. ⑤ The two generations that read more than the youngest are baby boomers and the silent generation.

※ 주어진 글 다음에 이어질 글의 순서로 가장 적절한 것을 고르시오. [34~35]

34

2점

Twentieth-century medicine has been marked by the emergence of medical specialties and the focus on an organ systems approach to treat disease.

(A) Changes in one tissue or organ can lead to physiological effects in other subsystems. Integration also means therapy can have broad-ranging effects. Treatment of disease in one tissue may have complicating effects in another tissue, for instance.

(B) This local systems approach is now giving way to an integrative methodology to medical management. A sick patient does not represent a biochemistry problem or an anatomy problem or a genetics problem or an immunology problem.

(C) Instead, each person is the product of multiple molecular, cellular, genetic, environmental, and social influences that interact in complex ways to determine health and disease. The human body is a highly integrated set of subsystems.

① (A) − (C) − (B)

② (B) − (A) − (C)

③ (B) − (C) − (A)

④ (C) − (A) − (B)

⑤ (C) − (B) − (A)

35

3점

There are certain rules that, to break them, would give us such intense pain that we don't even consider the possibility. We will rarely, if ever, break them. I call these rules **threshold rules**.

(A) Conversely, we have some rules that we don't want to break. I call these **personal standards**. If we do break them, we don't feel good about it, but depending upon the reasons, we're willing to break them in the short term. The difference between these two rules is often phrased with the words **must** and **should**.

(B) We have certain things that we must do, certain things that we must not do, certain things that we must never do, and certain things that we must always do. The "must" and the "must never" rules are threshold rules; the "should" and "should never" rules are personal standard rules. All of them give a structure to our lives.

(C) For example, if I asked you, "What's something you would never do?," you'd give me a threshold rule. You'd tell me a rule that you would never violate. Why? Because you link too much pain to it.

① (A) − (C) − (B)

② (B) − (A) − (C)

③ (B) − (C) − (A)

④ (C) − (A) − (B)

⑤ (C) − (B) − (A)

36 (A), (B), (C)의 각 네모 안에서 문맥에 맞는 표현으로 가장 적절한 것은?

2점

Even in today's modern society, many people still perform rituals on a daily basis ; they knock on wood to ward off bad luck or throw salt over their shoulders to (A) accept / repel evil spirits. Every culture has its own superstitions, and now anthropologists and psychologists think they know why. It is because our brains are always working to find the causes of the significant events that we perceive. When something strange happens that we can't explain, our minds are (B) uncomfortable / satisfied with the uncertainty. However, we fill this cognitive gap with whatever explanations are available to us, and superstitions provide a simple way to explain mysterious events. They believe that spirits that live in wood have to be appeased, or that throwing salt blinds the devil. Superstitions may seem silly to nonbelievers not sharing them. To believers those rituals on the other hand are providing a sense of control over situations otherwise which would be (C) secure / unsettling.

	(A)	(B)	(C)
①	accept	uncomfortable	secure
②	accept	satisfied	unsettling
③	repel	uncomfortable	unsettling
④	repel	satisfied	secure
⑤	repel	uncomfortable	secure

37 다음 글의 내용을 한 문장으로 요약하고자 한다. 빈칸 (A)와 (B)에 들어갈 말로 가장 적절한 것은?

3점

Here is an interesting experiment which was conducted on a group of elementary students in the U.S. over thirty years ago. The teacher who partook in the experiment told her students : "According to a recent study, children with blue eyes have a higher learning aptitude than children with brown eyes." After telling her students this bit of uncertified information, she had the children write the color of their eyes on a card and hang them around their necks. The children were monitored for a week and the results were as follows. Learning motivation for children with brown eyes dropped, and the blue-eyed children became drastically better in class. Then, the teacher told the students, "There have been reports that the experimental results were wrong. In fact, brown-eyed children do better in class than blue-eyed children." What were the results?

This time the children with brown eyes excelled in class and learning ambition for the children with blue eyes dropped.

⬇

According to the experiment above, ___(A)___ projected by teachers can determine students' ___(B)___ .

	(A)	(B)
①	self-images	academic achievement
②	self-images	career choice
③	traditional values	psychological wellbeing
④	traditional values	academic achievement
⑤	prejudices	career choice

※ 다음 글을 읽고, 물음에 답하시오. [38~39]

For many children, their first experiences with print occur in the home. Children from families that make literacy development a focal point of home activities via shared reading are at an advantage. ___(A)___ , there is little research on the precise mechanisms by which early literacy experiences influence children's subsequent language and print skills. A variety of factors, including cultural beliefs, socioeconomic status, parenting styles and parental beliefs may affect children's reading development. Moreover, establishing directional causality among these factors is difficult.

It is also difficult to disentangle the effects of children's genetic make-up from the effects on them of their biological parents. Although parents' motivations, enthusiasm, and willingness to read are behavioral influences on their children, their effects may be minimal relative to a child's own wants and needs. Parents who read a lot to their children may primarily be responding to the fact that their children are interested in reading. Such influence is, at least in part, genetically determined. ___(B)___ , parents who read little to their children may be responding to their children's lack of interest or to the fact that, genetically, both parents and children find reading-related activities boring or difficult. Children's genetic endowments strongly influence how their parents interact with them. Given the confounds of parents' behaviors with the family genetic make-up, experiments on parent-child shared reading are perhaps the clearest evidence thus far that home environment can affect reading-related skills.

*confound 혼동 요인

38 윗글의 제목으로 가장 적절한 것은?

[2점]
① Children Are Inherently Good Readers
② What Influences Children's Literacy Development?
③ Relationship Between Literacy Skills and Cultural Beliefs
④ Social Intelligence : etermined by Home Environment
⑤ What Makes Your Children Unwilling to Read?

39 윗글의 빈칸 (A), (B)에 들어갈 말로 가장 적절한 것은?

[2점]

	(A)	(B)
①	Therefore	Otherwise
②	However	Similarly
③	As a result	Moreover
④	However	Otherwise
⑤	As a result	Similarly

※ 다음 글을 읽고, 물음에 답하시오. [40~41]

As Jim Collins pointed out in Good to Great, ___(A)___ and a failure to see the situation as it is can be not only unhelpful—it can be fatal. He called this the Stockdale paradox, after James Stockdale, a U.S. military officer. Stockdale was held captive for eight years during the Vietnam War. He was tortured numerous times and had little reason to believe he would live to see his wife again. Although Stockdale understood his predicament, he also never lost hope that he might endure it and not only survive his ordeal but use it as a defining experience in his life. And here is the paradox:

While Stockdale had remarkable faith in the unknowable, he noted that it was always the most optimistic of his prisonmates who failed to make it out of there alive. "They were the ones who said, 'We're going to be out by Christmas.' And Christmas would come, and Christmas would go. Then they'd say, 'We're going to be out by Easter.' And Easter would come, and Easter would go. And then Thanksgiving, and then it would be Christmas again. And they died of a broken heart." What the optimists failed to do was confront the reality of their situation. They ___(B)___ the ostrich approach, sticking their heads in the sand

and hoping for the difficulties to go away. That self-delusion might have made it easier on them in the short term, but when they were eventually forced to face reality, it had become too much and they couldn't handle it.

And, of course, such unfounded optimism often precluded taking action to deal with the situation as best one could, which is precisely what Stockdale did.

*predicament 곤경

40 윗글의 빈칸 (A), (B)에 들어갈 말로 가장 적절한 것은?

3점

	(A)	(B)
①	irrational negativity	criticized
②	irrational negativity	preferred
③	unrealistic optimism	rejected
④	unrealistic optimism	preferred
⑤	unconditional devotion	rejected

41 윗글의 James Stockdale에 관한 내용과 일치하지 않는 것은?

2점
① 그의 이름을 따서 Stockdale paradox라는 표현이 생겨났다.
② 베트남 전쟁 중에 8년 동안 포로로 잡혀 지냈다.
③ 자신이 처한 곤경을 견뎌낼 수 있다는 희망을 잃지 않았다.
④ 가장 낙관적인 수용소 동료들이 살아 나오지 못하는 것에 주목했다.
⑤ 수용소 동료들에게 곧 풀려날 것이라는 희망을 불어 넣어주었다.

※ 다음 글을 읽고, 물음에 답하시오. [42~43]

The trend which has impacted the application of the laws of armed conflict is the increasing civilianisation of modern conflict. This trend is taking place through a number of processes, including the escalating prominence of internal armed conflicts in which the majority of war fighters are civilians, and the (A) shift / removal of the conduct of hostilities into civilian population centres. In addition, modern militaries increasingly outsource support and even core functions to contractors—some of whom, like private military or security firms, are engaged in armed tactical roles.

In the three − and − a − half centuries since the Treaty of Westphalia, the nation state has been the defining actor in international relations, and has held the monopoly on power and military force. The emergence of transnational armed groups, the increasing number of non-international armed conflicts and the (B) reduction / expansion of the battlespace to encompass entire territories have all meant that civilians are involved in conflicts more than ever.

Militaries are also under pressure to downsize and reduce budgets. As part of this trend, civilian contractors and employees are increasingly used to augment defence forces as an easy and flexible way to maintain military strength according to constantly changing needs. Further, as weapons and equipment become more technologically advanced, civilians are (C) excluded / recruited to provide essential maintenance and support functions, sometimes from the 'factory to the foxhole'. Civilians are an easy and less expensive way of maintaining access to the latest technical expertise; they can be hired when needed and discharged when the need is no longer urgent.

*hostilities 교전

42 윗글의 주제로 가장 적절한 것은?

2점

① conflict resolution without military intervention

② civilian involvement in a variety of military affairs

③ maintenance of military power for national security

④ competition between private sectors and public sectors

⑤ how military technological advancement benefits civilians

43 (A), (B), (C)의 각 네모 안에서 문맥에 맞는 표현으로 가장 적절한 것은?

	(A)	(B)	(C)
①	shift	expansion	recruited
②	shift	reduction	excluded
③	shift	reduction	recruited
④	removal	expansion	excluded
⑤	removal	reduction	excluded

※ 다음 글을 읽고, 물음에 답하시오. [44~45]

(A)

One summer when he was in high school, Colin attended church camp and made some new friends who proved to be a bad influence. They talked (a) him into sneaking out of camp with them to buy beer, and then they hid it in one of the toilet tanks to keep it cold. They thought no one would ever find out. But they were wrong.

(B)

He stood silent as she lectured (b) him about trust and responsibility, knowing there was no good defense for his actions. Then it was his father's turn to tell Colin how disappointed he was in his son. In the middle of the family crisis, Father Weeden — the priest at St. Margaret's — called to tell Colin's parents the whole story — about how their son had stood up like a man and taken responsibility for (c) his actions. The family was proud that Colin had done the right thing.

(C)

Because of his honesty, two other boys also admitted their guilt. All of their parents were notified, and the boys were sent home in disgrace. Riding on the train, Colin thought about what (d) he had done and regretted his involvement. How embarrassing for him and his parents! To get kicked out of church camp was worse than anything he could imagine. After walking slowly home from the train, Colin was met at the door by his scowling mother.

*scowl 얼굴을 찌푸리다

(D)

The camp director called all the boys together to confront them with the fact that the beer had been discovered. The priest didn't yell or scream. (e) <u>He</u> firmly asked the guilty parties to stand up and act like men and to accept the responsibility for their misdeed. Colin Powell, because of his mother's firm hand throughout his childhood years, was the one who came clean first. "Father, I did it," Colin confessed.

44 주어진 글 (A)에 이어질 내용을 순서에 맞게 배열한 것으로 가장 적절한 것은?

2점

① (B) − (D) − (C)

② (C) − (B) − (D)

③ (C) − (D) − (B)

④ (D) − (B) − (C)

⑤ (D) − (C) − (B)

45 밑줄 친 (a)~(e) 중에서 가리키는 대상이 나머지 넷과 다른 것은?

2점

① (a) ② (b)

③ (c) ④ (d)

⑤ (e)

▶ 해설은 p. 115에 있습니다.

01 Based on the following dialogue, which one is NOT true?

2점

> Jimmy : Let's go camping this weekend.
>
> Joanne : Not again. We just went last weekend and the rain soaked us.
>
> Jimmy : Yes, the tent leaks a bit, but the forecast says there won't be a cloud in the sky this weekend.
>
> Joanne : Can't we just go to see a play, or something else cultural?
>
> Jimmy : Fair enough. Since we did what I wanted last weekend, you get to make the plan this time. So what do you want to do?
>
> Joanne : I heard about an amazing ballet performance at the cultural center downtown. You'll love it.
>
> Jimmy : Sorry, but please don't make me go to a ballet! Ballet is the worst. How about anything else?

① Joanne is not interested in camping this weekend.

② It rained last weekend.

③ Their tent is not completely waterproof.

④ The weather is expected to be good this weekend.

⑤ Jimmy is a fan of the ballet.

02 Which is the best sequence of sentences for the blanks?

Janet : I must say I really like this apartment, but I do have some concerns. First of all, I have a young son and don't want him to walk too far to school.

Dave : I totally understand. There's a good school very near here. _____

Janet : How about the utilities? We don't have a lot of money to spend, actually.

Dave : This building is quite modern and energy-efficient. _____

Janet : Oh, that's a relief. And what about the neighbors? We prefer to live in a quiet place.

Dave : There are currently only a young family with no kids and some older couples living in the building. _____

Janet : Great! I think this may be the place.

〈보기〉

a. There's nothing available.

c. It's just a block away.

b. It shouldn't be noisy at all.

d. They're very affordable.

① a − b − d

② b − c − d

③ c − d − b

④ c − b − a

⑤ d − c − a

03 Where is the dialogue most likely taking place?

Aaron : Good morning. I was wondering if you have anything available for today. I'm in town for the day, flying out tonight, and was hoping to visit some of the sites.

Krista : Well, it is short notice, but I do have several options to offer you. Did you have any preferences?

Aaron : Actually, I was kind of hoping that you would have something compact that gets good mileage.

Krista : That shouldn't be a problem. I have the perfect one. And would you like the extra insurance? I would recommend it.

Aaron : I sure would. Better safe than sorry.

Krista : Great. I just need to see your license, and then I can prepare the contract. Just make sure the tank is full when you return it.

Aaron : No problem. I'll drop it off sometime this evening.

① at a gas station   ② at a car repair shop

③ at a car rental agency   ④ at a travel agency

⑤ at an insurance company

04 Based on the following dialogue, which one is true?

> Bill : Honey, on this day, our first wedding anniversary, I wanted to get you something special. I think you'll love it. Please, open it up.
>
> Diane : Oh my lord, a puppy! We can't keep a dog. It just costs too much to raise one, and it's a huge responsibility.
>
> Bill : It really doesn't cost that much, and now with me working at home these days it'll be quite easy for me to take care of him. You won't have to do a thing.
>
> Diane : Are you sure? Do you promise that you'll take full responsibility for him?
>
> Bill : Absolutely. Plus, look at him! He's adorable, and he seems to have bonded with you already. He's snuggling right up to you.
>
> Diane : To be honest, he is awfully cute. You may have a point. Let's give it a try.

① Bill forgot their anniversary last year.

② Diane got Bill a pet for their anniversary.

③ Diane thinks raising a dog will be a piece of cake.

④ Bill doesn't work at home these days.

⑤ Bill and Diane are going to keep the dog.

05 Choose the most appropriate sentence for the blank.

[2점]

> Taxi Driver : Hi there. Where are you headed?
>
> Passenger : Across town to the Smythe Building. And please hurry.
>
> Taxi Driver : Don't worry, there shouldn't be much traffic at this time.
>
> *[5 minutes later]*
>
> Passenger : Sorry to bother you, but why are you going through the city instead of using the expressway? I have to be at a meeting in just 40 minutes.
>
> Taxi Driver : There's major construction clogging up the expressway, and I know all the short cuts. I'll get you there in time.
>
> Passenger : Okay, I hope you know what you are doing.
>
> *[25 minutes later]*
>
> Taxi Driver : Here we are sir, at your destination with time to spare.
>
> Passenger : Apologies for my skepticism. _____

① Here's the fare and a well-earned tip.

② I'm not going to make it on time.

③ I should've taken the subway.

④ Let's take the expressway, then.

⑤ I'm going to complain to your supervisor.

06 Choose the sentence that best describes the situation.

3점

> Father : I can't believe my oldest is finally leaving the nest and moving out on his own. It's going to be so hard.
>
> Tim : Don't worry, dad. You and mom will do fine without me. I'm only two hours away, so we can visit each other anytime.
>
> Father : I'm not worried about us, son. I'm worried about you being able to take care of yourself like doing your laundry, cleaning your apartment, and paying your bills.
>
> Tim : Actually, I was kind of hoping that I could bring my laundry here for you guys to do, that mom would come visit to clean my place, and that you would pay my bills.
>
> Father : You must be joking. You're on your own young man. This is independence.
>
> Tim : Of course I'm kidding. I'm more than capable of doing my own housework. Plus, my new job pays me more than enough. You don't have to worry about a thing.

① Tim moved back home so that he could take care of his parents.

② Tim's parents decided to visit Tim regularly to take care of him.

③ Tim's father is happy to have Tim back home after a long absence.

④ Tim is moving away and thinks he is prepared for his independence.

⑤ Tim is going away to university but will still need his parents' support.

07 밑줄 친 부분이 가리키는 대상이 나머지 넷과 다른 것은?

Dr. J. F. Cowan once told the story of a small college that was having financial difficulties, even though their academic standards had been exceptionally high. One day a very wealthy man came on the campus, found ① a white-haired man in overalls painting the wall, and asked where he could find the president. The painter pointed out a house on the campus and said ② he was sure the president could be seen there at noon. At the designated time the visitor knocked at the president's door and was admitted by the same man ③ he had talked to on the grounds, though now he was attired differently. The visitor accepted an invitation to have lunch with ④ the painter-president, asking a number of questions about the needs of the college, and told him he would be sending a little donation. Two days later a letter arrived enclosing a check for $50,000. The humility of a man who was fitted for ⑤ his position as a college president, but who was not too proud to put on the clothes of a workman and do the job that needed doing so badly, had opened the wealthy man's purse strings.

※ 다음 글에서 전체 흐름과 관계 없는 문장을 고르시오. [8~9]

08

When the first Olympic victor was recorded in 776 B.C., Rome was a mere farm community surrounded by warring tribes. ① By 500 B.C., as the athletic program at Olympia settled into a fixed, predictable pattern, the Romans were rising up against the rule of the Etruscans, their hostile neighbors to the north. ② Within two centuries Roman military might, administrative officials, language, and culture dominated all of Italy. ③ Then began their imperial conquest of Sicily, Carthage, and Greece. ④ Furthermore, Greek sports and games were too individualistic, too geared to the participants rather than to spectator appeal. ⑤ By the end of the first century B.C., the Roman empire covered the entire rim of the Mediterranean, extending to the northern reaches of Britain, to the Danube in Europe, and east to the Caspian Sea.

09

3점

The fact that most organizations, large and small, are now filled with data is no bad thing. ① In fact, it is a huge opportunity for businesses to acquire insight and understanding in ways never before considered possible. ② However, what is a problem is that most organizations don't step back to consider how the data should be explored and understood. ③ Understanding data relating to human behavior is a long-standing skill of marketers and social scientists. ④ Analysis processes designed to uncover new insights are confused and mixed with those used to measure performance. ⑤ There is a lack of attention to which methods of analysis actually make a difference to the business—there is still too much focus on measurement as a function of ease for accessing the number rather than relevance to business outcomes.

※ 다음 글의 밑줄 친 부분 중, 어법상 틀린 것을 고르시오. [10~11]

10

2점

For years, psychology turned its attention to the study of negative emotions or negative affect, including depression, sadness, anger, stress and anxiety. Not surprisingly, psychologists found them ① interesting because they may often lead to, or signal the presence of, psychological disorders. However, positive emotions are no less fascinating, if only because of many common-sense misconceptions that ② exist about positive affect. We tend to think, for example, that positive affect typically, by its very nature, distorts or disrupts orderly, effective thinking, that positive emotions are somehow "simple" or ③ what, because these emotions are short-lived, they cannot have a long-term impact. Research has shown the above not to be the case, but it took it a while ④ to get there. It is only relatively recently that psychologists realized that positive emotions can be seen as valuable in their own right and ⑤ started studying them.

11

2점

In Ancient Rome, messages sent over short distances, for which a quick reply was expected, were written with a stylus on wax tablets ① <u>mounted</u> in wooden frames that folded together like a book. To modern eyes these tablets, with their flat writing surfaces surrounded by a wooden frame, look strikingly ② <u>similar</u> to tablet computers. The recipient's response could be scratched onto the same tablet, and the messenger who had ③ <u>delivered</u> it would then take it straight back to the sender. The tablets could be erased and reused by smoothing the colored wax with the flat end of a stylus. Within the city, this was a handy way to send a quick question to someone and ④ <u>get</u> a reply within an hour or two. Letters sent over longer distances ⑤ <u>written</u> on papyrus, which was more expensive but lighter and therefore more suitable for transport. A single sheet of papyrus typically measured about six inches wide by ten inches tall, which was enough for a short letter.

*stylus 철필

※ (A), (B), (C)의 각 네모 안에서 어법에 맞는 표현으로 가장 적절한 것을 고르시오. [12~13]

12

2점

The personal computer can be thought of as a commodity, as an everyday object. It can end its days as a piece of junk, a "bygone object," (A) are / to be disposed of somehow, either by literally throwing it away, or by resale, or by passing it on to someone else, or by keeping it somewhere out of sight. Christine Finn (2001) has written a brilliant book on computers-as-junk, (B) which / in which she looks at the ways they are disposed of, all the activities that take place at the supposed end of a PC's days, whether that means having its reusable bits removed, or being snapped up by a vintage computer collector. People from my generation don't like to think about computers as junk, because to us they're still such new things. I find (C) it / them much harder to throw one out than, say, a tumble drier, and I can see much more (symbolic) value in a 20-year-old computer than I can in a 20-year-old car.

	(A)		(B)		(C)
①	are	· · · · · ·	which	· · · · · ·	them
②	are	· · · · · ·	in which	· · · · · ·	them
③	to be	· · · · · ·	in which	· · · · · ·	it
④	to be	· · · · · ·	in which	· · · · · ·	them
⑤	to be	· · · · · ·	which	· · · · · ·	it

13

2점

Fairy stories are filled with frogs turning into princes, or pumpkins turning into coaches drawn by white horses (A) transformed / are transformed from white mice. Such fantasies are profoundly unrealistic. They couldn't happen, not for biological reasons but mathematical ones. Such transitions would be virtually impossible, which means that for practical purposes we can rule them out. But for a caterpillar (B) to turn / turns into a butterfly is not a problem: It happens all the time, the rules having been built up over the ages by natural selection. And although no butterfly has ever been seen to turn into a caterpillar, (C) it / which should not surprise us in the same way as, say, a frog turning into a prince. Frogs don't contain genes for making princes. But they do contain genes for making tadpoles.

*tadpole 올챙이

	(A)		(B)		(C)
①	transformed	· · · · · ·	to turn	· · · · · ·	it
②	transformed	· · · · · ·	to turn	· · · · · ·	which
③	are transformed	· · · · · ·	turns	· · · · · ·	it
④	are transformed	· · · · · ·	turns	· · · · · ·	which
⑤	are transformed	· · · · · ·	to turn	· · · · · ·	it

※ 다음 글을 읽고, 빈칸에 들어갈 말로 가장 적절한 것을 고르시오. [14~17]

14
[2점]

By examining the various functions of religion, we can see that religion is a(n) _____ force in a society. In a general sense religions support the status quo by keeping people in line through supernatural sanctions, relieving social conflict, and providing explanations for unfortunate events. Moreover, some of the major world religions, through both philosophical convictions and political interpretations, have tended to inhibit social change. To illustrate, orthodox Hindu beliefs, based on the notion that one's present condition in life is determined by deeds in past lives, have had the effect of making people so fatalistic that they accept their present situations as unchangeable. Such a worldview is not likely to bring about major revolutions or even minor initiatives for change. Likewise, some Muslim leaders have taken a strong stand against the introduction of new values and behaviors, particularly from the Western world.

① conservative
② democratic
③ impartial
④ intellectual
⑤ stimulating

15
[3점]

Imagine that you are standing in a large, square field. On one side of the field a noisy road crew is doing some repairs with a jackhammer. On an adjacent side of the field a street vendor with a food cart is playing a loud, repetitive jingle. With your eyes closed, you could wander around in the field and work out your distance from either the road crew or the food cart by gauging the loudness of the sounds. Knowing both distances would allow you to triangulate your position on the field with an accuracy limited only by your ability to discriminate loudness. What is even more interesting about this example is that you could work out your position in the field even from locations that you had never visited before, provided you had a basic understanding of the principle—two sources of sound in two different locations _____.

① keep you alert for longer periods
② provide unambiguous cues to position
③ hinder your positional awareness
④ lead to higher distraction levels
⑤ diminish auditory functions

16

3점

Like speech, most forms of nonverbal communication are symbolic behaviors: A particular body motion or distance does not inherently convey a certain message but does so only because of conventions, or common understandings. Because much nonverbal communication is arbitrary and conventional, there is great potential for misunderstanding when people do not share the same meanings for nonverbal messages —that is, when people have learned different conventions. Probably the potential for misunderstanding is even greater with nonverbal messages than with spoken language. When two people from different cultures converse, both generally know that they do not understand the other's language, so at least each person is aware of his or her own ignorance. However, both are more likely to think they understand nonverbal messages, so they _____.

① have to focus on verbal messages more carefully

② might give or take offense when none is intended

③ might end communication by clarifying the other's intention

④ will make their feelings clear to each other verbally

⑤ will be better at communicating with each other

17

2점

When people are stressed they react differently. It is difficult for them to eat and sleep. They become irritable and short-tempered. They may say things in the heat of the moment they would not otherwise say. As couples tend to react differently under stress, one partner may be affected far more than the other and so the relationship is damaged. The answer is to identify the source of stress and see what can be done about it. First, you must accept that you are under stress and that this is causing problems in the relationship. Then sit down together and talk about the issues. That alone is often enough to relieve some of the stress. Whatever the cause of the stress, it is not likely to be resolved easily or quickly, but just recognizing it and having some sort of plan to tackle it is reassuring. Much more important, by sitting down with your partner and talking about it you can work together to resolve it. There is a lot of truth in the saying "_____."

① Too many cooks spoil the broth   ② A bad workman blames his tools

③ Absence makes the heart grow fonder   ④ A problem shared is a problem halved

⑤ Better a live coward than a dead hero

18 다음 글이 시사하는 바로 가장 적절한 것은?

2점

Quite often, people will come up to me after a seminar and say that they have decided upon their financial goal. When I ask them what it is, they tell me that they have decided to become a millionaire or even a billionaire in the next year or two. In almost every case, these people turn out to have no money or very little. They are often in their thirties or forties and have a lifetime of financial mismanagement behind them. Nonetheless, they think that they can neutralize all their past experiences and somehow leap into wealth and affluence with little preparation, few resources, and no clear idea of how to get there. They believe that all they need to do is to think happy thoughts and they will magically attract everything they need to overcome decades of frustration and failure. When people say to me that they want to be a millionaire as soon as possible, I suggest that they first become a "thousandaire." After they have managed to save a thousand dollars and get out of debt, they can then become a "ten thousandaire," and so on.

① Positive thinking can lead one out of debt.

② Each person must walk before he or she can run.

③ If you work really hard, you will get rich in a short period of time.

④ You must develop multiple courses of action before leaving your job.

⑤ One's quality of life depends on how he or she neutralizes past experiences.

19 다음 글에서 필자가 주장하는 바로 가장 적절한 것은?

2점

Some of the biggest fears of pre-service teachers include what they are required to teach and whether or not they know enough of the subject matter to teach the class. Your jurisdiction's department of education will have mandated a curriculum for you to follow. Treat the curriculum as the stepping stones of information you are required to teach and your students are to learn. While you are required to follow the curriculum's learning outcomes, curriculum documents don't say how to teach them or how to assess them. Along with the curriculum, there are often approved textbooks that align with the jurisdiction's vision of student learning. Some of the best teachers do not solely rely on the curriculum and textbooks, but will expand on some areas based on student interest. Remember, although you should use the curriculum and textbooks as your guide to lesson planning and instruction, they shouldn't be everything.

*jurisdiction 관할구역

① 예비교사를 위한 교육실습 기회가 확대되어야 한다.
② 교사는 교과과정과 교과서에 전적으로 의존해서는 안 된다.
③ 교육청은 교사들에게 교과과정과 평가방법을 제시해야 한다.
④ 교과과정을 수립할 때 교사들의 의견을 충분히 수렴해야 한다.
⑤ 교과서를 집필할 때 학생들의 관심 분야를 적극 반영해야 한다.

※ 다음 글의 빈칸 (A), (B)에 들어갈 말로 가장 적절한 것을 고르시오. [20~21]

20

3점

Both internationally and domestically, tourism is seen as an effective means of transferring wealth and investment from richer, developed countries or regions to less developed, poorer areas. This ___(A)___ of wealth occurs, in theory, as a result of both tourist expenditures in destination areas and also of investment by the richer, tourist-generating countries in tourism facilities. In the latter case, developed countries are, in principle, supporting the economic growth and development of less developed countries by investing in tourism. However, it has long been recognized that the net retention of tourist expenditures varies considerably from one destination to another, while overseas investment in tourism facilities more often than not may lead to ___(B)___. This can be seen in profits often largely being diverted away from the less developed countries, potentially leaving them subject to the investor nations and corporations.

	(A)		(B)
①	concentration	······	exploitation and dependency
②	redistribution	······	exploitation and dependency
③	imbalance	······	prosperity and security
④	redistribution	······	prosperity and security
⑤	imbalance	······	collaboration and development

21

2점

A kind of personal knowledge that we have stored in our memory is the knowledge of our likes and dislikes. This is a highly personal kind of knowledge, dependent on individual taste. If we ask you,   (A) , what your favorite kind of soup is, you might tell us that it's Borscht or Chicken Noodle or Egg Drop. You know because you have eaten many kinds of soup before, and you remember which one you liked the best. Based on that memory, you probably ask for it over and over again at home or in restaurants.   (B) , you can easily tell us who your best friend is, who your favorite singer is, and which soccer team you like best, as well as what your favorite color or book or television program is. All of these things you remember because you have had extensive direct experience with them in the past, and you can easily compare and contrast the various experiences to determine which one gave you the most pleasure.

	(A)	(B)
①	for example	Similarly
②	for example	Therefore
③	on the contrary	Similarly
④	on the contrary	Otherwise
⑤	in other words	Therefore

※ 다음 글의 밑줄 친 부분 중, 문맥상 낱말의 쓰임이 적절하지 <u>않은</u> 것을 고르시오. [22~23]

22

Domesticated animals were frequently utilized as weapons and equipment in ancient wars. The Greeks often used elephants as war equipment. Intended primarily to ① <u>terrify</u> the enemy, elephants were elaborately decorated with ornaments, such as headpieces and clanging bells. They were occasionally given fermented wine to drink, ② <u>encouraging</u> fierce behavior. However, the use of elephants on the front lines was probably more a ③ <u>display</u> of strength than of their practical use as a war animal. Elephants are not ④ <u>effective</u> in fighting human wars; if bombarded by arrows, an elephant will simply turn around and retreat, often inflicting more damage on his own army than on the enemy. Further, a female elephant will refuse to fight if separated from her young, and she would immediately ⑤ <u>assume</u> all military duties and rush to the rescue if her offspring cried out when wounded or trampled upon.

23

Firms exist in capitalistic societies to make a profit. If the firm's product were viewed as a one-time-only purchase by consumers (e.g., novelty items such as the pet rock), if the level of performance were not subject to regulation, and if only ① <u>limited</u> cross-communication channels were open to consumers, then customer satisfaction would be an unimportant goal for the purely profit-oriented firm. Few producers, however, ② <u>encounter</u> these conditions. Most find that repeat purchasing is essential to a continued stream of ③ <u>profitability</u>. Even for products with long purchase intervals (e.g., major appliances, automobiles), satisfaction is important because of word of mouth and the activities of numerous watchdog organizations, such as Consumers Union, that ④ <u>track</u> reports of satisfaction over time. Now becoming more available, empirical data on the influence of satisfaction, quality, and other such measures are ⑤ <u>contradicting</u> the long-held assumption that customer satisfaction is one key to profitability.

24

Psycholinguistic researchers have found that a person will understand a positive statement in approximately two-thirds the time it takes to understand a negative one. Even if your only objective in life is to motivate others to do what you want them to do, constructive criticism will carry you much further than a negative attack. If someone has done something half right and half wrong, emphasize how great the end product would be if he consistently employed the techniques that worked well. If someone's clothing is attractive and stylish, but his hair looks like it was cut by a blind barber, compliment him on the tastefulness of his attire; and if you have a legitimate need to change his appearance, suggest that he would look even better if he conformed his hairstyle to his clothing style. Offer solutions, not just criticism; and give others the chance to take the hint. If they don't, you can always turn up the criticism until they do.

① Keep Your Criticism Positive

② Why Criticism Is So Hard to Take

③ Accept Negative Criticism for Growth

④ How to Recognize Empty Compliments

⑤ The Value of Offering Negative Feedback

25

People unconsciously signal that they are lying through inconsistencies in their nonverbal behavior. If you have ever caught someone in a lie, you might have noticed that statements made later in the conversation contradicted statements made at the beginning, or perhaps his or her gestures seemed to contradict the words being spoken. The person may have acted calm and aloof, but at the same time kept tapping his or her foot, playing with a button or piece of jewelry, and speaking with a higher pitch. Examinations of people's perceptions of courtroom testimony reveal that stereotypically deceptive behaviors don't necessarily trigger suspicion, but inconsistent nonverbal behaviors are frequently interpreted as deceptive regardless of the specific actions that are performed. Research has also shown that familiarity with a person's typical nonverbal behaviors makes it easier to detect deception. In particular, people are better able to tell whether a partner is telling the truth or lying when they have previous experience with that person's truthful behavior.

*aloof 초연한, 무관심한

① Patterns of Behavior That Reveal Deception

② Psychological Factors That Lead to Deception

③ Common Characteristics of Nonverbal Messages

④ Developing a Strong Relationship Free of Deception

⑤ Inaccurate Assessments of People's Truth or Deception

26

However, the same sport can have different meanings to different groups of people.

2점

As with education, sport has a common core of shared meaning and a periphery of additional meanings that are very much context-dependent. (①) In other words, although most of us have a common understanding of what sport is, it can still mean different things to different people. (②) In general terms we recognize that football is sport, but that ballroom dancing is not; motor racing is sport, but driving to work is not; sailing a boat on an ocean is sport, but sailing on a tanker delivering oil is not. (③) It is not necessary to define what we mean by sport whenever the word is used. (④) As an example of these differing meanings let us consider the sport of tennis. (⑤) To a professional tennis player tennis is a job; to a club player, however competitive, tennis is essentially a recreation; to a spectator at Wimbledon, tennis may be a temporary diversion or an all consuming vicarious passion.

*vicarious 대리의

27

3점

In a stable, fully occupied habitat, there may not be enough nest sites or food available in a given year for new breeders to strike out on their own.

Flamingos, penguins, ostriches, giraffes, dolphins, crocodiles, and many other species leave their young in the care of other adults for a while. This gives parents the freedom to track down the most nutritious foods for their growing family. (①) Just who are these surrogate parents that care for the young? (②) The sitters may be parents taking random turns, or they may be nonbreeding individuals that are related to the parents. (③) Though it may look like altruism, the sitters are merely promoting their own genes tied up in the young nieces, nephews, or siblings that they are caring for. (④) If their aim is to further their genes, you may ask, why not just have their own brood? (⑤) Rather than be forced into a marginal nesting site, they might hold off for a year, learning tricks in the meantime that will make them better parents.

*surrogate 대리의

※ 다음 글의 요지로 가장 적절한 것을 고르시오. [28~29]

28

[2점]

In everyday life, people are repeatedly exposed to different aspects of consumption. Advertising, traveling on a train, grocery shopping, watching television, listening to music, surfing the Internet, clothes shopping, and reading a book are all examples of things that people consume. Almost all behaviors that humans engage in are directly or indirectly linked to consumption. Even traditional holidays such as Christmas are these days mainly about consumption. What was originally a religious holiday has mainly been overtaken by aspects of consumption with the most typical example of this being Santa Claus delivering presents. Basically there is no way of escaping the fact that consumption is a part of humans' everyday lives. Hence, without studying how consumption affects individuals and groups, one can never truly say that we understand humans.

① 다양한 제품 개발로 소비 활동이 촉진될 수 있다.
② 개인의 선호에 따라 서로 다른 소비 양상이 나타난다.
③ 소비자는 자극적인 광고에 영향을 많이 받는 경향이 있다.
④ 인간을 이해하기 위해서는 소비에 대한 연구가 반드시 필요하다.
⑤ 크리스마스와 같은 종교적인 휴일에는 더 많은 소비가 발생한다.

29

2점

Complications arise when an artist attempts to illustrate a story from outside his or her realm of cultural experience. If the artist has little or no background in a particular area and is unwilling or unable to do thorough research, he or she is in danger of misrepresenting the story through illustrations, especially if an attempt is made to imitate "native" styles. It is very difficult for an outsider to extract details effectively without an understanding of the overall context from which they come. That is not to say it can't be done. Ed Young, for example, is known for his attention to authentic detail in the artwork he creates for traditional stories from other cultures. In Kimiko Kajikawa's Tsunami!, for example, Young accurately depicts the clothing, hairstyles, and architecture characteristic of mid-nineteenth-century Japan.

① 예술작품에 관해서는 문화 간의 우열을 가리는 것이 무의미하다.
② 삽화는 독자가 이야기의 세부내용을 이해하는데 많은 도움을 준다.
③ 타문화를 제대로 이해하려면 그 문화를 모방하려는 노력이 필요하다.
④ 배경지식이 부족하면 타문화권 이야기의 삽화를 정확하게 그리기 어렵다.
⑤ 타문화를 무분별하게 받아들이면 자국 문화에 부정적인 결과가 초래된다.

30

[2점]

Sports marketing is not new. The first known athletic event that required paid admission was a baseball game in Long Island, New York, in 1858, where spectators were charged 50 cents. Sports organizers soon realized the financial potential of sporting events and professional athletes. Golfer Gene Sarazen signed an endorsement deal with Wilson Sporting Goods in 1923. The original agreement was for $6,000 a year plus an equal amount for travel expenses. In 1949 Babe Didrikson Zaharias signed the first significant female endorsement with Wilson Sporting Goods for $100,000 a year. Coca-Cola partnered with the Summer Olympics in 1928 and remains a sponsor to this day. The first pay-per-view athletic event was a boxing match, the "Thrilla in Manila," with Muhammad Ali taking on Joe Frazier in the Philippines in 1975. It was broadcast to 276 closed-circuit locations. Capitalizing on the popularity of sports, ESPN made its debut in 1979, offering advertisers a new way to reach their target markets. Today many high schools and colleges offer sports marketing programs.

① the emergence and expansion of sports marketing
② effective budgeting for sports marketing activities
③ social changes affecting sports marketing
④ misconceptions about sports marketing
⑤ the dark side of sports sponsorship

31

2점

At the start of the century, interest in advertising was growing and it was not only manufacturers who could see its potential. Politicians also became interested when they realized that "how to sell products" could be applied to sell their own ideas. This was particularly evident during World War I when propaganda campaigns were used as tools to encourage people to continue fighting. For example, the British and Americans spread rumors about the appalling behavior of the Germans, such as making soap out of enemy soldiers. This was done so that people would feel that they could not possibly let such a horrible nation win the war and hence think that it was worth continuing to fight. Many so-called "atrocity stories" were used, and while some did contain an element of truth, many were invented solely for the benefit of the British and American governments. Nevertheless, they appeared to be effective in selling political agendas to the people.

*atrocity 잔학 (행위)

① different methods of advertising in different cultures

② political and social conflicts caused by propaganda

③ increasing influence of propaganda on advertising

④ differences between advertising and propaganda

⑤ the application of advertising to political matters

32 Romain Rolland에 관한 다음 글의 내용과 일치하지 <u>않는</u> 것은?

2점

Romain Rolland was a French dramatist, novelist, and art historian who was awarded the Nobel Prize for Literature in 1915 as a tribute to the lofty idealism of his literary production. He was born at Clamecy, Niévre in 1866. An excellent student, he entered the École Normale Supérieure, where he studied philosophy before gravitating toward the arts and music. After graduation in 1889, he spent several years in Italy studying the Italian masterpieces of the Renaissance. Upon his return to France, Rolland earned a doctorate in the study of early European opera in 1895. That same year, he earned a master's degree for a thesis on Italian oil paintings of the 16th century. He then taught at the university level until 1912, when he resigned his position to turn his full attention to writing. His greatest literary contributions came in the form of plays. He firmly believed that theater should be physically and intellectually welcoming to the masses. He favored plays that reminded audiences of France's revolutionary history.

① 프랑스인으로서 1915년에 노벨문학상을 수상했다.

② École Normale Supérieure에서 철학을 공부했다.

③ 16세기 이탈리아 유화에 관한 논문으로 박사학위를 받았다.

④ 저술 활동에 전념하기 위해 가르치는 일을 그만두었다.

⑤ 관객들에게 프랑스의 혁명 역사를 상기시키는 희곡을 선호했다.

33 다음 도표의 내용과 일치하지 않는 것은?

2점

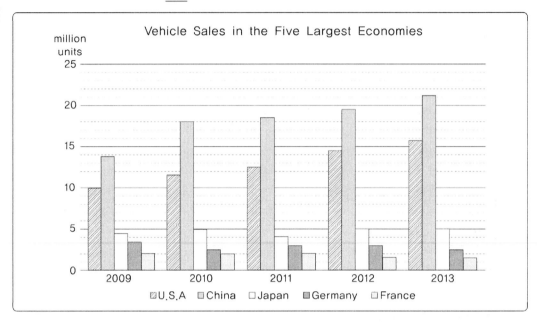

Vehicle Sales in the Five Largest Economies

☑U.S.A ☐China ☐Japan ■Germany ☐France

The above graph shows the number of vehicles sold in each of the five largest economies between the years of 2009 and 2013. ① Each year during the 5-year period China showed the largest vehicle sales, consistently followed by the U.S.A. ② The number of vehicles sold in China continued to increase from year to year with close to 14 million units sold in 2009 and over 21 million units sold in 2013. ③ The gap in the numbers of vehicles sold in China and the U.S.A. was more than 3 million units in 2009 and over 5 million units in 2013. ④ While the third most vehicles were sold in Japan each year, the number of vehicles sold there in 2013 was a third of what was sold in China in the same year. ⑤ Each year the fourth most vehicles were sold in Germany, with the number of vehicles sold in the country failing to reach 4 million units in any of the 5 years, and France had the smallest vehicle sales each year.

34

2점

You see your friend running towards you. As he approaches he gets larger and larger. However, you know your friend is coming closer, not actually growing.

(A) Likewise, as a car passes you and moves off into the distance, it appears to get smaller. However, it is known that perception of size does not vary as much as would be expected from the change in size of the retinal image.

(B) This is because you have knowledge in your memory about the size of people and know that people do not rapidly change size. In fact, the retinal image is expanding, and the rate of expansion is an indication of how fast something, in this case your friend, is approaching.

(C) These are the examples of perceptual constancy. Basically we experience a car moving away, or a person coming nearer. We do not concern ourselves with the changing size; we interpret the information as giving movement in the depth plane.

*retinal 망막의

① (A) − (C) − (B)

② (B) − (A) − (C)

③ (B) − (C) − (A)

④ (C) − (A) − (B)

⑤ (C) − (B) − (A)

35
3점

One of the most valuable outcomes from coaching people is that you also develop yourself in the process of coaching. It is the genuine passion and intention to grow others that spurs us on to transform ourselves.

(A) This cycle of learning returns over and over again throughout the entire coaching relationship. As we coach more people, we inculcate knowledge, skills, and competencies in coaching that will help us in many aspects of our professional and personal lives.

(B) During the coaching session, we gain hands-on experience and practice coaching skills and techniques. After coaching, we reflect on what happened during the dialogue and what went well, what didn't, and how we can do better next time.

(C) To develop others, we have to first develop ourselves. And to continuously change others, we can't help but continuously transform ourselves. Before we coach, we learn, we prepare, and we reflect on how we can be an effective coach.

*inculcate 되풀이하여 가르치다

① (A) − (C) − (B)

② (B) − (A) − (C)

③ (B) − (C) − (A)

④ (C) − (A) − (B)

⑤ (C) − (B) − (A)

36 (A), (B), (C)의 각 네모 안에서 문맥에 맞는 표현으로 가장 적절한 것은?

In the past, economy and thrift were the order of the day. Nothing was thrown away no matter how little value it seemed to have. Every purchased product was important and every dollar was worth saving. Today, products are less (A) durable / fragile and are meant to be disposed of. Cigarette lighters, contact lenses, and even watches and cameras have become throwaways. Similarly, clothing and accessories are perishables in the sense that once they are out of style their usefulness (B) expires / prevails. In regard to the new shopping trend this means that consumers, young and old, are becoming more used to living in a world where things are disposed of quickly and readily, and new things are bought to replace them. As the pace of life increases steadily there is more demand for more throwaway products. Our emotional (C) attachment / aversion to personal products is becoming less over time and that means that there is ever more demand for more products.

	(A)		(B)		(C)
①	durable	· · · · · ·	expires	· · · · · ·	attachment
②	durable	· · · · · ·	prevails	· · · · · ·	attachment
③	durable	· · · · · ·	expires	· · · · · ·	aversion
④	fragile	· · · · · ·	expires	· · · · · ·	attachment
⑤	fragile	· · · · · ·	prevails	· · · · · ·	aversion

37 다음 글의 내용을 한 문장으로 요약하고자 한다. 빈칸 (A)와 (B)에 들어갈 말로 가장 적절한 것은?

2점

In a psychological study, researchers gave questionnaires to two groups of students and asked them to respond by email. All the questions had to do with some mundane task, such as opening a bank account. But the two groups were given different instructions for answering the questions. The students in the first group were to write about what the activity implied about some intangible information such as personal traits—what kind of person has a bank account, for example. The second group wrote simply about the specific steps in the process—speaking to a bank teller, filling out forms, making an initial deposit, and so forth. There proved to be a significant difference between the response times of the two groups. The students in the first group tended to delay—in fact, some never completed the task at all. By contrast, the students in the second group, who were focused on the how, when, and where of the task, completed the task sooner than the first group.

*mundane 일상적인

⇩

In the study, the first group of students, who were given a task requiring thinking in more _____(A)_____ terms, turned out to _____(B)_____ their answers to a greater extent than the other group of students.

	(A)		(B)
①	abstract	· · · · · ·	postpone
②	abstract	· · · · · ·	emphasize
③	quantitative	· · · · · ·	postpone
④	practical	· · · · · ·	exaggerate
⑤	practical	· · · · · ·	emphasize

※ 다음 글을 읽고, 물음에 답하시오. [38~39]

Ecological approaches to human health consider human beings as part of a broader ecosystem. Disease ecologists focus on interactions between humans and the environments in which they live, helping to describe and explain patterns of health and disease across space. Humans interact with their environment in many ways that make them more or less susceptible to ill-health. Staying out too long in cold weather can lead to hypothermia, a condition of dangerously low body temperature, or too much exposure to the sun may promote the development of skin cancer, for instance. ____(A)____, not all connections are this direct. One of the main ways in which disease ecology has been useful in explaining disease patterns is by considering how characteristics of the environment influence where disease-causing organisms, or the vectors that carry them, can live. ____(B)____, many diseases are restricted to tropical climates where year-round warm temperatures allow vectors such as mosquitoes to thrive. Warm temperatures can also speed up the reproduction rates of micro-organisms such as viruses and bacteria, as well as the invertebrates that transmit them, leading to more rapid transmission of disease among humans. Analyzing relationships between people and infectious agents of disease was one of the first focuses of disease ecologists and remains a fundamental part of disease ecology today.

*vector (병균의) 매개 곤충 **invertebrate 무척추 동물

38 윗글의 제목으로 가장 적절한 것은?

2점

① Effective Hygiene Practices to Combat Diseases

② The Origin of Disease Ecology as a Scientific Field

③ The Evolution of Typical Disease-Causing Organisms

④ Effects of Environmental Change on the Spread of Diseases

⑤ Disease Ecologists' Concerns: Environment and Human Diseases

39 윗글의 빈칸 (A), (B)에 들어갈 말로 가장 적절한 것은?

[2점]

	(A)		(B)
①	However	……	As a result
②	However	……	For example
③	Furthermore	……	As a result
④	In other words	……	Similarly
⑤	In other words	……	For example

※ 다음 글을 읽고, 물음에 답하시오. [40~41]

Machu Picchu is surrounded by the Urubamba River located 2,000 feet below the citadel. This river was considered sacred to the Inca partly because nature was sacred to them but also because of the advantages it brought. It curves around the mountain in which Machu Picchu is located and some of the agricultural terraces extend all the way down to the river. The river cannot be navigated at the location of Machu Picchu, but further down it is possible to use boats to navigate to the Amazon River and all the way to the Atlantic Ocean and move people and goods. This may have been purposeful to avoid having people navigate directly to Machu Picchu but still offer a relatively close route of ____(A)____. Proximity to the rainforest was certainly another advantage of the geography of Machu Picchu. The rainforest was the only source of rare products that were prized by the Incas such as colorful bird feathers, butterflies, coca leaves, exotic fruits and vegetables and healing herbs among other products. The Inca would exchange these products with tribes from the rainforest for things that they did not have such as potatoes, guinea pigs, precious stones, quinoa, and gold and use them for religious ceremonies. When building Machu Picchu, the Inca must have considered the benefits from being so close to the rainforest as a(n) ____(B)____ source.

*citadel 요새

40 윗글이 시사하는 바로 가장 적절한 것은?

2점

① With no written language, the Inca left no record of how Machu Picchu was built.

② In building Machu Picchu, the Inca took into account their surrounding geography.

③ Conservation efforts are necessary for the future of Machu Picchu's tourism industry.

④ Machu Picchu is set in a rainforest providing a stable habitat for some endangered species.

⑤ The lack of direct route from the Atlantic Ocean delayed the development of Incan civilization.

41 윗글의 빈칸 (A), (B)에 들어갈 말로 가장 적절한 것은?

2점

	(A)		(B)
①	invasion	......	trading
②	invasion	......	energy
③	tourism	......	labor
④	transportation	......	trading
⑤	transportation	......	labor

During World War II, the composer Dmitry Shostakovich and several of his colleagues were called into a meeting with the Russian ruler Joseph Stalin, who had commissioned them to write a new national anthem. Shostakovich heard meetings with Stalin were (A) fascinating / terrifying ; one misstep could lead you into a very dark alley. He would stare you down until you felt your throat tighten. And, as meetings with Stalin often did, this one took a bad turn: The ruler began to criticize one of the composers for his poor arrangement of his anthem. Scared silly, the man admitted he had used an arranger who had done a bad job. Here he was digging several graves: Clearly the poor arranger could be called to task. The composer was responsible for the (B) hire / dismissal , and he, too, could pay for the mistake. And what of the other composers, including Shostakovich? Stalin could be relentless once he smelled fear.

Shostakovich had heard enough: It was foolish, he said, to blame the arranger, who was mostly following orders. He then subtly redirected the conversation to a different subject— whether a composer should do his own orchestrations. What did Stalin think on the matter? Always eager to prove his expertise, he swallowed the bait. The dangerous moment passed.

Shostakovich maintained his presence of mind in several ways. First, instead of letting Stalin intimidate him, he forced himself to see the man as he was: short, fat, ugly, unimaginative. So the dictator's famous piercing gaze was just a trick, a sign of his own (C) creativity / insecurity . Second, Shostakovich faced up to Stalin, talking to him normally and straightforwardly. By his actions and tone of voice, the composer showed that he was not intimidated.

42 (A), (B), (C)의 각 네모 안에서 문맥에 맞는 표현으로 가장 적절한 것은?

3점

	(A)		(B)		(C)
①	fascinating	· · · · · ·	hire	· · · · · ·	creativity
②	fascinating	· · · · · ·	dismissal	· · · · · ·	insecurity
③	terrifying	· · · · · ·	hire	· · · · · ·	insecurity
④	terrifying	· · · · · ·	dismissal	· · · · · ·	insecurity
⑤	terrifying	· · · · · ·	hire	· · · · · ·	creativity

43 윗글의 내용으로 적절하지 않은 것은?

2점

① Shostakovich와 그의 동료들은 Stalin으로부터 국가를 작곡하라는 의뢰를 받았다.

② Stalin은 국가를 잘 편곡하지 못한 작곡자 중 한 명을 비난했다.

③ Shostakovich는 지시를 따른 편곡자를 나무라는 것은 어리석은 일이라고 말했다.

④ Stalin은 자신이 전문적 지식을 지녔음을 입증하는 것을 원하지 않았다.

⑤ Shostakovich는 Stalin을 두려워하지 않는다는 것을 보여줬다.

(A)

When Don was 25, he went backpacking around South East Asia. For three of those weeks, he traveled around Indonesia, including a stop in a lovely town called Bukittinggi. At his guesthouse, he met a nice fellow from Sweden, Stephen, who recommended that (a) he explore a nearby lake atop a long inactive volcano.

(B)

In starting (b) his trek around the lake, Don knew that the last bus down the mountain left at 5:00 p.m., so he had to be sure to be back at the bus stop by then. As it was 1:00 p.m., he figured he had loads of time to make it all the way around the lake and back in time to catch the last bus down the mountain. It was an amazing hike. However, at about 4:00 p.m. he realized that (c) he was nowhere near half-way around the lake.

(C)

He decided to race back the way he came. As he neared the bus stop, he saw the last bus driving away without (d) him. Breathless, he had no choice but to start walking down the mountain and hope that some kind person would pick him up. He walked for hours before any vehicles even came by. Fortunately, eventually, a wonderful Indonesian gentleman stopped to help. He was very sympathetic to the situation and offered Don a ride all the way back to his guesthouse. Don was more grateful than words could express.

(D)

Following (e) his advice, Don found a bus that would take him up there. It turned out to be not so close, but rather a four-hour ride up steep, windy, and rather dangerous roads. It was worth it, though, because the view was unbelievable at the top. There was an absolutely majestic lake at the top of the mountain where the mouth of the volcano once was. It was surrounded by a lovely walking path, which according to Stephen, would take about two hours to walk around.

44 주어진 글 (A)에 이어질 내용을 순서에 맞게 배열한 것으로 가장 적절한 것은?

2점

① (B) − (D) − (C)　　　② (C) − (B) − (D)

③ (C) − (D) − (B)　　　④ (D) − (B) − (C)

⑤ (D) − (C) − (B)

45 밑줄 친 (a)~(e) 중에서 가리키는 대상이 나머지 넷과 다른 것은?

2점

① (a)　　　② (b)

③ (c)　　　④ (d)

⑤ (e)

▶ 해설은 p. 130에 있습니다.

01 Based on the following dialogue, which one is true?

2점

> Ms. Smith : OK, class, it's time to look at the solar system again!
>
> Sunny : Oh, Ms. Smith, do we have to? We just did that last week, and it's so boring, all planets and moons and stuff.
>
> Ms. Smith : Well, Sunny, then perhaps you can answer some questions. If you get them all right, we can study whatever you want. Does it sound good?
>
> Sunny : Yes, that's great! Ms. Smith, you're the best teacher! Ask away.
>
> Ms. Smith : First question: how many moons does Mars have?
>
> Sunny : That's easy! There's one.
>
> Ms. Smith : Sorry, Sunny, you're wrong on the first try. There are two.
>
> Sunny : Aw, how could I know that? I've never been there!

① Ms. Smith doesn't think students have to learn about the solar system again.

② Sunny is very interested in the planets and moons.

③ Sunny doesn't understand why she has to answer Ms. Smith's questions.

④ Sunny gives the right answer to Ms. Smith's first question.

⑤ Ms. Smith tells Sunny that Mars has two moons.

02 Which is the best sequence of answers for the blanks?

2점

> Julie : I'm starving. There are lots of places down by the river that sell good chicken.
> Rachel : That sounds great. It's pretty far from here, though, right? _____
> Julie : Well, there's the subway. I've got my transit pass. Do you have yours?
> Rachel : No, and besides, my feet already hurt from all the running around we've done.
>   We'd have to walk all the way to the subway station.
> Julie : _____ That would be easier, if not cheaper.
> Rachel : Oh, no. I don't have that much money.
> Julie : Then, I think we should just hop a bus. _____

〈보기〉

a. We could grab a taxi.   b. I'm not sure how to get there.
c. There's one right there.   d. It's not that far.

① a — b — d   ② b — a — c
③ b — d — a   ④ c — a — b
⑤ c — b — d

03 Where is the dialogue most likely taking place?

2점

> Dan : Look at that, over there! Have you ever seen anything like it?
> Paul : Well, on TV of course, but the plant looks kind of scary when I see it with my
>   own eyes. It looks like it has teeth.
> Dan : Yes, it does. But they're not teeth. They're just special leaves. That's one of the
>   most unique plants here.
> Paul : Well, then, let's get a closer look.
> Dan : Fine, but you know what? Now that I think of it, if the smell is too much, I'm
>   leaving. I had a big breakfast and I don't want to lose it.
> Paul : Grow up! It's nature, man! Some flowers smell bad.
> Dan : Have it your way, then, but I'm holding my nose.

① at a haunted house   ② at a botanical garden
③ at a recycling center   ④ at a cosmetics store
⑤ at an aquarium

04 Based on the following dialogue, which one is NOT true?

> Nick : I really liked that movie we saw last night. It was fantastic!
> John : Really? It didn't meet my expectation. Sequels are never as good as the originals.
> Nick : No, I disagree. I think the second *Avengers* movie was just as good as the first.
> John : Okay, I'll grant you that, but what about the *Iron Man* movies? *Iron Man* 2 wasn't good.
> Nick : You may be right, but the other *Iron Man* sequel, the third one, was excellent!
> John : Okay, that's true. You've got a point about that.
> Nick : And ... *Ant—Man* 2! Ha! It was also just as good as, and maybe even better than, the first one, right?
> John : Okay, you're right. I should think more before making generalizations.

① The two people saw a movie together last night.

② Nick doesn't agree with John's idea that sequels are worse than the originals.

③ John admits that the second *Avengers* movie was as good as the first.

④ The two people agree that *Iron Man 2* was excellent.

⑤ John accepts Nick's idea that *Ant—Man 2* was a good movie, like the first one.

05 Choose the best answer for the blank.

> Doctor : What seems to be the trouble?
> Patient : Well, I have this pain in my stomach, down here on the right side.
> Doctor : Lie down here. *[Pause]* Does it hurt when I push on it, like this?
> Patient : Ow! Yes! It's very painful. Please don't do that again.
> Doctor : Well, let's take your temperature. Hmm. Yes, it's pretty high, as I expected.
> Patient : As you expected? Do you already know what the trouble is, Doctor?
> Doctor : I'm pretty sure what it is. I think you need surgery, but to be certain, there's one more step before we schedule it. _____

① We should do another test.

② I want to apply for health insurance.

③ I need to go have lunch with my staff.

④ Can I get something for my stomachache?

⑤ Don't worry, your temperature is not high.

06 Choose the sentence that best describes the situation.

3점

> Lisa : John and I are going to open a restaurant!
>
> Suzy : That's pretty brave. I've heard that 50% of all restaurants fail within the first year.
>
> Lisa : You've got to have faith. We've been cooking for a long time, and we think we'll be able to create a great place.
>
> Suzy : What kind of cuisine are you thinking about offering?
>
> Lisa : We've got it narrowed down to Mexican or Vietnamese.
>
> Suzy : Wow, those are quite different styles. What made you consider those two particularly?
>
> Lisa : Mexican is super popular, but there's a lot of competition. Vietnamese is rather unusual, so that's good, but on the other hand, people aren't familiar with it.
>
> Suzy : Well, you'll have to make up your minds before you go to the bank for a loan.

① Suzy is going to open a new restaurant and is trying to find a good cook.

② Lisa and John will open a restaurant, but haven't made a final decision on the cuisine.

③ Lisa and Suzy are trying to decide what kind of food to eat tonight in the restaurant.

④ Suzy will go to the bank with Lisa so that Lisa can get a loan for her restaurant.

⑤ Suzy is confident that Lisa's new restaurant will succeed, but Lisa is not sure.

07 다음 글에서 필자가 주장하는 바로 가장 적절한 것은?

2점

Not all decisions are made from perfect data. Even though it is important to use all data at hand to render the best possible solution, sometimes you are still missing information and the solution doesn't seem clear. In cases like this, your intuition needs to be your guide. This means having faith in yourself and listening to what you believe is truth, regardless of what direction the data may point. When you are going through the decision-making process and you are sifting through the net to weed out the garbage and gather only the good information, remember to ask yourself how you feel about the information you have gathered. This is extremely important. The best decisions are the ones that combine good data that points to an obvious choice and that gut feeling that says, "You did the right thing."

① 반론을 제기할 때 타당한 근거를 제시하라.
② 연구 주제와 무관한 정보를 과감하게 버려라.
③ 자료를 선정하고 결정을 내릴 때 직관을 동원하라.
④ 객관적인 자료를 바탕으로 합리적인 결정을 내려라.
⑤ 자료 수집 과정에서 정보의 양보다 질을 중요시하라.

08 다음 글이 시사하는 바로 가장 적절한 것은?

2점

There are difficulties that we cannot deal with right away, or perhaps ever. As well as remembering to have the patience to bear what cannot be changed, there are other ways of adjusting to seemingly impossible situations. Many spiritual teachers regard afflictions, trials, sufferings, and deprivations as "blessings in disguise" through which our inner spiritual powers are stimulated, purified, and ennobled. Confucius stated that "the gem cannot be polished without friction, nor man perfected without trials," while Helen Keller wrote, "I thank God for my handicaps, for, through them, I have found myself, my work, and my God." If we use them correctly, the failures, tests, and difficulties in our lives can become the means of purifying our spirits and strengthening our characters. A quote from 'Abdu'l-Bahá illustrates this particularly well: "We should try to make every stumbling block a stepping stone to progress."

① The more educated, the more civilized.

② Adversity can lead to achievement.

③ Do as you would be done by.

④ Cooperation works miracles.

⑤ Look before you leap.

※ 다음 글의 요지로 가장 적절한 것을 고르시오. [9~10]

09

2점

When websites ask you to check a box saying "Don't ask me again," a lot of people are happy to check that box. If public officials, or doctors, ask you to fill out numerous forms with the same questions, registering choices of multiple kinds, you may get immensely frustrated and wish that at least some of those choices had been made for you. People would be better off if public and private institutions cut existing form-filling requirements dramatically. And if a cab driver insists on asking you to choose which route you want to take in an unfamiliar city, you might wish he hadn't asked, and just selected the route that he deems best. When you are having lunch or dinner with a friend, it's often most considerate to suggest a place, rather than asking the friend to choose.

① 사람들은 선택의 부담이 줄어드는 것을 더 좋아한다.

② 사람들은 자신이 직접 선택한 것에 더 애착심을 갖는다.

③ 고객 선호도 조사를 통해 서비스의 질을 개선할 수 있다.

④ 인터넷상에서는 개인 정보 보호 의식이 여전히 미흡하다.

⑤ 사람들은 선택의 기회가 많을수록 자신의 의사를 잘 표현한다.

10

2점

There are those who think that the skill is everything and they evaluate a work of art entirely on the amount of skill involved. Such people are more interested in realism in painting because of the skill associated with painting a subject realistically. They also are usually more interested in crafted items and are awed by the skill involved in making the item. Certainly we should give credit for many elements that go into making a piece of art, but there is a distinction between those elements and the aesthetic element. We can give credit for effort, for technique, for skill, for material, for scale, and the time it took to make the work. The value of art should not be measured by such qualities. No matter how hard one tries to make a work of art, it still may fail aesthetically. One could make a work out of gold, but it could also fail aesthetically. There is nothing worse in bad art than big, bad art. What a shame to work for years on one piece of art that is not successful in the end. If the skill is not developed well enough to get the aesthetic elements of the art across, then the value of the work lessens.

① 기술적 요소에 미학적 요소를 더해야 예술 작품의 가치가 높아진다.
② 위대한 예술 작품은 기존의 틀에서 벗어난 새로운 양식을 추구한다.
③ 비평가에게는 예술 작품의 진가를 알아보는 심미안이 필요하다.
④ 많은 시간과 자원을 투입해야 예술 작품의 수준이 높아진다.
⑤ 예술 작품을 평가하는 기준이 사람에 따라 다를 수 있다.

※ 다음 글의 주제로 가장 적절한 것을 고르시오. [11~12]

11

2점

Knowledge transfer has received a tremendous amount of publicity recently with advances in groupware and networking tools, designed to enable the flow of knowledge among groups and individuals. The goal of such tools is ultimately shared memory and understanding. In fact, this is difficult to achieve because knowledge is "sticky," alive, and rich. It is "sticky" because it is very tightly bound to the context which gives it meaning; without context it is just information. Knowledge can be thought of as being alive in that it must be constantly attended to as it is ever-changing and growing. It also dies, goes out of date, becomes irrelevant and must be discarded, but who is its rightful steward? Lastly, it is rich in its multi-dimensionality, containing a tremendous amount of content, context, and experience. All three of these factors make it very difficult to distribute knowledge.

① protection of traditional cultural knowledge

② close relationship between knowledge and context

③ importance of experience as a source of knowledge

④ characteristics of knowledge that make its transfer difficult

⑤ easier knowledge distribution with information technology

12

A number of unique security problems are associated with carrying air cargo. Air cargo often contains more expensive items than those shipped by other freight-carrying methods; hence, the potential for loss is greater. It is also more difficult to identify where losses occur. In other methods of shipment, items are simply picked up, moved, and delivered to loading docks. Air cargo movement is much more complex: cargo is first moved from freight terminals to flight terminals, then loaded onto freight aircraft before shipping, with opportunities for theft all along the way. When freight is placed on a passenger airplane, risk is increased because it must go to a passenger terminal and is exposed to additional handlers. At many airports, carts travel to and from flights along unlit routes, creating still more opportunities for theft. Moreover, 90 percent of air cargo is shipped at night, the time period when most crime occurs.

① factors that make air cargo more vulnerable to theft

② problems of airline passenger security screening

③ benefits and drawbacks of air freight transport

④ a brief history of air freight delivery service

⑤ different methods of transporting cargo

13

2점

What is truly arresting about human beings is well captured in the story of the Tower of Babel, in which humanity, speaking a single language, came so close to reaching heaven that God himself felt threatened. A common language connects the members of a community into an information-sharing network with formidable collective powers. Anyone can benefit from the strokes of genius, lucky accidents, and trial-and-error wisdom accumulated by anyone else, present or past. And people can work in teams, their efforts coordinated by negotiated agreements. As a result, *homo sapiens* is a species, like blue-green algae and earthworms, that has made far-reaching changes on the planet. Archaeologists have discovered the bones of ten thousand wild horses at the bottom of a cliff in France, the remains of herds stampeded over the clifftop by groups of paleolithic hunters seventeen thousand years ago. These fossils of ancient cooperation and shared ingenuity may shed light on why saber-tooth tigers, mastodons, giant wooly rhinoceroses, and dozens of other large mammals went extinct around the time that modern humans arrived in their habitats. Our ancestors, apparently, killed them off.

* stampede (동물 등을) 우르르 몰다

① Breaking the Language Barrier : A Hard Task

② Language : A Basis of Cooperative Human Power

③ Changes in Languages from Ancient to Modern Times

④ Communicating with Animals, Understanding Animal Language

⑤ How Language Began : Gesture and Speech in Human Evolution

14

2점

Education, either formal or informal, plays a major role in the passing on and sharing of culture. Educational levels of a culture can be assessed using literacy rates and enrollment in secondary or higher education, information available from secondary data sources. International firms need to know about the qualitative aspects of education, namely, varying emphases on particular skills, and the overall level of the education provided. The Republic of Korea and Japan, for example, emphasize the sciences, especially engineering, to a greater degree than do Western countries. Educational levels will have an impact on various business functions. Training programs for a production facility will have to take the educational backgrounds of trainees into account. For example, a high level of illiteracy will suggest the use of visual aids rather than printed manuals. Local recruiting for sales jobs will be affected by the availability of suitably trained personnel. In some cases, international firms routinely send locally recruited personnel to headquarters for training.

① Education as a Means of Social Mobility

② Educational Background and Economic Status

③ Trends in Education and Occupational Structure

④ Education : One Vital Consideration for Foreign Businesses

⑤ Educated Labor Force : A Driving Force for Economic Growth

15 다음 도표의 내용과 일치하지 않는 것은?

2점

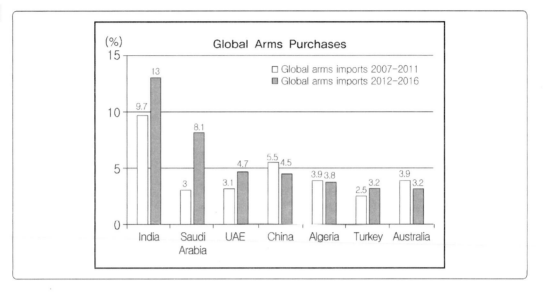

The graph above shows the global shares of arms purchases of seven countries over two time periods, 2007–2011 and 2012–2016. ① In the 2012–2016 period, India accounted for the largest share of global arms imports, followed by Saudi Arabia, the United Arab Emirates (UAE), China, Algeria, Turkey and Australia. ② Compared with the 2007–2011 period, the global shares of arms imports of India, Saudi Arabia, the UAE, and Turkey increased in the 2012–2016 period. ③ In contrast, the global shares of arms imports of China, Algeria, and Australia fell in the 2012–2016 period, compared with the previous period. ④ Specifically, China's share of global arms imports fell the most, from 5.5 percent to 4.5 percent, between the two periods. ⑤ The gap in global shares of arms purchases between 2007–2011 and 2012–2016 was the largest in Saudi Arabia, and the smallest in Turkey.

16 Bertolt Brecht에 관한 다음 글의 내용과 일치하지 않는 것은?

_{2점}

Bertolt Brecht was a major influence on 20th century drama. He explored a new style of drama, using unusual staging and different styles of acting in order to achieve his aim of making audiences think about the moral and political implications of his plays. Brecht was born in Augsburg, Germany, and studied medicine and philosophy at the universities of Munich and Berlin. After serving in World War I, he achieved success with his play *Drums in the Night*. Throughout the 1920s and early 1930s he wrote many more plays. In 1933 Brecht and his wife were forced to flee from Germany after Hitler came to power. Brecht eventually reached America, but there he was investigated for having Communist beliefs. He left America and returned to East Berlin in 1947, where he founded The Berliner Ensemble, a theater company that became world famous.

① 독특한 연출 및 다른 연기 방식을 이용하여 새로운 양식의 연극을 탐구했다.

② 뮌헨 대학교와 베를린 대학교에서 의학과 철학을 공부했다.

③ 1차 세계대전 이전에 연극 *Drums in the Night*로 성공을 거두었다.

④ 히틀러가 집권한 후 아내와 함께 독일을 떠나야 했다.

⑤ 1947년에 동베를린으로 돌아와 그곳에서 극단을 세웠다.

17 밑줄 친 he가 가리키는 대상이 나머지 넷과 다른 것은?

2점

At the height of the Civil War, President Lincoln and his Secretary of War visited the battle side house of General George McClellan on some urgent business. Since ① he was not at home, they waited in his parlor. When the General finally returned home, he saw that he had visitors but did not acknowledge them. Instead, he went straight to his room. Assuming that ② he would come out soon, they waited for him. An hour later, when he had still not appeared, they sent the maid to inquire. A minute later, she returned and said, "I am sorry, Mr. President, but the General has asked me to tell you that ③ he is very tired and has gone to bed." The Secretary of War was shocked and said, "Mr. President, this is unacceptable. You must immediately dismiss him from the post of General!" Lincoln thought about it for a minute and then ④ he said, "No, I will not dismiss him. He is a good general. He wins battles. I would hold his horse and wash the dirt from his boots if ⑤ he could shorten this bloodshed even by one hour."

※ 다음 글의 밑줄 친 부분 중, 어법상 틀린 것을 고르시오. [18~19]

18

2점

Given the dominance in Western cultures of naturalistic views of the body, the concept of the body in culture is ① potentially a difficult one to grasp. The bodies of accident victims, transplant patients and others ② undergoing cosmetic surgery are literally and physically reconstructed every day by surgeons. Such commonplace practices make ③ it relatively easy to think of the body as a machine. Like machines, bodies have components that can, up to a point, be taken apart and reassembled. The workings of the body can in similar fashion to other machine-like objects ④ be examined and malfunctions diagnosed and remedied. Mary Shelley's monster, literally constructed by Dr. Frankenstein, is the classical working out of the body-as-machine idea. So familiar are these ways of thinking about the body ⑤ which to some of us the ideas of the social construction of the body and of the body in culture may seem to be nonsense.

19

3점

Adolescence is a period of rebellion and of striving for independence; consequently, there will be many areas ① <u>where</u> children will disagree with you or not see things exactly the way you do. Remember, *what* they say ② <u>is</u> not as important as *how* they say it. If they communicate their disagreements with family policies and the way they are treated, certainly listen to them and when ③ <u>possible</u> try to respond positively. The child who says to his parent rationally, "I think I should be able to spend more time on the phone. Fifteen minutes a day is not enough. I've been doing all my homework and my grades are good," should ④ <u>respond</u> to in a very different manner from the child who begins by shouting and complaining angrily about his lack of phone time. It should be acceptable for a teenager to tell his mother that he does not like eating liver on Monday nights. However, it would be totally unacceptable for him to come into the kitchen on Monday evening and ⑤ <u>start</u> threatening that he will not eat this "garbage" and that his mother had better learn to cook something "decent."

※ (A), (B), (C)의 각 네모 안에서 어법에 맞는 표현으로 가장 적절한 것을 고르시오. [20~21]

20

3점

If you want something to happen in your life, you need to focus on it. Without focusing, and believing in what you want to achieve, you cannot accomplish the task at hand. This law of focus reminds you not to give up, no matter how (A) exhausted / exhausting the task may seem. By continuing to believe in it and focusing on it, you clearly stand a better chance of achieving the desired results. Through the law of energy and attraction, you will attract into your life (B) that / what you give energy to and focus on. A magnifying glass used to focus the sun's energy can start a fire. You can manifest what you want through your focused energy of thought and belief. You will continue to be faced with challenges, struggles and mishaps as other laws, such as the law of ups and downs, (C) are / is working in the background. You give power and life to whatever you focus on. You bring magic into what you want as you increase its vibration through your focus.

	(A)		(B)		(C)
①	exhausted	······	that	······	are
②	exhausted	······	what	······	is
③	exhausting	······	what	······	are
④	exhausting	······	what	······	is
⑤	exhausting	······	that	······	are

21

2점

Although hunter-gatherers had previously led semi-settled rather than entirely nomadic lives, moving between a number of temporary or seasonal shelters, the ability to store cereal grains began to encourage people to stay in one place. An experiment carried out in the 1960s shows why. An archaeologist used a flint-bladed sickle to see how (A) efficient / efficiently a prehistoric family could have harvested wild grains, which still grow in some parts of Turkey. In one hour he gathered more than two pounds of grain, which suggested that a family (B) worked / that worked eight-hour days for three weeks would have been able to gather enough to provide each family member with a pound of grain a day for a year. But this would have meant staying near the stands of wild cereals to ensure the family did not miss the most suitable time (C) harvested / to harvest them. And having gathered a large quantity of grain, they would have been reluctant to leave it unguarded.

* sickle 낫

	(A)		(B)		(C)
①	efficient	······	worked	······	harvested
②	efficient	······	that worked	······	to harvest
③	efficiently	······	worked	······	harvested
④	efficiently	······	that worked	······	to harvest
⑤	efficiently	······	that worked	······	harvested

※ 다음 글의 밑줄 친 부분 중, 문맥상 낱말의 쓰임이 적절하지 않은 것을 고르시오. [22~23]

22

2점

The embedding of reporters, as ground-breaking as it may have been, proved to be a ① <u>controversial</u> policy. Some critics charged that embedded reporters might endanger the troops or the mission. Others were concerned that journalists would become "too close" to those they covered, and naturally identify more directly with those whom they lived with and were protected by, thereby ② <u>gaining</u> their objectivity. This phenomenon was likened to Stockholm Syndrome, where hostages come to empathize with their captors. Nevertheless, advocates of embedding argue it has several advantages. It provides an "up close and personal" view and ③ <u>allows</u> journalists to experience war as the troops do, so that they can portray the efforts of those doing the fighting. It provides ④ <u>direct</u> access to the battlefield and the war's events in ways not otherwise possible. The live footage and "real time" reporting provide a ⑤ <u>realistic</u> "first cut of history" and document the war as it happens.

* embed (종군 기자 등을) 파견하다

23

3점

Stand at the edge of your favorite beach and look out. You are seeing one of the most unusual sights our universe has to offer: large amounts of liquid water. This perception of the oceans of the Earth as a ① <u>unique</u> phenomenon is fairly new. Those who read science fiction will have vivid memories of the "canals of Mars" and the "swamps of Venus." Less than a quarter century ago the best scientific guess as to the nature of our planetary neighbors presupposed the ② <u>presence</u> of large amounts of water. On Mars, the white polar caps indicated that the temperature might be too cold for the water to be liquid, so that it was thought to be ③ <u>locked</u> in ice sheets. On Venus, the cloud cover prevented us from seeing the surface, but it didn't prevent us from ④ <u>imagining</u> the planet as an overgrown version of the Amazon rainforest. In both cases, our view of neighboring planets was shaped by the expectation that water, so plentiful on the Earth, must be ⑤ <u>scarce</u> everywhere else in the solar system.

24

3점

According to Nassim Taleb, author of the brilliant book Black Swan, we try to make sense of all the data around us because there are costs attached to information storage. So the more orderly we can make that information, the easier and less costly it is to store in our minds. This means that we prefer our data to be more ordered and less random. We have a drive to (A) [increase / reduce] the number of dimensions that we handle, so we place complex data into a much simpler order as a way to achieve this. Taleb considers that this is not only the purpose of narrative but also causality. We will try to attribute causality to events so that we can explain and understand, rather than leaving us to deal with the complexity and randomness of the world. And the purpose of (B) [denying / imposing] a narrative is that it can generate a sense of chronology, so both move in a single direction. The narrative means that we tend then to recall those facts that fit the story, that meet the requirements of the causality the narrative has perpetuated. We then don't recall the true sequence of events but a reconstructed one that makes the causality appear much more (C) [complicated / straightforward] than it was.

* perpetuate 영속화하다

	(A)		(B)		(C)
①	increase	······	denying	······	complicated
②	increase	······	imposing	······	complicated
③	reduce	······	denying	······	straightforward
④	reduce	······	imposing	······	complicated
⑤	reduce	······	imposing	······	straightforward

25

[3점]

Alongside the wounded, ill, and injured service members and veterans exists a group of individuals who help care for them, whom we term *military caregivers*. Military caregivers are heroes in their own right, but their efforts are often (A) honored / unrecognized . They serve in the shadow of war, as their caregiving responsibilities persist for months and years after conflicts end. The men and women of the military who have made sacrifices for their country often receive honors, awards, and benefits in recognition of their service—accolades and opportunities that they (B) hardly / rightly deserve. However, their caregivers help the disabled walk and eat, tend to wound care, or take them to their medical appointments, and rarely receive honors and awards. These caregivers are an incidental population, one that has received policy attention only as a consequence of the focus on the ones for whom they provide care. Yet their value is (C) enormous / insignificant . Military caregivers provide benefit not only to their loved one, but also to society. The care they render helps reduce health care costs to the government and society.

* accolade 표창

	(A)		(B)		(C)
①	honored	⋯⋯	hardly	⋯⋯	enormous
②	honored	⋯⋯	hardly	⋯⋯	insignificant
③	unrecognized	⋯⋯	rightly	⋯⋯	enormous
④	unrecognized	⋯⋯	rightly	⋯⋯	insignificant
⑤	unrecognized	⋯⋯	hardly	⋯⋯	enormous

26

2점

Several historians declare that the foreign correspondent—the reporter covering events outside the country—is _____. This description applies to traditional mass media correspondents in particular. Since 1980, American networks have closed most of their overseas bureaus and have decreased their international news coverage. Neither the terrorism of September 11, 2001, nor the war in Iraq has reversed these trends. In a review of the year 2007, for example, the *Tyndall Report*, which monitors network television news, found that while the war in Iraq was the story of the year by a wide margin, the networks' foreign bureaus had their lightest workload since 2001. Economic pressures, global interdependence, and technological innovations—and a perception of public disinterest—have changed the way foreign news is reported and consumed.

① an endangered species

② an amateur ambassador

③ a fountain of exotic ideas

④ a particularly hated figure

⑤ the storyteller of a secret war

27

3점

If you live in a country like the United States, it is easy to say that population is the major problem for preserving the environment. But if you think about it a little more deeply, you could rapidly come to understand that consumption and the kinds of technology that we use are also very important in setting the stage for the world of the future. For example, people in rural Brazil or rural Indonesia, like most of their counterparts in developing countries, live at about one-fortieth of the consumption level of people in the United States. If you consider that we've added 135 million people to the population of the United States since the end of World War II, then you realize that the impact of the extra people in the United States on the world—in terms of levels of consumption, levels of pollution, uses of inappropriate technologies that may themselves be destructive—is about equal to the impact on the world of all the entire population of developing countries—4.2 billion people. It is not justifiable to say that population is the only factor. It's _____ that is truly significant.

① our way of dealing with the world

② our viewpoint on the welfare problem

③ humanitarian aid to developing countries

④ how to put an end to poverty and violence

⑤ how to measure the degree of economic equality

28

Personality characteristics are important not only for how we define ourselves, but also for _____. Social psychologists have shown that when we form impressions of others we try to extract information about their personality attributes from how they look and act: whether they are friendly, trustworthy, emotional, dominant, and so on. Impression formation is all about making what are known as 'dispositional inferences' about other people's personalities. Similarly, the stereotypes that we hold about particular social groups are saturated with personality characteristics. Whether accurate or inaccurate, these stereotypes represent personality portraits of group members, such as whether they are happy-go-lucky, aggressive, socially awkward, greedy, and so on. Once again, personality characteristics matter to us as social perceivers because they are such centrally important aspects of people.

① how we form our character

② sorting out false information

③ how we perceive other people

④ making inferences about causality

⑤ finding a career fit for our personality

29

Due to the efforts of Renaissance artists to elevate their profession as a liberal art, the Western world has popularized the idea of a lone individual creating his or her own art to express something very personal. In the nineteenth and twentieth centuries it became more common for artists to determine individually the appearance and content of their own work, and, in their search for new forms of self-expression, to make art that was often very controversial. This remains true today. But for many centuries before this, very few artists worked alone. Even Renaissance artists who promoted the idea of creative genius operated workshops staffed by artist assistants who carried out most of the labor involved in turning their master's design into a work of art. Even today, some famous artists, such as Jeff Koons, _____.

① employ other artists to realize their ideas
② work within the confines of a frame
③ want their work to incite controversy
④ get thousands of step-by-step solutions
⑤ depend on patrons for financial support

30

Of all the thinkers of antiquity, Aristotle was perhaps the most comprehensive, his works ranging over the landscape of knowledge, such as physics, politics, and ethics. But the very scale of Aristotle's achievement left a problematic legacy. There are authors like Aristotle who are too clever for our own good. Having said so much, they appear to have had the last word. Their genius inhibits the sense of irreverence vital to creative work in their successors. Aristotle may, paradoxically, prevent those who most respect him from behaving like him. He rose to greatness only by doubting much of the knowledge that had been built up before him, not by refusing to read Plato or Heraclitus, but by mounting significant critiques of some of their weaknesses based on an appreciation of their strengths. To act in a truly Aristotelian spirit may mean allowing for some _____.

① opportunities to work together across disciplines
② credits to humanities such as politics, ethics, and literature
③ significant ties based on the values shared by philosophers
④ generalizations to be made about the features of individual cases
⑤ intelligent departures from even the most accomplished authorities

※ 주어진 글 다음에 이어질 글의 순서로 가장 적절한 것을 고르시오. [31~32]

31

2점

To parents and the general public, class size seems to be the "litmus test" of the quality of a school. Schools with small class sizes are perceived as being better than schools with large class sizes. Surveys show that parents care more about class size than anything else except school safety.

(A) Furthermore, discipline is much more difficult: for example, students may be able to doze in class without the teacher knowing it, and surely the teacher cannot correct every student who shows evidence of daydreaming.

(B) After all, if a teacher has only fifteen or so students in a class, it is far more possible for that teacher to provide individual attention to each student. None will be left behind, and none will have to move forward on their own.

(C) On the other hand, teachers of class sizes of thirty or so students simply cannot teach to each individual student. These teachers have huge numbers of papers to grade, grades to calculate, makeup work for students who are absent, parents to contact, and e-mails to answer.

① (A) − (C) − (B)　　　　② (B) − (A) − (C)

③ (B) − (C) − (A)　　　　④ (C) − (A) − (B)

⑤ (C) − (B) − (A)

32

2점

Eating is still fun for the one-year-old, but it is no longer the main interest in the child's life. Children's need for food is determined mostly by their activity level and by the rate at which they are growing in height and weight.

(A) If this happens everybody loses. The parents lose because they never get over their frustration at the way their children eat. The children lose because they really do become picky, difficult eaters or else chronic overeaters.

(B) That concern often leads parents to try to force children to eat more. When parents force and children resist, a chronic battle is set up which may become more important to all concerned than the question of food which started it all in the first place.

(C) Because this rate slows down greatly in the second year of life, many children are actually eating less at 15–18 months than they were at 8–10 months. Not unexpectedly this concerns a great many parents who feel it is obvious that the bigger and older children are, the more they should eat.

① (A) − (C) − (B)　　　　② (B) − (A) − (C)

③ (B) − (C) − (A)　　　　④ (C) − (A) − (B)

⑤ (C) − (B) − (A)

33

3점

> That prompted the military to take the chemical−repelling technology that it had developed to protect soldiers against biological weapons and apply it to T−shirts and underwear.

Who knew that the largest number of casualties from Operation Desert Storm in the 1991 Gulf War would be from bacterial infections? Soldiers in combat don't always have the luxury of being able to change into fresh underwear, if they even have a clean pair to change into. (①) Underwear worn day after day in those hot desert conditions turned out to be a significant cause of bacterial infections and discomfort. (②) The underwear is manufactured by using microwave energy to bond tiny "nanoparticles" to the fibers in the underwear fabric. (③) Then chemicals that repel oil, water, bacteria, and other substances are bonded to the nanoparticles. (④) The result was underwear that is very, very difficult to get dirty, because virtually nothing will stick to it. (⑤) And because bacteria never gets established, undergarments made with the stuff can be worn for weeks without washing and without risk to the wearer's health.

34

2점

> However, private property rights are not sacred, even in societies with strong views on this subject.

Landscape−level restoration will almost always involve public property (especially where water is concerned) and a mixture of organizational and personal private property. (①) Consequently, a formidable barrier to a landscape approach is the inevitable conflicts between environmental protection and property rights. (②) The individual property owner with a small wetland is likely to be angry when told that filling, draining or altering the wetland in major ways is illegal. (③) This property, the owner sometimes says, is private "and I will do as I wish with my property." (④) Each person lives not only on private property, but in a larger ecological landscape shared with others. (⑤) So, a key question is: to what extent should individual, organizational or national behavior and attitudes be modified for the betterment of others of the human species and for other species as well?

※ 다음 글에서 전체 흐름과 관계 없는 문장을 고르시오. [35~36]

35

2점

Gifted children, with their extreme emotional sensitivity and idealism, often notice great gaps between how things are and how they ought to be—in their family, their school, their community, and the larger world. ① Because of their keen minds and their sharp thinking and reasoning abilities, they find themselves sharply aware of mediocrity, greed, poverty, corruption, violence, abuse, pollution, hypocrisy, and other flaws in society. ② They become discouraged and disillusioned that no one else cares or that these problems can never be fixed. ③ They may feel relieved and act swiftly to conform to the social or behavioral norms of their age group. ④ As a result of this "What's the point?" attitude, many intellectually gifted youngsters choose to underachieve in school, and some drop out of high school, college, or even society altogether. ⑤ They may search for a life or career where they don't have to deal with social hypocrisy or other aspects of society that make them uncomfortable.

36

2점

Scientific evidence is mounting that some animals use tools, live by moral codes, use complex communication systems, and have culture. ① These findings fit squarely within Charles Darwin's theory of evolution, which predicts that differences between humans and other animals are in degree, not kind. ② Yet there is an ongoing debate about the nature and sufficiency of the evidence for culture among animals. ③ Some scholars aren't convinced that ecological and genetic explanations for animal behavior have been ruled out in all cases, while others define culture in ways that exclude nonhuman animals. ④ In order to understand the legal status of nonhuman animals it is necessary to understand what is fundamental about how legal systems work. ⑤ The unresolved debate makes this an active, exciting field of study, with new discoveries and important advances appearing regularly.

37

다음 글의 내용을 한 문장으로 요약하고자 한다. 빈칸 (A)와 (B)에 들어갈 말로 가장 적절한 것은?

2점

Consider a new manager who wants to test her employees' planning skills. She may ask her employees to develop a written plan for a particular project. The manager could use very concrete and specific language to describe the assignment: "I want you to develop a five-page plan for this proposed project. First, make sure you include an overview of the project in the introduction. Second, I want a section that highlights your analysis of why we have embarked on this project. Third, I want a solutions section in the report. Finally, I want a description of the criteria and benchmarks for assessing the success of your proposed solution." This request uses very concrete and specific language, but does it meet this manager's needs? By outlining the length and format for the project proposal, the manager clearly specifies what she wants, and in doing so, she reduces her chances to assess her employees' planning abilities. She could have made her request more ambiguous: "Please develop a proposal for this project. I don't want to tell you too much more, because I don't want to limit your creativity." Although this language is more abstract, it may give the manager better insight into how each employee thinks and plans.

⇩

When assessing employees' planning skills, a manager can provide them with an opportunity to show their ____(A)____ by adjusting the level of ____(B)____ in the instructions for an assignment.

	(A)		(B)
①	creativity	......	agreement
②	creativity	......	abstraction
③	experience	......	frequency
④	experience	......	abstraction
⑤	enthusiasm	......	frequency

※ 다음 글을 읽고, 물음에 답하시오. [38~39]

You never know when a so-called bad idea will contain the seeds of greatness within it. We've seen it countless times in our work. A bad, even absurd, idea is offered up, and within minutes it has transformed into a brilliant example of innovative thinking. We make use of some effective idea generation methods that invite participants to come up with the worst, most ridiculous, even distasteful ideas imaginable—and then to turn around or transform those ideas into great ones.

Consider the extreme "what if we all jumped out of the window" example. From this bad idea, you might develop an innovative emergency personal parachute product for individuals working in tall city buildings. Or conceive an improved process for evacuation from high floors during a fire. A new "team hang-gliding" extreme sports event. A breakthrough advertising concept where a group of people are able to fly after consuming a new beverage. An infinite number of other possibilities could be born from the bad idea that everyone in the room should jump out of a window. That is, unless the idea is shot down prematurely before the great idea within it has a chance to blossom. So, _____ until an idea has had a fair chance to show all it's got.

38 윗글의 제목으로 가장 적절한 것은?

① Creative Ads Will Inspire You

② Bad Ideas Can Lead to Big Ideas

③ Why Doesn't Group Brainstorming Work?

④ Good Intentions Can Have Bad Outcomes

⑤ Are People More Creative Alone or Together?

39 윗글의 빈칸에 들어갈 말로 가장 적절한 것은?

① detect errors

② follow tradition

③ suspend judgment

④ punish wrongdoing

⑤ reduce daydreaming

※ 다음 글을 읽고, 물음에 답하시오. [40~41]

As an example of the ability of language to direct our attention, think about the term 'politically correct,' or PC, language. Its proponents argue that we can rid our minds of discriminatory thoughts by removing from our language any words or phrases that could offend people by the way they reference differences and handicaps. Los Angeles County in California asked suppliers to stop using the terms *master* and *slave* on computer equipment, even though these are commonly used terms that refer to primary and secondary hard disk drives, because of cultural sensitivity. Other substitutions, such as *police officer* for *policeman*, are intended to highlight that such positions are held by both men and women.

Using PC language and being PC have come to be viewed negatively,   (A)   , and even ridiculed and satirized because they overcompensate for others' sensitivities. One reason that PC language is fairly easy to ridicule is that its political agenda is not always connected to large social and cultural institutions.   (B)   , it is one thing to say that we need to rid the workplace of sexist language in an effort to create equal relationships between men and women, but unless this directive is connected to a broader agenda of fostering gender pay equity and equal opportunity for promotions and advancement, merely ridding the workplace of sexist language may not generate the hoped-for effect.

40 윗글의 주제로 가장 적절한 것은?

2점

① grounds for supporting political correctness

② effects of social progress on language changes

③ pros and cons of using politically correct language

④ differences between male and female language use

⑤ necessity of getting a clear idea with a clear expression

41 윗글의 빈칸 (A), (B)에 들어갈 말로 가장 적절한 것은?

2점

	(A)		(B)		(A)		(B)
①	however	······	For example	②	however	······	In contrast
③	that is	······	For example	④	thus	······	In contrast
⑤	thus	······	Furthermore				

A boy was born in England to parents from Ghana. Because he was born in England, the boy was automatically a British citizen. As a youngster, he returned to Ghana to live with his father, leaving behind his mother, two sisters, and a brother. Some years later he returned, intending to live with his mother and siblings. At this point, the story gets (a) complicated. Immigration authorities suspected that the boy was an impostor and thought he was either an unrelated child or a nephew of the boy's mother. On the basis of their suspicions, the boy's application for residency was (b) denied. The boy's family fought to establish his identity so that he could live in the country of his birth. The first round of medical tests used blood types as well as genetic markers normally employed to match organ donors and recipients. The results (c) confirmed that the boy was closely related to the woman he claimed was his mother, but the tests could not tell whether she was his mother or an aunt.

The family turned to Alec Jeffreys, a scientist at the University of Leicester, for help. They asked if DNA fingerprinting, a technique developed in Jeffreys's research laboratory, could establish the boy's identity. However, the mother's sisters and the boy's father were not available for testing. Despite these problems, Jeffreys agreed to take on the case. He took blood samples from the boy, the children he believed were his brother and sisters, and the woman who claimed to be his mother. The pattern of bands, known as a DNA fingerprint, was analyzed to determine the boy's identity. The results showed that the boy had the same father as his brother and his sisters because they all (d) shared DNA fragments associated with the father. The most important question was whether the boy and his "mother" were related.

Jeffreys found that 25 fragments of the woman's DNA matched those of the boy, indicating that she was in fact the boy's mother. Faced with this evidence, immigration authorities had to (e) maintain their position. They allowed the boy to live in England with his family.

* impostor 남의 이름을 사칭하는 사람

42 윗글에 관한 내용으로 적절하지 않은 것은?

[2점]

① 소년은 영국에서 태어나 자동적으로 영국 시민이 되었다.

② 소년은 어렸을 때 아버지와 살려고 Ghana로 갔다.

③ 소년의 가족은 소년이 영국에서 살 수 있도록 그의 신원을 증명하려고 애썼다.

④ 소년의 가족은 Alec Jeffreys에게 DNA 지문 검사를 요청했다.

⑤ Alec Jeffreys는 소년의 아버지의 혈액 샘플을 받았다.

43 밑줄 친 (a)~(e) 중에서 문맥상 낱말의 쓰임이 적절하지 않은 것은?

3점 ① (a) ② (b)

③ (c) ④ (d)

⑤ (e)

※ 다음 글을 읽고, 물음에 답하시오. [44~45]

(A)

It was summer and Mary was 14. Her whole family spent weekend after weekend at the river, waterskiing and swimming and just having a great time. But Mary couldn't ski like her big brothers and sisters. She was too embarrassed to try. (a) She was horrified at the idea of looking ridiculous, and looking like a novice next to her skilled and experienced siblings. One day she told her mother all about this.

(B)

On that day, Mary learned to ski. Her mother was patient and careful. It wasn't nearly as difficult as Mary had thought it would be, and with no audience (b) she had no discomfort about being hunched over her skis. As the afternoon wore on, she stood up straighter and straighter on the skis. The next weekend river trip would see Mary happily skiing along with her brothers and sisters, (c) her embarrassment erased by her mother's kind act.

(C)

Mary explained that when beginning skiers got up out of the water for the first time, they started off crouched over their skis with their bottoms stuck out, looking absolutely absurd. And there were so many people on the river on any sunny weekend. Some of them were boys, and they would all see Mary as (d) she adopted that humiliating pose. Mary told her mom that she was not willing to risk this shame.

(D)

One Thursday soon after this talk, Mary's mother left work after lunch and came home. Mary didn't understand why her mom was home, but Mary's mom just told her to help hook the boat trailer to the car. Her mother was offering something, and Mary had to accept (e) her offer. Before she knew what had happened, Mary and her mom were in the boat, heading up the river in the warm sunshine on quiet water. It was a Thursday, so no one else was about. No one was there to see Mary look ridiculous.

44 주어진 글 (A)에 이어질 내용을 순서에 맞게 배열한 것으로 가장 적절한 것은?

2점

① (B) – (D) – (C) ② (C) – (B) – (D)

③ (C) – (D) – (B) ④ (D) – (B) – (C)

⑤ (D) – (C) – (B)

45 밑줄 친 (a)~(e) 중에서 가리키는 대상이 나머지 넷과 다른 것은?

2점

① (a) ② (b)

③ (c) ④ (d)

⑤ (e)

10 | 2020학년도 영어영역

▶ 해설은 p. 147에 있습니다.

1 Based on the following dialogue, which one is true?

Ron : I don't think I can go any further.

Dan : Come on, man! Push it, we have about one more kilometer to the top. Don't quit now!

Ron : That's easy for you to say! You're in great shape, and your bike is carbon fiber! It must weigh 10 kilograms less than my bike!

Dan : If you make it without stopping, I'll buy you dinner after the ride. Anything you want.

Ron : I can't even think about eating. My legs feel like they're going to fall off and my throat is drier than a desert. Seriously I've got to stop and rest. I want to get in better shape, but I'm too tired. This is too hard.

Dan : You have to push yourself. You're not going to lose all that fat by taking rests. You're the one that asked me to help you.

Ron : I see. You're right.

① Ron and Dan managed to reach the top together.

② Ron's bike is lighter than Dan's.

③ Ron says that he can eat anything after the ride.

④ Ron desperately wants to take a break.

⑤ Ron is helping Dan to lose weight.

02 Choose the best answer for the blank.

2점

> Salesman : Well, I think this SUV is exactly what you're looking for.
> Bob : It looks nice, but it's much bigger than I expected.
> Salesman : In that case, maybe this sedan is more to your interest? It's smaller and the price is reasonable.
> Bob : That sounds great. Does it come in navy blue?
> Salesman : We have one in navy blue here in the showroom. The sticker price is $75,000. Would you like to take it for a test drive?
> Bob : No, I drove the same car at another dealership last week. I think I'm going to just go ahead and buy it.
> Salesman : _____

① Great. Let me get the paperwork together and you can get on the road.

② Okay. I can introduce you to another car dealer in your neighborhood.

③ No problem. I can give you enough time for your test drive.

④ Don't worry. Both cars will be within your price range.

⑤ I'm sorry, but we don't have the car in navy blue.

03 Which is the best sequence of answers for the blanks?

2점

> Randy : What should we have for dinner?
> Martha : Actually, I can't think of anything I really want to eat.
> Randy : How about Mexican food? A new Mexican restaurant called El Gordo's has opened nearby.
> Martha : _____ Last time I ate spicy food in a Mexican restaurant, my stomach hurt for two days.
> Randy : Then what about the Waffle Shack? _____
> Martha : So do I, but there's always a really long wait for a table.
> Randy : You may be right. What about pizza?
> Martha : I can't eat it again. _____
> Randy : Mmm.... How about trying El Gordo's? We can choose unspicy food.
> Martha : Okay. If you want.

<보기>

a. I don't think it's a good idea.

b. I really love their dinner menu.

c. I'm so hungry.

d. I've already had it three times this week.

① a − b − d   ② a − c − d

③ b − a − d   ④ d − b − c

⑤ d − c − b

04 What is the relationship between the man and the woman?

2점

> Man : So I think it's exactly what you're in the market for. What do you think?
>
> Woman : Well, honestly, I love it. The neighborhood seems fantastic and it is within my budget.
>
> Man : So, should we make an offer to the owner? I know there are several other people interested in the house.
>
> Woman : Yes, but I have one concern. Does the house next door always look like that? It looks empty and untidy.
>
> Man : In fact, no one lives there. It needs renovating but the owner doesn't have the mind to do it.
>
> Woman : I don't want to live next to the deserted house. I'd like to see some other places in the area.

① security guard − visitor   ② real estate agent − homebuyer

③ tour guide − tourist   ④ house owner − tenant

⑤ architect − reporter

05 Based on the following dialogue, which one is NOT true?

2점

> Jeff : I was hoping we'd get some nice waves today.
>
> Paul : Yeah, but it doesn't look like they'll be any good. You just missed it. They were fantastic yesterday. We had overhead waves.
>
> Jeff : It seems like I'm always missing the good surf. Last month on the Baja Peninsula was the last time I had a great surfing day.
>
> Paul : I've had those slumps before as well. Sometimes the surf gods smile upon us, and sometimes they don't!
>
> Jeff : What does the forecast look like for tomorrow?
>
> Paul : Rain and no surf, but the day after tomorrow looks like there'll be clear skies and fantastic waves! When are you leaving?
>
> Jeff : Tomorrow night. The surf gods must hate me.

① Paul says that the waves were fantastic yesterday.

② Jeff is having terrible luck with surfing.

③ Jeff had great surf on the Baja Peninsula last month.

④ The forecast says it will rain tomorrow.

⑤ Jeff is going to leave the day after tomorrow after enjoying surfing.

06 Choose the sentence that best describes the situation.

3점

> Tom : Sorry but all of those plastic pipes have to be ripped out and replaced. Then we are going to have to build a new shower in there.
>
> Jane : Oh no! That sounds expensive! How much is something like that going to cost?
>
> Tom : Well, I'd have to write up an estimate, but off the top of my head, I'd say around $2,000. I did a job like this last year.
>
> Jane : Oh boy! That's too expensive. I expected a few hundred maybe. I paid the last person $500. Couldn't you do it for that?
>
> Tom : The reason I'm here is because you paid the last guy $500. He did a terrible job. That's why all your pipes are leaking and your shower has to be replaced.
>
> Jane : Well, I just don't know. I guess I don't really have a choice. How about $700?
>
> Tom : If I did the work for $700, I'd be losing a ton of money. It is going to be at least $1,800.

① Jane is asking Tom where the shower facility is.

② Tom broke Jane's shower, and now she wants him to fix it.

③ Tom and Jane are negotiating the fee for building a new shower.

④ Tom is trying to sell Jane some pipes, but she doesn't want to buy them.

⑤ Jane is willing to pay as much as Tom asks for the repair job.

07 다음 글에서 필자가 주장하는 바로 가장 적절한 것은?

Thought stopping, a term coined by Richard Rawson of UCLA, who works with recovering drug addicts, is a definitive decision not to respond to the pull of a reward: Encounter a stimulus, and shut off the action it provokes. "Think of it like television," says Rawson. "Change the channel." Turning off a thought has to be almost immediate. "You're not helpless about this; you can make a decision, but you have to make the decision quickly," said Rawson. The more seconds you spend thinking about what to do in the face of an urge, the greater the chance that you'll ultimately give in to it. Once you begin to debate "Should I or shouldn't I?" you've lost the battle. Experience a cue, switch off the associated thought. No ambiguity, no maybes. Don't waste time in debate; don't struggle with your response. Just get it out of your working memory. Internalize a response to urges that is absolute, even rigid, leaving no room for doubt.

① 결정을 내리기 전에 심사숙고하라.

② 자신의 생각을 남에게 강요하지 말라.

③ 다른 사람의 의견보다는 자신의 판단을 따르라.

④ 주관적인 판단보다는 전문가의 견해를 들어 보라.

⑤ 유혹에 빠지게 하는 생각을 단호하게 중단하라.

08 다음 글에서 시사하는 바로 가장 적절한 것은?

The collective mind of any cultural group, accumulated over time, is typically smarter than any individual human mind. This is why cultural learning is so important, and also why such techniques as crowdsourcing are so effective. Xunzi, a thinker in early China, compares the Confucian Way inherited by his generation to markers used to indicate a ford over an otherwise deep and swift river. People with experience have, through careful trial and error, figured out the best place to cross the river and have left markers to help us find it. We could ignore them and just wing it, but that would be counterproductive and even dangerous. In other words, if a respected member of the local community tells you to boil this root vegetable for two hours, then strain it, and then pound it with a stick blessed by a priest until you've sung this sacred song twenty times, you should probably just shut up and do it, exactly the way you are told.

* ford : (강 따위의) 얕은 곳, 여울

** wing it : 즉흥적으로 하다

① Learn from old wisdom.
② Easy come, easy go.
③ To err is human.
④ Pride comes before a fall.
⑤ Nothing ventured, nothing gained.

※ 다음 글에 요지로 가장 적절한 것을 고르시오. [9~10]

09

Many decisions that you make will turn out to be wrong in the fullness of time. When you made the decision or commitment, it was probably a good idea, based on the circumstances of the moment. But now the situation may have changed, and it is time to zero-base it again. You can usually tell if you are in a zero-based-thinking situation because of the stress that it causes. Whenever you are involved in something that, knowing what you now know, you wouldn't get into again, you experience ongoing stress, aggravation, irritation, and anger. Sometimes people spend an enormous amount of time trying to make a business or personal relationship succeed. But if you zero-base this relationship, the correct solution is often to get out of the relationship altogether. The only real question is whether or not you have the courage to admit that you were wrong and take the necessary steps to correct the situation.

① 상황이 바뀌면 원점에서 다시 시작하는 수고를 감내할 필요가 있다.
② 스트레스를 유발하는 상황을 가급적 만들지 않는 것이 좋다.
③ 순간적인 판단이 고심 끝에 내린 판단보다 좋을 수 있다.
④ 합의를 통해 결정한 사항은 쉽게 번복해서는 안 된다.
⑤ 의사결정을 내리는 것을 무한정 미루는 것은 바람직하지 않다.

10

2점

Our natural response to reading or hearing about the darker qualities in human nature is to exclude ourselves. It is always the other person who is narcissistic, irrational, envious, grandiose, or aggressive. We almost always see ourselves as having the best intentions. If we go astray, it is the fault of circumstances or people forcing us to react negatively. Stop once and for all this self-deluding process. We are all cut from the same cloth, and we all share the same tendencies. The sooner you realize this, the greater your power will be in overcoming these potential negative traits within you. You will examine your own motives and look at your own shadow. This will make it that much easier to spot such traits in others. You will also become humbler, realizing you're not superior to others in the way you had imagined. This will not make you feel guilty or weighed down by your self-awareness, but quite the opposite. You will accept yourself as a complete individual, embracing both the good and the bad, dropping your falsified self-image as a saint. You will feel relieved of your hypocrisies and free to be more yourself. People will be drawn to this quality in you.

① 다른 사람의 긍정적인 면을 본받으려는 노력이 필요하다.
② 사람에게는 개별적인 특성뿐만 아니라 보편적인 특성도 있다.
③ 자신의 부정적인 면을 인정하면 그것을 극복하는 데 도움이 된다.
④ 결과뿐만 아니라 의도를 고려하여 행동의 정당성을 판단할 필요가 있다.
⑤ 자신감을 갖고 상대방을 대할수록 자신의 의견에 대한 동의를 얻기 쉽다.

※ 다음 글의 주제로 가장 적절한 것을 고르시오. [11~12]

11

[2점]

> For all its size and grandeur, the Inca Empire lasted only a century before it was conquered by the Spanish, beginning in 1532. Even before the Spanish Conquistadors arrived in central South America, the Inca had begun to suffer from the European arrival in the New World, for the Europeans brought diseases with them that peoples in the Americas had no immunity to. Shortly after Europeans landed in South America, smallpox, measles, typhoid, influenza, malaria, whooping cough and other diseases killed the indigenous peoples of the Americas. These Old World diseases spread to the Inca Empire by the 1520s. Just before the arrival of the Spanish in the Andes, epidemics killed many Inca leaders, including their Emperor and his successor. Eventually an estimated one－third to one－half of the total population of the Inca Empire died of these viral killers. Those who survived were demoralized, which contributed to the relatively easy Spanish conquest of the Inca.
>
> * conquistador : 정복자

① Spanish conquerors of the New World and their cruelties

② European diseases as a cause of the collapse of the Inca Empire

③ impact of the collision of the Old and New World on Europeans

④ a scientific method to track the rise and fall of the Inca Empire

⑤ Incan natural therapies to treat diseases from the Old World

12

2점

If people know an attack is coming, they can prepare to defend themselves. High school students in a study were forewarned either 2 or 10 minutes in advance that they would hear a speech on "Why Teenagers Should Not Be Allowed to Drive" (not a very popular message, as you might guess). The remaining students heard the same talk, but received no forewarning. The results showed that students who received no forewarning were persuaded the most, followed by those who received 2 minutes' warning, followed by those who received 10 minutes' warning. When people believe that someone is trying to persuade them (and take away their freedom of choice), they experience an unpleasant emotional response called psychological reactance, which motivates them to resist the persuasive attempt. Often people will do exactly the opposite of what they are being persuaded to do. The parents of Romeo and Juliet in Shakespeare's play found this effect out when their efforts to end the romance only drove the young lovebirds closer together.

① effect of forewarning on persuasion
② characteristics of persuasive speeches
③ importance of an interactive presentation
④ necessity of giving warning signs in advance
⑤ functions of persuasive communication in education

※ 다음 글의 제목으로 가장 적절한 것을 고르시오. [13~14]

13

2점

To reconstitute democracy in line with our present situation, we need to challenge the frightening, but false, assumption that increased diversity automatically brings increased tension and conflict in society. Indeed, the exact reverse can be true. Conflict in society is not only necessary, it is, within limits, desirable. But if one hundred men all desperately want the same brass ring, they may be forced to fight for it. On the other hand, if each of the hundred has a different objective, it is far more rewarding for them to trade, cooperate, and form symbiotic relationships. Given appropriate social arrangements, diversity can make for a secure and stable civilization. It is the lack of appropriate political institutions today that unnecessarily sharpens conflict between minorities to the knife-edge of violence. The answer to this problem is not to stifle dissent or to charge minorities with selfishness. The answer lies in imaginative new arrangements for accommodating and legitimating diversity—new institutions that are sensitive to the rapidly shifting needs of changing and multiplying minorities.

① Does Diversity Harm Democracy?

② Are Democracy's Weaknesses Inherent?

③ The Rise of Diversity Is a Threat to Democracy

④ The Majority Rule: A Basic Principle of Democracy

⑤ Democracy Is Contagious: Democratization in Progress

14

2점

Imagine that on your first day working at a record store, your manager says, "Our records are organized alphabetically." Under this direction, you file your first pack of albums with ease. Later, you overhear a coworker saying, "Sorry, it looks like we're sold out of Michael Jackson right now." Your manager looks under "J" and checks the inventory, which says the store should have a single copy of Thriller. You remember that it was part of the shipment of records you just filed. Where else could you have put that record, if not under "J"? Maybe under "M"? The ambiguity that's wrapped up in something as simple as "alphabetize these" is truly amazing. We give and receive instructions all day long. Ambiguous instructions can weaken our structures and their trustworthiness. It's only so long after that first album is misfiled that chaos ensues.

* ensue : (결과로서) 일어나다

① Alphabetical Classification Makes It Easy

② Leave Complexity, Stay with Simplicity

③ A Manager : Coworker or Enemy?

④ Old Albums Are Hard to Collect

⑤ Ambiguity Hides in Simplicity

15 다음 도표의 내용과 일치하지 않는 문장은?

[2점]

The above graph shows the percentages of men and women in occupational roles in the U.S. military in 2010. ① Active-duty women were much more heavily concentrated in administrative roles than were active-duty men : the percentage of women was more than twice that of men in administrative positions. ② And while only 6% of men in the military held medical roles, 15% of women had these types of jobs. ③ In the electrical field, the percentage of men was larger than that of women : while 22% of men were in electrical positions, only 12% of women served the same roles. ④ Compared to 19% of servicemen in the infantry, gun crews and seamanship, only 3% of servicewomen were in these roles. ⑤ No occupational role showed the same distribution of men and women in the military.

* infantry : 보병
** active-duty : 현역의

16

2점

Herbert Marcuse에 관한 다음 글의 내용과 일치하지 않는 것은?

Born in Berlin in 1898, Herbert Marcuse served with the German army in World War I before completing a PhD in literature in 1922 at the University of Freiburg. After a short spell as a bookseller in Berlin, he studied philosophy under Martin Heidegger. In 1932, he joined the Institute for Social Research, but he never worked in Frankfurt. In 1934 he fled to the US, where he was to remain. While he was in New York with Max Horkheimer, the latter received an offer from Columbia University to relocate the Institute there and Marcuse joined him. In 1958 Marcuse became a professor at Brandeis University, Massachusetts, but in 1965 he was forced to resign because of his outspoken Marxist views. He moved to the University of California, and during the 1960s gained world renown as a social theorist, philosopher, and political activist. He died of a stroke, aged 81.

① 1차 세계대전 중 독일군에서 복무했다.
② Martin Heidegger의 지도하에 철학을 공부했다.
③ 1934년에 미국으로 피신하여 그곳에 머물렀다.
④ California 대학에서 교수가 되어 Brandeis 대학으로 옮겼다.
⑤ 1960년대에 사회이론가, 철학자, 정치활동가로 세계적인 명성을 얻었다.

17

2점

밑줄 친 부분이 가리키는 대상이 나머지 넷과 다른 것은?

Four-year-old Betsy loved to spit. Every time someone said, "Hello, Betsy," she would pucker up and get ready to spray the person with a cloud of saliva. Her parents were embarrassed and couldn't understand how she started such a "bad" habit. ①They were both very respectful people and didn't understand where Betsy learned to do such a "naughty and disgusting" thing. All ② their efforts to get Betsy to stop fell on deaf ears. One day they visited a friend of the family, and when Betsy puckered up to spit, the friend smiled broadly and said, "Betsy, I bet you love to spit. Let's both go in the bathroom and spit into the toilet. I think it's fun to do too." Betsy's parents watched in a mixture of shame and amazement as Betsy took her friend by the hand and the two disappeared into the bathroom. After a few minutes, ③they returned and Betsy stopped spitting. What Betsy's parents realized is that ④they had been creating a power struggle by trying to control Betsy's behavior. Now ⑤they had an option and could tell Betsy, "Spitting is okay as long as you do it in the toilet." It didn't take long for Betsy to give up her "habit."

* pucker up : 입술을 오므리다

18

2점

For women in leadership positions, ① what often works best is a calm, confident expression, warm yet businesslike. Perhaps the best example of this would be current German chancellor Angela Merkel. Her smiles are even less frequent than the average male politician, but when they occur they are especially meaningful. They never seem ② fake. She listens to others with looks of complete absorption, her face remarkably still. She has a way of getting others to do most of the talking while always ③ seeming to be in control of the course of the conversation. She does not need to interrupt to assert herself. When she wants to attack someone, it is with looks of boredom, iciness, or contempt, never with blustering words. When Russian president Vladimir Putin tried to intimidate her by bringing his pet dog into a meeting, ④ know Merkel had once been bitten and had a fear of dogs, she visibly tensed, then quickly composed herself and looked him calmly in the eye. She put ⑤ herself in the one-up position in relation to Putin by not making anything of his ploy. He seemed rather childish and petty in comparison. Her style does not include all of the alpha male body posturing. It is quieter and yet extremely powerful in its own way.

* blustering : 호통치는

19

3점

Rules and incentives are an inevitable and necessary part of our social and political life – the banking crisis would have been far less serious ① had Depression-era regulations not been removed and had existing regulations been enforced. For all the importance of rules and incentives, however, a debate that focuses only on the proper mix of these two mechanisms ② leave out an important ingredient. The kind of work that most practitioners want to do, and ③ that those they serve also want them to do, demands practical wisdom. Rules and incentives may improve the behavior of those who don't care, though they won't make ④ them wiser. But in focusing on the people who don't care—the targets of our rules and incentives—we miss those who do care. We miss those who want to do the right things but ⑤ lack the practical wisdom to do them well. Rules and incentives won't teach these people the moral skill and will they need. Even worse, rules can kill skill and incentives can kill will.

20

3점

Biodiversity as a whole forms a shield protecting each of the species that together compose it, ourselves included. What will happen if, in addition to the species already extinguished by human activity, say, 10 percent of those remaining (A) $\boxed{\text{are / is}}$ taken away? Or 50 percent? Or 90 percent? As more and more species vanish or drop to near extinction, the rate of extinction of the survivors accelerates. In some cases the effect is felt almost immediately. When a century ago the American chestnut, once a dominant tree over much of eastern North America, (B) $\boxed{\text{being / was}}$ reduced to near extinction by an Asian fungal blight, seven moth species whose caterpillars depended on its vegetation vanished, and the last of the passenger pigeons plunged to extinction. As extinction mounts, biodiversity reaches a tipping point (C) $\boxed{\text{which / at which}}$ the ecosystem collapses. Scientists have only begun to study under what conditions and when this catastrophe is most likely to occur.

* blight : 마름병

	(A)		(B)		(C)
①	are	······	being	······	which
②	are	······	was	······	which
③	are	······	was	······	at which
④	is	······	being	······	at which
⑤	is	······	was	······	which

21

2점

In the 1970s, Stanley Schachter, a Columbia University social psychologist, became convinced that overweight people did not respond (A) [appropriate / appropriately] to internal signals, such as hunger, satiety, or a need for fuel. He hypothesized that overweight people ate in response to external cues, rather than internal signals. Schachter's cracker study compared the eating behaviors of thin and overweight subjects. He first divided his participants into two groups, offering one all the sandwiches they wanted to eat and (B) [ask / asking] the other only to fill out a questionnaire about food. Then he gave everyone the same opportunity to sample five different types of crackers. Not surprisingly, the thin people who had already eaten the sandwiches ate fewer crackers than the thin people who had simply completed the questionnaire. But those who were overweight ate about the same number of crackers whether or not they had eaten the sandwiches first. Schachter theorized that the sight of food was (C) [exerted / exerting] more pull on the overweight population than any internal messages reporting an absence of hunger.

	(A)		(B)		(C)
①	appropriate	......	ask	......	exerted
②	appropriately	......	asking	......	exerting
③	appropriately	......	asking	......	exerted
④	appropriate	......	asking	......	exerting
⑤	appropriately	......	ask	......	exerted

※ 다음 글의 밑줄 친 부분 중, 문맥상 낱말의 쓰임이 적절하지 않은 것을 고르시오. [22~23]

22

3점

Joseph Schumpeter expressed the view that the essence of capitalism is the process of "creative destruction"— the perpetual cycle of destroying the old and less efficient product or service and ①replacing it with new, more efficient ones. Andy Grove took Schumpeter's insight that "only the paranoid survive" and made it in many ways the business model of globalization capitalism. Grove helped to popularize the view that dramatic, industry-transforming ②innovations are taking place today faster and faster. Thanks to these technological breakthroughs, the speed by which your latest invention can be made ③obsolete is now lightning quick. Therefore, only the paranoid, only those who are constantly looking over their shoulders to see who is creating something new that will destroy them and then staying just one step ahead of them, will survive. Those countries that are most willing to let capitalism quickly destroy inefficient companies, so that money can be freed up and directed to more innovative ones, will ④perish in the era of globalization. Those which rely on their governments to ⑤protect them from such creative destruction will fall behind in this era.

* paranoid : 편집증적인 사람

23

2점

Boston and Cambridge are cities where many people do not stay for too long. Many people here are graduate students and postdoctorals, which means that by definition their positions have an ①expiration date. Boston and Cambridge are melting pots, but also cities where you make new friends at farewell parties. The combination of high resident turnover and friendships produces a situation in which the best apartments in Cambridge never ②reach the market. When someone moves out of a good apartment, there's always a friend looking to move in, and landlords usually are okay with this hand-me-down dynamic because it ③causes them the burden of finding a new tenant. So the lesson is that, at least in the case of Boston and Cambridge, the real estate market for apartments is ④secondary to the social network. According to Mark Granovetter, a sociologist who has studied the economic relevance of social networks throughout much of his life, we can say that in Cambridge the market for student apartments is ⑤embedded in the network of social interactions.

24

2점

Behavior is not infinitely flexible, easily moved in any direction. Rather, organisms are born with natural behavior systems and tendencies that (A) constrain / expand how learning occurs and what changes one may expect from a training procedure. These limitations were described elegantly in an analogy by a researcher, who compared learning to sculpting a wooden statue. The sculptor begins with a piece of wood that has little (B) contrast / resemblance to a statue. As the carving proceeds, the piece of wood comes to look more and more like the final product. But the process is not without limitation since the sculptor has to take into account the direction and density of the wood grain and any knots the wood may have. Wood carving is most successful if it is in (C) conflict / harmony with the preexisting grain and knots of the wood. In a similar fashion, learning is most successful if it takes into account the preexisting behavior structures of the organism.

	(A)		(B)		(C)
①	aconstrain	......	contrast	......	conflict
②	constrain	......	resemblance	......	conflict
③	constrain	......	resemblance	......	harmony
④	expand	......	contrast	......	conflict
⑤	expand	......	resemblance	......	harmony

25

3점

Plants are great chemists — and alchemists: they can turn sunbeams into matter! They have evolved to use biological warfare to repel predators — poisoning, paralyzing, or disorienting them — or to reduce their own digestibility to stay alive and protect their seeds, (A) enhancing / reducing the chances that their species will endure. Both these physical and chemical defensive strategies are remarkably effective at keeping predators away, and even sometimes at getting animals to do what they wish. Because their initial predators were insects, plants developed some lectins that would paralyze any unfortunate bug that tried to dine on them. Obviously, there is a quantum size difference between insects and mammals, but both are (B) resistant / subject to the same effects. Clearly, most of you won't be paralyzed by a plant compound within minutes of eating it, although a single peanut (a lectin) certainly has the potential to kill certain people. But we are not immune to the long — term effects of eating certain plant compounds. Because of the huge number of cells we mammals have, we may not see the (C) beneficial / damaging results of consuming such compounds for years. And even if this is happening to you, you don't know it yet.

* lectin : 렉틴(주로 식물에서 추출되는 단백질)

	(A)		(B)		(C)
①	enhancing	……	resistant	……	beneficial
②	enhancing	……	subject	……	damaging
③	enhancing	……	subject	……	beneficial
④	reducing	……	subject	……	damaging
⑤	reducing	……	resistant	……	beneficial

26

2점

Observers have repeatedly noticed that animals in the wild do not live solely by "tooth and claw" but regularly show _____. Once, when an old bull elephant lay dying, human observers noted that his entire family tried everything to help him to his feet again. First, they tried to work their trunks and tusks underneath him. Then they pulled the old fellow up so strenuously that some broke their tusks in the process. Their concern for their old friend was greater than their concern for themselves. Elephants have also been observed coming to the aid of a comrade shot by a hunter, despite their fear of gunshots. The other elephants work in concert to raise their wounded companion to walk again. They do this by pressing on either side of the injured elephant and walking, trying to carry their friend between their gigantic bodies. Elephants have also been seen sticking grass in the mouths of their injured friends in an attempt to feed them, to give them strength.

① self − treatment for injury

② compassion for their fellows

③ family ties for their offspring

④ tricks of deceiving their predators

⑤ collaboration for finding food in the wild

27

3점

A factor which helps people to withstand fear is _____. The front − seat passenger in a car, for example, is usually more anxious than the driver. In the studies of American servicemen this was revealed when aircrew in the European theater of operations were asked in June 1944: "If you were doing it over again, do you think you would choose to sign up for combat flying?" Pilots were always more willing to answer "Yes, I'm pretty sure I would"(51−84 percent) than other enlisted men (39−51 percent), and fighter pilots flying their planes single−handed (84 percent) more so than bomber pilots (51−74 percent). Heavy bomber crews showed increasing reluctance the more missions they had flown, and the reason is not hard to discover. The casualty rates (over 70 percent killed or missing in action after six months and 17.5 percent wounded or injured in action) were dreadful.

* theater : 작전 구역

① being in control　　　　　　② to wait and see

③ recalling good events　　　　④ being with a companion

⑤ proper training and practice

28

2점

Some contemporary technologies seem to open new and deeply troubling ethical issues, issues of a kind that humankind has never had to address before. The emerging technology of genetic engineering, for instance, creates the prospect of our designing our own children and turning humanity itself into a kind of artifact. Some authors seem to welcome this prospect, but others believe that we are at a crossroads that requires that we relinquish the opportunity to acquire the knowledge that would enable us to create such a brave new world. Others believe that we can place reasonable limits on how biotechnology and genetic engineering will be employed on human beings that will allow some uses but prohibit others. Genetic engineering of plants and some animal species is already in widespread use, and it may already be impossible to put this particular genie back in the bottle. Hans Jonas believes that technologies such as these that give us the capability _____ should be approached with a sense of "long-range responsibility" and, above all, a sense of humility.

① to make aesthetic use of science

② to alter nature in fundamental ways

③ to produce materials with little variation

④ to detect and locate hidden defects in complex systems

⑤ to defend the organism from external and internal dangers

29

2점

You can almost certainly recall instances when being around a calm person leaves you feeling more at peace, or when your previously sunny mood was spoiled by contact with a grouch. Researchers have demonstrated that this process occurs quickly and doesn't require much, if any, verbal communication. In one study, two volunteers completed a survey that identified their moods. Then they sat quietly, facing each other for a two-minute period, waiting for the researcher to return to the room. At the end of that time, they completed another emotional survey. Time after time, the brief exposure resulted in the less expressive partner's moods coming to resemble the moods of the more expressive one. It's easy to understand how emotions _____. In just a few months, the emotional responses of both dating couples and college roommates become dramatically more similar.

* grouch : 불평이 많은 사람

① can be best managed for optimal functioning

② can operate independently of external stimuli

③ can be even more infectious with prolonged contact

④ are influenced by social and cultural norms

⑤ are related to the whole creative process

30

3점

There is much evidence that the use of language enables us＿＿＿＿＿＿＿, because the stimulation associated with the use of language facilitates a further spurt of brain development. There have been extended attempts to teach chimpanzees the use of language by bringing them up in human family environments. Since they do not have the vocal apparatus for speech, they have been taught using American sign language. It has proved possible to teach chimpanzees up to a few hundred words in their first five years of life, a tiny fraction of what human children achieve. The comparative abilities of human children and chimpanzees are rather similar until the point at which language develops in the children, somewhere between their first and second birthdays, after which our mental development accelerates away from that of chimpanzees. A related point is that we have very few memories of the period before we learn the use of language. It is obvious that our use of language does not merely enable us to communicate, but that it also profoundly affects the way we perceive the outside world.

① to express our curiosity about nature

② to memorize events much more precisely

③ to share our perceptual experiences with others

④ to communicate with animals around us

⑤ to put creative thoughts into action

31

2점

Today, the secret of success of many profitable businesses lies in their ability to process the data using advanced analytical methods. The business of information management encompasses more than just storing the data. It also covers 'data mining' or acquiring information by processing data using a new form of business intelligence.

(A) This ability of knowing 'why' will therefore empower the organization to make the necessary strategic changes. For example, the organization should capitalize on the newfound knowledge by building a stronger, one－to－one relationship with its customers.

(B) However, a report aided by data mining or business intelligence, is not only able to identify the best－selling product in a supermarket but the report is also able to explain the reasons why the product is the best.

(C) Hence, organizations need to invest in data mining techniques (aided by statistical analysis, visualization and neural networks) to uncover hidden patterns, discover new knowledge, and as a consequence gain more insight into the current business situation. For example, a typical report is able to identify the best－selling product in a supermarket.

① (A) － (C) － (B)　　　　　② (B) － (A) － (C)

③ (B) － (C) － (A)　　　　　④ (C) － (A) － (B)

⑤ (C) － (B) － (A)

32

2점

As the case on the Canada–US Free Trade Agreement shows, it was important for Canada to gain the attention of US political leadership to increase Canadian power in the negotiation. Lack of attention by the stronger party is often a statement that it does not consider the other side particularly powerful or significant.

(A) This action provoked a diplomatic crisis between the two long – time allies and succeeded in getting US attention, which led to high – level American participation in the negotiations. Canada enhanced its power by playing on the historically strong relationship between the two countries.

(B) Such lack of attention may manifest itself in many ways, but it is almost always demonstrated by entrusting the negotiations to relatively low – level officials who have limited authority and access to their country's political leadership.

(C) Canada faced this problem in this negotiation. The tactics of attention – getting may include stalling and walking out of the negotiations. In the Canada – US Free Trade Agreement talks, Canada walked out when they felt that the United States was not taking the negotiations seriously.

* stall : (교묘하게) 시간을 벌다

① (A) – (C) – (B)　　　　② (B) – (A) – (C)

③ (B) – (C) – (A)　　　　④ (C) – (A) – (B)

⑤ (C) – (B) – (A)

33

3점

> An alternative use, however, treats law generally as a means of enforcing norms or standards of social behavior.

The term 'law' has been used in a wide variety of ways. In the first place, there are scientific laws or what are called descriptive laws. These describe regular or necessary patterns of behavior found in either natural or social life. (①) The most obvious examples are found in the natural sciences; for instance, in the laws of motion and thermodynamics advanced by physicists. (②) But this notion of law has also been employed by social theorists, in an attempt to highlight predictable, even inevitable, patterns of social behavior. (③) This can be seen in Engels's assertion that Marx uncovered the 'laws' of historical and social development, and in the so-called 'laws'of demand and supply which underlie economic theory. (④) Sociologists have thus seen forms of law at work in all organized societies, ranging from informal processes usually found in traditional societies to the formal legal systems typical of modern societies. (⑤) By contrast, political theorists have tended to understand law more specifically, seeing it as a distinctive social institution clearly separate from other social rules or norms and only found in modern societies.

34

3점

Another, unexpected, consequence is the ability of bacteria to overcome the mechanisms that give antibiotics their efficacy, rendering them useless.

Initially seen as miracle drugs, antibiotics, once they became widely available, were used not only for bacterial infections, but for everything from the common cold to headaches. (①) Indeed antibiotics were a godsend, drastically improving medicine and contributing significantly to the increase in life expectancy achieved during the twentieth century. (②) Like many technological fixes, along with the positive benefits of antibiotics came negative side effects. (③) Antibiotics can kill the many beneficial bacteria in the human body, for instance those that promote digestion, along with invasive bacteria. (④) Antibiotic resistance, first a curiosity seen in the laboratory, became common among populations of bacteria exposed to antibiotics. (⑤) In a matter of years following the introduction of penicillin, penicillin-destroying staphylococci appeared in hospitals where much of the early use of penicillin had taken place.

* staphylococci : 포도상구균

35

Far from existing inertly, the inhabitants of the pasture – or what the ancient Hellenes called botane – appear to be able to perceive and to react to what is happening in their environment at a level of sophistication far surpassing that of humans ① The sundew plant will grasp at a fly with infallible accuracy, moving in just the right direction toward where the prey is to be found. ② Some parasitical plants can recognize the slightest trace of the odor of their victim, and will overcome all obstacles to crawl in its direction. ③ Plants are in trouble because they are rooted to the ground and therefore unable to pick up and move when they need something or when conditions turn unfavorable. ④ Plants seem to know which ants will steal their nectar, closing when these ants are about, opening only when there is enough dew on their stems to keep the ants from climbing. ⑤ The more sophisticated acacia actually enlists the protective services of certain ants which it rewards with nectar in return for the ants' protection against other insects and herbivorous mammals.

* inertly : 비활동적으로

36

Transport geography is a topical branch of geography that evolved out of economic geography. Like tourism, transportation is, of course, inherently geographic because it connects places and facilitates the movement of goods and people from one place to another. ① Transport geography fundamentally depends on the geographic concepts, such as location or scale. ② For example, location shapes patterns of movement, including whether movement is possible from and/or to a given location and how that movement might occur. ③ Transportation networks exist at local and regional scales and, in the modern world, are increasingly being connected into a global system. ④ With much faster personal and organized transport, afternoon drives, day trips, overnight stays and weekends have added a considerable scope to the tourism industry but also to tourists themselves. ⑤ In addition, there are many geographic factors of places – both physical and human – that either allow or constrain transportation.

37

다음 글의 내용을 한 문장으로 요약하고자 한다. 빈칸 (A)와 (B)에 들어갈 말로 가장 적절한 것은?

2점

Consider a household that dumps sewage into a public lake rather than purchasing a septic system to process and store the waste. This "straight pipe" method of disposal damages the lake's appeal for water sports and as a source of drinking water. Although the social cost of dumping sewage is larger than the cost of a septic system, the household's private cost of dumping is not, because the household bears only a fraction of the overall damage of dumping. If the lake area belonged to the household dumping the sewage, that household would internalize the full social cost of dumping and invest in a septic system. If the lake area belonged to someone else, that person would have an incentive to prohibit and carefully monitor dumping. Biologist Garrett Hardin felt that by assigning property rights to land, water, and air, society could avoid externalities caused by everything from factories to loud music. As evidence of his point, poaching is a far greater problem in countries where property rights are weak than in countries where they are well - defined and strictly enforced.

* septic system : 오수정화 시스템

** poach : (남의 영역을) 침해하다

According to Garrett Hardin, environmental damage to open—access areas, such as lakes, could be _____(A)_____ if the areas were _____(B)_____ held.

	(A)		(B)
①	caused	⋯⋯	exclusively
②	caused	⋯⋯	commercially
③	disclosed	⋯⋯	commonly
④	prevented	⋯⋯	publicly
⑤	prevented	⋯⋯	privately

※ [38 ～ 39] 다음 글을 읽고, 물음에 답하시오.

We cannot divorce emotions from thinking. The two are completely intertwined. But there is inevitably a (a) <u>dominant</u> factor, some people more clearly governed by emotions than others. What we are looking for is the proper ratio and balance, the one that leads to the most effective action. The ancient Greeks had an appropriate metaphor for this: the rider and the horse.

The horse is our emotional nature continually (b) <u>impelling</u> us to move. This horse has tremendous energy and power, but without a rider it cannot be guided; it is wild, subject to predators, and continually heading into trouble. The rider is our thinking self. Through training and practice, it holds the reins and guides the horse, transforming this powerful animal energy into something (c) <u>productive</u>. The one without the other is useless. Without the rider, no directed movement or purpose. Without the horse, no energy, no power. In most people the horse dominates, and the rider is weak. In some people the rider is too strong, holds the reins too tightly, and is (d) <u>willing</u> to occasionally let the animal go into a gallop. The horse and rider must work together. This means we consider our actions (e) <u>beforehand</u>; we bring as much thinking as possible to a situation before we make a decision. But once we decide what to do, we loosen the reins and enter action with boldness and a spirit of adventure. Instead of being slaves to this energy, we channel it. That is the essence of rationality.

38 윗글의 주제로 가장 적절한 것은?

① necessity of finding the optimal balance of thinking and emotion
② traditional skills of taming and harnessing wild animals
③ effects of emotional suppression on physical health
④ difficulties of getting the right technique to win horse races
⑤ ancient Greek concepts about the importance of philosophy in sports

39 밑줄 친 (a)～(e) 중에서 문맥상 낱말의 쓰임이 적절하지 않은 것은?

① (a)   ② (b)
③ (c)   ④ (d)
⑤ (e)

Yesterday's Observer features two pieces about human enhancement in the prospect of the FutureFest festival in London in September. The articles mention Bertolt Meyer, a Swiss man born without a left hand who was recently fitted with a state-of-the-art bionic one (which he controls from his smartphone), and include quotes from well-known authors associated with the topic of human enhancement, such as Nick Bostrom and Andy Miah. At the moment, prosthetic devices like Meyer's are used to restore normal human functions among those who lack them. Yet as such devices become ever more (A) _____, to the point that they eventually outperform "natural" limbs in terms of speed, strength, executive control etc., "will it become the norm to have one of these?" Meyer asks. Also, as the author of the Observer editorial worries, "what happens when these technologies and machines get so smart that humans can be written out of the equation altogether?" For instance, what if we could simply turn to our smartphone rather than a human doctor to get a diagnosis for our ailments as well as appropriate treatment recommendations? Such suggestions can (B) _____ fears of a dystopian future where humans are pressured to become "cyborgs," whether they like it or not, if they are to remain competitive on the job market (including competitive sports) and in other contexts; or where they are increasingly made useless by more effective machines, and real-life human interaction is reduced (machines replacing staff at supermarket checkouts, but also general practitioners, etc.), and becomes less accessible than it is now (think of having to pay a significant premium to see a human doctor).

* prosthetic : 인공 기관의

40 윗글의 제목으로 가장 적절한 것은?

2점

① Where Machines Could Replace Humans and Where They Can't

② Human Enhancement Technologies: Blessing or Curse?

③ Disabled Persons and Their Right to Equal Treatment

④ Artificial Intelligence: Science Fact vs. Science Fiction

⑤ Science Fiction Foretells Future Technologies

41

윗글의 빈칸 (A), (B)에 들어갈 말로 가장 적절한 것은?

	(A)		(B)
①	expensive	······	calm
②	expensive	······	reflect
③	outdated	······	trigger
④	sophisticated	······	calm
⑤	sophisticated	······	trigger

※ 다음 글을 읽고, 물음에 답하시오. [42~43]

When Mario came to me for therapy, he explained that he worried about everything. He was newly married and in the midst of purchasing an expensive home that would require investing his life savings, barely leaving money for the necessary renovations. "Did I marry the right person? Am I going crazy? Is my mind working? I seem forgetful. What if the plane I take to Miami crashes? Will my father develop Parkinson's like my grandfather?" The worries were (a) underline{endless}, and Mario noticed that the more he worried the more he felt depressed. To ease his tortured mind, he spent time (b) underline{distracting} himself by eating.

Over the course of cognitive behavioral therapy with an emphasis on mindfulness and acceptance, Mario began to learn to not panic over his feelings of panic. He became able to bring awareness to his worries as mental processes rather than get (c) underline{stuck} in his mind, where he would live in the worst-case scenarios. He practiced asking himself, "Is this worry productive or unproductive?" If a worry was productive, he came up with an action plan. If it was unproductive, he noticed the feelings and thoughts in his body and mind and practiced returning to the present moment. When he noticed urges to reach for sweets and salty foods as he tensed up, he chose to sit with his feelings instead, seeing his feelings as meaningful.

What sat behind his worries? He deeply (d) underline{valued} serving as a provider, establishing a secure, loving home, and protecting his father. His feelings (e) underline{denied} what mattered to him, though his relationship with his feelings – profound fear and confusion about feeling too much and not understanding his feelings – got in the way of his willingness to accept and learn from his emotions. During our last session, he said, "I feel because things matter to me. I can talk to my wife about our difficulties, take action to solve financial problems, and show my dad how much I care. That tastes sweet in my heart."

42 Mario에 관한 윗글의 내용으로 적절하지 않은 것은?

 2점

① 평생 저축한 돈을 투자해야 하는 비싼 집을 구입하는 중이었다.

② 자신의 공황 상태의 감정에 당황하지 않는 법을 배우기 시작했다.

③ 자신의 걱정이 생산적인지 아닌지 스스로에게 질문하는 것을 연습했다.

④ 단것과 짠 음식을 먹고 싶어 하는 충동을 이겨내는 데 결국 실패했다.

⑤ 재정적인 문제를 해결하기 위한 조치를 취할 수 있다고 말했다.

43 밑줄 친 (a)~(e) 중에서 문맥상 낱말의 쓰임이 적절하지 않은 것은?

3점

① (a)

② (b)

③ (c)

④ (d)

⑤ (e)

(A)

Bibs the canary lived with an elderly lady who had a niece who lived next door and checked on her each night to make sure she was all right. A warm and sweet friendship had blossomed between the old woman and the tiny bird. At breakfast each morning, they shared toast and Bibs liked to sip whatever beverage the woman was having. One rainy night, seeing that her aunt's lights were on and assuming everything was fine, the niece retired with her husband for the night rather than going over to the aunt's house.

(B)

The tiny yellow bird had escaped from the aunt's house and flown through the storm to the next house. There it had pecked at the window with such desperate fury that it collapsed in exhaustion and died before their eyes. Now completely alarmed, the niece and her husband raced over to the aunt's house.

(C)

They found the old lady lying unconscious on the floor in a pool of blood. She had slipped and fallen, striking her head on a table corner. Her niece rushed her to the hospital. Because of her little bird's loyalty and determination to get help, even at the sacrifice of his own life, the woman's life was saved.

(D)

As the couple relaxed cozily by a fire, they were startled by an odd tapping at the window. At first they assumed it was a windblown branch, but the tapping grew louder and continued persistently, followed by a strange cry. Finally, the niece went to the window, pulled back the curtains and found Bibs, who had been furiously beating on the window and chirping.

44 주어진 글 (A)에 이어질 내용을 순서에 맞게 배열한 것으로 가장 적절한 것은?

① (B) – (D) – (C)

② (C) – (B) – (D)

③ (C) – (D) – (B)

④ (D) – (B) – (C)

⑤ (D) – (C) – (B)

45 윗글에 관한 내용으로 적절하지 않은 것은?

① 노부인의 조카딸은 노부인의 옆집에 살았다.

② 노부인과 Bibs는 토스트를 나눠 먹었다.

③ Bibs는 폭풍우를 뚫고 옆집으로 날아갔다.

④ 노부인은 의식을 잃고 바닥에 쓰러져 있었다.

⑤ 조카딸 집의 창문에 나뭇가지가 부딪쳐 소리가 났다.

정답 및 해설

ANSWER

01	02	03	04	05	06	07	08	09	10	11	12	13	14	15	16	17	18	19	20
⑤	①	④	③	②	③	③	②	④	④	④	①	③	①	④	①	①	①	⑤	④
21	22	23	24	25	26	27	28	29	30	31	32	33	34	35	36	37	38	39	40
③	②	①	②	⑤	④	③	④	⑤	⑤	⑤	②	②	③	②	④	②	⑤	①	⑤
41	42	43	44	45															
③	③	②	①	④															

01 어휘 pack 포장하다, 소지하다 / summit 산꼭대기, 절정, 정상 / thirsty 목이 마른, 갈증이 나는 / view 견해, 시야, 전망 / steep 가파른, 비탈진, 급격한 / climb 오르다 / gradual 점진적인, 완만한 / binocular 쌍안경 / trail market (산에서 길을 잃지 않기 위해 만든) 표지판

해설 'summit', 'view', 'climb' 등을 통해 두 사람이 산을 오르고 있다는 것을 알 수 있다.

보기 ① 사무실 ② 동물원 ③ 해변 ④ 체육관 ⑤ 산

해석 Tom : 물 갖고 왔니?
Jane : 물론이지. 정상까지 2시간 걸리니까, 우린 목이 마를 거야. 게다가 난 우리 점심도 싸왔어.
Tom : 정상에서 점심 먹을 수 있겠다. 전망이 아주 좋다고 들었어. 오르막이 가파를까?
Jane : 내 생각엔 끝에만 그럴 것 같아. 대체로 완만해. 좋은 운동이 될 거야.
Tom : 우리 나무를 봐야 돼. 사람들이 이 지역에 흥미로운 새들이 있대.
Jane : 네 생일 날 누나가 준 쌍안경 가지고 왔니?
Tom : 응, 가지고 왔어. 봐, 여기 길 표지판이 있다.

02 어휘 itinerary 여행 일정표 / statue of liberty 자유의 여신상

해설 예술 박물관은 화요일부터 일요일까지 개장한다.

보기 ① • 미술 박물관
  • 월요일 오전 9시
② • Periguino's에서 저녁식사
  • 월요일 오후 8시
③ • 자유의 여신상
  • 화요일 오전 9시
④ • 브로드웨이 공연
  • 화요일 오후 8시
⑤ • 시 역사 박물관
  • 수요일 오전 10시

Sue : 뉴욕엔 볼거리가 매우 많아. 우리 여행 일정표 짜는 거 끝났니?

Joe : 응, 근데 재확인 좀 할게. 너 Periguino's에서 우리 저녁식사는 예약했어?

Sue : 월요일 저녁 8시로 예약했어.

Joe : 박물관은 어때? 언제 열어?

Sue : 시 역사 박물관, 예술 박물관 그리고 Longfellow Gallery는 화요일에서 일요일까지 열어. 자연사 박물관과 영화 박물관은 월요일에서 금요일까지 열고.

Joe : 우리는 자유의 여신상도 봐야해. 화요일 아침에 열 때 보자. 긴 줄이 늘어서기 전에 말이야.

Sue : 그리고 우리 브로드웨이 뮤지컬은 언제 보지?

Joe : 내가 화요일 밤 공연 티켓을 예약해놨어.

Sue : 이번 여행 매우 기대돼!

03 **어휘** attend 참석하다 / conference 회의, 회담 / fully 완전히 / book 예약하다 / standby 예비품, 대기하다 / route 길, 노선 / layover 도중하차

해설 12시에 파리에 도착해서 2시간을 기다린 후 런던행 비행기를 타야한다고 했으므로 ④가 정답이다.

보기 ① 여자는 수요일 오후 6시 비행기를 원한다.

② 여자는 런던에서 열리는 회의를 중요하게 생각하지 않는다.

③ 여자는 런던으로 가는 직행 비행기만 원한다.

④ 여자는 화요일 오후 2시에 파리에서 런던으로 가는 비행기를 탈 것이다.

⑤ 여자는 파리에서 4시간을 기다려야 한다.

해석 Woman : 런던으로 가는 다음 비행기가 언제 있죠?

Man : 수요일 오후 6시에 있습니다, 손님.

Woman : 전 수요일 아침에 런던에서 열리는 회의에 참석해야 해요. 화요일에 떠나는 다른 비행기가 있는지 재확인 해주실래요?

Man : 죄송하지만, 런던으로 가는 비행기는 전부 예약되어 있습니다. 원하신다면, 손님 이름을 대기명단에 올려드릴 수는 있습니다.

Woman : 이번 회의에 참석 못하면 기회가 없어요. 다른 도시를 통해서 런던으로 가는 노선을 알려주시겠어요?

Man : 확인해 보죠, 손님. 파리행 피행기가 런던행 비행기와 연결되는 것 같네요. 화요일 오전 10시에 출발해서 정오에 파리에 도착하는데, 런던행 비행기를 타기 전에 2시간을 기다렸다가 가야합니다. 이 티켓을 예약해드릴까요?

Woman : 네. 그렇게 할게요. 감사합니다.

04 **어휘** up the whole 구토를 하다, 전체를 삼키다 / vomiting 구토, 토하기 / nauseous 메스꺼운, 역겨운 / feverish 열이 나는, 과열된 / green salad 야채 샐러드 / food poisoning 식중독 / prescribe 처방을 내리다, 처방하다 / meanwhile 그 동안에, 한편 / plenty of 많은, 풍부한 / persist 집요하게 계속되다, 계속되다, 지속되다 / appointment 약속, 임명, 직위

해설 아내와 스프는 같은 것을 먹었지만 메인 요리에서 아내는 닭고기를 남편은 생선요리를 먹었다고 했으므로 ③을 유추할 수 있다.

보기 ① 환자와 그의 아내는 6시에 저녁식사를 끝냈다.

② 환자의 아내 역시 식중독에 걸려 아프다.

③ 생선이 아마도 식중독을 야기했을 것이다.

④ 물을 많이 마시는 것은 그의 통증에 좋지 않다.

⑤ 환자는 내일 의사와 새로운 예약을 할 것이다.

해석 의사 : 무슨 문제죠?

환자 : 밤새 아프고 구토를 했어요. 속이 계속 메스껍고 열이 나요.

의사 : 언제 이 증상이 시작됐죠?

환자 : 밤 10시 정도예요. 아내와 시내에 있는 레스토랑에서 저녁을 먹은 후 2시간이 지나서요.

의사 : 아내분도 아픈가요?

환자 : 아니요, 그녀는 괜찮습니다.

의사 : 거기서 무엇을 드셨죠?

환자 : 우린 둘 다 야채 샐러드와 야채 스프를 먹었어요, 하지만 메인 요리는 서로 다른 것을 시켰어요. 전 생선을 먹었고 그녀는 닭요리를 먹었어요.

의사 : 식중독 같군요. 속을 부드럽게 하고 열을 내려주는 처방을 내릴게요, 물을 많이 드시고 휴식을 많이 취하세요. 만약 증상이 3일 후에도 계속된다면, 연락하세요. 다시 진료 예약을 잡아드릴게요.

05 어휘 lost 잃어 버린, (길을) 잃은 / central post office 중앙 우체국 / intersection 교차로, 교차점

보기 ⓐ 그리고 시의 지도를 갱신하지 않았나봐요

ⓑ 그런다음 신호등 앞에서 왼쪽으로 가세요

ⓒ 경찰서 옆으로 오른쪽에 있습니다

ⓓ 하지만 제 지도가 약간 헷갈려서요

ⓔ 하지만 그는 그 곳에 가려면 택시를 타야할 거에요

해석 Woman : 길을 잃었나요? 도와드릴까요?

Man : 중앙 우체국을 찾고 있습니다. 그런데 제 지도가 좀 헷갈려서요.

Woman : 무슨 문제가 있는지 알 것 같네요. 중앙 우체국은 2달 전 다른 건물로 이전했는데, 시의 지도를 갱신하지 않았나봐요.

Man : 새로운 곳이 여기서 먼가요?

Woman : 아니요, 그렇지 않아요. 약 15분 정도 걸으면 돼요.

Man : 어떻게 가는지 알려주실 수 있나요?

Woman : 물론이죠. 일단, 세 번째 교차로까지 이 길을 따라가셔서 신호등 앞에서 왼쪽으로 가세요. 약간의 언덕을 오르셔야 할 거에요. 꼭대기에 공원이 있습니다. 새로운 중앙 우체국 건물은 공원의 남쪽 모퉁이에 있어요.

Man : 정말 감사합니다.

06 어휘 tough 힘든, 어려운, 굳센 / pay attention ~에 주의를 기울이다 / nod off 깜박 졸다 / exactly 정확히, 꼭, 틀림없이 / complain 불평하다 / manage 다루다, 간신히 해내다 / wisely 현명하게, 꾀를 부려 / in order 적절한, 제대로 된 / stay up 안자고 깨어 있다

해설 기주가 민주의 충고에 수긍하는 대답이 왔으므로 ③의 내용이 오는 것이 적절하다.

보기 ① 넌 다음 시험을 위해 더 열심히 공부해야만 해.

② 우린 둘 다 토요일과 일요일에 늦게까지 안 자는 걸 좋아해.

④ 난 항상 내가 좋아하는 컴퓨터 게임에서 가장 높은 점수를 얻어.

⑤ 이 수학 수업이 화요일 오후라면 더 좋을 텐데.

해석 기주 : 이번 영어 수업은 너무 어려워. 난 우리 교수님이 학교에서 우리가 겪는 힘든 생활을 이해하지 못하시는 것 같아.

민지 : 아무래도 넌 더 집중해야 할 것 같아. 난 수업시간 동안 네가 몇 번이나 졸고 있는 걸 봤어.

기주 : 그런데 그 수업은 월요일 아침 첫 수업이잖아. 가끔 주말 후유증으로 너무 피곤해.

민지 : 주말 내내 공부하느라고 피곤한거니?

기주 : 음… 그런 건 아니고. 때때로 난 일요일 여가시간 동안 컴퓨터 게임을 해. 고등학교에 입학한 후로 컴퓨터 게임을 해왔어.

민지 : 내 생각엔 네가 수업에 대해 투덜거리는 걸 멈추고 네 시간을 더 현명하게 관리해야 할 것 같아. 여가시간에 휴식을 하는 것은 잘못이 없지만 네 공부를 제대로 하고 나서 해야지. 그리고 나서 쉬어야 해.

기주 : 좋은 조언이야. 이번 일요일에는 공부를 하고 일찍 잠자리에 들어야 겠어.

---

07 `어휘` aborigine 원주민 / native (사람이) 태어난 곳의, 토박이의 / throughout 도처에, ~동안, 내내 / sprit 정기, 정신 / wherever 어디에나, 어디든지 / whatever 어떤 것이라도, 어떤 ~라도 / supposedly 아마, 추정상 / essence 본질, 정수, 진수 / spring up 갑자기 생겨나다 / ensure 반드시 ~하다, 보장하다 / generate 발생시키다

`해설` 나머지는 Aborigine을 가리키고, ③은 spirit(영혼, 정기)를 가리킨다.

`해석` Aborigine은 호주의 원주민이다. 그들의 역사 동안, 그들은 그들의 종교적 믿음을 반영하는 예술을 해왔다. 그들은 그들의 문화와 환경이 jugurrba나 꿈의 결과라고 믿는다. 꿈을 꾸는 동안, 영혼은 인간과 동물의 형상을 갖추었고, 땅과 동물을 창조했다. 그 영혼들이 어디를 창조하든지, 무엇을 믿든 그들은 그들의 정수를 좀 남겨 두었던 것 같다. Aborigine은 영혼의 정수가 생명을 샘솟게 한다고 믿는다. 그들은 아직도 동물과 장소의 정령에게 좋은 날씨나 성공적인 사냥 같은 것들을 보장해 달라고 청한다. 1960년대 이래로, 예술 세계는 Aboriginal의 나무껍질 그림에 관심을 갖기 시작했다. 이러한 관심은 Aborigine 사이에서 대형 시장을 발생시켰고, 그들은 전보다 더 많은 예술품을 팔기 위해 더 많은 예술품을 생산하고 있다.

---

08 `어휘` punctuation 구두점, 구두법, 문장부호 / mainly 주로, 대부분, 대개 / aloud 소리 내어, 크게 / pause 잠시 멈추다 / emphasize 강조하다 / likewise 똑같이, 마찬가지로 / comma 콤마, 쉼표 / master 달인, 명수 / printing press 인쇄기 / firmer 날이 얇은 끝 / guideline 안내선

`해설` ②는 쉼표에 관한 설명으로 punctuation(구두점)과는 관련이 없는 내용이다.

`해석` punctuation은 "점"을 뜻하는 라틴어인 Punctus에서 왔다. punctuation이 생기면서, 그것은 사람들이 주로 소리 내어 읽는 것에 도움이 됐다. 몇 백 년 전까지, 적은 사람들만 읽는 법을 배웠고, 그래서 읽을 수 있는 소수의 사람들에 의해 큰 소리로 읽히는 경우가 많았다. 고대 세계에서 큰 소리로 읽기를 돕기 위해, "점"이라고 알려진 표시들을 쓰기 페이지에 추가하였다. 이러한 점들은 잠시 멈추거나 숨을 쉴 때, 강조해야 하는 것을 독자들에게 알린다. 마찬가지로, 보통 글쓴이가 대부분의 문제를 야기하는 문장부호인 쉼표는 완벽히 배우기 어렵다. 세기 초부터 유럽에서는 비록 모두가 같은 것을 위해 같은 "점"을 사용하진 않았지만 이러한 "점"들은 넓게 사용되었다. 그러나, 15세기에 인쇄기가 발명되었을 때, 인쇄업자들은 무엇을 어디에 놓아야 할지에 대한 정확한 지침을 원했다. 그래서 모든 사람들이 같은 것을 사용하게 되었다. 그 이후로, 수많은 구두법이 발견되었고 창조되었으며, 심지어 그에 대해 논쟁되고 있다.

---

09 `어휘` benefit 이익, 특혜, (회사에서 급여 외에 주는) 특전 / experiment 실험, 실험하다 / retain 유지하다 / variation 변화, 변형 / permit 허용하다, 가능하게 하다 / portion (음식) 1인분, 몫 / compute 계산하다 / immediate 즉각적인, 당면한 / pass away 사망하다 / individual 각각의, 개인용의

`해설` 전체적으로 '선택적으로 복지제도'에 대한 설명인데, ④는 휴가에 관한 설명으로 관련없는 내용이다.

`해석` 대부분 모든 기업에서 수당의 범위가 넓어지고 있어서, 그 비용을 충당하는 것에 대한 관심도 늘고 있다. 많은 기업들이 여전히 매력적이고 가치 있는 직원을 유지하는 한에서 예산 절감 계획을 실험하고 있다. 한 가지 방법은 선택적 복지제도 계획인데, 각 직원 당 일정액의 수당을 챙겨 놓는 것이다. 그래서 각각의 직원들은 다양한 대안들 중에서 선택할 수 있다. 최근의 선택적 복지제도로의 변화는 직원들이 세금을 계산하기 전이나 후에 그들의 급여로부터 그들의 수당의 몫을 선택할 수 있도록 허용한다. 대부분의 기업들은 가족 구성원이 사망한 즉시 일주일의 휴가를 주도록 법적으로 규정하고 있다. 대부분 개인은 제대로 선택을 하면, 수당 자체는 세금이 계산되지 않으므로 실제로 세금 절약의 결과를 가져온다.

10 어휘 occasion 때, 행사 / after-dinner speech 식후 탁상 연설 / rally 집회 / banquet 연회, 만찬 / kickoff 시작, 개시 / nature 성격, 본질 / digest (음식을) 소화하다, (어떤 내용을) 소화하다 / radical 근본적인, 철저한 / rethink 다시 생각하다, 재고하다 / negativity 부정적 성향, 소극성 / savor 맛, 풍미

해설 'S + V + C'가 완전한 문장에서 주어가 도치되면서 명사의 기능을 하는 none이 오는 것은 문법적으로 옳지 않다.

해석 특별한 행사를 기념하거나 절차의 시작과 끝을 기념하는 행사에는 종종 만찬 후 연설을 필요로 한다. 정치적인 집회, 시상 연회, 기금모금 캠페인, 또는 학년말이 그러한 연설을 필요로 하는 경우이다. 행사의 성격을 유지하기 위해, 만찬 후 연설은 너무 어려워서 소화를 어렵게 해서는 안 된다. 연설자는 이러한 연설에서 청중에게 그들의 가치를 재고할 것을 유구하거나 믿음과 행동에 극적인 변화를 요구하는 급진적인 사상을 전해서는 안 된다. 그러한 경우는 이것은 그들을, 그들이 하는 것을, 또한 그들이 원하는 것을 만끽하는 시간이다.

11 어휘 defeate 패배시키다, 무산시키다 / tactic 전략, 전술 / phalanx (사람들이 밀집해 있는) 집단 / derive 끌어내다, 얻다 / frontal 정면의, 전선의 / assault 폭행, 공격, 죄 / penetrating 뚫고 들어가는, 마음속을 꿰뚫는 듯한, 귀를 찢는 듯한, 날카로운 / rank 계급, 지위, 사병 / consist of ~로 구성되다 / tightly 단단히, 꽉, 빽빽이 / blockade 봉쇄, 봉쇄하다 / station 움직이지 않는, 정지된 / rectangular 직사각형의, 직각의 / offensive 모욕적인, 불쾌한, 공격적인 / posture 자세 / spear 창 / pike 창 / collective 집단의, 공동의 / formidable 가공할, 어마어마한 / mowing down 살육하다

해설 'with + 명사 + 보어'의 형태를 취해 '~하는 상태로'를 뜻한다. 무기를 적을 향해 겨눈 것이므로 현재분사 'pointing'을 써야 올바른 표현이 된다.

해석 알렉산더 대왕은 전쟁에서 절대 패배하지 않았고, 집단 대형이라고 불리는 그의 전술은 오늘날 여전히 연구되고 있다. 손가락을 뜻하는 그리스어 'phalangos'에서 유래된 것으로, 적이 공격자들의 대열을 뚫는 것을 막으면서 동시에 적에 대항하는 전면공격을 기본으로 한 대형이었다. 이것은 직사각형의 공격적인 포즈를 취한 군인들이 단단히 연결되어 봉쇄막으로 구성되어 있다. 각각의 군인들은 적들을 찌를 수 있는 긴 창이나 짧은 창과 같은 무기를 가지고 옆 사람과 어깨를 나란히 하고 서 있다. 집단 대형은 집단 병력 중 한 부대를 앞으로 나아가게 하여 뚫는 것이 거의 불가능한 가공할 만한 전술 체제를 만들어 냈다. 그리고 전진하는 병사와 무기의 벽으로 적을 대량 살육하였다. 집단의 힘 조직을 발전시켰고, 가공할만한 전략시스템을 뚫는 것이 거의 불가능했으며 사람과 무기의 움직이는 벽은 적을 살육했다.

12 어휘 kindness 친절, 다정함 / first of all 우선, 가장 먼저 / sense 감각 / show up 나타내다, 눈에 띄다 / caged (우리에) 갇힌 / bully 약자를 괴롭히는 사람 / imitative 모방적인 / admire 존경하다, 감탄하며 바라보다 / disapprove 탐탁찮아 하다

해설 (A) '그들이 느끼는 것'이라는 의미가 되어야 하므로, 선행사를 포함하는 관계대명사로 '~하는 것'의 의미로 쓰이는 'what'이 와야 한다.
(B) 'who says ~ another child is bullied'까지는 'A grade school child'를 수식하는 수식어이다. 따라서 문장의 동사가 와야 하므로 3인칭 단수 동사인 'shows'가 와야 한다.
(C) 'taught' 뒤에 'that'이 생략된 형태이다. 'that'절의 주어는 'hitting'이 되고 동사가 와야 하므로 'is wrong'이 와야 한다.

해석 세 가지 다른 유형의 친절이 연구로 밝혀졌다. 우선, 타고난 친절이다. 다른 사람들과 동일시하여 그들의 기분을 파악할 수 있는 능력을 기반으로 한 자연스러운 친절이다. 이 친절은 매우 어린 나이에 나타난다. 우리에 갇힌 고릴라가 슬퍼 보인다고 말하거나 다른 아이들이 약자를 괴롭힐 때 화를 내는 초등학생은 이러한 타고난 친절을 나타낸다. 친절의 두 번째 유형은 지침을 교육 받은 친절이다. 지침을 교육받은 사람들은 "그렇게 하는 것은 잘못된 거야"라고 배웠다. 예를 들어, 규칙 안내자인 아이들은 그들이 때리는 것이 잘못된 것이라고 배워왔기 때문에 다른 사람을 때리지 않는다. 친절의 마지막 유형은 모방하는 것이다. 우리는 우리가 존경하는 사람들의 행동을 모방한다. 예를 들어, 그들의 부모를 존경하는 모방하는 아이들은 그들의 부모가 탐탁치 않아 하는 행동을 피할 것이다.

13 어휘 fall in love 사랑에 빠지다 / antique 골동품인, 골동품 / bowl 그릇, 통 / bidding 호가, (경매에서) 값을 부르는 / row 열, 줄, 행 / skyrocket 급등하다 / realize 깨닫다, 알아차리다

해설 (A) 앉고 있는 중이 아닌, 다른 곳에 앉혀진 것이므로 수동태인 'were seated'형태가 되어야 한다.
(B) 장소를 나타내는 접속사가 아닌, 계속적 용법의 관계부사가 와야 하므로 'when'이 와야 한다.
(C) 'motion'은 to와 함께 쓰여 '~하도록 신호하다'의 뜻으로 쓰인다. 따라서 'to stop'이 오는 것이 적절하다.

해석 내 아내는 경매에서 골동품 그릇에 빠졌고, 그녀의 여동생에게 그것을 얻을 수 있게 도와달라고 부탁했다. 입찰이 시작되었을 때, 우리는 방의 다른 부분에 앉고, 나는 맨 뒤에서 그들을 기다렸다. 그릇의 가격은 급등하기 시작했고, 나는 문제가 있다는 것을 알아차렸다. 내 아내와 인척 관계인 여동생은 서로 경쟁적으로 입찰가를 부르고 있었다. 나는 재빨리 그들에게 멈추라는 동작을 취했지만, 너무 늦었다. 경매사는 망치를 두드리며 "팔렸습니다", "뒤의 신사분에게"라고 말했다.

14 어휘 mention 말하다, 언급하다 / feasibility study 예비 타당성 조사 / extend 연장하다 / operation 영업, 작전 / board of director 이사회 / expansion 확대, 확장 / out of date 구식의, 구식인, 오래된 / prove 입증하다, 증명하다 / look forward to ~을 기대하다

해설 사업확장을 위한 예비타당성 조사를 수행해줄 것을 위임하고 있는 글이다.

보기 ① 연구 사업을 위임하기 위해서
② 개인적인 조언을 얻기 위해서
③ 특별한 회의를 알리기 위해서
④ 공식적인 초대를 하기 위해서
⑤ 재정적 기부에 감사를 표하기 위해서

해석 제가 지난 회의에서 언급했듯이, 저는 당신이 태평양 연안 시장을 포함하여 영업을 확장하자는 우리의 제안에 대해 한 달간의 예비 타당성 조사를 수행해주었으면 합니다. 만약 결과가 긍정적이라면, 당신의 보고서는 이번 확장에 대한 안정적인 자금 조달을 할 수 있도록 이사회에 먼저 보고될 것입니다. 우리가 현재 예산 내에서 일을 해야 하기 때문에 당신에게 할당된 예산은 빠듯할 것입니다. 하지만 저는 당신이 신중한 선택을 할 것을 압니다. 저는 이 문제에 대한 Neumann의 보고서 사본을 동봉했습니다. 이 보고서는 약간 시대에 뒤떨어지긴 했지만, 여전히 본보기로서 유용할 것입니다. 저는 주간 보고서는 물론, 늦어도 당신의 최종보고서를 7월 14일까지 볼 수 있기를 기대합니다.

15 어휘 humiliating 굴욕적인, 면목 없는 / peer 또래, 귀족 / embarrass 당황스럽게 만들다, 난처하게 만들다 / gossip 수다, 험담 / regarding ~에 관하여 / playdate 아이들이 함께 놀 수 있도록 부모들이 정한 약속 / humiliate 굴욕감을 주다 / considerate 사려 깊은, 배려하는 / tenderheart 다정한, 다감한, 상냥한 / stranger 낯선 사람 / tolerate 용인하다, 참다, 견디다 / compliment 칭찬, 찬사

해설 Mary 엄마의 모습을 보면서 어린 소녀의 감정을 존중해 주는 것이 사려깊은 일이라고 생각했음을 알 수 있다.

보기 ① 낯선 사람에게 다정하게 대하는 것
② 다른 엄마들의 지원에 감사하는 것
③ 내 딸의 잘못된 행동을 참는 것
④ 어린 소녀의 감정을 존중하는 것
⑤ 아이들을 친구 앞에서 칭찬하는 것

해석 나는 아이들을 또래 친구들 앞에서 창피를 주는 것을 싫어한다. 우리 엄마가 친구들 앞에서 나에게 "그렇게 행동 하지마!" 또는 "수다 떨지마!"라고 했을 때 당황스러웠다. 이것에 관해서, 내 딸 Jane을 키우는 데 나를 도와주었던 다른 엄마들로부터 많은 것을 배웠다. 그녀가 어렸을 때, 우리는 그녀의 친구 Mary와 함께 만나서 시간을 보냈다. Mary가 무언가를 잘못했을 때, 그녀의 엄마는 "잠깐 실례해도 될까(자리 좀 비켜주실래요)?"라고 말한다. 후에 내가 "무슨 일 있었어?"라고 물으면, 그녀는 "나는 Mary가 그렇게 행동하는 것을 좋아하지 않지만 Mary가 Jane 앞에서 굴욕감을 당하는 것은 원하지 않아."라고 말했다. 나는 어린 소녀의 감정을 존중하는 것이 배우 사려 깊다고 생각했다.

16 어휘 structure 구조 / debate 토론, 토의, 논쟁 / theory 이론, 학설 / roughly 대략, 거의, 거칠게 / refer to ~을 나타내다, ~을 언급하다 / determinist 결정론자, 결정론자의 / primary 주된, 주요한, 초기의 / strictly 엄히, 엄격히, 절대적으로 / reliant 의존하는, 의지하는 / latter 후자의, 마지막의 / notion 개념, 관념, 생각 / frequently 종종, 자주 / imperative 반드시 해야 하는, 긴요한, 위엄 있는 / interdependent 상호의존적인 / heavily 심하게, 아주 많이

해설 마지막 문장에서 조직과 기술이 상호 영향을 미친다고 했으므로 ①의 내용을 유추할 수 있다.

보기 ① 기술과 구조는 상호의존적이다
② 구조는 기술에 크게 의존한다
③ 새로운 기술은 얻는 것은 매우 비싸다
④ 어떠한 조직은 기술 없이 기능할 수 있다
⑤ 기술은 많은 조직들에 의해 공유되어야 한다

해석 조직의 구조에 대한 기술의 영향은 1950년대 이래로 논쟁의 중심이 되어 왔다. 이 분야에 대한 이론과 조사는 대략 두 그룹으로 나뉜다. 한 그룹은 때로 기술적인 결정론을 언급하는데, 이 그룹은 조직의 구조의 주요 결정론자로서 기술을 바라본다. 이 그룹은 다른 구조들은 다른 기술들을 필요로 한다고 주장하며, 전자가 절대적으로 후자에 의존한다고 주장한다. 이 생각은 종종 기술의 위엄을 언급한다. 두 번째 그룹은 개방된 시스템으로서 조직을 바라보며, 기술과 구조가 상호의존적이라고 주장한다. 따라서 기술은 조직에 영향을 미치고 조직에 의해 영향을 받는 것이 지속된다.

17 어휘 nonprofit 비영리적인 / agency 대리점, 대행사, 단체 / disaster 참사, 재난, 재해, 구호 / relief 안도, 안심, 경감 / increasingly 점점 더, 갈수록 더 / come under fire 비난을 받다 / accusation 혐의, 비난, 고소 / mismanagement 그릇된 처리, 실수 / corruption 부패, 오염, 변질 / stung by 쏘이다, (벌에) 쏘이다 / galvanize 충격 요법을 쓰다 / grant 인정하다, 수락하다, 보조금 / composed of ~로 구성되다 / debit card 직불(현금) 카드 / administer 관리하다, 운영하다, 부여하다 / eliminate 없애다, 삭제하다 / stimulate 자극하다, 활발하게 하다, 고무하다 / boost 신장시키다, 북돋우다 / whereas 반면에

해설 전통적인 구호 방법인 현물 지원이 아니라 현금 지원의 장점을 설명하고 있다.

보기 ① 현금 ② 곡물 ③ 의복 ④ 의약품 ⑤ 고용

해석 최근 몇 년간 재난 구호에 참여했던 비영리 단체들은 구호물자가 단체의 잘못된 관리와 수령 국가들의 부패로 인해 피해자들에게 도달하지 못하고 있다는 비난에 직면한 채, 점점 더 빈축을 사고 있다. 그 후 구호 단체들은 충격 요법을 쓰고 있다. 이러한 움직임이 비정상적으로 보일 수도 있지만, 그들은 조력의 전통적인 형식을 현금으로 대체하고 있다. 지금까지 대부분의 사람들은 구호가 음식과 담요와 같은 재난 피해자에게 실질적으로 필요한 것으로 구성되어야 한다고 인정해왔다. 하지만, 현금 카드 형식의 실제 돈을 제공하는 시스템은 관리하기에 더욱 저렴하고 교통비를 줄이기 때문에 장점이 된다. 이것은 또한 농부가 소상인들에게 부양책을 제공하여 지방 경제를 자극하지만, 식량 기부는 지역 매출을 축소하는 결과를 가져올 수 있다.

18 어휘 primitive 초기의, 원시의 / commonly 흔히, 보통 / harsh 가혹한, 혹독한 / existence 존재, 생활, 생계 / dominate 지배하다, 군림하다 / incessant 끊임없는, 쉴새없는 / quest / 탐구, 탐색 / contemporary 현시대의, 당대의, 현대의 / labor 노동, 수고, 애씀, 노력 / inhabitant 주민, 서식동물 / materially 실질적으로 / desire 욕망, 욕구 / material 재료, 작물 / wealth 부, 부유한, 풍부한 / relatively 상대적으로 / exchange 교환하다

해설 빈칸의 뒷문장을 통해서 더 많은 것을 얻기 위해서 애써 일하지 않는다는 것을 알 수 있다.

보기 ① 그들에게는 욕심이 많지 않다.
② 그들은 가장 자원이 많은 곳에서 산다.
③ 그들의 생산성은 상대적으로 낮다.
④ 그들은 시간 개념이 없다.
⑤ 그들은 서로 물건을 교환한다.

원시인들의 생활은 보통 고달플 것이라고 생각된다 – 그들의 존재는 끊임없는 음식 찾기에 의해 지배당하기 때문에. 실제로, 몇몇의 원시 부족들은 거의 일을 하지 않는다. 당대의 기준에 의하면, 우리는 그들을 매우 게으르다고 판단해야 한다. 만약 파푸아의 Kapauka가 하루 일을 하면, 그들은 다음날 노동을 하지 않는다. Kung 부시맨들은 오직 일주일에 이틀하고 반나절만 일하며, 하루에 6시간만 일을 한다. 하와이의 샌드위치섬에서, 원주민들은 하루에 단지 4시간만 일한다. 우리처럼 그들이 더욱 많은 것들을 얻기 위해 더 많은 일을 하려고 하지 않는 이유를 이해하기 위한 열쇠는 그들에게 욕심이 많지 않다는 것이다. 원하는 것과 소유하는 것 사이의 경쟁에서, 그들은 그들의 소유욕을 낮게 유지한다 – 그리고 이러한 방법으로, 일종의 자기만족을 보장한다. 그들은 동시대의 기준으로 볼 때 물질적으로 가난하지만, 적어도 한 가지 면 –시간 –에 있어서 우리는 그들이 더욱 부자라고 인정해야 한다.

19 **어휘** sentence 문장, 형벌, 선고 / childlike 아이 같은, 순진한 / subject matter 주제 / profound 엄청난, 깊은, 심오한 / letter 글자, 문자 / frisky 기운찬, 팔팔한 / put together 조립하다, 만들다 / intricate 복잡한 / glittering 눈부신, 성공적인, 화려한 / admirable 감탄스러운, 존경스러운 / sacred 성스러운, 종교적인, 신성시되는 / no matter how ~라고 해도, ~이지만 / illuminate 비추다, 밝히다, 분명히 하다 / clever 똑똑한, 기발한, 재치있는 / scratch 긁다 / accuracy 정확, 정확도 / simplicity 간단함, 소박함, 순박함

해설 복잡하고 화려한 문장보다는 단순한 문장이 오히려 효과적이라는 예를 들어 설명하고 있다. 빈칸에 들어갈 말은 ⑤가 적절하다.

보기 ① 드라마를 쓰는 것
② 고전 작품을 읽는 것
③ 문법의 정확성
④ 인물에 대한 이해
⑤ 언어의 간결성

해석 당신의 언어 사용에 있어서, 주제가 매우 심오할 때 거의 아이처럼 보이는 문장을 쓴 William Shakespeare와 James Joyce 두 명장을 기억하라. "죽느냐 사느냐?" 셰익스피어의 햄릿은 묻는다. 가장 긴 단어가 단 세 글자이다. Joyce는 한창 때, 클레오파트라를 위한 목걸이만큼 복잡하고 화려한 문장을 만들 수 있었지만, 내가 그의 단편 소설 Eveline에서 가장 좋아하는 문장은 이것이다 : "그녀는 피곤했다." 이야기의 그 부분에서, 다른 어떠한 단어들도 이 세 단어처럼 독자의 심장을 때릴 수 없었다. 언어의 간결성은 감탄스러울 뿐만 아니라 성스럽기까지 했다. 당신의 법칙은 이러할 것이다 : 만약 문장이 아무리 훌륭하다고 해도 당신의 주제를 몇몇 재치 있고 효과적인 방법으로 분명하게 드러내지 않으면, 그 문장은 지워버려라.

20 **어휘** unfortunately 불행하게도 / unhealthy 건강하지 못한, 유해한 / direction 방향 / obsession 강박관념, 집착 / at any cost 무슨 일이 있어도 / extreme 극단적인, 극단의 / pressure 압박, 압력 / focus on 집중하다, 전념하다 / cheating 속임수, 사기 / penalize 처벌하다, 주의를 주다 / come up with 찾아내다 / ingenious 기발한, 독창적인 / bend 구부리는, 휘는

해설 부정행위가 하나의 "전략"처럼 보이고, 선수와 감독이 부정행위를 저지르고 있다는 내용을 통해 ④의 내용을 유추할 수 있다.

보기 ① 실질적인 제공하지 않는 것
② 경기의 실제 시간을 줄이는 것
③ 부정한 행위로 배제되는 것
④ 경기의 일부로 받아들여지는 것
⑤ 감독들과 선수들이 더욱 포기하도록 만드는 것

해석 스포츠는 경쟁이다. 모든 운동선수, 모든 팀의 목표는 승리이다. 불행하게도 두 가지 요인이 오늘날의 스포츠를 불건전한 방향으로 이끌고 있다. 하나는 무슨 일이 있어도 이겨야 한다는 강박관념이다. 다른 하나는 돈이다. 이러한 두 가지 요소는 선수들과 감독들이 오직 승리에만 집중하도록 극단적인 압박을 주었다. 이것은 만연되고, 더욱 심각해지는 문제를 야기했다. 그 문제는 부정행위이다. 물론, 모든 스포츠에는 부정행위에 대해 처벌을 하는 규칙이 있다. 하지만 몇몇 감독들과 선수들은 규칙을 악용하기 위해 기발한 방법을 찾아냈다. 불공평한 경쟁력에서 우위를 얻는 것은 부정행위라기보다는 "전략"처럼 보여진다. 부정한 행동은 현재 경기의 한 일부로 받아들여지고 있다. 몇몇 감독들은 경기 도중 선수들이 불법적인 행동을 저지른다는 것을 알고 있을 때, 상대 선수가 다른 곳을 보고 있다면, 선수들에게 부정행위를 하도록 장려한다.

21 **어휘** author 작가, 저자 / figure of speech 비유법 / vivid 생생한, 선명한, 강렬한 / hyperbole 과장법 / exaggeration 과장 / interpret 설명하다, 이해하다 / exhaust 기진맥진하다, 고갈되다 / overstatement 과장 / convey 전달하다, 실어나르다 / extremely 매우, 극히

해설 ③ 'literally'은 '글을 읽고 쓸 줄 아는'이라는 뜻으로 '과장된 단어가 글자 그대로를 의미하지 않는다'는 문맥에 사용하기에 부적절하다. 따라서 '글자 그대로'라는 단어인 'literally'가 들어가야 문맥의 의미가 통한다.

해석 작가들은 독자의 마음에 선명한 그림을 그리기 위해 또는 강조 혹은 유머와 같은 몇 가지 다른 특별한 효과를 얻기 위해 비유법을 사용한다. 비유법의 한 가지 예는 과장법이다. 과장법은 작가가 강조를 위해 명백한 과장을 하는 비유법이다. 독자들은 단어가 작가가 말하려 하는 것을 글자 그대로 의미하지 않는다는 것을 깨달아야 한다. 다시 말해서, 독자들은 작가의 의도된 뜻을 이해해야 한다. 과장법의 일례로, "난 기진맥진해서 일주일동안 잘 수 있을 거야." 과장은 "난 일주일 동안 잘 수 있을 거야."이다. 이 부분에서 작가가 전달하기 원하는 것은 그나 그녀가 매우 피곤하다는 것이다.

22 **어휘** institute 기관, 협회, 연구소 / modeling 모형제작, 모형화 / turn down ~을 거부하다, 거절하다 / proclaim 선언하다, 선포하다 / praise 칭찬, 찬사 / forge 구축하다, 나아가다 / spread with 퍼지다, 널리 퍼지다 / appearance 등장, 나타남 / apparel 의류, 의복 / barrier 장애물, 장벽 / mainstream 주류, 대세 / grace 꾸미다, 장식하다, 빛내다 / disgrace 먹칠하다, 실각하다 / embrace 포괄하다, 아우르다, 수용하다

해설 (A) 피부색이 검다고 칭찬(praising)한 것이 아니라 선언(proclaiming)하였다.
(B) 그녀의 옷(apparel)이 아니라 모습(appearance)이 장벽을 무너뜨렸다.
(C) 소녀들이 치욕(disgrace)스럽게 생각하도록 한 것이 아니라 받아들일(embrace) 수 있도록 하였다.

해석 나오미 심즈는 1966년 패션 기술 연구소에 참여하기 위해 뉴욕시에 도착해서 독립생활을 하기 위해 모델 일을 하기로 결심했다. 대부분의 기업들이 그녀의 피부색이 너무 검다고 선언하면서 그녀를 거절한 후에 그녀는 자신의 신념을 고수하여 앞으로 나아갔고, 사진 작가와 직접적으로 계약함으로써 New York Times에 실리는 사진을 따냈다. 1968년 Ladies' Home Journal 표지에서 그녀의 모습은 주요 여성 잡지에서 피부색의 장벽을 깨뜨렸고, 그녀는 Cosmopolitan, essence 그리고 life의 표지를 빛냈다. 그녀는 다른 슈퍼모델인 나오미 캠벨을 포함한 다른 사람들을 위한 패션쇼의 문을 열었다. 그리고 그녀는 모든 피부색의 소녀들이 그들 자신의 내면의 아름다움을 받아들일 수 있게 만들었다.

23 **어휘** throughout ~을 통해서, ~동안, 내내 / ongoing 진행 중인 / controversy 논란, 논쟁 / school of thought 학설, 관점 / contradiction 모순, 반박 / in particular 특히 / theorize 이론을 제시하다 / eternal 영원한, 끊임없는 / internal 내부의, 체내의 / no matter what 비록 무엇이 ~이 일지라도 / static 고정적인, 고정의, 잡음의, 정전기 / statistical 통계적인, 통계상의 / motionless 움직이지 않는

해설 유사한 형태의 단어지만 뜻이 서로 전혀 다르므로 주의하여야 한다.

해석 기록된 역사 동안 우주의 기원은 진행 중인 논란의 주제가 되어왔다. 특히, 논쟁은 어떻게 우주가 생겨났는가가 중심이 되어왔다. 특히 유대교, 기독교, 이슬람교에 의해 받아들여진 한 가지 학설은 우주가 창조되었다는 것이다. 따라서 우주가 아니었던 시간이 있었고, 동일하게 우주가 사라지는 시간이 있을 것이다. 반면에, 그리스의 철학자인 아리스토텔레스와 같은 몇몇 사람들은 우주가 시작되었다고 믿지 않는다. 그는 우주는 존재해왔고 영원히 존재할 것이며 영원하고 완벽하다는 이론을 제시했다. 원래 이 두 학설에서 공통적이었던 한 가지는 비록 우주의 기원이나 끝이 존재할지라도 우주 그 자체는 고정되어 있다는 것이다. 그러나 19세기 이후, 우주는 움직임이 없고, 불변하다는 생각에 도전하는 증거가 나타나기 시작했다.

24 **어휘** armed 무기가 사용되는, 무장한 / conflict 갈등, 충돌 / globe 지구의, 세계의 / mortality rate 사망률 / decline 감소하다 / lead to 이끌다 / span 시간 / motivate 이유가 되다, 동기를 부여하다 / humanitarian 인도주의적인 / vaccinate 예방주사를 맞히다 / measles 홍역 / initiative 계획, 결단력, 주도 / malnutrition 영양실조 / silver lining 밝은 희망 / warrior 전사 / deadly 극도의, 치명적인 / epidemic 유행성, 급속한 확산

해설 전쟁으로 인해 국제 인도 단체들이 공중 보건 계획을 통해 빈곤 국가들을 도운 긍정적인 효과를 말하고 있다.

보기 ① 아프리카의 자유를 위한 외침
② 현대 전쟁의 긍정적인 측면
③ 현대 전쟁의 젊은 용사들
④ 아프리카 내전의 어두운 면
⑤ 삽시간에 퍼지는 치명적인 유행성 질병

해석 새로운 연구에 따르면, 1970년대 이래로 세계에서 일어나는 대부분의 무력 충돌이 벌어지는 동안 사망률은 사실상 감소했다고 한다. 전쟁 자체가 수명 연장을 가져온 것은 아니다. 대신에, 사망률 감소의 주요 원인은 무력 충돌이 국제 인도 단체에게 빈곤 국가에서 그들의 노력을 더욱 강화하도록 동기부여를 해왔고, 그들이 짧은 시간에 공중 보건 기적을 배우도록 했다는 것이다. 예를 들어, 콩고 민주 공화국에서 10년간의 긴 내전이 시작된 1997년에는 단지 20%의 아이들만이 홍역 예방 주사를 맞았다. 하지만 2007년에 그 수치는 80%가 되었다. 영양실조의 치료에서 모기장을 제공하는 것까지, 다른 보건 계획들의 역사는 유사한 이야기를 말해 준다.

25 **어휘** guided missile 유도 미사일 / target 표적, 목표 / unerringly 틀림없는, 항상 정확한 / no matter where 어디서 ~하더라도 / sophisticated 세련된, 복잡한, 정교한 / lock onto (공격 대상을) 추적하다, 따라가다 / evasive 얼버무리는, 회피하는 / destruction 파괴, 말살, 파멸 / launch 착수하다, 시작하다 / distraction 집중을 방해하는 것, 오락

해설 목표를 정해 나아가되, 피드백을 통해 수정해나가라고 말하고 있으므로 ⑤가 적절하다.

보기 ① 최선의 도주는 속도다.
② 피드백은 쓸모없는 방해물이다.
③ 같은 실수를 다시 하지 말라.
④ 많은 시간을 들여 당신의 목표를 설정하라.
⑤ 결단력과 유연함은 목표를 이끌어 낸다.

해석 한번 표적을 향해 프로그램 된 유도 미사일은 어디서 표적이 움직이더라도 항상 정확하게 표적을 향할 것이다. 크루즈 미사일이나 엑조세 미사일과 같이 정교한 무기는 표적을 추적하고 미사일이 표적을 맞출 때까지 항로와 방향을 계속해서 조정할 것이다. 어떠한 회피 작전도 표적이 파괴를 면할 수 있도록 허락하지 않을 것이다. 당신 또한 유도 미사일과 유사하다. 크게 성공하고 당신의 미래를 만들기 위해, 당신은 당신의 목표를 향하여 나아가야 한다. 일단 당신이 무엇을 원하는지에 대한 확실한 생각을 가지고 움직이기 시작하면, 당신은 당신의 항로를 조정할 수 있도록 하는 지속적인 피드백을 받을 것이다. 어려움과 장애물 형태로 보이는 이 피드백은 당신이 전진할 수 있는 정확한 항로를 만들도록 할 것이다. 이러한 항로 교정은 결국 당신을 목표한 곳으로 이끌어 줄 것이지만, 당신은 계속해서 움직여야 한다.

26 어휘 initial 초기의, 처음의 / reaction 반응, 반작용, 반발 / downturn (매출 등의) 감소, 하강 / cash flow 현금 유동성 / defer 미루다, 연기하다 / maintenance 유지, 생활비 / capital 자산, 자본, 수도 / modernize 현대화하다 / halt 멈추다, 중단하다 / diagnose 진단하다 / profitability 수익성, 이윤율 / temporary 임시적인, 임시의 / turn around 회전하다, 바꾸다, 뒤돌아보다

해설 단기적 대응이 아니라 경기 침체의 원인 분석 등을 통해 조직의 기능을 호전시켜야 한다고 말하고 있다.

해석 경기 침체에 있어서 많은 성공적인 조직 관리자들의 초기 반응은 가능한 한 적게 하고, 이 상황이 지나가길 기다리는 것을 뜻하는 "폭풍을 뚫고 나오는 것"이다. 현금 유동성을 증가시킴으로써 경기 침체의 증상을 처리하는 가벼운 조치의 예로는 유지·보수의 연기, 신제품 개발에 대한 소비의 감소, 공장과 장비를 현대화 하는 데 따르는 소비의 감소, 새로운 인력 고용의 중단, 그리고 조사·개발 재정의 축소 등이 있다. 수익성의 감소 또는 현금 유동성의 감소의 원인 진단에는 거의 관심을 기울이지 않는다. 이러한 반응은 경기 침체가 일시적이지 않다면 문제가 된다. 관리자들은 조직의 기능을 호전시킬 수 있는 가치 있는 시간과 자원을 낭비하고 있다. 만일 그러한 징후 "치료"에 대한 반응이 초기에 성공적으로 보일지라도, 환경 변화를 이해하고자 하는 열의가 감소한다면, 보통 얼마 지나지 않아 중대한 위기를 초래할 것이다.

27 어휘 opponent 경쟁 상대 / relative 비교적인, 상대적인 / take up (시간·공간을) ~하는 데 쓰다 / critical edge 결정적인 이점 / retreat 후퇴하다

해설 반인치 전진하는 전략이 필자에게도 자신감과 전략을 심어 주었다. 적절한 것은 ③이다.

보기 ① 항상 의외의 반전에 준비되어 있어라.
② 기회는 때론 인식하기 어렵다.
③ 앞으로 움직이는 것은 당신에게 결정적인 이점을 준다.
④ 최고의 선수는 가장 신중한 선수이다.
⑤ 당신은 더 멀리 나아가기 위해 한 발 후퇴하는 전략을 세울 수 있다.

해석 몇 년 전 내가 태권도 시합에 나갔을 때, 나는 세계 최고의 명장 중 한 분으로부터 중요한 기술을 배웠다. 그분은 태권도 경기에서 내가 상대를 향해 앞으로 갈 때 한 번에 반인치만 전진하면 상대는 우리 사이의 상대적 거리를 유지하기 위해 뒤로 움직일 것임을 가르쳐 주셨다. 내가 상대에게 다가가는 동안, 나의 힘과 집중력의 100%가 그에게 집중되었다. 하지만 상대가 뒤로 물러나면, 그의 힘 중 거의 절반이 그의 뒤엔 무엇이 있고 매트의 끝엔 무엇이 있을지에 대해 생각하는 데 사용되었다. 이 전략 덕분에, 나는 좋은 상대들에게 대항하여 성공적으로 경쟁을 펼칠 수 있었고 몇몇 국제 챔피언십 경기에서 상을 탔다. 그 전략은 내가 충만한 자신감을 갖게 해주었으며 모든 것이 달라지도록 도와주었다.

28 어휘 comforting 안락, 위안, 편안 / infancy 유아기, 초창기 / phrase 구, 구절 / feeding 수유, 먹이 주기 / distress 고충, (정신적) 고통 / over and over 거듭하여 / generally 대개, 일반적으로, 보통 / reassuring 안심시키는, 걱정을 없애주는 / after a while 잠시 후 / internalize (사상, 태도 등을) 내면화하다 / compassion 연민, 동정심 / cock 수탉 / crow 수탉 울음소리

해설 부모가 아이를 달래려고 했던 말을 아이가 그대로 따라 하는 것을 보여주고 있다. 어른을 보고 아이가 배운다는 뜻의 ④가 적절하다.

보기 ① 작은 문제도 소수의 사람들에게 큰 문제가 된다.
② 좋은 일과 나쁜 일은 같이 일어난다.
③ 건강 없이, 아무도 진정하게 행복해질 수 없다.
④ 늙은 수탉이 울 때, 어린 수탉이 배운다.
⑤ 샘이 마르고 나서야 물이 귀한 줄 안다.

해설 우리의 첫째 딸 로라가 유아기 동안 달래주어야 할 때, 내 아내와 나는 보통 2개의 어구 중 하나를 사용했다. 로라가 울고 있을 때 우리는 왜 우는지 알지 못해서, 처음에 우리는 로라에게 수유를 하거나 위생상 문제를 해결해주는 것과 같은 모든 확실한 해결책은 모두 시도해 보았다. 아이가 여전히 괴로워하고 있을 때, 우리는 아이를 잡고 가장 감정적인 어조로 "아가야, 아가야, 아가야," 또는 "알아, 알아" – 마치 우리가 정말 안다는 듯 고개를 끄덕이며 거듭하여 반복하였다. 우리는 대개 알지 못했지만, 우리가 한 말이 안심을 시키는 것처럼 보였다. 얼마 후, 로라는 이것을 자기 것으로 만들었다. 그녀의 첫 번째 생일이 다가오고 있을 때쯤, 그녀는 때론 아침에 일어나 울기 시작했다. 하지만 다른 아기들처럼 단지 우는 소리를 내는 대신, 로라는 스스로 "아가야, 아가야, 아가야… 알아, 알아."의 단어를 거듭 말하며 울었다. 로라는 강한 동정심을 갖고, 마치 우리가 하는 것을 봤던 것처럼 그녀의 작은 머리를 끄덕이며 그녀 스스로 그 말들을 하며 울었다.

29 어휘 debt 빚, 부채 / dip 살짝 담그다, 내려가게 하다 / overall 전반적인

해설 ⑤ 2011년 정부 부채 비율은 그리스가 이탈리아보다 약간 높다.

해석 이 차트는 각 국가의 연도별 GDP당 정부의 부채율을 나타낸다. 이 차트는 4개의 모든 국가에서 2006년과 2007년에 약간의 하락이 있었음을 보여준다. 하지만, 2007년 이후 각 국가는 전반적인 상승을 경험했다. 2007년부터 2011년까지 가장 극적으로 눈에 띄는 증가는 GDP당 정부 부채 비율이 3배 이상이 된 아일랜드에서 나타날 것이다. 2011년에, 독일의 GDP당 정부 부채 비율은 4개 국가 중에 가장 낮을 것으로 예상된다. 이탈리아와 그리스는 매우 유사한 곡선을 따르는데, 이탈리아는 2011년 그리스보다 정부 부채 비율이 약간 높은 것이 눈에 띈다.

30 어휘 tend to ~하는 경향이 있다 / overlook 간과하다 / measure 측정하다, (가치, 중요성 등을) 판단하다 / fulfillment 성취, 달성, 획득, 처리 / optimism 낙관론, 낙관주의 / marriage 결혼 상태, 결혼 / marital 결혼 생활의 / shortcut 지름길, 간단한 방법 / invisible 무형의, 보이지 않는, 볼 수 없는

해설 행복한 삶을 사는 것이 신체적 건강에 긍정적인 영향을 미친다고 하였다.

보기 ① 보이지 않는 즐거움을 측정하는 것에 대한 어려움
② 일에 대한 생각을 공유하는 것에 대한 중요성
③ 당신의 혈압을 조절하는 것의 필요성
④ 결혼과 스트레스 사이의 관계
⑤ 신체적 건강에 대한 행복한 삶의 영향

해석 환자와 그들의 의사는 건강에 있어서 즐거움의 중요성을 간과하는 경향이 있다. 왜 그런가? 아마도 이러한 사실을 측정하는 수치가 없기 때문일 것이다. 대신에, 우리는 콜레스테롤, 혈압, 체중 등등 "명백한" 평가에 초점을 맞춘다. 이것들은 모두 중요하다 – 하지만 관계, 개인적인 성취, 그리고 낙관주의 또한 중요하다. 좋은 건강과 낙관주의, 행복, 그리고 즐거움을 연결 짓는 많은 의학 연구들이 존재한다. 연구는 또한 좋은 결혼 생활로 건강함을 기대할 수 있는 반면, 결혼 생활의 스트레스로 그 반대(건강하지 못함)일 수 있다는 것을 보여준다. 그렇게 볼 때 나는 내가 건강할 수 있는 비밀 방법을 갖고 있는 것 같다. 그녀의 이름은 Rita이고 우리는 43년 동안 결혼 생활을 해오고 있다.

31 어휘 attribute ~의 결과로 보다, ~것이라고 보다 / outcome 결과 / distinguish 구별 짓다, 차이를 보이다 / scholar 학자, 장학생, 모범생 / practitioner 전문직 종사자, 현역 / competent 능숙한, 수준 있는 / increasingly 점점 더, 갈수록 더 / conform 일치하다, (관습, 규칙 등을) 따르다 / passive 수동적인, 소극적인 / describe 말하다, 묘사하다 / conformity 따름, 순응 / followership 지지, 충성

해설 지도력뿐만 아니라 용기있고, 책임감 있으며, 활동적인 추종자의 역할도 조직적 성공에 영향을 준다고 하였다.

보기 ① 재정적 지원으로 추종자들에게 동기 부여
② 리더십에 있어서 실패의 이유 조사
③ 순응과 수동적인 충성 장려
④ 전통적인 충성심과 현대적인 충성심의 결합
⑤ 효과적인 충성에 의한 조직적 성공의 획득

해석 조직적 성공과 실패는 비록 추종자들이 결과의 실제 이유를 가지고 있을지라도 주로 효과적이거나 비효과적인 리더십의 결과로 보여 진다. 평균적인 팀이나 조직들과 높은 업무 수행을 보이는 팀과 조직들을 구분 짓게 하는 것이 무엇인지에 대한 질문에 대해 조사했을 때, 대부분의 학자들과 전문직 종사자들은 높은 업무 수행 조직이 좋은 지도자와 좋은 추종자를 갖고 있다는 것에 동의 했다. 능숙한, 자신감 있는, 그리고 동기부여 된 추종자들은 어떠한 지도자의 업무 그룹 혹은 팀의 성공적인 수행을 위한 핵심적 존재이다. 점점 더, 많은 사람들이 추종자들의 늙고 부정적인 개념을 긍정적인 개념으로 대체하고 있다. 규칙을 따르고 규칙에 수동적인 추종자 대신, 용기 있고, 책임감 있고, 활동적인 추종자로 묘사된다.

32 **어휘** severe 심각한, 가혹한 / bring down 무너뜨리다 / squeal 끽, 꽥하는 소리 / thud 쿵, 턱하는 (둔탁한) 소리 / fox terrier (개의 종, 털이 짧고 작은) 강아지 / dense 빽빽한, 복잡한 / gently 부드럽게 / attentively 주의를 기울이는 / wounded 부상을 입은 / erect 똑바로 선, 일어선 / unbowed 지칠 줄 모르는, 패배하지 않는 / screeched 꽥하는 소리를 내다 / companion 동반자, 친구 / fortunately 다행스럽게도/ splendid 아주 인상적인, 훌륭한 / reunite 재회하다, 재회하게 하다

해석 심각한 폭풍은 우리 동네 전부의 나무와 울타리를 무너뜨렸다. 내가 우리 앞마당을 살펴보고 있을 때, 나는 브레이크의 끽하는 소리와 쿵하는 둔탁한 소리를 들었다. 공포에 질린 나는, 도로 한 복판에 누워있는 작은 폭스테리어 한 마리를 보았다. 차들은 빽빽했고, 어떤 운전자도 멈추지 않았다.
(B) 갑자기, 독일 세퍼트가 혼잡한 도로의 차를 피하며 나타나 작고 부상을 입은 강아지를 지키고 섰다. 차들이 그의 주변에서 끽소리를 내고 있었지만 세퍼트는 고개를 똑바로 세운 채, 굴하지 않고 용감하게 강아지를 지켰다. 난 나중에 그 강아지가 세퍼트의 친구라는 것을 알았다.
(A) 한 대의 차가 마침내 멈췄고 운전자는 독일산 세퍼트가 유심히 지켜보는 가운데 조심스럽게 폭스테리어를 보도로 옮겼다. 나는 그에게 약간의 물과 음식을 주었고 경찰을 불렀다.
(C) 다행스럽게도, 아주 인상적인 개와 그의 친구는 다음 날 그들을 걱정하던 주인과 재회했다. 폭풍이 몰아칠 때 개들의 울타리가 무너졌고 두 마리의 개는 함께 탈출했던 것으로 드러났다.

33 **어휘** medieval 중세의 / vehicle 차량, 수단 / promote 촉진하다, 홍보하다 / spirituality 정신, 정신성 / devotion 헌신, 전념, 기도 / aesthetic 심미적, 미학적 / secular 세속적인 / theme 주제, 테마 / portray 그리다, 나타내다, 표현하다 / consequently 그 결과, 따라서 / lifelike 실물과 똑같은 / propagate 전파하다, 번식시키다 / intent 강한 관심을 가지는, ~에 몰두하는 / proportion 비율, 균형 / humanity 인류, 인간애 / endow 기부하다 / dignity 위엄, 품위, 존엄성

해설 (B) − (A) − (C)의 순서로 나열되는 것이 자연스럽다.

해석 중세 시대 동안 예술의 목적은 종교를 가르치는 것이었다. 중세 시대에 사는 많은 사람들은 글을 읽지도, 쓸수도 없었기 때문에 그림들과 조각품들은 종교적 지도자가 신에 대한 정신과 헌신을 촉진시키는 수단으로 제공되었다.
(B) 그 결과, 중세의 예술가들은 모습과 형태를 실물과 똑같이 나타내는 것에 대해 관심이 없었다. 그들은, 종교적 정신과 의미를 전파시키는 것을 더욱 중요시했다.
(A) 그러나, 르네상스 시대의 예술가들은 예술을 개인적이고 심미적 표현의 수단으로 바라보았고 세속적인 주제에 많은 흥미를 느꼈다. 그들은 이를 통해 세계를 표현하길 원했다.
(C) 그들의 강한 관심은 실제적으로 정확한 외형과 비율의 성취를 이루었을 뿐만 아니라, 자연과 인간성을 기릴수도 있었다. 그래서, 그들은 주로 아름다움과 존엄성으로 그들의 주제를 표출했다.

34 **어휘** while ~인데 비하여, ~에 반하여 / feast 연회, 잔치 / social class 사회 계층 / nobility 귀족, 고결함 / gentry 상류층, 신사들 / knight (중세의) 기사 / landowner 지주, 토지 소유주 / servant 하인, 종업원 / merchant 상인, 무역상 / farmhands 농장 노동자 / impoverished 빈곤한, 저하된, 결핍된 / countryside 시골 지역, 전원지대 / sewer 하수관, 수채통 / sanitation 위생시설 / outbreak (전쟁, 사고, 질병 등의) 발생 plague 전염병 / rarity 진귀한, 희귀성

③ 튜더 시대의 최상위 계층은 귀족이며, 법률가들은 세 번째 상위 계층에 속한다.

해석 튜더 시대는 셰익스피어와 영웅적 모험가들이 살았던 시대인데 비하여, 커다란 축제와 아름다운 음악이 있던 시대는 아니었다. 튜더 왕조 때 영국에서의 삶은 최소한이라고 불릴 만큼 힘들었다. 튜더 영국에서 4개의 주요한 사회 계층은 중요했다. 귀족은 가장 소수이면서 가장 부자인 계급으로 이루어져있다. 그 바로 밑의 계층은 기사와 많은 하인을 거느린 저택에 사는 부유한 지주를 포함하는 상류층이다. 다음 계층은 상인과 법률가들과 같은 전문인들이다. 가장 광범위하고 가장 낮은 계급은 농장 노동자들, 하인들, 그리고 빈곤한 사람들을 포함한다. 대부분의 사람들은 시골 지역에 살았는데, 그 곳엔 하수관이 없었다. 위생시설의 부족은 많은 전염병을 발생시켰고, 의학적 지식의 부족으로 많은 사람들이 병과 죽음에 직면했다. 목욕을 하는 것이 드물었던 튜더 왕조 시대의 영국에서 살고 있지 않았던 당신은 매우 행복한 것이다.

35 어휘 virtual 사실상, 가상의 / originally 원래, 본래 / distraction 방해하는 것, 오락, 활동 / umpire 심판, 심판을 보다 / backstop 백네트 / slogan 구호, 슬로건 / broadcast 방송하다, 널리 알리다 / plastered 더덕더덕 붙은 / pitcher 투수

해설 ② 가상 광고는 실제 광고가 선수들의 집중력을 떨어뜨릴 염려가 있을 대 사용된다고 하였으므로 ②는 옳지 않은 설명이다.

해석 가상 광고 창조의 기술은 약 1955년부터 시작되었다. 원래, 이러한 유형의 광고는 스포츠 중계에서 사용되었다. 가상 광고는 실제 광고가 선수들의 집중을 방해할 수 있는 곳에 놓여졌다. 예를 들어, 야구 경기에서, 타자와 심판 뒤의 벽은 백네트라고 불린다. 컴퓨터 기술을 사용하여 제품의 그림과 구호가 이 벽에 투영될 수 있고, 그렇게 되면 경기 동안 널리 방송된다. 집에 있는 경기의 시청자들은 백네트 전체에 걸쳐 더덕더덕 붙은 코카콜라의 거대한 적백색의 광고를 볼 것이지만, 경기장에 있는 투수는 오직 빈 백네트만 본다. 광고는 컴퓨터에 의해 축구 경기를 하는 잔디가 덮고 있는 센터 필드에 그려질 수 있고, 또한 경기장 위에 가상의 소형 비행선 옆에 놓여 질 수도 있다.

36 어휘 deprive 허용하지 않다, 박탈하다 / reward 보상, 보상하다 / shaping 성형 / a series of 일련의, 연속하여 / disturb 방해하다 / cataract 백내장, 폭포 / physician 의사, 내과 의사 / vision 시력, 눈, 시야 / deteriorate 악화되다, 더 나빠지다 / permanently 영구히, 불변으로 / temper 성질, 기분, 울화통 / tantrum 짜증을 냄, 성질을 부림 / ease 덜해지다, 편안함, 편의성 / gradual 점진적인, 서서히 일어나는

해설 형성법의 구체적 방법이 제시되고 있으므로 ④에 들어가는 것이 가장 자연스럽다.

해석 "형성법"은 지속해서 '전체 중 작은 부분'을 장려함으로써 새로운 행동을 가르치는 방법이다. 예를 들면, 이러한 접근법은 백내장 수술 수 안경을 쓰게 된 Dickey라는 이름의 정신장애가 있는 작은 소년을 가르치는 데 사용되었다. 그의 의사는 Dickey가 안경이 없으면, 그의 시력이 영구적으로 상실될 것을 걱정했다. 하지만, Dickey는 안경이라는 단순한 언급에도 지독하게 짜증을 내며 성질을 부렸다. 그래서 조사원들은 그가 안경을 착용할 수 있게 하기 위해 형성법을 사용하기 시작했다. 그들은 Dickey의 아침 식사를 빼앗아 음식을 보상으로 사용하도록 했다. 그리고 Dickey는 안경을 잡을 때마다 약간의 음식을 받았다. 이러한 과정 후에, 그는 다른 보상을 받기 위해 안경을 써야만 했다. 18일 안에, Dickey는 점차적인 단계를 통해 하루에 12시간 동안 안경을 쓸 수 있게 되었다.

37 어휘 daydream 공상에 잠기다, 백일몽 / take note 주목하다 / alert 기민한, 정신이 초롱초롱한 / wandering 돌아다니는, 헤매는, 방랑하는 / needle 바늘, 침, (기계의) 바늘 / preoccupy 뇌리를 사로잡다 / paragraph 단락, 절 / refrigerator 냉장고, 냉각기 / concentrate on ~에 집중하다 / stimulus 자극제, 자극 / perception 지각, 인식

해설 사람은 모든 것에 집중할 수는 없으며, 보통 필요한 것에 집중된다.

만일 당신이 강의시간 동안 무언가에 대해 공상에 잠겼다면, 당신의 머릿속에는 강의 내용의 거의 남지 않거나 아무 것도 남지 않을 것이다. 당신은 주목하고 정신을 차리도록 노력할 것이지만, 마음이 산란하다는 것을 찾을 수 있을 것이다. 당신은 기름이 거의 "비어있음"을 가리킬 때 고속도로를 따라 운전한 적이 있는가? 주유소의 위치만이 당신의 뇌리를 사로잡을 가능성이 있다. 다른 날 당신의 연료통은 가득하지만 배가 고플 때, 주유소를 지나쳐도, 모든 음식과 레스토랑이 당신의 눈을 사로잡을 것이다. 만일 당장 당신이 배가 고프거나 목이 마르다면, 당신은 냉장고보다 이 글을 읽는 데 계속해서 정신을 집중하기 어려울지도 모른다. 당신은 단순히 당신 주변에 있는 모든 자극에 다 (A) 집중할 수는 없으며, 오직 (B) 필요한 것만이 집중된다.

✧ [38~39]

carry it off 멋지게 해내다 / put off 미루다, 연기하다 / confess 인정하다, 자백하다 / sullen 뚱한, 시무룩한 / drop 떨어지다, 그만두다, 중단하다 / stick it out 참다 / assignment 과제, 임무 / dawn 분명해지다, 이해되다, 시작되다 / marine biology 해양 생물학 / quite 꽤, 상당히 / fate 운명, 운명에 따라 / classmate 급우, 반, 친구 / chip away 서서히 사라지다 / reveal 드러내다, 드러내 보이다

「Jimin은 언제가 있을 공개 발표 수업에 대해 걱정이 있었다. 그녀는 그녀 스스로를 공개 발표자로 보지 않았고 그녀가 그것을 멋지게 해낼 것이라고 확신하지 않았다. 하지만 그녀가 더 이상 그 수업을 미룰 수 없는 시간이 다가왔다. 그녀의 첫 수업에서, 그녀는 그녀가 느끼는 것만큼 불편한 얼굴의 돌처럼 굳은 표정을 짓고 있는 20명의 학생들을 보았다. 그녀의 선생님은 나중에 그녀가 뚱한 표정의 학생들을 보았을 때 의욕이 꺾이는 것을 느꼈다고 인정했다. Jimin은 수업을 중단할까 생각했지만, 그것은 선택사항이 아니라는 것을 깨달았다. 그래서 그녀는 참아보기로 결정했다. Jimin의 첫 과제는 자기소개를 하는 것이었다. 그녀는 이 과제를 하면서 그녀의 가장 좋아하는 과목을 떠올렸고 해양 생물학에 흠뻑 빠져있는 이유를 분명히 알게 되었다. 그녀가 연설을 할 때, 좋아하는 과목에 대한 흥분으로 그녀의 불안감을 잊었다. 그녀의 연설이 완벽하지는 않았지만, 그녀는 몇 가지 것들은 상당히 잘했다. 그녀는 다른 학생들이 자신에 대해 알 수 있도록 도왔고, 바다의 운명에 대해 수업시간에 했던 한 유용하고 설득력 있는 연설로 존경을 받았다. 그녀는 반 친구들이 그녀가 했던 연설에 대해 긍정적으로 토론해 주었을 때 기뻤다. 그녀는 반 친구들의 연설을 들으면서, 수업을 즐기기 시작하고 있다는 것을 깨달았다. 몇몇 연설은 매우 흥미로웠고, 그녀는 연설에서 무엇이 좋았고 향상된 것은 무엇인지에 대한 토론에 참여하였다. "돌처럼 굳은 얼굴"은 서서히 사라져갔고 그들이 가지고 있었던 진정한 인간의 모습을 드러냈다.」

38 해설 ① 수업을 듣기 전에는 연설에 자신이 없었다.
② 첫 과제로 자기소개를 했다.
③ 첫 발표 준비를 하면서 해양 생물학이 좋은 이유를 분명하게 알게 되었다.
④ 첫 발표를 하는 동안 발표에 대한 불안감을 잊었다.

39 해설 ⓐ는 Jimin의 선생님을 가리키며, 나머지는 Jimin을 가리킨다.

rationality 순리성, 합리성, 합리적인 행동 / calculation 계산, 산출, 추정 / underlie 기저를 이루다 / if so 그렇다면 / explanation 해설, 이유, 설명 / exploit 부당하게 이용하다, 착취하다, 활용하다 / incompetence 무능, 무능함 / awkward 어색한, 거북한 / thieving 도둑질, 절도 / proposition 제의, 문제 / rational 합리적인, 이성적인 / shoplifter 가게 좀도둑 / roundly 강력하게, 대대적으로

「(A) 합리성과 계산이 경제적 행동의 기저를 이룬다는 것은 강조되어 왔다. 그렇다면, 왜 많은 가격이 0.99달러로 끝나는가? 고객들은 정말 18.99달러가 단 18달러와 같다고 생각하는 것인가? 이러한 가격은 무능함을 이용하기 위해서가 아니라 부정행위와 싸우기 위해 설계된 것이라고 설명할 수 있을 것이다.

(D) 전형적인 가게는 많은 좀도둑질을 경험할 것이다. 계산원보다 좀도둑질로 이익을 얻을 수 있는 위치는 아무도 없다. 만일 책들 – 또는 어떤 제품들 – 은 10달러, 15달러, 20달러로 크게 가격이 붙어 있고, 그러면 고객들은 종종 정확한 양의 가격을 낸다.

(C) 이러한 경우, 계산원들이 금전등록기에 그것을 기록하지 않고 물건을 포장해서, 돈을 주머니에 넣는 것은 간단하다. 책은 고객들에 의해 도난당한 것처럼 보일 것이다. 이것은 훔친 책을 판매하는 것보다 훨씬 더 매력적인 제안이며, 적발될 위험도 더 적을 것이다. 합리적인 좀도둑들은 가게에서 직업을 구하기를 원할 것이다.

(B) 그러나, 가격 책정이 더 어설플수록 도둑질하는 계산원이 속임수를 사용할 수는 없을 것 같다. 고객이 거스름돈을 원할 것이므로 출납원이 이 거스름 돈을 착복할 가능성은 적다. 계산원은 정확한 교환을 위해 금전 등록기를 통해 그 품목을 기록해야만 한다.」

40 해설 (A)에서 가격이 .99로 끝나는 이유에 대해 문제를 제시하고 가격이 떨어질 경우 (D)에서 좀도둑질을 할 수 있는 가능성을 말하고 있다. (C)는 (D)를 구체화하였으며, (B)에서 .99로 끝나는 경우 좀도둑질이 줄어들 수 있다고 하고 있다.

41 보기 ① 세금 포함
② 판매 촉진
③ 부정직과의 싸움
④ 거스름돈 갖기
⑤ 더욱 많은 직업 창출

dolphin 돌고래 / intelligence 지능 / alike 비슷한, 비슷하게 / whistle 호루라기, 호각 / nevertheless 그럼에도 불구하고 / pod (물개·고래 등의) 작은 떼, 무리

「돌고래에 관한 많은 과학 연구들은 돌고래들이 생각하고, 이해하고, 물체에 대해 빠르게 배우는 것이 가능해 보인다는 것을 밝혀왔다. 그러면, 그들은 인간만큼 지적이거나, 고양이 혹은 강아지보다 지적인가? 돌고래는 사람들이 하는 것과는 다르게 그들의 두뇌를 사용한다. 그러나, 과학자들은 돌고래의 지능과 인간의 지능이 어떤 면에서는 매우 유사하다고 말한가? 어떻게?

인간과 마찬가지로, 모든 돌고래들은 자신의 "이름"을 갖는다. 이 이름은 특별한 호각이다. 각각의 돌고래는 이 특별한 호각을 보통 첫 번째 생일쯤에 스스로 선택한다. 실제로 과학자들은 사람과 마찬가지로 돌고래가 그들의 나이, 그들의 감정, 또는 음식을 찾는 것 등과 같이 많은 것들에 대해 서로 "이야기"를 한다고 생각한다. 게다가, 인간과 마찬가지로, 돌고래는 대화를 하기 위해 소리 체계와 몸짓 언어를 사용한다. 그럼에도 불구하고, 그들의 대화를 이해하는 것은 인간에게 쉽지 않다. 아직 "돌고래의 말"을 하는 사람은 없지만, 몇몇 과학자들이 배우려고 시도 중이다. 돌고래들은 또한 사회적 동물이다. 그들은 pods라고 불리는 집단 내에서 살며 사람과 마찬가지로 종종 다른 떼의 다른 돌고래들과 게임을 하고 놀이를 한다. 사실, 함께 노는 것은 지능을 가진 동물들만이 할 수 있는 것이다. 돌고래와 인간은 다른 면에서도 유사하다 : 둘 다 원하는 것을 얻기 위한 계획을 세운다.

예를 들어, 브라질 남해의 돌고래는 음식을 얻기 위해 흥미로운 전략을 사용한다. 물고기가 배 근처에 있을 때, 돌고래는 어부에게 물에 그물을 던지라는 신호를 보낸다. 이러한 수단을 사용하여 어부들은 많은 물고기를 잡을 수 있다. 무엇이 돌고래에게 이점인가? 왜 돌고래들은 사람을 도와주는 것일까? 어부는 그들이 잡은 고기 중 일부를 돌고래에게 나눠준다.」

42 해설 '과학자들은 돌고래의 지능이 인간과 어떤 면에서는 유사하다고 말한다.'고 본문에 제시되어 있다.
보기 ① 돌고래는 인간이 가장 좋아하는 동물이다.
② 돌고래는 독립적으로 살아가는 경향이 있다.
③ 돌고래는 매우 지능적이라고 입증되었다.
④ 돌고래는 많은 다른 기후에서 산다.
⑤ 돌고래는 물고기를 잡기 위한 특별한 방법을 가지고 있다.

43 해설 돌고래들은 첫 번째 생일 즈음에 스스로 이름을 선택하며, 소리 체계와 몸짓 언어를 사용해 이야기한다. 또 '돌고래 말을 하는 사람은 없지만 과학자들이 배우려고 시도 중이며 물고기를 얻기 위해 어부가 고기 잡는 것을 돕는다.
보기 ① 돌고래는 어미로부터 이름을 얻는다.
② 돌고래는 많은 것들에 대해 이야기하기 위해 언어를 사용한다.
③ 돌고래는 호각을 불지만, 몸짓 언어는 사용하지 않는다.
④ 돌고래 대화는 인간이 이해하기에 쉽다.
⑤ 돌고래는 그들의 무리를 보호하기 위해 어부가 고기 잡는 것을 돕는다.

psychologist 심리학자 / set out 시작하다, 착수하다 / abandoned 버려진, 유기된 / suburban 교외의, 따분한 / secretly 몰래, 숨어서 / stripper 스트리퍼, 페인트 등을 긁어내는 도구 / lookout 망보는 사람 / glove compartment 수납함 / handed 손을 사용하는, 도움의 손길을 주는 / radiator 방열기, 냉각기 / destructive 파괴적인 / vandalize 공공기물을 파손하다 / seemingly 외견상으로 보기에는, 보아하니 / hunk 덩이, 조각 / in contrast ~와 대조하여 / passerby 통행인, 지나가는 사람 / crucial 중대한, 결정적인

「사회 심리학자 Philip Zimbardo는 한 가지 이론을 실험에 착수했다. 그는 다른 두 지역에 버려진 자동차를 준비했다 : 뉴욕시와 캘리포니아의 가장 작은 시골 마을인 팰러 앨토에. 차의 번호 표지판은 제거되고 차의 후드는 버려졌다는 신호를 보내기 위해 올려졌다. 그리고 각각의 차들은 64시간 동안 비밀리에 관찰되었다. 뉴욕시의 차를 관찰하는 임무를 할당받은 사람은 오래 기다리지 않았다. 10분이 안되어서 차는 첫 번째 약탈자인 아빠, 엄마, 8살 난 아들을 맞이했다. 엄마는 망보는 역할을 했고, 아들은 아빠가 트렁크, 수납함, 그리고 엔진을 찾는 것을 도왔다. 그는 그리고 나서 배터리와 방열기를 제거하는 데 필요한 도구를 그의 아빠에게 건넸다. 파괴하는 데 걸린 총 시간은 7분이었다. 하지만 이것은 첫 번째 시도이다. 64시간의 마지막쯤에, 차는 24번 파손되었는데, 주로 잘 차려입고, 보기에는 중산층으로 보이는 어른들에 의해서였다. 실험이 끝나고 남아 있는 것은 쓸모없는 철 덩어리였다. 이와 대조적으로, 팰러 앨토의 차에 접근한 것은 단 한 번이었다. 비가 내리기 시작했을 때, 지나가던 사람이 차의 후드를 내리기 위해 멈췄을 때였다. Zimbardo에 따르면, 두 차량의 다른 양상의 중요한 요인은 익명성이라고 한다. 대도시에서, 밖에서 자신의 이웃에게 인식될 가능성은 극히 적어서, 정직한 시민들이 일시적으로 도둑 또는 공공기물파손자로 변한다. 반면, 작은 마을에서 인식되고 잡힐 가능성이 더 높은 사람들은 정직함을 지킨다.」

44 [해설] 두 지역에서 차이가 나는 이유가 'recognized'라고 뒷 문장에서 나타난다.
[보기] ① 익명성 ② 호기심 ③ 불복종, 반항, 거역 ④ 탐욕 ⑤ 과신

45 [해설] 각각의 차들은 64시간 동안 관찰되었고, 뉴욕시에서 한 가족이 자동차를 파괴했지만 다른 곳으로 몰지는 않았다. 이 중 감시자는 엄마였다. 작은 마을에서는 인식되거나 잡힐 확률이 높아서 정직을 고수한다.
[보기] ① 뉴욕시에서 Philip Zimbardo의 실험은 단 10분만에 끝났다.
② 뉴욕시에서, 자동차를 긁어내는 한 가족은 버려진 차를 다른 곳으로 몰았다.
③ 뉴욕시에서, 자동차를 긁어내는 가족의 아들은 누가 다가오는지 감시한다.
④ 팰러 앨토에서, 보행자는 비가 올 때 버려진 자동차의 후드를 닫았다.
⑤ 작은 도시의 시민들은 그들의 사회적 지위와 상관없이 범죄를 저지른다고 입증 받았다.

ANSWER

01	02	03	04	05	06	07	08	09	10	11	12	13	14	15	16	17	18	19	20
②	③	④	③	②	④	③	④	④	②	⑤	③	①	②	①	②	⑤	⑤	②	⑤
21	22	23	24	25	26	27	28	29	30	31	32	33	34	35	36	37	38	39	40
⑤	④	③	③	①	①	③	②	⑤	⑤	①	③	②	⑤	③	③	①	④	①	③
41	42	43	44	45															
④	⑤	①	⑤	①															

01 어휘 runny nose 콧물이 나는 코 / hack 난도질하다

해설 ③ 누워서 조금 쉬라고 했으므로, ② that he get some rest가 맞다

보기 ① 스미스 의사 선생님을 방문할 것
③ 주사 맞을 것
④ 병원 갈 것
⑤ 약 먹을 것

해석 Julie : 너 몸 되게 안 좋아 보여. 무슨 일 있어?

Frank : 콧물이 나고 자꾸 기침 나고, 그리고 머리가 너무 아파. 병원 가야 될 것 같아.

Julie : 약은 먹었어?

Frank : 아직, 스미스 선생님께 진료 받으려고 해.

Julie : 그냥 감기면 굳이 병원 갈 필요는 없어. 차라리 누워서 조금 쉬는 게 어때? 내가 차 끓여줄게. 금방 괜찮아질 거야.

02 어휘 vehicle 탈 것 / public transportation 대중교통 / senior 고령자의

해설 ③ ⓑ 뒷부분에 가격 이야기가 나오므로 빈 칸에 임대료를 물어보는 것이 자연스럽다.
ⓒ 뒷부분에 차가 없다는 이야기가 나오므로 빈 칸에 대중교통을 물어보는 것이 자연스럽다.
ⓐ 다음 문장에 이웃들의 특징에 대해 설명해주므로 빈 칸에 이웃들에 대하여 물어보는 것이 자연스럽다.
ⓔ 다음 문장에 날짜에 대해 언급하므로 빈 칸에 언제 입주하냐고 물어보는 것이 자연스럽다.

해석 Gary : 나 이 아파트 마음에 들어요. 임대료가 어떻게 되죠? 비싸 보이네요.

Landlord : 그렇게 비싸지는 않아요. 한 달에 950 달러에요.

Gary : 대중교통은 어때요? 저는 차가 없어서요.

Landlord : 두 블록 쯤 나가면 버스 정류장 있어요. 편리하죠.

Gary : 이웃들은요? 저는 좀 조용하신 분들이면 좋겠어요.

Landlord : 대부분 노인분들이라 일찍 주무세요. 그건 걱정하지 않으셔도 될거예요.

Gary : 좋아요. 계약하죠. 언제 들어오면 되죠?

Landlord : 청소할 시간 며칠만 주세요.

03 해설 ④ Jane의 네 번째 말에서 알 수 있다.

보기 ① 선물을 교환한다.
② Tom의 형 생일파티에 간다.
③ Tom의 처남 생일파티에 간다.
⑤ Tom과 Jane의 결혼기념일 파티에 간다.

해석 Tom : 자기야, 아직 멀었어?
Jane : 방금 선물 골랐어. 이게 부모님 마음에 들까? 다른 걸로 바꾸는 게 나을까?
Tom : 아냐, 좋아하실 거야. 그리고 우리 시간도 없잖아. 30분 이내로 도착해야 하는데 지금 시간에 교통 상황 최악이야. 서둘러
Jane : 진정해. 우리 늦어도 아무도 뭐라고 하지 않을 거야. 부모님 결혼기념일은 매년마다 있는걸!
Tom : 나도 알아, 그렇지만 40주년 기념일은 큰 행사잖아. 그리고 늦으면 너희 오빠가 엄청 화내실걸? 이 파티 준비하느라 제일 고생하셨잖아.

04 어휘 excitement 흥분 / best-looking 잘생긴

보기 ① Mike와 Sarah는 두 달 안에 아이를 출산할 것이다.
② Mike는 그들의 아이가 똑똑할 것이라 믿는다.
③ Mike와 Sarah는 아이의 성별에 대해 생각이 다르다.
④ Mike는 아빠가 되기를 고대하고 있다.
⑤ Sarah는 딸을 원한다.

해석 Sarah : 우리가 두 달 있으면 부모가 된다는 게 믿겨져?
Mike : 나 너무 흥분돼서 벽도 뚫어버릴 것 같아. 우리의 아기 아인슈타인이 빨리 나왔으면!
Sarah : 잠깐만, 우리 아기가 정말 천재일 거라고 생각해? 그리고 만약에 여자아이면 어떡해?
Mike : 자기야 그거는 당연히, 난 아빠니까 우리 아이가 세상에서 가장 똑똑한 아기일 거라고 믿는 거지. 그리고 내 느낌에 아들 같아! 그리고 엄마의 미모를 닮아서 가장 잘생긴 아이가 되겠지?
Sarah : 아냐, 당신 틀렸어. 나는 우리 아이에게 예쁜 분홍 아가 옷을 사주고 싶어. 그리고 나를 닮아 아주 아름 다운 아기가 되겠지.

05 어휘 good shape 몸매가 좋은 몸 / diabetes 당뇨병

해설 친구가 당뇨의 위험에 대해 걱정했고, 이를 받아들이고 있으므로, '네 말이 맞아. 나 오늘부터 운동해야겠어.'라 는 뜻의 ②가 맞다.

보기 ① 좋은 생각이야. 피자 시키자.
③ 아니, 아내는 몸매가 좋아.
④ 나 어릴 때 운동선수였어.
⑤ 그렇게 먹어야한다고 생각하지 않아.

해석 Dave : 아내가 나보고 살 빼라고 구박했어. 내 생각에는 몸매 괜찮은 것 같은데 말이야. 네 생각은 어때?
Brett : 몇 파운드 정도만 빼는 게 어때? 우리 나이가 젊은 것도 아니잖아. 그리고 너희 아버지 당뇨이시지 않았 어? 네가 관리 제대로 안하면 남들보다 몇 배는 더 병 걸릴 확률이 높아.
Dave : 맞는 말이네. 우리 아버지 살찌셨을 때, 당뇨가 여러 건강 문제들을 발생시켰지. 몇 년이나 병원에 계셔 야했어.
Brett : 그것 봐. 아내 말 듣는 게 나을 것 같아. 아내가 현명하시네.

06 어휘 couple of months 몇 달간 / maintenance 관리 / tune-up 정비

해설 자동차에서 이상한 소리가 나서 점검을 받기 위해 이곳으로 왔다. 답은 ④ 자동차 정비소이다.

<보기> ① 경찰서
② 치과
③ 철물점
⑤ 컴퓨터 수리점

<해석> Joe : 문제가 뭐야?
Bob : 몇 달째 이상한 소음을 내고 있어.
Joe : 몇 달씩이나! 좀 더 일찍 오지 그랬어? 문제가 무엇이든, 심각한 손상이 있었을 거야.
Bob : 적절한 관리를 신경 쓸 여유가 없었어. 계속 운전해야 했거든.
Joe : 관리를 신경 쓰는 게 가장 우선순위가 되었어야지. 마지막으로 오일 바꾸고 정비 받은 게 언제야?
Bob : 글쎄, 3년 전부터 한 번도 안 한 것 같은데?
Joe : 세상에나!

07 <어휘> hail 우박 / armory 무기고 / meteorologist 기상학자

<해설> 다른 it은 모두 우박을 가리킨다. 그러나 ③의 it은 thunderstorm을 가리킨다.

<해석> 우박은 자연의 무기 중 가장 잔인하고 예측 불가능한 장치이다. 우박은 순식간에 수확에 대한 농부의 기대를 짓밟을 수 있다. 그 주변 논밭은 파괴하지 않고서 말이다. 우박 때문에 평야의 양 떼가 다친 후에 다시 햇살이 밝게 비치는 날이 될 수도 있다. 기상학자들은 천둥번개보다도 우박이 더 교묘하다고 말한다. 물론, 천둥번개에 대한 기상예보도 어렵지만 적어도 천둥번개가 발생하면 어디로 갈지, 얼마나 지속될지는 알 수 있다. 그러나 우박 같은 경우에는 땅에 떨어진 후에 그 크기에 대해서나 조사 가능할 뿐이다. 더구나 우박은 기상학자가 조사하려 보관하는 즉시 녹기 시작하기 때문에 조사도 어렵다. 우박이 어떻게 형성되었는가도 확실히 단정 짓기 어려우니 우박이 언제 어디서 떨어질지 예측하기란 매우 힘들다.

08 <어휘> disturb 혼란스럽게 하다 / out-of-date 구식의 / exasperate 분노하게 하다 / unflatter 변형하지 않다

<해설> 인터넷이 잘못된 정보로 가득 차 있고, 한 번 웹상에 오른 정보는 계속 인터넷에 남아 지워지지 않는다는 것이 글의 주 내용이다. ④는 내용과 관련 없는 인터넷의 부작용을 언급하고 있다.

<해석> 인터넷이 구식 정보, 모순되고 부정확한 자료들로 가득 차 있다는 것은 매우 혼란스러운 진실이다. 소문은 부풀려지고, 믿을만한 사이트들은 사실과 자료를 갱신하는 데 굼뜨다. 정보 제공자와 수용자 모두가 이로 인해 분노한다. 어떤 사람들은 더 큰 문제는 오래되고 변형되지 않은 사진들이 인터넷 검색 엔진에서 그대로 제공된다는 것이라 지적한다. 웹상에서 조작된 부정적이고 거짓된 정보들을 좇아 없애기란 쉬운 일이 아니다. (인터넷은 사람들이 정보를 찾는 다양한 시각을 축소시키고 있다. 돈이 많든 적든, 훌륭한 문학 지식이 있든 없든 모두 똑같은 결과를 얻는 것이다.) 친구의 어릴적 사진들이 아직도 인터넷 상에서 검색되는 것이다.

09 <어휘> improvement 개선 / billion 십억 / toxic 독성의

<해설> DIY의 성과에 대한 글이다. ④ DIY로 인한 건강 문제 우려는 글과 무관하다.

<해석> 집안 꾸미기를 위한 DIY 사업이 미국 시장에서 매년 2조의 수입을 거두고 있다. 집이 훨씬 적고 가구가 드물게 배치되는 일본의 경우도 300억 이상의 수입을 거뒀고, 독일에서 DIY 회사들은 330억을 벌었다. 이전과 비교했을 때 이는 놀라운 성과이다. 2008년에 텔레비전 DIY 프로그램이 인기를 끌면서 이 사업은 빠르게 성장하기 시작했다. (DIY 제품들은 독성물질들을 포함하기 때문에 유아에게 건강 이상을 유발할 확률이 높다.) 영국에서는 DIY 사용자들에게 쉽고 간편한 도움말을 주는 Changing Rooms and Ground Force라는 프로그램이 높은 시청률을 기록했다.

10 <어휘> isolate 격리하다 / colleague 동료 / personnel 직원

<해설> 6번째 줄 이후의 내용을 확인한다. 체육관 건설이 직원의 건강과 회사의 단합을 위해 좋다는 근거를 들어 체육관 건설을 주장하고 있다

해석 큰 회사에서 일하는 것은 오히려 격리된 삶을 조장한다. 다른 운 좋은 회사원들처럼, 현장에 나갈 수 있다면 우리는 활동적으로 새로운 사람을 만나고 돌아다닐 것이다. 그러나 사무직 직원이기 때문에, 우리는 지하주차장에 차를 세우고 사무실로 엘리베이터를 타고 올라와 하루 종일 일할 좁은 책상으로 향할 뿐이다. 식당이 만남의 장소일 수 있겠지만, 대부분의 직원들은 같은 사무실 직원들과 함께 모여 앉는다. 체육관을 건설하는 것은 나이와 배경이 다른 다양한 부서 사람들과의 편안한 만남을 가능케 할 것이다. 만약 체육관을 지을 생각이 있다면, 지금은 창고로 쓰이는 지하실 뒷방이 적절할 것이다. 아니면 잘 이용되지 않는 10층 라운지도 괜찮다. 체육관에 대한 투자는 직원의 건강뿐만 아니라 회사의 단합을 위해서도 큰 가치가 있을 것이다.

11 어휘 roughly 대략 / definitive 명확한 / motivation 동기

해설 ⑤ '예측이 믿을 만하지 않다면'의 의미로, 'relying'으로 고쳐 쓰는 것이 옳다.
① 'turn out + to be + 형용사'의 형태로, '~이 밝혀지다'의 의미이다.
④ '지각동사 + 목적어 + 동사원형'의 형태로, '포장마차의 벨소리를 듣다'는 의미이다.

해석 미래에 대한 정확한 예견은 불가능할 지라도, 일상의 경험으로 어떤 일이 일어날 것인지 대략 추측하는 것은 가능하다. 과거부터 미래까지 지속되는 일정한 형식이 존재하지 않는다면, 인간을 포함한 어떤 동물도 지구상에 존재하기 어렵다. 크든 작든 끊임없이 결정을 내릴 때, 우리는 인간 행동의 동기가 무엇이었고 과거 사건들이 어떠한 공통 형식이 있었는지를 기본으로 생각한다. 절대적인 법칙은 없다. 그러나 가능성과 경향성은 존재한다. 예를 들어, 우리 동네에 수요일마다 어김없이 fish-and-chip 포장마차가 벨을 울리며 온다면, 수요일에 우리는 그 포장마차를 기다릴 것이다. 과거 경험에서 비롯된 예측들마저 신뢰할 수 없다면, 우리는 밥 먹는 것부터 게임을 하는 것, 자전거를 타는 사소한 일까지 확신을 할 수가 없을 것이다.

12 어휘 sail 나아가다, 항해하다 / figure 인물 / humanize 고상하게 만들다

해설 ③ He is even one of only two people 과 the United States honors him by name ~의 합성으로 목적격 관계대명사가 생략되며 한 문장이 되었다. 따라서 him은 삭제하는 것이 옳다.
② '다른 어떤 인물보다도'의 의미로, any 뒤에는 단수명사가 맞다.
④ '사실상'의 뜻으로, 문장 전체를 받아 부사를 쓰는 것이 맞다.

해석 '1492년, Columbus는 청해를 향해 나아갔다.' 모든 미국 어린이들은 이 운율을 알 것이다. 미국 교과서는 미국 역사상 다른 어떤 인물보다 Christopher Columbus를 부각시켜 다루고 있다. 교과서에서, 그는 미국의 훌륭한 영웅인양 묘사되고 있다. 사람을 이름을 딴 국가기념일이 미국에 단 두 개 있는데, 그 중 하나 역시도 Columbus이다. 그러나 모든 교과서가 그에 대해 설명하고 모든 아이들이 1492년을 기억함에도 불구하고, Columbus와 유럽 개척자들이 아메리카에 저지른 잔혹한 일들은 교과서에 하나도 설명되지 않았다. 교과서들은 좋은 이야기들만 아름답게 꾸며내어 Columbus를 고상하게 보이게 하였고, 이러한 과정을 통해 독자가 그와 동화되도록 유도했다.

13 어휘 evidence 증거 / composition 구성물질 / orbit 궤도

해설 (A) 달로부터 표본이 수집되어야 하는 것이므로 수동형인 'collected'가 맞다 (B) '현재의 이론'이라는 뜻이 되어야 하므로 형용사인 'current'가 맞다. (C) 본래 뒷 문장은 'The moon was formed from an iron-free outer layer'이므로 'from which'가 맞다.

해석 이제 과학자들은 달이 초록 치즈로 만들어졌다는 오래된 미신이 사실이 아니라는 증거를 확보했으므로, 관심을 달의 구성 물질에서 달의 생성 기원으로 돌리고 있다. 초기 이론 중 하나는 달이 지구와 동일한 시기에, 같은 구성 요소들로 생성되었을 것이라 추측한다. 달의 정찰정이 달 표면에서 추출한 표본들을 확인했을 때, 지구의 가장 흔한 구성성분인 철이 달에서는 관찰되지 않았다. 현재의 이론은 지구가 타 행성과 충돌했을 때 튀어나온 파편이 궤도를 벗어나 달을 형성했다고 말한다. 달에 철 성분이 없는 것에 대해서는, 지구의 철성분이 핵심부에 집중되어 있어 바깥쪽에는 철 성분이 없는 부분이 형성되었고, 바로 여기에서 분리되어 나온 것이 달이라고 설명한다.

14 어휘 security 보안 / employ 이용하다 / plainclothes 사복의

해설 (A) 목적어 'such cameras'를 취해야하므로 동명사 형태의 'employing'이 맞다. (B) '자격을 갖춘 사람'이라는 뜻으로 수동형인 'qualified'가 맞다. (C) 'is watching the moniters'의 주어가 필요하므로 'whoever'가 맞다.

해석 감시카메라는 보안 분야에 있어서 가장 획기적인 발명품 중 하나이다. 이것은 '하늘에 있는 눈'이고 '등 뒤에 있는 눈'이다. 감시카메라는 거의 모든 장소에서 다양하게 이용된다. 백화점, 도서관, 학교, 은행 그리고 심지어는 거리에도 카메라가 설치되어 있다. 어떤 이들은 감시카메라가 사생활을 침해한다고 주장한다. 그러나 감시카메라를 설치하는 것은 분명 장점이 많다. 다른 어떤 방법보다도 감시카메라의 설치는 범죄의 방지와 범죄인의 체포에 효과적이다. 문제점이라면 오직 카메라 감시자가 충분한 자격을 갖춘 사람이어야 한다는 것이다. 감시되는 매 구역을 훈련된 사복 경찰들이 번갈아가며 경계해야 효과적으로 작동할 수 있다. 누가 모니터를 지켜보고 있든 그들은 긴밀하게 협력하며 감시를 진행한다.

15 어휘 admission 허가 / trap 덫 / mundane 일상적인 / embellish 꾸며내다

해설 경험과 교훈을 꾸며내어 멋 부릴 것이 아니라 사실에 기반을 둔 글을 써야한다는 것이 글의 주제이다. 보기 중에서는 '과장하기'라는 뜻의 ①이 맞다.

보기 ② 개인화하기
③ 재조직하기
④ 평가절하하기
⑤ 단순화하기

해석 학생의 경험과 경력을 보여 줄 대학 지원 에세이를 쓸 때 중요한 것은 경험과 그를 통해 얻은 교훈을 과장하지 않는 것이다. 대신, 평범한 경험 속에서도 비판적으로 교훈을 찾고 그 경험이 왜 특별했는가를 명확히 표현해내야 한다. 진실에 기반을 두지 않은 과장과 허풍의 복잡한 문장은 피해라. 스스로를 뽐내려 들수록, 감독관의 눈에는 더 거만해 보인다. '진실에 기반을 둔 글쓰기'를 할 때, 경험을 꾸며내지 않고서도 인상 깊은 에세이를 쓸 수 있을 것이다.

16 어휘 on-the-spot 현장에서의 / audible 들을 수 있는 / accompany 수반하다

해설 뮤직비디오는 영상 위에 음악이 덧입혀지기 때문에 소리를 찍을 필요가 없다. 따라서 ② '소리가 아닌 영상을 찍는다'가 맞다.

보기 ① 촬영 중 정숙한다
③ 다른 예술 장르를 합친다
④ 생생한 음악을 듣는다
⑤ 원하는 음악가를 고용한다

해석 영화를 찍는 것에 비해 뮤직비디오를 찍는 것은 소리가 아닌 영상만 찍는다는 대단한 장점을 가진다. 패션 사직작가가 모델에게 끊임없이 포즈를 요구하는 것처럼, 뮤직비디오 감독은 연기자에게 연기를 주문한다. 카메라를 통해서 사람들은 현장감을 느껴 감독이 지시하는 사항들을 직접 수행하려 들기도 한다. 촬영장에 있을 때 현장감은 증폭된다. 뮤직비디오의 한 장면에서 기타 연주자가 음을 잘못 짚었다고 해서, 감독이 '컷'을 외치고 재촬영할 필요는 없다. 뮤직비디오 영상 촬영이 끝나면 그 위에 음악이 덮히기 때문에 뮤직비디오 감독은 이미 녹음된 음악과 함께 할 이미지들을 만들어내기만 하면 되는 것이다.

17 어휘 dismay 경악, 당황 / overturn 뒤집어엎다 / hazardous 위험한

해설 상급심이 하급심의 판결을 뒤집어엎었다고 했다. 즉, 기업이 무죄라 판결한 것이다. 따라서 ⑤ '기업은 책임이 없다'가 맞다.

보기 ① 본래 판결이 유지되다
② 보상금으로 사망이 무마되다
③ 미래에는 이러한 홍수가 예측 가능하다
④ 보다 엄격한 채굴 기준이 제정되다

해석 1987년 한 광산 업체는 Montana 지방 샛강 상부의 급경사 지대에 서식하는 식생들을 12 에이커 정도 제거했다. 그러자 홍수가 발생해 채굴 파편들이 거대한 강물 속으로 유입되었다. 홍수로 실종된 사람은 없었지만, 물의 범람은 계곡의 집들을 파괴했다. 계곡 근처 주민들은 광산 업체에 소송을 제기하였고 승소하여 상당한 보상금을 받아내었다. 그러나 기업은 하급심의 판결을 항소하여 사건을 보다 기업에 우호적인 상급법원으로 보냈다. 주민들은 경악했다. 처음의 판결이 뒤집어진 것이다. 법원은 토양 성분과 뿌리 뽑힌 나무들, 바위 조각들은 본래 무해한 것이라고 선언했다. 그저 홍수가 왔기 때문에 위험해진 것이다. 결국 법원은 기업은 주민의 피해에 책임이 없다고 선언했다.

18 **어휘** publicity 명성, 인지도 / affiliate 회원이 되다, 회원으로 참여하다 / ambush 잠복

해설 경기장 관중석에 똑같은 미니스커트를 입은 36명의 여성들이 등장하는 것은 사람들의 시선을 끈다. 'Ambush marketting'은 이를 노린다. 따라서 ⑤ '큰 행사 진행 중에 상품에 이목을 집중시킨다'가 맞다.

보기 ① 제품을 크게 할인해준다
② 상대 회사의 이미지를 악화시킨다
③ 제품 광고 예산을 증대시킨다
④ 행사에 공동 후원을 한다.

해석 중요 행사에 대한 후원은 중요한 사업이다. 그러나 공식 후원사가 아님에도 중요 행사로부터 사업 이익을 얻고 싶다면 어떻게 할 것인가? 간단하다! 'Ambush marketing'을 하면 되는 것이다. 'Ambush marketing'은 중요 행사가 진행되는 중에 제품에 대한 관심을 얻는 것을 뜻한다. 맥주 회사 A가 큰 스포츠 행사를 후원한다고 가정해보자. 막대한 돈을 투자한 대가로, 그 회사는 행사에 참여할 권리를 얻게 된다. 맥주 회사 B 역시도 행사에 참여하기를 원한다. 그러나 그 비용은 지불하고 싶지 않다. 인지도를 얻으려면, 카메라와 대중들의 눈길을 끌 획기적인 무언가가 필요하다. 그들은 이벤트를 잠복시킨다. 최근 'Ambush marketing' 대표적 사례는 월드컵 매치에서 확인할 수 있다. 독일의 한 맥주 회사는 36명의 어리고 매력적인 여성들에게 회사 로고가 그려진 미니스커트를 입혀 관중석에 앉아있도록 했다. 카메라들이 그 여성들을 찍었고, 그들의 로고를 전 세계에 광고했다. 큰돈을 들이지 않으면서 회사는 귀중한 마케팅 기회를 얻어내었다.

19 **어휘** primate 영장류 / dominance 지배 / chip 깎다, 조각하다

해설 사람들이 가까이 올 것을 미리 예측하여 기다리고 있던 침팬지에 대한 설명이다. ② '미래에 대한 계획을 세우다'가 맞다.

보기 ① 다른 이들과 공유하다
③ 감사를 표현하다
④ 분노를 조절하다
⑤ 배우자를 위해 먹이를 모으다

해석 스웨덴의 한 동물원에 있는 똑똑한 침팬지는 사람이 아닌 영장류도 미래에 대한 계획을 세울 수 있다는 것을 보여주었다. 최근 몇 년 동안, 수컷 침팬지 Santino는 매일 오전 11시에 고함을 치고 뛰어다니는 지배의 과시적 표현을 해왔다. 이 것 말고도 이 침팬지는 관광객들에게 놀라운 광경을 보여줬다. 직원들은 이른 아침 침팬지가 그의 서식지 주변에 해자를 두르고 둥근 원반 모양이 되도록 그 서식지를 조각하는 것을 발견했다. Santino는 몇 시간이고 관광객들이 다가올 때까지 기다렸다. 그들이 다가오자 침팬지는 쌓아올린 더미들을 그들을 향해 날렸다.

20 **어휘** temperature 온도 / revolt -에 반하다, 반항하다 / liquid 액체

해설 ⑤ (A) 액체를 끓여 기체를 얻는 방법이므로 '증류'라는 뜻의 'distillation'이 맞다. (B) 증류를 통해 액체 속 여러 화학물질들을 분리시키므로 'seperate out the chemicals'가 맞다.

보기 ① 혼합 …… 다양한 요소들을 섞는다

② 합금 …… 두 개의 다른 금속을 합한다

③ 정제 …… 찌꺼기로부터 물을 추출한다

④ 살균 …… 박테리아를 없앤다

해석 증류는 화학에서 가장 흔하게 이용되는 기술이다. 증류를 하기 위해서는 다만 액체가 끓어 기체가 발산될 때까지 기다리기만 하면 된다. 기체가 액체로부터 발생해서 보관용기로 이동하는데, 여기서 기체는 다시 액화된다. 다른 화학물질들은 다른 온도에서 기화되므로, 화학물질들이 복합된 액체를 끓이면 이것들이 차례로 기화할 것이다. 따라서 어떤 물질은 보관용기로 이동한 것이고 어떤 물질은 채 끓지 않아 용기 바닥에 머물러 있을 것이다. 간단히 말하면, 이 기술은 액체가 포함하는 여러 화학물질을 분리하는 데에 이용된다.

21 어휘 hobbyist 취미에 열중인 사람 / gourmet 미식가, 고급음식

해설 문맥상 Famous Amos Chocolate Chip Cookies를 버리는 것이 아니라 사업을 착수하는 것이므로 ⑤ 'abandoned'가 문맥상 맞지 않는 단어이다.

보기 ① 이전에

② 고무시키다. 영감을 주다

③ 도착하다

④ 심각하게

⑤ 버리다

해석 전 세계의 수천가지 작은 사업들은 사실 몇몇 취미에 열중인 사람들이 이전에 그들이 자기 자신을 위해 또는 그들의 친구, 이웃을 위해 만들던 것을 팔기 시작한 것에서 기원한다. 예를 들어 Wally Mos가 그의 고모 Della 에게 영감 받아서 취미로 제빵을 하기 시작했고 친구들과 가족에게 쿠키를 나누어 주었다. 그는 "이것은 사람들이 나를 보았을 때 '안녕'이라고 말하지 않는 지점에 도착했다. 그들은 '내 쿠키 어디 있어?'라고 말했다. 모두들 나에게 쿠키 사업을 해야 한다고 말했다." 라고 말했다. 그는 "그러나 나는 그때 이것을 심각하게 받아들이지 않았다." 라고 덧붙였다. 그가 결국 이 아이디어를 심각하게 받아들였을 때 Wally Mos는 Famous Amos Chocolate Chip Cookies를 버렸고(→ 열었고) 지금은 미국에서 가장 유명한 브랜드들 중 하나이며 고급 쿠키 사업에서 선구적인 힘이다.

22 어휘 seduce 유혹하다 / intoxicate 중독시키다

해설 교사가 학생들과의 친밀감을 중요시 하는 교실은 구조와 규율이 무너져 학생들에게 혼란이 올 수 있으므로 교사는 항상 친절하려고만 해서는 안 되고 적당한 규칙과 규율이 필요하다는 것을 시사하고 있다. 그러므로 ④ '교사는 체계와 규율을 강조할 필요가 있다.'가 맞다.

해석 교사가 항상 친절하려고 노력하는 교실은 어떨까? 우리는 그들을 가르치고 리더십을 보이는 것 보다 학생들과 친구가 되는 것에 더 가치를 두는 교사와 이야기하고 있다. 시작할 때 느낌이 정말로 좋다. 그 아이들은 그들이 어른들과 가지려는 이 조금 더 가까운 관계에 대해 흥미로워 한다. 이 학기의 몇 주 동안에 그들은 이 모든 것에 대해 의구심을 갖기 시작한다. 책임자가 아무도 없는 것처럼 느껴진다. 곧 혼란이 온다. 아이들은 구조와 규율을 원하고 요구한다. 과제는 명확해야 하며 규칙은 집행되어야 한다. 아이들은 어떻게 그것들을 직접적으로 요청해야 하는지 모른다. 약한 시스템에서 그들은 약한 구조와 규율에 유혹 될 수 있고, 이것에 익숙해지며 심지어 이것에 중독될 수 있다. 이 문제가 일어났을 때 교사와 학생들의 궁극적인 딜레마는 그 둘 모두 서로를 돌보지만 그 둘 모두 구조와 규칙을 필요로 한다는 것이다. 확실하게 그것들(규칙과 규율)을 제공하는 것은 학생들의 직업이 아니다.

23 어휘 informative 유용한 정보를 주는 / contract 계약하다 / distinctive 독특한 / comprise 구성되다 / compromise 타협

해설 문맥상 (A)는 독자들을 끌어들인 다는 뜻이므로 attract이고 (B)는 기사들로 구성되었다는 뜻이므로 comprising이고 (C)는 사진, 일러스트 등을 동반한다는 뜻이므로 accompany 이다. 그러므로 정답은 ③이다.

해석 TIME 잡지는 매주 전 세계의 수백만의 사람들이 읽으며 수백 이상이 인정한다. 최근 유용한 정보를 주는 기사들은 미국인들과 미국의 생활에 관심이 있는 사람들의 특정한 관심사의 주제뿐만 아니라 국제적인 흥미의 이슈로 독자들을 끌어당긴다. 원래의 출판물인 TIME이 미국과 이 사람들의 독창적인 관점을 제공하는 것처럼, 이것의 특별판인 TIME: Reaching for Tomorrow는 영어를 쓰는 학생들에게 독특한 읽을 기회를 준다. 이미 TIME 지와 친한 이들은 이것이 43개의 최근 출판된 기사들로 구성된 모두 새로운 호라는 것을 보게 되어 기뻐할 것이다. 그 기사들은 미국에서 생활의 긍정적면과 부정적인 면, 영구적인 면과 일시적인 면 모두를 포함하는 넓은 개요를 주기 위해 선택되었다. 각각의 기사는 간소화 없이 이것의 원래 형식이다. 사진, 일러스트, 차트 그리고 다른 그래픽이 기사에 동반된다.

24 어휘 plunder 약탈하다 / vigilant 바짝 경계하는 / crippled 무능한 / infest 들끓다 / unacquainted 경험이 없는 / nautical 선박의

해설 문맥상 (A)는 바짝 경계하는 이라는 뜻이고 (B)는 번영하다, (C)는 들끓는 이란 뜻이므로 정답은 ③이다.

해석 해적들은 뱃사람들을 천년동안 괴롭혀 왔다. 16, 17세기, Blackbeard와 같은 범법자들이 금과 은을 약탈하며 해로 장식된 섬들을 지배하던 때에 해적행위가 성행하였다. 그러나 해적행위는 점점 더 바짝 경계하는 군인들과 증기기관의 발전 덕분에 다음 세기에 하락하기 시작했다. 그러나 해병 순찰대의 감소와 냉전 종전에 따른 국제 무역의 부흥 가운데, 해적 행위가 특히 홍해와 아라비아 해를 잇는 아시아의 말라카 해협과 아덴만과 같은 좁은 과문에서 번창하였다. 빠른 배와 무시무시한 무기 그리고 고급 기술의 통신 장비를 갖추면서 해적들은 2007년 보고된 강탈 263을 저질렀으며 이것은 소말리아의 무법해안에서 일어난 범죄의 28%를 차지한다. 이 거대한 해안과 무능한 정부를 가진 나라는 해적들이 가장 들끓는 나라이다. 지금은 배들은 해안에서 200해리 멀리서 머물도록 경고 받는다.

25 어휘 feel at ease 마음이 편안하다 / savor 맛보다 / rejoice 기뻐하다

해설 주어진 순간을 감상함으로써 삶의 기쁨을 얻으라는 글의 내용으로 보아 ① "너의 행복한 순간을 찾아라"가 제목으로 가장 적절하다.

보기 ② 당신의 하루를 체계화하라
③ 너무 감성적이지 말라
④ 정착하고 가정을 꾸려라
⑤ 당신의 건강을 돌보아라

해석 긍정적인 감정을 조성하는 한 가지 방법은 그 순간을 음미할 시간을 갖는 것이다. 그저 당신의 하루를 음미할 기회를 제공하는 두세 가지 간단한 활동을 해보아라. 예를 들어 아침에 열 가지를 한 번에 하려고하기보다는, 커피 한잔을 창가로 가져가 당신의 아이들이 뒤뜰에서 노는 모습을 보며 천천히 커피를 마셔보아라. 주위를 둘러보며 그 순간을 음미하라. 이것이 당신의 삶을 바꾸게 될까? 아마도 아니겠지만, 아마도 마음은 편안해질 것이다. 더 쉽게 이러한 것을 할 수 있는 방법은 매 한 시간 중 10초 동안 네가 하고 있는 일을 더 높은 곳에서 바라보는 것이다. 네가 얼마나 멋진 삶을 살고 있는 지 헤아릴 시간을 갖고, 함께 기뻐할 수 있는 누군가와 그 환희를 함께하라. 이것들이 바로 삶에서 좋은 점을 붙잡을 두 가지 방법이다.

26 어휘 life savings 일생 동안 저축한 돈, 노후대비 자금 / paranoid 편집증, 망상 / certificate of deposit 예금 증권 / live off someone 누구에 의존해서 살아가다

해설 값비싼 자동차를 소유하면서 발생한 문제점들과 차를 팔게 된 이후의 좋은 점에 대한 글이므로 ① "더 적은 게 낫다"가 적절한 제목이다.

보기 ② 너의 자동차가 네가 누구인지 말해준다
③ 삶을 간소화해서 지구를 보존하라
④ 누가 경제의 적인가?
⑤ 대중교통 : 자동차 문제의 해결책

해석 내가 열일곱 살이었을 때, 나는 일생동안 모은 돈을 내가 본 가장 멋진 차였던 1969 Chevy Camaro를 사는 데에 썼다. 몇 달 뒤, 쇼핑몰 주차장에서 이것을 도둑맞았다. 경찰이 찾았을 때 이것은 손상돼있었고 아무 바퀴도 없는 채 길에 놓여있었으며 겉칠을 절실히 필요로 하고 있었다. 보험금으로 자동차는 복구되었고 제법 가치 있어졌다. 하지만 이번에는 차가 지나치도록 멋있어보였고, 지난 번 절도로 인해 나는 차를 아무 곳에나 두는 것에 대해 편집증이 생겼다. 이건 더 이상 기본적 교통수단이 아니라 값비싼 골칫덩어리에 불과했다. 난 이것을 꽤 괜찮은 가격에 팔았고, 두 가지 예금 증권에 돈을 넣어두고, 몇 년 뒤 대학원 다닐 때 그 돈에 의지해서 살았다. 오늘날 난 그저 작고 평범한 국산 자동차를 몰고 다니는 모습을 볼 수 있다.

27 **어휘** relief 원조물자 / refugee 난민, 망명자 / unprecedented 전례 없는

해설 여러 국가의 봉사활동을 예시로 보여주고 봉사자들의 사회적 필요성에 대해 강조하고 있으므로 ③ "봉사 활동의 중요성"이 적절하다.

보기 ① 봉사 활동의 불리한 면
② 봉사 활동을 구축하기 위한 어려움
④ 유능한 봉사자가 되는 방법
⑤ 국제적인 봉사 기관의 유형

해석 대한민국에는 대략 6백5십만 명의 거주자들이 봉사를 한다. 그들은 태풍 홍수피해 이후 원조물자를 제공하고, 보살핌이 필요한 고령자들을 돌보고, 고아원에서 아이들과 시간을 보내며 일하고, 탈북자들이 남한 생활에 적응할 수 있도록 가르치기도 한다. 이탈리아에서 봉사자들은 암 환자 간호를 돕고 요양원에서 일한다. 또 전례 없는 홍수가 2002년 독일을 강타했을 때, 수만 명의 봉사자들이 전국적으로 몰려와 넘쳐나는 물과 투쟁했다. 봉사자들은 각 국가의 경제, 사회적 분위기, 전반적인 복지를 위해 반드시 필요한 부분이다. 봉사자들은 필수적인 서비스를 제공하고 공공 부문의 막대한 부담을 경감시킬 뿐만 아니라, 공동체와 협동의 환경을 창조하기까지 한다.

28 **어휘** enticing 유혹적인 / propensity 경향, 습성 / endear 사랑받다 / vermin 해로운 동물(해충 등)

해설 고대 문명지 시절부터 고양이들이 인간들과 상부상조하며 살게 된 내용을 담고 있으므로 ② "고양이들이 가축화된 요인"이 적절하다.

보기 ① 초기 정착자들이 직면한 어려움
③ 고양이의 크기에 가해진 진화의 힘
④ 고양이들이 사냥 기술을 발달시킨 방법
⑤ 고양이와 쥐가 어떻게 천적이 되었는지

해석 9000~10000년 전 비옥한 초승달 지대에의 이른 정착은, 충분히 적응력 있고 호기심 많은 야생 동물 종들에게 완전히 새로운 환경을 형성했다. 이러한 정착지 변두리의 쓰레기 더미들은 고양이들을 크게 유인한 것으로 드러났는데, 고양이들은 쓰레기 자체에서 뿐만 아니라 유혹적인 냄새에 이끌려온 쥐들을 먹을거리로 삼았다. 쥐들은 병을 옮기고 집 모퉁이마다 기어 다니는 습성으로 인해 아마도 사람들에게 사랑받지는 못했던 반면에, 사람들은 훨씬 따뜻한 환영을 받았다. 새끼 고양이들의 타고난 귀여움과, 병을 옮겨 다니는 설치류 또는 혐오스런 뱀 같은 그 지역의 해로운 동물들을 제거하는 데 도움을 주는 그들의 실용적인 도움을 생각하면, 고양이들은 '머무르는' 것이 장려됐다. 이런 적응력과 대담한 천성으로, 새로운 '이웃들'과의 조화로운 관계를 형성하면서, 고양이는 그때부터 사람들의 문명 중심지에 영원히 환영받게 되었다.

29 **어휘** hover 맴돌다 / downtrend 하락세 / take a hit 타격 입다

해설 도표에서 자가용과 소형트럭의 격차는 더 벌어지므로 shrink(줄어들다)가 도표와 일치하지 않는다.

해석 위의 도표는 2007~2010년 캘리포니아 주에서 팔린 소형 트럭과 자가용의 수를 비교하고, 2010년 판매량을 예측하고 있다. 2007년에 두 가지 운송수단 판매량이 거의 같았고 1백만 대를 상회했다. 2008년 자가용 판매는 약간 상승했고 다음해부터 잇달아 하락했다. 소형 트럭은 2007년부터 2010년까지 계속 하락세를 보였다. 소형 트럭은 심지어 2010년의 80만에서 2011년 60만 대로 떨어지며 큰 타격을 입을 것으로 예측된다. 도표에 의하면 전체적인 운송 수단들의 2011년 판매량은 전반적으로 떨어질 것이고, 자가용과 소형 트럭 판매량 간의 격차는 계속 줄어들 것이며 자가용이 시작에서 훨씬 큰 비중을 차지하게 될 것이다.

30 어휘 idiom 숙어

해설 숙어에 대한 이해의 차이로 인해 생긴 사건을 예로 들어 만화영화 대본에서 숙어를 사용했을 경우의 문제점을 이야기하고 있다. 문단 마지막 부분의 It has become necessary to avoid using idioms in animation scripts because they usually go overseas for production. They are sometimes too obscurely language-specific and might mean nothing to an overseas animator. 라는 두 문장에서 주제를 유추할 수 있다.

해석 요즘 거의 모든 텔레비전 만화영화들은 해외에서 만들어진다. 이는 곧 비영어권 국가의 만화영화 소비자들을 위해 대본을 일본어, 한국어, 불어, 독일어 등의 외국어로 번역해야 한다는 것을 의미한다. 이러한 상황은 꽤 재미난 문제를 일으키기도 하는데, 특히 숙어를 사용할 때를 들 수 있다. 내 친구는 자신이 번역했던 G. I. Joe 대본에서 등장인물들이 사막에서 언쟁을 벌이는 장면을 이야기하는 것을 좋아한다. 그는 등장인물 X가 자신의 의견을 내길 결정했다는 뜻에서 'X decides to stick his oar in the water'라는 숙어를 사용했었다. 그런데 만화영화가 돌아왔을 때, 사막에 서 있던 주인공들이 갑자기 물 위의 나룻배에 노와 함께 나타나는 장면이 있었다. 만화영화들은 보통 해외에서 생산되기 때문에 만화영화 대본에 숙어 쓰는 것을 피할 필요가 있게 되었다. 숙어는 때때로 너무 애매하게 언어 밀착적이어서 해외의 만화영화 생산자들에게는 아무 의미가 없을 수도 있다.

31 어휘 identical 동일한

해설 ESL국가에서는 영어가 행정과 교육 전반에서 쓰이는 의사소통 수단이고, EFL국가에서는 영어를 외국어로 여겨 학교에서만 배운다고 이야기하고 있다. ESL국가와 EFL국가에서 영어를 가르치는 의도가 다르다는 것을 알 수 있다.

보기 ① ESL과 EFL국가에서 영어 교육의 의도가 다르다.
② ESL과 EFL국가에서 영어 교육 환경은 동일하다.
③ ESL과 EFL국가에서 영어가 쓰이는 범위는 비슷하다.
④ EFL국가에서 영어는 의사소통의 매개체로 사용된다.
⑤ 프랑스와 일본은 ESL국가의 예이다.

해설 ESL국가의 전통적인 의미는 영어를 모국어로 사용하지 않지만 교육, 행정 등의 영역에서 영어를 의사소통의 수단으로 널리 사용하고 있는 국가이다. 이러한 나라에는 나이지리아와 싱가포르가 있다. 또한 ESL이라는 용어는 제 1언어가 영어가 아닌 사람들에게 영어를 가르치는 프로그램을 의미하기도 한다. EFL국가에서는 영어가 교육이나 행정에 쓰이는 언어는 아니지만 프랑스나 일본의 경우처럼 영어로 말하거나 쓰기 위해 학교에서 영어를 배운다. ESL국가와 EFL국가는 학교 밖에서 영어에 노출되는 정도가 다르고 교육 체계나 더 넓은 사회에서의 영어의 역할도 다르기 때문에 꽤나 다른 영어 교육 수요와 방법이 존재한다.

32 어휘 pioneer 개척하다 / siege 포위 공격, 끈덕진 권유, 많음 / aloft 위에, 높이 / watchful 경계하는

해설 전쟁 중 의사소통 수단의 부재 → 비둘기를 이용한 방법 제안 → 메시지의 무게 해결과 결과의 순서로 이어져야 하므로 (B) - (C) - (A)의 순서가 맞다.

해석 보내야 하는 메시지의 크기를 줄이기 위한 사진술의 사용은 프랑코-프러시아 전쟁 중 프랑스인들에 의해 개척되었다.

전쟁 중에 파리는 철저히 포위당했고 모든 외부 연락이 끊긴 상태였다. 도시를 포위한 프러시아 인들은 모든 전보를 끊고 편지가 오가지 못하도록 하였다. 이러한 상황에서 파리 사람들이 외부 세계와 소통하는 것은 불가능했다.

파리 사람들은 공식 서신이 든 방수 공을 세느 강에 띄우거나 풍선 안에 메시지를 높이 띄워 보내는 등 많은 방법으로 프러시안을 피해 의사소통을 하려 했으나 어떤 것도 효과가 없었다. 그 때, 한 비둘기 비행 클럽이 새들의 날개 깃털에 메시지를 묶자고 제안했다.

그러나 그것이 효과를 거두기 위해서는 메시지가 작고 가벼워야 했다. 해법은 원본 메시지를 복사하는 것이었다. 이것들은 약 1.5인치짜리의 종이에 인쇄되어 둥글게 말아 비둘기의 다리에 묶였다. 8개월의 포위 공격 기간 동안 거의 60개의 메시지가 경계의 시선과 총, 그리고 프러시아 인들을 지나쳐갔다.

33 **어휘** stimulating 고무적인

해설 However, also 등의 표현에 유의하여 해석한다. 제시된 문장과 일맥상통하는 부분을 찾고 그 후에 상반된 내용이 나오는 것이 흐름상 자연스러우므로 ② (B) - (A) - (C)가 답이다.

해석 홈스쿨링은 아이들이 학교에 등하교하고 붐비는 교실에서 지내며 겪는 문제들과 그 외 모든 것들에 노출되는 부담을 지지 않아도 된다는 점에서 점점 더 바람직하다고 여겨지는 추세이다.

또한 보다 효율적이고 더 나은 학습 환경을 조성하는 부모님과 지도자의 개인적인 관심 또한 존재한다. 사회적 기준이 점점 더 유연해짐에 따라 홈스쿨링은 사실 미래의 일반적인 현상이 될 수도 있다.

그러나 많은 결과에서 학생들은 교실 안에서 더 많은 혜택을 얻는 것으로 나타났는데, 다른 학생들과의 상호작용과 대화가 고무적인 학습 환경을 조성하기 때문이었다.

게다가 교실에 학생이 많을수록 집단은 더 다양해지고 피드백도 다양해진다. 좋은 선생님과 함께 교실은 학생의 인지 발달에 매우 큰 혜택을 줄 수 있다.

34 **어휘** indigenous 토착의 / fibrous capsule 섬유질의 삭과, 섬유피막 / Old Testament 구약 성서

해설 마지막 문장에 의하면 아랍 국가에서는 Cardamom을 커피와 함께 끓여 'Cardamom 커피'로 만들어 마신다고 하였으므로 ⑤의 내용과 일치하지 않는다.

해석 Cardamom은 사프란과 바닐라에 이어 세계에서 세 번째로 비싼 향료다. 이는 생강과에 속하는 씨앗으로 남서 인도 산지의 토착 식물이고 1900년까지만 그 곳에서 길러졌다. 독일 이민자들이 그때 과테말라로 이것을 가져가 지금 최대 생산지가 됐다. Cardamom 씨앗은 서로 다른 시간에 익는 섬유질 열매 송이에서 나기 때문에 열매는 하나씩 손으로 따야만 한다. 이들은 완전히 익어서 열매가 터지기 약간 전에 수확되어야 한다. Cardamom은 구약 성서에 계피와 함께 언급되어 있지만, 중세 시대까지 유럽에 전파되진 않았다. 오늘날 북유럽 국가가 주로 제빵용으로 세계 무역량 10퍼센트를 소비하는 반면, 아랍 국가들이 Cardamom커피를 위해 80퍼센트를 차지한다. 이 커피는 신선하게 로스팅된 굵게 간 커피와 Cardamom의 초록 꼬투리를 함께 끓여서 만든다.

35 **어휘** accuse A of B A를 B 때문에 체포하다 / open-housing policy 주거 개방 제도(주택 매매에서 인종/종교에 의한 차별 금지) / ethnic 인종의

해설 네 번째 줄에 따르면 Daley 시장이 Martin Luther King을 불렀다 하였으므로 ③은 잘못되었다.

해석 Daley 시장과 다른 시카고의 백인 정치/종교적 지도자들은 Martin Luther King 박사가 문제를 야기하였다며 체포했다. 그들은 Martin Luther King 박사에게 또 다른 행진 계획을 철수할 것을 요구했다. 그러나 킹 박사는 그들이 자신의 행진을 멈추고 싶다면 정의를 실현화시켜야한다고 말하였다. 그래서 Daley는 지역 노동 및 사업 리더들과의 회의에 King 박사를 불렀다. 그들은 시카고 인권 위원회가 부동산 매매 중개인들이 도시의 주거 개방 제도를 게시하도록 하여 모든 인종들이 본래 제지되었던 주택에 접근할 수 있도록 시에서 집행할 것에 대해 동의했다. 또한, 시카고 은행은 자격 있는 가정이라면 인종적 배경을 불문하고 돈을 빌려줄 것에 동의했다. King 박사는 비폭력 항거가 북부에서 통한다는 것을 입증했다.

36 **어휘** bottom-up 세부적인 원리에서 출발하는 방식의 / Top-down 일반적인 것에서 시작해 세부적인 사항으로 진행 되는 방식의 / syntactic 구문론적인 / endorse 시인하다, 찬성하다

해설 주어진 보기는 독자들의 기존 지식을 글에 끼워 맞춘다는 내용이므로 top-down 이론에 부합한다. 따라서 가 장 적절한 위치는 Top-down 이론의 정의 직후에 위치한 ③이다.

해석 읽기가 발생하는 세 가지 주요 모범이 있다. Botto-up 이론은 독자가 작은 단위로부터 글을 구성해 나가고(글 자에서 단어에서 구에서 문장으로 등), 글을 작은 단위로부터 구성하는 것이 아주 자동적으로 되어 독자들이 이것이 어찌 작용하는지 의식하지 못하게 된다고 주장한다. Top-down 이론은 독자가 거대한 양의 지식, 예상, 가정, 의문을 글에 적용시키고, 어휘에 대한 기초적인 이해를 바탕으로, 글이 그들의 기대를 확정시키는 한 계 속 읽어나간다고 주장한다. 이 이론은 독자들이 이미 가지고 있는 (문화적, 구문론적인, 언어적인, 역사적인) 지식에 글을 끼워 맞추어 나가고 새롭거나 예상 밖의 정보가 나타나면 되돌아가 확인한다고 주장한다.) 이러한 대부분의 연구자들이 최근 찬성하는 상호적인 이론가들의 학파는, top-bottom과 bottom-up 과정 모두가 번 갈아서 또는 동시에 발생한다고 주장한다. 이 이론가들은 글의 종류와 독자의 배경 지식, 언어적으로 유창한 정도, 동기, 전략의 이용, 문화적으로 형성된 읽기에 대한 믿음에 따라 bottom-up과 top down 과정들이 작동 한다고 설명한다. Bottom-up과 top-down 과정은 독자가 글로부터 의미를 구성할 때 상호적으로 발생하는 것이다.

37 **어휘** conventional wisdom 사회적 통념 / stoop 몸을 구부리다 / off-limits 접근 금지의

해설 "가게 제품의 (배열)을 바꾸면, 고령층의 (증가된 구매)를 기대할 수 있다"라는 문장의 내용을 성립시키는 arrange와 increased sales가 정답이다.

제품의 크기(size), 포장(packaging)을 증가시키거나, 노인의 충동구매(impulsive purchase), 신체 운동 (physical exercise), 마케팅 조언(marketing advice), 감소된 불평호소(decreased complaint)를 기대할 수 있다는 것은 주요 내용에 어긋난다.

해석 쇼핑 몰에서 가장 천천히 팔리는 배터리는 보청기에 쓰이는 것이었으므로 사회적 통념상 이들이 다른 흥미를 끌지 않는 상품들과 함께 선반 애래 쪽에 들여놓아야 한다고 지시되었다. 하지만, 당연히 몸을 구부리기 가장 어려운 노인들이 이를 구입한다. 그 배터리들은 그 뒤로 선반의 더 높은 곳으로 이동해서, 판매량의 네 배가 늘어났다. 몇몇 제품들의 주요 구매자는 고령층이다. 그것들을 허리 높이보다 높지도 낮지도 않게 특별한 주의 를 기울여 비치한다면 어떨까? 대부분의 슈퍼마켓에서, 너무 낮거나 높은 곳에 놓인 제품은 사실상 고령 구매자 들에게 접근 금지다. 고령 구매층의 생활을 편하게 만드는 것은 종종 소매상에게 나쁜 대접을 받는 집단에게 따뜻한 느낌을 불러일으킬 것이다. 더불어, 이렇게 함으로써, 입소문이 날 것이다. 보청기 배터리를 사러 온 사람들이 아마도 전화나 컴퓨터를 살 필요가 있는 자신의 친구들을 데려오게 될 것이다.

concave 오목한 / lay down 규정하다 / 11th commandment 11번째 계명(성경의 십계명 뒤에 덧붙여야 할 만큼 중요한 규칙) / impertinent 뻔뻔한

「소음에 대한 나의 혐오감을 설명해보려 한다. 만일 거대한 다이아몬드를 잘게 자른다면, 다이아몬드는 전체로서의 가치를 완전히 잃게 되고, 작은 부대로 나누어진 군대는 힘을 잃게 된다. 그래서 훌륭한 지성은 저지되고 방해되는 즉시, 주의력이 흩뜨려지고 문제에 당면하면서 평범한 것으로 전락하고 만다. 이것의 우월함은 마치 오목거울에 비추어지는 모든 광선을 한 점으로 모으듯 집중력에 달려있기 때문이다.

시끄러운 방해는 하나의 장애물이다. 그래서 유명한 지성인들이 자신들의 생각에 침범하고 저지하는 어떠한 형태의 방해이든지 항상 극도의 혐오감을 드러내어온 것이다. 특히 그들은 소음에서 야기되는 격렬한 방해를 혐오해왔다. 보통 사람들은 그런 종류의 무엇에 의해서든 그다지 성가셔하지 않는다. 유럽에서 가장 현명하고 지성적인 모든 국가들이 '절대 방해하지 말라!'는 규칙을 11번째 계명으로 정해놓았다. 소음은 모든 방해 형식 중에서도 가장 뻔뻔하다. 이는 단순한 방해일 뿐만 아니라 생각의 와해이다. 당연히 방해할 것이 없다면 소음은 특별히 고통스러울 것은 아니다. 때때로 가볍고 지속적인 소음이 내가 뚜렷하게 인지하기 전까지 나를 괴롭히고 방해하곤 한다. 나는 지적 노동이 끊임없이 불어나는 것을 느낄 뿐이다. 마치 내가 발에 추를 달고 걷는 것처럼 말이다. 마침내 나는 이게 무엇인지 알아냈다.」

38 해설 빈칸 다음에 오목거울이 광선을 한 점으로 모은다는 비유가 나오고, 앞의 전반적인 내용이 방해에 의해 주의력이 흩뜨려진다는 내용을 담고 있으므로, '집중'을 뜻하는 ④ concentration이 빈칸에 가장 알맞다.

39 해설 이 글의 주제로 ① "소음은 지성적인 이들을 방해한다"가 가장 알맞다.
보기 ② 소음에 대한 포용력은 국가별로 크게 다르다.
③ 식별하기 어려운 환경적인 소음이 건강을 해친다.
④ 적절한 수준의 소음이 사고 작용을 향상시킨다.
⑤ 일이 재미있을수록 소음을 차단해내기 쉽다.

⟐ [40~41]

economic depression 경제 위기, 공황 / cancer 암 / surgeon 외과 의사 / incident 사고

「Washington D. C.에서 전 내각이 채택한 화폐 정책이 야기한 경제 공황의 중심부에 미국이 있다. 미국은 안정성이 필요했고, 인플레이션을 끝내고 일자리를 되돌려줄 강한 리더를 원했다. 이러한 이슈들을 가지고 미국인들은 Stephen Grover Cleveland를 24대 대통령으로 추대했다. 그 해 8월 그는 취임 선언을 하기로 예정되었다.

그러나 문제가 있었다. Cleveland가 그의 입천장에 흑점이 생긴 것을 발견한 것이다. 그는 그 병에 대해 크게 신경 쓰지는 않았지만, 그렇다고 무시하고 넘어갈 수도 없었다. 곧, 의사에게 검진을 받았다. 그는 25센트 크기의 상처를 관찰했고 대통령에게 즉시 수술해야 하는 암이 있다고 진료했다. 그리 간단한 문제가 아니었다. 8월에 의회에서 선언한 기로 이미 약속 잡혀 있었던 것이다. 일정을 연기하면 심각한 타격을 입게 될 것이었다. 더욱이, 국가는 건강한 지도자에 의해 운영되어야 했다.

뉴욕으로의 짧은 휴가동안, 대통령은 비밀리에 수술을 진행했다. 의사들은 왼쪽 위턱의 이 두개와 입천장 조직의 절반 가량을 제거했다. 종양은 골프공만큼 커져있었다. 혹이 제거된 빈자리는 거즈로 채워졌다. 수술이 성공적이었고 겉으로 보기에는 아무 이상도 없었으므로 대통령은 일하는 데 어떠한 이상도 보이지 않았다. 그의 연설 역시 사고 없이 마무리 되었다. 그는 의회와의 약속을 지켰고 대중들은 그의 병에 대해 알지 못했다.

그 사실이 알려진 것은 사건이 있은 25년 후, 즉, 대통령이 죽고 10년이 지난 1917년 Saturday Evening Post 기사를 통해서였다. 대통령 가족의 허락을 받아 당시 담당의사가 공개한 것이다.」

40 해설 나머지는 모두 Cleveland 대통령을 가리키는데, ③은 진료 의사를 가리킨다.

41 보기 ④ 기사는 가족의 동의를 얻어 공개되었다.
① 연설은 연기 없이 진행되었다
② 휴가 기간 동안 수술하였다
③ Cleveland가 살아있는 동안에는 수술 사실이 알려지지 않았다
⑤ Cleveland가 경제 위기를 극복할 수 있으리라 여겨졌다

✥ [42~43]

---

one-dimensional 일차원적인 / airborne 공수의

「어디선가 우리는 우리를 예상치 못한 긍정적이고 활기찬 방향으로 변화시켜 줄 특별한 사람을 만나게 된다. 축복스럽게도 나에게 그러한 사람은 비행 선생님이었다. 수업을 받기 시작했을 때, 나는 십대였다. 훈련을 끝냈을 때, 선생님은 나에게 모든 요구 조건을 충족해서 자격증을 받을 수 있을 것이라 말해주셨다.

그러다가 갑자기, 그는 감명 깊은 한 마디를 내뱉었다. "Mike, 너는 기본 기술을 익혀서 비행기를 위아래로 움직일 줄 알게 되었어. 솔직히 너의 실력은 나쁘지 않았다. 그러나 비행기가 너를 위험에 빠지게 할 위험성은 언제나 존재해. 네가 비행 중일 때는 네가 가진 모든 기기들이 곧 네 자신이란다. 충분히 준비하지 않으면 너는 죽을 수도 있어. 위험에 대해 언제나 생각하고 대비하렴. 위험이 발생할 때 너는 살아남아 무용담을 들려주거나 그렇지 않으면 생존하지 못해 사라지게 되겠지. 어느 쪽이 되어야할지 생각하렴."

나는 그 말이 얼마나 중요한 것인지를 알아차렸다. 그가 그 때보다 한 번에 많은 말을 하는 것을 본 적이 없었기 때문이다. 빠르게 4년이 지났다. 나는 자정 전에 고성능의 단엔진 비행기를 타고 이륙하여 강한 겨울 폭풍을 지나가고 있었다. 갑자기 엔진이 정지했을 때, 나는 10,000 피트 상공에 있었다. 하늘은 달도 없이 새까맣고 땅에는 2 피트 두께의 눈이 쌓여있어 모든 것이 하나인 듯 보였다.

주어진 시간은 단 5분이었다. 되돌아보면, 나는 그 기회를 통해 '국제적인 조종사가 될 수 있음을 알고 있었던 것 같다. 배워왔던 모든 기술과 준비들을 이용하기 시작했다. 그동안의 수많은 연습과정에서, 나는 비상시 착륙을 낮이고 밤이고 수십 번 연습했다. 그리고 조종실에서 나는 완벽히 외로움을 느꼈다. 그러나 나는 모든 연습이 되어있다는 말로 스스로를 진정시켰다. 위기 상황의 발생은 그동안의 연습이 의미 있다는 것을 뜻했다. 그것은 쇼 타임이 아니었다. 나는 비행기를 버리고 탈출했고 지금 이 이야기를 쓰고 있다. 따라서 그것은 훌륭한 착륙이었다.」

---

42 해설 ⑤ 나를 변화시킨 선생님에 대한 이야기가 나와야하므로 우선 (D)가 필요하다. 그 다음으로 그 말이 나의 삶에 실제 끼친 영향을 보여주어야 하므로 (C)를 통해 위기 상황의 발생을 설명하고 이어 (B)로 상황의 해결을 보여준다.

43 해설 외롭고 무서웠지만 할 수 있다고 스스로를 다독인 것이므로, ① '나는 이 상황에 만반의 준비를 해두었다'가 맞다.

보기 ② 나는 철저히 혼자였고 누구도 나를 방해할 수 없었다.
③ 내 면허는 오래 유효하지는 않았다
④ 이전에 충돌하면서 착륙한 적이 있다
⑤ 계획대로 비행기는 목적지에 도착해야 했다

database 자료 체제 / district 구역 / implementation 수행 / homicide 살인

「1994년 William J. Bratton이 뉴욕경찰의 수장이 되었을 때, 경찰의 공공 분야는 크게 변화하였다. 그는 더 이상 경찰이 범인 검거에만 그치는 것이 아니라 미래의 범죄를 예방하는 데에도 초점을 맞추겠다고 선언했다.

Bratton이 부임하기 전에, 뉴욕 경찰은 FBI가 매 6개월마다 조사한 각 경찰의 평가자료를 가지고 다른 곳과 비교하였다. 그러나 Bratton은 이에 만족하지 않고 그들의 구역에서 어떤 범죄가 증가하고 감소하는지를 일주일 단위로 조사할 것을 명령하였다. 그리고 매주 경찰들은 범죄가 증가할 동안 무얼하고 있었느냐는 Bratton의 질책에 대답해야 했다. 현장으로부터의 더 나은, 더 빠른 피드백이 업무 수행 능력을 개선시켰다.

가장 잘 알려진 그의 혁신은 '깨진 창문' 정책이었다. 창문을 깬다던가 그래피티 낙서를 하는 것, 운전자들을 방해하는 것과 같은 경범죄도 엄하게 다스리라 명령한 것이다. 장기적으로 이 정책은 중범죄들을 예방하는 것에 효과가 있다는 사실일 밝혀졌다.

모든 수준에 있어서의 혁신으로 Bratton은 임기 27개월간 살인을 44% 감소시키고 중범죄를 25% 감소시켰다. 이후 그는 Los Angeles 경찰로 가서 똑같은 방법의 혁신을 단행했다.」

44 해설 ⑤ 자살 감소가 아니라 살인 감소이다. 자살은 suicide이다.

45 해설 ① Bratton이 뉴욕 경찰을 변화시킨 이야기이다. 따라서 '새로운 수장이 어떻게 뉴욕 경찰을 바꾸었나?'가 맞다.

보기 ② Los Angeles는 중범죄로부터 안전한가?

③ '깨진 유리창'정책은 무엇인가?

④ 뉴욕의 경범죄를 막는 방법

⑤ 살인 없는 뉴욕을 만들기 위한 장기적인 방안

ANSWER

01	02	03	04	05	06	07	08	09	10	11	12	13	14	15	16	17	18	19	20
④	③	②	④	④	③	③	④	③	①	④	④	⑤	⑤	②	②	⑤	①	①	③
21	22	23	24	25	26	27	28	29	30	31	32	33	34	35	36	37	38	39	40
④	⑤	④	⑤	①	⑤	③	②	③	①	①	①	⑤	④	②	②	②	⑤	①	②
41	42	43	44	45															
①	⑤	①	③	②															

01 어휘 entire 전체의 / can't think of~ ~가 생각나지 않다.

해석 Thomas와 Sarah의 관계는 무엇인가?

Sarah : 어머, 귀여워라! 전 Thomas가 아기였을 때의 저 사진이 좋아요.

Carolyn : 그래, 좋은 날이었지. 그의 세 번째 생일이었던 것 같아. 가족과 많은 친구들과 함께 저 날을 보냈어.

Sarah : 저도 함께했으면 좋았을 텐데. 제 평생 동안 그와 알고지낸 것 같아요.

Carolyn : 너희는 인생의 가장 멋진 부분을 함께 해 오고 있잖니. 나는 그 아이가 어렸을 적을 빼고는 네가 곁에 없었을 때를 모르겠다.

Sarah : 네, 전 Thomas를 중학생 때부터 알고 지냈어요. 음, 이제 우리는 아플 때나 건강할 때나 평생을 함께 보내요.

02 어휘 impersonal 비인간적인 / could (제안)~해볼 수 있다 / resort to ~에 의지하다

해설 ③ John은 여자 친구에게 무엇을 사줄지 결정하는 데 어려움을 겪고 있다.

해석 상황을 가장 잘 묘사 한 문장을 고르시오.

Paul : 안녕, John. 무슨 일 있니? 너 걱정스러워 보여.

John : 내 여자 친구에게 크리스마스 선물로 무엇을 줘야 할지를 모르겠어. 그녀는 까다로운데(그녀를 위한 선물을 사는 것은 어려운데), 나는 올해 그녀가 무엇을 원할지 모르겠어.

Paul : 그녀가 무엇을 좋아하니? 취미나 흥미가 있어? 한가할 땐 뭘 하니?

John : 그녀는 책 읽는 걸 정말 좋아하고, 친구들이랑 어울려 지내기, 그리고 물론 쇼핑도 가지.

Paul : 그녀가 가장 좋아하는 가게들 중 한 군데의 상품권을 주는 것은 어때? 그 방법이면 그녀는 너에게서 선물을 받을 수 있지만, 자기가 특별히 갖고 싶은 것을 고를 수도 있어.

John : 좋은 생각이지만, 잘 모르겠어. 상품권은 너무 인간미가 없는 것 같아.

Paul : 상품권이 인간미가 없다는 건 그럴 수 있겠다. 음, 보석에 의지해 볼 수도 있겠다.

03 어휘 check (수하물을) 부치다 / strand 오도 가도 못 하게 하다 / upcoming 다가오는 / exit (고속도로의) 출구 램프

해설 '고속도로 출구', '다시 되돌아간다', '팁을 드린다' 등의 표현에서 Scott의 마지막 말에 나오는 'he(him/his)'가 택시 운전수임을 짐작할 수 있다.

해석 대화가 이루어지는 장소로 가장 적절한 곳은?

Susan : 오, 이런! 내 수하물을 부치면서 매표소에 지갑을 놓고 온 것 같아.

Scott : 뭐라고? 잃어버리면 큰일인데. 언제 잃어버렸다는 것을 알았어?

Susan : 방금 전에. 잠깐만, 나 계속 핸드백을 뒤지고 있어. 아니, 여기 없다. 어떻게 하지? 여기서 발이 묶이긴 싫은데.

Scott : 빨리! 그에게 다음 출구로 나가서 지갑이 발견 되었는지 볼 수 있게 되돌아가 주실 수 있는지 여쭤보자. 신경 쓰지 않으실 거야. 우리가 그의 수고의 대가로 추가 팁을 드리면 될 것 같아.

Susan : 정말 그게 매표소에 있었으면 좋겠다. 내가 마지막으로 그걸 가지고 있었던 곳인데. 나는 이 여행을 정말 오랫동안 계획 했다고.

04 어휘 pricey 값비싼 / sales tax 판매세

해설 ① 판매원은 매니저가 코트 가격을 더 할인해 주지 않을 것이라고 말했다.

해석 다음 대화에 의하면 올바른 것은 무엇인가?

Herbert : 안녕하세요, 간판에 따르면 세일 중이고, 최대 50%까지 할인된다고 하던데요.

판매원 : 우리 매장에 오신 것을 환영합니다! 네, 저희의 올해 최대 세일이 오늘 시작했습니다. 무엇을 찾으시나요?

Herbert : 음, 저는 새 겨울 코트가 필요해요. 사이즈는 38이나 40인 것 같아요.

판매원 : 좋아요! 고객님께 딱 어울리는 코트가 있어요! 외피가 100% 울로 만들어 졌어요. 정상 가격은 400달러 인데, 할인해서 200달러 밖에 안 한답니다.

Herbert : 음, 입어 봐도 되나요? (코트를 입어 본 후)와, 이거 정말 마음에 드는데요! 불행하게도, 여전히 저한 테는 다소 비싸군요. 가격을 더 할인해 주실 수는 없을까요?

판매원 : 죄송합니다만, 매니저께서 최종 가격이라고 명시하셨어요. 다음 주에 판매세가 5%에서 7%로 인상 될 거예요. 만약 오늘 구매 하시면 세금으로 10달러를 내면 되세요. 만약 다음 주 까지 기다리신다면, 세 금으로 14달러를 내셔야 할 겁니다.

Herbert : 오늘 몇 시까지 영업하시죠? 아내랑 같이 와서 그녀의 의견을 들어 봐야겠어요.

05 어휘 for ~ sake ~를 위해 / plan B 제2안 / fall back on ~에 의지하다 / cooperate 협력하다

해설 ④ Robert는 Peter에게 원래 계획을 고수할 것을 추천하고 있다.

해석 다음 대화에 따르면 옳지 않은 것은 어느 것인가?

Peter : 이번 주말 일기 예보를 아세요?

Robert : 음, 확실하지는 않은데, 기상 캐스터가 비가 올지 모른다고 한 것을 들었어.

Peter : 정말요? 아니면 좋겠는데. 이번 주말에 해변에 가려고 계획 중이거든요.

Robert : 음, 널 위해 그 때 비가 오지 않길 빌어.

Peter : 네, 저도요. 가장 친한 친구를 만날 거예요. 저희가 대학교에 가기 전 마지막으로 만날 기회거든요. 저희는 초등학교 때부터 친구였어요.

Robert : 의지할 다른 대책을 세우는 게 좋겠는데. 날씨가 협조하지 않더라도 실망하지 않게 말이야.

Peter : 그런 것 같아요. 지금 가장 친한 친구에게 해변 대신 다른 어떤 것을 선택할지 확인하러 전화할 거예요.

Robert : 좋은 생각이야. 그나저나, 이번 주말에 새로운 영화가 개봉한다더구나. 블록버스터인 것 같더라고.

06 어휘 pocket book 재정형편 / handle 다스리다, 취급하다 / alternative 대안 / attraction 명소, 명물 / time off 한 가한

빈 칸에 들어 갈 대화의 알맞은 순서는 무엇인가?

Krista : 올 여름 휴가에 어디를 가야 할지를 모르겠어.

Darren : 염두에 두고 있는 것은 뭐야? 열대지방? 유럽은 어때? 항상 여행 가고 싶어 했던 곳은 어디야?

Krista : 거의 어디든지 다니곤 했어. 추천해 준 것은 둘 다 좋아 보인다. 그런데 내 주머니 사정이 그런 비싸고 먼 장소들을 감당할지 모르겠네.

Darren : 음, 항상 대안들이 있기 마련이지. 너 "staycation"에 대해 들어 봤니?

Krista : 아니. 뭐야?

Darran : 새로운 표어야. 휴가 때 집에 머무르면서 지역의 장소들과 명소, 평소에는 가지 않던 식당을 탐험하는 거지. 재정 형편에도 무리가 가지 않고 너희 지역에 이미 있던 것들을 보고 놀랄 거야.

Krista : 그거 정말 재미있겠다. 일단은 내 staycation을 위한 계획을 세워야겠어. 다음에 일이 없을 때, 내가 늘 꿈꿔 오던 열대지방 섬으로 가는 계획을 세우면 되겠다.

07 **어휘** unload (짐을) 내리다 / light up (담배를) 물다 / inclined 하고 싶은 / disturb 방해하다

해설 ① 영국인 남성이 먹고 싶은 것을 물은 대상은 당연히 영국인 여성일 것이다.

② 칸막이 안에 이미 누군가 앉아 있다는 것을 눈치챈 것도 영국인 여성이며, 이 문장의 someone이 미국인 여성에 해당한다.

③ 영국인 여성의 담배 냄새에 자리를 옮기고 한 것은 미국인 여성이다.

④ 담배를 피우고 있던 것은 영국인 여성.

⑤ 담배를 끄는 행동을 함으로써 다른 사람을 눈치 챘다는 것을 어필하는 것으로 미루어 보아 담배를 피우고 있던 영국인 여성임을 알 수 있다.

해석 Deborah Tannen에 따르면, 문화가 다르면 예의를 나타내는 방식도 다르다. 예를 들어, 미국인 여성이 기차역 구내매점에 있는 한 칸막이 안에 앉아 있었다. 잠시 후에, 어떤 영국인 부부가 같은 칸막이 속의 맞은편 좌석에 자리를 잡기 시작했다. 그들은 짐을 내렸다. 그는 ①그녀에게 무엇이 먹고 싶은지 물은 뒤 사러 가고 그녀는 미국인 맞은편 자리인 칸막이로 미끄러져 들어갔다. 이 모든 것이 일어나는 동안, ②그녀는 칸막이 안에 이미 누군가 앉아 있다는 것을 눈치챘다는 것에 대한 신호를 전혀 보내지 않았다. 영국인 여성이 담배를 피워 물었을 때, 그 미국인에게는 명확한 분노의 대상이 있었다. ③그녀는 자리를 옮길 다른 테이블이 있는지 주변을 둘러보기 시작했다. 물론, 전혀 없었다. 그래서 그 영국인 부부가 바로 그녀의 칸막이 안에 앉았던 것이다. ④그녀는 곧장 담배를 끄고 사과했다. 이것이 ⑤그녀가 칸막이 속에 누군가 있다는 것을 눈치 챘다는 것을 나타냈다. 그리고 그녀는 그녀를 방해하고 싶지 않았던 것이다.

08 **어휘** inevitably 필연적이다시피 / aspect 측면 / consequence 결과, 중요함 / pedagogical 교육학적인 / application (컴퓨터의) 응용 프로그램 / obtain 얻다 / implement 시행하다 / significant 중요한 / with respect to ~에 대하여

보기 ① 대부분 학습이 일어나는 학교와 기관들은 이제 컴퓨터와 인터넷에 접속한다.

② 학생들은 그들의 숙제를 워드 프로세서를 이용하고 인터넷을 정보의 입수처로 생각한다.

③ 선생님들은 또한 자료를 만들고 수업을 시행할 때 컴퓨터에 의존한다.

④ 컴퓨터의 발전은 최근 하드웨어와 소프트웨어에 대하여 중요한 성장을 경험 해오고 있다.

⑤ 전 세계의 많은 국가들이 컴퓨터를 통해 배달되는 원격 교육을 제공하고 있다.

해석 기술은 필연적으로 인간의 삶의 모든 측면과 연결되어 있는 듯하다. 컴퓨터들은 특히, 우리가 사는 방식과 극적으로 영향을 미치고 있고, 이것은 자연적인 결과로, 또한 교육적인 프로그램에도 영향을 미쳐오고 있다.

09 **어휘** accounting 회계 / expand 확장시키다 / basis 근거 / firm 회사 / interest rate 이율 / controversial 논란이 많은 / given ~을 고려해 볼 때 / taxation 조세 / declared 공표한 / bankrupt 파산자

해석 회계는 사업의 언어라고 일컬어진다. 경영자들은 그들이 잘 하고 있는지, 확장을 시켜야 할지, 혹은 그들이 잘 못하고 있는지, 축소시켜야 할지를 보기 위해 영업 이익과 손실 장부를 사용한다. ① 회계는 다른 이유에서 금전적인 판단의 근거이다. 외부인의 회사 재정 형편에 대한 관점은 그 장부에 근거한다. ② 그것은 주식 가격의 근거

가 된다. 그것은 또한 그 회사에 대출을 내어주는 사람들이 이자를 얼마나 청구할지 혹은 그렇지 않으면 전혀 빌려주지 않을 것인지 결정하는 근거가 된다. ③ 논란이 되는 회계의 역할을 고려 해 볼 때, 우리는 무엇이 이러한 토론의 동기가 되었는지를 판단하기 위해 새로운 이론을 정립시킬 필요가 있다. ④ 장부들은 또한 회사의 조세 금액의 근거이다. ⑤ 그들은 또한 회사가 언제 파산 선고를 받을지, 혹은 파산 선고를 받을지 그렇지 않을지를 알아내는 역할을 수행한다.

10 어휘 devalue 평가 절하하다 / enhance 높이다 / helpless 무력한 / inequality 불평등 / imply 넌지시 나타내다

해석 많은 사람들은 다른 사람들을 도와주는 것을 좋아한다. 그들은 노인들을 검사하고 어린 아이들을 돌본다. 그러나 그들은 그것으로 돈을 받을 수도 있고 그렇지 않을 수도 있다. 확실히 해라. 만약 네가 대가를 요구하더라도, 너의 일을 깎아내리지 마라. 사실, 너는 그것의 가치를 높인다. 만약 네가 도움이 필요한 사람을 어떠한 대가 없이 돕는다면, 너는 불평등을 만든다. 그것은 네가 강하고 상대방이 약하다는 것을 암시한다. 만약 네가 그 사람이 사리에 맞는 액수의 돈을 지불하도록 허락한다면, 불평등은 감소된다. 그것은 양쪽 모두에게 좋은 일이다. 당신이 도움을 주었을 때 대가로 돈을 받는다는 것을 알아차리는 것은 현명한 일이다. 나는 당신이 절대 "저는 양심상 돈을 받을 수 없습니다."라고 말하지 않기를 바란다. 그렇게 함으로써 당신은 당신의 도움에 대해 기꺼이 대가를 지불하고 싶어 하는 사람을 기분 상하게 하지 않아도 된다.

11 어휘 laughter 웃음 / severe 심각한 / genuine 진짜의 / numbing 망연자실하게 하는, 감각을 마비시키는

해설 ④의 경우 'ten minutes of ~'절이 discovery라는 명사를 수식하는 것이 아니라, discovery가 어떤 발견인지 부가 설명을 하는 역할을 한다. 따라서 부가 설명의 기능을 하는 명사절을 이끄는 that(~라는)을 사용하는 것이 옳다.

해석 18세기에, Sebastian Chamfort는 "가장 낭비 된 날은 우리가 웃지 않은 날이다."라고 썼다. 최근 며칠이나 낭비하였는가? 마지막으로 배꼽을 잡고 실컷 웃은 날은 언제인가? 유명한 편집자이자 작가인 Norman Cousins는 그의 베스트셀러인 〈Anatomy of an Illness〉에서 웃음이 그가 극심한 질병의 고통을 극복할 수 있도록 얼마나 도왔는지 설명하였다. "나는 10분간의 진심어린 배꼽 웃음이 통각을 마비시키는 효과를 가졌다는 것과 나에게 최소한 두 시간의 고통 없는 수면을 선사하곤 했다는 기쁜 발견을 했다. 그가 자신을 위해 고안한 치료의 일부분은 Marx Brothers의 영화를 보고 웃긴 책을 읽는 것을 포함하고 있었다.

12 어휘 rabies 광견병 / infected 감염된 / administer 관리하다, 투여하다 / proceed 나아가다 / injection 주사 curative

해설 ③의 경우 administer를 명사로 착각하기 쉽지만 동사 '투어하다'로 'call on to 동사원형(~하도록 요청하다)'구문이 되므로 옳다. ④ Following은 전치사로 '~후에', '~에 따라'라는 의미를 가진다.

해석 1881년, Pasteur는 감염된 동물에게 물림으로써 확산되는 고통스럽고 치명적인 병인 광견병을 연구하기 시작했다. Pasteur와 그의 조수는 연구실에서 많은 시간을 보냈다. 그리고 그 의지는 보답 받았다. Pasteur는 동물 실험에서 광견병의 진전을 예방하는 백신을 만들어냈던 것이다. 그러나 1885년 7월 6일, 그 과학자는 미친개에게 물린 한 어린 소년에게 백신을 투여하도록 부탁 받았다. Pasteur는 치료제를 주는 것을 망설였다. 그러나 그 소년이 광견병으로 인해 명확하고 고통스러운 죽음에 직면했기 때문에, Pasteur는 치료를 진행했다. 몇 주간에 걸쳐 배에 힘들게 주사를 맞은 후에, 소년은 광견병에 걸리지 않았다. Pasteur의 치료는 성공적이었다. 우리가 오늘날 알고 있는 광견병에 치유력이 있으며 예방에 효과적인 치료법은 당국이 그 질병의 확산을 통제할 수 있게 한 Pasteur의 백신에 기초한 것이다.

13 어휘 astonishingly 놀랍게도 / cease 중단하다 / boundary 경계 / territorial 영토의

해설 (A) strange는 뒤의 happened가 아니라 앞의 명사 something을 수식하므로 형용사 형태로 쓰는 것이 옳다. thing, body 등으로 끝나는 명사는 형용사의 수식을 뒤에서 앞으로 받는다.

(B) and라는 등위 접속사를 끼고 반복되는 주어인 they(불개미들)가 생략 된 형태이다. 따라서 동사 형태인 began을 써야한다.

(C) 'with+명사구 형태의 문장으로 erase는 boundaries를 수식하는 형태의 분사로 고쳐써야 한다. boundaries 는 의미상 능동적으로 사라지는 것이 아니라 사라지게 된 것이므로 수동의 의미를 나타내는 형용사인 과거 분사로 쓰는 것이 옳다.

해석 그들의 본래 서식지에서, 불개미들은 그 중앙에 단 한 마리 혹은 여러 마리의 여왕개미들을 놓고 개별적인 군락들을 만들어 낸다. 이것이 개미가 사는 방법이다. 그러나 미국에 도착한 후, 불개미들에게 무언가 매우 이상한 일이 일어난다. 그들은 순결한 여왕개미들의 비행을 배웅하던 전통 방식의 식민지 설립을 포기했다. 그리고 대신 최초의 몸의 확장자들을 만들어 나감으로써, 아메바 생식을 통해 식민지를 퍼뜨리는 많은 작은 여왕들을 만들어내기 시작했다. 놀랍게도 동시에 개미들은 다른 불개미들에 대한 식민지 경계선의 방어를 중단했다. 영토의 경계가 사라짐에 따라 지역 개체군은 이 거주지 전역에 걸쳐 공존하는 단일한 개미군과 하나로 통합된다.

14 **어휘** enroll 접수하다 / respond 대응하다

해설 (A) 반복되는 주어와 동사인 'triplets were'가 생략된 형태로 등장하는 동사는 모두 수동태 be pp의 모양에 따라 pp형태로 써 주는 것이 옳다.
(B) 셋 중 한 명이 A를 받아서 부정 대명사 one을 사용하였고, 나머지 둘이 C를 받았으므로 빈 칸에는 '나머지 모두'라는 의미의 부정 대명사 'the others'써야 한다.
(C) like와 alike는 의미는 거의 같지만, alike는 주로 동사 뒤에서 서술적인 용법으로 사용되는데 비해, like는 뒤에 명사를 덧붙여 'like + 명사(~처럼, ~같이)'의 형태로 사용하는 것에 주의한다.

해석 나는 세쌍둥이 중 하나로 태어났다. 그 때 세쌍둥이들은 똑같이 입혀지고, 똑같은 장난감을 받고, 똑같은 교외 활동에 등록되는 등이었다. 사람들은 심지어 우리가 개인이 아니라 한 묶음인 것처럼 반응했다. 우리 셋이 학교에서 아무리 착하게 있었든, 내가 빨리 익혔건, 열심히 했건 아니건 간에, 우리는 항상 C를 받곤 했다. 우리 중 하나가 A를 받고 나머지들이 F를 받으면, 선생님들은 항상 우리를 헷갈려 하셔서, 전체한테 C를 주는 것이 더 안전했다. 때때로, 내가 아빠의 무릎에 앉아 있을 때, 나는 아빠가 내가 어느 쪽인지 알아차리지 못하신다는 것을 알았다. 이러한 것들이 너의 정체성에 무슨 짓을 할지 상상이 되니? 요즘 우리는 개인을 인식한다는 것이, 우리들 각자가 얼마나 다른지를 알아차린다는 것이 얼마나 중요한지를 안다. 최근에는 다태(多胎)가 흔하다. 부모님들은 자기 자식들을 똑같이 입히거나 대해서는 안 된다는 것을 배웠다.

15 **어휘** staple 스테이플러, 주요소 / irrelevant 무관한

보기 ① 반복 ② 삽입 ③ 대용 ④ 치환 ⑤ 생략

해석 옛날에, 금전 등록기가 거의 모든 가게의 필수품이 되기 전에는, 상인들은 각 상품의 가격을 봉투 바깥에 써서 금액을 더하곤 했다. 하지만 고객들이 전화로 주문을 했을 때, 몇몇 상인들은 실수인지 일부로인지 주소나 아파트 호수를 봉투 윗부분에 적고 그 숫자도 총 합계에 더해버렸다. 이런 상관없는 정보를 집어넣는 것은 삽입 오류이다. 실수로 햄릿의 독백을 "확실히 할 것이냐, 신뢰를 잃느냐, 그것이 문제로다."로 인쇄한 어느 출판인이 이와 유사한 실수를 한 것이다.

16 **어휘** furrowed 주름진 / sullen 시무룩한 / be true with ~도 마찬가지이다 / to wear one's heart on one's sleeves 숨김없이 드러내다

보기 ① 확실한 ③ 긍정적인 ④ 예리한 ⑤ 간단한

해석 당신이 어렸을 때, 당신의 어머니가 문에서 가슴팍에 양 팔을 팔짱 끼고, 그녀의 발을 탁탁 치면서, 눈썹은 찌푸리고, 입술은 굳게 다문채로 맞이해 주시면 당신은 혼잣말을 했을지도 모른다. "엄마가 화나셨구나." 그녀는 당신에게 한마디도 하지 않았다. 우리는 누군가가 시무룩하거나, 불안하거나, 행복해하거나, 다른 어떤 기분일 것이라고 느낀다. 왜냐하면 그렇게 보이기 때문이다. 그러나 겉모습은 속여질 수 있다. 어린 아이가 웃으려다 실수로 얼굴을 찡그리는 것처럼, 어른도 마찬가지이다. 불안한 웃음은 기쁨의 표현이 아니다. 눈물은 실망이나 행복에서 흐를 수 있다. 몇몇 사람들은 그들이 무슨 생각을 하는지 다른 사람들보다 더 많이 내보인다. 그들은 숨김없이 드러낸다. 그러나 다른 사람들은 확실치 않은 것처럼 하지 않거나 항상 불확실하게 한다.

17 어휘 fundamental 근본적인 / distinction 대조 / refer to ~와 관련 있다 / probability 개연성 / objective standard 객관적 기준

보기 ① 사전 실험 ② 미래를 향한 중요한 도약 ③ 전략적이고 심리적인 ④ 논리적 사고에 입각한

해석 사업가들은 미래에 대한 근본적인 불확실성을 결정한다. Frank Knight는 그의 책 〈Risk, Uncertainty and Probability〉에서 경제학자의 위험에 대한 개념과 거의 모든 사업 결정상에서 다른 종류의 불확실성을 구별했다. 그가 말하길 위험은, 수학적인 개연성에 의해 측정될 수 있는 무엇인가와 관련 있다. 대조적으로, 불확실성은 측정될 수 없는 무엇인가와 관련 있다. 왜냐하면 개연성을 나타낼 객관적인 기준이 없기 때문이다. 이론적인 경제학자들은 그 후로 사람들이 어떻게 그런 진정한 불확실성을 다루는지를 이해하기 위해 발버둥치고 있다. Jack Welch의 표현 "가슴으로부터의 고백"은 그들의 노력을 보여준다. 투자에 문제가 되는 결정들은 분석적인 것보다 직관적인 것이다. 그 직관력은 심리학적인 순리에 따르는 사회적 절차이다. 그리고 특히, 사회 심리학이라는 집단 결정이 이루어지고 있기 때문이다.

18 어휘 contrary 반대되는 / by-product 부산물 / grasp 완전히 이해하다 / implication 영향

해석 대중적인 인식과 반대로, 지도자들은 항상 스스로나 그들이 지시에 대해 확신을 가지는 사람들이 아니다. 더 정확히 말하자면, 지도자들은 열린 마음의 학습자들이다. 한술 더 떠서, 그들은 다른 사람들이 이렇게 생각하는 것을 두려워하지 않는다. 사실, 배우는 것과 그것의 자연스러운 부산물인 실수들이 괜찮다는 환경을 만드는 것은 집단을 구성하고, 창의성 북돋기, 위험감수, 그리고 노력에 강한 도구가 될 수 있다. 오늘날, 이러한 리더쉽을 연습하는 사람들은 그들의 동료와 추종자에 대해 배우기를 받아들여야 한다. 그것은 그들의 개인적인 차이점과 일하는 방식, 그들의 생활양식과 같이 노력이 영향을 미치는 것과 나이, 인종, 종교, 그리고 성별과 같은 요인들의 상호작용을 포함한다. 아무도 그런 넓은 범위의 차이를 완전히 이해 받으리라 기대하지 않는다. 그러므로 지도자들은 특히 그들이 기꺼이 배우며, 배울 수 있다는 것을 보여주어야만 한다.

19 어휘 demonstrate 입증하다 / literate 읽고 쓸 수 있는 / artificially 인공적으로 / primitive 원시 사회의 / sophisticated 세련된 / indicate 나타내다 / abacus 주판 / numeral 숫자

해석 어느 정도 지식을 가지고 있었던 선사시대의 사람들, 아이들, 그리고 심지어 동물들은 물체, 동작, 수량, 혹은 다른 현실적인 측면을 나타내기 위해 인공적으로 꾸며낸 상징을 쓰는 학식 있는 자가 될 필요가 없다는 것을 입증 해왔다. 원시시대 사람들이나 교양 있는 사람들 모두에게, 돌무덤이 어떤 지역을 나타내는 동안, 화살표는 어떤 특정한 방향을 나타낸다. 두 손가락을 세워 드는 것은 크레파스 두 개, 영화 표 두 장, 혹은 소다 두 잔을 의미할 수 있다. 유사하게, 주판에서 각 구슬 알은 무엇이든 세어지거나 계산되고 있다는 것을 나타낸다. 더 많은 추상적인 상징들은 더 훌륭한 복잡성과 지성을 요구한다. 이제 우리는 우리가 간단한 산술을 수행하는 방법을 알기 훨씬 전에 몇몇 원시사회는 숫자를 사용했다는 것을 인정하고 추측했다. 우리는 그것들을 결합해 무한한 범위의 가능한 의미들을 습득하기 전에 기본적인 상징에 익숙해지도록 한다.

20 어휘 engage in ~에 종사하다 / esteem 존경하다 / authentic 진품인 / phrase 표현하다 / quantity 양 / transient 일시적인, 순간적인 / likewise 똑같이 / persevere 인내하다

해설 사랑의 대상이 '일시적'이고 '순간적'이라는 것은 그 대상의 '양이 아니라 '질'을 나타낸다. 따라서 quantity 대신 quality를 사용하는 것이 적절하다.

해석 17세기에, 철학자 Benedict de Spinoza는 그의 중년기 재포장에 관여하였다. 그는 대부분의 사람들이 가장 좋은 것으로 여겼던 부, 명성, 그리고 기쁨의 감각들을 추구하는 데 관여된 활동을 고려하는 것으로 시작했다. Spinoza는 이것들이 매력을 가진 반면에 그들은 결코 그가 찾고 있던 진정한 기쁨을 제공할 수 없다고 판단했다. 그는 자신이 "행복이나 불행은 전적으로 우리가 사랑하는 대상의 양에 의존해 만들어진다."라고 표현 한 위대한 발견을 했다. 만약 우리가 순간적인 끌림과 가치들을 사랑한다면 우리의 행복 또한 일시적이고 덧없어 질 것 이다. 반면, 만약 우리가 우리의 사랑을 더 오래 지속되는 가치에 정착시킨다면, 우리의 행복도 마찬가지로 지속되는 경향을 나타낼 것이다.

21 어휘 evoke 떠올려주다 / enchanted 마법에 빠진

해석 우리 아이들이 아주 어렸을 때, 나는 그들에게 A. A. Milne이 쓴 곰돌이 푸 이야기를 읽어 주었다. 이 동화는 자연을 마법에 걸린 존재, 의미와 목적으로부터 활기를 받는 존재처럼 보게 하는 유아적 관점을 부추긴다. 책 앞부분에서, 곰돌이 푸는 숲으로 걸어가다가 큰 오크나무와 마주친다. 그 나무의 꼭대기에서 "시끄러운 윙윙거리는 소리가 들려왔다." 곰돌이 푸는 나무 발치에 앉아서 머리를 두 손 사이에 끼고 생각하기 시작했다. 무엇보다, 그는 "저 윙윙거리는 소리는 뭔가를 의미해. 만약 윙윙거리는 소리가 있다면, 누군가 윙윙거리는 소리를 만든다는 것이고 내가 아는 윙윙거리는 소리를 낼 유일한 이유는 바로 네가 꿀벌이기 때문이지." 라고 혼잣말을 했다. 그 후 그는 또 한참을 생각하고 말 했다. "그리고 내가 아는 꿀벌이 존재할 유일한 이유는 꿀을 만들기 위해서야." 그 후 그는 일어서서 말 했다. "그리고 꿀을 만드는 유일한 이유는 내가 맛 볼 수 있게 하기 위해서지." 그리고 그는 나무를 기어오르기 시작했다.

22 어휘 reveal 드러내다 / call for 요청하다 / incident 사건 / credibility 신뢰성 / savvy 지식 / conventional 관례적인

해석 최근 일어난 파워 블로거 사건은 온라인상의 권위자들의 추잡한 면을 폭로한다. 총 4,983명의 사람들이 온라인 기사 전문가에 대항하여 사이버 반대 운동을 펼치고 일반인들을 속인 것에 대해 사과와 보상을 요구했다. 이 사건은 전문적인 블로거들의 권력의 범위와 책임감을 조명했다. 설문에 따르면, 블로그 게시물을 포함한 온라인 매체는 TV의 뒤를 이어 신뢰성 순위 2위를 차지했다. 이것은 그들이 급격히 옛 매체들을 대신하고 기술적 지식을 가진 사람들 사이에서 그들의 영향력이 커진다는 것을 나타낸다. 이러한 블로거들은 그저 독자들을 즐겁게 해주는 것만은 아니다. 그들은 사람들의 쇼핑 패턴에 영향을 주고 광고 효과를 만들어 낸다. Online Today는 이러한 파워 블로거들이 일반적인 매체 광고보다 10배 이상의 광고 효과를 만들어 낼 수 있다고 보도했다. 이제 사회가 블로거들이 지휘하는 사업에 다른 온라인 사업가들만큼 책임감을 부가할 방법을 찾을 시간이다. 우리는 먼저 그들이 게시물과 행위에 책임감을 가지게 할 방법을 생각해야 한다.

23 어휘 decline 감소 / bring under 억압하다 / bring about 야기하다, 유발하다 / result in ~ 결과가 되다 / result from 원인이 되다 / improvement 향상 / prolong 연장시키다 / add to 늘이다 / offset by 상쇄하다

해석 전 세계 인구가 종합적으로 증가한다는 것을 의미하는 사망률의 감소는 산아제한 운동을 야기한다. 18세기와 19세기 동안의 과학적 발전은 선진국에서의 생활에 더 나은 음식 제공, 질병의 통제, 그리고 더 안전한 근무 환경의 결과를 유발했다. 이런 향상은 의약 발전과 결합되어 인간의 생명을 구하고 수명을 연장시켰다. 1800년대 동안, 이전까지는 사망률에 상쇄되어 왔던 출생률은 인구 성장이 생명을 유지할 수 있을 만큼 적절한 자원을 제공할 이 행성의 능력을 앞지를 것인가에 대한 많은 사람들의 걱정거리가 되었다.

24 어휘 conscious 의식하는 / eventually 결국 / attend to 처리하다 / inquire 묻다 / require 요구하다 / disrupt 방해하다 / erupt 분출하다 / disclose 밝히다 / distort 비틀다

해석 어떤 행동은 그것을 배울 때 완전히 의식해서 집중하기를 요구한다. 그러나 결국 그들은 우리가 다른 일을 하면서 안전하게 수행할 수 있는 아주 일상적이며 자동적인 것이 된다. 예를 들어, 핵심적인 기술을 습득한 후에, 우리는 대화하거나 음악을 들으며 자동차를 운전할 수 있다. 그러나 우리는 사실 그것들을 수행하는 동안에 그런 기술들을 아주 조금 처리한다. 오직 무언가가 일상적인 반복을 방해할 때만 이제는 자동적으로 된 일에 다시 집중을 한다. 또한, 대부분 사람들이 길을 잃었다고 알아차렸을 때 하는 처음의 것은 자동차의 라디오를 끄는 것이다. 마치 오디오 주파수가 길에 집중하는 우리의 능력을 뒤튼 것처럼. 우리의 의식적인 집중은 한 번에 하나의 행동에 제한되어 있다.

25 어휘 tempt 부추기다 / statistically 통계상으로 / regardless 개의치 않고 / crave 열망하다 / veneer 겉치장

보기 ① 확률과의 화해
② 행운은 항상 기쁜 일이다.
③ 허리케인 : 끔찍한 경험들
④ 무작위성 : 문제해결에 대한 장애물들
⑤ 통계와 확률 간의 차이점들

해석 우리가 누군가 "운이 좋다"거나 "운이 나쁘다"고 생각하는 것은, 결국 이른바 확률에서 오는 운에서 유래한다. 그것은 그런 방식의 확률의 결과가 무언가 "일어나도록 의도 된"것처럼 해석하기를 부추긴다. 그러나 사실은 복권에 당첨되거나 허리케인으로부터 직접적인 타격을 받는 것은 그 경험이 얼마나 기쁠지, 끔찍 할지와 관계 없이 통계적으로 설명 가능한 사건이다. 이것은 특히 확실성을 갈망하는 인간의 뇌에게는 받아들이기 힘든 것이다. 확률은 우리가 하는 모든 것의 기저를 이룬다는 것을 아는 것은 꼭 더 받아들이기 쉬운 결과를 만든다는 것은 아니다. 그러나 그것은 신비성으로 겉치장하지 않았다는 것을 사실로 받아들임으로써 만족 할 것이다.

26 어휘 identical 동일한 / perception 지각, 자각 / tangible 실존하는

보기 ① 시간과 인간의 관계
② 천문대에서의 시간
③ 가상현실 속의 시간
④ 시간을 제어하는 방법
⑤ 시간의 상대성

해석 시간은 당신이 가만히 있느냐, 움직이느냐에 따라 다른 비율로 흘러간다. 만약 당신이 우주선을 타고, 아니면 비행기나 지하철을 타고 여행한다면 시간은 다르게 흐른다. 1975년 해군은 두 개의 시계를 사용하여 어떤 실험을 했다. 그들은 하나를 땅에 놓고, 하나를 비행기에 실었다. 시간을 비교하기 위해 두 시계 사이로 레이저가 쏘아지는 동안 비행기가 열다섯 시간 동안 비행했다. 결과는 움직이는 비행기 안의 시간이 느리게 갔다고 나왔다. 시간은 또한 지각에 좌우된다. 여자는 그 영화를 좋아하는데 반해 남자는 싫어한다는 사실을 제외하고는 함께 같은 영화를 보는 남녀를 상상해 보아라. 그녀에게는 그 영화가 너무 빨리 끝나는 것처럼 느껴질 것이다. 남자에게는, 평생 동안 계속되는 것처럼 느껴졌을 것이다. 영화가 7시에 시작했고 엔딩 크레디트가 8시 57분에 올라왔다는 사실에는 둘 다 동의한다. 그러나 그들은 그 한 시간 오십칠 분의 경험에 대해서는 동의하지 않는다. 실제로 어떤 사람의 시간은 다른 사람의 시간과 같지 않다.

27 어휘 compost 퇴비 / dirt 먼지, 때, 흙

해석 퇴비는 정원의 토양에 더해질 수 있는 자연적인 물질 혹은 전반적인 질이 향상된 흙이다. 그것은 여러모로 유용하다. 먼저, 정원의 토양에 퇴비를 뿌리는 것은 식물을 더 건강하게 만든다. 이것은 퇴비가 매우 중요하고 식물에게 음식과 같은 역할을 하는 영양분을 함유하고 있기 때문이다. 게다가, 토양에 퇴비를 더하면 물을 더 오랫동안 머금고 있다. [이것은 물이 토양에 더 오래 머무른다는 것과 식물이 길어진 건기를 이겨낼 수 있도록 한다는 것을 의미한다.] 퇴비의 다른 장점은 가정에서 처리해야 할 쓰레기의 양이 줄어든다는 것이다. 미국 가정의 24퍼센트의 가정 쓰레기들은 내다 버리는 대신 퇴비화 시킬 수 있는 자연 물질로 구성되어 있다. 이것은 커피찌꺼기, 바나나 껍질, 그리고 오래된 신문과 같은 물건들을 포함한다. 이러한 물건들이 쓰레기통에 들어가는 대신 퇴비화 되었을 때 이것은 전체 지역사회에게 이득을 준다.

28 어휘 satellite (인공) 위성 / communications 정보통신 / pest 해충

해석 수백 개의 위성들이 우주에서 지구 주위를 맴돈다. 그들은 로켓으로 우주로 쏘아 보내어 졌고 아마 10년이나 그 이상 거기에 머무를 것이다. 이러한 위성들은 지구, 혹은 날씨 살피기, 그렇지 않으면 우주로 나아갈 각각의 역할들이 있다. 날씨 위성들은 기상 캐스터들이 날씨가 어떨지를 말 해주는 것을 돕는다. 이러한 위성들은 구름이 어디에 형성되어 있는지, 어디로 그들이 갈지를 볼 수 있다. 그들은 바람과 비를 살피며 공기와 지면이 얼마

나 뜨거울지를 잰다. [정보통신 위성들은 TV 프로그램과 전화 메시지를 세상에 옮긴다.] 이러한 것들은 우리가 지구 반대편에 있는 사람들과 이야기 할 수 있게 해 주고 멀리 떨어진 나라에서 일어나는 일들을 볼 수 있게 해 준다. 지구 감시망 위성들은 공해를 감시한다. 바다의 기름 유출과 도시의 공해를 이러한 위성들을 통해 선명한 사진으로 보여준다. 그들은 농작물들이 얼마나 잘 자라는지, 해충과 질병을 찾아냄으로써 농부를 도울 수 있다. 위성 망원경은 천문학자들이 우주 너머 멀리를 볼 수 있게 해 주고 그 너머에 무엇이 있는지 알아낼 수 있게 해 준다. 그들은 또한 천문학자들에게 블랙홀이 어디에 있을지에 대해서도 알려준다.

29 어휘 stroke 뇌졸중 / fluctuate 등락을 거듭하다 / diabetes 당뇨병 / distribute 나누어주다 / regardless 개의치 않고

해설 여기 과체중인 모든 사람들을 위한 훌륭한 장려책이 있다. 살을 빼는 것은 즉각적으로 당신이 심장마비나 뇌졸중을 앓을 확률을 감소시킬 수 있다. 만약 당신의 혈중 콜레스테롤이 높으면 그것은 제일 먼저 해야 할 일이다. 그러나 요요현상이 올 만큼(다시 살이 찔 수 있을 만큼) 너무 빨리 많이 살을 빼지는 마라. 연구원은 만약 당신의 몸무게가 10파운드 이상 쪘다 빠졌다 하기를 반복한다면 당신은 심장마비로 죽을 확률을 두 배 높이는 것이라고 시사했다. 만약 당신이 과체중이면 뇌졸중을 일으킬 가능성이 높은 심장병, 당뇨병, 고혈압을 가지고 있을 가능성이 높다. 그러나 당신의 몸무게가 어떻게 분포 해 있느냐는 당신이 몇 킬로그램이냐 보다 더 중요할 수 있다. 사과 형 몸매(지방이 복부에 집중되어 있는 것)인 사람들은 배 형 몸매(엉덩이와 허벅지에 지방이 있는 것)인 사람들 보다 뇌졸중의 위험이 두 배 높다. 그러나 연구자들은 사람의 몸매와 상관없이 과체중이 남성보다 여성에게 더 많은 뇌졸중의 위험을 가져다준다는 것을 발견했다.

30 어휘 acquire 얻다 / opt 택하다 / explicitly 명쾌하게 / implicitly 암암리에 / ownership 소유 / comfort 안락, 위안 / increasingly 점점 더

해설 ① 우리는 이동통신 기술로부터 이득을 얻기 위해서는 최소한 몇 가지 우리의 개인적인 부분은 포기해야 할지도 모른다.

해석 인류의 이동성 추적과 모형화는 인류의 삶을 발전시킬 훌륭한 가능성을 가지고 있으나 논란이 많은 목적으로 사용될 수 있다. 요즘, 연구원, 기업, 그리고 정부가 우리의 개인적인 위치와 움직임에 대한 정보를 얻고 이로부터 이익을 얻을 수 있을지 아닌지는 대체로 우리에게 달려 있다. 어느 정도는 우리는 이러한 단체들이 우리에 대한 정보를 모으는 것을 허락하도록 선택한다. 우리의 위치와 움직임이 기록될 수 있는 이동통신 기술과 어플리케이션을 사용할 것을 선택함으로써 우리는 동의한다. 명백하게든 은연중에든 간에 다른 사람들에게 우리의 개인정보로부터 이득을 취할 것을 허가하는 것이다. 한때 우리는 우리의 위치 정보에 대한 소유권을 잃고 있었다. 다른 사람들은 법의 범주 안에서 이익을 얻기 위해 그 정보를 우리의 허락 없이 사고팔았을 수 있다. 지금은 우리가 스위치를 "꺼짐"으로 돌릴 수 있다는 것을 앎으로 위안을 받을지라도 점점 늘어나는 유비쿼터스 환경의 이동통신 기술은 곧 피하기 어려울 것이라는 점을 시사하고 있다.

31 어휘 yield 내다 / alternative 대안 / indisputably 명백하게 / composite 합성물 / inconclusive 결정에 이르지 못한 / installation 설치 / committed 헌신적인 / ongoing 계속 진행 중인

해설 ① 충전재의 소재

해석 여러 해 동안, 아말감(아연, 구리, 주석, 은, 수은의 복합체)과 금, 오직 두 종류의 충전재만이 가능했다. 그러나 플라스틱 기술의 발전은 이러한 오래 된 대비책들에게 몇몇 멋진 대안들을 내 놓았다. 충전재로 가장 훌륭한 것은 명백히 금이다. 그러나 그것은 아말감이나 플라스틱 합성물을 이용하는 것보다 열 배 이상 비용이 들 수 있다. 금 충전재는 다른 것들보다 더 긴 20년까지 유지될 수 있다. 아말감 충전재의 안전성에 대한 결말이 나지 않은 연구들에도 불구하고 (수은이 들었기 때문), 대부분의 치과 의사들은 아직도 비교적인 내구성, 시술의 편리함, 저렴한 비용 때문에 그들을 깊이 신뢰한다. 미국치과협회 또한 여전히 그들의 역할에 대해 헌신적이며 그 물질이 안전하다고 한다. 아마 아말감 논란 때문에 플라스틱 합성물 충전재들은 인기를 얻고 있는 것 같다. 그들 또한 치아 색과 같으며, 사실상 보이지 않게 만들 수 있다는 장점이 있다. 계속 진행되는 조사는 그들의 내구성과 설치의 간편함을 개선시킬 수 있다.

32 **어휘** salaries 급료 / effectiveness 유효 / associate 연상하다 / frequently 자주 / evaluation 평가 / adjustment 수정

해설 ① 업무수행 수준에 따른 급료의 수정

해석 급료는 고용자가 하는 일의 수준과 얼마나 그들이 책임감을 잘 수행하느냐 두 가지 모두와 관련 있다. 모든 직업 임무들은 유효성, 생산성, 그리고 질적으로 다른 수준으로 수행될 수 있다. 그래서 각 직업의 급료 범위가 그것과 관계있다는 것은 타당하다. 높은 수준으로 많은 일을 해내는 고용자는 그저 최소 기준을 달성하고 자주 오류를 저지르는 고용자보다 더 많이 받아야 한다. 연간 업무수행 능력 평가는 고용자들의 월급을 그들의 업무 수행에 관련시키는 이상적인 방법을 제공한다. 개인적인 업무 수행 평가를 결과의 질에 관련시키고 업무수행 수준을 직접적으로 급료에 관련시킴으로써 당신은 개인에게 성과급을 지급한다.

33 **어휘** organism 유기체 / acorn 도토리 / mature 어른스러운 / figuratively 비유적으로 / invariably 변함없이 / accumulation 보이지 않는

해설 ⑤ 성공은 보이지 않는 이점들로부터 생겨난다.

해석 생물학자들은 "생태"의 유기성에 대해 자주 말한다. 숲에서 가장 큰 오크나무는 가장 단단한 씨앗에서 자라났기 때문에 가장 큰 것은 아니다. 그것은 다른 나무들이 햇빛을 가로막지 않았고, 그것을 둘러싼 토양이 풍부했고, 나무껍질을 물어뜯는 토끼가 없었으며 그것이 완전히 성장하기 전에 베어버리는 벌목꾼이 없었기 때문이다. 비유적으로 말해서, 우리는 모두 성공한 사람들이 강인한 씨앗에서부터 왔을 것이라고 생각할 수 있다. 그러나 우리가 그들을 따뜻하게 비추어주는 햇빛과, 뿌리 위에 내려앉은 토양, 토끼들, 그리고 벌목꾼들을 피할 만큼 운이 좋았다는 것에 대해 충분히 아는가? 왕 앞에 서 있는 사람은 모든 것을 스스로 하는 것처럼 보일지 모른다. 그러나 사실, 그들은 변함없이 배우고, 열심히 일하고, 다른 사람은 못할 방식으로 이 세상을 이해할 수 있게 하는 보이지 않는 장점, 놀라운 기회, 그리고 문화유산의 수혜자이다.

34 **어휘** cognitive 인지적

해설 ④ 65~74세의 사람들은 인지적 여가 활동 시간을 35~44세의 사람들 보다 52분 많이 보냈다. (98 - 46 = 52)

해석 위의 그래프는 평균 여가활동 시간을 활동의 종류와 연령에 따라 나타낸다. ① 15~24세의 사람들은 다른 연령의 그룹보다 여가활동에 더 많은 시간을 보냈다. 반면 33~44세의 그룹은 여가활동에 가장 적은 시간을 보냈다. ② 하루에 여가활동으로 사용한 시간의 평균 양은 45세까지는 줄어드는 경향이 있다가, 그 지점을 넘어서면 다시 늘어났다. ③ 15~24세의 사람들은 사회적인 활동에 많은 여가활동 시간을 보냈다. 그리고 또한 육체적인 활동에 다른 연령의 그룹보다 많은 시간을 할애했다. ④ 65~74세의 사람들은 인지적 여가 활동에 35~44세의 사람들 보다 하루에 31분 많이 보냈다. ⑤ 인지적 여가활동에 보낸 시간은 45세 이후에 증가하였고 65~74세 그룹에서 가장 극적으로 증가하는 경향이 있었다.

35 **어휘** gradually 서서히 / empathize 공감하다 / crucial 중대한 / hatred 증오 / autonomous 자주적인 / rejoice 크게 기뻐하다 / exasperating 매우 짜증내다 / milestone 중요한 단계 / consequence 결과

해석 많은 청소년들이 Jean Piaget이 구체적 조작적 사고라고 불렀던 것에서 형식적 조작으로 서서히 바꿀 것이다. 형식적 조작은 다른 사람들에게 둘러싸이는 것을 포함하여, 진실 되게 가설할 수 있는 능력과 다른 사람들과 더 깊이 공감할 수 있는 능력이다.
(B) 이러한 변화의 일부분은 질문하고 궁금해 하기 위해 중요히 필요하다. 그리고 특히 우리가 어렸을 때 받은 많은 가치와 신념에 대한 질문들에게 그러하다. 다시 말해, 청소년이 "정말 착한 사람도 증오심을 느낄 수 있나요?"같은 것들을 묻는 것은 평범할 뿐 아니라, 필수적인 일이다.
(A) 이 최근 생겨난 자주적인 질문들로 그들의 자녀가 건강하고 정상적이며 "예정대로"라는 것을 인식한 부모들은 매우 기뻐하고 안심 할 것이다. 심지어 때때로 그들의 자녀가 짜증스럽게 구는 것을 발견한다 해도 말이다.
(C) 반면, 이것이 건강하고 정상적이라는 것을 이해하지 못하는 부모들은 아마 어떤 것이 그들을 제어하고 이 흥미진진한 사건을 예방하게 할 수 있을지에 대해 불행한 결과를 야기하며 걱정하고 있을 것이다.

36 **어휘** pedestrian 보행자 / cyclist 자전거 이용자 / linear 직선의 / fatality 사망자 / caput(복수 capita) 머리 / neatly 깔끔하게

해석 너는 거리에 보행자나 자전거 이용자가 더 늘어남에 따라 그들이 사고를 당할 확률도 높아진다고 생각할지 모른다. 당신이 옳다.

(A) 다시 말해, 보행자나 자전거 이용자들이 늘어남에 따라, 1인당 사망률이 떨어지기 시작한다. 보행자들이 더 많은 보행자 동료들에게 둘러싸여 더 안전하게 움직이기 시작했기 때문은 아니다. 사실, 그 반대이다.

(B) 미국의 다른 어떤 곳 보다 New York시에서 더 많은 보행자들이 자동차에 의해 부상을 당하거나 사망에 이른다. 그러나 California의 공중위생 자문가인 Peeter Jacobsen은 이러한 관계들이 일직선상에 있지 않다는 것을 알아냈다.

(C) 운전자의 태도가 변화한 것이다. 갑자기 그들에게 어디서나 보행자들이 보인다. 그들은 더 많이 볼수록, 더 천천히 운전한다. 그리고 딱 들어맞게 순환 고리를 이루어 그들은 더 천천히 운전하고, 더 많은 보행자들을 효과적으로 발견한다. 왜냐하면 보행자들이 더 오래 시야에 들어오기 때문이다.

37 **어휘** participant 참가자 / altruistic 이타적인 / doubtful 의심스러운 / conservative 보수적인 / prudent 신중한 / rational 합리적인

해석 심리학자들이 흥미로운 실험을 고안했다. 이 실험의 서두에, 그들은 참가자들에게 다음 질문에 답하도록 요청했다. '만약 어떤 회사가 각 1,200달러에 컴퓨터 열다섯 대를 구입한다면, 당신이 계산하기에 회사는 총 얼마를 지불해야 하는가?' 이것은 수학적인 문제가 아니었다. 그것의 목표는 참가자들을 더 계산적으로 준비시키려는 것이었다. 다른 참가자들은 그들의 감정을 준비시키는 질문을 받았다. 질문에 답한 후에, 참가자들은 한 아프리카 소녀의 개인적인 슬픈 이야기에 대한 것과 아프리카의 식량 부족과 같은 일반적인 것에 대한 정보를 받았다. 그 후, 그들은 다음과 같은 경우에 얼마나 많은 돈을 기부할지 질문 받았다. 결과는 감정을 느낄 준비가 된 사람들이 전반적인 식량 부족 문제의 해결을 돕는 것보다 그 아프리카 소녀에게 훨씬 더 많은 돈을 기부했다는 것을 보여주었다. 그리고 더 많이 계산적으로 생각한 사람들은 양쪽의 경우 모두에 거의 똑같이 적은 양의 돈을 기부함으로써 평등한 구두쇠가 되었다.

→실험에 따르면, 감정을 느낄 준비가 된 사람들이 더 계산적인 방식으로 생각한 사람들보다 더 이타적이 되었다.

⊕ [38~39]

sympathetic 동정어린, 호의적인 / anticipate 예상하다, 기대하다 / convince 납득시키다 / in good hands 안심할 수 있는 / opportunity 기회 / portray 그리다 / in place 제 자리에 있는
「Martin은 모여 있는 군중들 앞에 서 있었다. 그는 거대한 건설 프로젝트를 위해 가장 적합한 건축 회사를 선택하기를 바라는 호의적이며 기대어린 미래 고객의 청중들에게 말을 하려는 참이었다. Martin은 건설 회사의 주요 설계사 중 하나였다. 그리고 그는 그의 청중들을 그의 회사와 함께라면 안심할 수 있으며 그가 그 일과 의뢰인의 요구사항을 그들이 여태까지 입찰에 초대 한 다른 누구보다 잘 이해하고 있다고 확신시킬 필요가 있었다. 그런데, 청중에게 발표를 할 기회를 주어서 감사하며 그들에게 자기 회사의 비전을 공유하게 되어 흥분된다고 그가 말하기 시작했을 때, 그의 얼굴은 그를 배신했다. 기쁨의 흔적도, 심지어 흥분의 자국도 아닌 어떤 긍정의 감정도 그의 얼굴에는 깃들어 있지 않았다. 그의 말은 그가 느끼고 묘사하는 감정과 극명한 대조를 이루었다. Martin은 자신의 얼굴 근육이 얼어붙어 꼼짝 않는 것을 느꼈다. 그는 소개하는 동안 애써 웃거나 하다못해 편안히 무표정을 짓는 것조차 불가능했다. 그는 긴장되고, 불편하고, 걱정스러워 보였다.」

38 **해설** ⑤ 흥분의 감정을 나타내며 고객을 안심시켜 주어야 했으나 편안한 표정을 지을 수 없었다.

① 그의 얼굴은 그를 배신했다.

② 그는 대단히 안도하였다.

③ 그의 눈은 눈부시게 반짝거렸다.

④ 그는 그의 손가락을 교차시켰다.

⑤ 그는 그의 머리를 높이 치켜세웠다.

[40~41]

stationary 정지된 / presence 존재, 장소 / constantly 거듭되는 / herd 무리, (짐승 등을) 몰다 / school(고래 혹은 생선) 떼 / revealing 흥미로운 / glimpse 언뜻 봄

「해양 생물학자들은 종종 바다 속에서 실제로 어떤 일이 일어나는지 확인하는 것이 얼마나 어려운지 때문에 좌절한다. 바다표범, 바다사자, 그리고 고래들과 같은 거대한 해양 동물의 복잡한 습성을 관찰하는 것은 항상 그런 문제를 가져온다. 우리가 아는 대로, 그들은 인간 잠수부들에게는 너무 빠르게, 너무 멀리 이동한다. 하물며 정지된 카메라는 도저히 그들이 움직임을 기록할 수 없다. 어떻게 사람들이 그들을 따라잡을 수 있다 하더라도, 그들은 거의 확실히 거추장스러운 존재가 되어 있을 것이다. 그리고 그 동물들은 평소처럼 행동하지 않을 것이다. 그러면 동물들이 스스로 사진을 찍게 내버려 두는 것은 어떤가? 이것은 이러한 동물들에게 부착시킬 수 있는 작고 간결한 수중 비디오카메라, "Crittercam"의 숨겨진 이야기이다. 이러한 동물들의 습성에 대한 우리의 지식은 한때 대부분 전적으로 그들을 육지와 수면에서 관찰한 것에서부터 왔다. Crittercam은 우리가 그들을 대부분의 시간을 보내는 물속에서도 관찰할 수 있게 해주었다. 이것은 우리에게 새롭고 끊임없는 성장을 주었으며 그들이 물속에서 무엇을 하는지 꿰뚫어 볼 수 있게 해주었다. 예를 들어, 최근에, Crittercam은 혹등고래들이 먹이를 제공하기 위해 무리로 쏘아들어가기 전에 청어 떼를 단단한 거품 속으로 몰기 위해 거품 막을 사용하는 최초의 수중 영상을 기록하였다. 이것은 우리에게 흥미롭고 새로운 바다 속의 삶을 살짝 경험하게 해주었다.」

40 해설 나머지는 모두 해양 동물들을 가리키지만 ②는 해양 동물들을 관찰하기 위해 다이빙한 'People'을 가리킨다.

41 해설 해양 동물에게 부착하는 방식의 비디오카메라이다.

[42~43]

Arbor Day 식목일 / appreciate 인정하다

「(A) 식목일은 1800년대 Nebraska에서 시작 되었다. 이 특별한 날의 이름은 'arbor'라는 단어에서 유래했는데, 그 단어는 몇 가지 다른 언어에서 나무라는 뜻을 가지고 있다. 그 당시 미국 중심부에 있는 주인 Nebraska는 나무가 거의 없었다. 다른 주에서 Nebraska에 이주 해 온 사람들은 나무 보기를 즐겨했고 집과, 공원, 들판에 나무가 있었으면 했기 때문에 매우 불만족스러웠다.

(B) Morton씨와 그의 아내는 모든 이들에게 본보기가 되기를 원했기 때문에 그들은 많은 나무들을 그들의 땅에 심었다. Morton씨는 또한 그가 일하는 신문에 나무에 대한 기사를 썼다. 사람들은 그의 아이디어에 매우 흥미를 가지고 나무의 중요성을 깨닫기 시작했다.

(C) 그가 기사를 작성하기 시작한 후 얼마 지나지 않아, Nebraska의 사람들은 나무를 심기 시작했다. 1870년대쯤에는 Nebraska에 백만 그루 이상의 나무가 있었다. Morton씨는 그의 아이디어가 도움이 된 것을 알고 매우 자랑스러워했다.

(D) Nebraska로 이주해 온 사람들 중에 미국 북쪽에 있는 주인 Michigan주에서 온 한 남자와 그의 아내가 있었다. Sterling Morton씨 부부는 전원을 사랑했으며 나무의 중요성을 잘 알고 있었다. 그들은 Nebraska가 더 나은 미래를 위해 나무가 필요할 것이라고 보았다.」

42 해설 문맥상 Nebraska로 이주해온 사람들 중 Sterling Morton씨 부부가 나무의 중요성을 알리기 위해 나무를 심고 기사를 썼으며, 그 이후 마을 사람들에게 알려져 많은 나무를 심게 되었다는 내용이 되어야 하므로 (D) – (B) – (C)가 자연스럽다.

43 해설 (B)의 'they began to plant large numbers of trees on their own land.'를 미루어 보아 공원이 아닌 자신의 땅에 나무를 심었다는 사실을 알 수 있다.

✧ [44~45]

---

fraction 분수 / conjecture 추측 / rectangle 직사각형 / numerator 분자 / astonished 크게 놀란 / extinguished 끝내다, 불을 끄다

「학기가 끝날 무렵, Deborah Ball은 3학년 수학 수업이 진전되어 가는 것에 전반적으로 만족했다. 그러나 오늘 오후, 시계가 하루의 끝을 향해 째깍거렸을 때, 그녀에게 문제가 생겼다. 그것은 작은 금발머리 소녀 Nancy가 분자가 커질수록 더 큰 값을 얻어낸다는 것을 알아차렸을 때 시작되었다. Ball 선생님은 학생들에게 Nancy의 추측이 맞는지 알아내도록 시켰다. 한 학생이 4/4와 5/5를 제시했다. Ball 선생님은 단순히 이 두 분수들이 똑같다고 말할 수 있었다. 하지만 대신에 그녀는 학생들에게 공책에 하나는 4등분 된, 그리고 나머지 하나는 5등분 된 두 개의 직사각형을 그리도록 했다. 그 후에 분자를 색칠하라고 했다. 그녀는 곧 모두가 5/5가 더 많이 칠해지지 않은 것을 알아차리리라 자신했다. 그러나 그녀가 학생들에게 물어보았을 때, 그녀는 화들짝 놀랐다. 키가 큰 소녀 Cassandra는 그들이 다른 숫자라고 말했다. Ball 선생님이 이런 상황에서 무엇을 할지를 계산하는 것은 확실히 몇 가지 수학적 지식이 요구된다. 그러나 그것은 더 많은 것을 필요로 했다. 학생들을 가르치기 위해서 Ball 선생님 자신이 수학을 이해하는 것은 충분치 않았다. 그녀는 학생들을 어떻게, 그리고 왜 올바르게 고쳐줘야 하는지, 그리고 그녀가 그들에게 알아내 보라고 할지 혹은 올바른 답을 말 해 줄지에 대해 생각했다. 마침내, 그녀는 학생들은 선생님이 문제를 해결할 수 있도록 연습하는 것을 북돋아 줄 때만 학습할 수 있다는 John Dewey의 입장에 마음이 기울었다. 그녀는 편지 봉투 두 개를 뽑아 들고 그것을 상상속의 쿠키라고 가정했다. 그리고 그 중 하나를 네 조각으로, 하나는 다섯 조각으로 잘랐다. 그녀와 학생들은 조각들에 대해서 대화를 하고 다시 조각들을 테이프로 붙였다. 수업이 끝날 무렵, 여전히 반대 의견들은 사라지지 않았지만, 그녀는 학생들에게 수학적으로 사고하고 스스로 답을 구하는 것을 가르칠 수 있었다.」

---

44 해설 ③ 실천을 통해 학생들이 배울 수 있도록 북돋아 주다.

45 해설 ② 칠판이 아닌 공책에 사각형을 그려 두 개의 분수 값이 같음을 설명했다.

2014학년도 정답 및 해설

ANSWER

01	02	03	04	05	06	07	08	09	10	11	12	13	14	15	16	17	18	19	20
④	④	③	②	⑤	①	③	④	④	⑤	②	②	③	⑤	①	①	①	③	③	①
21	22	23	24	25	26	27	28	29	30	31	32	33	34	35	36	37	38	39	40
②	③	①	④	⑤	④	④	④	③	②	③	②	④	⑤	⑤	③	①	④	③	①
41	42	43	44	45															
⑤	①	⑤	②	②															

---

01 **어휘** freezing 꽁꽁 얼게 추운 gruesome 끔찍한, 섬뜩한

해설 사라는 끔찍한 장면을 보면 토할 것 같다고 했지 현재 기분이 그렇다고 한 건 아니므로 ④번이 옳지 않다.

해석 Sarah : 나는 우리가 오늘 공원에 갈 계획을 세운 걸로 알고 있는데, 너무 춥다. 영화 보는 게 어때?

Megan : 좋은 생각이야! 지난주에 새로운 공포 영화가 나왔다고 들었어.

Sarah : 만약 끔찍한 걸 보면 난 토할지 몰라. 넌 다른 사람이랑 가는 게 나을걸.

Megan : Jim에게 나중에 전화해야겠다. 근데, 오늘은 네가 알아서 해. 네 기분은 어떤데?

Sarah : 내가 좋아하는 배우가 피겨 스케이팅에 관한 영화를 만들었어, 그거 확인해 보자.

02 **어휘** demographic 인구학의 extensive 광범위한 qualification 자격

해석 Karen : 당신의 회사와 인터뷰하게 되어 정말 감사합니다.

면접관 : 와주셔서 감사합니다. 간단한 질문으로 시작해 볼게요. 우선, 광고에 대해 어떤 경험을 가지고 계신가요?

Karen : 사실, 이 분야에는 생소합니다. 단지 TV광고를 만드는 2주간의 계약직을 마쳤을 뿐입니다. 그러나 그 전에, 저는 주로 아이 돌봄과 교육 분야에서 일했습니다.

면접관 : 그것에 대해 더 얘기해 주시죠. 당신의 아이 돌봄 경험이 광고 경력에 도움이 된다고 생각하십니까?

Karen : 물론이죠! 젊은 사람들은 광고주들에겐 가치 있는 인구학인걸요. 그래서 그들의 생각과 의견을 이해하는 것이 중요합니다.

면접관 : 전적으로 동의합니다. 저도 두 아이가 있고 그들은 항상 그들이 TV에서 보는 새로운 전자기계를 사달라고 조르거든요.

03 **어휘** get involved with ~에 참여하다 draft 선발하다, 징병하다 step into one's shoes 후계자가 되다 memorabilia 기념품 tribute to ~에 대한 헌사

해설 전쟁에 관한 내용의 언급으로 보아 전쟁 박물관임을 알 수 있다.

해석 Gina : 어떻게 여기를 돕는 것에 참여하시게 되었나요?

Suzie : 사실, 두 가지 대답이 있습니다. 첫째, 나의 대학에서 우리가 지역의 교육, 문화 센터를 지원하도록 격려하고 있습니다.

Gina : 구체적으로 당신은 여기 무엇에 끌리셨나요?

Suzie : 그것이 두 번째 대답입니다. 나의 증조부께서 내 나이 이었을 때, 해외로 싸우기 위해 징병되셨어요. 그는 이미 돌아가셨지만, 나는 그의 오래된 일기에 마음을 쏟아 부었고, 여기에 참여하는 것이 그의 전쟁 경험을 이어갈 또 다른 방법입니다. 나는 여기 전쟁 기념품에 관한 최근의 전시회를 계획했을 때 그의 자리를 대신하는 것처럼 느꼈어요.

Gina : 그것이 제복을 입은 사람들의 용감한 희생에 대한 딱 맞는 헌사군요. 그리고 당신의 여행이 얼마나 유익한지에 대해 제가 기뻐하고 있다고 꼭 말하고 싶네요. 제 갤러리를 당신에게 보여주는 것으로 어떤 보답을 하고 싶군요. 여기 제 카드입니다.

04 어휘 catch up on 만회하다, 따라잡다 freak out 놀라다, 흥분하다 breeze 산들바람, 식은 죽 먹기 exorbitant 지나친, 비싼 buck 달러

해설 Molly는 그 수업에 결석하여 다른 곳에서 보충을 했다고 말하였으므로 ②번이 옳다.

해석 Roger : 너의 필기를 볼 수 있겠니? 나는 Willis 교수님이 낭만시대의 예술 작품에 대해 설명하려고 하신 것을 이해 못하겠어.

Molly : 나 그 날 결석했어, 기억나? 나중에 나는 스터디 센터에서 Hannah와 그 수업에 대해 보충을 해야 했어. 그래서 그 강의에 대한 필기가 없어.

Roger : 오, 이런! 내가 이해 못한 한 가지가 바로 네가 놓친 거라니.

Molly : 흥분하지 마! Willis 교수님은 교과서대로 말씀하셔. 그러니 네가 그 장을 다시 살펴보면 시험은 식은 죽 먹기 일거야.

Roger : 음, 사실 책도 없어. 신간의 가격이 너무 비싸. 그래서 나는 돈을 조금 절약하고 수업에 의지하려고 했지.

05 어휘 embarrassed 당황스러운 inflexible 변경할 수 없는 confused 혼란스러운 attendance 출석 participation 참여 submit 제출하다 leeway 만회

해석 교수 : 안녕, Pierre. 사무실에 들러 주어 고맙군. 오늘은 무엇을 도와줄까?

Pierre : 음, 여기에 오게 되어 저는 좀 당황스러운데요. 그러나 제 성적에 대해 논의하고 싶어서요. 사실, 당신의 역사 수업에 대한 제 기말 점수에 대해 제가 조금 혼란스럽고 실망스러워서요. 제가 그것에 대해 제기할 방법이 있을까요?

교수 : 모든 학생들이 공평하기 위해서, 내 규칙은 변경할 수가 없다네. 너는 시험은 잘 봤지만, 강의의 거의 반을 빠졌어. 출석과 참여가 너의 성적의 30%야. 또한, 너는 발표 보고서도 기한 보다 2주 늦게 제출했어.

Pierre : 만약 제가 추가 에세이를 제출한다면 어떨까요? 저는 만기일이 지난주인줄 알았어요. 저에게 약간의 만회의 여지를 주실 수 없나요?

교수 : 너는 기회를 놓쳤어. 내가 예외를 둘 수 없어 유감이군.

06 어휘 bet 내기 pickpocket 소매치기

해설 Anthony는 길 가다 부딪힌 Bert를 소매치기로 의심하였다.

해석 Anthony : 이봐, 길 좀 조심하지!

Bert : 정말 미안합니다. 부딪히려고 한 건 아니었어요.

Anthony : 그래! 내가 보기에 너는 소매치기임에 틀림없어. 많이 들어봤거든. 고향에서 모든 사람들이 내가 뉴욕으로 이사하기 전에 나에게 너 같은 사람에 대해 경고해 주었지.

Bert : 정말 실수였어요.

Anthony : 음, 다행인줄 알아. 내 지갑이 아직 내 주머니에 있으니. 그러나 내가 이 주변에서 너를 또 보게 된다면 나는 경찰을 부를 거야.

07 어휘 composer 작곡가 outstanding 눈에 띄는, 뛰어난 be destined to ~할 운명이다 secure 얻다

해설 ①②④⑤는 Bach를 가리키며, ③은 그의 형을 가리킨다.

해석 역대 가장 훌륭한 작곡가로 여겨지는 Johann Sebastian Bach는 그의 생애 동안 주로 뛰어난 오르간 연주자이며 기술자로 알려져 있었다. 음악적인 부모님의 8남매 중 막내로 태어나, 그는 음악가가 될 운명이었다. 어렸을 때, 그는 오르간과 바이올린을 익혔고, 또한 훌륭한 가수였다. 열 살의 나이에, 그의 부모님 두 분 다 서로 일 년 이내에 돌아가셨다. 그의 형인 Johann Christoph가 Johann Sebastian을 데려가, 그의 동생의 음악적 훈련을 계속하게 해주었다. 15세의 나이에, Bach는 뤼네부르크의 St. Michael의 학교 성가대에서 첫 직책을 얻게 되었다. 그는 평생 한 번도 독일을 떠나지 않으며 거의 여행을 하지 않았지만, 그의 경력동안 전국의 궁중과 교회에서 다양한 직책을 맡았다.

08 어휘 oppressed 억압받는 conscience 양심 clarity 명확성 wickedness 사악, 부정 thy 당신의 prominent 뛰어난, 현저한 protest 항의, 시위

해석 억압받는 사람들의 문학은 인간의 양심을 반영한다. 이것을 아프리카계 미국인들의 문학에서보다 더 명확하게 보여주는 곳은 없다. 아프리카계 미국인들의 필수 요소는 전체로써의 문학이 – 이따금 있는 작가들의 작품이 아니라 – 구체적인 악에 대항하는 운동이라는 것이다. 따라서 아프리카계 미국인들의 문학에는, 미국 문학과는 별개의 곳에서 드물게 발견되는 슬픔이 있고, 종종 다른 미국인의 편지에서 드물게 발견되는 범위가 있다. 아프리카계 미국인 작가들이 펜을 들 때 마다, 그의 목표는 미국인들의 인종주의인 경향이 있고, 그의 주제는 그의 국민들의 고통이며, 핵심 요소는 그 자신의 슬픔과 그의 국민들의 슬픔인 것 같다. 몇몇 작가들은 뛰어난 아프리카계 미국인 지도자인 Martin Luther King, Jr.의 "당신의 이웃을 사랑하라."라는 비폭력적인 접근을 다룬다. 거의 모든 아프리카계 미국 문학은 항의에 대한 짐을 다룬다.

09 어휘 sediment 침전물, 퇴적물 sequence 연속 molten 녹은 lava 용암 dike 제방, 둑, 수로 limestone 석회암 adjacent 인접한

해석 퇴적물의 층은 시간이 지나면서 쌓이고, 바위의 형태를 만들 때 까지 계곡과 바다를 채우기 위해 강화된다. 가장 오래된 바위들은 만약 접히거나 결함이 있음으로써 바위의 바닥이 뒤집혀 지지 않는다면 항상 바다에 있다. 땅 아래에, 혹은 화산 안에 너무 많은 녹은 용암이 있을 때, 녹은 바위는 퇴적물의 층을 통과하여 물리적인 힘을 받게 된다. 이것은 화성관입으로 알려져 있고 그것들은 화성암의 많은 층을 지나 화산 수로 안으로 굳어진다. 대리석은 석회암으로 시작하고, 인접한 층의 압력으로 인하여 변화되고, 녹은 바위의 흐름이나 마그마류에서 가열될 것이다. 그러므로, 화성관입이 화성암의 생성을 뚫고 나가는 곳은 항상 주변 층보다 더 최근에 생성된 곳이다.

10 어휘 urge 재촉하다 subsidiary 자회사 give in to ~에 굴복하다 far and away 단연코, 훨씬 encyclopedic 해박한 skeptical 회의적인

해석 자동차 액세서리의 한 프랑스 제조업자가 독일에 있는 자회사의 독일 관리이사에게 독일 TV에 대한 그들의 제품을 광고하도록 계속해서 재촉했다. 그 독일 관리자는 두 가지 이유로 거부했다: 그는 목표 고객이 거의 TV를 보지 않는다는 것과, 그 제품이 독일에서는 생소하다는 것을 알고 있었다. 그는 대신에 인쇄된 광고를 제안했다. 결국, 그는 파리 본사로부터의 지속적인 압박에 굴복하게 되었으나, 다른 4개의 매체 – 텔레비전, 라디오, 광고판, 인쇄된 광고 – 로 동시에 광고를 함으로써 통제된 실험을 해보기로 결정했다. 인쇄된 광고가 단연코 가장 효과적이었다. 이유는? 인쇄된 광고는 회사가 새로운 제품의 많은 특징들을 아주 자세하게 묘사하도록 해주었고, 그것의 새로움 때문에 회의적이었을 독일 소비자들에게 호소력을 얻게 된 해박한 세부사항으로 그 묘사를 뒷받침할 수 있게 해 주었다.

11 어휘 satellite 위성 swirl 소용돌이 cartographer 지도 제작자 serpent 큰 바다뱀 coincidence 우연의 일치 eddy 소용돌이, 회오리 Hanseatic League 한자동맹

해설 ② was의 주어는 the rounded swirls로 주어가 복수의 형태이므로 were가 올바르다.

① to부정사의 부사적 용법중 목적의 용법으로 '~하기 위해로 해석된다.

③ 동사 matches를 수식하므로 부사 closely는 올바르다.

④ current를 수식하는 과거분사로 '발견되는'의 수동으로 해석되므로 올바르다.

⑤ It is believed that '~라고 믿어진다.'

해석 위성영상은 1539년만큼이나 오래 전에 만들어진 바다해류의 지도에서 그려진 물 온도 소용돌이를 일치시키기 위해 이용되었다. 그 지도는 스웨덴의 지도 제작자, Olaus Magnus에 의해 만들어졌다. 바다뱀과 바다 괴물의 사진 사이에 위치한 둥근 소용돌이는 순전히 예술적인 이유로 거기에 있었다고 생각되었다. 그러나 그 소용돌이의 크기, 모양, 위치는 이것이 우연의 일치라고 하기에는 물의 온도 변화에 너무 가깝게 일치한다. 그 지도는 아이슬란드의 남쪽과 동쪽에서 발견된 바다 소용돌이 흐름의 정확한 표현일 가능성이 있다. 그 지도 제작자는 한자동맹의 독일 선원들로부터 그의 정보를 수집했다고 믿어진다.

12 **어휘** fabled 전설적인 seize 장악하다, 움켜잡다 speculate 추측하다 extraterrestrial 외계인 be grounded in ~에 근거를 두다 geomagnetic 지구자기의 flux 흐름 treacherous 위험한, 기만적인 navigation 항해 foul 아주 안 좋은

해설 such as 전치사 뒤에는 동명사가 와야 한다. 따라서 동명사의 의미상의 주어 extraterrestrials 뒤에 capturing 의 형태가 올바르다.

① Bermuda Triangles를 수식하는 형용사

③ disappearances라는 명사를 받는 수량 형용사

④ 뒤의 절을 이끄는 접속사

⑤ '치명적인'이라는 뜻의 형용사로 뒤에 명사 place를 수식하고 있다.

해석 수십 년 동안, 대서양의 전설적인 버뮤다 삼각지대는 배, 비행기, 사람들의 설명할 수 없는 사라짐으로 인간의 상상력을 장악해 왔다. 몇몇은 알려지지 않은 신비한 힘이 연구를 위해 외계인이 인간을 잡아가는 것, 또는 아틀란티스의 사라진 대륙의 영향과 같은 사라짐에 대한 설명을 해준다고 추측한다. 다른 설명들은 분명하진 않지만, 지구자기의 흐름의 붕괴와 같은 과학에 근거를 더 두고 있다. 환경적인 고려는 대부분은 아니지만 많은 사라짐에 대해 설명할 수 있다. 대서양의 열대 폭풍과 허리케인의 대부분이 버뮤다 삼각지대를 지나고, 발전된 기상 예측 이전의 시대에는, 이 위험한 폭풍들이 많은 (사라진) 배들을 뒷받침해 주었다. 또한, 캐리비안 바다의 많은 섬들이 배 항해에 위험할 수 있는 많은 얕은 물의 지대를 만드는 동안, 멕시코 만류가 날씨에 있어서 빠르고 극심한 변화를 유발할 수 있다. 바다는 인간에게는 항상 신비로웠다. 그리고 매우 나쁜 날씨나 서투른 항해가 관련 있을 때는 매우 치명적인 장소가 될 수 있다. 이것은 전 세계적으로 사실이다.

13 **어휘** occupation 직업 demonstrate 입증하다, 증명하다 undecided 결정하지 못한

해설 (A) 앞의 skills를 꾸미므로 형용사 necessary가 와야 한다.

(B) 관련성(The link)이 증명된 것이므로 수동의 has been이 와야 한다.

(C) 주어 more ~ group에 대한 동사가 와야 하므로 enrolled가 옳다.

해석 학생들의 최종 직업 선택은 그들의 흥미와 능력에 영향을 받을 수 있다. 만약 학생들이 특정 직업에 있어서 성공을 위한 필수적인 기술을 갖고 있다고 믿는다면, 그들은 그 직업에 대한 흥미를 더 발달시키고, 그 안에서 직업을 찾으려고 할 것이다. 성공에 대한 기대와 직업 선택 사이에 연관은 전공 선택을 결정하지 못했던 대학생들과 함께 한 실험실에서 증명되었다. 실험실 그룹의 학생들은 간단한 수학 시험을 치르고 통과했다(또는 통과했다고 들었다). 따라서 수학에 있어서 성공에 대한 그들의 기대는 증가했다. 시험을 치르지 않은 학생들과 비교하여, 실험 그룹의 더 많은 학생들이 다음 학기에 수학이나 과학 과목을 등록했거나, 또는 수학이나 과학 전공을 선택했다.

14 어휘 far-reaching 지대한 영향을 끼칠 ample 충분한 deprived 부족한 elusive 찾기 힘든 interminable 끝없이 계속되는 insomnia 불면증

해설 (A) 전치사구 형태로 comparing이 옳다.
(B) 앞의 employees를 선행사로 받기 때문에 목적격 관계 대명사 whom이 와야 한다.
(C) 뒤에 절이 온 형태로 접속사가 와야 하는데 의미상 whether는 적절하지 않다.

해석 "일찍 자고 일찍 일어나는 것은 사람을 건강하고 부유하고 현명하게 만든다."라고 벤자민 프랭클린은 말했다. 그리고 실제로, 연구는 밤에 잘 자는 것에 대한 지대한 영향을 가져 올 이점을 반복적으로 보여주었다. 충분한 잠을 잔(하룻밤에 약 7, 8시간) 성인들과, 만성적으로 피곤한(밤마다 5시간미만의 잠을 자는) 성인들을 비교한 장기간의 연구에서 보면, 휴식을 잘 취한 사람들이 전형적으로 수면이 부족한 또래들보다 약 10년 정도 까지 더 산다. 그러나 "휴식을 가져라"라는 익숙한 조언은 종종 하기보단 말이 더 쉽다. 건강한 수면 습관은 겉보기에 끝없이 계속되는 야간 근무를 하거나, 스케줄이 자주 바뀌는 많은 직장인들에게는 찾기 힘들다. 트럭 운전사나 항공사 종사자들은 특히 그들의 수면에 있어서 규칙적인 혼란에 빠지기 쉽다. 그리고 심지어 일하지 않는 사람들조차도 역시 수면 부족으로 고통을 겪을 수 있다. 예를 들어, 직장에 다니지 않고 있는 신생아의 부모들은 그들의 아기가 태어난 지 일 년 동안은 깊게 잠자기 어렵다는 것을 알 것이다. 불면증과 다른 수면 장애는 매년 수백만 명의 사람들에게 영향을 끼친다. 그러나 좋은 소식은 안전하고 효과적인 치료법이 있다는 것이다.

15 어휘 openly 드러내 놓고 despise 경멸하다 proceed 나아가다, 진행하다 literate 읽고 쓸 줄 아는, 교육 받은 nonliterate 미개의 exterminate 몰살시키다 controversial 논란이 많은

해설 지나 온 역사 속에서 서로 다른 사회들을 나열하며 사회의 불평등을 이야기 하고 있다.

해석 많은 백인 식민지 개척자들은 뉴기니 사람들을 대놓고 "원시적인"것으로 경멸했다. 심지어 1972년에 여전히 칭해지고 있는 것처럼, 최소의 뉴기니의 백인 "주인들"은 뉴기니 사람들보다 훨씬 더 높은 삶의 수준을 즐겼다. 우리 모두는 역사가 세계의 다른 지역의 사람들에게 매우 다르게 나아갔다는 것을 안다. 마지막 빙하기가 끝난 지 13,000년이 지나 세계의 몇몇 지역들은 금속 도구로 교육 받은 산업 사회를 발달시켰고, 다른 지역들은 오직 미개의 농경 사회를 발달시켰고, 여전히 다른 지역들은 돌 도구를 가지고 수렵, 채집 사회를 유지했다. 그러한 역사적인 불평등은 현대 사회에 긴 그림자를 드리우고 있다. 왜냐하면, 금속 도구를 사용하는 교육 받은 사회는 다른 사회를 정복하거나 몰살시켜왔기 때문이다. 그러한 차이들이 세계 역사의 가장 기본적인 사실을 구성하는 반면, 그에 대한 이유는 불확실하고 논란이 많은 상태로 남아 있다.

16 어휘 summit 정상 incident 사고 restrict 제한하다 considerable 상당한

해설 노인들의 산행이 안전하게 계속 되기 위한 방법을 제시했으므로 ①번이 적절하다.

해석 최근에, 노인들 사이에서 산행에 대한 붐이 있어 왔다. 불행히도, 이러한 많은 노인들이 이 취미를 인생에 늦은 시기에 시작했기 때문에 그들은 보통 경험을 통해 얻어지는 기술들이 부족하다. 대신에, 그들은 그들의 꿈의 정상으로 그들을 데려가는 산악 가이드에 의해 이끌어지는 상업적인 단체 여행에 의존한다. 그러나 늘어나고 있는 많은 비극적 사고가 보여주는 것처럼, 여행에 합류하는 것이 뭔가가 잘못 되었을 때 그들의 안전을 보장해 주지는 못한다. 분명히, 노인들이 산에 오르는 것을 막으려고 노력하는 것은 현실적이지 않다. 사실, 사람들은 자연의 야생에서 자유로움을 경험하기 위해 산에 가고, 규칙과 규정으로 산악 활동을 제한하는 것은 활동성의 정신을 파괴하는 것이다. 산에 대한 더 많은 안전 교육과 개인적인 책임감이 앞으로 나아갈 수 있는 한 방법이 될 수 있다. 만약 안전하게 수행된다면, 산행은 육체적, 정신적 건강에 유익하다. 또한 산악지역에서의 관광과 관련된 상당한 경제적 이익들도 있다.

17 어휘 alien 이방인, 외국인, 외계인 obvious 분명한, 명백한, 뻔한 seize up 멈추다 abandon 버리다, 포기하다 obstructively 폐쇄적으로 cynical 냉소적인

해설 첫 번째 이론을 가정하고 검토와 관찰을 한 후 새로운 이론을 언급했기 때문에 내용상 ①번이 적절하다.

해석 이방인으로써, Ford Prefect가 인간에 대해 항상 이해하기 가장 어렵다고 생각했던 것들 중 하나는 "좋은 날이야." 또는 "너는 정말 크다.", "맙소사, 너 30피트나 되는 우물에 빠졌었던 것 같구나, 괜찮아?"와 같은, 당연한 것을 계속적으로 언급하고 반복하는 그들의 습관이었다. 처음에, Ford는 이 이상한 행동을 설명하기 위해 이론 하나를 형성했다. 만약 인간이 그들의 입술을 계속해서 연습하지 않는다면, 그가 생각하기에, 그들의 입은 멈춘다. 몇 달 간의 검토와 관찰 후에, 그는 <u>새로운 이론을 위해 이 이론을 버렸다.</u> 만약 그들이 그들의 입술을 계속해서 연습하지 않으면, 그가 생각하기에, 그들의 뇌는 작동하기 시작한다. 얼마 후 그는 폐쇄적으로 냉소적인 이 생각을 버리고 결국 인간을 좋아하기로 결심했다.

18 **어휘** in proportion to ~에 비례하여 illustrate 설명하다 convenient 편리한, 알맞은 previous 이전의

해설 어떤 것에 관심을 가질 때, 상대적으로 그 관심을 방해하는 다른 관심 대상이 없을 때 관심을 끌 가능성이 높아진다고 설명한다.

해석 관심을 끄는 것에 관해서라면, 관심을 주는 어떤 상황들과 그것을 방해하는 다른 상황들이 있다. 다른 것들은 같은 상태로, 어떤 특별한 것이 관심을 끌 가능성은 경쟁적인 끌어당기는 요소의 부재에 비례한다. 이것은 다음의 구체적인 경우에서 설명될 수 있다: 나는 알맞은 크기의 카드 한 장을 가지고 있고, 그 위에는 네 개의 글자들이 있다. 이 카드는 1/25초 동안 보도록 노출되었고, 그 시간 안에 모든 네 개의 글자들이 관찰자들에게 읽혀졌다. 그리고 나서 나는 네 개의 다른 글자들을 추가했고 전과 마찬가지로 1/25초 동안 그 카드를 노출했다. 그 관찰자들은 이전의 시도에서처럼 오직 네 개의 글자만 읽을 수 있었지만, 이번 노출에서 어떤 특별한 글자라도 읽혀질 확실성은 없었다. 나는 그리고 나서 카드를 네 개 더 추가했고 이전의 시도에서처럼 글자들을 노출시켰다. 구체적인 글자들이 무작위로 알려졌고, 관찰자들은 여전히 12개 중 네 개만 기억할 수 있었다. 말하자면, 어떤 지점까지는 모든 것이 보일 수 있다. 물체의 수가 두 배가 되었을 때, 어떤 특정한 물체가 보일 가능성은 50%로 줄어든다. 물체의 수가 세 배로 증가했을 때, 어떤 특정한 물체가 보일 가능성은 33%로 줄어든다.

19 **어휘** interfere 방해하다 autonomy 자율성, 자주성 extraordinary 놀라운, 비범한 loop 고리 nurture 양육하다, 키우다 exceedingly 대단히 nag 잔소리 하다 aversive 혐오의, 꺼리는, 유해한

해설 아이가 하는 일에 부모가 개입하면 아이의 자기 숙달 능력을 키워주는 것이 아니라 오히려 방해하거나 해치는 것이 되므로 본문에 나오는 'interfere'의 의미를 쓰는 것이 적절하다.

해석 어른들이 자유와 자율성에 대한 아이의 욕구를 방해하지 않고 지지해 주는 것을 배우는 것은 어려울지도 모른다. 예를 들어, 만약 당신이 세 명중 한 소년이 그의 신발 끈을 묶으려고 하는 모습을 본다면, 당신은 비록 고리가 맞지 않지만 놀라운 동기로 그가 시도하는 것을 보게 될 것이다. 그리고 그가 마지막 매듭을 시도할 때면, 그는 각각의 손에 하나씩 두 개의 분리된 끈으로 그 일을 끝마치게 된다. 아이들이 이와 같은 일을 시도하는 것을 그들의 부모가 보고 있을 때, 부모들을 지켜보아라. 너무 자주 부모들은 개입하고 빼앗아서 신발을 올바른 방법으로 묶어 주며, 아이들의 성장하는 자기 숙달을 키워준다(→방해한다). 부츠나 코트를 입을 때, 심지어 장난감을 가지고 놀 때도 마찬가지다. 이 연령의 아이에게 거의 항상 부정적으로 반응하는 덫에 걸리기는 대단히 쉽다. 흔히, 부모는 이 단계에서 하루에 200번까지 아니라고 말할지 모른다. 그러한 잔소리는 극도로 유해할 뿐만 아니라 아이에게 자신의 자기통제의 부족에 대해 지속적으로 상기시켜주는 것이 되기도 한다.

20 **어휘** alliance 동맹, 연합 strategic 전략적인 commonality 공통성 permanent 영구적인 sovereign 자주적인 arrangement 방식, 배열 operative 가동되는 converge 집중하다, 모으다 adversary 상대(국) ideological 이념적인 orientation 성향 cohesive 응집력 있는 invincible 천하무적의 robust 원기 왕성한 brittle 불안정한 eternal 영원한

해설 서로의 이익이나 관심사를 기초로 만들어진 것이 동맹이므로 내용상 (A)에는 편의(convenient)가 적절하고 동맹을 맺고 있으나 서로의 이익을 계산하고 있어 언제든 대립할 수 있으므로 (B)에는 깨지기 쉽다(fragile)는 내용이 적절하다.

해석 동맹은 단기간의 이해일지도 모른다; 그들은 쟁점에 근거되었을지도 모른다; 그들은 또한, 만약 전략적 목적이나 공통의 관심사로 만들어진다면 오랜 기간 동안 생존할 수 있다. 동맹은 성격상 영구적이지 않다. 국가들은 독립적이고 자주적이기 때문에, 필요할 때마다 동맹을 만들거나 깰 수 있다. 동맹은 실질적으로 편의에 의해 만들어진 방식이다. 그들은 국제적 정치에서 어떤 국가나 국가의 그룹이 충분히 강력해지는 것을 막기 위해 주로 형성된다. 그리고 따라서 힘의 균형을 유지하는데 있어서 중요한 역할을 한다. 동맹의 일시적인 성격은 실제로 힘의 체계의 균형이 잘 이루어지는 것을 도와준다. 대부분의 동맹들은 관심사, 공통의 상대국으로부터의 위협, 비슷한 이념적인 성향을 모으는 것을 기초로 형성된다. 국가적인 관심사가 동맹으로 모일 때, 그들은 훨씬 더 응집력 있고, 조직적이 되는 경향이 있다. 그러나 일반적으로, 힘의 체계의 균형 안에 있는 대부분의 동맹들은 천성적으로 <u>깨지기 쉽다</u>. 왜냐하면 그들은 참여 국가들에 대한 정치적인 계산을 기초로 하고 있기 때문이다.

21 **어휘** attraction 명소, 볼거리 transport 운송하다 marine 해양의 commando 특공대 quarry 채석장, 원천

해석 Bethesda의 Penryhn Quarry에 있는 The Big Zipper는 탑승자들을 1마일 이상의 거리를 100mph까지의 속도로 옮길 수 있다. 첫 탑승자들은 - 주로 기자들 - 어제 도착했다. 그러나 안 좋은 날씨와 심한 바람 때문에 주요 볼거리는 영업을 하지 않았다. 대신에, 그들은 아쉬운 대로 The Little Zipper를 탈 수 있었다. - 더 작은 zip wire지만, 여전히 길이 500미터 정도로, 탑승자들을 약 50mph 속도로 운송해준다. The Big Zipper가 볼거리를 대중에게 공개하는 3월 29일까지는 실행되기를 기대한다. Zip World라는 명소 뒤에 회사는 Sean Taylor라는 사람의 소유이다. - 근처의 Tree Top Adventure 명소를 운영하는 과거의 해양 특공대. 두 개의 zip wire를 타는 것뿐만 아니라, 그 곳에 오는 방문객들은 또한 예전의 군용차량에 대한 안내 관광을 받게 된다.

22 **어휘** zoned 구획화된 reserve 보호구역 extensive 대규모의 undisturbed 방해받지 않은 buffer zone 완충지대 alteration 개조, 변형 in turn 결국 artificial 인공적인 intrusion 침입 unsuitable 적합하지 않은 compatible 양립할 수 있는 viability 생존 능력 disagreeable ~에 맞지 않는 stability 안정성

해설 (A) 훼손되지 않은 지역 안에 인공적인 침입이 들어오는 것을 막는다는 의미이므로 into가 적절하다.
(B) 사회적이고 경제적인 풍토를 조성하면서 보호 구역의 장기간의 생존 능력도 중요하므로 양립할 수 있다 (compatible with)는 내용이 적절하다.
(C) 보호구역에서는 파괴적인 행위들이 행해져서는 안 되므로 discourage가 적절하다.

해석 구획화된 보호 구역은 인간에 의해 훼손되지 않은, 하나 또는 그 이상의 지역을 포함하는 대규모의 땅이다. 구획화된 보호구역을 둘러싸고 있는 땅들은 완충지대라고 불리어 진다. 이것들은 인구를 지탱하기 위해 계속적으로 사용되면서, 또한 훼손되지 않은 지역으로의 인공적인 침입을 막으면서 거대한 개조로부터 보호를 받는다. 구획화된 보호 구역의 접근은 주로 보호되는 지역의 장기간의 생존력과 양립할 수 있는 완충지대에서 사회적이고 경제적인 분위기를 발전시키는 것을 추구한다. 예를 들어, 거대한 벌목이나 대규모의 단일 작물 농업과 같은, 보호된 지역에서의 생태학적 안정성에 맞지 않는 파괴적인 관행은 완충지대에서는 막아진다.

23 **어휘** startling 놀랄만한 transformation 변화, 변형 fundamentally 근본적으로 genetic 유전적인 axiomatic 자명한, 공리적인 formula 공식 demographer 인구통계학자 serialist 작곡가

해설 (A) manipulation 조작, subtraction 삭감, 뺄셈
(B) rule 우세하다, waver 약해지다
(C) scatter 흩뿌리다, scan 훑어보다

해석 우리는 승리감의 시대에서 산다. 수학, 물리학, 음악, 예술 그리고 사회 과학에서, 인간의 지식과 그것의 진보는 놀랍고 강력한 방법으로 필수적인 형식적 구조와 그것들의 변형에 관한 문제로 축소되어지고 있는 것 같다. 컴퓨터의 마술은 1과 0의 빠른 조작이다. 만약 그것들이 더 빨라지면, 그것들이 우리를 대체할거라는 소리를 듣게 된다. 모든 풍부함과 복잡성 속의 삶은 유한한 유전적 코드의 조합과 재조합으로써 근본적으로 설명될 수 있다고 말하여 진다. 공리적인 방법은 수학에서 뿐만 아니라 경제학, 언어학, 그리고 때때로 심지어 음악에

서도 우세하다. 이러한 승리에 대한 관행적 제품들은 이제 우리의 일상생활과 문화의 일부이다. 우리는 유전적으로 조작된 옥수수를 먹는다. 우리는 인터넷으로 탄생을 알리고 결혼 축하를 보내고 차를 산다. 우리는 신용카드를 스캔하여 식료품을 산다. 우리의 세금은 인구 통계학자와 경제학자들에 의해 만들어진 공식으로 결정된다. 우리는 양을 복제한다. 작곡가들은 수학적 원리에 따라 그들의 음을 선택한다.

24 **어휘** daunting 벅찬 strive 애쓰다, 분투하다 guidance 지도

해설 인생을 살면서 실패를 하지만 시간이 지나 실패가 인생의 교훈이 될 것이므로 극복해야 한다는 내용이다.

해석 많은 십대들은 벅찬 일을 맡으려고 시도하고 그것들에 실패하는 것에 대해 그들의 또래에게 거절당하는 매우 실질적인 두려움을 경험한다. 이 두려움은 많은 십대들이 그들이 삶에서 원하는 것들을 위해 애쓰는 것을 멈추게 한다. 삶은 실패에 대한 가능성을 걱정하기에는 너무 짧다. 십대들은 실패에 대한 그들의 불안감을 극복하는 것을 배워야 한다. 왜냐하면 많은 인생의 교훈들은 실패로부터 배워지기 때문이다. 이러한 걱정에 대해 십대들에게 줄 수 있는 최고의 조언은 시간이 모든 상처를 치료해 줄 거라는 것이다. 그들의 또래들로부터 많은 세월은 그들이 시도했고 실패했던 것들조차도 기억하지 못할 것이다. 몇몇 십대들은 위대한 일을 하거나 이루기를 원할지도 모르지만, 그들은 실패에 대한 두려움을 극복하는데 힘든 시간을 보낸다. 이런 경우, 학교 지도 상담사, 부모, 또는 다른 신뢰할 만한 어른들이 이 두려움에서 나오도록 그들을 도울 수 있을 것이다.

25 **어휘** malicious 악의적인 facility 기능, 장치 acute 극심한 wipe out 소진되다, 몰살되다 inflict 가하다 disgruntled 불만을 품은 power failure 전기 고장 uninterrupted 중단되지 않은

해설 의도적이든, 우연적이든 컴퓨터와 자료의 손상을 막기 위해서 보안이 필요하다고 주장한다.

해석 우리는 지속적으로 컴퓨터 바이러스와 악의적인 프로그램들에 의해 행해지는 손상에 대해 듣는다. 그러나 심지어 최고의 바이러스 보호 소프트웨어조차도 개인 컴퓨터가 도난 당하는 것을 막지는 못한다. 따라서, 컴퓨터 보안은 컴퓨터와 자료를 저장하는 장치를 보호함으로써 시작된다. 이 문제는 특히 산업에서 극심하다. 많은 회사는 만약 회사의 컴퓨터나, 특히 만약 민감한 자료가 도난당하거나 손상된다면 무너질 수 있다. 손상은 범죄적이거나 불만을 품은 직원에 의해 가해지는 의도적인 것일 수도 있고, 화재나 전기 고장, 고장 난 에어컨에 의해 유발되는 우연한 것 일수도 있다. 해결책은 물리적으로 이 민감한 자산을 보호하는 것이다. 가정은 경보시스템을 가져야 하고, 컴퓨터 전력은 중단되지 않는 전력 공급을 통해 처리되어야 한다. 상업적인 독립체는 통제된 접근, 단단한 문, 카드로 작동되는 자물쇠, 보안 카메라, 그리고 자동 화재 시스템을 갖춘, 보안 컴퓨터 장치를 가져야 한다.

26 **어휘** stateroom 개인 전용실 theft 절도 deck 갑판 perpetrator 범인 suspicion 의심 suspect 용의자 call someone's bluff 할 테면 해보라고 허세를 부리다 accusation 혐의 dock 정박하다 detective 탐정, 형사 pawnshop 전당포 proprietor 주인, 소유주 pawn 전당포에 물건을 잡히다 pawnbroker 전당포 주인 graphically 생생하게

해설 배가 정박하고 형사를 고용한 후 그 형사가 조사를 시작한 내용이 뒤에 이어지므로 ④번이 적절하다.

해석 1879년 6월, 미국 철학자이면서 과학자인 Charles Sanders Peirce는 보스턴에서 뉴욕으로 가는 증기선에 타고 있었는데, 그 때 그의 금시계가 개인 전용실에서 도난당했다. Peirce는 그 절도를 보고했고, 배의 선원들을 갑판에 일렬로 세워야 한다고 주장했다. 그는 그들 모두를 인터뷰했지만, 어디에서도 찾을 수 없었고 얼마 동안 걸은 후, 그는 이상한 뭔가를 했다: 그는 비록 그의 의심 말고는 아무것도 없었지만 누가 범인인지 추측해보기로 결심했다. Peirce는 자신 있게 용의자에게 다가갔으나, 그는 마음대로 해보라고 허세를 부렸고 혐의를 부인했다. 그의 주장을 뒷받침해 줄 증거나 노리적인 이유가 없는 상태로, 할 수 있는 것은 아무것도 없었다. ― 배가 정박할 때 까지. 배가 정박했을 때, Peirce는 즉시 택시를 타고 지역 관할 경찰서에 가서 조사할 형사를 요청했다. 그 형사는 전당포에서 Peirce의 시계를 발견했고, 다음 날 Peirce는 주인에게 그것을 전당포에 맡긴 사람을 묘사해달라고 부탁했다. Peirce에 따르면, 그 전당포 주인이 용의자를 너무 생생하게 묘사해서 틀림없이 그것이 용의자였을 거라는 것에 의심할 여지가 없었다.

27 　**어휘**　colloquial 구어의, 일상적인 대화체의 distinction 구별, 뛰어남 self-identification 자아 일체 의식 relevant 관련 있는 aspire 열망하다 seep into 침투하다, 침범하다 exclusive 특권층의 extravagant 사치스러운

　해설　집단에 대한 소속감을 위해 재정적인 희생을 한다는 전제에 대한 구체적인 예를 언급한 것으로 보아 ④에 들어가는 것이 적절하다.

　해석　과학자들은 사람들이 일부라고 느끼는 어떤 집단을 내집단이라고 부르고, 그들을 배척하는 집단을 외집단이라고 부른다. 일상적인 대화체에서의 사용과는 반대로, 전문적인 의미에서의 내집단과 외집단이라는 용어는 집단 내에 있는 사람들의 인기를 언급하는 것이 아니라 단순히 "우리와 그들"이라는 구분을 말한다. 우리 모두는 많은 내집단에 속해 있고 그 결과, 우리의 자아 일체 의식은 상황마다 다르다. 다른 상황에서 똑같은 사람이 어떤 것이 관련 있는지에 따라 그녀 스스로를 여자로써, 경영진으로써, 또는 엄마로써 생각할 수 있다. 사실, 실험적 연구와 현장 연구 둘 다는 사람들이 그들이 일부가 되기를 열망하는 내집단에 대한 소속감을 만드는 것을 돕기 위해 커다란 재정적인 희생을 할 것이라는 것을 발견했다. 예를 들어, 사람들이 비록 그 기능을 활용하지 못하더라도, 사치스러운 컨트리클럽이나 특권층의 구성원이 되기 위해 너무 많은 돈을 지불하는 이유가 바로 그것이다. 일단 우리가 컨트리클럽이나 경영진의 지위에 대한 소속감으로써 우리 스스로를 생각하게 된다면, 집단 안에 있는 다른 사람들의 관점이 우리의 생각을 침범하게 되고, 우리가 세상을 인식하는 방식을 색칠하게 된다. 심리학자들은 그러한 관점을 "집단 규범"이라고 부르고, 집단의 구성원으로써 우리 스스로를 보는 것은 자동적으로 우리 모두를 "우리" 또는 "그들"중 하나로써 나타내는 것이다.

28 　**어휘**　erosion 침식 foremost 가장 중요한 divert 방향을 바꾸게 하다 discharge 방류 gutter 도랑 contain 억누르다 velocity 속도 erode 침식시키다 be bound to ~할 것 같다 storm drain 빗물 배수관

　해설　Never redirect ~의 문장에서 빗물 배수관이나 도랑으로 다시 보내지 말라고 말했다.

　해석　토양 침식은 산사태에 대한 가장 흔한 이유 중 하나이다. 그러므로 그것을 예방하는 것이 산사태의 위험을 줄이는데 도움을 줄 수 있다. 우선적으로 해야 할 것은 도랑을 만들고 모래주머니를 사용함으로써 비탈로 내려가는 물길을 돌리는 것이다. 만약 방향 전환이 불가능하면, 작은 댐을 세워서 그것의 속도를 줄일 수 있다. 물의 속도는 얼마나 많은 토양이 침식 되었는지를 결정하며, 그러므로 그것의 속도를 줄이는 것은 도움이 될 수 있다. 물의 흐름의 방향을 바꾸거나 속도를 줄이고 그것을 완전히 막지 않도록 하는 것이 중요하다. 왜냐하면 그것을 막으면 시간이 지나 압력이 증가하게 될 것이고, 곧 어느 정도 무너지게 된다. 비록 쉬운 방법처럼 보일지라도 비탈 아래에 빗물 배수관이나 도랑으로 다시 보내지 마라. 대신에 너는 유연성 있는 파이프를 이용하여 안전한 방법으로 이 물의 방향을 돌릴 수 있다.

29 　**어휘**　conduct 수행하다 vegan 엄격한 채식주의자

　해설　사람들이 자신의 믿음에 대해 덜 확신을 가질 때, 그들은 훨씬 더 열심히 몰입하여 논쟁한다는 내용이다.

　해석　Gal과 Rucker는 최근에 사람들이 불확실하다고 느끼게 만드는 짜 맞추기 기법을 사용하는 연구를 수행했다. 예를 들어, 그들은 한 집단에게 확실성으로 가득 찼을 때를 기억하라고 말했고, 다른 집단에게는 의심이 가득 찼을 때를 기억하라고 말했다. 그리고 나서 그들은 참가자들에게 그들이 육식주의자인지, 채식주의자인지, 엄격한 채식주의자인지를 묻고, 이것이 그들에게 얼마나 중요한지, 그들의 의견에 얼마나 확신이 있는지를 물었다. 그들이 불확실했던 때를 기억하도록 요구받은 사람들은 그들의 식성 선택에 대해 덜 확신했다. 그러나 다른 누군가에게 그들이 먹는 방식을 설득하기 위한 신념을 쓰라고 요구 받았을 때, 그들은 선택에 대해 확실한 집단보다 더 많이 그리고 더 강한 주장을 썼다. 연구는 선호도에 대한 다른 주제로 수행되었고(예를 들어, 컴퓨터 또는 노트북), 비슷한 결과가 발견되었다.

30 　**어휘**　determined 완강한 alternative 대체의, 대안의 co-ordination 합동, 협동 discipline 규율, 훈육 abundance 풍부함 receptive 수용적인 inhibition 어색함, 거리낌 insecure 불안정한

　해설　어린 나이에 발레를 배우면 좋은 점을 설명하고 있다.

해석 심지어 가장 완강한 부모들조차도 그들의 아이들이 TV나 컴퓨터 앞에서 너무 오래 앉아 시간을 보내지 않도록 격려하는 것이 도전이라는 것을 안다. 게다가 아이들이 재미를 찾을 수 있는 대안적인 활동을 찾는 것이 매우 어려울 수 있다. 발레를 배우는 것은 훌륭한 해결책이 될 수 있는데 왜냐하면 그것은 아이들에게 많은 이점을 제공하기 때문이다. 어떤 좋은 댄스 학교나 댄스 아카데미라도 안전하고 잘 갖춰진 환경에서 이루어지는 잘 관리된 수업을 할 것이다. 이러한 수업들은 너의 아이가 육체적으로, 정신적으로 도전하게 할 것이고, 이것은 그들이 정신 집중을 하고 그들의 관심을 유지하는데 도움이 될 것이다. 그들의 능력이 향상됨에 따라 그들의 협동성, 자기 통제, 규율도 향상될 것이고, 결국 그들의 자신감이 향상될 것이다. 게다가 그것은 아이들의 풍부한 에너지의 긍정적이고 자연스러운 돌파구를 제공해 줄 것이다. 이른 나이에 발레를 배우는 것은 특히 유익하다. 왜냐하면 어린 아이들이 어른들보다 훨씬 더 잘 받아들이기 때문이다. 그들은 배우는 것이 더 쉽다는 것을 알고 거리낌도 훨씬 적으며, 그래서 특정한 동작을 수행함에 있어서 불안정하거나 당황스러움을 훨씬 덜 느낄 것이다.

31 **어휘** cognitive psychology 인지 심리학 sensorimotor 지각 운동의 underlie 바탕이 되다 abstract 추상적인, 추상적 개념 embodied 형상화된, 상징화된 concrete 구체적인 theoretical 이론적인 empirical 실증적인

해설 인간의 감각 인식과 운동 동작이 개념에 대한 이해를 지지한다는 내용으로 보아 '지각 운동 체계를 통한 개념의 표현'이 주제로 적절하다.

해석 인지 심리학에서의 핵심 질문 중 하나는 어떻게 사람들이 '축구', '사랑'과 같은 개념에 대해 지식을 표현하는지이다. 최근에, 몇몇 연구자들은 개념은 바깥세상과의 상호작용에 바탕이 되는 지각 운동 체계에 의해 인간의 기억 속에서 표현된다고 제안했다. 이 이론들은 인지를 더 이상 추상적인 정보 처리에 관해서 보는 것이 아니라 인식과 행동에 관해서 보는 인지 과학의 최근 발달을 보여준다. 다시 말해서, 인지는 형상화된 경험을 바탕으로 하고 있다. 연구는 감각 인식과 운동 동작이 단어와 물체의 개념에 대한 인간의 이해를 지지한다는 것을 보여준다. 게다가, 심지어 추상적 개념과 감정 개념에 대한 이해조차도 더 구체적이고 형상화된 경험에 의존하는 것으로 볼 수 있다. 결국, 언어 그 자체는 지각 운동 처리 과정에 기반을 둔 것으로 볼 수 있다. 우리는 이 체계를 지지하기 위해 이 분야의 여러 핵심 연구자들로부터 이론적인 주장과 실증적인 증거를 종합할 수 있다.

32 **어휘** miraculous 기적적인 huddled 웅크리는 boldness 대담 devoid ~이 전혀 없는 embrace 껴안다, 아우르다 exuberance 풍부, 윤택

해설 두려워하지 말고 모험을 즐기라는 내용이므로 "구하지 않으면 찾는 것도 없다."는 속담이 적절하다.

해석 당신의 인생을 만드는 것은 당신에게 달려 있기 때문에, 당신은 기적적인 모험으로 가득 찬 인생을 만들 수도 있고, 대담하게 당신의 세상 밖으로 나가 즐거운 일을 경험하지 못하고 웅크리거나 안전하게 있을 수도 있다. 모험이 전혀 없는 삶은 안전할 수 있겠지만, 질감이나 색이 부족한 것이 된다. 만약 당신이 앞으로 모험을 하지 않는다면, 당신은 절대로 커지지도 성장할 수도 없다. 당신이 평생 가져왔던 모험에 대해 생각해 봐라. 당신이 신념을 가지고 당신의 안전지대를 넘어 넓혀 나가는 그러한 순간들은 귀중한 선물이다. 왜냐하면 그것들은 당신에게 당신이 삶을 윤택하게 아우를 때, 이용할 수 있는 즐거움을 떠오르게 해 준다. 이러한 순간들은 당신의 개인적인 역사의 전환점이 될 수 있고 당신이 선택할 때마다 스스로 새로운 현실을 만들도록 당신을 격려해 줄 수 있다.

33 **해석** 위의 그래프는 편도 여행의 장거리 출장에서 개인 차량과 항공 여행의 비율을 보여준다. (이 그래프는 다른 운송 수단은 반영하지 않는다.) ① 개인 차량을 탈지 목적지까지 비행할지에 대한 결정은 여행의 거리에 변화를 준다 ; 거리가 더 길수록, 항공으로 하는 출장의 퍼센트가 더 크다. ② 100-249 마일의 출장에서, 개인 차량은 소수의 다른 운송 유형과 함께 운송의 지배적인 수단이다. ③ 만약 목적지가 250-499 마일이라면 출장의 60% 이상은 개인 차량으로 이루어진다. ④ 반면에, 만약 목적지가 500-749 마일 이라면 출장의 3분의 2이상(一般)이 항공으로 이루어진다. ⑤ 750-999 마일과 1,000-1,499 마일의 출장 사이에는 항공을 선호하는 여행자들의 퍼센트에 있어서 분명한 차이가 없다.

34 **어휘** shot down 격추시키다 seize 체포하다 installation 장치, 시설 feign ignorance 모른 체 하다 collapse 붕괴되다 escalate 확대되다 confrontation 대립 overshadow 그림자를 드리우다 embarrassingly 당황스러울 정도로 confession 자백 undercover 비밀리에 하는 authorize 권한을 부여하다, 인정하다

해설 미국의 스파이 비행에 대한 거짓 보고에 대해 소비에트가 사실을 폭로하는 내용인 (C)가 이어지고 (C)의 정상회담에 대한 내용에 이어 소비에트가 미국의 사과를 요구하는 (B)가 뒤를 잇고, 미국이 사과하기를 거부하면서 정상회담이 무산된 내용인 (A)가 이어진다.

해석 1960년 5월 1일, 소비에트 연방은 미국의 U2 스파이 비행기를 격추시키고 소비에트 군 시설에 대한 불법적인 사진으로 조종사를 체포했다. 소비에트 정부가 그들의 체포에 대해 모른 체 하고 있는 동안, 미국은 기상 연구 비행기가 사라졌다는 보고를 냈다.

(C) 물론 이것은 당황스러울 정도로 잘못된 것이었고 그 때 소비에트는 미국 조종사의 비밀 임무에 대한 자백을 폭로했고, 미국은 어쩔 수 없이 그 비행을 인정하게 되었다. 그 당시 두 국가는 영국과 프랑스와 함께 Big Four 정상회담에 참여하기로 되어 있었다.

(B) 몹시 기다려 온 그 회의는 냉전의 긴장을 약화시키기 위해 만들어졌는데, 스파이 비행기 사건이 전체적인 행사에 그림자를 드리웠다. 소비에트 연방의 후르시초프는 만약 아이젠하워가 사과를 하지 않는다면 정상회담 진행을 거절하기로 했다.

(A) 정상회담은 미국이 그렇게 하기를 거절했을 때 하루 만에 부너지고 말았다. 즉, 냉전은 베틀린 상벽의 선설과 쿠바 미사일 위기에 대한 대립으로 확대되었다.

35 **어휘** motivational 동기가 부여된 lofty 아주 높은 starve 굶다 declared 공표한 bask 누리다 knock off 해치우다

해설 너무 높은 목표를 세우는 전략이 실망감을 준다는 전제 문장 뒤에, Bob의 체중감량 프로그램에 대한 언급이 나오는 (C)가 오고, 비현실적인 목표인 "5파운드"를 언급한 (B), 결국 체중감량은 했으나 목표치가 아니어서 실망감을 받았다는 내용의 (A)가 온다.

해석 하나의 보편적인 동기 부여 전략은 먼저 아주 높은 목표를 세우고 스스로에게 그것을 이루도록 압박하는 것이다. 그러나 이 전략은 만약 당신이 도달하기에 너무 높은 비현실적인 목표를 만족시키려고 노력한다면, 대신에 잠재적으로 실망감으로 이끌 수 있다.

(C) 예를 들어, Bob은 누군가가 정말 그에게 열의를 불어넣어 준 새로운 체중감량 프로그램에 대해 말하는 것을 듣는다. 회의가 끝날 무렵, 모든 사람들은 그 주 동안 얼마나 많은 체중을 감량할 것인지에 대해 이야기하기로 했다.

(B) 너무 고무되어, Bob은 "5파운드!"라고 소리치고 박수갈채를 받았다. 그가 전에 6개월 동안 전혀 체중을 줄이지 않았다는 것을 기억하지만, 지금 그는 단 1주의 짧은 시간 안에 많은 체중을 감량할 것이라고 선언했다.

(A) Bob은 그의 목표를 만족시킬 거라고 결단하면서 매일 굶었으나, 몸무게를 잴 시간이 왔을 때, 그는 "오직" 3파운드만 줄었다. 이것은 사실 놀라운 성취이다. 그러나 그는 마치 그가 실패한 것처럼 느꼈다. 왜냐하면 그는 그가 선언한 목표를 충족시키지 못했기 때문이다.

36 **어휘** integrated 통합된 take an active part in ~에 능동적으로 참여하다 commonsense 상식적인 excess 과잉, 초과

해설 건강을 위해서 몸과 마음을 잘 유지하는 것이 필요하다는 내용이다.

해석 현대 의학의 진보는 고통을 덜어주고 인간의 복지를 발전시키는데 많은 일을 해 왔지만, 좋은 건강을 보장해주지는 못한다. 건강은 단지 질병이 없는 상태 이상이다; 그것은 몸과 마음이 하나의 통합된 단위로써 효과적이고 조화롭게 기능을 하는 상태이다. 결과적으로, 우리는 우리 자신의 육체적, 감정적 행복을 위해 어느 정도의 책임감을 가정함으로써 좋은 건강을 이루는데 능동적으로 참여해야 한다. 이것은 적절하게 먹기, 규칙적으로 운동하기와, 육체적 또는 감정적 행복을 파괴할 수 있는 과식, 흡연, 과음 또는 약물 사용 등과 같은 해로운 과함을 피하는 것과 같은 상식적인 방법을 실행하는 것을 의미한다. 자신의 건강에 대한 책임감을 갖는 것은 또한 자신의 정신을 건설적으로 사용하고, 감정을 표현하고, 스스로를 기분 좋게 하는 것을 필요로 한다.

37 **어휘** intimately 친밀하게 diagram 도표 renowned 명성 있는, 유명한 revolutionize 대변혁을 일으키다 visible 시각적인 contemporary 동시대의, 동시대인 spatial 공간적인 formulate 표현하다

해설 천재들은 사고를 단지 언어적이거나 수학적으로 표현하지 않고 시각적 공간적으로 표현함으로써 동시대의 다른 사람들과는 달랐다는 내용이다.

해석 르네상스 시대에 창의력의 폭발은 그림, 그래프, 그리고 다 빈치와 갈릴레오의 유명한 도표와 같은, 도표들에 대한 방대한 지식의 전달과 기록에 친밀하게 연결되어 있었다. 그의 동시대인들이 오직 전통적인 수학적, 언어적 접근을 사용하는 반면, 갈릴레오는 그의 생각을 생생하게 시각적으로 만듦으로써 과학의 대변혁을 일으켰다. 일단 천재들은 어떤 최소한의 언어적 장치를 얻고 나면, 그들은 그 기술을 그들에게 다른 방법으로 정보를 보여주는 융통성을 주는 시각적, 공간적 능력으로 발달시키는 것 같다. 아인슈타인이 어떤 문제에 대해 숙고했을 때, 그는 도표 사용을 포함하여 가능한 한 많은 방법으로 그의 주제를 표현하는 것이 필요하다는 것을 항상 알았다. 그는 매우 시각적인 마음을 가졌다; 그는 단지 순수하게 수학적이고 언어적인 추론을 생각하기 보다는, 시각적이고 공간적인 형태에 관해 생각했다. 사실, 아인슈타인은 단어와 숫자들은, 그것들이 쓰여 지고 말하여 지는 것처럼, 그의 사고 과정에 중요한 역할을 하지 못했다고 믿었다.

→ 그들의 사고를 <u>시각적</u>으로 만듦으로써, 천재들은 좀 더 관습적인 또래들과는 <u>구별되었다</u>.

✧ [38~39]

sophomore 2학년생 / presently 지금, 곧 / intimidated 겁먹은 / devilishly 지독하게 / feverishly 열중하여 / stumped 당황한 / retract 물리다 / inept 서투른 / bewildered 당황한 / enlightened 계몽된

「어느 날, 2학년생인 Joe Kohn이 공대 학생 회관에서 혼자 신문을 읽고 있었다. 교수이면서 유명한 수학자인 Norbert Wiener교수가 방으로 들어와 주변을 걸어 다니기 시작했다. 곧, 그는 다소 겁먹은 Joe Kohn에게 다가가 말했다. "젊은이! 장기 게임 할 줄 아나?" Kohn은 그렇다고 했고 Wiener는 외쳤다. "그럼 한 판 하지!" Kohn은 너무 무서웠고, Wiener 교수가 그를 놀릴 것이라고 확신했다. 약 15분 정도 게임을 한 후, Wiener는 그의 여왕 말을 움직였고 Kohn의 졸이 그것을 잡았다. Kohn은 당황했다. 분명히 Wiener는 지독히 현명한 희생을 하고 있었고, 곧 궁지에 몰릴 것이다. Kohn은 장기판을 열중하여 응시하며 그가 무엇을 할지 결정하려고 노력하며 20분을 보냈다. 마침내 그가 말했다. "Wiener 교수님, 좀 당황스러운데요. 왜 여왕 말을 희생하고 계신가요?" Wiener의 눈이 커지며 그는 말했다. "오, 이런. 실수네! 내가 한 번 물려도 될까?" 물론 Kohn은 Wiener가 그의 말을 물리는 것을 허락했다. Wiener가 정말 서투른 장기 선수였다는 것이 빠르게 분명해졌고, 그는 곧 졌다.」

38 **해설** Wiener가 장기 게임을 잘 할 거라고 생각하고 있었는데 여왕 말을 빼앗기는 것에 Kohn은 당황한 심정이었다.

39 **해설** Wiener가 실수로 여왕 말을 움직였고 물려달라고 말한 상황을 보아 퀸을 희생시켜 게임을 빨리 끝내려는 의도를 가진 것은 아니다.

utter 완전한, 전적인 / persist 고집하다, 계속하다 / impulsiveness 충동성 / blurt out 무심결에 말하다 / outrageous 충격적인 / instance 사례, 경우

「부모와 선생님들은 종종 ADHD(주의력 결핍 및 과잉 행동 장애)를 가진 아이들에 대한 전적인 불만을 보고한다. 왜냐하면, 그들은 명백한 사건에 대해 거짓말을 하기 때문이다. 예를 들어, 선생님이 한 아이가 다른 아이의 책상에서 물건을 가져가 그녀의 책상에 놓는 것을 볼 것이다. 선생님이 그것에 대해 학생에게 물을 때, 그 아이는 가져갔다는 것을 부인하고 다른 누군가를 탓하거나 어깨를 움츠리는 경향이 있다. 그 학생은 또한 숙제가 있다는 것이나, 선생님이 시험에 대해 그녀에게 말해 준 것에 대해 부정할 지도 모른다. 그러한 행동이 지속될 때, 그것은 아마 그녀의 충동성과 관련이 있을 것이다. 다시 말해, 아이는 그것에 대한 의식 없이 마음에 들어오는 생각대로 행동 할 것이다. 예를 들어, 그녀는 다른 학생의 책상 위에 있는 샤프를 보고 혼잣말을 할 것이다. "나는 저 샤프 가질 거야." 그 다음 그녀는 그것이 그녀의 손 안에 있다는 것을 알고, 다른 아이의 책상에서 그것을 가져 온 그 과정에 대해서는 알지 못한다. ADHD를 가진 아이들이 당황스럽고 충격적인 말을 무심결에 뱉어내거나 그들의 손이 다른 아이들의 물건을 만지는 것에 대해 보고되는 것을 일으키는 것이 바로 이와 같은 행동에 대한 의식적 관찰의 부족이다. 이러한 장애의 결과로, ADHD를 가진 아이들은 그들의 행동 관찰에 서투르고, 그러므로 그들이 말한 것이나 많은 경우에 그들이 하는 행동에 대해 완전히 모를지도 모른다.」

40 해설 (a)는 선생님이고, (b), (c), (d), (e)는 ADHD를 가진 아이를 지칭한다.

41 해설 위 내용으로 보아 그들이 높은 불만감 때문에 부적절하게 행동한다는 내용은 적절하지 않다.

bitterly 몹시 / drop in 들르다 / apparently 분명히, 명백하게

「"Hee Haw"의 유명한 코미디언이자 스타가 되기 전에, Archie Campbell은 Tennessee의 Knoxville의 몹시 추운 밤에 집도, 옷도, 돈도 없었다. 그가 잠을 잤던 버스 정류장에서 쫓겨난 후에, Campbell은 따뜻하게 하지 못하고 돌아다니기 시작했다.

(B) 밤새 여는 식당을 보고, 그는 들어가서 난방기 근처에 서 있었다. Nick이라는 이름의 그리스인 주인은 그에게 무엇을 하고 있냐고 물었다. Campbell은 그가 근처에 살고(그는 집이 없기 때문에 거짓말이다), 그의 코트를 깜박 잊었고(그는 코트가 없기 때문에 거짓말이다), 몸을 녹이려고 들렸다고(거짓말이 아니다) 말했다.

(D) Nick은 그가 어디 사는지를 물었고, Campbell은 생각나는 첫 아파트 단지의 이름을 댔다. 분명히 만족하여, Nick은 그에게 자리에 앉아서 몸을 녹이도록 해 주었다. Campbell은 자리에서 잠이 들었고, 일어났을 때, Nick은 그 앞에 많은 따뜻한 아침식사를 차려 주었다.

(C) Campbell은 그가 식사에 대한 돈을 지불하지 못한다고 설명했으나, Nick은 그럴 필요 없다고 말했다. - 그는 Campbell이 이름을 댄 아파트 단지에 살고 있었기 때문에 Campbell이 집이 없다는 것을 알았다. 부자가 되고 유명해진 후, Campbell은 그가 Knoxville에 있을 때마다 그 식당을 들렀다.」

42 해설 Campbell이 가난하고 집이 없었을 때의 일화로, 처음 Nick의 식당을 알게 되었고(B), Nick의 대접을 받고(D), 유명해 진 후 Nick의 식당을 찾아간다(C)는 내용이다.

43 해설 다음에 이어지는 식사에 대한 돈을 지불할 수 없다는 내용으로 보아 Nick이 식사를 대접했다는 것을 알 수 있다.

awkward 서투른, 어색한 / ask out 데이트 신청하다 / content 억누르다, 막다 / inevitable 불가피한, 필연적인 / mediocrity 보통 사람, 평범함 / brush off 무시 / convinced 확신하는 / chronic 만성의, 매우 안 좋은 / phenomenon 현상

「그가 어렸을 때, 그의 삼촌은 Spark Plug라는 이름의 연재만화의 말 이름을 따서 그를 "Sparky"라고 불렀다. 학교는 Sparky에게는 힘들었다. 8학년 때, 그는 체육을 포함하여 모든 과목에 낙제했다. 어렸을 때, Sparky는 사교적으로 서툴렀다. 다른 학생들이 그를 싫어해서가 아니었다; 단지 아무도 정말 그것에 대해 신경 쓰지 않아서였다. 그는 한 번도 고등학교에서 여학생에게 데이트 신청을 해 본적이 없다. 그는 거절당할 것을 너무 두려워했다. Sparky는 실패자였다. 모두가 그것을 알았다. 그래서 그는 그대로 살아가는 것을 배웠다. 그는 만약 어떤 일들이 되려고 한다면, 될 것이라고 일찍 마음을 먹었다. 그렇지 않으면 그는 무엇으로 그를 불가피한 보통의 사람으로 보이게 할지에 그 자신을 가둘 것이다.

그러나 한 가지는 Sparky에게 중요했다. ─ 그림. 그는 그의 미술 작품을 자랑스러워했다. 어느 누구도 그것을 감상하지 않았다. 그러나 그에게는 그것은 중요한 것 같지 않았다. 고등학교 상급생이었을 때, 그는 학교 졸업앨범에 약간의 만화를 올렸다. 편집자는 그 콘셉트를 거절했다. 이런 무시에도 불구하고, Sparky는 그의 능력을 확신했다. 그는 심지어 화가가 되기로 결심했다. 그래서 고등학교를 마치고, Sparky는 월트 디즈니 스튜디오에 지원했다. 그들은 그의 작품에 대한 샘플을 요청했다. 꼼꼼한 준비에도 불구하고 그것은 또 거절당했다.

그러나 Sparky는 여전히 포기하지 않았다. 대신에, 그는 만화에 자신의 인생에 대한 이야기를 말하기로 결심했다. 주인공은 매우 안 좋은 낙제생을 상징화하는 소년이었다. 그의 만화는 일종의 문화적 현상이 되었다. 사람들은 쉽게 이 사랑스러운 등장인물에 동일시되었다. 그는 사람들에게 그들 자신의 과거의 고통스럽고 당혹한 순간이나, 그들의 고통과 그들의 공유되는 인간성을 떠올리게 해주었다. 그 인물은 전 세계적으로 유명해졌다. 그리고 당신이 Charles Schultz로 더 잘 알지도 모르는 Sparky는 매우 성공한 만화가가 되었다. 그의 연재만화는 인생은 어쨌든 우리 모두, 심지어 실패자를 위해서도 방법을 찾아준다는 것을 보여주었다.」

44 해설 어렸을 때, 실패자였던 Sparky가 포기하지 않고 결국 만화가로 성공했다는 내용이다.

45 해설 본문에 사교적으로 서툴렀다는 내용으로 보아 ②번은 일지하지 않는다.

05 2015학년도 정답 및 해설

ANSWER

01	02	03	04	05	06	07	08	09	10	11	12	13	14	15	16	17	18	19	20
①	②	④	①	⑤	①	③	③	②	②	⑤	⑤	④	②	③	①	⑤	②	③	②
21	22	23	24	25	26	27	28	29	30	31	32	33	34	35	36	37	38	39	40
①	①	⑤	④	④	④	③	⑤	③	⑤	⑤	③	⑤	③	④	②	①	②	③	④
41	42	43	44	45															
③	⑤	④	④	①															

01 어휘 figure out 생각해 내다, 계산해 내다 soaring 날아오르는 vast 광활한 traverse 횡단하다 brochure 안내용 책자

해설 대화가 일어나는 장소를 묻는 문제이다.
① 모병센터
② 군인 식당
③ 사관생도 기숙사
④ 관제탑
⑤ 전쟁 기념관

해석 심 대령 : 아가씨, 무엇을 도와드릴까요?
Sonya : 잘 모르겠어요. 저는 제가 제 삶에서 원하는 것을 알아내기 위해 노력하고 있고, 제 친구가 여기에 가 보기를 추천했어요.
심 대령 : 현명한 결정이에요. 우리는 당신처럼 똑똑하고 어린 사람에게 제공할 훌륭한 직업 선택지들을 가지고 있습니다. 어떤 분야의 근무 대해 생각하고 계신가요?
Sonya : 저는 정말 모르겠어요. 조언 해 주시면 감사하겠어요.
심 대령 : 음, 눈을 감고 당당하게 제복을 입고 국가를 위해 일하는 당신의 모습을 상상해 보세요. 자신의 모습 이 높은 바다를 항해하고 있나요, 광활한 하늘을 향해 날아오르고 있나요, 그렇지 않으면 이국적인 외국 땅을 횡단하고 있나요?
Sonya : 음... 나는 것이 멋진 것 같아요.
심 대령 : 그럼 우리의 공군 안내 책자를 보여드리죠.

02 어휘 transfer 옮기다, 환승 resign 사임하다

해설 대화와 일치하지 않는 보기를 고르는 문제이다.
Perez 부인의 대사 ...I'd(=would) have to resign from work...를 미루어 볼 때 would have to RV(~해야 한다) 표현을 사용하여 현재의 직업을 그만두어야 할 것에 대해 걱정하고 있음을 알 수 있다.
① Perez씨는 전근을 승낙한다면 승진 할 것이다.

② Perez 부인은 현재 실업자이다.

③ Perez 부인은 스웨덴어를 할 수 없다.

④ Perez씨는 그 일을 맡는다면 더 많은 돈을 벌 것이다.

⑤ Perez부인은 스웨덴으로 가기를 망설이고 있다.

해석 Mr. Perez : 잠깐 말 할게 있어.

Mrs. Perez : 응, 여보. 무슨 일이야?

Mr. Perez : 나 오늘 승진을 제의 받았어. 굉장한 기회라 흥분이 되지만, 그것은 몇 년간 스웨덴으로 이동해야 한다는 뜻이야.

Mrs. Perez : 와! 하지만... 잘 모르겠어. 나는 일을 그만둬야 해. 게다가, 내가 거기서 어떻게 새로운 직업을 얻을 수 있겠어? 나는 언어도 모르잖아.

Mr. Perez : 그것에 대해서는 걱정 할 필요가 없어, 승진에는 상당한 월급 인상이 동반되기 때문에 당신은 일 할 필요가 없어.

Mrs. Perez : 정말 우리가 집과 친구들을 그렇게 오래 떠날 수 있을까? 우리는 이것에 대해 꼭 생각 해 봐야해.

03 어휘 leak 새다 in no time 당장

해설 a. 무엇이 문제인가요?

b. 제가 할 수 있는 일이 없군요.

c. 간단한 수리면 되겠군요.

d. 정말 죄송합니다.

해석 Mrs. Won : 드디어 와 주셔서 감사해요! 3일 동안 전화를 했어요.

Frank : 정말 죄송합니다. 하지만 폭염 때문에 이 동네의 모든 분들이 에어컨 수리를 필요로 하시더군요. 저는 이번 주 내내 하루에 열 두 시간씩 일하고 있어요.

Mrs. Won : 전 다 이해해요. 하지만 저희 가족과 저는 여기서 구워지고 있답니다.

Frank : 음, 그럼 이걸 고쳐서 최대한 빨리 식혀드려야겠군요. 무엇이 문제인가요?

Mrs. Won : 제가 이걸 켜면, 그저 따뜻한 바람이 나와요.

Frank : 간단한 수리면 되겠군요. 아마 프레온 가스만 채워 넣으면 될 겁니다. 만약 아무것도 새지 않는다면 즉시 수습할 수 있어요.

Mrs. Won : 좋아요. 하지만 부디 서둘러 주세요. 녹아내릴 것 같아요.

04 어휘 get arrested 체포되다 leave out 빼놓다

해설 상사에게 신고 당해 체포 된 여성이 변호사에게 변호를 의뢰하고 있다.

① 의뢰인 – 변호사

② 판사 – 피의자

③ 가해자 – 피해자

④ 경찰 – 용의자

⑤ 고용주 – 종업원

해석 여자 : 제가 곤란한 일이 있어 도움이 필요해서 전화를 드렸어요.

남자 : 무엇을 도와드릴까요?

여자 : 상사가 제가 자신의 사무실에서 절도를 했다고 신고해서 체포당했어요. 이제 경찰은 저에게 법정에 가야 한다고 말 하고요.

남자 : 전체 이야기를 말 해 주세요, 아무것도 빼 놓지 마시구요.

여자 : 저는 확실히 그런 짓을 저지르지 않았어요. 그건 큰 착오에요. 저는 그저 돈을 빌렸을 뿐이에요. 전 그걸 갚을 것이었어요.

남자 : 걱정 마세요. 제가 맡겠습니다. 하지만 제가 법정에서 제대로 당신을 대변하려면 우리는 만나서 이것에 대해 이야기를 해야 해요.

05 어휘 distracted 산만해진 late with ~에 늦은 suspend 정학시키다 consistently 지속적으로 disinterest 무관심

해설 Sam이 특별한 잘못을 저지른 것은 아니기 때문에 ①은 정답이 될 수 없다.
① 만약 그가 그런 짓을 한 번만 더 한다면, 그는 정학 당할 수 있습니다.
② 저는 그가 학교 성적을 현재 수준으로 유지할 수 있기를 바랍니다.
③ Sam은 학기가 진행 되어 감에 따라 지속적으로 향상되고 있습니다.
④ 처음부터 그의 수업에 대한 무관심 때문에, 저는 그를 포기했답니다.
⑤ 그와 이야기를 나눠 주세요. 만약 그가 나아지지 않는다면, 낙제 할 수도 있습니다.

해석 Sam의 선생님 : 오늘 학교에 와 주셔서 감사합니다. 전화로 말씀 드린 대로 저는 Sam이 조금 걱정되는군요.
Sam의 아버지 : 제가 듣기로 했지요. 그가 무슨 잘못을 했나요?
Sam의 선생님 : 아니오, 전혀요. 단지 최근에 조금 산만해져서 집중을 못 하는 것 같아요. 학기가 시작할 때, 그는 제 최고의 학생 중 한 명이었어요. 하지만 최근 그는 숙제도 제 때 하지 않고, 성적은 떨어지고, 학급 친구들과도 멀어진 것 같아요. 집에서 무슨 일이 있나요?
Sam의 아버지 : 이상하군요. 저는 항상 그가 학교에서 잘 하고 있다고 생각했습니다. 무슨 문제가 있는지 모르겠군요. 사실, 가정생활도 좋고요.
Sam의 선생님 : <u>그와 이야기를 나눠 주세요. 만약 그가 나아지지 않는다면, 낙제 할 수도 있습니다.</u>

06 어휘 explore 탐험하다 entertain 즐겁게 해 주다

해설 ① 할아버지는 Bobby를 돌봐주고 계신다.
② Bobby의 부모님은 늦게까지 일하고 계신다.
③ Bobby는 스마트 폰으로 게임을 하고 있다.
④ Bobby와 할아버지는 함께 여행 중이다.
⑤ 할아버지는 Bobby와 밖에서 놀기를 원치 않으신다.

해석 Bobby : 할아버지, 저 지겨워요. 할아버지의 스마트 폰으로 게임을 해도 되나요?
Grandpa : 그 게임들은 너무 큰 시간과 에너지 낭비란다. 나가서 노는 것이 어떠니? 오늘 날이 좋구나.
Bobby : 하지만 밖에는 아무 것도 없어요. 엄마와 아빠는 언제 여행에서 돌아오시나요?
Grandpa : 밖에는 탐험 할 온 세상이 있단다. 내가 어렸을 때, 나는 해가 뜰 때부터 해가 질 때까지 밖에서 놀았지. 나는 항상 스마트폰이나 비디오 게임 없이 즐길 방법을 찾았어. 우리는 일주일을 더 같이 지내야 한단다. 그러니 우리 자신을 즐겁게 해 줄 방법을 최고로 잘 찾아보자꾸나.
Bobby : 나가서 저랑 같이 놀아 주실 거예요?
Grandpa : 그러자꾸나. 나가자.

07 어휘 fabricate 날조하다 convinced 확신하는 personage 저명인사 incident 사건 in an attempt to ~하기 위해 exquisitely 절묘하게

해설 유모의 얼굴에 상처를 입힌 것은 Piaget이 아닌 그를 유괴하려고 한 어떤 남자였다.

해석 기억은 쉽게 날조될 수 있어서 사람들은 결코 일어나지 않은 일의 현실에 대해 확신하게 된다. 유명한 예가 다름 아닌 저명인사 스위스인 심리학자인 Jean Piaget에게 일어났다. ① <u>그의</u> 생에 동안, Piaget는 종종 그가 어렸을 때 일어난 사건의 생생한 기억에 대해 말했다. 어느 날, 그의 보모가 ② <u>그를</u> 유모차에 태워 산책시키는 동안, 어떤 남자가 Piaget을 유괴하기 위해 수풀에서 뛰쳐나왔다. 그 남자는 유모와 분투했는데, 그녀는 성공적으로 그를 물리쳤다. 하지만 ③ <u>그가</u> 그녀의 얼굴에 상처를 입히기 전에 물리치지는 못했다. Piaget의 그 무서운 사건에 대한 기억은 절묘하게 상세했다. ④ <u>그는</u> 그 현장에 있던 사람들의 얼굴, 경찰관의 제복, 유모의 얼굴에 있던 상처, 그리고 공격이 일어난 정확한 장소를 기억했다. 그럼에도 불구하고, Piaget와 ⑤ <u>그의</u> 가족은 그 사건은 결코 일어난 적 없었다는 것을 나중에 알게 되었다. 시간이 지난 후, 유모는 Piaget의 부모에게 편지를 써서 상처를 포함한 모든 이야기를 꾸며냈다는 것을 고백했다.

08 어휘 run counter …에 어긋나다 unconventional 변칙적인 conform (집단의 양식에) 따르다

해설 나머지 보기는 사회 규범에 순응하는 것에 대한 부정적인 견해를 나타내고 있지만 ③은 사회 규범에 따름으로써 안정된 사회를 만들 수 있다고 설명하고 있다.

해석 Muhammad Ali는 일반적인 방법으로 싸우는 것을 거부했다. Ali의 스타일은 거의 모든 면에서 그 당시 복싱의 통념에서 어긋나 있었다. 하지만 이런 변칙적인 스타일이 바로 그를 전설적인 복싱 선수로 만들어 준 것이었다. ① 어린이와 청소년으로서, 우리는 남들과 다르다는 것은 사회적 대가를 수반한다는 것을 배우면서, 어떤 행동 규칙과 일 처리 방식에 순응하도록 가르침을 받는다. ② 하지만 맹목적 순응에는 치러야 할 더 큰 대가가 있다. 우리는 진정 자기 자신만의 방식에서 나오는 개성에서 오는 힘을 잃는다. ③ 사회적 관습을 따르는 것은 안전하고 안정된 사회를 만드는데 근본적인 기초 작업을 형성한다. ④ 진정 관습에 얽매이지 않는 방법은 아무도 모방하지 않고 당신 자신만의 리듬에 따라 맞서 싸우고 운용하는 것이다. ⑤ 만약 당신의 특성이 충분히 진정하다면, 그것은 당신에게 사람들이 색다르고 비범한 사람들에게 항상 나타내는 종류의 관심과 존경을 가져다 줄 것이다.

09 어휘 stable 안정된 entity 독립체

해설 문맥상 성인은 이미 안정된 사회적 독립체이기 때문에 대면 대화 능력에 문자 메시지는 크게 영향을 주지 않음을 알 수 있다.

해석 문자 메시지를 보내는 것에 대한 영향을 연구하는 발달 심리학자들은 특히 젊은이들을 걱정하고 있다. 왜냐하면 그들의 대인관계 기술들이 아직 완전히 형성되지 않았기 때문이다. ① 아이들과 다르게, 대부분의 어른들은 그들이 처음으로 문자 메시지를 보낼 수 있는 모바일 기기를 손에 쥐었을 때 이미 안정된 사회적 독립체들이다. ② 게다가 그들의 대면 대화 능력은 문자 메시지에 크게 의존한 뒤로 대폭 감소한다. ③ 하지만, MIT의 대인관계 연구자인 Sherry Turkle에 따르면 아이들은 그렇지 않다. ④ 그녀는 아이들이 과도하게 문자 메시지 연락에 의존한다면 그들의 대면 대화 능력은 발달하지 않을 것이라고 생각한다. ⑤ 이것은 또한 그들이 생각하고, 추론하고, 자아를 찾는 법을 배우는 것을 방해할 수 있다. 왜냐하면 이러한 기술들은 충분한 언어적 소통의 경험 없이는 습득하기 어렵기 때문이다.

10 어휘 continuous 지속적인 continuous 보도 term 용어

해설 사람들은 본인이 겪은 자연재해라 할지라도 TV에 의해 제공되는 정보로 이해의 틀을 다진다.

해석 카트리나는 24시간 내내 텔레비전으로 보도 된 미국을 강타한 최초의 허리케인이었다. 사회 과학 용어에서, TV는 시청자들과 의사 결정자들이 카트리나를 파악할 수 있게 한 이해의 틀을 세웠다. 해안을 따라 몇몇 사람들에게는 카트리나에 대한 개인적 경험이 도움이 되었을지 모른다. 만약 당신이 Dauphin섬, Biloxi 만, St. Louis, 혹은 Bourbon 거리의 어느 술집에 있었다면, 그 태풍은 조금 달랐을 것이다. 하지만 우리들 대부분에게, 그 태풍의 현실은 텔레비전 네트워크를 통해 와 닿았다. 심지어 전력을 잃은 "희생자들"에게도, 전기가 다시 돌아 왔다면 커피 주전자와 텔레비전이 그들 자신의 경험을 미디어에 의해 제공되는 정보의 전후사정에 따라 이해시키고 확인시킬 수 있도록 다시 전원을 켤 최초의 기기들이었을 것이다.

11 어휘 self 본모습 strategy 전략

해설 ⑤의 are designed가 선행사인 defensive strategies를 수식하기 위해서는 관계대명사가 필요하다. which are designed 또는 수동의 의미를 나타내는 과거 분사의 수식형태로 나타내기 위해 designed로 고쳐 쓸 필요가 있으며, 이는 주격 관계대명사 + be동사가 생략 된 형태로도 볼 수 있다.

해석 당신의 타인과의 의사소통은 몇몇 종류의 위험을 수반한다. 의사소통은 다른 사람에게 당신의 본모습, 당신의 역할, 상황, 그리고 그들이 거부할지도 모르는 것들에 대해 보여주는 것을 의미하기 때문이다. 의사소통의 분위기는 당신이 주어진 상황에서 얼마나 많은 위험이 수반될지를 추측하는 부분에서 중요하다. 당신은 자신이 얼마나 안전하다고 생각하는지를 근거로 행동한다. 만약 당신이 안전하다고 느끼지 않는다면, 당신은 아마 방어적인 전략을 사용할 것이다. 어쩌면 당신이 선생님께서 학생들이 문제를 터놓고 토의함으로써 참가해야 한다고

계속 주장하고, 그런 다음 학생들이 그렇게 하면 그들의 견해를 비난하거나 조롱하는 상황의 교실에 있다 치자. 당신이 공개적으로 빈정댐에 의해 쓰러뜨려 넘어지는 것이 편안하지는 않다는 것을 알아내는데 오래 걸리지 않을 것이다. 당신은 그 분위기가 안전하지 않다는 것을 재빠르게 배울 것이다. 당신의 의사소통은 당신을 보호하기 위해 고안된 방어적인 전략을 취할 것이다.

12 어휘 agony 고통 heliocentric 태양을 중심으로 하는 cling to ~을 고수하다

해설 마지막 문장에 동사가 존재하지 않는다는 점에 주목한다. But Galileo 뒤의 whom people considered the father of the experimental method는 선행사인 Galileo에 대한 추가적인 정보를 제공하는 관계대명사 절이므로 ⑤번의 to praise는 주어의 동작을 나타내는 동사 praised로 사용되어야 한다.

해석 과학 탐구는 많은 성취와 고통을 겪어 왔다. 그들은 보통 함께 관련되어 있었고 과학에서의 믿음의 역할을 똑같이 잘 입증했다. 첫 번째 주요한 성취는 코페르니쿠스의 행성의 순서에 대한 개요였다. 그는 오히려 태양을 중심으로 하는 명제를 확실히 증명하려 하지 않았다. 하지만 그는 부족했던 물적 증거들을 자연에 대한 믿음으로 보충했다. 자연은 조물주의 작품이라는 그의 믿음으로부터, 그는 손쉽게 자연은 단순하다는 결론을 지을 수 있었다. 그의 행성계는 프톨레마이오스가 한 것 보다 더 훌륭한 행성의 움직임에 대한 예측을 제공해 주지는 않았다. 코페르니쿠스가 제시한 가장 매력적인 증거는 행성의 새로운 배열의 기하학적 단순함에 있었다. 그것은 대담한 관점이었고, 그는 사람들이 불신으로 머리를 내젓는 사이에서 그것을 고수했다. 하지만 갈릴레오는, 사람들은 그를 그 실험 방식의 아버지로 여기는데, 정확히 코페르니쿠스가 한 일, 즉 자신의 믿음을 유지한 것에 대해 그를 칭찬했다.

13 어휘 obstacle to ...의 장애물 breakthrough 돌파구

해설 (A) obstacle to의 to는 to부정사의 to가 아니라 전치사이므로 to + 동명사형태가 올바른 답이다.

(B) 문장의 의미를 잘 파악했다면 능동 – 수동 관계를 금방 이해 할 것이다. 주어인 whose extra energy storage는 목적어인 the battery's weight를 감소시키는 능동 관계이다. 수동태는 주어가 행위자에 의해 동사의 행위를 당하는 경우에 사용한다.

(C) 행위자인 주어와 주어에게 동사를 당하는 대상인 목적어가 일치할 경우 그 목적어는 재귀대명사를 이용해 나타낸다. (C)에 해당하는 자동차를 움직이는 것은 주어인 cars of this sort로 동일하다.

해석 하이브리드 자동차의 폭을 증가시키는데 가장 큰 장애물은 배터리의 무게이다. 더 강력한 배터리는 차를 더 먼 거리로 움직일 수 있지만 그들은 또한 더욱 무겁다. 하이브리드 자동차의 새롭게 등장한 개념은, 문, 후드, 그리고 여러 곳에 전기를 저장할 수 있는데, 이런 문제를 처리할 잠재적 돌파구로 관심을 끈다. 몇몇 연구자들은 이미 에너지 저장 트렁크 플로어를 가진 시험판의 전기 운송 수단의 실험을 시작했는데, 그것의 여분 에너지 축적은 배터리의 무게를 15퍼센트까지 감소시킬 수 있다. 궁극적으로, 만약 이런 새로운 기술이 현재의 리튬 이온 전지의 효율에 도달한다면, 이런 종류의 차는 지붕이나 문과 같은 배터리가 아닌 부품으로 80마일은 갈 수 있는 충분한 전력을 저장할 수 있을 것이다.

14 어휘 priority to ...에게 우선권을 주다 finding 결과

해설 (A) 현재 분사와 과거 분사 사이에서 알맞은 표현을 고르는 문제이다. 수식받는 명사의 능동적인 동작을 나타낼 경우 현재 분사를, 수동적인 동작을 나타 낼 경우 과거 분사를 사용하면 된다.

(B) but으로 연결된 절의 동사인 rated sales most important를 받는 대동사가 필요하다. 과거시제이므로 대동사 did가 올바른 답이다.

(C) 일견 명사인 the conclusion을 수식하는 관계대명사절로 해석 할 가능성이 있지만 lead to the conclusion (결과를 이끌어 내다)의 목적어가 되는 명사절이 나와야 하므로 which는 사용할 수 없다.

해석 다음은 지각에 대한 고전 연구를 나타낸다. 스물세 명의 중간 관리자들이 한 제철 회사의 조직 활동에 대해 서술한 포괄적인 사례를 읽도록 요청 받았다. 스물셋의 관리자 중 여섯은 판매부서에, 다섯은 생산에, 넷은 회계에, 그리고 여덟은 여러 가지 기능 부서에 속해 있었다. 그 사건을 읽은 다음 각 관리자는 새로운 사장이 먼저

해결해야 할 문제를 확인하기 위한 질문을 했다. 83퍼센트의 판매 관리자들은 판매에 우선순위를 매겼지만, 다른 사람들은 겨우 29퍼센트에 그쳤다. 마찬가지로, 생산 관리자들은 생산 부문을 우선시했지만, 회계 부서의 종사자들은 회계 문제에 집중했다. 이러한 결과들은 참가자들이 사례의 우선순위를 관리자들이 소속 된 기능적 부서의 활동과 목표 면에서 해석했다는 결론을 이끌어 낸다.

15 어휘 make good use of 적절히 사용하다

해설 Not only ..., but also ~로 연결되어 의미상 부정적인 내용, 즉 학습에 대한 부정적인 자세를 만들어 낸다는 의미의 단어를 사용해야 자연스럽게 이어진다.

해석 변변치 않은 학습은 당신이 배우고 있는 것에 집중하지 않을 때 일어난다. 집중이라는 것은 기본적으로 생각하는 것이다. 집중은 당신의 정신적, 물리적 작업 능력을 ① 향상시킬 수 있다. 이것이 학교에서의 많은 실패들이 ② 낮은 지능보다 집중력 부족 때문이라는 이유이다. 연구원들은 집중력의 한 가지 적은 망설임이라는 것에 주목한다. 언제 공부할지, 어느 과목을 먼저 공부할지에 대한 망설임은 시간을 대단히 낭비하게 할 뿐 아니라, 학습을 향한 부정적인 자세를 ③ 없애는 방법이기도 한다. 개인적인 문제 또한 집중력에 개입한다. 당신이 만약 개인적인 문제에 ④ 사로잡혀 있다면 당신은 지능을 적절히 사용하지 못 할 것이다. 당신의 문제점에 대해 어떤 ⑤ 건설적인 행동을 한 다음에야 당신은 잘 학습하거나 수행하는데 있어서 더 나은 위치를 잡을 수 있을 것이다.

16 어휘 linear 1차적인 around the clock 24시간 내내

해설 삶의 질을 향상시키는 행동은 그 효과나 행복이 누적되는 것이 아니기 때문에 무조건 많은 시간을 보낸다고 해서 행복한 것은 아니라는 것을 알 수 있다.
① 누적되는
② 환원적인
③ 일시적인
④ 즉각적인
⑤ 회피 가능한

해석 행동에 있어서의 심리적 효과들은 1차적인 것이 아니라 우리가 하는 모든 다른 일의 조직적 관계에 의존한다. 예를 들어, 음식이 기쁨의 원천이라 할지라도, 우리는 24시간 내내 식사를 함으로써 행복해 질 수는 없다. 우리가 노동시간의 약 5퍼센트를 식사하는데 사용할 때에만, 식사는 우리의 행복 지수를 높여준다. 만약 우리가 하루의 100퍼센트를 식사하는데 사용한다면, 음식은 빠르게 보람을 잃을 것이다. 우리 삶에서 대부분의 나머지 좋은 것들도 마찬가지이다. 조금씩 휴식을 취하고 텔레비전을 보는 것은 일상생활의 질을 향상시키는데 이바지 하지만, 수확 체감의 문제는 빠르게 도달하기 때문에 효과가 누적되는 것은 아니다.

17 어휘 a range of 다양한 travelogue 여행기

해설 National Geographic이 신기하고 이국적인 사진과 이야기로 미국에 있는 독자들이 가정에서도 제3세계의 문화를 느낄 수 있다.
① 그들의 전통
② 지역 경제 사안
③ 환경 운동
④ 노동 조건의 현실
⑤ 자신의 것과 다른 문화

해석 앞선 세기 동안, National Geographic 잡지는 자신의 경계 밖에 있는 세계에 대한 정보와 화상을 받아들이는 미국인들에게 가장 중요한 의미 중 하나가 되었다. National Geographic은 미국의 지리적이고 문화적인 경이, 야생동물과 자연의 이야기, 그리고 우주 탐험의 이야기, 대양, 그리고 극지방의 만년설을 포함하여 다양한 주제를 다루기는 하지만, 대부분의 내용과 사진이 신기하고 이국적인 제3세계의 사람들과 문화의 모습을 나타내는데 전념하고 있다. National Geographic은 직원이 멀리 떨어진 사람들과 장소의 이야기와 사진을 가져오도록

원정을 보내기 때문에 오랜 여행기의 전통에 입각한다. 그 사진과 이야기가 자신의 집에 있는 독자들에 의해 감탄의 대상이 되는 동안, 그것은 사람들을 <u>자신들의 것과는 다른 문화</u>에 접할 수 있도록 끌어들인다.

18 어휘 desirable 바람직한 scarcely 거의 …않다 take into account 고려하다

해설 Were the foreign supplies…부터 …workers can't share its benefits?까지의 의문은 투표에 참가한 응답자들이 고려한 사회적 가치의 예를 나타내고 있다.
① 다가 올 선거
② 친근한 사회적 가치
③ 최대의 생산성
④ 국가 경쟁력
⑤ 새로운 기술 발전

해석 만약 다섯 개의 경쟁적인 회사가 모두 겨우 그들이 모두 생산하는 표준 제품의 생산 가격과 판매 가격을 모두 낮출 수 있었다고 가정 해 보자. 어떤 회사는 그것을 노동자들의 임금을 절감함으로써 해냈다. 어떤 회사는 노동시간을 늘임으로써 해냈다. 어떤 회사는 자재를 더 가난한 국가에서 더 낮은 가격에 입수함으로써 그것을 해냈다. 어떤 회사는 노동자를 로봇으로 대체함으로써 해냈다. 하나는 누구에게도 생산량, 이익, 일자리, 혹은 임금 손실과 같은 아무런 해 없이 시간을 질김힐 수 있도록 히는 기계 개선을 발명해 냄으로써 해냈다. 어떤 변화가 가장 바람직한지 물어 보아라. 그러면 앞의 두 가지를 지정하는 사람은 거의 없을 것이다. 나머지 세 회사에서는 비록 조건부라 할지라도 투표가 있었을 것이다. 해외 공급은 잔혹하게 이용되는 노동자에 의해, 혹은 오염 폐기물로 생산되었는가? 로봇으로 대체 된 노동자들이 다른 직업을 찾을 수 있다는데 기댈 수 있는가? 기계 개선을 발명한 사람은 다른 회사와 노동자가 그 이점을 공유하지 못하도록 그것의 특허를 받았는가? 이와 같이 응답자들은 그 문제에 대해 생각할 때 <u>친근한 사회적 가치</u>를 고려했다.

19 어휘 screening 상영,심사 contract 약정

해설 Hart씨는 이력서, 면접, 시험의 단계를 모두 통과하여 최종 합격 하였다. 정직원이 되기 위해서는 무급 인턴 프로그램을 마쳐야 하니 이달 말까지 인턴 프로그램에 참가 할지 여부를 알려주기를 요구하고 있다.
① Hart씨가 ACME 컨설틴트 회사에 지원하도록 격려하기 위해
② Hart씨가 인턴을 완료한 것을 축하하기 위해
③ Hart씨에게 ACME 컨설틴트 회사의 일자리를 제안하기 위해
④ Hart씨에게 다가올 약정 개편을 알리기 위해
⑤ Hart씨에게 구직서가 거부되었음을 공지하기 위해

해석 Hart씨께
백 명이 넘는 지원자들의 심사가 완료된 후, 우리는 우리가 당신의 이력서, 면접, 그리고 시험 결과에 큰 감동을 받았음을 알려드리게 되어 기쁩니다. 따라서 당신은 현재 ACME 컨설틴트 회사에 채워 질 다섯 자리 중 중 하나로 선택 받으셨습니다. 만약 당신이 받아들이시려면, 즉시 6개월짜리의 무급 인턴 프로그램에 참여하셔야 합니다. 성공적으로 수행이 끝난 뒤 당신은 모든 일반 수당을 포함하여 정식 월급을 받는 정직원이 될 수 있을 것입니다. 또한 전 세계의 많은 지점 중 한 곳으로 전근을 하거나, 여기 도심부의 본사에 머무를 기회가 있습니다. Hart씨, 축하합니다! 이달 말까지 당신의 결정을 알려주십시오.
친애하는 Cheryl Smith
ACME 컨설틴트 회사 인사부

20 어휘 encode 암호화하다 accuracy 정확도

해설 ① 어마어마한 – 제거하다
② 어마어마한 – 복제하다
③ 보통의 – 제거하다

④ 대수롭지 않은 - 개선하다

⑤ 대수롭지 않은 - 복제하다

해설 유전자는 어떠한 의미의 변화 없이 암호화되고, 재 부호화되고, 그리고 부호화 될 수 있는 순수한 정보이다. 순수한 정보는 복제될 수 있다. 그리고 복제물의 정확도는 (A) 어마어마하다. 사실, DNA의 기질은 현대의 다른 엔지니어들이 하는 다른 어떤 것들에 필적하는 정확성으로 복제된다. 그들은 세대를 통해 다양성이라고 소개될 딱 필요한 만큼의 간헐적 오류만을 가지고 복제된다. 이 다양성 중에서, 세계적으로 더 많아지는 부호화된 조합들은 신체 내에서 부호화되고 복종되었을 때, 확실히 그리고 자동적으로 같은 DNA 메시지를 보호하고 전파시키기 위한 적극적인 조치를 취하도록 만드는 것이 될 것이다. 우리, 즉 모든 생명체들은 그렇게 프로그램 한 데이터베이스를 (B) 복제하도록 프로그램 된 생존 기계들이다. 다윈설은 이제 순수한 코드 수준에서 생존자의 생존인 것으로 보여 진다.

21 **어휘** alternate 교체의 deposit 매장 층 extract 추출하다

해설 ① 예를 들어 - 그러므로

② 반면 - 그럼에도 불구하고

③ 예를 들어 - 대조적으로

④ 반면 - 그러므로

⑤ 같은 방법으로 - 그럼에도 불구하고

해설 대체 에너지로의 변천은 화석 연료의 결핍에서 우러나올 수 없다. 수십 년간, 에너지 생산자들은 지속적으로 새로운 화석 연료의 비축 분을 찾고 종전에는 너무 어려워서 접근할 수 없다고 여겨지던 매장 층에서 석유와 가스를 경제적으로 만회할 기술을 개발했다. (A) 예를 들어, 최근 일본은 해저의 수화된 매장 층에서 메탄가스를 추출할 수 있게 되었다고 발표했는데, 그것은 온 지구상의 화설 연료를 결합 시킨 것 보다 두 배 이상 많은 탄소를 함유하고 있는 것 같다고 한다. 이것은 인류가 지금까지 화석 연료의 아주 적은 양만을 태워왔다는 것을 의미한다. 우리의 화석 연료 중 그렇게 적은 부분을 사용했다 하더라도, 지구는 이미 심각한 온난화 문제를 겪고 있다. 만약 우리가 에너지 공급을 위해 계속해서 화석연료에 심각하게 의존한다면, 기후 변화에 관련된 피해는 화석 연료의 공급에 실질적인 압박이 생기기 전에 극심히 장기화 될 것이다. (B) 그러므로, 대체 에너지 운동은 기후를 살기 좋고 정상적으로 유지하기 위핸 일치단결의 노력으로 이끌어져야 한다.

22 **어휘** autotrophic 자가의 photosynthesize 광합성하다 ensure 반드시 ...하게 하다

해설 ① 극대화하다 - 융통성 있는 - 변화

② 극대화하다 - 융통성 있는 - 불변성

③ 최소화하다 - 융통성 없는 - 불변성

④ 최소화하다 - 융통성 있는 - 변화

⑤ 최소화하다 - 융통성 없는 - 변화

해설 식물의 자가 영양의 성질은 그들이 빛에 의존하도록 하고 광합성을 할 수 없는 식물의 종은 소수에 그친다. 따라서 식물이 빛을 느끼고 그에 반응하는 것은 중요하다. 식물은 광원을 찾아내고 그들을 향해 자랄 필요가 있다. 또, 그들은 광합성 기관이 (A) 최대한의 빛에 노출될 수 있도록 잎사귀가 올바른 방향을 잡게 할 필요가 있다. 하지만 식물이 빛을 감지하는 것으로 부터 얻는 이보다 더 상세한 정보가 있다. 식물은 변화하는 환경에서 산다. 밤낮이 변화하고, 계절이 변화하고, 날씨가 변화하고, 그리고 서식지가 변화한다. 이것은 식물이 이런 반응에 응답하기 위해 그들의 주변 환경을 알 수 있어야 하고 반응 면에 있어서 매우 (B) 융통성 있어야 할 필요가 것을 의미한다. 심지어 광합성도 계속 변화하는 불빛에 맞서기 위해 계속 변경되어야 한다. 태양은 한낮에 가장 밝지만, 드물게 일시적으로 해를 막아 줄 구름이 없는 날도 있다. 이것은 식물이 대처할 수 있어야 하는 빛의 세기의 큰 (C) 변화를 이끈다.

23 어휘 irrelevant 무관한 reward 보상

해설 ① 무관한 – 끈질기게 계속하다 – 중단된
② 무관한 – 그치다 – 중단된
③ 중요한 – 그치다 – 착수된
④ 중요한 – 끈질기게 계속하다 – 착수된
⑤ 중요한 – 끈질기게 계속하다 – 중단된

해석 당신이 일단 사람들을 통제하기 위해 보상을 이용하기 시작한다면, 당신은 쉽게 되돌릴 수 없을 것이다. 행동에 금전적인 보상이 (A) 중요해질 때, 다른 말로 사람이 보상을 받기 위해서 일을 할 때, 이런 행동은 오직 보상이 곧 주어질 때만 지속 될 것이다. 어떤 경우에는 괜찮겠지만, 대부분의 경우에는 우리가 보상하는 행동들은 보상이 끝난 후에도 오래도록 (B) 끈질기게 계속 되기를 바라는 것들이다. 예를 들어 당신이 만약 아이들에게 성적표에서 A 하나당 1달러의 공부에 대한 보상을 제공한다면, 당신은 아이들이 당신의 보상 체계가 (C) 끝난 다음에도 공부에 대한 열정을 유지하기를 원할 것이다. 하지만 그것은 만약 그들이 보상을 위해 공부를 한다면, 보상이 더 이상 존재하지 않을 때 공부하기를 멈출 가능성이 꽤 크다.

24 어휘 widen 넓히다 archaeologist 고고학자 fuss 법석을 떨다

해설 매일 양치하거나 빗질하는 등의 습관을 늘림으로써 노동자들이 규범에 익숙해지도록 했다는 새로운 관점을 제시하고 있다.
① 아나폴리스 : 고고학자를 끌어당기는 웅장한 곳
② 영어에서 "칫솔"의 등장
③ 치아 보호 산업에서의 칫솔의 영향
④ 산업 노동자의 발달에 대한 칫솔의 역할
⑤ 산업 혁명이 야기한 경제의 변화

해석 우리는 매일 양치를 하도록 길들여 져 있다. 우리는 그것이 우리의 치아와 잇몸을 지키고 활짝 웃을 수 있게 하는 건강에 좋은 일이라는 것을 안다. 그것의 장점은 개인적이면서 마찬가지로 사회적인 것이기도 하다. 하지만 신흥 계급의 사람들이 일 하기를 열망했던 18세기 아나폴리스 유적 사이에서 일 하고 있는 고고학자들은 어떻게, 그리고 왜 우리가 칫솔질하고 이 사이를 닦고 야단법석을 떨게 되었는지에 대한 새로운 관점을 제시했다. Mark Leone과 그의 도시 고고학 팀은 아나폴리스 거리 아래에서 많은 칫솔들을 발견했다. 18세기 칫솔들은 개인 위생용품과 자기 관리 개념에 대한 새로운 강조를 제안했다. 노동자들이 제시간에 와서 일을 하도록 하는 것은 중요해서, 그들은 규율을 발전시켜야 한다. 그래서 산업 사회는 칫솔과 빗, 시계와 같은 사람들이 자기 자신을 정돈시킬 수 있도록 도와주는 다른 많은 것들 강조한다. 칫솔은 산업 혁명이 일어났을 때, 우리가 쉽게 그것을 받아들이게 하는데 중요한 역할을 했다.

25 어휘 undesirable 원하지 않는 superficial 얄팍한

해설 진짜 설탕이 아닌 다이어트 음료 속의 감미료를 섭취함으로써 더 이상 호르몬이 분비되지 않을 가능성에 대해 경고하고 있다.
① 소다 중독의 예방과 치료
② 다이어트 음료 속의 감미료 보급
③ 최근 소다 시장에서의 소비자 선호도
④ 다이어트 음료의 보호 호르몬에 지장을 주는 효과
⑤ 과도한 당 소비에 뇌가 대항하는 법

해석 연구원들은 다년간에 걸쳐 다이어트 음료 소비와 허약한 건강 사이의 연관성을 알아차렸다. 하지만 사람들은 이 달갑지 않은 연관성은 이미 건강치 않거나 뚱뚱한 사람들이 먼저 다이어트 음료를 먹으려 하는 경향이 있다는 사실 때문이라고 단순히 생각한다. 하지만 Purdue 대학의 Susan Swithers는 이 얄팍한 행동적 설명은 다이어트 음료에 대한 근거 없는 믿음이 야기한 건강 문제들을 짚어주지 않는다고 주장한다. 그녀는 신체가 정상적

으로 당분에 반응할 때, 열량과 당분 모두의 증가된 섭취에 대비하는데 필요한 호르몬을 분비한다고 지적했다. "당신이 다이어트 음료를 섭취했을 때 무슨 일이 일어나느냐면, 당신은 단 맛은 느끼지만 열량과 당분은 섭취하지 않습니다." Swithers는 말했다. 그런 이유로, 그녀는 만약 이런 부자연스러운 상황이 계속 일어난다면, 사람의 뇌와 신체는 당신이 진짜 실제로 진짜 당분을 섭취했을 때조차 보호하기 위한 호르몬을 더 이상 내보내지 않도록 훈련될지 모른다고 경고한다.

26 **어휘** collective 집단의

해설 Even so의 의미를 단서로 앞부분에는 현대 일기 예보의 한계나 단점에 대해서 서술했을 것이다. 주어진 문장을 기점으로 이후에는 일기 예보의 장점에 대해 서술된다.

해석 오늘날의 현대의 일기예보는 컴퓨터 모델링의 발전과 인간 집단의 통찰력이 결합되어 있다. 함께, 그들은 1933년 3월의 "세기의 폭풍"과 2012년 10월의 대폭풍 Sandy 때처럼 점점 더 정확한 예측을 통해 인명을 구하고 재산을 지킨다. 앙상블 예보(종합적 분석에 기반한 기상 예보)는 기상학자들이 훨씬 더 나은 예보를 근거로 해 많은 "차선책"을 가질 수 있게 해 준다. 그러나 일기 예보가 얼마나 좋아질 수 있는지에 대한 한계는 존재한다. 대기가 어떻게 작용하는지에 대한 불완전한 정보와 불완전한 지식, 컴퓨터 연산 능력의 한계, 그리고 심지어 카오스 이론은 부정확한 예보를 야기한다. **그렇기는 하지만, 현대 일기 예보는 현대 기상학과 모든 과학을 통틀어 가장 훌륭한 성취 중 하나이다.** 날씨를 예측하는 우리의 능력은 10년마다 약 하루 이상의 비율로 미래를 향해 정교하게 향상 되었다. 그것은 앙상블 예보와 같은 새로운 기술을 통해 당신이 살아있는 동안 지속적으로 향상 될 것이다.

27 **어휘** diversity 다양성 inhabitant 주민

해설 Rather라는 부사를 미루어 보아 앞부분에는 문화적 균일화와 상반되는 문화적 다양성에 대한 내용이 언급되었을 것이다.

해석 세계화가 전 세계의 사람들을 더욱 비슷하게 만드는가, 혹은 더욱 다르게 만드는가? 이것은 문화 세계화의 주제에서 가장 자주 제기되는 질문이다. 한 그룹의 사람들이 불행히도 전자의 것이 사실일 것이라고 언쟁을 벌인다. 그들은 우리가 지구상에 존재하는 문화들의 다양성을 반영하는 문화적인 무지개에 가까워지고 있지 않다고 말한다. **오히려, 우리는 점점 더 균일화 된, 서양의 "문화 산업"에 의해 인수 된 대중문화의 성공을 목격하고 있다.** 그들의 설명에 대한 증거로, 이런 사람들은 아마존 원주민들이 나이키 운동화를 신고, 남부 사하라 주민들이 양키즈의 모자를 구입하며, 팔레스타인의 젊은이들이 자랑스럽게 자신의 시카고 불스 스웨터를 라말라 시내에서 내보이는 점을 든다. "전 세계의 미국화"로서의 영미계의 가치와 소비재의 전파와 관련해서, 이 문화적 균일화론의 지지자는 서구 표준과 생활양식은 다른 취약한 문화들을 압도한다고 주장한다. 비록 "문화 제국주의"의 힘에 저항하려는 몇몇 국가들의 심각한 저항이 있지만, 미국 대중문화의 전파는 막을 수 없을 것이다.

28 **어휘** bankruptcy 파산 somewhat 약간

해설 당시 그의 사상을 진지하게 받아들여 주는 사람은 few, 즉 거의 없었다.
a few 약간의 few 거의 없는

해석 식민 시대 Boston의 젊은이로서, Samuel Adams(1722-1803)는 한 가지 꿈을 키웠다. 그는 아메리카 식민지는 언젠가 영국으로부터 독립을 완료하고 영국인 철학자 John Locke의 글을 근거로 정부를 세워야 한다고 믿었다. Locke에 따르면, 정부는 시민의 의지를 반영해야만 하고, 그렇게 하지 않은 정부는 존재 할 권리를 잃는다. Adams는 아버지로부터 맥주 양조장을 물려받았으나 사업에 대해서는 신경을 쓰지 않았다. 양조장이 파산하는 동안, 그는 Locke의 견해와 독립의 필요성에 대한 기사를 쓰는데 시간을 보냈다. 그는 기사가 출판 될 만큼 훌륭한 작가였다. 하지만 당시 그의 견해를 심각하게 받아들이는 사람은 거의 없어서 그는 세상과의 접촉을 끊는 듯 했다. Adams는 자청한 임무가 가망이 없었기 때문에 침체에 빠지기 시작했다.

29 [어휘] relatively 비교적 longhand 손으로 쓰기

[해설] 노트북으로 필기를 하는 것 보다 손으로 직접 필기를 하는 것이 학습에 더 이로움이 시험 성적으로 증명 되었다.
① 키보드로 필기하는 것은 더 나은 사실 내용 암기를 산출한다.
② 자필 필기의 우수함에 대한 증거가 없다.
③ 자필 필기는 더 나은 학업 성취를 위해 추천된다.
④ 종이와 연필로 필기를 하는 것은 일반적으로 더 완벽하고 상세한 필기를 이끌어 낸다.
⑤ 노트북으로 작성 된 문자 그대로인 필기는 일반적으로 더 높은 시험 점수를 보증한다.

[해석] Mueller와 Oppenheimer에 의해 시행된 최근 연구는 사람들이 타자로 치는 것 보다, 자필로 된 필기를 할 때 더 나은 학습 결과를 가진다는 새로운 증거를 시사했다. 연구원들은 수업시간에 노트북으로 필기하는 사람들은 일반적으로 길고, 문자 그대로인 필기를 하는데 반해, 자필로 필기하는 사람들은 비교적 짧은 필기를 한다는 것을 관찰했다. 더 엄청나고 상세한 필기들이 낮은 질의 사실 인출과 개념의 이해를 이끈다는 사실이 시험 성적으로 밝혀졌기 때문에 세심한 주의가 기울여 졌다. 노트북으로 필기를 하는 사람들은 키보드는 문자 그대로 기록 할 만큼 충분히 빠르기 때문에 무엇을 입력할지 고르지 않았다. 반면, 수기 필기자들은 그들의 필기는 빠르지 않아서 무엇을 받아 적을지 고르기 위해 정보를 더 신중히 처리해야만 했다. 이 최초의 선택이 장기적인 강의 자료의 이해에 대한 이유로 여겨진다.

30 [어휘] consequently 따라서

[해설] 협력 연계, 즉 사회 연결망을 발전시키는 것은 창의력 향상에 도움을 준다고 하였으므로 정답은 ⑤번이다.
① 독창성을 묶는 강한 그물망의 해로운 영향
② 소외 계층을 지원하기 위한 사회 연결망의 필요
③ 작업 공간 내의 개성 존중의 중요성
④ 창조적 결과물에 대해 지나친 강조를 주는 것에 대한 위험성
⑤ 창의력 향상을 도와주는 사회 연결망의 가치

[해석] 사회 연결망은 종업원을 다양한 지역과 수준의 전문 기술을 가진 개인으로의 접근을 증가시키기 때문에 특히 중요한 것으로 여겨진다. 따라서, 협력 연계 발전의 촉진, 특히 취약한 연계는, 창의력에 긍정적인 영향을 받을 것이다. 그것은 또한 작업 공간 내에서, 동료들의 정보적이고 감정적인 도움 둘 다 더 높은 수준의 창의력과 관련이 있다는 것은 명확하다. 그러므로 창의력을 만드는데 관심이 있는 기관들(혹은 지도자들)은 종업원들 사이에서의 깊은 관계를 장려해야 한다. 마지막으로, 창의적인 동료의 존재는 지도자에게 창의력을 향상시키기 위한 그들 자신의 노력의 영향을 자각하기 위해 필요할지 모른다. 개인은 창의적인 동업자가 있을 때 감독관 피드백에 대응하여 가장 높은 수준의 창의력을 보여준다. 명확히, 개인 창의력의 발전은 그저 개인이 아닌, 그들의 사회적 맥락의 고려를 필요로 한다.

31 [어휘] satellite 위성, 졸졸 쫓아다니는 사람

[해설] 로마 제국 시절, 개인 경호원을 의미하는 satellite는 중세에 접어들어 위성이라는 의미로 사용되기 시작했다.
① 목성의 위성들의 발견
② 로마 제국의 흥망성쇠
③ 공식 화법으로의 고전 라틴어의 부활
④ 로마 시민들의 무장 경호원에 대한 필요
⑤ satellite라는 단어의 의미의 발전

[해석] 천 년이 넘는 기간 동안, 로마는 서양 문명의 중심지였다. 하지만 결과적으로, 제국에서의 삶이야말로 경제적 불안과 정부의 급격한 변화의 연속으로 위협받는 것이었다. 사태는 satellites라고 불리는 무장한 경호원 없이는 감히 수도의 거리를 걷는 중요 인물이 없을 정도에 도달했다. 제국이 몰락했을 때, 고전 라틴어는 상업과 과학의 언어가 되기를 중단했다. 하지만 10세기 후 지식인들은 고대 언어를 돌려놓고 그것을 가장 격식을 차린 화법으로 사용하였다. 부활한 단어들 중 satellite는 중세 통치자들이 자신의 개인 경호원에게 적용했다.

Johnnes Kepler가 목성 주변을 도는 이상한 물체에 대해 들었을 때, 그는 왕을 둘러싼 경비들과 신하를 떠올렸다. 그래서, 1611년 Kepler는 그들을 satellite라고 이름 붙였고, 곧 그 용어는 주된 덩어리 주변을 맴도는 모든 하늘의 물체에 적용 되었다.

32 **어휘** ruthless 가차 없는   deed 행위

해설 많은 말 보다 행동이 중요하다는 것을 강조하고 있다.
① 돌다리도 두드려 보고 건너라.
② 대접 받고 싶은 대로 행동해라.
③ 행동이 말보다 더 중요하다.
④ 펜은 칼보다 강하다.
⑤ 제비 한 마리가 왔다고 해서 여름이 되는 것은 아니다.

해석 전쟁의 탁월한 점은 아무리 많은 웅변이나 말도 전쟁터에서의 실패를 해명할 수는 없다는 것이다. 어느 장군이 자신의 병사들을 패배로 이끌었다, 목숨들이 낭비되었다. 그리고 그것이 역사가 그를 판단하는 방법이다. 당신은 일상생활에서 이 가차 없는 기준을 적용하기 위해 노력 해야만 한다. 자신의 행동의 결과, 보여 지고 평가될 수 있는 행위들, 그리고 그들의 목표를 성취할 수 있게 해 주는 걸어 온 발자취로 사람들을 판단하기 때문이다. 사람들이 자기 자신에 대해 말 하는 것을 중요하지 않다. 사람들은 아무렇게나 말 할 것이다. 그들이 무엇을 했는가를 보아라. 행위는 거짓말을 하지 않는다. 당신은 또한 이 논리를 스스로에게도 적용해야만 한다. 떠벌리는 것을 멈추고 노력의 결실로 당신의 가치를 증명해 내라. 사람들은 당신이 한 말이 아니라 행동으로 판단할 것이다.

33 **어휘** prescription 처방전   drastic 극단적인

해설 2005년에서 2008년 사이 45세에서 64세의 연령에 해당하는 남성의 수는 9%인데 반해 여성의 수는 22%로 여성이 남성보다 두 배 이상 많은 처방전을 받았음을 알 수 있다.

해석 위의 그래프는 "당신은 과거 1개월간 항우울제 처방을 받은 적 있나요?"라는 질문에 그렇다고 대답한 미국인의 백분율을 성별과 연령을 1988년에서 1994년, 2005년에서 2008년 사이의 두 기간에 따라 나타낸다. ①일반적으로 항우울제 처방의 사용은 두 기간 사이에 성별과 연령 두 그룹 모두에 걸쳐 증가했다. ②고연령 군에 해당하는 두 남성 계층에서는, 18세에서 44세에 해당하는 남성들이 1%에서 4%로 조금 더 완만한 증가세를 보인 것과 달리, 각각 2%에서 9%로, 2%에서 10%라는 도드라지는 증가세가 있었다. ③대조적으로, 모든 여성 그룹은 18세에서 44세 그룹에서는 10%, 45세에서 64세 그룹에서는 17%, 그리고 최고령 그룹에서는 13%라는 더욱 극단적인 증가세를 보였다. ④남성들은 최고령 그룹에서 가장 많은 증가세를 나타낸데 반해, 여성의 경우에는 45세에서 64세에 걸쳐 그러하였다. ⑤2005년에서 2008년의 기간 동안, 45세에서 64세에서는, 여성에 비해 두 배 이상의 남성들이 항우울제 처방전을 받았다.

34 **어휘** universally 일반적으로

해설 아름다워지기 위해, 사물은 반드시 일반인에게 감탄의 감정을 불러일으키는 분명한 특색을 가져야 한다. 예술적 판단력이 모든 사람에게 똑같이 존재하지 않고, 최소한 모든 사람이 똑같이 발달되지도 않는다는 것은 사실이다.
(B) 하지만 일반적으로 화음이라고 불리는 소리의 조합이 있고, 불협화음이라고 불리는 것들이 있다. 좋은 배합이라고 여겨지는 어떤 색의 조합이 있고, 좋지 않은 배합이라고 여겨지는 것들이 있다.
(C) 마찬가지로 아름다운 기하학적 형태나 공간이 있고, 조화롭지 않은 것들이 있다. 음악가들은 어떤 음조가 조화로울 것인지, 그리고 어떤 것이 그렇지 않을 것인지를 안다.
(A) 음악적 교육을 받지 않은 사람에게는 그런 지식이 존재하지 않지만, 그것을 들었을 때 그에 대해 감탄한다. 색채 전문가는 색을 이용하여 좋은 효과를 만드는 방법을 안다. 그는 다른 사람이 그의 작업물에 대해 감탄은 할 수 있지만, 가지고 있지는 않은 이 지식을 습득하고 있다.

35 **어휘** split second 짧은 시간

해설 어느 날 John이 자전거를 타고 출근하고 있었을 때, 그의 휴대전화가 울리기 시작했다 .그는 오른손으로 주머니에서 휴대전화를 , 그는 왼손으로는 브레이크를 걸었다. 그는 제어 할 수 없게 되어 자신의 자전거 앞으로 고꾸라지게 되었다.

(C) 그 찰나의 시간에, 그의 본능은 자신의 신체적 안녕을 대가로 피해로부터 전화를 보호하려 했다. 그의 손은 자신의 얼굴이 낙하를 정지시키기 위해 사용되는 대신, 자신의 전화가 인도에 부딪히는 것을 막기 위해 든 채였다.

(A) John은 그렇게 많은 고통을 느끼지는 않았지만, 그의 자존심은 상처를 입었다. 그는 재빨리 몸을 일으키고 자신의 부끄러운 나자빠짐을 본 사람이 아무도 없다는 것을 확인하기 위해 주변을 둘러보았다. John에게는 다행히도, 목격자는 아무도 없었다. 그는 얼굴의 먼지를 털고 가던 길을 다시 갔다.

(B) 직장에 도착한 뒤, John은 얼굴에 심하게 긁히고 뺨을 가로지르는 큰 상처가 생겼음을 알아차리게 되었다. 그는 병원으로 달려가서 붕대를 감고 상처를 꿰매었다. 심각한 상처가 아니었음에도 불구하고, 그는 여전히 자신의 가족에게 사고에 대해 설명해야 하는 수치에 직면했다.

36 **어휘** affection 애착 treacherous 기만적인 color 영향을 끼치다

해설 감정의 끌어당김은 불가피하지만 감정은 현실을 바로 볼 수 없게 하므로 주의해야한다는 요지의 글이다.

해석 공포는 당신으로 하여금 문제를 과대평가하게 하고 지나치게 소극적으로 행동하게 만든다. 분노와 초조는 당신의 선택을 차단하는 무분별한 행동으로 끌어내릴 것이다. 자신감 과잉, 특히 어떤 성공의 결과는 당신이 도를 넘게 만들 것이다. 사랑과 애착은 겉보기에는 당신편인 것 같은 사람들의 기만적인 행위를 알지 못하게 할 것이다. 이러한 감정들 중 가장 미세한 단계들조차 당신이 사건을 바라보는 관점에 영향을 끼칠 수 있다. 유일한 해결책은 감정의 끌어당김은 불가피하다는 것을 인식하고, 감정의 끌어당김이 일어났을 때 주목하고, 그것을 벌충하는 것이다. 당신이 성공했을 때, 각별히 우려해라. 당신이 화가 났을 때, 아무런 행동도 취하지 마라. 당신이 겁을 먹었을 때, 당신이 직면한 위험을 과장할 것이라는 것을 기억해라. 당신의 정서 반응을 더 많이 한정짓거나 벌충할 수 있다면, 당신은 더욱 면밀히 사물을 있는 그대로 볼 수 있을 것이다.

37 **어휘** convince 납득시키다

해설 Alemseged 박사는 인내심을 가지고 갈등을 벌이는 부족들을 설득해 화석 연구를 진행할 수 있게 되었다. 그리고 그 결과 인류의 선조는 기존 연구보다 늦은 시점에 나무를 오르는 능력을 버렸다는 것을 알 수 있게 되었다.

① 인내 – 버렸다
② 너그러움 – 버렸다
③ 인내 – 얻었다
④ 너그러움 – 향상되었다
⑤ 독창성 – 얻었다

해석 Zeray Alemseged 박사는 인류학 분야에서 놀라운 기여를 했다. 에티오피아 국립 박물관에서 일 했던 경험에서 영감을 받아, Alemseged는 파리 대학의 박사과정을 밟았다. 그가 에티오피아로 돌아 온 후, 그는 외떨어진 지역을 새로운 화석을 찾을만한 최적의 장소로 겨냥했다. 수백 년 된 부족 갈등 탓에 그곳에서 일 하는 것은 너무나 위험했기 때문에, 다른 과학자들은 이 지역을 기피하였다. 하지만 그는 양측 모두가 자신이 그 곳에서 일 하는 것을 허락하도록 설득하는 것을 포기하지 않았다. Alemseged와 그의 팀은 마침내 삼백 삼십만 년 된 여자 아이의 화석화 된 유골을 발견했다. 거의 완전한 상태인 견갑골도 포함되어 있었는데, 그것은 종이 정도의 두께라 화석화 된 채로 발견 된 적이 없었다. 이 견갑골의 형태를 근거로, Alemseged와 그의 동료들은 오스트랄로 피테쿠스 아파렌시스는 삼백 삼십만 년 전에는 훌륭한 등반가였고, 그것은 우리의 선조들이 많은 연구자들이 이전에 제시했던 것 보다 훨씬 나중에 나무에 오르는 것을 포기했다는 것을 의미한다는 연구를 발표했다.

→ 그의 인내 덕분에, Zeray Alemseged는 인류의 선조가 기존의 연구자들이 주장한 것 보다 상당히 나중에 그들의 나무를 오르는 능력을 버렸다는 증거를 찾음으로써 인류학의 상당한 발전에 공헌할 수 있었다.

virtuoso 고도의 기교를 보이는 run (음악)악구 blunder 실수

「내가 들은 중 가장 감동적인 피아노 연주회는 Rudolf Serkin의 것이었는데, 그는 베토벤의 발트슈타인 소나타와 슈베르트의 방랑자 환상곡을 생생히 연주했다. 슈베르트의 작품을 이루고 있는 고도의 기교를 보이는 악구 동안, Serkin의 손가락은 들릴 정도로 흐트러졌다. 두드러지는 실수에도 불구하고, Serkin은 방해받지 않고 계속 연주하였다. 악보가 끝나 그가 의자에서 일어났을 때, 그는 친절히도 자신의 주먹을 피아노에서 흔들어 보임으로써 솔직하게 자신의 실수를 인정했다. 당황스러울 수 있는 상황에서, Serkin은 재치 있는 행동으로 관중들에게서 웃음을 끌어냈다. 말 할 필요도 없이, 청중들은 모두 멋진 퍼포먼스에 감동했다. 그것은 내가 전까지, 혹은 지금까지 들었던 이 악보의 다른 어떤 음악가들의 "완벽한" 것보다 더 흥미롭고 더 아름다운 버전이었다. 이 교훈은 전체적으로 좋은 퍼포먼스를 보여 주면, 명백한 것이라 할지라도 한두 가지 실수 정도는 용서 받을 것이라는 것을 보여준다. 오히려 당신의 실수가 당신의 퍼포먼스를 방해하지 않도록 해라. Serkin의 청중들이 그의 실수를 잡아내기 위해 공연에 참석한 것이 아니듯, 당신의 청중 또한 당신이 실수하는 것을 보기 위해 일부러 모일 가능성은 없을 것이다. 그리고 만약 당신이 공연 중 실수를 한다면, 그 실수를 받아 들여라. 그리고 <u>공연을 계속 하라</u>.」

38 해설 Serkin과 같이 실수를 하더라도 흔들림 없이 공연을 마치도록 권하고 있다.
   ① 짧게 쉬도록 하여라.
   ② 공연을 계속 하라.
   ③ 분노에 차 당신의 주먹을 흔들도록 해라.
   ④ 처음부터 다시 시작해라.
   ⑤ 연주 할 다른 곡을 골라라.

39 해설 Serkin은 연주가 끝난 후 재치 있는 동작으로 자신의 실수를 인정하고 청중에게 사과했다.

⊹ [40~41]

> entrepreneur 사업가 mundane 재미없는
>
> 「나는 항상 청중을 사로잡을 흥미진진한 방법을 만드는 전달자를 찾고 있다. 나는 젊은 이탈리아인 사업가이자 텔레비전 진행자인 Marco Montemagno보다 소품을 더 많이 쓰는 사람을 거의 보지 못했다.
>
> Montemagno는 인터넷 문화를 주제로 자주 말하는데, 그것은 이탈리아인들에게 왜 인터넷을 받아들여야 하고 두려워해서는 안 되는지 보여준다. 그는 로마, 밀라노, 그리고 베니스와 같은 장소에서 3천명의 사람들이 모인 그룹에게 발표를 한다. 그의 주된 청중은 인터넷을 갓 사용하기 시작한 초심자이기 때문에, (a) 그는 모든 사람들이 이해할 수 있는 말을 사용한다. (음, 당신이 이탈리아어를 안다고 가정하면 말이다.) 그의 슬라이드는 매우 간결하고 시각적이다. 그는 종종 사진이나, 애니메이션, 비디오만을 사용한다. 그러나 진정 Montemagno를 다른 주된 발표자를 구분 짓는 것은 바로 (b) 그의 수많은 소품과 설명들이다.
>
> 그의 발표에 대해서는, Montemagno는 자신의 청중에게 무대에서 함께 해 주기를 요청한다. 예를 들어, (c) 그는 무대에서 티셔츠를 갤 자원자를 한 명 모집한다. 대부분의 사람들처럼, 자원자는 일반적인 방법으로 약 20초를 소요하여 셔츠를 갤 것이다. (d) 그가 완료한 뒤, 청중은 누군가가 5초 만에 셔츠를 개는 법을 보여주는 유명한 유튜브 비디오를 보게 된다. 그리고 나서 Montemagno는 청중이 환호하는 동안 그것을 다시 해 보인다. (e) 그의 요점은 인터넷은 심층적이고 지적인 수준까지 가르쳐 줄 수도 있지만, 재미없는 일도 더 쉽게 만들어 줄 수 있다는 것이다.」

40 해설 (a), (b), (c), (e)는 Montemgagno를 가리키지만 (d)는 무대에서 티셔츠 개기를 완료한 자원자이다.

41 해설 로마, 밀라노, 베니스는 이탈리아이다. 그는 이탈리아에서 이탈리아인을 대상으로 인터넷 교육을 실시한다.
① 그는 사업에 종사하면서 TV 프로그램의 진행자를 맡고 있다.
② 그는 자신의 청중들로 하여금 인터넷에 대해 두려움을 갖지 않도록 격려한다.
③ 그는 영국에서 대단히 규모가 큰 모임에게 발표를 한다.
④ 그는 발표에서 소품과 다른 시각적 자료들을 활용한다.
⑤ 그는 청중을 자신의 발표에 참여 시킨다.

objection 반대   persist 집요하게 계속하다

「(A) 하이든은 여러 측면 때문에 런던에 대해 만족했다. 하지만 그가 사랑하는 비엔나로 다시 돌아갈 때 기꺼이 떼어 놓고 가고 싶은 한 명의 문하생이 있었다. 어느 날 어떤 귀족이 그를 방문하여 음악에 대한 자신의 음악에 대한 열정을 늘어놓았다. 그리고 하이든이 한 번의 수업 당 1파운드에 작곡에 대한 가르침을 주었으면 한다고 말 했다.

(D) 하이든은 동의하고 언제부터 수업을 시작할지 물어 보았다. "일단, 이의가 없으시다면," 주머니에서 하이든의 4중주 곡 중 하나를 꺼내며 그가 말했다. "첫 수업에서는 이 4중주를 검토 해 보죠. 그리고 작곡법에 반하는 몇몇 조음과 어떤 진행에 대한 이유를 설명 해 주세요."

(C) 하이든은 이것에 이의를 제기하지 않았다. 그리고 그들은 그 음악의 검토를 시작하였다. 몇몇 곳들이 발견 되었는 데, 그가 왜 이렇게 하고 저렇게 했는지를 질문 받았을 때, 하이든은 그저 좋은 효과를 얻기 위해 그렇게 했다고 말 할 수밖에 없었다. 하지만 그 귀족은 그런 이유에는 만족할 수 없었고, 작곡가(하이든)가 자신의 획기적인 발전 을 위해 더 좋은 답을 주지 않는다면, 아무짝에도 쓸모없다고 선언했다.

(B) 그러자 하이든은 문하생에게 자신의 취향대로 음악을 고쳐 써 볼 것을 제안했는데 그는 이를 거절했다. 대신 그는 집요하게 하이든의 작곡 선택에 대해 캐물었다. 마침내, 하이든은 이 귀족 비평가에게 인내심이 사라져 "당신은 너무나 훌륭한 분이시라 저에게 가르침을 주실 수 있을 정도라는 것을 알았습니다. 저는 당신 같은 대가의 수업을 받을만한 자격이 되지 않기 때문에, 당신의 수업을 원치 않습니다. 작별을 고해야겠군요."라고 말 했다. 그리고 그 귀족에게 문을 안내했다.」

43 [해설] 하이든의 제자가 되기 위해 찾아 온 귀족이 가르침을 받을 자세는 갖추지 않은 채 불평과 비평만 늘어놓고 있다.

① 돈이 인내심을 사다
② 음악 검토의 기쁨
③ 런던에서의 가장 아름다운 추억
④ 좋은 제자는 아니되, 가혹한 비평가
⑤ 도전적인 질문에서 온 영감

⊕ [44~45]

> brittle 잘 부러지는 milestone 이정표, (중요) 단계
> 「지구 온난화를 막기 위한 많은 친환경 운동에도 불구하고, 북극의 얼음은 이미 보이지 않는 속도로 융해되고 있다. 융해는 캐나다와 알래스카 해안 곳곳의 얼음들을 상당히 (A) 잘 부서지게 하고 있다. 그 얼음은 쉽게 부서져서 큰 덩어리를 이루고 (이 과정은 분리빙하라고 알려져 있다) 탁 트인 대양에서 녹는다.
> 또한 북극해에는 해빙이 적은데 이는 얼음이 대서양으로 흘러 들어갔기 때문이다. 북극해 해빙의 사상 최저 기록은 2005년 8월 15일이었다. 하지만 북극은 2007년 여름 또 다른 중대 시점을 겪었다. 8월, 북서항로에는 유빙이 거의 없었다. 항해 할 항로가 완전히 열린 것은 1972년 기록이 시작 된 이후 처음이었다.
> 예전에는 (B) 영원할 것이라고 여겨졌던 북극해의 얼음은 이제 급격히 사라지고 있다. 얼음의 소실은 심각히 주목되어야 한다. 그것은 전 세계의 온도를 낮추는데 중요한 역할을 하기 때문이다. 해빙은 태양 광선의 80퍼센트를 반사하여 대기로 돌려보내는 반면, 해수는 90퍼센트를 흡수한다. 해빙되는 얼음은 더 많은 대양이 태양 광선에 직접 드러나게 하기 때문에, 과학자들은 수온이 훨씬 더 상승할 것이고, 이는 더욱 빠른 속도로 녹고 있는 얼음을 소실시킬 것으로 예상한다.」

44 해설 지구 온난화로 인해 해빙이 융해되어 더 많은 대양이 태양 광선에 노출됨에 따라 수온은 더욱 상승하게 되고, 상승한 수온으로 인해 해빙의 융해가 가속화 되는 악순환에 대해 이야기하고 있다.
① 북극 얼음 융해에 맞서기 위한 계획의 구상
② 지구 온난화를 관찰하는 과학적인 방법들
③ 육지와 대양에 대한 햇빛의 다른 영향
④ 지구 온난화와 북극 해빙 융해의 악순환의 고리
⑤ 지구 온난화에 따른 원양 항해의 변화

45 해설 (A) 융해의 결과 얼음이 잘 부서지게 되었다는 단어가 적절하다.
(B) 과거에는 영원할 것이라고 여겨졌지만 현재는 사라지고 있다는 내용이 문맥상 적절하다.
① 잘 부러지는 – 영구적인
② 잘 부러지는 – 연약한
③ 단단한 – 무방비의
④ 단단한 – 영구적인
⑤ 부드러운 – 연약한

ANSWER

01	02	03	04	05	06	07	08	09	10	11	12	13	14	15	16	17	18	19	20
③	①	①	②	⑤	④	③	③	④	⑤	③	④	①	⑤	③	④	②	②	⑤	②
21	22	23	24	25	26	27	28	29	30	31	32	33	34	35	36	37	38	39	40
④	⑤	①	②	②	⑤	②	①	⑤	③	②	③	③	①	④	⑤	①	④	①	④
41	42	43	44	45															
③	①	②	②	②															

01 **어휘** keep in suspense ~를 초조하게 하다 objectively 객관적인 견지에서 decent 품위 있는 skeptical 의심 많은, 회의적인

해설 대화 내용에 대한 내용일치 판단에 관한 문제이다.
　Mrs. Sanders는 딸애의 남자친구를 만난 적이 없으므로 ③번이 옳지 않다.
① Sanders 씨네 딸은 바이올린을 배우고 있다.
② Sanders 씨네 딸은 데이트 중이다.
③ Sanders 여사는 그 남자애를 좋아하지 않는다고 말한다.
④ Sanders 여사는 그 남자애를 만난 적이 없다.
⑤ Sanders 씨는 그 남자애에 관해 원래 의심이 많았다.

해석 Mr. Sanders : 바이올린 레슨을 끝낸 우리 딸을 오늘 데리러 갔다가, 내가 누구를 만났는지 당신은 전혀 상상도 못 할 거예요?

Mrs. Sanders : 애간장 태우지 마세요. 누구였는데요?

Mr. Sanders : 우리 딸의 첫 번째 남자친구였지. 그 애가 벌써 데이트를 한다는 게 믿을 수가 없어.

Mrs. Sanders : 오, 하느님 맙소사! 하긴, 그 애는 이제 어른이 됐잖아요, 그렇지 않아요? 당신 생각에는 그 남자애가 어땠어요?

Mr. Sanders : 난 아빠라고! 물론, 첫눈에 봤을 때, 그렇게 인상적이지 않았어. 어느 누구도 우리 소중한 딸에게 충분히 멋지지 않아.

Mrs. Sanders : 이봐요! 객관적으로 말 좀 해봐요, 그 남자애 어떤 애 같았어요?

Mr. Sanders : 솔직히, 잠시 얘기를 나누었을 때, 남자애가 아주 예의바르게 보였어. 그래도, 난 여전히 그 남자애에 대해 모든 것을 알고 싶어.

02 　**어휘**　librarian 사서(司書)　digit 숫자, 손(발)가락

　해설　대화의 문맥에 적합한 어휘를 찾는 문제, 컴퓨터에는 제목(title), 계단과 관련 있는 것은 층(floor), 책장의 숫자를 확인하는 것과는 선반(shelf)이 적합하므로 ①번이 정답이다.

　해석　사서 : 안녕하세요, 뭘 도와드릴까요?

　　톰 : 솔직히 말씀드리면, 제가 처음으로 도서관을 방문했는데요, "밥의 Big Barbecue"라는 책을 찾을 필요가 있지만요, 누가 그 것을 썼는지는 모르겠어요.

　　사서 : 걱정하지 마세요. 우선, 컴퓨터의 이곳에다가 우리는 책의 제목을 입력할 것입니다. 그러면, 일련의 숫자들이 나오죠. 첫 번째 숫자는 우리들이 몇 층에서 찾아야 할 것인 가를 알려줄 거예요. 그래서, 그것이 우리가 저편에 있는 계단을 이용해야만 한다는 것을 우리들에게 보여주는 거예요.

　　톰 : 그 다음 숫자는 무엇인가요?

　　사서 : 이것들은 찾아봐야 할 선반을 나타내는 것이죠, 그래서, 당신은 정확한 범위의 숫자들을 찾을 때까지 각각의 책장에 있는 번호들을 확인하세요.

　　톰 : 도와주셔서 대단히 감사합니다.

03 　**어휘**　limp 발을 절뚝거리다　paw (동물의) 발　surgery/operation 수술　cone 원추형　veterinary clinic 동물병원진료실　veterinarian = vet 수의사

　해설　단서가 되는 어휘와 선택지를 참고로 대화의 장소를 추론하는 문제이다.
　　① 동물병원 진료실 ② 치과 진료실 ③ 약국 ④ 의약품 공급소 ⑤ 병원 안내 데스크

　해석　Mr. Gupta : Mia를 치료하시려고 데려오셔서 기쁘군요. Mia가 괜찮아질 것이라는 것은 좋은 소식이지만, Mia의 상처가 수술이 필요하다는 것은 나쁜 소식이죠.

　　Susan : 그런 점이 무서웠어요. 사고 이후로 계속해서, Mia가 심하게 절뚝거리고 있어요. 그리고, 그 뒷발이 완전하게 낫지를 않는 거예요.

　　Mr. Gupta : 그래요. 유감스럽게도, Mia는 뒷다리에 수술을 필요로 하는 골절이 있어요.

　　Susan : 하지만, 수술 후에, 괜찮아질까요?

　　Mr. Gupta : 그런 다음에, Mia는 집에서 몇 주일간의 회복기를 갖게 될 것이고, 그동안에는 Mia가 상처부위를 핥지 않게 하려고 머리 둘레에 큰 플라스틱 깔때기를 쓰고 있어야만 할 거예요. 하지만, 그렇게 하고 나면, Mia는 100% 회복될 거예요.

　　Susan : 좋아요! 안심이 되네요!

04 　**어휘**　stalk (사냥감에) 몰래 접근하다　reasonable (가격 등이) 비싸지 않은　be fond of = like accommodation 숙박시설

　해설　대화내용과 일치하는 것을 고르는 문제, Dean의 마지막 대화를 참고하면 ②번이 정답임을 알 수 있다.
　　① Dean은 물가에 텐트를 치고 싶어 한다.
　　② Dean은 야외에서 취침하는 것을 좋아하지 않는다.
　　③ Steve와 Dean은 텐트에서 취침할 예정이다.
　　④ Steve는 야생동물을 두려워한다.
　　⑤ Steve는 숙박비를 지불할 것이다.

　해석　Steve : 와우! 정말 멋진 곳이네! 난 여기서 영원토록 지낼 수 있을 것 같아. 자, 너는 어디에 텐트를 치고 싶은 거야?

　　Dean : 너 확실히 여기서 취침하기를 원하는 거야? 길 아래에 비싸지 않은 호텔이 있잖아.

　　Steve : 아, 왜 그래. 저기 물 근처는 어떻게 생각해? 땅이 근사하고 평평해 보이네.

　　Dean : 난 모르겠는데. 그늘도 없이 햇볕이 바로 드는 곳이네.

　　Steve : 그렇다면, 저기서 약간 뒤편 나무 아래는 어떤 것 같니?

Dean : 거긴 훨씬 더 나쁘네, 벌레들에 둘러싸여 있고, 어둠속에서 몰래 접근해 오는 야생 동물들에게 더 가까운 곳이잖아.

Steve : 너 완전 애구나! 좋아. 내가 포기하지. 하지만, 방 값은 네가 지불하는 거야.

Dean : 전혀 문제될 것 없어. 우리가 옥외 취침을 하지 않는 한.

05 **어휘** loan application 대출 신청서   convinced 확신하는   fool-proof 아주 간단한, 실패할 염려가 없는   desirability 바람직함   viable 성공 할 수 있는

해설 대화 내용의 일관성을 추론하는 문제, 아이스크림 가게를 알래스카에서 열려고 하는 대출 신청자의 신청에 대해 가게의 위치를 문제 삼고 있으므로, 부정적인 견해인 ⑤번이 정답이다.

① 그 거 멋진 생각처럼 들립니다. 당신의 행운을 빕니다.
② 당신의 대출신청을 시작하기 위해 이 서류를 작성해주세요.
③ 우리는 장기적이고 건전한 사업 관계를 학수고대 합니다.
④ 당신의 대부가 승인되었음을 말씀드리게 되어 저희는 기쁩니다.
⑤ 죄송합니다만, 저희는 당신의 대부 신청을 처리할 수 없을 것 같습니다.

해석 은행 지점장 : 우리는 당신의 소규모 사업 대출 신청서를 검토해 봤습니다만, 당신 계획의 가능성을 완전히 확신하지 못하고 있습니다.

대출 신청인 : 무슨 말씀이세요? 그건 실패할 염려가 전혀 없는 일입니다. 모든 사람이 아이스크림은 좋아하는데, 수백 마일 부근에 다른 아이스크림 가게는 없죠.

은행 지점장 : 당신 상품에 대한 일반적인 바람직함이 사실은 문제가 아닙니다.

대출 신청인 : 저는 이해가 안 됩니다. 제 경험 부족이 문제인가요? 제가 당신께 약속했기 때문에 저는 아이스크림에 관해 알아야만 하는 모든 것을 배웠습니다.

은행 지점장 : 아니요, 진짜 문제는 위치입니다. 당신은 거의 일 년 내내 겨울인 알래스카의 작은 마을에서 당신의 가게를 열겠다고 선택을 했습니다. 우리는 아이스크림 가게가 그런 장소에서 성공할 수 있는 사업이라고는 생각하지 않습니다. 유감스럽지만, 우리는 당신의 대출신청서를 처리할 수 없을 것 같습니다.

06 **어휘** get to the bottom of ~의 진상을 규명하다. (문제)를 해결하다   fill an order 주문을 충족시키다

해설 대화 내용의 상황을 파악하는 문제로서 배송문제의 불만을 제기하는 Donna에게 Sam은 문제의 원인을 파악하여 즉시 조치를 취한다는 대화의 내용이므로 ④이 정답이다.

① Donna는 Sam의 배달 서비스에 완전히 만족하였다.
② Donna는 Sam이 수 주일 동안 그녀의 불만사항을 무시해 왔던 것이 유감스럽다.
③ 주문을 적절하게 충족시켰기에 Sam이 할 수 있는 일이 없다.
④ Sam은 문제를 해결해서 그의 고객을 기쁘게 만들려고 노력할 것이다.
⑤ Donna는 Sam의 사무용품점에 대한 주문을 취소하려고 계획하고 있다.

해석 Sam : Sam의 사무용품점입니다, 무엇을 도와 드릴까요?

Donna : 한 달 전에 A4 프린트 용지 주문했던 것 때문에 전화 드립니다. 그런데, 그때, 배달이 단지 1주일 걸릴 것이라고 들었습니다.

Sam : 물론입니다. 우리의 주문품은 배송위치에 따라 1주일 혹은 그 이전에 배달되도록 보장하고 있습니다. 어떤 문제가 있으신 지요?

Donna : 문제는 배송이 2주일 늦었을 뿐만 아니라, 단지 절반만 배달되었으며, 여전히 저는 나머지를 기다린다는 것입니다.

Sam : 대단히 죄송합니다. 저희 기록에 의하면 10박스 모두 배달되었다고 나옵니다만, 제가 문제를 해결해서 나머지 5박스가 즉시 배송되도록 할 것입니다.

Donna : 감사합니다. 그리고, 이런 일이 다시 발생하지 않도록 확실히 해주세요.

07 어휘 retrieve ~을 되찾다 rake 갈퀴질 하다 awe 경외(敬畏)감 mandatory 의무적인, 필수적인 sign autograph 서명하다, 사인해주다

해설 지칭하는 They(they)가(이) 가리키는 것이 나머지 넷과 다른 것을 고르는 문제로서 ①②④⑤는 Misty May-Treanor와 Kerri Walsh를 지칭하고, ③은 자원봉사자들을 지칭한다.

해석 Misty May-Treanor와 Kerri Walsh는 훌륭한 운동선수이며 멋진 사람들이다. 2008 북경올림픽의 비치발리볼 준결승에서 그들은 매우 훌륭한 브라질 팀을 이겼다. 그 후에, 그들은 브라질 팀의 선수들과 악수를 나누며 고맙습니다 라고 말했다. 그런 다음에, 그들은 공을 되찾아오고, (경기장) 모래를 정리(갈퀴질)하는 것과 같은 일을 하는 많은 자원봉사자들과 악수를 했다. 저널리스트 Mike Celizic는 경탄하면서, "그들이 자신들의 노력이 얼마나 고맙게 생각되고 있는지를 모르는 채 떠나가도록 하는 것을 원하지 않았기 때문에, 그들은 몇몇의 자원봉사자들이 코트를 떠날 때 글자 그대로 그들의 뒤를 쫓아갔다"라고 썼다. 그들은 또한 팬들에게 손을 흔들어 인사를 했으며 의무적인 약물테스트 후에 다시 돌아오겠다고 약속했다. 그들은 정말 돌아왔고, 사진포즈를 취해주었고 정말 많은 팬들에게 사인을 해주었다. 그리고 물론, 팬들은 그들과 악수했던 것을 진실로 고맙게 생각했다.

08 어휘 MSG 글루탐산 소다(monosodium glutamate) concentrate 농축하다 extract 추출하다 beet 사탕무 a small fraction of 소량의 a number of ~ 많은, 다수의 the number of ~의 수

해설 문단의 일관성을 추론하는 문제로서, MSG의 안전성에 대한 내용과 어울리지 않는 것은 요리사들이 MSG를 좋아하지 않는다는 ③번이 정답이다.

해석 MSG는 본질적으로 농축된 나트륨의 형태로서 해초, 사탕무, 곡물로부터 추출된다. ① 글루탐산 협회는 MSG는 완전히 안전하다고 주장한다. ② 그들은 MSG는 우리가 음식으로 단백질을 섭취할 때 우리 몸에서 나오는 글루탐산염과 전혀 다르지 않고, 음식에 첨가된 MSG는 대부분의 음식에 자연적으로 포함된 아주 소량의 글루타민산염에 해당하는 것이라고 주장한다. ③ 똑같은 많은 이유 때문에, 다수의 요리사들은, 그것이 음식의 맛을 떨어뜨리고 너무도 종종 저급한 제품을 보상하기 위해 사용된다고 생각하면서 MSG를 좋아하지 않는다. ④ 예를 들면, 대부분의 요리법들은 고기 1파운드당 티스푼 절반의 MSG를 요구하고 있다. ⑤ 이러한 비율로는, 1회분 치킨요리의 MSG는 이미 닭에서 발견된 글루타민산염의 10퍼센트보다 적은 부분을 차지한다.

09 어휘 on behalf of ~을 대신해서 employ 사용하다 on a daily basis 매일 come in contact with 와 접촉하다, 만나다 tactic 전략, 수단 objective 목표 prevalent 만연한, 널리 퍼진 counterproductive 비생산적인 First World 제 1세계(서방 선진국)

해설 광고에서 유머는 자주 사용되는 전략적인 방법이라는 내용과 어울리지 않는 것은 유머가 비효과적이고 비생산적이라는 ④번이다.

해석 전통적인 광고는 알아 볼 수 있는 광고주들을 대신하여 대중매체를 통하여 소비자들에게 전달되는 설득적이며, 개인적이지 않은 의사소통으로 전형적으로 정의되며, 유머는 종종 사용되는 중요한 도구이다. ① 대부분의 소비자들은 매일 많은 광고에 노출되기 때문에, 유머러스한 광고는 많은 사람들이 의도적인 유머를 접하는 가장 빈번한 방식일 수 있다. ② 광고자(주)들은 다양한 전략적 목표를 달성하기 위하여 광고의 잠재력을 끌어올린다는 의도를 갖고 유머를 메시지 전략으로 사용한다. ③ 유머는 현대 광고의 초기 동안에는 다소 드물게 사용되었다. 하지만, 연구자들은 현대광고에 유머의 사용은, 특히 방송매체에서, 널리 유행한다는 것을 확인했다. ④ 유머는 아주 비효율적이고 비생산적이다라는 것이 광고 산업에서 널리 받아들여지고 있다. ⑤ 이것이 비록 제1세계, 즉 아주 선진화된 나라들에서는 사실이라 하더라도, 유머는 동양 국가에서보다 서양국가의 광고와 문화에서 다소 더 빈번하게 발견된다.

10 어휘 opposing 반대되는 ubiquitous 도처에 존재하는 architectural features 건축 상의 특징 obligatory 의무적인 domestic props 가정의 소품 prevalence 유행, 널리 행하여짐 intimate 친구, 친밀한 사람 penetrate 관통하다, 뚫고 들어가다

해설 요지추론의 문제로서 사람들은 사생활과 사회생활에 대한 정반대의 욕구가 있다는 글의 흐름으로 보아 ⑤번이 정답이다.

해석 대부분의 사람들은 잠재적으로 두 개의 서로 반대되는 욕구가 있다. 그 하나는 사회적 접촉을 위해 다른 사람들에게 이용가능해지는 것이며, 다른 하나는 사생활을 갖는 것이다. 어떤 사람들은 더 많은 사생활을 필요로 하고, 다른 사람들은 더 많은 사회적 접촉을 필요로 한다. 만약 우리가 환경에 대하여 생각한다면, 공적인 공간이든, 가정 내의 공간이든 간에, 우리는 이러한 두 가지 욕구를 반영하고 있는 특징을 볼 수 있다. 서구사회에서는 문은 어디에나 있는 건축 상의 특징이며, 커튼은 거의 의무적인 가정 내 소품의 일부분이다. 문과 커튼을 열고 닫는 가능성은 이용가능성을 알리는 장치이다. Goffman은 가정 내와 공적인 환경 둘 다에서 뒤쪽(사적인) 공간(영역)과 앞쪽(공적인) 공간(영역)이 널리 퍼져있는 것에 주목했다. 침실, 욕실, 그리고 때로는 부엌 등이 포함되는 가정에서의 뒤쪽 공간(영역)은 단지 친밀한 사이의 사람들만이 초대받지 않고서 들어 갈 수 있는 공간(영역)이다. 앞쪽 공간(영역)은 일반 사람들에게 개방되어 있다.

11 어휘 antibiotics 항생제 blunt 약하게 하다, 무딘 complications 합병증 infections 감염, 전염병 outwit ~을 앞지르다 spur 박차를 가하다 purge 제거하다, 추방하다

해설 어법상 틀린 것을 고르는 문제로서, ③번은 대동사 do(that 앞에 나온 have 의 과거형 had를 대신함)의 과거형 did가 와야 한다.
①번은 one of ~ 복수형 명사, ②번은 평행구조가 와야 하므로, have + 과거분사형, ④번은 선행사 + 관계대명사, ⑤번은 목적보어로 형용사 difficult가 올바른 형태이다.

해석 질병을 야기하는 박테리아에 대한 항생제의 승리는 현대 약의 가장 위대한 성공 이야기 중 하나이다. 이러한 약들은 2차 세계 대전 시대에 처음으로 널리 사용된 이래로, 그것들은 셀 수 없이 많은 생명을 구했고, 많은 두려운 질병과 감염의 심각한 합병증을 약화시켰다. 하지만 50년 이상 널리 사용된 후에, 많은 항생제들은 한때 가졌던 것과 똑같은 효과를 갖고 있지 않다. 시간이 지나면서, 약간의 박테리아는 항생제의 효과보다 앞지를 수 있는 방법을 발달시켰다. 널리 퍼진 항생제 사용은 박테리아들이 이러한 강력한 약보다 오래 살아남을 수 있도록 하는 그들의 진화적인 변화를 자극했다고 여겨진다. 항생제의 저항성이 미생물들에는 도움이 되는 반면에, 인간에게는 두 가지 큰 문제를 제기한다. 그것은 감염을 신체에서 제거하는 것을 더 어렵게 만들고, 병원에서 감염에 걸릴 위험을 증가시킨다.

12 어휘 assume 가정하다 primacy effect 초두 효과(처음 입력된 정보가 나중에 습득하는 정보보다 더 강한 영향력을 발휘하는 것) murky 매우 어두운, 애매한 recency effect 신근성 효과(최신 효과)(최신의 정보에 의해서 좌우되는 것)

해설 어법상 틀린 것을 고르는 문제로서, ④ stop ~ing와 stop to ~는 의미가 완전히 다른 구문으로, 문제에서는 '조사자가 읽기를 멈출 때'가 문맥에 맞는 것이므로, stop reading이 와야 한다. ① and로 연결되는 평행구조이므로 현재형 동사가 와야 하며, ② those는 앞에 나온 복수명사 options을 지칭하는 것이며 ③ quickly 부사가 동사를 수식하고 있고, ⑤ 내용상 수동형이 와야 한다.

해석 설문조사에서, 응답 선택지가 시각적으로 제시되었을 때, 응답자가 전형적으로 목록의 위에서 시작해서 순서대로 나머지 선택지를 해나간다고 가정하는 것은 합리적인 것처럼 보인다. 그러므로 초두 효과가 법칙인 것처럼 보인다. 응답자는 끝에 있는 선택지보다 목록의 처음에 있는 선택지를 선호하는 경향이 있다. 하지만, 설문 조사자가 응답자에게 응답 선택지를 읽어 줄 때 상황은 다소 더 애매해진다. 설문 조사자는 보통 다음 선택지로 넘어가기 전에 응답자가 일반적으로 첫 번째 선택지를 평가할 시간을 갖지 않도록 질문을 빠르게 읽는 경향이 있다. 응답자는 조사자가 읽기를 멈출 때 마지막 선택지가 작동 기억에 남아있게 될 것이기 때문에, 그 선택지를 고려하면서 시작할 가능성이 아주 크다. 결과적으로, 질문이 응답자에게 소리 내어 제시될 때, 우리는 목록의 끝에 있는 선택지를 선택하는 경향, 즉 신근성(최신) 효과를 예상해야 한다.

13 어휘 tremendous 엄청난, 굉장한 feat 업적, 위업 blower(크리켓에서) 투수 successive 연속적인, 연이은 honor 존중하다, 예우하다 proceeds 결과, 수익금 National Hockey League 북아메리카 프로 아이스하키 리그 surface 나타나다

해설 어법에 알맞은 어휘를 고르는 문제로서, (A)는 주어가 단수인 The reward이므로 was, (B)는 '전치사 + 관계대명사'의 구문이 와야 한다. 'scoring is relatively infrequent'라는 문장에서 선행사인 other sports가 이 문장에 올 수 있기 위해서는 'in other sports'의 형태로 와야 한다. (C)는 another goal (being scored) by other player에서 goal과 by other players 사이의 관계를 생각해보면, 수동형이 나와야 하니까 being scored가 올바른 형태이다.

해석 "해트트릭"은 원래 투수가 연속 투구로 세 명의 타자를 아웃시키는 굉장한 업적을 묘사하기 위해 사용되었던 영어의 크리켓 용어였다. 많은 크리켓 클럽에서 이 업적에 대한 보상은 새 모자였다. 다른 클럽들은 팬들 사이에 "그 모자를 전달하고" 득점자에게는 그 결과물(모자)을 주는 것에 의해서 그들의 영웅을 존중하였다. 이 용어는 비교적 득점이 좀처럼 일어나지 않는 다른 스포츠로 퍼지게 되었다. 그래서 "해트트릭"은 또한, 축구에서 3골을 득점한 업적을 묘사하기 위해서 사용된다. 북아메리카 프로 아이스하키 리그의 Belinda Lerner에 따르면, 1900년대 초반에 하키에서도 이 표현이 등장했다. "하키에서는 이것의 진짜 의미에 대해 약간의 혼동이 있어요. 오늘날, '진정한' 해트트릭은 한 선수가 경기에서 다른 선수가 다른 골을 득점하는 일이 없이 연속적으로 3골을 득점할 때 발생합니다."

14 어휘 barren 황량한, 불모의, 불임의 apparently 명백히, 외관상으로는 vague 막연한, 애매한(ambiguous) constantly 언제나, 계속적으로

해설 어법에 알맞은 어휘를 고르는 문제로서, (A)는 whether ~ or not의 구조이며, (B)는 문장의 구조가 guided primarily by a sense of ~이다. guide가 올 경우에는 guide 뒤에 목적어 형태가 와야 한다. (C)는 that절 속의 동사형이 필요하므로, influences가 와야 한다.

해석 대부분의 우리들은 우리가 보내는 삶의 종류를 선택한다. 비록, 우리가 그것을 인식하지 못할지라도, 매일 우리는 우리가 행복할지 불행할지, 건강할지 아플지, 창의적일지 비생산적일지를 결정하는 선택을 한다. 우리는 주로 과거에 우리에게 일어났었던 것과 미래에 우리에게 일어날 수도 있는 것에 대한 감각에 의해 이끌려, 무의식적인 수준에서 이러한 많은 선택을 한다. 이 명백하게 자동적인 의사결정 과정은 우리가 계속적으로 선택을 한다는 사실을 숨기는 경향이 있다. 시간이 지나면서, 우리는 삶의 매 새로운 순간에서 선택을 한다는 느낌을 잃어버린다. 그 결과, 우리는 운명, 숙명, 또는 운과 같은 막연한 외부의 힘이 우리가 어떻게 사는지, 우리가 무엇을 성취하는지, 그리고 때때로 우리가 어떻게 죽는지에 영향을 미친다고 믿게 된다.

15 어휘 melting pot 용광로 equity 공평, 공정 eliminate 제거하다 fashion 방법, 방식 homogeneous 동종의, 동질의(⇔ heterogeneous 이종의, 이질의) ingredient 성분, 요소 metaphor 은유(隱喩) wherein 어디에서, 어떤 점에서 dilute 희석하다, 묽게 하다

해설 빈칸에 들어갈 낱말을 추론하는 문제로서, 이글은 사회를 용광로에 비유하는 관점에 대한 글이므로, 마지막 문장에서 용광로의 결과는 동질의 생산물이라는 내용으로 보아 용광로 비유는 동일함(③ sameness)에 대한 욕구를 반영한다는 내용이 와야 한다.

해석 사회를 용광로라고 보는 관점은 모든 사람들이 충분히 열심히 노력만 한다면 성공할 수 있다는 것을 나타내기 때문에 약간의 호소력이 있다. 하지만, 어느 시점에서 우리는 이러한 종류의 공평함은 차이와 다양성을 제거함을 의미한다는 것을 인식해야 한다. 이상적인 용광로(사회)는 개인은 일반적으로 존재하는 체제에 꼭 들어맞기 위해 자신의 독특함을 희생할 것을 요구한다. 적어도 사회적으로 용인될 수 방식(유명한 갱스터가 되는 것과는 정반대로) 으로 성공적이 되기 위한 유일한 방법은 자신의 문화적 배경을 포기하면서 적응하는 법을 발달시킬 것을 필요로 한다. 우리는 다른 요소가 섞이는 방식으로서 용광로라는 개념을 사용하지만, 우리는 이 용광로의 결과는 독특한 특징들이 희석되는 동질의 생산물이라는 것을 인식해야만 한다. 간단히 말하면, 용광로의 비유는 동일함에 대한 욕구를 반영한다.

16 어휘 dimension 차원 conceive 마음에 그리다, 생각하다 empirical 경험에 의거한, 실증적인 theoretical 이론적인 fabric 구조 accord 일치하다, 부합하다 common-place 흔한 on this account 이런 까닭에 imperceptible 지각할 수 없는 manifest 명시하다, 분명히 나타내다 tangible 실재하는, 명백한 embed 깊이 새겨두다, 박아 넣다

해설 물리학에서 다루어지는 시간의 개념을 다룬 글의 내용에서, 시간은 우리가 거주하는 환경을 지배하는 물리적 법칙 안에 시간의 개념이 반영되고 있다는 문장에서 추론해 볼 때, ④번이 정답이다.
① 그 자체의 추진력으로 지나가다.
② 물리적으로 지각될 수 없다.
③ 물리학 분야에서 다루어지지 않는다.
④ 객관적으로 외부세계에 내장되어있다.
⑤ 가상의 인간경험의 구성개념이다.

해석 시간은 우리가 세상과 세상 속에서의 우리의 위치를 이해함에 있어서 중요하고 필수적인 차원을 더한다. 우리의 경험의 세계가 시간이 부재한다면 어떨 것인가에 대해 생각하는 것은 거의 불가능한 것처럼 보인다. 결국, 사건들은 시간 안에서 일어난다. 이것은 물리학자들이 이론적이며 경험적인 원형으로서, 공간과 함께 시간을 다루도록 야기했다. 어느 수준에서, 시간이 우주의 물리적 구조의 일부를 구성하고, 그러한 것으로서(우주의 물리적 구조의 일부를 구성하는 것으로서) 물리적으로 실재한다는 관점은 내가 시간의 평범한 관점이라고 칭한 것과 일치한다. 대부분의 사람들은 물리적인 의미에서 실제로 존재하는 '진짜' 시간이라는, 시간에 대한 이러한 관점을 믿는다. 그런 이유에서, 우리가 거주하는 환경을 지배하는 물리적 법칙에 반영되고 있는 것처럼, 시간은 객관적으로 외부 세계에 내장되어 있다. 시간은 그 자체로 "지각 할 수 없는" 것일 수 도 있는 반면에, 시간은, 그럼에도 불구하고, 진짜로, 실재하는 결과물을 나타낸다. 시간의 "경과(흐름)" 없이, 연속은 없고, 그래서 지속의 경험도 있을 수 없다.

17 어휘 vastness 광대함 tedious 지루한, 싫증나는 piecemeal 조금씩 하는 a first bite 첫 단계 immeasurable 셀 수 없을 만큼의 magnitude 규모, 중요도 therapeutic 긴장을 푸는 데 도움이 되는 a good cause 대의명분

해설 빈칸에 들어갈 낱말을 추론하는 문제로서, 우리는 큰 꿈과 야망을 갖고 살아가지만, 그것을 실현하기 위해서는 작고, 지루한 단계들을 밟아 나가는 일이 어려우며, 욕망의 광대함은 우리를 압도한다고 한다. 목표를 향해서는 작은 일들이 관련되어 연속성을 갖게 되는 과정을 거치면서, 우리의 욕망이 실현가능한 것처럼 보이게 된다는 내용이므로, ②번 '그 작은 단계를 내딛는 것'이 빈칸에 와야 한다.

해석 많은 우리들이 직면하는 문제는 우리가 큰 꿈과 야망을 가지고 있다는 것이다. 우리 꿈의 감정과 욕구의 광대함에 사로잡혀 있어서, 우리는 그것을 달성하기 위해 주로 필요한 작고 지루한 단계에 집중하는 것이 어렵다는 것을 알게 된다. 우리는 우리의 목표를 향한 거대한 도약의 관점에서 생각하는 경향이 있다. 하지만 자연에서처럼 사회적 세계에서는 규모와 안정성의 무엇이든지 천천히 성장한다. 조금씩 하는 전략은 우리의 타고난 성급함에 대한 완벽한 해독제이다. 이것은 작고 즉각적인 것인, 첫술 뜨기(첫 번째 단계)에, 그런 다음, 두 번째 단계가 어떻게, 어디에서 우리를 우리의 궁극적인 목표에 더 가까워지게 할지에 우리를 집중시킨다. 이것은 아무리 작은 것이라 하더라도, 우리가 관련된 단계와 행동의 연속, 즉 과정의 관점에서 생각하게끔 하며, 이것은 또한, 측정할 수 없을 정도의 심리학적인 이점을 지닌다. 너무 자주 우리 욕망의 규모가 우리를 압도한다. 그 작은 첫 단계를 내딛는 것이 그 욕망들이 실현 가능한 것처럼 보이게 만든다. 행동보다 더 도움이 되는 것은 없다.

18

어휘 no ~ whatever ~ 은 전혀 없는 tolerate 묵인하다, 참다 ward off 피하다, 물리치다 vigilant 방심하지 않는, 경계하고 있는 panicked 공포에 사로잡힌 perceive 인식하다, 인지하다 instill 주입시키다 inhibit 억제하다, 금지하다

해설 빈칸에 들어갈 낱말을 추론하는 문제로서, 우리는 불안을 느끼기 때문에 공격받을 상황이 닥쳐왔을 때, 그 상황을 벗어나기 위한 조치를 취하고 덕분에 그 위험에서 벗어날 수 있다는 내용이므로, 빈칸에 들어갈 말로 가장 적절한 것은 ②번 '당신을 살아 있고 편안하게 하는 것을 돕는다'이다.

해석 믿거나 말거나, 불안은 <u>당신을 살아 있고 편안하게 하는 것을 돕는다</u>. 왜냐하면 당신은 욕구, 선호, 목표를 갖고 태어나고 키워졌기 때문에, 만약 당신이 전혀 불안감이 없다면, 그리고 당신의 욕구를 성취하는 것에 대해 완전히 무관심하다면, 당신은 모든 종류의 불쾌한 것을 묵인하고, 그것들로부터 피하거나 도망치기 위해 아무것도 하지 않을 것이다. 기본적으로 불안은 당신의 욕구에 반대되는 것을 의미하는 불쾌한 일들이 일어나고 있거나, 일어날 가능성이 있음을 깨닫게 하고, 당신이 그것에 대해 무언가를 하는 편이 좋을 것이다 하고 경고하는 일련의 불편한 감정과 행동 경향이다. 따라서, 만약 당신이 공격받을 위험에 처해 있고, 당신이 다치지 않기를 바란다면, 당신은 도망치기, 공격자와 싸워 물리치거나, 경찰에 신고하기 등 몇 가지 가능한 행동을 선택한다. 하지만 만약 당신이 걱정을 하거나, 신경을 쓰거나, 불안해 하거나, 긴장하거나, 조심스러워 하거나, 경계심을 갖거나, 혹은 공포감에 사로잡히지 않는다면, 아마도 이러한 일들 중에서 아무것도 하지 않을 것이다. 당신은 아마 공격의 위험을 인지할 것이지만, 그것에 대해 아무것도 하지 않을 것이다.

19

어휘 AI 인공 지능(artificial intelligence) correspond to 일치하다, 해당하다 autonomous 자주적인, 자율적인 natural language(프로그램 언어에 대한) 자연 언어 agent 행위자, 대리 specification (자세한) 설명서, 설계명세서 strictly 철저히, 엄격히 flexible 유연한, 융통성 있는 perspective 관점, 견해 constraint 제약, 강제

해설 필자가 주장하는 것을 고르는 문제로서, 인공지능의 한계에 대한 필자의 견해는 문단의 마지막에서 창의적 행동을 수행할 수 없는 한계가 있다고 필자는 주장하고 있으므로, ⑤번이 정답이다.

해석 처음부터 전적으로, 인공지능 연구의 주된 초점은 항상 문제 해결의 문제에 있었다. 이러한 관점에서 볼 때, 지능은 정확하고 자율적인 로봇 팔의 움직임부터 자연 언어 문장의 이해까지 복잡한 문제를 해결하는 능력에 해당한다. 가장 좋은 환경은 지적인 대리인이 최고의 선택을 찾는 곳, 즉 문제에 대한 해결책이 있는 공간에서 탐구하는 환경이다. 인공 지능의 문제 해결 방법에 대하여 가해지는 가장 흔한 비판 중 하나는 설명서에서 예측되지 않는 상황을 처리할 수 있는 그것들의 제한된 능력이다. 그 시스템이 아무리 융통성 있고, 복잡하고, 적응성 있는 것처럼 보이든 간에 탐색 공간은 일반적으로 엄격하게 한정되어 있다. 이러한 탐색 공간에서 전혀 만족할 만한 해결책이 없는 문제에 직면했을 때, 관점을 변화시키거나, 제한을 완화하거나, 새로운 상징을 추가하는 가장 간단한 조작을 통해 해결책이 성취 될 수 있을 때조차도, 인공지능 시스템은 그 탐색 공간에 존재하는 기껏해야 가장 성공적이지 못한 결과를 가지고 그저 돌아온다. 요컨대, 그러한 시스템은 지능의 근본적인 측면, 즉 우리가 일반적으로 창의적 행동이라고 부르는 것을 수행할 능력이 거의 없다.

20

어휘 aesthetic 미학의, 미적인 embody 상징[구현]하다, 구체화하다 pile up 축적하다, 쌓아 올리다 embodiment 구현 implication 영향, 결과 dualism 이원론 provocative 도발적인 objectionable 불쾌한, 무례한 come to grips with ~에 대처(직면)하다, ~을 이해하기시작하다 profound 심오한 far-reaching 광범위한 at odds with ~와 불화하여, ~와 상충하여

해설 우리 마음과 몸은 하나의 유기적인 과정의 결과물이므로, (A)에는 organic(유기적인)이 적절하고, (B)에는 인간의 마음의 모든 측면은 몸과 관련되어 있다는 내용이므로 'grounded in'이 적절함

해석 우리가 "마음"이라고 부르는 것과 "몸"이라고 부르는 것은 두 가지가 아니고, 오히려 하나의 <u>유기적인</u> 과정의 양상이다. 그래서 모든 우리의 의미, 생각, 언어는 이 구현된 활동의 심미적인 차원으로부터 나타난다. 이러한 심미적 차원 중에서 중요한 것들은 자질, 이미지, 감각운동 과정의 패턴, 그리고 감정이다. 적어도 과거 30년 동안, 많은 학문분야의 학자들과 연구자들은 마음과 의미의 구현에 대한 주장과 근거를 축적해 왔다. 하지만,

그들 연구의 영향은 대중의 의식에 들어가지 못했고, 그래서 몸과 마음의 이원론을 부인하는 것은 대부분의 사람들이 불쾌해 하고 심지어 위협적이라고 생각하는 여전히 매우 도발적인 주장이다. 당신의 구현을 이해하기 시작하는 것은 당신이 항상 직면하게 될 가장 심오한 철학적 과제 중 하나이다. 인간 마음의 모든 측면이 환경과 더불어 특정한 형태의 신체적 개입(관여)에 기초를 두고 있다는 점을 인정하는 것은 우리들에게 이어져 내려온 서양 철학과 종교적 전통의 많은 것과는 주로 대립하는 방식으로, 우리가 누구이고 무엇인지를 광범위하게 다시 생각하는 것을 요구한다.

21 **어휘** warfare 전쟁, 전투 alien 외국인의, 외국의 peculiar 이상한, 기이한 impenetrable mystery 불가해한 미스터리 outward 표면상의, 겉보기의 strategist 전략가

해설 문맥상 빈칸에 적절한 연결어 추론하는 문제로서, 정보가 부족했던 시기에 전쟁을 하는 상황에 대한 내용이다. (A)에는 the enemy often came from ~ 의 어구에서 추론이 가능한 'In addition'이 와야 내용상 일관성이 있고, (B)에는 정보가 부족한 장군이 적에 대한 정보를 알아내는 방법의 예를 들고 있으므로. 'For example'이 정답으로 오면 된다.

해석 전쟁의 초기 역사에서, 군 지도자는 다음과 같은 곤경에 직면했었다. 어떤 전쟁 시도의 성공은 상대방의 의도, 강점과 약점 등, 상대편에 대해 가능한 한 많은 것을 아는 능력에 달려 있었다. 하지만 적은 절대로 이러한 정보를 기꺼이 밝히려고 하지 않는다. 게다가, 적은 종종 독특한 사고와 행동 방식을 갖고 있는 이질적인 문화로부터 왔었다. 장군은 상대편 장군이 무슨 생각을 하고 있는지 정말 알 수 없었다. 외부에서는 적군은 대단히 불가해한 미스터리를 나타내고 있었다. 하지만 아직, 상대편에 대한 이해가 부족하기 때문에, 장군은 어둠 속에서 작전을 해야 할 것이다. 유일한 해결책은 안에서 무슨 일이 일어나고 있는지에 대한 외견상의 신호를 위해 적을 면밀히 조사하는 것이었다. 예를 들어, 전략가는 적군 기지의 조리하는 불, 그리고 시간에 따라 그 수의 변화를 셀 수도 있을 것이다. 그것은 군대의 규모를 나타내 줄 것이다.

22 **어휘** stop-motion 스톱 모션(물체의 움직임을 고정해 촬영하고 연속되는 다음 동작을 같은 방법으로 찍어 움직이는 영상을 만드는 기법. 애니메이션 제작에 많이 사용됨) still photograph 스틸 사진(정지된 사진) delicate 정교한, 섬세한 frame 틀, 구조 blur 흐릿함, 잔상 jerky 급격히 움직이는, 덜컥거리는

해설 스톱 모션 촬영 기법에 대한 내용으로, (A) 뒤에서 1초에 24장의 사진이 나올 만큼 정교한 작업이라고 설명하였기 때문에, 물체는 조금씩 움직여야 하므로 'slightly(약간)'가 와야 한다. (B)에는 점토 모델이 실제로 움직이는 것처럼 보인다고 해야 하므로, 'moving(움직이는)'이 적절하다. (C)에는 사실적인 움직임을 위해서는 '잔상' 효과가 있어야 한다는 내용으로 보아 'blurry'(흐릿한)가 적절하다.
(A) considerably 상당히, slightly 약간
(B) resting 정지하고 있는, moving 움직이고 있는
(C) blurry 흐릿한, jerky 급격히 움직이는

해석 스톱 모션 촬영 기법은 움직임을 보도록 눈을 속이기 위해 사용된다. 정지한 사진은 공룡의 점토 모델과 같은 물체로 만들어진다. 물체를 약간만 움직이고 또 다른 사진을 찍는다. 이 정교한 과정이 수천 번 반복된다. 사진, 즉 프레임이 1초에 24개의 프레임씩, 영화촬영 카메라의 속도로 보일 때, 점토 모델은 움직이고 있는 것으로 나타난다. 스톱 모션 촬영의 주된 문제는 "잔상"이 없다는 것이다. 만약 당신이 한 사람이 거리를 달려가는 것을 촬영한다면, 각 프레임에는 약간의 잔상이 있을 것이다. 비록 관객이 알아채지 못한다 하더라도, 잔상은 달리는 모습을 부드럽고 현실감 있게 만드는 것을 돕는다. 스톱 모션 영화에서, 달리는 생명체들은 급격히 움직이는 것처럼 보인다. 이 문제는 사실적인 움직임을 만들기 위해 프레임을 흐릿하게 만들어 주는 데 사용 될 수 있는 컴퓨터 애니메이션으로 해결해 왔다.

23 어휘 in a matter of seconds 순식간 동안에 subjectively 주관적으로 commodity 상품 bound 묶인, 구속된, 제본한 around the clock 24시간 내내 nomadic 유목의, 방랑의 herald ~을 알리다, 예고하다 crunch 위기, 긴장, 바삭바삭 소리를 내다, 아작아작 씹다
cut back on ~을 줄이다 juggle 곡예하다, 잘 양립하다

해설 시간을 절약해 주고 공간에서 우리들을 해방시킨다고 알려졌던 휴대폰과 같은 도구들에 의해서 오히려 시간이 점점 더 부족한 사람들의 상황에 대한 글의 내용으로 보아, (A)에는 휴대폰은 친구와 동료들과 대화하면서 출근 전쟁을 할 수 있다는 의미이므로 'allow', (B)에는 시간은 진실로 귀중한 상품이라는 의미이므로 'precious' (C)에는 휴대폰 등의 도구는 해방의 도구로 처음에는 알려졌다는 내용이므로 'liberation'이 와야 한다.
(A) allow 허용하다 forbid 금지하다
(B) common 보통의, precious 귀중한
(C) constraint 제약, liberation 해방

해석 현대 기술은 우리에게 수많은 시간 절약 장치들을 제공해 왔다. 헤드셋이 있는 휴대폰은 사람들이 친구나 동료와 이야기하면서 동시에 출근 전쟁을 할 수 있게 <u>허용해</u> 준다. 손으로 한다면 몇 달이 걸리는 계산을 컴퓨터는 순식간에 수행할 수 있다. 그럼에도 불구하고, 대부분의 우리들은 충분한 시간이 없다고 불평한다. 설문조사는 대다수의 사람들은 그들 스스로를 위한 시간이 점점 더 적어진다고 개인적으로는 느끼고 있음을 나타내고 있다. 시간은 정말로 <u>소중한</u> 것이다. 한 국내 설문조사는 성인 응답자의 51%가 돈보다는 차라리 더 많은 시간을 원한다는 것을 알아냈다. 이 문제의 일부는 우리 현대 사회에서는 사람들이 집에까지 와서 일을 한다(일이 집까지 사람을 따라온다)는 것이다. 그래서 사람들은 처음에는 해방의 도구로 알려졌던 휴대폰, 태블릿, 무선 이메일 등, 유목민들의 도구와 똑같은 것에 의하여 자신들 스스로가 24시간 내내 일에 묶여 있다고 생각한다. 이러한 시간의 위기를 대처하기 위해, 점점 더 많은 사람들은 일, 가족, 가정의 의무를 잘 양립하려고 노력하면서 자신들의 잠을 줄이고 있다.

24 어휘 capitalism 자본주의 inherent contradiction 내재된 모순 i.e. = id est(that is 즉, 바꿔 말하면) e.g.= exempli gratia(for example) inevitable 피할 수 없는 impose 부과하다 rationality 합리성 undermine 약화시키다 crucial 아주 중대한, 결정적인 agentive 행동적인

해설 문단의 제목을 추론하는 문제로서, 필자는 자본주의의에서 위기는 피할 수 없고 오히려 합리성의 회복 기능을 갖도 있다고 주장하고 있으므로, ② 자본주의 위기의 필요성 이라는 제목이 정답으로 적절하다.
① 위기의 파괴적인 본질
③ 자본주의 체제에서 위기를 피하기
④ 경쟁 : 자본주의의 추진력
⑤ 자본주의 : 위기와 혼돈에서 벗어나는 길

해설 자본주의에 대한 설명적인 비판 이론에 따르면, 자본주의의 내재된 모순이 불균형으로 이어질 때, 즉 존재하는 시스템이 계속 기능을 발휘하기 위하여 필요한 (예를 들면, 생산된 것과 소비된 것 사이의) 균형의 상실로 이어질 때, 위기는 발생한다. 불균형이 생길 때, 사람들은 붕괴와 혼돈의 상황에 약간의 질서를 부여해야하기 때문에, 위기는 불가피할 수밖에 없을 뿐만 아니라 필요하기도 하다. 우리는 위기는 합리화하는 기능, 즉 합리성이 약화된 곳에서 합리성을 회복하는 기능을 가지고 있다고 말할 수 있다. Harvey의 말에 따르면, 위기는 "항상 불안정한 자본주의의 비이성적인 합리주의자"이다. 위기는 객관적이고 체계적인 면을 가지고 있지만, 또한 필수적이며 진정으로 중요한 주관적인 면도 가지고 있는데, 이것은 행동적이고 전략적이다. 위기에서, 사람들은 균형과 합리성을 회복시킬 것으로 희망하는 특정한 행동방침 혹은 정책을 추구하기 위해 어떻게 반응하여 행동하고 어떻게 전략을 발달시켜야만 하는가에 대하여 결정을 해야만 한다.

25 founder 창시자 spontaneously 자발적으로 restrict 제한(금지) 하다 while away the time 여가를 보내다

해설 제목을 추론하는 문제로서, 필자는 철학자 몽테뉴, 정신분석학자 프로이드의 말을 예로 들면서, 아이들의 놀이는 단순한 시간보내기 장난이 아니며, 아이들은 놀이를 통해 자아를 표현하고 있다고 주장하고 있다. 그래서, ② 놀이 : 아이들의 내적 자아의 표현이라는 것이 제목으로 적절하다.
① 아이들의 폭력적인 놀이에 의해 야기된 피해
③ 아이들의 놀이 규제의 중요성
④ 신체적으로 건강한 아이들을 양육하는 법
⑤ 아이들의 놀이 : 친구 사귀기의 수단

해석 16세기 수필가 몽테뉴는 "아이들의 놀이는 장난이 아니고, 아주 신중한 행동으로 간주되어야만 한다."라고 썼다. 만약 우리가 아이들을 이해하길 바란다면, 우리는 그의 놀이를 이해할 필요가 있다. 현대 심리학의 창시자 프로이드는 놀이를 아이가 그것을 통해서 자기 자신을 표현 하는 수단으로 간주했다. 그는 또한 아이들이 놀이를 통해 그들의 생각과 감정을 얼마나 많이, 얼마나 잘 표현하는지에 주목했다. 아이의 놀이로부터, 우리는 그가 세계를 어떻게 바라보고 해석하는지, 즉 세계가 어땠으면 좋겠는지, 그의 관심사와 문제가 무엇인지에 관한 지식을 얻어낼 수 있다. 아이를 지켜보는 어른이 아이가 그렇게 한다고 생각할지라도, 아이는 단지 한가한 시간을 보내기 위해 자발적으로 놀지 않는다. 그가 비어있는 시간을 채우기 위해 부분적으로 놀이에 참여할 때조차도, 그가 놀려고 선택한 것은 내적 과정, 욕구, 문제, 걱정에 의해 동기가 부여된 것이다.

26 어휘 overdependence 과도한 의존 kick out of ~에서 쫓아내다 institution 기관, 제도 analogy 유사성, 비유 flaw 결점, 결함 transcend 초월하다, ~을 능가하다 mortality 언젠가 죽어야함, 죽음을 면할 수 없음 ⇔ immortality 불멸 first and foremost 무엇보다 먼저, 맨 먼저

해설 문단 내용의 일관성을 추론하는 문제로서, 모든 위대한 카리스마적인 지도자들에게는 결함이 있다는 주장, 즉 인간은 죽는다는 한계를 언급해야 하므로, 주어진 문장은 ⑤에 와야 적절하다.

해석 카리스마적인 지도자 모델을 볼 때, 우리는 세계가 정확히 반대 방향으로 향하고 있다고 생각한다. 21세기를 보라. 거의 전 세계가 민주주의를 향해 움직여 왔다. ① 민주주의의 바로 핵심은 어떤 한 명의 지도자에 대한 과도한 의존을 피하고 주된 초점을 과정에 두는 것이다. ② 아마 지난 세기의 가장 위대한 한 명의 지도자였던 처칠조차도 국가와 그 과정에서는 2차적(부차적)인 존재였으며, 2차 세계대전이 끝나고 사무실에서 쫓겨났다. ③ 히틀러, 스탈린, 무솔리니는 그들이 직무를 수행하였던 기관들보다 그들이 근본적으로 덜 중요하다는 사실을 이해하지 못했던 카리스마적인 지도자들이었다. ④ 그리고 당신이 민주주의로의 변화와 기업의 진화 사이에 유사성을 믿지 못한다 하더라도, 위대한 카리스마적인 지도자는 하나의 근본적인 결함을 가진다. 그리고 이것은 사라지지 않을 것이다. 지금도 아니고, 22세기도 아니고, 1,000년 후도 아니다. 모든 지도자는 죽는다. ⑤ 인간이 죽을 운명이라는 이 변하지 않는 현실을 초월하기 위해, 초점은 훌륭한 카리스마적 지도자가 되는 것 대신에, 다른 무엇보다도 조직의 특성을 확립하는 것에 맞추어져야만 한다.

27 어휘 transaction 거래, 매매 commitment 약속, 헌신 undertake 착수하다, 하다, 약속하다 implication 암시, 결과, 영향 ensue 잇따라 일어나다 encounter 만남, 접촉, 조우 minutes 회의록 outset 착수, 시초, 발단 agenda 의제 forthcoming 다가오는, 뒤따르는 cognitive 인지적, 인지의, 인식의

해설 문단 내용의 일관성을 추론하는 문제로서, 주어진 글의 내용에서 단서를 찾아보면, '만약 이 단계에서 이견과 혼돈이 있다면 ~ '의 내용과 그 뒤에 이어지는 '이러한 문제는 미팅의 회의록이 작성되는 ~ '의 내용을 참고해 보면, ②에 주어진 문장이 들어가는 것이 가장 적절하다.

대인관계의 많은 거래에서, 하나의 만남은 이전의 만남에서 내려진 결정과 행해진 약속에 의해 영향을 받는다. ① 다시 말하자면, 모든 당사자들이 현재의 논의를 위해 이전 교류에서 발생한 주요 내용과 이것의 결과에 대해 동의한다는 것을 분명히 하는 것이 중요하다. 만약 이 단계에서 이견과 혼돈이 있다면, 뒤따르는 만남이 유익할 것 같지는 않다. ② 이러한 문제는 미팅의 회의록이 작성되는 많은 사업적 환경에서 형식적으로 극복된다. ③ 현재의 미팅을 위한 주요 안건들이 논의되기 전에, 이전의 미팅 회의록이 검토되고 처음부터 동의된다. ④ 이러한 절차는 모든 참가자가 이전에 어떤 일이 진행되었는지에 대해 동의하고 있고, 그러므로 앞으로 다가올 미팅에 대한 공통의 기준 틀을 갖고 있음을 확실히 한다. ⑤ 게다가, 안건들은 대개 미팅이 있기 이전에 회람 된다. 그래서 이것은 그 자체로 개인들이 앞으로 논의될 주요 영역에 대해 스스로를 준비하도록 하게 해주는 인지적 틀의 한 형태이다.

28

어휘 unmanned 무인의 machine gun 기관총 warrior 전사, 병사 monopoly 독점 ripple 잔물결을 이루다, 파문이 퍼지다 warfare 전쟁, 전투 substantially 상당히

해설 문단의 내용을 추론하는 문제로서, 로봇공학이 전쟁의 양상을 변화시키며, 전쟁을 인류가 5천 년간 독점해왔던 것이 붕괴하고 있다고 주장하는 것으로 추론하여 볼 때 ①이 가장 적절하다.
① 로봇공학은 전쟁의 영향이 사회 깊숙이 미치는 전쟁 속의 혁명을 야기하고 있다.
② 무인 시스템이 전쟁터에서 인간 병사를 구하는 유일한 방법이다.
③ 급속하게 발달하고 있는 로봇공학은 언젠가는 전쟁을 종식시킬 것이다.
④ 전쟁에서 싸움을 하는 방식에는 거의 변화가 없을 것이다.
⑤ 정부는 로봇공학 투자를 우선사항으로 해야만 한다.

해석 역사가들이 이 시기를 볼 때, 그들은 우리가 다른 형태의 혁명, 즉 원자 폭탄의 발명과 같은 전쟁의 혁명 속에 있다고 결론내릴 것이다. 하지만 우리의 무인 시스템이 전투의 "방식"에 영향을 끼칠 뿐만 아니라, 아주 기본적인 수준에서 전투의 "대상"에도 영향을 끼치고 있기 때문에, 이보다는 훨씬 더 큰 문제일 수도 있다. 즉, 모든 이전의 전쟁 혁명은, 그것이 기관총이든 혹은 원자 폭탄이든지 간에 더 빨리 쏘고, 더 멀리 가거나 혹은 더 큰 폭발을 일으키는 것 중의 하나인 시스템에 대한 것이었다. 이것은 확실히 로봇공학에 관한 문제이다. 하지만 그들은 또한 전사의 경험, 심지어는 전사의 정체성까지 바꾼다. 이것을 달리 표현하자면, 전쟁의 싸움에 대한 인류의 5천년 독점이 우리 생전에 붕괴되고 있다는 것이다. 이것의 영향은 인류의 발전, 사회, 법, 윤리 등의 바로 그 방향을 상당히 바꾸면서 시간이 지남에 따라 파문을 일으키며 외부로 퍼져 갈 것이다.

29

어휘 barometer 지표, 기압계 self-indulgent 방종한, 제 멋대로 하는 consistent 일관된, 일치하는 preconception 선입관, 예상

해설 문단의 내용을 추론하는 문제로서, 마키아벨리의 실제적인 진실에 대한 말에서 단서를 찾아서 내용을 추론해 보면 의사소통은 타인에게 영향을 줄 수 있을 때만이 효과적이라는 ⑤가 문단의 내용과 일치하는 것이다.
① 당신의 원칙을 적용할 때는 일관성을 유지하는 것이 중요하다.
② 행동을 통한 진실 탐색은 어렵다는 것이 입증되었다.
③ 사람들은 자신의 예상에 따라 타인의 말을 해석한다.
④ 훌륭한 연사는 자신의 메시지 뿐 아니라 발표에도 초점을 둔다.
⑤ 의사소통은 그것이 타인에게 영향을 끼칠 수 있는 힘이 있을 때만이 효과적이다.

해석 "중요한 것은 사람들이 말하거나 의도한 것이 아니라 그들 행동의 결과이다." 이것은 마키아벨리가 "실제적인 진실" – 즉 진정한 진실, 다시 말해서, 말이나 이론 속에서가 아니라 사실 속에서 발생한 것 – 이라고 불렀던 것이다. 당신은 당신의 의사소통 시도에도 이와 같은 지표를 적용할 수 있다. 만약 한 사람이 그가 혁명적이라고 생각하고 그가 희망하기에 세상을 바꾸고 인류를 향상시키게 될 것을 말하거나 글을 쓰지만, 결국에 거의 어느 누구도 어떤 실제적인 방식으로 영향을 받지 않는다면, 그것은 결코 혁명적이거나 진보적인 것이 아니다. 대의를 주장하거나 원했던 결과를 만들어내지 못하는 의사소통은 단지 제멋대로 지껄이는 말이고, 사람들이 자신의 목소리를 사랑해주기를 반영할 뿐이다. 그들이 쓰거나 말했던 것에 대한 실제적인 진실은 아무것도 바뀌지 않았다는 것이다. 사람들에게 다가가고 그들의 의견을 변경시키는 능력은 중대한 일(문제)이다.

30 [어휘] exert 영향을 미치다, 행사하다, 가하다 commerce 사업, 무역 at interest 이자를 붙여 take on 떠맡다 the Prophet 이슬람교의 교조(Muhammad) vast sums of money 거액의 돈 prescribe 규정하다, 지시하다 caste 카스트 제도(인도의 세습적 계급) geographical features 지리적인 특징

[해설] 문단의 주제를 추론하는 문제로서, 종교가 무역에 영향을 미쳤던 중세시대, 힌두교 사회의 카스트 제도가 사람의 직업선택에도 영향을 준다는 등의 내용으로 보아 ③ '경제에 대한 종교의 상당한 영향'이 주제로 적절하다.

[해석] 종교는 무역에 강한 영향을 끼칠 수 있다. 예를 들어, 중세 유럽시대에 기독교 교회는 이자를 붙이는 대금업에 강하게 반대했다. 대인들은 이러한 종교 규범에 구속되지 않았기 때문에, 그들은 대금업자의 역할을 맡았다. 마호메트는 대출자로부터 이자를 받는 것을 금지했기 때문에, 아주 최근까지도 금융기관은 이슬람교도들 사이에서 발전하지 않았다. 그 이면에서는, 신성한 지역으로 가는 종교 순례자들에 의해, 글자 그대로 거액의 돈이 거래되었다. 순례는 사우디아라비아의 메카, 프랑스의 루르드, 인도의 베나레스와 같은 종교 중심지의 경제에서 중요한 역할을 한다. 종교는 또한 한 개인이 어떤 형태의 직업을 갖게 되는지에도 강하게 영향을 줄 수 있다. 특히 카스트 제도가 적합성보다는 생득권에 의해 특정한 의무와 직업을 규정하고 있는 힌두교 사회에서 그렇다.

31 [어휘] approve of 찬성하다, ~을 좋게 말하다 with reference to ~에 관하여 derive from ~에서 유래하다 ample 풍부한, 충분한 relevant 관련 있는, 연관된

[해설] 주제 추론의 문제로서, 비교의 대상이 적절해야 비교가 의미 있다는 내용이므로 ②번이 주제로 적절하다.
① 경쟁에 과도하게 초점을 두는 것의 해로운 효과
② 자기 평가에서의 적절한 비교대상의 역할
③ 높은 자존감을 갖는 것의 중요성
④ 경쟁적인 정신의 발달
⑤ 자기 가치 척도로서의 스포츠

[해석] 아마 우리가 우리 스스로에 대해 생각하는 방식의 가장 중요한 차원은 평가의 차원, 즉 자존감의 수준이다. 우리가 세계적으로 우리 스스로를 좋게 생각하는 정도는 우리가 행동하는 방식, 특히 타인과 함께 행동하는 방식에 영향을 끼친다. 어느 정도까지는 우리 자신에 대한 평가는 다른 사람과의 비교에 의존한다. 예를 들어, 특정한 능력을 평가할 때, 우리의 판단은 실제로는 단지 상대적일 수 있다. 테니스선수/음악가/요리사가 얼마나 훌륭한가에 대한 질문은 다른 사람의 수행으로부터 얻어진 등급과 관련 있어야 단지 의미 있는 것이 될 수 있다. 우리가 우리 스스로를 적절한 타인들과 비교할 기회를 찾고 있다는 충분한 증거가 있다. '적절한'이라는 말은 비교가 의미 있을 수 있는 약간의 전반적 척도의 관점에서 우리에게 충분히 근접할 것 같은 사람들을 의미한다. 예를 들어, 지역의 테니스 클럽은 국제 테니스 챔피언 대회가 할 수 있는 것보다는 우리의 테니스 실력에 대하여 보다 의미 있는 일련의 비교를 제공한다.

32 [어휘] lighthearted 근심 없는, 마음 편한 preacherly 설교적인 abrupt 갑작스러운 bizarre 기괴한, 별난, 이상한 mystifying 혼란스러운 metaphysical 형이상학적인, 철학적인 manifestly 명백하게 pretension 요구, 가식, 허세 crave 갈망하다 trophy wife or husband 과시할 수 있는 아내나 남편 for its own sake 그 자체를 위한

[해설] 문단의 사실적 이해를 묻은 문제로서, 내용과 일치하지 않는 것은 ③으로 러시아의 소설은 도덕적 교훈을 배우기 위해 읽혀졌다는 내용과 정반대이다.

해석 적절한 영어 번역이 존재했던 세기 동안에, 러시아의 진짜 소설과 희곡 작품들은 평판과 특성한 "색채"를 얻었다. 이것은 심각하고, (즉, 비극적이거나 불합리하지만, 좀처럼 마음 편하지 않은, 결코 사소한 내용은 아닌) 다소 설교적이면서, 종종 정치적으로 반대주의자가 등장하고, 그리고, 갑작스럽거나 이상한 시작과 끝을 가진 혼란스러운 형식으로 빈번하게 만들어진다. 소설들은 특히 너무 길고, 형이상학적인 생각으로 가득차고, 너무 명백하게 독자가 재미나 즐거움을 위해 소설을 읽지 않고 도덕적 교훈을 배우기를 갈망한다. 이러한 책들은 이러한 요구를 패러디할 때조차도 선과 악에 깊이 관여한다. 만약 희극이라면, 끝날 때쯤에는 당신을 오싹하게 만드는 급반전이 있다. 러시아 문학의 등장인물은 그 흔한 돈, 경력, 성공 그 자체를 위한 사회에서의 성공, 과시적 아내나 남편, 교외의 주택을 추구하는 것이 아니고, 그 대신 다른 성취할 수 없는 것들을 갈망한다.

33 **어휘** spike (꺾은선 그래프에서)(위로) 산 모양으로 꺾인 부분 fluctuation 변동, 요동 correlation 상관관계

해설 2013년에 불에 탄 면적이 약 4,00,000헥타르로 가장 넓었던 것은 맞지만, 그 이전 해인 2012년에는 약 2,00,000헥타르였으므로, 약 3배가 아닌 약 2배 이상 많으므로 ③의 3배 는 도표의 내용과 일치하지 않는다.

해석 위의 그래프는 2003년과 2013년 사이에 캐나다의 불에 탄 숲의 면적과 산불의 횟수를 보여 준다. ① 이 기간에 불에 탄 헥타르의 수치는 2004년과 2010년에 3백만 이상, 2013년에 4백만 이상이라는 3번의 상당한 급증이 있음을 보여주고 있다. ② 또한 2009년에는 불에 탄 숲 면직이 백만 헥타르 훨씬 미만으로 상당한 급락이 있었다. ③ 이 기간 동안에, 불에 탄 헥타르 수치는 2013년에 가장 많고, 그것은 그 이전 해보다 3배 이상 많았다. ④ 2006년에는 거의 10,000번의 높은 횟수였고, 2011년에는 5,000번 미만의 낮은 횟수였던 것처럼, 산불의 횟수에는 약간의 상당한 변동이 있었다. ⑤ 전체적으로, 매년 불에 탄 숲 면적과 산불의 횟수 사이에는 일관된 상호관련성은 없다.

34 **어휘** component 구성 요소, 성분, 부품 scrutinize 세밀히 조사하다 application 사용 supervise 감독(관리)하다 consequence 결과, 중요성

해설 주어진 글의 내용은 살충제의 환경오염에 대하여 언급하고 있으며, 이에 이어질 글의 내용으로는 (A)에서 언급하고 있는 추가적인 이유(면밀한 조사 및 곤충의 내성)가 와야 적절함. 이어서, (C)에서 언급하고 있는 'All of these issues'라는 어구가 단서를 제공하면서, 해충 규제에 대한 인식이 바뀌었다는 내용에 이어서 마지막으로 (B)에서 살충제를 안전하고 효과적으로 사용하기 위해 알아야 할 사실에 대해 설명하는 것이 글의 순서로 적절하다.

해석 살충제는 식품 생산과 대중의 건강을 위한 해충 관리 전략에 있어서 중요한 요소이다. 그것들의 중요성에도 불구하고, 이 화학물질은 종종 환경오염 때문에 비난받는다. (A) 사실, 우리 사회에서 흔히 사용되는 다른 화학물질들은 이것보다 더 면밀하게 조사되는 것이 거의 없다. 더욱이 곤충은 빈번한 살충제 사용 때문에 저항력을 키울 수 있다. (C) 이런 모든 문제들은 해충 규제를 옛날의 단순한 업무에서 오늘날의 복잡하고 대중들이 민감해하는 업무로 바꾸어 놓았다. 현대의 해충 규제 방법을 개발하고 관리하는 사람들은 살충제 사용법의 많은 분야에서 고도로 훈련받아야 한다. (B) 그러므로, 살충제를 안전하고 효과적으로 사용하기 위해서, 우리는 특정한 환경에서 어떤 살충제를 사용해야 하는지 알아야만 할 뿐만 아니라 또한 모든 생물학적, 생리학적, 환경적 결과도 이해해야만 한다.

35 **어휘** pathetic 불쌍한, 측은한 cower 움츠리다, 웅크리다 crawl 기다 snatch 낚아채다, 움켜쥐다 snuggle up to ~을 끌어안다 scour 찾아다니다 drastically 철저히, 심하게, 매우

해설 개를 좋아하지 않던 필자가 자신의 차 밑에서 털이 많은 개 한 마리를 만나면서 개를 좋아하게 되는 내용으로, 개를 처음 만나게 되는 장면 ⇒ (C) 차 밑의 개를 끌어내고 처음으로 유대감을 형성 ⇒ (A) 그리고, 출장을 가면서 친구에게 개를 돌봐 줄 것을 부탁하지만, 그 사이에 개가 사라짐 ⇒ (B) 포스터를 붙이며 개를 찾아다니고, 마침내 다시 만나게 되는 순서대로 배열하게 되면 내용이 적절하다.

해석 나는 개를 좋아하는 사람이 전혀 아니었다. 나는 심지어 개를 싫어한다고 말하곤 했었다. 내가 내 차 밑에서 웅크리고 있는 불쌍한 털북숭이 개를 발견한 어느 날까지는 그랬다. 그것은 겁먹은 작은 개였다. 몇 주 동안 먹지도 씻지도 못한 것처럼 보였다. (C) 개가 너무 겁을 먹어서 나는 개가 밖으로 나오게 할 수가 없었다. 그래서 내가 그 아래로 기어 들어가서 개를 움켜쥐었다. 그런데 그때가 그것이 일어난 순간이었다. 개가 내 품으로 달려들었다. 그 순간부터 연대감이 형성되었고, 개는 나의 것이고, 나의 책임이자, 나의 가장 친한 친구였다. (A) 나는 다음 날 출장을 가야 했지만 개는 너무 힘이 없어 혼자 남겨둘 수 없었고, 그래서 나는 친구한테 개를 돌봐 달라고 부탁했다. 내가 돌아와서, 개를 데리러 달려갔다, 하지만 보아하니 개는 "도망친"듯 했다. 나는 밤새 이웃 동네를 찾아다녔지만, 소득이 없었다. (B) 나는 개에 대한 묘사와 내 핸드폰 번호를 적은 포스터를 만들고, 지역 주변에 붙였다. 하지만 일주일 이상이나 아무 소식도 없었다. 마침내 전화가 울렸다. 개가 나에게 돌아왔고, 그 이후로 우리는 떨어진 적이 없다. 두 말할 필요도 없이, 개에 대한 나의 감정은 매우 철저하게 바뀌었다.

36 어휘 incoming (solar) radiation 일사량   deem 간주하다, 생각하다, 여기다   evaporative 증발의, 증발에 의한   perspiration 땀   provision 대비, 준비   conversely 정반대   accelerate 촉진시키다, 가속하다

해설 외부 온도의 변화가 우리가 느끼는 편안함과 관련 있다는 글의 내용으로, ⑤ 'accelerate(촉진하다)'를 'prevent(막다)'로 바꾸어야만 주변의 온도가 내려가면 체내의 열이 방출되는 것을 막는 것이 도움이 된다는 의미가 되어 글의 전체적인 내용과 일치한다.

해석 생리학적 편안함은 생리학적인 스트레스가 비교적 없는 상태에서 경험되는 느낌이다. 이러한 편안함은 정교한 기구에 의해 기분 좋게 여겨지는 온도, 일사량, 습도, 풍속의 특정한 범위 내에서 존재한다. 편안함을 측정하기 위해 사용되는 정교한 기구는 인간의 몸이다. 몸의 내부 온도가 바람직한 범위 안에 유지되는 한, 지각작용은 편안해진다. 환경적 상황이 이러한 내적인 상태를 유지해주는 범위를 초과할 때, 불편함은 발생한다. 환경의 온도가 상승할 때, 혹은 증가된 활동이나 열이 내부 온도를 끌어올릴 때, 피부표면에서는 증발에 의한 냉각작용(땀)이 증가하여 추가적인 신체의 열기를 없애준다. 증가된 공기의 속도나 낮아진 습도는 증발에 의한 냉각 작용의 이점을 증가시킴으로써 상승된 온도가 만들어 내는 스트레스를 줄일 수 있다. 이와는 반대로, 주위의 온도가 떨어질 때, 몸의 열이 방출되는 것을 촉진하거나(→막거나) 더 많은 태양 복사열을 붙잡아 둘 수 있기 위한 대비를 취해야만 한다.

37 어휘 vervet 긴꼬리원숭이의 일종   tint 색깔을 넣다, 염색하다   taint 더럽히다, 오염시키다   conformity 순응   abundance 풍부함

해설 글의 내용을 한 문장으로 요약하는 문제로서, 원숭이 집단에서도 동료(또래) 집단의 압력이 실행된다는 내용을 통해서 (A)에는 원숭이가 음식을 바꾸어 먹는 행위가, (B)에는 동료 압력을 사회적 순응으로 대체하면 적절한 요약문이 완성된다.

해석 많은 십대들은 학교 구내식당에 있는 모든 애들처럼 되고 싶어 한다. "우리는 우리가 생각하고 싶어 하는 만큼 독특하지 않아요."라고 원숭이 행동에 대해 연구를 수행했던 Erica van de Waal이 말했다. "우리는 동물들에게서 우리 행동의 많은 근원을 찾을 수 있어요." 그녀의 연구팀은 야생에서 무리 생활을 하는 109마리의 긴꼬리원숭이에게 분홍색이나 파란색으로 물들인 음식을 주었다. 각 그룹의 한 가지 색깔은 나쁜 맛을 내기 위해 알로에로 오염시켰다, 그러나, 단지 처음 몇 번의 식사 때만 그렇게 했다. 맛이 정상으로 돌아온 후 조차도, 원숭이는 그들이 나쁘다고 생각한 색깔은 먹으려하지 않았다. 그리고 나서 파란색을 먹는 약간의 원숭이는 분홍색을 먹는 원숭이 무리에게 갔고, 분홍색을 먹는 약간의 원숭이는 파란색을 먹는 원숭이 무리에게 갔다. 그 때에 연구자들은 동료 압력이 작용하는 것을 목격했다. 분홍색 음식을 먹는 원숭이로 가득한 곳으로 옮겨간 파란색 음식을 먹는 원숭이는 전에는 분홍색 음식을 먹는 것을 피했었음에도 불구하고 바뀌었다. 분홍색을 먹는 원숭이들도 또한 파란색 음식을 먹는 지역으로 옮겼을 때 바뀌었다. 그들은 다른 모든 원숭이들이 먹는 것을 먹었다.
→ 긴꼬리원숭이의 (A)음식을 바꾸는 행동은 새로운 집단에서 (B)사회적 순응의 결과로 여겨진다.

어휘 knock … off … …을 …으로부터 쳐서 떨어뜨리다 irreplaceable 무엇으로도 대체할 수 없는 shatter 산산이 부서지다 beyond repair 수리가 불가능한 stem from ~에서 생겨나다, 기인하다 unconscious impulses 무의식적인 충동 uncover 들추다, 드러내다 deliberate 의도적인, 계획적인 reckless 무모한, 신중하지 못한 self-inflicted 자초한, 스스로 초래한 inflict (고통 등을) 입히다, 가하다

해석 당신이 친구와 논쟁을 벌이고 있고, 당신이 "우연히" 선반을 쳐서 그 친구가 소유하고 있는 무엇으로도 대체할 수 없는 조각상을 떨어뜨렸다고 가정해보자. 그 조각상은 고칠 수 없을 정도로 산산조각이 났다. 당신은 그럴 의도는 아니었다고 말하며 사과한다. 하지만 이것은 정말로 사고인가? 프로이드의 관점에서는, 많은 명백한 사건들은 사실 무의식적 충동에서 유래하는 고의적인 행동이다. 프로이드는 당신이 그나 그녀의 소중한 물건을 깰 때, 친구를 아프게 하려는 무의식적인 욕구를 표출했다고 주장하는지도 모른다. 실수로 정기 치료 약속을 잊었다고 주장하는 고객은 프로이드가 '저항'이라고 부르는 것을 보여 주는 것일 수도 있다. 의식적으로는, 고객은 그들이 단순히 약속을 기억하지 못했다고 생각한다. 무의식적으로는, 위협적인 무의식의 내용을 밝혀내는 것에 근접해 있을 수 도 있는 치료사를 막으려고 하는 고의적인 노력이 있는 것이다. 이와 비슷하게, 무모한 운전자는 자기가 자초한 피해에 대한 무의식적인 욕구를 충족시키기 위해 자기 스스로를 사고에 처하게 할 수도 있다. 프로이드 학파의 심리학자들에게는, 많은 불운한 사건들은 사람들이 의식적으로 그것을 의도하지 않는다는 점에서는 사고지만, 그것들이 의도된 것이 아니라는 점에서는 사고가 아니다.

38 **해설** 제목을 추론하는 문제로서, 실수나 사고라고 생각했던 많은 일들이 사실은 행위자의 숨겨진 욕구를 충족시키기 위한 것일 수 있다는 프로이드의 관점을 서술하는 내용으로 ④ '사고에 숨겨진 무의식적인 의도'가 적절한 제목이다.
① 사고를 피하는 법
② 바람직하지 못한 충동에 대한 저항
③ 좋은 의도는 결과보다 더 중요하다
⑤ 안전과 편안함을 위한 무의식적인 욕구

39 **해설** 빈칸에 들어갈 적절한 어휘를 추론하는 문제. Freud가 resistance을 어떻게 정의하고 있는지를 이해하면 빈칸에 ① hinder(막다)가 적절하다.
② 지지하다 ③ 상담하다 ④ 감동시키다 ⑤ 동기를 유발시키다

어휘 anarchist 무정부주의자 keen 간절히 ~하고 싶은, 열망하는 be accompanied by ~을 동반하다 visionary 통찰력이 있는 boundless 무한한, 경계가 없는 disorganization 혼란, 질서의 파괴 grapple 붙잡고 싸우다 upset ~ 을 뒤엎다 vivid 활기에 넘치는, 생생한 derange 흐트러뜨리다, ~을 혼란시키다

해석 인생 후반기에, Arthur Rimbaud(아르튀르 랭보)는 무정부주의자, 사업가, 무기거래상, 자본가이자 탐험가였다. 하지만 10대였을 때, 그가 정말 되고 싶었던 것은 시인이었다. 1871년 5월, 16살의 Rimbaud는 그의 은사님이었던 Georges Izambard(이장바르)에게 한 통, 그리고 그가 감명을 주고 싶어 했던 출판업자 Paul Demeny(드므니)에게 한 통, 총 2통의 편지를 썼다. Rimbaud는 젊은 교수님께 그의 최근 시를 보여드리기를 갈망하며, 창백한 채로 학교 교문 밖에서 서성거리면서 Izambard를 매일 기다렸다. 그는 또한 자신의 시에 대해 설명하고 그 시들이 출판되어 나오는 것을 보고 싶다는 강력한 암시를 주는 메모와 함께, Demeny에게 그의 작품의 사본을 제출했다. Demeny에게 보낸 편지에서, Rimbaud는 새로운 종류의 시에 대한 그의 비전의 개요를 말했다. "시인은 모든 감각의 길고, 무한하며, 체계화된 해체를 통해 그 스스로를 예언자로 만든다."라고 Rimbaud는 그에게 설명했다. Rimbaud는 오직 그것만이 "향수, 소리, 색, 생각과 싸우는 생각, 이 모든 것을 포함할" 언어를 창조해 낼 수 있다고 주장했다. 그의 시적인 프로그램은 지각의 관습적인 순서를 뒤엎는 것, 보고 듣고 냄새

맡고 느끼고 맛보는 습관적인 방식을 혼란스럽게 하는 것, 그리고 그것들을 새로운 조합으로 다시 정리하는 것을 포함했다. 감각 인상이 감각 인상과 부딪칠 때, 생각이 생각과 싸울 때, 신선하고, 생생하고, 때때로는 충격적인 이미지가 생겨났다.

40 해설 (a), (b), (c), (e)는 Arthur Rimbaud를 가리키고, (d)는 Paul Demeny를 가리킨다.

41 해설 ③ 그가 스승으로부터 비전을 얻었다는 내용은 글의 내용과 일치하지 않는다.

⊕ **[42~43]**

어휘 densely 촘촘하게 mingle with ~와 섞이다, ~와 어울리다 embed 끼워 넣다, 박다 conducive 도움이 되는, 이바지 하는, 공헌하는 thrust upon ~에 떠맡기다 contempt 경멸, 멸시

해석 인간은 의도적으로 그들의 사회망을 항상 만들고 다시 만든다. 이것에 대한 기본적인 예는 우리를 닮은 사람과 어울리는 의식적이거나 무의식적인 경향인 homophily(단어는 글자 그대로 "비슷한 것에 대한 사랑"을 의미한다.)이다. 우표 수집가이든, 커피 마시는 사람이든, 번지점프를 하는 사람이든 간에, 진실은 우리는 우리의 관심사, 역사, 꿈을 공유하는 사람을 찾는다는 것이다. 속담에 있듯이, "유유상종"이다.
하지만 우리는 또한 세 가지 중요한 방식으로 우리의 사회망의 '구조'를 선택한다. 첫째, 우리는 얼마나 많은 사람과 관련을 맺을 것인지 선택한다. 당신은 체커 게임을 위한 한 명의 파트너를 원하는가 아니면 숨바꼭질을 위한 여러 명의 파트너를 원하는가? 당신은 미친 삼촌과 연락을 유지하고 싶은가? 둘째, 우리는 우리의 친구와 가족이 얼마나 촘촘하게 상호 연관되어 있는지에 영향을 준다. 당신은 결혼식에서 신랑의 대학 룸메이트를 당신의 들러리 옆에 앉혀야 하는가? 당신은 파티를 열어서 당신의 모든 친구들이 서로 만날 수 있게 해야 하는가? 당신은 당신의 사업 파트너를 소개해야 하는가? 그리고 셋째, 우리는 우리가 사회망 안에서 얼마나 중심적인지를 조절한다. 당신은 방의 중심에서 모두와 함께 어울리며 파티의 분위기를 뛰우고 있는가, 아니면 방관한 채로 있는가?
이러한 선택의 다양성은 우리가 뿌리를 내리게 되어있는 전체 사회망의 놀랍도록 다양한 구조를 만들어낸다. 그리고 바로 이러한 선택의 다양성이 우리들 각각을 우리 사회망의 특별한 장소에 위치시킨다. 물론, 때때로 이러한 구조적 특징이 선택의 문제는 아니다. 즉, 우리는 우정을 맺기에 다소 도움이 되는 장소에 살고 있을 수 있고, 혹은 대가족 혹은 소가족에서 태어났을 수도 있다. 하지만 이러한 사회망의 구조가 우리에게 억지로 떠맡겨졌을 때조차도, 그것들은 여전히 우리의 삶을 지배한다.

42 해설 우리가 사회망(사회적 인간관계)의 구조를 선택하는 방식은 다양하다는 내용으로 주제로 적절한 것은
① 우리가 사회망을 형성하는 방법이 적절하다.
② 온라인 사회망이 우리의 삶에 영향을 미치는 방식
③ 손상된 사회망을 복구하기 위한 조언
④ 당신의 사회망을 다양화 하는 것의 위험성
⑤ 직업을 구할 때 사회망의 필요성

43 해설 '비슷한 사람들끼리 어울린다'라는 속담은 ② '유유상종(같은 깃털의 새들은 함께 모인다)'이다.
① 잘 알면 무례해지기 쉽다.
③ 사공이 많으면 배가 산으로 간다.
④ 겉모습만 보고 판단하지 마라.
⑤ 구르는 돌에는 이끼가 끼지 않는다.

⊕ [44~45]

어휘 fold up 접다 look forward to ~ 을 학수고대하다, ~을 기대하다

해석 (A) 우리가 어렸을 때, 오빠와 나는 부모님으로부터 여러 개의 크리스마스 선물을 받곤 했다. 대개 우리 엄마와 아빠는 우리들 각각에게 몇 개의 덜 비싼 물건뿐만 아니라 매우 비싼 선물을 주곤 하셨다. 하지만 이것은 크리스마스 때 우리 집에서 일어나는 유일한 선물 주기가 아니었다.

(C) 우리는 또한 우리 가족만의 독특한 전통이 있었다. 매년 11월 쯤, 각자의 이름을 작은 종이에 쓰고, 그 종이를 접어서 모자에 집어넣었다. 다음에, 한 사람씩 각각 종이 하나를 고른다. 이름이 종이에 있는 사람은 그 종이를 선택한 사람이 선물을 사줘야 할 가족 구성원이었다.

(B) 종이가 접혀있었기 때문에, 누구도 자신들이 누구의 이름을 선택했는지를 알 수가 없었다. 또한, 자신들이 누구의 이름을 선택했는지 누구에게도 말하지 않았다. 이런 식으로, 우리 가족은 비밀스럽게 가족 중 누군가를 위해 무언가를 샀다. 우리는 누구한테 선물을 받을지를 궁금해 하며 진실로 크리스마스를 기대했었다.

(D) 그러던 어느 해에 생각하지도 못했던 일이 일어났다. 크리스마스 날, "비밀 선물"을 주는 시간이 왔을 때, 우리 부모님, 오빠, 그리고 나는 우리들 각자가 동생 Joe를 위한 선물을 샀다는 것을 알고는 크게 놀랐다. 그때서야 비로소 우리는 Joe가 종이를 준비했던 사람이었으며, 그가 모든 종이에 자기 자신의 이름을 썼다는 것을 깨달았다.

44 **해설** 글의 순서에 맞게 배열하는 문제

주어진 글의 (A) 내용이 크리스마스 때 부모님으로부터 받는 선물 받기가 유일한 선물 주기는 아니었음.⇒ (C) 이 가족만의 독특한 크리스마스 선물 주기 전통에서는 접혀진 종이를 선택하는 방식 소개 ⇒ (B) 종이가 접혀서 누군지 알 수 없음 ⇒ (D) 어느 크리스마스에 있었던 막내 동생과 관련된 일화가 나오므로 ②번 이 정답이다.

45 **해설** Joe를 위한 선물을 모든 가족이 준비했다는 글의 내용으로 보아, 빈칸에는 Joe가 모든 종이에 자신의 이름을 썼다고 생각하는 것이 내용과 일치하므로 ②번이 정답이다.

ANSWER

01	02	03	04	05	06	07	08	09	10	11	12	13	14	15	16	17	18	19	20
⑤	③	②	⑤	①	②	⑤	④	④	③	⑤	④	①	①	②	①	②	①	③	③
21	22	23	24	25	26	27	28	29	30	31	32	33	34	35	36	37	38	39	40
①	④	⑤	③	④	⑤	③	①	②	④	③	④	⑤	③	④	③	①	②	②	④
41	42	43	44	45															
⑤	②	①	⑤	⑤															

01 **해설** Rachel의 마지막 대화에 보면 밥(쌀)을 조금 줄이고 대신 생선을 더 먹으라는 대목이 있으므로 ⑤번은 본문 내용과 일치하지 않는다.

보기 ① Rachel은 헬스장 강사(트레이너)다.
② Dave는 수분섭취를 잘한다.
③ 균형 잡힌 식단은 다양한 종류의 음식을 포함해야 한다.
④ 일부 지방은 건강한 식단에 중요하다.
⑤ Dave는 밥(쌀)을 더 섭취해야 한다.

해석 Rachel : Dave씨 안녕하세요? 헬스장에 잘 오셨습니다. 운동 시작해도 될까요?
Dave : Rachel씨 좋은 아침입니다. 운동을 시작하기 전에 좋은 몸매를 가꾸는 데 도움이 될 만한 영양조언을 먼저 해주시겠어요?
Rachel : 좋아요! 오늘 아침 수분 섭취는 충분히 하셨나요?
Dave : 물론이지요! 지난 수업 때 수분 섭취가 얼마나 중요한지 알려주셨잖아요.
Rachel : 잘하셨습니다. 그럼 균형 잡힌 식사를 하셨나요? 균형 잡힌 식단은 빵과 밥(쌀)과 같은 곡물, 건강한 지방과 기름 그리고 충분한 과일과 야채로 이루어집니다.
Dave : 전 밥을 좋아합니다. 우리 몸에 어느 정도의 지방이 좋다는 것을 몰랐네요!
Rachel : 물론이지요! 건강한 지방은 생선에 많이 포함되어 있고 균형 잡힌 식단에 아주 중요합니다. 또한 밥(쌀)은 에너지원이 되지만 칼로리가 높은 편입니다. 다음에는 밥(쌀)을 조금 줄이고 생선으로 대체해 보세요.

02 **해설** 첫 번째 빈칸은 Empire State Building에 관련된 내용이므로 skyscraper를 유추할 수 있다.
두 번째 빈칸은 앞에 sports라는 단어가 나오고 유명한 야구팀은 Yankees가 나오는 것으로 봐서 보기의 baseball(야구)를 유추할 수 있다.
세 번째 빈칸은 Susan의 대답에서 서둘러야 한다는 내용이 나오므로 시간에 관련된 내용이 나왔음을 유추할 수 있다.

Ben : 안녕하세요? 길을 잃은 것 같은데 도와드릴까요?

Susan : 고맙습니다. 사실 New York City에 처음이라서 어디를 가야할지 모르겠네요.

Ben : 제가 기꺼이 도와드리겠습니다. 다행히 저쪽 코너에 관광명소가 있답니다. 엠파이어스테이트 빌딩(Empire State Building)에 가보셨나요? 엠파이어 빌딩은 최고의 초고층 건물 중 하나입니다.

Susan : 아직 가보지 않았는데 꼭 가봐야겠네요! 또 어디를 방문하면 좋을까요?

Ben : 혹시 스포츠를 좋아하신다면 5번가로 가서 36번 거리의 Yankees 가게를 방문해 보세요. 여행객들이 야구 기념품들을 많이 산답니다.

Susan : 좋습니다! 저는 또 독서를 좋아합니다. 독서와 관련해서 추천해 주실 곳이 있나요?

Ben : 네! 42번 거리에 뉴욕 공립도서관이 있습니다. 도서관이 6시에 닫으므로 염두해 두세요!

Susan : 오, 서둘러야겠군요. 알려주신 것들 너무 감사합니다!

03 보기 ① 화원 ② 과수원 ③ 비닐하우스, 온실 ④ 식료품점 ⑤ 과일 가공 공장

해석 Laura : 와 여기 너무 아름답군요! 저 과일들은 너무 신선해 보여요. 좀 따고 싶은데요. 저 과일들 어디서 찾으셨나요?

Steven : 과일에 따라 나르지요. 딸기나 사과 어떤 걸 말씀하시나요?

Laura : 딸기와 사과 둘 다요. 딸기는 제가 가장 좋아하는 과일이지만 또 애플파이 굽는 길 좋아해요. 우리 할머니의 애플파이 레시피가 우리 마을에서 아주 유명해요.

Steven : 좋아요! 그럼 제가 과일 따는 것을 도와드리면 저도 파이가 완성되면 맛볼 수 있나요?

Laura : 물론이지요. 딸기와 사과는 어디에서 딸 수 있고 얼마인가요?

Steven : 딸기는 1kg에 1달러이고 저쪽 개울가에 딸기 밭이 있어요. 사과는 1kg에 2달러이고 남쪽에 밭이 있어요. 갑시다!

04 보기 ① Joe는 전자기기 가게에서 일을 한다.
② 핸드폰 전원이 켜지지 않는다.
③ 핸드폰 보증기간이 만료되었다.
④ Joe는 휴대폰을 교체받기를 원한다.
⑤ Joe는 아침에 휴대폰 가게에 방문하기를 원한다.

해석 Sam : 여보세요? 좋은 아침입니다. Big Electronics의 고객서비스 부서입니다. 저는 Sam입니다. 무엇을 도와드릴까요?

Joe : 저는 Joe Lee입니다. 최근에 Big Electronics사 핸드폰을 구매했고 화면에 결함이 생겼습니다.

Sam : 저런 죄송합니다. 구매한 날짜와 장소를 말씀해주시겠어요?

Joe : 물론이지요. 2주 전인 7월 3일에 구매했습니다. 구매 장소는 San Pedro 거리의 LA Big Electronics 가게 중 가장 큰 곳에서 구매했습니다.

Sam : 네. 고객님의 핸드폰은 보증기간 중입니다. 고객님께서 제조업자에게 핸드폰을 보내셔서 교체 받으시거나, 고객님께서 우리 회사 분점(가게)에 방문하셔서 직접 수리 받으실 수 있습니다.

Joe : 저는 핸드폰을 빨리 고치고 싶습니다. San Pedro 가게로 10시까지 갈 수 있습니다.

Sam : 네 그럼 제가 San Pedro 가게에 고객님이 한 시간 내로 도착한다고 미리 알려두겠습니다.

05 보기 ① 정말 좋은 생각이야. 사업장 페이지 만드는 것을 도와줄래?
② 그런데 높은 비용이 걱정 돼.
③ 좋아 내가 한번 해볼게. 내 블로그는 사업장 페이지에 연동되어 있어.
④ 그런데 나는 TV광고를 하는 것이 더 나을 것 같아. 가격이 더 저렴해.
⑤ 그런데 나는 그 전략이 정말 효과적일지 걱정 돼. 리스크가 있어 보여.

해석	Emma : 안녕 Tom! 네가 광고 전문이라고 했지? 나에게 전문적인 마케팅 조언을 좀 해주면 너무 고마울 것 같아.

Emma : 안녕 Tom! 네가 광고 전문이라고 했지? 나에게 전문적인 마케팅 조언을 좀 해주면 너무 고마울 것 같아.

Tom : 물론이지 Emma. 내가 기꺼이 도와줄게. 어떤 종류의 사업이지?

Emma : 테이크-아웃(포장전문) 치킨 전문점이야. 나의 치킨 레시피는 정말 맛있지만 요즘에 치킨 집 경쟁이 너무 치열해. 게다가 TV 광고는 너무 비싸.

Tom : 그럼 온라인 마케팅 생각해본 적 있어? .그건 훨씬 더 저렴해.

Emma : 정말? 그런데 나는 컴퓨터를 잘 못 다뤄. 난 블로그도 없어.

Tom : 괜찮아. 온라인 마케팅은 간단하고 아주 효과적인 전략이야. 소셜미디어 사이트에 사업장 페이지를 만들고 구독자들에게 할인을 해주는 거야. 이 방법으로 사업장을 빠르게 널리 알릴 수 있어.

Emma : 조언 정말 고마워. 정말 좋은 아이디어야. <u>내가 사업장 페이지 만드는 것을 도와줄래?</u>

06 **해설** cook(요리), pet(애완동물), cleanliness(정리) 등의 키워드를 종합해 보면 roommate에 관련된 내용임을 유추할 수 있다.

보기 ① Julia는 애완동물을 키우는 것에 관한 Diana의 조언을 듣고 싶어 한다.

② Julia는 룸메이트를 찾고 있다.

③ Julia와 Diana는 취미에 관해 이야기하고 있다.

④ Diana는 새 친구를 사귀려고 하고 있다.

⑤ Diana는 직업을 얻기 위해 인터뷰를 받고 있다.

해석 Julia : Diana씨 안녕하세요? 제 광고에 응해주어 고마워요.

Diana : 별 말씀을요. 제 첫인상이 좋았으면 좋겠습니다.

Julia : 물론 첫인상은 매우 좋으세요. 그래도 우리가 같이 살게 된다면 제가 알아야 할 것들이 있어요. 우선 요리를 할 수 있나요? 그리고 애완동물을 소유하고 있나요?

Diana : 물론 요리를 합니다. 저는 건강하게 지내기 위해 노력하고 있답니다. 그리고 고양이를 기르고 있는데 아주 조용하고 잘 훈련되어 있고 애교도 많답니다.

Julia : 좋습니다. 저는 애완동물을 기르지 않지만 강아지보다는 고양이가 더 좋아요. 다음으로 Diana씨는 정리를 잘하나요? 저에겐 깨끗함(청결함)이 제일 중요하거든요.

Diana : 저도요. 전 지저분한 것을 정말 싫어합니다.

07 **어휘** adjacent 근접한/ cottage 오두막, 작은집/ paddle 노를 젓다/ puff 숨을 헉헉거리다/ bleat out 힘없는 소리로 이야기하다/ splutter 식식거리며 말하다.

해설 ①번부터 ④번까지는 Wiener를 가리키지만 ⑤번은 Kline을 가리킨다.

해석 J.R. Kline은 다른 수학학자에 관해 이야기하는 것을 좋아했다. Norbert Wiener에 관한 이야기가 Kline이 가장 좋아하는 이야기였다. 어느 여름 Kline 가족과 Wiener 가족은 New Hempshire 지역에 있는 작은 호숫가에 근접한 오두막을 소유하고 있었다. Wiener는 종종 부두에서 호수 가운데에 있는 섬까지 수영을 하곤 했다. Wiener가 수영을 할 때 Kline은 보트에 타고 노를 저으며 Kline의 옆을 지나가며 친구가 되어주었다. Wiener가 목표지점을 향해 빠르게 수영을 해나갈 때 Wiener와 Kline은 대화를 이어나갔다. Wiener는 수영을 하느라 숨을 헉헉거리면서도 대화를 주도해 나가려고 노력했다. 그러던 어느 날, 거의 끝 지점에 다다랐을 때 Wiener는 "Kline, 현존하는 위대한 5명의 수학자가 누구지?"하고 힘없이 물었다. Kline은 조용히 답했다. "그거 흥미로운 질문이네. 보자." Kline은 재빠르게 4명의 수학자(Wiener의 이름은 없었다)의 이름을 이야기했다. "계속 말해봐" Wiener는 식식거리며 말했다. Kline은 농담을 하며 다섯 번째 이름을 언급하지 않았다.

08 **어휘** sustain 유지하다, 지속되다/ trigger 촉진하다/ chronic 만성적인/ craving 갈망/ accumulate 축적하다/ abdominal 복부의/ region 영역, 지역/ immune 면역성 있는/ be associated with ~과 연관되다/ diabetes 당뇨

해설 글의 요지는 high level of cortisol → bad effect on health로 높은 코르티솔 수치가 건강에 좋지 않은 영향을 준다는 것이다. 하지만 ④번 내용은 운동으로 인해 단기적으로 높아진 코르티솔 지수가 건강에 좋은 영향을 준다는 내용이므로 전체적인 흐름에는 적절하지 않다. 또한 ③번 문장에서 abdominal region(복부)에 관련된 이야기를 하고 있고 ⑤번에서도 이어서 복부에 관한 이야기가 이어지고 있으므로 ④번 내용은 전체 흐름과 또한 어울리지 않는다.

해석 만성 스트레스에 의한 높은 코르티솔 수치는 장기적인 관점에서 건강에 부정적인 영향을 준다고 과학적 연구는 명백히 보여준다. ① 이러한 부정적인 영향 중 하나는 식욕 증가와 어떤 특정 음식을 계속 먹고 싶어 하는 것이다. ② 코르티솔이 스트레스 요인에 반응한 뒤 몸에서 스스로 영양을 재공급하도록 촉진하는 것이 코르티솔의 역할 중 하나이며, 높아진 코르티솔은 또 식욕이 증가하도록 만든다. ③ 게다가 스트레스 때문에 생긴 식욕증가의 결과로 축적되는 지방은 대부분 복부에 쌓이게 되는데 이 복부는 또 다른 스트레스에 반응하는 부위가 된다. ④ 운동은 코르티솔 수치를 증가시키는데 이러한 단기적인 증가는 면역체계, 기억력 그리고 체중 감소에 도움이 된다. ⑤ 복부 지방의 또 다른 큰 문제는 이러한 종류의 지방은 심장질환, 당뇨병, 암과 높은 관련이 있다는 것이다.

09 **어휘** efficacy 효험/ cognitive decline 인지력 감퇴/ placebo 위약 – 임상의약의 효과를 검정할 때 대조하기 위해 투여하는 약리학적으로는 전혀 효과가 없거나 약간 유사한 약효를 갖는 물질/ conclusion 결론/ supplementation 보충/ optimal 최적의/ cognitive impairment 인지장애

해설 이 글의 요지는 multivitamins → no effect on cognitive function으로 종합 비타민 섭취가 인지력(노인이나, 인지장애인, 혹은 치매환자)에 영향을 주지 않는다는 내용인데 ④번은 이에 반하는 내용(비타민이 두뇌기능에 필수라는)이다.

해석 한 연구는 5,947명의 남자 노인을 대상으로 인지력 감퇴를 막기 위해 매일 종합비타민을 섭취하는 것이 효과가 있는지 연구했다. ① 12년을 추적 조사해 본 결과 종합비타민을 섭취한 그룹과 위약을 섭취한 그룹 사이에 전체적인 인지력과 언어적 기억에서 거의 차이를 보이지 않았다. ② 연구가들은 영양 섭취가 잘 이루어지는 노인들에게는 종합비타민의 추가 섭취가 인지력 감퇴를 막을 수 없다고 결론지었다. ③ 이 결론은 다른 연구들에서도 지지되었는데 이 연구들은 종합비타민, 비타민B, 비타민E, 비타민C와 오메가3 지방산 등을 섭취한 약한 인지장애를 가진 사람들이나 약한 치매환자들에게서 이루어졌다. ④ 모든 비타민이 최적의 건강상태와 두뇌기능에 필수적이지만 이중에서도 몇몇은 두뇌건강에 필수다. ⑤ 어떠한 비타민도 인지력을 향상시켜주지 않았고 이는 비타민 섭취가 치매 치료에 어떠한 영향력도 없음을 암시한다.

10 **어휘** misaligned 정렬이 되지 않은, 어긋난

해석 한 실험에서 두 그룹의 쥐들이 특정한 장소에서 두려움을 느끼도록 훈련받았고 나중에 연구자들은 쥐들이 두려움을 느끼는지 보기 위해 그 장소에 다시 쥐들을 돌려놓았다. 흥미롭게도 정상적인 수면시간에 음식을 먹도록 스케줄이 바뀐 쥐들이 일반적인 스케줄로 먹는 쥐들보다 두려움을 덜 느꼈고, 이는 정상적이지 않은 식사와 잠자는 시간이 두려운 상황에서 쥐의 기억에 영향을 준다는 것을 암시한다. "스케줄이 뒤바뀌어 버린 쥐들은 그들이 훈련받았던 것을 상기시키는데 심각한 결함을 보였다"라고 Clowell은 이야기했다. Clowell의 연구팀은 시차가 사람과 쥐 모두의 기억에 영향을 준다고 밝혔다. 연구팀은 또한 신경 연결의 강도 – 뇌에서 학습을 측정하는 –도 측정해 보았다. 당연하게도 정상적인 수면 시간에 음식을 먹은 쥐들은 일반적인 식사시간에 음식을 먹은 쥐들보다 느리게 배우는 것이 밝혀졌다.

11 어휘 weaver 직공/ tailor 재단사/ covered wagon 서부개척 시대의 포장마차

해설 ⑤번에서 that 이하의 주어절(주절)은 dying neutral-colored denim pants dark blue to minimize soil stans까지이고 그 이하의 동사가 필요하므로 increasing은 동사인 increased로 바뀌어야 한다.

해석 이탈리아 제노바에서 생산되었고 "jeans" 단어의 기원인 Genes라 불리는 프랑스 직물 공들에 의해서였다. 그러나 청바지의 기원은 미국의 이민 재단사였던 Levi Strauss의 이야기에 있다. Levi Strauss가 1850년 골드러시 때 샌프란시스코에 도착했을 때 그는 텐트와 포장마차를 위한 캔버스 천을 팔았다. 똑똑한 관찰자였던 Strauss는 광부들의 바지가 빨리 닳는다는 것을 깨닫고 캔버스 천을 꿰매어 바지로 만들었다. 캔버스로 만든 바지는 다소 무겁고 뻣뻣했지만 정말 튼튼해서 Strauss는 재단사로서 인기가 높아졌다. 1860년대에 Strauss는 캔버스 천을 데님으로 대체했다. Strauss는 얼룩 자국을 잘 안보이게 하기 위해서이 데님을 어두운 파란색으로 염색한 것이 청바지의 인기를 높여주었음을 발견했다.

12 어휘 validity 타당성/ empowering 힘 돋우기/ scrutinize 면밀히 조사하다/ presupposition 예상, 추정

해설 ④번 문장은 주어가 many of our beliefs이고 뒷부분 by information이 나오는 것으로 보아 수동태 문장이다. 그러므로 ④번은 are supported로 바뀌어야 한다.

해석 새로운 실험은 그 실험이 우리의 믿음을 의심하게 만들 때 변화를 가져온다. 우리가 어떤 것을 믿고 있을 때 우리는 어떠한 식으로도 그것을 의심하지 않는다. 우리가 우리의 믿음에 관해 질문을 제기하기 시작했을 때 우리는 더 이상 그 믿음에 관해 완전히 확신하지 못하는 것이다. 우리는 우리의 인지맵의 연결고리들을 흔들기 시작하고 결과적으로 "확신감"을 잃게 된다. 당신은 당신이 어떤 것을 할 수 있는 능력을 의심해본 적이 있는가? 어떻게 해 보았는가? 당신은 아마도 자신에게 "그것이 안 되면 어쩌지?"와 같은 몇몇 질문들을 했을 것이다. 하지만 우리가 그 질문들을 우리가 맹목적으로 받아들이고 있던 믿음의 타당성을 시험해보기 위해 사용한다면 그 질문들은 아주 강력한 힘을 갖게 된다. 사실상, 우리의 믿음들은 우리가 질문을 하지 않았을 당시 다른 사람들에게 받았던 정보에 의해 지지된다. 만일 우리가 그 믿음들을 면밀히 조사해 본다면 우리는 수년간 우리가 무의식적으로 믿고 있었던 것이 잘못된 추정이었을 것이다.

13 해설 (A)는 how to send or (how to) receive로 ~을 하는 방법이라는 의미가 되므로 how가 와야 하고 what이 올 경우 send나 receive동사의 목적어로 오는 것인데 send와 receive의 목적어는 messages와 signals이므로 what이 올 수 없다.

(B) 문장을 풀어서 보면 Just as verbal languages differ from culture to culture, and nonverbal languages differ from culture to culture, too. 이다. 그러므로 so+동사+주어 (~도 역시 그렇다) 구문에서 일반 동사 differ를 받는 대동사 do가 와야 한다.

(C)는 Understanding cultural differences in nonverbal behavior is에서 문장 전체 동사는 is로 is 앞부분은 명사 역할을 해야 하므로 동명사 understanding이 되어야 한다.

해석 의사소통은 다양한 감각 내에서 언어적으로 혹은 비언어적으로 일어난다. 그러나 우리는 비언어적 행동이 중요한 것을 알고 있음에도 종종 비언어적 행동을 당연시 여긴다. 우리는 비언어적 메시지나 신호를 어떻게 주고받는지 어떠한 공식적인 훈련을 받지 않음에도 불구하고 어른이 되면 아주 능숙해져서 무의식적으로 그리고 자동으로 비언어적 행동을 하게 된다. 비언어적 행동은 언어와 여러 가지 면에서 비슷하다. 언어가 문화마다 다르듯이 비언어적 행동도 문화마다 다르다. 우리는 여러 가지 언어들이 다르다는 것을 알고 있기 때문에 다른 언어를 이해하기 위해서 사전이나 다른 도구들을 주저하지 않고 사용한다. 그러나 비언어적 행동에 있어서 우리는 종종 비언어적으로 의사소통하는 체계가 모두 같을 것이라고 종종 실수를 하게 된다. 비언어적 행동에 있어서의 문화적 차이점을 이해하는 것은 의사소통에서 문화적 차이점을 진심으로 이해하는 첫 단계이다.

14 어휘 water-based toilet 수세식변기/ sewage 하수, 오물/ outbreak 발병/ urban 도시의/ contaminate 오염시키다/ establish ~을 설립하다/ reservoir 저수지

해설 (A) 이하 절은 앞에 있는 선행명사인 pipes를 수식하고 있다. (A) sending 뒤에 목적어 the outflow가 있기 때문에 수동의 의미가 아니므로 sending이 되어야 한다.
(B) 이하의 문장은 완전한 절로 관계대명사를 필요로 하지 않는다. 그러므로 (B)에는 관계부사인 where이 와야 하고 이는 앞 문장의 전치사구 in the growing industrial-commercial cities를 받고 있다.
(C)는 and 앞부분에 있는 created 동사와 병렬관계를 이루고 있으므로 (C)에도 동사가 와야 하고 created와 같은 과거시제인 built동사가 와야 한다.

해석 선진국에서 19세기 중반부터 수세식 변기가 널리 사용된 것은 오물을 오물처리 공장으로 보내는 광범위한 하수 체계가 도시에 만들어졌다는 것을 의미했다. 이 체계는 19세기 초반, 산업화 도시의 많은 인구를 황폐화시킨 콜라라 발생의 문제를 해결하는데 도움을 주었다. 이 도시에서는 처리되지 않은 배설물들이 강에 버려지면서 지하수와 지역에 공급되는 물을 오염시켰다. 전염병의 발생과 배설물로 오염된 물 공급 간의 연결 관계를 찾아내는데 많은 시간이 걸렸지만 대부분 선진국의 도시들은 저수지로부터 물을 공급받는 체계를 만들어냈고 건물들마다 늘어나는 화장실에서 나오는 오물을 가져가는 격리된 오물처리 체계를 만들어냈다. 이는 해로운 물질을 걸러내는 오물 처리 체계의 발달을 이끌었다.

15 어휘 flexibility 유동성/ ingredient 재료/ source 얻다, 공급자를 찾다/ sweetener 감미료/ derive 끌어내다, 얻다 / starch 녹말, 전분/ argofood 농식품

보기 ① 통합 ② 대치, 대체 ③ 보존 ④ 간소화 ⑤ 과소비

해석 가공식품 생산자들은 농장의 생산품을 사고 어떤 재료를 사용할지, 어디서 그 재료를 얻을 것인지에 관한 유동성을 갖고 있기 때문에 농부들 보다 유리하다. 예를 들어 가공식품에 감미료가 필요할 때 그것이 반드시 설탕농장에서 생산된 설탕일 필요는 없다. 가공식품에 기름을 필요할 때 그것이 반드시 옥수수에서 나오는 기름일 필요는 없다. 가공식품에 전분이 필요할 때 그것은 감자, 밀, 다른 곡물로부터 나올 수 있다. 감자 칩의 생산이 이 대체 효과의 좋은 예가 될 수 있다. 생산자들은 생산 당시 가장 싼 기름으로 감자 칩을 튀길 수 있다. 이는 왜 농부들이 종종 농식품 생산 체계에서 불리한 위치에 있는지를 설명해준다.

16 어휘 transform 변형시키다

해설 Berger의 실험은 쥐의 뇌의 해마 부분(장기기억이 저장되어 있는)을 컴퓨터 칩(특별한 과정을 통해 쥐의 장기기억을 옮겨놓은)으로 대체함으로 장기기억이 보존되고 있음을 보여주고 있으므로 빈칸에는 장기기억의 재현 내용이 와야 한다. 문단에서 rat's memories could be fully restored가 memory regeneration으로 paraphrase되었다고 볼 수 있다.

보기 ① 장기기억의 재현
② 기억 용량의 증가
③ 기억의 선택적 왜곡
④ 충격적 기억의 삭제
⑤ 기억 전달 속도의 향상

해석 Theodore Berger는 쥐의 해마(뇌의)의 손상된 부분을 이식된 칩을 사용함으로써 <u>장기기억을 재현</u>하는데 성공을 거두었다. Berger와 Southern California대학 연구팀은 쥐의 해마에 오랜 시간 동안 축적된 기억들을 컴퓨터 코드로 기록하고 변형하는데 성공했다. 그들은 쥐가 기억 과업을 수행하도록 했다. 그 후 그들은 그 과업의 기억을 디지털 코드로 다운받고 변형시켰다. 마침내 그들은 이러한 기억을 가지고 있는 쥐의 해마(뇌의)를 제거했고 그 부분을 컴퓨터의 특별한 칩으로 대체했다. 그 컴퓨터 칩에는 쥐의 저장된 기억들이 인위적으로 재적재되어 있었다. 그들은 쥐의 기억이 이 기술을 이용하여 완전하게 복구되는 것을 밝혀냈다.

17 어휘 exotic 외래의, 이국적인/ contagious 전염성이 있는/ be ignorant of ~에 무지한/ pertaining to ~와 관계된
/ hygiene 위생/ as a consequence 결과적으로

해설 이 글의 요지는 foreign-ness(외래성)가 질병을 퍼뜨린다는 것이고 그에 관한 두 가지 이유가 제시되고 있다.
그러므로 이글의 말미의 밑줄에는 외국인(이방인)들이 전염병의 위협이 된다는 내용을 유추할 수 있다.

보기 ① 지역 사람들을 고립시키다
② 전염병의 위협을 증가시키다
③ 새로운 기술을 전달하다
④ 지역 경제를 해를 끼치다
⑤ 지역의 위생 조건을 충족시키다

해석 "외래성"이 암묵적으로 병을 퍼뜨릴 가능성이 있다는 것에는 최소한 두 가지 이유가 있다. 첫째로 역사적으로
이국적인 사람과의 접촉을 하면 낯선(이국적) 세균에 노출을 높였고 이는 지역(나라) 사람들에게는 특별히 전염
이 되는 경향이 있다. 두 번째로 이방인(외국인)들은 종종 그 지역의 전염병 예방을 위한 행동 규칙을 잘 모른다.
그 규칙들은 예를 들면 위생이나 음식 준비 등에 관련된 규칙들이다. 그 결과 이방인들은 이러한 규칙들을 어길
가능성이 높고 이로 인해 지역 사람들에게 전염병을 퍼뜨릴 위험이 증가한다. 그러므로 이방인들에 의해 생기는
다른 위험 요소들뿐만이 아니라 외래 사람들은(외국인들) 암묵적으로 전염병의 위협을 준다고 판단된다.

18 어휘 seduce 유혹하다, 꾀다/ seductive 유혹적인

해설 이 글의 요지는 이방인들이 새로운 집단(나라)에서 그 집단(나라)의 삶의 방식을 따름으로 그 집단(나라)에 융화
되며 사람들에게 매혹적인 존재가 된다는 내용이며 그 예로 프랑스 가수 Jesephine Baker와 영국 보수당 지도
자인 Benjamin Disraeli를 들고 있다. 마지막 문장은 다시 한 번 요지를 강조하는 문장이므로 그 나라(집단)의
관습을 더 좋아한다는 내용을 유추할 수 있다.

보기 ① 당신이 얼마나 그들의 취향과 관습을 당신의 것보다 더 좋아하는지
② 당신이 오해되는 것에 관해 불평하지 않는 것이
③ 당신이 특별한 취향, 의견, 경험을 가지고 있는 것이
④ 당신이 고상하고 자비로운 행실을 하기 위해 얼마나 열심히 노력하는지
⑤ 당신의 정체성을 기꺼이 밝혀내는 것이

해석 Josephine Baker는 1925년 흑인 음악극을 선보이며 파리로 이주를 했고 그녀의 이국성은 하룻밤에 그녀를 스
타로 만들었다. 그러나 Baker는 그녀를 향한 프랑스인들의 관심이 곧 다른 사람에게 갈 것이라는 사실을 알았
다. 관중을 매혹시키기 위해 Baker는 프랑스어를 배웠고 프랑스어로 노래했다. Baker는 마치 그녀가 미국인의
삶보다 프랑스인들의 사는 방식을 훨씬 더 좋아한다고 말하듯이 화려한 프랑스인처럼 옷 입고 연기하기 시작했
다. 나라들도 사람들과 똑같다 : 다른 관습을 위협적으로 느낀다. 이방인들이 그들의 삶의 방식을 바꾸어 가는
것을 보는 것은 사람들에게 매우 매혹적이다. Benjamin Disraeli은 영국에서 태어나서 자랐지만 유대인 출신이
고 이국적인 특징들을 지니고 있었다. 이에 영국인들은 그를 이방인이라 여겼다. 하지만 Disraeli는 행동방식이
나 취향 등이 많은 영국인들보다 훨씬 영국적이었고 이것은 그의 매력의 일부였다. 이는 그가 영국 보수당의
지도자로 선출되면서 증명되었다. 만약 당신이 어떤 집단에 이방인이 된다면, 그 집단에게 <u>당신이 얼마나 그들
의 취향과 관습을 당신의 것보다 더 좋아하는지</u> 보여줌으로써 이점을 얻을 수 있다.

19 어휘 caregiver 양육자/ martyr 순교자/ self-sacrifice 자기희생

해설 이 글의 요지는 [As a parent, you have to balance your role as a caregiver with your needs as an individual.] 이다. 즉 부모로서 양육자의 역할과 본인의 욕구를 적절히 조화를 이루는 것이 본인 뿐 아니라 가족에게도 도움이 된다는 내용이다.

해석 가족의 모든 구성원은 가족의 일부일 뿐만 아니라 개인이기도 하다. 부모는 양육자로서의 역할과 개인의 욕구 사이에 균형을 잘 잡아야 한다. 만일 당신이 다른 사람들과 어울리지도 않고, 지적으로 자극을 받으려고 하지도 않고 건강한 몸과 마음을 유지하기 위한 노력도 하지 않은 채 오로지 가족만을 위해 모든 시간과 에너지를 희생 한다면 그것은 가족 모두에게 고통이 될 것이다. 기억해라 : 당신은 당신의 아이들에게 성인으로서 모델이다 -- 아이들에게 부모로서 순교자역할을 하는 모델을 하지마라. 당신은 아이들이 텅 비고 자기희생만 하는 껍데 기뿐인 역할 모델을 보기를 원하지 않을 것이다. 물론 매일 이 모든 욕구를 만족시키며 살아가기란 매우 어렵 다. 부모가 된다는 것은 어느 정도의 희생이 필요하지만 당신과 당신 가족을 적당히 조화를 이룰 필요가 있다.

20 어휘 comprehend 이해하다/ metaphorical 비유적인, 은유적인/ be inconsistent with ~와 일치하지 않는/ attack 공격하다 ↔ defend 방어하다/ cooperative 협력적인

보기
	(A)	(B)
①	~을 숨기다	~에게 무관심한
②	~을 밝혀내다	~에 관여된
③	~을 숨기다	~에 사로잡힌
④	~을 밝혀내다	~에 사로잡힌
⑤	영향을 미치다	~에 무관심한

해석 우리로 하여금 어떤 개념의 한 측면을 다른 면에서 이해하도록 하는 체계성은 반드시 그 개념의 다른 측면을 숨긴다. (예를 들면 논쟁의 한 측면을 싸움으로 이해하는 것) 비유적 개념은 우리로 하여금 어떤 개념의 한 측면 에만 초점을 두게 하고 그 비유와 일치하지 않는 개념의 다른 측면은 보지 못하도록 한다. 예를 들면 우리가 과열된 논쟁 중에 상대의 의견을 공격하고 자신의 의견을 방어하기 하고 있을 때, 우리는 논쟁의 협력적인 측면 은 보지 못하게 되는 것이다. 당신의 편에 서서 논쟁을 하는 사람은 상호 이해를 만들어내기 위해 그 사람의 시간과 가치 있는 것들을 당신에게 주는 것으로 보일 것이다. 하지만 우리가 논쟁에서 "싸움" 측면에만 지나치 게 사로잡혀 있으면 우리는 논쟁의 협력적인 측면은 보지 못하게 된다.

21 해설 (A)의 앞부분 에서는 긍정적인 보디이미지를 발달시키는 내용이 나오고 있는 반면 (A)의 뒷부분에서는 부정적 인 보디이미지를 얻게 되는 내용이 나오므로 대조 접사인 On the other hand(반면)가 온다.
(B)는 이 글의 결론에 관한 내용이므로 therefore(그러므로)가 온다.

보기
	(A)	(B)
①	반면	그러므로
②	반면	예를 들면
③	같은 방식으로	그럼에도 불구하고
④	그 결과	그럼에도 불구하고
⑤	그 결과	예를 들면

해석 당신의 보디이미지는 하룻밤에 만들어지지 않는다. 보디이미지는 오랜 시간 천천히 발달하며 많은 요소들이 영향을 끼친다. 예를 들면, 수년 동안 스포츠 활동을 하거나 운동을 해왔을 경우 힘과 신체 능력 면에서 보디이 미지에 자신감을 가지면서 긍정적인 보디이미지를 발달시킬 수 있다. 반면, 어떤 사람에게서 당신의 보디이미 지에 관해 무심한 좋지 않은 평을 들으면 이는 당신의 보디이미지에 오랫동안 부정적인 영향을 줄 수 있다. 더 나아가 보디이미지는 사람의 일생에 거쳐 진화하고 변화한다. 대부분의 사람들은 신체적으로 정신적으로 정서적으로 나이 들고 성숙해 가면서 그들의 보디이미지를 변화시킨다. 당신의 삶의 어떤 시점에서 부정적인 보디이미지를 가질 수 있지만 또 다른 시점에서는 긍정적인 보디이미지를 가질 수 있다. 그러므로 긍정적인 보디이미지를 만드는 것은 끝이 없는 과정이다.

22 **어휘** uncover ~을 밝혀내다/ deficit 결손, 결점/ significantly 상당히/ lag 지연/ adolescence 성인/ emerge 나타나다/ counter 대응하다/ compulsion 충동/

해설 본문의 내용에 따르면 ADHD 장애를 가지고 있는 아이들이 성인이 되면 두뇌가 회복이 된다는 내용이기 때문에 이시기가 되면 문제 행동이 ④ 나타나는(emerge) 것이 아니라 반대로 사라지다(disappear) 등의 의미가 된다.

해석 2007년 11월 미국 국립정신건강센터와 McGill 대학 연구팀은 ADHD(주의력 결핍 과잉행동장애) 두뇌의 특정 결손을 ① 밝혀냈다고 발표했다. 그 결손은 발달상 문제인 것으로 판명되었다. 종종 ADHD 증상을 보이는 아이들의 두뇌는 상당히 ② 느린 속도로 발달된다. 이 발달 지연은 전전두엽 피질에서 가장 명백히 나타나는데 이는 정신적인 근육이 부족한 이 아이들은 유혹되는 자극에 저항해야 할 필요가 있다는 것을 의미한다. 그러나 좋은 소식은, 천천히 발달하기 시작한 뇌는 항상 ③ 회복이 된다는 것이다. 어른이 되면 이 아이들의 전두엽이 정상 크기가 된다. 그 시점이 되면 이 아이들의 문제 행동이 ④ 나타나기 시작한다는 것은 우연의 일치가 아니다. 발달 지연을 갖고 있던 이 아이들은 결국 욕구와 충동에 ⑤ 대응할 수 있게 된다. 그들은 맛있는 마시멜로우를 보았을 때 기다리는 것이 더 좋다고 결정할 수 있다.

23 **어휘** represent ~을 나타내다/ camouflage 위장술/ aerial 항공의, 안테나/ collaboration 합동, 협력

해설 ⑤번은 지금 시대에는 옛날 전쟁 시대에 입었던 군복이 시대에 뒤떨어진다는 내용이 적절하므로 up-to-date가 아니라 out-of-date가 와야 한다.

해석 옷이 사람을 만든다(옷이 날개다)라는 말이 있고 군에서 만큼 이 말이 더 진실인 곳은 없다. 군인의 군복은 충성심에서부터 직책, 직위까지 모든 것을 ① 나타낸다. 위장을 할 때 군복은 삶과 죽음의 차이를 의미할 수도 있다 – 미국 입법자들이 아프가니스탄의 병력이 입을 70,000개의 새로운 군복의 ② 자금을 위한 긴급 전쟁 비용 1060억 달러가 필요하다는 조항을 통과시키기 위해 주장했던 것이 이점이다. 명백히 아프가니스탄의 진흙투성이와 산세가 험한 지형은 바그다드와 같은 먼지로 뒤덮인 사막도시를 위해 고안되었던 "보편적인 위장 무늬"와는 ③ 어울리지 않는다. 1차 세계대전 동안 항공기와 참호의 등장은 위장술의 전략이 생기게 했는데, 이 전략은 군인, 예술가, Abbot Thayer와 같은 자연주의자의 ④ 합동 전략으로 생겨났다. Thayer가 1909년 저술한 책 – Concealing Coloration in the Animal Kingdom – 동물왕국에의 은폐색-보호색-은 위장술 고안자들에게 필수로 읽어야 할 책이 되었다. 이제 병사들은 사방에서 날아오는 폭탄과 총알을 피해야 하기 때문에 예전 전쟁 시대에 입었던 전통적인 군복은 완전히 위험하지는 않더라도 ⑤ 최신식처럼 보인다.

24 **어휘** disparity 차이/ simply put 간단히 말해서

보기 ① 자기만족의 덫에 빠지지 마라.
② 주관성은 객관성으로부터 온다.
③ 행복은 각각 사람들에게 다르다.
④ 다른 사람들의 눈으로 너 자신을 평가하라.
⑤ 네가 더 많이 획득할수록(가질수록) 너는 더 행복해질 것이다.

해설 우리가 행복에 관하여 말할 때 "비교하기"는 전혀 도움이 되지 않는다. 행복이란 주관적인 현상이다. 행복은 모든 사람들이 다르게 경험하고 행복은 다른 사람들에게 다른 의미로 작용한다. "한 사람에게는 고기가 다른 사람에게는 독이 될 수 있다"는 말처럼 우리의 욕구는 다양해서 한 사람을 행복하게 만들어주는 것이 다름 사람에게 같은 영향을 줄 수는 없을 것이다. 우리 대부분이 우리의 개인적인 욕구들 사이의 차이점을 깨닫고 있음에도 불구하고 담장 너머를 내다보고는 이웃들이 가지고 있는 것들이 우리도 필요할 것이라고 생각하는 덫에 빠지기 쉽다. 간단히 말해서 이는 전혀 도움이 되지 않고 불행으로 가는 지름길임에 틀림없다. 한 연구는 가장 행복한 사람들은 자신이 가진 것에 감사하고 그들이 가지지 못한 것에 관심을 두지 않는다고 강하게 주장한다. 장기적인 행복은 그들 자신을 다른 사람들과 관련지어 판단하는 것이 하니라 그들에게 중요한 것을 명백히 하고 그들 자신의 우선순위를 달성하는데 초점을 두는 것이다.

25 어휘 sodium 나트륨/ significant 중요한/ cardiovascular 심혈관/ stroke 뇌졸중/ trigger ~을 촉진하다/ osteoclast 파골세포/ osteoporosis 골다공증/ bone density 골밀도

보기 ① 뼈 약화의 노령화의 중요한 영향
② 몸무게 감소와 뼈 약화의 관련성
③ 비정상적인 소변 나트륨 배출의 간과된 원인들
④ 뼈 약화 : 과도한 나트륨 섭취의 위협
⑤ 칼슘 균형 : 건강한 심장을 유지하기 위해 새롭게 밝혀진 팁(지름길)

해석 많은 사람들은 나트륨의 주원인 소금을 지나치게 많이 섭취하는 것이 뇌졸중이나 심장마비와 같은 심혈관 질환의 주요 원인이라는 것을 알고 있다. 하지만 지나친 나트륨 섭취가 뼈에도 해롭다는 사실을 아는 사람은 많지 않다. 소변을 통해 당신의 몸이 손실하는 칼슘의 양은 당신이 소금을 섭취함으로 인해 증가한다. 낮은 혈중 칼슘농도에 의해 촉진되어지며 파골세포라 불리는 세포들은 칼슘을 혈중으로 내보내기 위해 뼈를 쪼개고 이는 잠재적으로 뼈 손실을 가져온다. 그러므로 나트륨이 높은 식단은 부가적으로 원치 않는 결과를 가져오는데 이는 골다공증이라 알려진 뼈가 약해지는 질환이다. 예를 들면 2009년도에 노인 여성들에게 실시된 연구는 2년간 엉덩이 골밀도의 손실이 연구 초반에 시행했던 24시간 소변의 나트륨 배출과 관련이 있었고, 그 관련성은 뼈 손실과 칼슘 섭취의 관계만큼 강하다는 것을 보여주었다. 다른 연구에서는 나트륨 섭취를 줄이는 것이 칼슘 균형을 유지하는데 도움이 된다는 것을 보여주었고 이는 소금을 적게 섭취하는 것이 나이가 들면서 생기는 뼈의 칼슘 손실을 늦춘다고 제안하고 있다.

26 어휘 immense 엄청난, 어마어마한/ resentment 분개/ dictatorial 독단적인, 독재의/ obedient 복종적인/ automaton 로봇 같은 사람

해설 주어진 문장은 Bergman의 감독 방식이 변화된 내용이고 그렇게 된 계기가 ⑤번 문장 앞에 제시되고 있으므로 주어진 문장은 ⑤에 들어가야 한다.

해석
> 그것은 Bergman의 명령을 적게 하게했다. Max von Sydow와 같은 배우들과 함께 Bergman은 단지 그가 생각하는 것을 제안했고, 위대한 배우(Sydow)가 감독의 생각에 어떻게 생명을 불어넣는지 지켜볼 수 있었다.

위대한 스웨덴의 영화감독인 Ingmar Bergman은 감독 일을 하던 초반에는 종종 좌절에 빠졌다. ① Bergman은 그가 만들고자 했던 영화의 비전을 갖고 있었지만 영화감독이 되는 것은 매우 까다롭고 부담감이 너무 커서 배우들이나 직원들을 꾸짖거나 그가 원하는 것을 해내지 못하는 것에 관해 소리를 지르거나 공격적인 발언을 하곤 했다. ② 몇몇 사람들은 감독의 독단적인 방식에 분개를 했고 다른 사람들은 그저 복종하는 로봇처럼 되기도 했다. ③ Bergman이 만드는 거의 모든 영화에서 그는 늘 새로운 배우, 직원들과 시작해야 했고 이는 모든 상황을 더욱 악화시켰다. ④ 그러나 결국 Bergman은 스웨덴의 최고의 촬영기사들, 편집자들, 예술 감독들과 배우들의 팀을 꾸렸고 이들은 감독의 높은 기대수준을 함께 공유하며 감독을 믿어주는 사람들이었다. ⑤ 최고의 통솔은 흘러가게 두는 것(통제를 덜하는 것)으로부터 나온다.

27 어휘 import(수입) ↔ export(수출) / theoretically 이론적으로 / interstate 주 간, 주 사이/ undercut ~보다 저가로 풀다 / eliminate ~을 제거하다

해설 주어진 문장은 수입을 제한하는 내용이고 이것의 예가 ③번의 미국의 토마토 수입 제한에 관한 것이므로 주어진 문장이 ③번에 들어가야 한다.

해석
> 그러나 국가들은 다양한 이유로 어떤 상품의 수입을 제한하는 경향이 있다.

다른 나라의 회사들과 사업을 진행하는 크고 작은 회사들이 점점 늘어나고 있다. 어떤 회사들은 외국에 있는 회사에 물건을 팔고, 다른 회사들은 자신의 나라에 물건을 수입해오기 위해 물건을 산다. ① 그들이 국경을 넘어서 물건을 사거나 파는 것은 세계의 경제에 불을 붙이는 국제무역에 공헌한다. ② 이론상으로 국제 무역은 캘리포니아 주와 워싱턴 주 사이의 주 간 거래만큼 논리적이고 가치가 있다. ③ 예를 들면 2000년대 초반에 미국은 멕시코로부터 토마토를 수입하는 것을 제한했는데 이는 토마토 수입이 미국의 토마토 가격을 저하시켰기 때문이다. 그러한 제한에도 불구하고 국제무역은 2차 대전 이후로 꾸준히 증가해 왔다. 산업화된 국가들은 국제 무역의 문제점을 제거하고 후진국의 국제 거래 참여를 돕는 무역 협정에 서명을 했다.

28 어휘 evaluation 평가/ curiosity 호기심

해설 비판적인 질문을 통해 비판적인 사고능력과 비판적인 듣기, 읽기 능력을 향상 시킬 수 있다는 것이 내용의 요지이다.

해석 비판적 듣기와 읽기 -즉, 당신이 듣는 것과 읽는 것을 체계적으로 평가하며 반응하는 것 -는 일종의 기술과 태도를 필요로 한다. 이러한 기술과 태도는 일련의 관련된 비판적 질문으로 생겨난다. 우리가 그러한 기술과 태도를 하나씩 배울지라도 우리의 최종 목표는 그것들을 함께 사용하여 최고의 결정을 내리는 것이다. 우리는 그것들을 당신이 해야만 하는 것들의 리스트로 표현할 수도 있지만, 질문을 하는 것은 비판적인 사고의 핵심인 일종의 호기심, 궁금함 그리고 지적인 모험들과 훨씬 더 부합한다. 주의 깊게 사고하는 것은 끝나지 않는 과업이며 도달할 수 없는 결말을 찾는 이야기이다. 비판적인 질문은 비판적인 사고를 위한 자극과 방향을 제공한다. 비판적인 질문은 우리로 하여금 계속해서 더 나은 의견, 결정 또는 판단을 위하여 움직이도록 해준다.

29 어휘 spatial 공간적인/ fundamental 기초적인/ requirement 필요조건, 요건/ unspectacular 특별하지 않은

해설 인간의 공간 인지 능력이 보편적인 것이 아니라 다소 가변적이고 문화적인 요인에 의지한다는 것이 이 글의 요지이다.

해석 공간 인지 능력은 본거지를 지닌 모든 움직이는 매개체에게 기초적으로 필요한 것이다. 그리고 공간 인지 능력이 사람의 생각과 이성에 중요한 역할을 한다는 사실에는 의심할 여지가 없다. 사실상 공간 인지 능력이 중심적 역할을 하는 것에 관한 증거는 우리 주변에 있고, 우리 언어에서도 공간적인 비유가 많은 다른 영역을 위해 사용되며, 기억장소에서도 특별한 역할을 하고 있다. 공간 인지가 우리의 본성에 만들어진 기초적인 직관이라는 생각은 최소한 칸트 시대로 거슬러 올라가며, 우리의 공간 지각 능력이 인지적 보편성에 의해 지배된다는 것은 현대 인지과학을 만들어 낸다. 그러나 어떤 면에서 인간의 공간 인지 능력은 수수께끼이다. 첫째로, 우리 인간은 벌이나 비둘기, 박쥐나 고래 등에 비교해봤을 때 우리 주변의 길을 찾아내는 것에 있어서 특별하지 못하다. 두 번째로 인간의 공간 인지 능력은 가변적이다 – 사냥꾼들, 항해자들, 택시 운전수들은 일반적으로 도시에 사는 사람들과는 다른 능력을 지니고 있다. 이는 다음과 같은 사실을 제안한다. 효과적인 공간 사고력은 문화적인 요인에 의존하고, 이는 다시 말해 공간적인 능력에 있어서 인지적 보편성을 주장하기에는 한계가 있다는 것이다.

30 어휘 deliberate 고의적인/ convey ~을 전달하다, 나르다/ vague 모호한

해설 이 글의 주제는 초보 작가들이 모호한 생각 때문에 글이 써지지 않는 것이 단순히 어휘가 부족하다고 착각하고 있다는 내용이다.

보기 ① 몇몇 작가들이 그들의 작품에서 진실하지 못한 이유들
② 학생들이 생각을 체계적으로 발달시키는 것을 훈련시키는 방법
③ 글쓰기를 효과적으로 하기 위한 풍부한 어휘력의 중요성
④ 초보 작가들의 모호한 생각과 부족한 어휘를 혼동하는 실수
⑤ 충분한 어휘 없이 명확한 생각을 얻는 것의 어려움

해석 숙련되지 않은 작가들은 그들이 확고한 생각을 가지고 있다고 생각하는 실수를 종종 범한다. 그들은 종종 이렇게 불평을 한다. "나는 내가 말하고자 하는 바를 잘 알고 있지만 그것을 표현하는 그 단어를 찾지 못 하겠어" 이 불평은 거의 다 진실이 아닌데 이는 초보 작가들이 의도적으로 거짓말을 하기 때문이 아니라 그들이 말하고자 하는 직관과 그것이 무엇인지 그들이 이미 정확히 알고 있다는 잘못된 감각 사이를 혼동하기 때문이다. 작가가 단어에서 막혔을 때 그 문제는 단순히 단어 때문인 경우는 거의 없다. 숙련되지 못한 작가들은 그들이 좀 더 명확한 아이디어가 필요할 때 그들은 더 풍부한 어휘력이 필요하다고 생각할 것이다. 단어에서 막혔다는 것은 작가가 전달하고자 하는 생각이 아직 모호하고 확실치 않고 혼란스럽다는 것이다. 만일 당신이 어떤 구체적인 의미를 찾아냈다면 동시에 그것을 표현하는 적절한 단어도 찾아낼 것이다.

31 해설 이 글의 주제는 스포츠를 어떻게 정의 내릴 것인가에 관한 것이다.

보기 ① 스포츠에 내재된 여가활동들
② 경쟁력 높은 활동들의 인기
③ 스포츠를 정의하는 기준에 관한 논쟁
④ 스포츠가 인간의 정신건강에 주는 영향
⑤ 당구를 스포츠로 정의하는 특징들

해석 겉보기에 간단해 보이는 질문인 "무엇이 스포츠를 정의하는가?"는 수년 동안 전문적인 운동선수들과 스포츠 보는 것을 좋아하는 사람들 사이에서 논쟁과 대화의 주제가 되어 왔다. 야구, 축구, 미식축구와 같이 격렬하고 매우 경쟁적인 활동을 스포츠라 하는 것은 의심의 여지가 없다. 하지만 다트, 체스, 셔플보드와 같은 활동에 관해서 이야기 할 때 우리는 그 논쟁의 중심에 서게 된다. 만약 당구가 스포츠가 아니라고 한다면 그것은 정확히 무엇일까? 당구가 스포츠라는 것을 반박하는 사람들은 그것이 단순 여가 활동이라고 응답할 것이다. 그들은 진정한 스포츠는 신체적인 활동(노력)이 필수라고 주장할 것이다. 좀 더 정확히 하자면 만일 선수가 땀을 흘리지 않는다면 그것은 스포츠가 아니다. 그것을 넘어서 조금 더 중요한 기준은 정확한 손과 눈의 협응이 필요하고 부상의 위험성이 있다는 것이다. 당구는 이중 오로지 한 가지만을 만족시킨다(손과 눈의 협응). 그러므로 위와 같이 주장하는 사람들에 따르면 당구는 진짜 스포츠가 아닌 것이다.

32 어휘 impersonate ~을 가장하다, ~을 흉내 내다

해설 Warhol은 예술을 전혀 모르는 배우인 Allen Midgette를 골라 대신 강연하게 했으므로 ④번은 일치하지 않는다.

해석 1967년 Andy Warhol은 여러 대학교에서 강의 제안을 받았다. Andy Warhol은 이야기 하는 것을 싫어했고, 특별히 자신의 예술에 관해 이야기하는 것은 더욱 싫어했다. "예술이란 더 적게 이야기할수록 더 완벽해진다."고 그는 생각했다. 그러나 강의료 때문에 Andy Warhol은 강의 제안을 거절할 수 없었다. 그의 해결책은 아주 간결했다. Andy Warhol은 배우인 Allen Midgette에게 그를 가장해 줄 것을 부탁했다. Midgette는 머리색이 짙고 피부가 검은 반 체로키 인디언이었다. Midgette는 Andy Warhol과 조금도 닮지 않았다. 그러나 Warhol과 친구들은 Midgette의 얼굴을 화장하고 갈색머리를 은색으로 바꾸고 어두운 안경을 씌우고 Warhol의 옷을 입혔다. Midgette은 예술에 관해 전혀 몰랐기 때문에 학생들의 질문에 대한 대답은 짧고 수수께끼 같았다. Midgette의 가장은 성공적이었다. Warhol은 시대의 우상이었지만 어느 누구도 그에 대해 정말로 알지는 못했다. 심지어 Warhol이 어두운 안경을 쓰고 다녔기 때문에 그의 얼굴조차도 상세히 알려지지 않았다.

33 **어휘** visibly 눈에 띄게, 분명히/ counterpart 상대

해설 텔레비전이 가장 인기 있지 않은 세대는 Z 세대 뿐 아니라 silent generation(노인 세대)도 해당이 되기 때문에 ③번은 도표의 내용과 일치하지 않는다.

해석 위의 그래프는 세 개의 레크리에이션 매체 활동에 대한 세대별 참여 비율을 보여주고 있다. ① 세 개의 레저 활동 중에 음악은 Z 세대 사이에 가장 인기 있었고, 반면 읽기는 65세 이상 노인 세대에게 가장 인기 있었다. ② 읽기에 여기 시간을 소비하는 새천년 세대(21세-34세)의 비율은 다른 세대들 보다 현저히 작았다. ③ 텔레비전은 Z 세대를 제외하고 모든 세대에게 가장 인기 있었는데, Z 세대 중 텔레비전을 가장 좋아하는 레저 활동으로 고른 비율이 1/4 이하였다. ④ X 세대, 베이비 붐 세대, 노인 세대들에게는 음악이 읽기보다 인기가 적었다. ⑤ 가장 어린 세대(Z 세대)보다 더 많이 읽는 두 세대는 베이비 붐 세대와 노인 세대이다.

34 **어휘** tissue 조직/ organ 장기/ physiological 생리학적인/ give away 내주다/ biochemistry 생화학적인/ genetics 유전학적인/ immunology 면역의/ molecular 분자의/ cellular 세포의

해설 (B)의 this local systems approach는 주어진 글의 organ systems approach를 받고 있다. 그러므로 주어진 글 다음에 (B)가 오며 글의 요지는 병 치료에 있어서 국부 접근법이 통합 접근법으로 바뀌고 있다는 내용이다. (B)의 말미에 인간의 몸은 어떤 국부적인 문제를 나타내는 것이 아니라 (C) Instead (대신에) 통합적인 문제를 나타낸다는 내용으로 이어진다. 다음으로는 (A)에서 통합접근법을 부연 설명해주고 있으므로 순서는 (B)-(C)-(A)가 된다.

해석

> 20세기 의학은 병을 치료하기 위해 의료 전문화와 장기 조직 접근법에 의해 큰 발전을 이루어왔다.

(B) 이 국부 조직 접근법은 이제 의학 치료에서 통합 접근법이 대신하고 있다. 아픈 환자는 각각의 생체 화학적 문제, 해부학적 문제, 유전학전인 문제, 면역학인 문제는 나타내지 않는다.

(C) 대신에 각각의 사람은 분자의, 세포의, 유전자의, 환경의 그리고 사회적 영향은 받는 생산물이며, 건강이나 질병을 결정하기 위해 복합적인 방식으로 통합된다. 인간의 몸은 하부조직들의 통합체인 것이다.

(A) 한 개의 조직이나 장기의 변화는 다른 하부조직들에 생리학적인 영향을 줄 수 있다. 통합은 또한 치료가 다양한 영역에 영향을 준다는 것을 의미한다. 예를 들면, 한 조직에서 발견된 병의 치료는 다른 조직에 복잡한 영향을 줄 수 있다는 것이다.

35 **어휘** conversely 반대로

해설 주어진 글에는 threshold rules에 관한 설명이 나와 있고 (C)에서 그 예를 들어 쉽게 부연 설명하고 있다. 그리고 (A)의 Conversely(대조적으로)의 등장으로 threshold rules와 대조적인 personal rules가 등장하고 있고 이 차이점을 must와 should를 사용하여 설명하고 있다. 그리고 (B)에서는 이 차이점을 조금 더 자세히 설명해주고 있으므로 순서는 (C)-(A)-(B)가 된다.

해석

> 어떤 규칙들은 그것들을 어기면 너무 심한 고통이 따르기 때문에 그 규칙을 깨는 것을 고려조차 하지 않는 규칙들이 있다. 우리는 거의 그 규칙을 어기지 않을 것이다. 나는 이러한 규칙들을 "threshold rules"(한계 규칙)이라 일컫는다.

(C) 예를 들어 만일 내가 당신에게 "당신이 절대로 하지 않는 어떤 일은 무엇인가요?"라고 묻는다면 당신은 나에게 threshold rule(한계 규칙)을 이야기 할 것이다. 당신은 당신이 절대로 어기지 않는 규칙을 나에게 이야기할 것이다. 그 이유는? 그 규칙을 어기는 것은 너무 많은 고통이 따르기 때문이다.

(A) 반대로 우리는 우리가 어기지 않는 몇몇 규칙을 가지고 있다. 나는 이러한 규칙들은 personal standard(개인 규칙)이라고 일컫는다. 만일 우리가 이 규칙을 어기면 기분이 좋지는 않지만 경우에 따라서 단기적으로 이 규칙들을 어길 수는 있다. 이 두 규칙(threshold rules와 personal standard) 사이의 다른 점은 종종 must와 should 사이의 차이점으로 비유된다.

(B) 우리는 우리가 반드시 하는(must do) 어떤 것, 우리가 해서는 안 되는 어떤 것(must not do), 우리가 절대로 해서는 안 되는 어떤 것(must never do) 그리고 우리가 항상 해야만 하는 어떤 것(must always do)들이 있다. 반드시 해야만 하는 것(must)과 절대로 하면 안 되는 것(must never)의 규칙이 바로 threshold rule(한계규칙)이다. "should"와 "should never" 규칙은 personal standard rules(개인 규칙)이다. 이 모든 것들은 우리의 삶에 체계를 준다.

36 어휘 ward off ~을 막다/ repel ~을 쫓아내다/ anthropologist 인류학자/ appease ~을 달래다

해설 (A) accept(~을 받아들이다)/ repel(~을 쫓다) 중 소금을 뿌리는 행위는 악령을 쫓는 의미가 되므로 repel이 답이 된다.

(B) uncomfortable(불편한)/ satisfied(~에 만족하는) 중 uncertainty(불확실성)에 관해서는 불편함을 느끼는 것이므로 uncomfortable이 답이 된다.

(C) secure(안전한)/ unsettling(불안한) 중에 미신을 행하지 않으면 불안한 상황이 되는 것이 어울리므로 unsettling이 답이 된다.

보기
	(A)	(B)	(C)
①	~을 받아들이다	불편한	안전한
②	~을 받아들이다	만족스러운	불안한
③	~을 쫓다	불편한	불안한
④	~을 쫓다	만족스러운	안전한
⑤	~을 쫓다	불편한	안전한

해석 현대사회에서도 많은 사람들이 일상적으로 어떤 의식 행위를 한다. 이는 불운을 막기 위해서 나무를 두드리거나 악령을 (A) 쫓아내기 위해 어깨 너머로 소금을 뿌리는 등의 행위이다. 모든 문화는 그 문화의 미신을 가지고 있고 이제는 인류학자들과 심리학자들은 그 이유를 알고 있다고 생각한다. 이는 우리의 뇌는 늘 우리가 감지하는 어떤 중요한 사건들의 이유를 찾기 위해 일하기 때문이다. 우리가 설명하지 못하는 어떤 이상한 일이 일어나면 우리의 마음은 불확실성 때문에 (B) 불편해진다. 그러나 우리는 이 인지적 차이를 우리가 할 수 있는 설명으로 채우거나 그 이상한 사건을 아주 간단하게 설명해주는 미신으로 채운다. 그들은 나무 안에 살고 있는 나쁜 영이 위로를 받거나 소금을 던지는 것이 악귀를 막는다고 믿는다. 미신은 그것을 믿지 않는 사람들에게는 우스꽝스러워 보인다. 하지만 미신을 믿는 사람들에게는 (C) 불안한 상황을 해결할 수 있는 해결책을 주는 의식이 되는 것이다.

37 어휘 aptitude 적성/ uncertified 보증되지 않은

해설 주어진 글은 선생님이 학생들에게 주는 자아상이 학업성취도에 영향을 준다는 내용이다.

보기
	(A)	(B)
①	자아상	학업성취도
②	자아상	직업선택
③	전통적 가치	심리학적 행복
④	전통적 가치	학업성취도
⑤	편견	직업선택

해석 미국에서 30년 전에 수행되었던 흥미로운 실험이 있다. 실험에 참여했던 선생님은 학생들에게 "최근의 연구에 따르면 파란 눈동자를 가진 아이들이 갈색 눈동자를 가진 아이들보다 학습 적성이 더 뛰어나다"라고 이야기했다. 학생들에게 이 확실치 않은 정보를 이야기 한 후에 선생님은 학생들에게 눈동자의 색깔을 카드에 써서 목에 걸도록 했다. 일주일 동안 관찰해 본 결과는 다음과 같았다. 갈색 눈동자를 가진 아이들의 학습 동기는 떨어졌고 파란 눈동자를 가진 학생들은 수업시간에 훨씬 더 잘했다. 그 후 선생님은 학생들에게 "지난 번 이야기 했던 연구결과가 잘못되었다. 사실 갈색 눈동자를 가진 학생들이 파란 눈동자를 가진 학생들보다 학습에 더 뛰어나다"라고 이야기를 했다. 결과는 어떠했을까? 이번에는 갈색 눈동자를 가진 학생들이 수업에서 훨씬 뛰어났고 파란 눈동자를 가진 학생들의 수업 동기는 떨어졌다.

위의 실험에 따르면 선생님에 의해 주어진 (A) <u>자아상</u>은 학생들의 (B) <u>학업성취도</u>를 결정지을 수 있다.

✧ [38~39]

어휘 literacy 문해, 문자/ causality 인과관계/ disentangle ~을 구분하다/ endowment 자질

해석 많은 아이들은 대부분 집에서 처음 문자를 접하게 된다. 함께 읽기를 통해 문해발달을 가정 활동 중 중요한 활동으로 여기는 가족에서 자란 아이들은 유리한 입장에 있다. (A) 그러나 조기 문자경험이 아이들의 언어 발달과 문해 발달에 영향을 주는지에 관한 정확한 관계에 관한 연구는 거의 없다. 문화적 신념, 사회 경제적인 지위, 양육 방식과 부모의 신념 등을 포함한 다양한 요인이 아이들의 읽기 발달에 영향을 줄 수 있다. 게다가 이 요소들 중 정확한 인과관계를 찾기는 어렵다.

또한 아이들의 유전적인 구성과 그들의 생물학적 부모가 그들에게 주는 영향을 구분해내기는 어렵다. 책을 읽어주고자 하는 부모의 동기, 열정, 의지가 그들의 아이들에게 행동학적인 영향을 준다 할지라도, 그 영향은 아이들 스스로의 욕구에 비한다면 사소할 것이다. 그들의 아이들에게 책을 많이 읽어주는 부모들은 아마도 그들의 아이가 읽기에 흥미가 있다는 사실에 반응하는 것이다. 최소한 그러한 영향력은 유전적으로 결정되어진다. (B) 유사하게 아이들에게 책을 별로 읽어주지 않는 부모들은 그들의 아이들이 책을 읽는 것에 흥미가 없음에 반응하거나 유전학적으로 부모와 아이 둘 다 독서와 관련된 활동이 지루하고 어렵다고 느끼는 사실에 반응하는 것이다. 아이들의 유전적인 자질은 그들의 부모가 그들에게 어떻게 상호작용하는지에 강한 영향을 준다. 부모의 행동과 가족의 유전적인 구성간의 혼동 요인들을 가정해보면 부모와 아이 간의 함께 읽기에 관한 연구는 가장 환경이 읽기와 관련된 능력에 영향을 줄 수 있다는 가장 명백한 증거가 될 것이다.

38 **보기** ① 아이들은 선천적으로 좋은 독서가이다.
② 아이들의 문해발달에 무엇이 영향을 주는가?
③ 문해능력과 문화적 신념과의 관계
④ 가정환경에 의해 결정되는 사회적 지능
⑤ 무엇이 아이들로 하여금 읽기를 꺼리게 만드는가?

해설 (A)의 앞 뒤 문장은 상반된 내용이 나오고 있으므로 상반 접속사인 However가 적절하고 (B)의 앞 뒤 문장은 비슷한 예시가 나오고 있으므로 Similarly가 어울린다.

39 **보기**

	(A)	(B)
①	그러므로	반면에
②	그러나	유사하게
③	과적으로	더욱이
④	그러나	반면에
⑤	결과적으로	유사하게

[40~41]

어휘 captive 포로/ ordeal 시련/ defining 결정적인/ unfounded 근거 없는/ preclude 불가능하게 하다

해석 Jim Collins가 Good to Great(좋은 기업을 넘어 위대한 기업으로)에서 지적한 것처럼 (A) 비현실적인 낙관주의와 상황을 직시하지 못하는 것은 도움이 되지 않을 뿐 아니라 치명적일 수도 있다. Collins는 이를 미군 장교 James Stockdale에 따라 스톡데일 패러독스(Stockdale Paradox)라고 일컬었다. Stockdale은 베트남 전쟁 중에 8년 동안 포로로 잡혀 지냈다. 그는 수많은 고문을 받았지만 그의 아내를 다시 만나기 위해 살아 나갈 것이라고 믿었다. Stockdale은 곤경을 겪으면서도 그 곤경을 견딜 수 있을 것이라는 희망을 잃지 않았다. 그는 시련을 견디었을 뿐 아니라 그의 인생에서 결정적인 경험으로 여겼다. 여기에 패러독스(역설)가 있다.

Stockdale은 놀라운 신념을 가지고 있었지만, 그는 가장 낙관적인 수용소 동료들이 살아 나가지 못한다는 사실에 주목했다. 낙관적인 동료들은 "크리스마스 때 나갈 수 있을 거야."라고 이야기를 했다. 그리고 크리스마스가 왔지만 그들은 나가지 못했다. 그러면 그들은 "부활절에는 나갈 수 있을 거야."라고 이야기를 했고 부활절이 왔지만 그들은 또 나가지 못했다. 그리고 추수 감사절, 그 다음 크리스마스도 지나갔다. 그리고 그들은 상심에 가득차서 죽게 된다. 낙관주의자들은 그들의 상황의 현실을 직시하지 못했다. 그들은 현실 도피 기법(ostrich approach-그저 모래에 머리를 박고 어려움이 지나가 버리길 희망하는)을 (B) 선호했다. 이 자기기만은 단기적으로는 그 상황을 좀 쉽게 만들 수 있지만 그들이 결국 현실을 직시하게 되었을 때 현실이 너무 힘들어 그들은 그 상황을 견디지 못하는 것이다.

물론 그러한 근거 없는 낙관주의는 그 상황을 최선을 다해 처리하는 것을 불가능하게 한다. Stockdale은 그 상황에서 최선을 다하는 것이 바로 Stockdale이 했던 것이다.

40 **해설** (A) 이하에서 설명되고 있는 내용은 비현실적인 낙관주의관한 내용이므로 unrealistic optimism이 와야 한다. (B)의 주어인 they는 앞 문장의 수용소에서 가장 낙관적이었던 사람들을 가리키는 것이고 이 사람들은 현실도피(ostrich approach)를 선호했다는 내용이므로 preferred가 와야 한다.

보기

	(A)	(B)
①	비이성적인 비관주의	비난했다
②	비이성적인 비관주의	선호했다
③	비현실적인 낙관주의	거절했다
④	비현실적인 낙관주의	선호했다
⑤	무조건적인 헌신	거절했다

41 **해설** James Stockdale은 비현실적인 낙관주의나 단기적인 낙관주의는 지지하지 않았으므로 ⑤번의 "곧 풀려날 것이라는 희망을 불어 넣어주었다."라는 내용은 일치하지 않는다.

어휘 civilianisation 민간화/ prominence 중요성/ shift 이동/ removal 제거/ outsource 위탁하다/ contractor 계약자/ tactical 전술의, 전략의/ transnational 초국가적 reduction 감소/ expansion 팽창, 증가/ encompass ~을 포함하다/ augment 증가하다 exclude ~을 배제하다/ recruit ~을 고용하다/ foxhole 참호

해석 무력분쟁법의 적용에 영향을 주고 있는 새로운 동향은 점점 증가하고 있는 현대 전쟁의 민간화이다. 이 동향은 다양한 절차를 통해 일어나는데, 이는 전쟁에 참여하는 사람들의 대다수가 민간인으로 무장된 전쟁이 증가하고 있다는 사실과 교전의 통솔력이 민간 중심으로 (A) 옮겨지고 있다는 사실을 포함한다. 게다가 현대의 군대는 점점 민간군사나 보안회사와 같은 계약자들에게 도움을 위탁하고 심지어 전술의 핵심기능을 위탁하는데 이 민간군사나 보안회사는 무장된 전술 역할을 담당하고 있다.

웨스트팔리아 조약이 맺어지고 350여 년이 지난 후 민족 국가는 국제 관계에 있어 결정적인 역할을 하고 있고, 군사력을 독차지하고 있다. 초국가적으로 무장된 그룹의 등장과 점점 증가하는 국경을 넘어선 무장된 갈등과 전체 영토를 어우르는 전투가 (B) 증가하는 것은 민간인들이 이전보다 훨씬 더 많이 전쟁에 개입된다는 것을 의미한다.

군대들 또한 예산을 줄여야 하는 압박을 받고 있다. 이 동향의 일부로 민간 계약자들과 고용인들은 점점 변화하는 욕구에 따른 군사력을 유지하기 위한 쉽고 유동적인 방법으로써 방어력을 증진시키기 위해 사용된다. 더욱이 무기와 설비들이 기술적으로 진보되면서 민간인들은 때로는 "공장에서 참호까지" 전투력을 지지하고 유지하기 위해 (C) 고용된다. 민간인들을 고용하는 것은 최신의 전문기술에 접근하기 위한 쉽고 비용이 덜 드는 방법이다. 민간인들은 필요할 때 고용되고 필요가 없어질 때 해고될 수 있다.

42 **해설** 현대의 전쟁(전투)에 민간인이 참여하는 추세(동향)에 관한 내용이다.
보기 ① 군사 방해 없는 갈등해결
② 민간인들의 군사 참여
③ 국가 안보를 위한 군사력의 유지
④ 기적 지구와 공적 지구 사이의 경쟁
⑤ 군사 기술 진보가 민간에게 어떻게 이득을 주는지

43 **해설** (A)는 shift A into B는 A가 B로 이동의 의미가 되는데 이 글에서 conduct of hostilities(교전의 통솔력이) civilian population(민간세력)으로 이동해 가는 의미이다.
(B)는 앞부분에 transnational(초국가적인, 국가를 넘어선)이 나오는 것으로 보아 battlespace(전투공간)가 점점 넓어지고 있는 의미가 되므로 expansion이 와야 한다.
(C)civilians(민간들)이 뒤의 역할을 위해 고용되고 있는 의미가 되므로 recruited가 되어야 한다.

보기

	(A)	(B)	(C)
①	이동	증가	~을 고용하다
②	이동	감소	~을 배제하다
③	이동	감소	~을 고용하다
④	제거	증가	~을 배제하다
⑤	제거	감소	~을 배재하다

⊕ [44~45]

해석 (A)

한 여름 Colin이 고등학생이었을 때 그는 교회 캠프에 참여를 했고 평판이 좋지 못한 친구들과 어울리게 되었다. 그들은 Colin에게 캠프를 몰래 빠져나가 맥주를 사와서 맥주를 차갑게 하기 위해 변기 수조에 숨기자고 했다. 그들은 아무도 맥주를 찾지 못할 것이라고 생각했다. 그러나 그렇지 않았다.

(D)

캠프지도자는 모든 소년들을 불렀고 맥주를 발견한 사실을 알렸다. 신부님(성직자)은 소리를 지르거나 고함치지 않았다. 신부님은 잘못을 저지른 소년들에게 똑바로 서서 어른처럼 행동하고 그들의 잘못에 대한 책임감을 갖으라고 했다. 유년 시절 매우 엄격하게 자란 Colin Powell은 제일 먼저 앞으로 나왔다. "제가 그랬습니다."라고 Colin은 고백했다.

(C)

그의 정직함 덕분에 다른 소년들도 그들의 잘못을 인정했다. 소년들의 부모들도 이를 알게 되었고 소년들은 불명예스럽게 집으로 보내졌다. 기차를 타고 가면서 Colin은 그가 했던 행동에 관해 생각했고 그 일에 관해 후회했다. 그의 부모와 그에게 얼마나 부끄러운일인가! 교회 캠프에서 쫓겨난다는 것은 그가 상상할 수 있는 그 어떤 일보다 최악의 일이다. 기차에서 내려 천천히 집으로 걸어오면서 Colin은 화가 난 엄마를 문 앞에서 만났다.

(B)

Colin의 엄마가 그에게 신뢰와 책임감에 관해 이야기를 할 때 Colin은 조용히 서서 그의 행동에는 어떠한 변명도 있을 수 없음을 알았다. 그리고 Colin의 아버지의 차례가 되었을 때 Colin의 아버지는 그가 아들에게 얼마나 실망을 했는지 이야기했다. Colin이 부모님께 혼나고 있는 동안 세인트 마가렛 교회의 Weeden 신부님이 전화가 와서 Colin이 그의 행동에 얼마나 책임감 있게 행동했는지 이야기를 했다. Colin의 가족은 Colin이 올바른 행동을 한 것에 관해 매우 자랑스러워 했다.

44 **해설** 내용의 흐름에 따라 순서대로 배열하면 (A) − (D) − (C) − (B)이다.

45 **해설** (a)~(d)는 Colin이고 (e)는 신부이다.

ANSWER

01	02	03	04	05	06	07	08	09	10	11	12	13	14	15	16	17	18	19	20
⑤	③	③	⑤	①	④	③	④	③	③	⑤	③	①	①	②	②	④	②	②	②
21	22	23	24	25	26	27	28	29	30	31	32	33	34	35	36	37	38	39	40
①	⑤	⑤	①	①	④	⑤	④	④	①	⑤	③	④	②	⑤	①	①	⑤	②	②
41	42	43	44	45															
④	③	④	④	⑤															

01 **어휘** soak 흠뻑 적시다 / fair enough 괜찮다

해석 Jimmy : 이번 주말에 캠핑 갑시다!

Joanne : 싫어요. 우리 지난주에 갔다가 비 맞았잖아요.

Jimmy : 맞아요. 텐트에 비가 조금 샜지요. 하지만 이번 주말에는 일기예보가 말하길 하늘에 구름 한 점 없을 거래요.

Joanne : 그냥 연극이나 다른 문화를 보러 갈 순 없을까요?

Jimmy : 괜찮아요. 지난 주말에 제가 원하는 걸 했으니까, 이번엔 당신이 계획을 세워 보세요. 그래서 당신은 뭘 하고 싶어요?

Joanne : 시내 문화센터에서 놀라운 발레 공연에 대해 들었어요. 당신은 분명 좋아할 거예요.

Jimmy : 미안해요. 발레를 보러가고 싶지 않아요. 발레는 정말 싫어요. 다른 걸 하는 게 어때요?

보기 ① Joanne는 이번 주말에 캠핑에 흥미가 없다.

② 지난 주말에 비가 내렸다.

③ 그들의 텐트는 완전히 방수가 되지 않는다.

④ 이번 주말에는 날씨가 좋을 것으로 예상된다.

⑤ 지미는 발레의 팬이다.

02 **어휘** utilities 공공요금

해석 Janet : 나는 정말 이 아파트가 맘에 들지만, 걱정이 좀 있어요. 우선, 저는 어린 아들이 있는데 학교에 너무 멀리 걸어가는 걸 싫어해요.

Dave : 이해합니다. 이 근처에 좋은 학교가 있어요. 학교는 여기서 한 블록 떨어져 있어요.

Janet : 공과금은 어떤가요? 사실 우리는 쓸 돈이 많지 않아요.

Dave : 이 건물은 꽤 신축이고 에너지 효율적입니다. 공과금은 아주 적당합니다.

Janet : 오, 그거 안심이네요. 이웃들은 어떤가요? 우리는 조용한 장소에 살고 싶어요.

Dave : 현재는 아이가 없는 젊은 한 부부와 몇몇 노인부부가 살고 있어요. 전혀 소음이 없을 거예요.

Janet : 좋네요. 아마도 이곳이 좋을 거 같아요.

a. 이용가능 한 것이 없네요.
b. 전혀 소음이 없을 거예요.
c. 학교는 여기서 한 블록 떨어져 있어요.
d. 공과금은 아주 적당합니다.

03 어휘 contract 계약(서)

해석 Aaron : 좋은 아침입니다. 오늘 이용가능한 차가 있을까요. 저는 오늘 낮에 시내에 있고 밤에 비행기를 탑니다. 몇몇 장소를 좀 방분하기를 원해요.
　　　Krista : 음, 짧은 공지이지만, 당신에게 제공할 약간의 옵션이 있네요. 선호하는 게 있나요?
　　　Aaron : 사실, 저는 연비가 좋은 소형차를 희망합니다.
　　　Krista : 물론이죠. 완벽한 차가 있네요. 당신 추가적인 보험을 희망하시나요. 저는 이것을 추천합니다.
　　　Aaron : 그럼요. 안전한 게 좋지요.
　　　Krista : 좋아요. 면허증 좀 보여주시겠어요. 저는 계약서를 준비할게요. 차를 반납할 때 기름을 가득 채울 것을 확인해주세요.
　　　Aaron : 네. 제가 오늘 저녁쯤에 차를 가져올게요.

보기 ① 주유소
② 자동차 수리점
③ 자동차 렌트점
④ 여행사
⑤ 보험회사

04 어휘 snuggle 바싹 파고들다, 달라붙다

해석 Bill : 여보. 우리 오늘, 첫 번째 결혼기념일에 내가 특별한 걸 준비했어. 당신도 좋아할 거야. 열어봐.
　　　Diane : 강아지네! 우리는 강아지를 키울 수 없어. 강아지를 키우는 데 너무 비용이 많이 들어. 그리고 큰 책임이 필요해.
　　　Bill : 그렇게 비싸지 않을 거야. 내가 요즘 집에서 일하니까, 강아지를 돌보는 것은 쉬울 거야. 당신이 할 건 없어.
　　　Diana : 확실해? 당신이 강아지를 책임질 거라고 약속할 수 있어?
　　　Bill : 물론이지. 게다가 쟤를 봐봐. 너무 사랑스러워. 이미 당신과 친해진 것 같은데. 당신에게 잘 붙어 다니잖아.
　　　Diana : 솔직히 말해서, 정말 귀엽다. 당신 말대로 한번 키워보자.

보기 ① Bill은 작년에 기념일을 잊어버렸다.
② Diana는 기념일 선물로 Bill에게 애완동물을 주었다.
③ Diana는 강아지를 기르는 것이 쉬울 거라고 생각한다.
④ Bill은 요즘 집에서 일하지 않는다.
⑤ Bill과 Diana는 강아지를 키울 것이다.

05 어휘 clog 막다 / skepticism 회의론

해석 택시운전사 : 안녕하세요. 어디로 가시나요.
　　　승객 : 마을을 지나 Smythe Building으로요. 서둘러 주세요.
　　　택시운전사 : 걱정 마세요. 이 시간에는 교통이 혼잡하지 않습니다.
　　　[5분 후]
　　　승객 : 죄송한데, 고속도로를 두고 왜 도시를 지나쳐 가나요? 저는 40분 안에 미팅에 가야해요.
　　　택시운전사 : 고속도로를 막히게 만드는 큰 공사가 있어요. 저는 모든 지름길을 알고 있어요. 당신을 제시간에 모셔다 드릴게요.

승객 : 알겠습니다. 그러길 희망합니다.
[25분 후]
택시운전사 : 조금 일찍 목적지에 도착했습니다.
승객 : 회의적이었던 것에 대해 사과드릴게요. <u>여기 요금과 충분한 팁이 있습니다.</u>

보기 ① 여기 요금과 충분한 팁이 있습니다.
② 정시에 도착하지 못할 것 같아요.
③ 지하철을 타는 게 나을 것 같네요.
④ 그냥 고속도로로 갑시다.
⑤ 당신의 간섭이 불편하네요.

06 어휘 on your own 혼자

해석 아빠 : 벌써 첫째가 스스로 집을 떠나고 나간다니 믿을 수 없구나. 힘들텐데.
Tim : 걱정하지마, 아빠. 엄마 아빠는 나 없이 잘 지낼 거야. 두 시간 떨어져 있을 텐데, 언제든지 볼 수 있어.
아빠 : 난 우리에 대해 걱정하지 않는단다. 나는 네가 혼자서 빨래, 청소, 세금납부를 할 수 있을지 그게 걱정이란다.
Tim : 나는 사실 빨래를 여기로 가져와서 아빠가 해 주고, 엄마가 내 집에 와서 청소해 주고, 아빠가 세금을 내줬으면 좋겠어.
아빠 : 농담하니. 너는 너 독립한 젊은이란다. 이것이 바로 독립이라는 거야.
Tim : 물론 농담이에요. 저 혼자서 집안일을 할 수 있어요. 게다가, 제 일은 보수가 충분히 좋아요. 아빠는 걱정할 필요 없어요.

보기 ① Tim은 부모님을 돌보기 위해 다시 집으로 돌아왔다.
② Tim의 부모님은 그를 돌보기 위해 규칙적으로 그의 집에 방문하기로 결정했다.
③ Tim의 아빠는 Tim이 오랜만에 집에 와서 기쁘다.
④ Tim은 이사할 것이고, 그는 충분히 독립할 준비가 되었다.
⑤ Tim는 대학으로 떠나지만, 여전히 부모님의 도움이 필요하다.

07 어휘 attired 복장의

해설 ③은 캠퍼스를 방문한 부유한 남자이고, 나머지는 모두 총장을 가리킨다.

해석 J. F. Cowan 박사는 학업 기준이 예외적으로 높았음에도 불구하고 재정적인 어려움을 겪고 있는 작은 대학에 관한 이야기를 전했다. 어느 날 부유한 남자가 캠퍼스에 와서 벽에 그림을 그려 넣은 ① 하얀 머리의 남자를 발견하고 그가 어디에서 총장을 찾을 수 있는지 물었다. 그 화가는 캠퍼스에 있는 한 집을 가리키며 총장을 정오에 그곳에서 볼 수 있을 것이라고 ② <u>그는</u> 확신한다고 말했다. 지정된 시간에 방문객이 총장 집 문을 두드렸고 지금은 다르게 옷을 입고 있었지만 ③ <u>그가</u> 캠퍼스에서 이야기했던 같은 사람에 의해 입장되었다. 방문객은 초대를 받아들이고 ④ <u>그 화가-총장</u>과 점심을 같이하고 대학의 필요에 대해 여러 가지 질문을 하고 나서 약간의 기부금을 보내겠다고 그에게 말했다. 이틀 후에 5만 달러 수표가 동봉된 편지가 도착했다. 대학총장으로서의 ⑤ <u>그의</u> 지위에 적합하면서도 작업복을 입은 채 절실히 필요한 작업을 수행하지 못할 정도로 자존심이 세지 않은 한 인물의 겸손함이 그 부자의 지갑 끈을 열었다.

08 어휘 spectator 관중

해석 첫 번째 올림픽 승리자가 기원전 776년에 기록되었을 때, 로마는 전쟁 종족들로 둘러싸인 단순한 농장 공동체였다. ① 기원전 500년경 올림피아에서의 운동 프로그램이 고정적이고 예측 가능한 패턴으로 정착됨에 따라, 로마인들은 북쪽에 있는 적대적인 이웃인 에트루리아인의 통치에 대항해 일어나고 있었다. ② 2세기 동안 로마 군대, 행정 공무원, 언어 및 문화가 이탈리아 전체를 지배했다. ③ 시칠리아, 카르타고, 그리스의 제국 정복을 시작했다. [④ 또한, 그리스의 스포츠와 게임은 너무 개인주의적이었고, 관중의 호소보다는 참가자들에게 적합했다.] ⑤ 기원전 1세기가 끝날 무렵, 로마 제국은 지중해 전역을 덮어 영국 북부, 유럽 다뉴브, 동쪽 카스피해까지 이어졌다.

09 어휘 long-standing 오래된

해석 크고 작은 대부분의 조직이 현재 데이터로 가득 차 있다는 사실은 나쁜 것이 아니다. ① 실제로 이것은 기업은 이전에는 불가능했던 방식으로 통찰력과 이해를 얻을 수 있는 커다란 기회다. ② 그러나 문제는 대부분의 조직이 데이터를 어떻게 탐구하고 이해해야하는지 고려하지 않는 것이다. [③ 인간 행동과 관련된 데이터를 이해하는 것은 마케터와 사회 과학자의 오랜 숙련된 기술이다.] ④ 새로운 통찰력을 발견하도록 고안된 분석 과정은 혼란스럽고 성과 측정에 사용된 분석 과정과 혼합된다. ⑤ 분석 방법이 실제로 비즈니스에 변화를 가져오는 것에 대한 관심이 부족하다. 비즈니스 결과와 관련이 있는 것보다는 숫자를 측정하는 용이성의 기능으로써의 측정에 너무 많은 초점을 두고 있다.

10 어휘 fascinating 대단히 흥미로운 / distort 왜곡하다

해설 ③의 what은 문장 내의 본동사 think의 목적어이며, 완벽한 절을 이끎으로 명사절 that으로 바꿔야 한다.

해석 수년간 심리학은 우울증, 슬픔, 분노, 스트레스 및 불안 등 부정적인 감정이나 부정적인 영향에 대한 연구에 관심을 돌렸다. 놀랍지 않게도, 심리학자들은 그것들이 심리적 장애 존재의 신호를 보내거나 이끌지도 모른다는 것 때문에 그것들을 종종 흥미롭다고 생각했다. 그러나 긍정적인 감정에 대해 존재하는 많은 상식적인 오해 때문에 긍정적인 감정은 덜 매혹적이다. 예를 들어 우리는 긍정적인 감정이 전형적으로 본질적으로 질서 정연하고 효과적인 생각을 왜곡하거나 분열시키는 경향이 있다고, 긍정적인 감정들은 어느 정도 단순하다고, 또는 이러한 감정들은 수명이 짧기 때문에 긍정적인 감정들은 장기적인 효과를 가질 수 없다고 생각하는 경향이 있다. 연구 결과에 따르면 위와 같은 결과는 나타나지 않았지만 거기에 도달하는 데는 어느 정도 시간이 걸렸다. 비교적 최근에는 심리학자들이 긍정적인 감정을 자신들의 권리 속에서 귀중한 것으로써 보일 수 있다고 깨달았고 그것들을 연구하기 시작했다.

11 어휘 strikingly 두드러지게

해설 ⑤의 written은 문장의 주어인 Letters의 수동의 의미를 가지고 있는 동사임으로 were written으로 고쳐야 한다.

해석 고대 로마에서 빠른 답장이 기대되는 짧은 거리에서 보내진 메시지들은 책과 같이 접힌 목제 틀에 고정된 납판에 철필과 함께 적혀있었다. 현대의 눈에 이 납판은 평평한 필기 면이 나무틀로 둘러싸여 있어 태블릿 컴퓨터와 비슷하다. 수신자의 응답이 동일한 납판에 새겨질 수 있으며, 그것을 전달했던 메신저가 발신자에게 곧바로 다시 가져갈 수 있었다. 그 납판은 철필의 평평한 끝으로 유색 납을 부드럽게 하여 지워지고 재사용될 수 있다. 도시 내에서 이것은 빠른 질문을 누군가에게 보내는 편리한 방법이고, 1~2시간 내에 답변을 얻을 수 있었다. 더 먼 거리를 통해 보내졌던 편지는 더 비싸지만 가볍고 운송에 더 적합했던 파피루스에 기록되었다. 한 장의 파피루스는 일반적으로 폭이 약 6인치, 높이가 10인치인 것으로 측정되어 짧은 편지에 적합했다.

12 dispose of somebody/something ~을 없애다(처리하다)

해석 개인용 컴퓨터는 일상의 물건으로서의 필수품이라고 생각할 수 있다. 그것은 문자 그대로 쓰레기로 버리거나, 재판매하거나, 누군가 다른 사람에게 건네거나, 보이지 않는 어딘가에 버려두는 등 쓰레기, 지나간 물건으로 끝날 수 있고 어떻게든 처리된다. 크리스틴 핀(Christine Finn, 2001)은 컴퓨터 쓰레기(computer-as-junk)에 대한 훌륭한 책을 저술했다, 그 책에서 그녀는 컴퓨터들이 처분되는 방법과, 골동품 컴퓨터 수집가에 의해 처리되든지 재사용가능한 비트를 없애버리든지, PC의 시대가 끝날 때 이루어지는 모든 활동을 살펴본다. 제 세대의 사람들은 컴퓨터가 쓰레기라고 생각하는 것을 좋아하지 않는다. 왜냐하면 우리에게는 여전히 새로운 물건들이기 때문이다. 예를 들어 나는 회전식 건조기보다 컴퓨터를 던져 버리는 것이 훨씬 어렵다고 생각한다. 그리고 나는 20년 된 자동차에서 내가 볼 수 있는 것보다 훨씬 더 상징적인 가치를 20년 된 컴퓨터에서 볼 수 있다.

해설 (A)는 to부정사 부사적 용법의 결과 "~그래서 ~하게 되었다"로 사용되었다.
(B)는 완벽한 절을 이끎으로 in which가 와야 한다.
(C)는 가목적어 it

13 caterpillar 애벌레

해석 요정 이야기는 개구리가 왕자로 변신하거나, 호박이 흰색 쥐에서 변형된 흰 말들이 끄는 마차들로 변한다. 그러한 환상은 심오하게 비현실적이다. 그들은 생물학적인 이유가 아니라 수학적인 이유 때문에 일어날 수 없었다. 그러한 변환들은 사실상 불가능하다. 그리고 그것은 실용적인 목적에서 우리는 그것들을 배제한다는 것을 의미한다. 그러나 애벌레가 나비로 변하는 것은 문제가 되지 않는다. 그것은 항상 발생해 왔고, 자연 선택에 의해 시대에 걸쳐 규칙들이 수립되었다. 나비가 애벌레로 변한 적이 없다고 하더라도 개구리가 왕자로 변하는 것과 같은 방식으로 우리를 놀라게 하지는 않는다. 개구리는 왕자를 만들기 위한 유전자를 가지고 있지 않고, 그들은 올챙이를 만들기 위한 유전자를 가지고 있다.

해설 (A)는 horses를 꾸며 주는 과거분사 transformed
(B)는 문장의 주어이므로 to turn
(C)는 앞 문장을 받아주는 대명사 주어 it

14 orthodox 정통의

해석 종교의 다양한 기능을 검토함으로써, 우리는 종교가 사회 안에서 보수적인 힘임을 알 수 있다. 일반적인 의미에서 종교는 초자연적인 제재를 통해 사람들을 일직선으로 유지하고, 사회적 갈등을 해소하고, 불행한 사건에 대한 설명을 제공함으로써 현상 유지를 지지한다. 더욱이, 몇몇 주요 세계 종교는 철학적 신념과 정치적 해석을 통해 사회적 변화를 억제하는 경향이 있다. 예를 들어, 삶의 현재 상태가 과거 삶의 행위에 의해 결정된다는 개념에 기초한 정통 힌두교의 신념은 사람들이 현재 상황을 변할 수 없는 것으로 받아 들일만큼 너무나 운명적으로 만드는 효과를 가져왔다. 그러한 세계관은 큰 혁명이나 변화를 위한 사소한 계획을 불러일으키지 않을 것 같다. 마찬가지로, 일부 무슬림 지도자들은 특히 서구 세계에서 새로운 가치와 행동의 도입에 맞서 싸우는 강한 입장을 보였다.

보기 ① 보수적인 ② 민주적인 ③ 공정한 ④ 지적인 ⑤ 고무되는

15 gauge 측정하다

해석 당신이 커다란 정사각형 필드에 서 있다고 상상해 보라. 그 필드의 한쪽 편에서 시끄러운 도로 일꾼이 착암기로 수리를 하고 있다. 필드의 인접한 쪽에서 음식 장바구니가 있는 거리 상인은 시끄럽고 반복적인 종소리를 울리고 있다. 눈을 감고 필드에서 돌아 다니면서 당신은 소리의 크기를 측정하여 도로 일꾼이나 음식 카트로부터 당신의 거리를 계산할 수 있다. 두 거리를 아는 것은 소리의 크기를 구분할 수 있는 당신의 능력에 의해서만 제한된 정확도로 필드에서의 당신의 위치를 삼각화하도록 허락해 준다. 이 사례에 관한 더 흥미로운 점은 당신이 두 다른 장소에서 소리의 두 가지 근원들이 위치에 대한 모호하지 않은 단서들을 제공한다라는 원리의 기본적인 이해만 가지고 있다면, 이전에 방문한 적이 없는 위치에서도 필드에서 자신의 위치를 파악할 수 있다는 것이다.

16 **어휘** inherently 선천적으로 / convey 전달하다

해석 말하기와 마찬가지로 대부분의 비언어적인 의사소통은 상징적인 행동이다: 특정 신체 동작이나 거리는 본질적으로 특정 메시지를 전달하지 않지만 관습이나 일반적인 이해로 인해서 특정 메시지를 전달한다. 많은 비언어적인 의사소통이 자의적이며 관습적이기 때문에 사람들이 비언어적인 메시지에 대해 동일한 의미를 공유하지 않을 때, 즉 사람들이 다른 관습들을 배웠을 때 오해 할 큰 가능성이 있다. 아마도 오해의 가능성은 음성 언어보다 비언어적인 메시지에서 더 크다. 서로 다른 문화권의 두 사람이 대화할 때, 둘 다 일반적으로 상대방의 언어를 이해하지 못한다는 것을 알고 있으므로 적어도 각 사람은 자신의 무지를 알고 있다. 그러나 둘 다 비언어적인 메시지들을 이해한다고 생각할 가능성이 높으므로 그들은 <u>아무것도 의도되지 않을 때 불쾌감을 주거나 받을 수 있다.</u>

17 **어휘** reassuring 안심시키는, 걱정을 없애주는

해석 사람들이 스트레스를 받을 때, 그들은 다르게 반응한다. 그들이 먹고 자지 않는 것은 어렵다. 그들은 짜증이 나고 성질을 낸다. 그들은 그렇지 않으면 말하지 않을 것들을 순간 화가 나서 말지도 모른다. 부부가 스트레스를 받으면 다르게 반응하는 경향이 있을 때, 한 파트너가 다른 파트너보다 훨씬 더 많은 영향을 받을 수 있으므로 관계가 손상된다. 해답은 스트레스의 근원을 확인하고 그것에 대해 행해질 수 있는 것을 확인하는 것이다. 첫째, 당신은 스트레스를 받고 있고 이것이 관계에 문제를 일으킨다는 사실을 인정해야 한다. 그런 다음 함께 앉아서 문제에 대해 이야기해라. 그것만으로도 스트레스를 덜어주기에 충분하다. 스트레스의 원인이 무엇이든 쉽고 빠르게 해결되지는 않을 것이다. 다만 그것을 인식하고 그것에 대처할 계획을 갖고 있는 것이 걱정을 없애준다. 훨씬 더 중요하게, 당신의 파트너와 함께 앉아서 그것에 대해 이야기함으로써 당신은 그것을 해결하기 위해 함께 일할 수 있다. "<u>고통을 나누면 반이 된다.</u>"는 말에는 많은 진실이 있다.

보기 ① 요리사가 너무 많으면 스프를 망친다.(= 어떤 일에 관여하는 사람이 너무 많으면 일을 망친다.)
② 서투른 일꾼이 연장을 탓한다.
③ 옆에 없으면 더 애틋해지는 법이다.
④ 고통은 나누면 반이 된다.
⑤ 위험할 땐 도망가는 것이 최선이다.(= 목숨이 위태로운 상황에서는 명분을 버리고 도망치는 것이 좋다.)

18 **어휘** neutralize 무효화시키다

해석 자주, 세미나를 마친 사람들은 나에게 다가와 재정 목표를 결정했다고 말한다. 내가 그것이 무엇인지 물어 보면, 그들은 내년이나 2년 안에 백만장자나 억만장자가 되기로 결심했다고 나에게 말한다. 거의 모든 경우에 이 사람들은 돈이 없거나 거의 없다고 판명된다. 그들은 종종 30대 또는 40대를 살고 있으며 평생 재무적인 관리가 이루어지지 않았다. 그럼에도 불구하고 그들은 과거의 모든 경험을 무효화할 수 있으며 조금 준비하고, 자원도 부족하고, 어떻게 부를 얻을지에 대한 명확한 생각 없이 어떻게든 부유함으로 도약할 수 있다고 생각한다. 그들은 그들이 해야 할 일은 행복한 생각을 생각하는 것 뿐이라고 믿고, 수십 년의 좌절과 실패를 극복하기 위해 필요한 모든 것을 그들은 마술처럼 끌어들일 것이라고 믿는다. 가능한 한 빨리 백만장자가 되기를 바라는 사람들이 나에게 말하면, 그들은 처음으로 "천 달러를 가진 사람"이 되라고 나는 제안한다. 그들이 천 달러를 모으고 부채에서 벗어나면, 그들은 "만 달러를 가진 사람"이 될 수 있고, 이어서 나갈 수 있다.

보기 ① 긍정적인 사고는 빚을 갚을 수 있다.
② 사람들은 달릴 수 있기 전에 걸어야 한다.
③ 만약 여러분이 정말 열심히 일한다면, 여러분은 짧은 시간 안에 부자가 될 것이다.
④ 당신은 직장을 떠나기 전에 여러 가지 행동 과정을 개발해야 한다.
⑤ 삶의 질은 어떻게 그가 과거의 경험을 무시하느냐에 달려 있다.

19 **어휘** stepping stone 초석, 디딤돌

해석 예비 교사의 가장 큰 두려움 중에는 그들이 가르치도록 요구되는 것과 그들이 수업을 가르치는 데 필요한 주제를 충분히 알고 있는지 여부가 포함됩니다. 귀하의 관할구역의 교육부는 귀하가 따라야 할 교과과정을 지시할 것입니다. 교과과정을 당신이 가르치도록 요구되고 학생들이 배워야 하는 정보의 초석으로 간주하십시오. 교과과정의 학습 결과를 따라야 하지만, 교과과정 문서들은 학생들을 가르치는 방법이나 평가방법을 밝히지 않습니다. 교과과정과 함께, 관할 지역의 학생 학습 비전과 일치하는 승인된 교과서가 종종 있습니다. 최고의 교사들은 교과과정과 교과서에만 의존하지 않고 학생들의 흥미에 따라 일부 영역을 확장합니다. 교과과정 및 교과서를 수업 계획 및 교육 지침으로 사용해야 하지만 이것이 전부는 아니어야 함을 기억하십시오.

20 **어휘** diverted 전환시키다, 전용하다

해석 국제 그리고 국내에서도, 관광은 더 부유하고 개발된 나라(선진국) 또는 지역에서 덜 개발되고 가난한 지역으로 부와 투자를 이동시키는 데 효과적인 것처럼 보인다. 이러한 부의 재분배는 이론적으로 목적지에서 여행객들의 지출과 관광시설에서 관광객을 발생시키는 더 부유한 나라들의 투자로 발생한다. 후자의 경우, 선진국은 원칙적으로 관광에 투자함으로써 저개발국의 경제 성장 및 개발을 지원한다. 그러나 여행자 지출의 순 보유액은 한 목적지에서 다른 곳으로 상당히 다양한 반면, 관광시설에 대한 해외 투자는 종종 착취와 의존으로 이어질 수 있다고 오랫동안 인식되어 왔다. 이것은 보통 후진국들로부터 상당히 전용된 이익으로 보일 수 있으며 잠재적으로 그들을 투자자 국가와 기업에 종속되게 만든다.

21 **어휘** extensive 광범위한

해석 우리가 기억 속에 저장해 온 일종의 개인적인 지식은 우리가 좋아하는 것과 싫어하는 것들의 지식이다. 이것은 개별적인 취향에 따른 매우 개인적인 지식이다. 예를 들어, 우리가 당신에게 좋아하는 종류의 수프가 무엇인지 물어 보면, 당신은 보르시치(폴란드 수프), 치킨 누들 또는 계란 수프라고 말할지도 모른다. 당신은 전에 많은 종류의 수프를 먹어보았기에, 당신이 가장 좋아하는 것이 무엇인지 기억하고, 알 수 있다. 그 기억을 바탕으로 집이나 식당에서 반복해서 그 음식만을 요청할 것이다. 마찬가지로 당신의 가장 친한 친구가 누구인지, 좋아하는 가수가 누구인지, 가장 좋아하는 축구팀은 무엇인지, 좋아하는 색상이나 책 또는 TV 프로그램은 무엇인지 쉽게 우리에게 말해줄 수 있다. 과거에 직접적으로 광범위한 경험을 했기 때문에 이러한 모든 것들을 기억할 수 있으며 다양한 경험을 쉽게 비교하고 대조하여 어느 것이 가장 즐거움을 주는지 확인할 수 있다.

22 **어휘** domesticated animal 가축 / utilize 활용하다

해설 코끼리가 그들의 임무를 다하는 것이 아니라 무시하거나 거절하는 것임으로 assume을 refuse나 ignore로 고쳐야 한다.

해석 가축들은 고대 전쟁에서 무기와 장비로 자주 이용되었다. 그리스 사람들은 종종 코끼리를 전쟁 장비로 사용했다. 주로 적에게 ① 겁을 주기 위한 의도로, 코끼리들은 머리 장식과 소리가 나는 종과 같은 장식품으로 정교하게 장식되었다. 그들은 때로 발효된 포도주를 받아 마셨고, 그것은 맹렬한 행동을 하도록 ② 고무시켰다. 그러나, 전선에서 코끼리를 사용하는 것은 전쟁 동물로서의 실용적 사용보다는 아마도 힘의 ③ 과시를 위한 것이었다. 코끼리는 인간들의 전쟁을 치르기에 ④ 효과적이지 않았고, 화살에 포격 당하면 코끼리가 돌아 서서 퇴각하여 종종 적군보다 자신의 군대에 더 많은 피해를 입혔다. 더 나아가, 여성 코끼리는 어린 아이와 헤어지면 싸우기를 거부하고, 즉시 모든 군대의 의무를 ⑤ 완수하고[→ 무시하고] 자식들이 부상당하거나 짓밟혀 운다면, 구출에 돌입할 것이었다.

23 어휘 firm 회사 / encounter 맞닥뜨리다 / watchdog 감시인, 감시 단체

해설 고객의 만족도가 수익성에 핵심효소라는 견해에 소비자들의 경험적 데이터는 일치하고 부합하는 것임으로, contradicting이 아닌 consistent with나 coincide with가 적합하다.

해석 회사들은 이익을 창출하기 위해 자본주의적 사회 속에서 존재한다. 만약 그 회사의 상품이 단지 소비자에게 단 한 번의 구매로만 비춰진다면(애완돌과 같은 비실용적인 물건들), 그 물건의 성능 수준이 규제에 대상이 아니라면, 그리고 오직 ① 제한된 상호간의 의사소통 채널이 소비자에게 열려있다면, 소비자의 만족도는 단순히 이익을 지향하는 회사에게서는 중요한 목표가 아닐 것이다. 그러나, 몇몇 생산자들인 이러한 조건들에 ② 마주친다. 대부분은 반복되는 구매가 ③ 수익성의 지속되는 흐름에 필수적이라고 생각한다. 구매주기가 긴 제품(예 : 주요 가전 제품, 자동차)의 경우에도 입소문과 소비자 동맹(Consumers Union)과 같은 지속적으로 만족보고들을 ④ 추적하는 수많은 감시 기관의 활동으로 인해 만족이 중요하다. 이제는 더욱 용이해지고 있는 만족도, 품질 및 기타 측정치들의 영향에 관한 경험적 데이터는 고객 만족도가 수익성의 핵심 요소라는 오랜 견해에 ⑤ 모순된다.[일치한다]

24 어휘 emphasize 강조하다 / legitimate 정당한

해석 심리 언어학 연구자들은 사람이 부정적인 것을 이해하는 데 걸린 시간의 약 2/3의 시간으로 긍정적인 진술을 이해할 수 있음을 발견했다. 당신의 인생의 유일한 목적이 다른 사람이 자신이 원하는 것을 할 수 있도록 동기를 부여하는 것이라 할지라도 건설적인 비판은 부정적인 공격보다 훨씬 더 멀리 당신을 옮겨놓을 것이다. 만약 누군가가 반쯤 옳고 반쯤 잘못된 상태로 무언가를 끝냈다면, 그가 제대로 작동하는 기술을 지속적으로 사용하기만 한다면 최종 결과가 얼마나 훌륭할지를 강조해라. 누군가의 옷이 매력적이고 세련된 것 같지만 그의 머리카락이 눈먼 이발사에 의해 잘려진 것처럼 보이면 그의 옷차림의 세련됨을 칭찬해라. 당신이 그의 외모를 바꿔줄 정당한 필요성이 느낀다면, 자신의 헤어스타일을 자신의 옷 스타일에 맞추면 더 좋아 보일 것이라고 제안해라. 비판만이 아니라 해결책을 제공해라. 다른 사람들에게 힌트를 얻을 수 있는 기회를 제공해라. 그렇지 않으면 당신은 그들이 그렇게 할 때까지 지속적으로 비판받을 것이다.

보기 ① 당신의 비판을 긍정적으로 유지하라.
② 왜 비판은 받아들이기 힘든가.
③ 성장에 대한 부정적인 비판 수용
④ 공치사를 인식하는 방법
⑤ 부정적인 피드백 제공의 가치

25 어휘 stereotypically 진부하게, 틀에 박힌

해석 사람들은 무의식적으로 자신의 비언어적인 행동의 모순들을 통해 거짓말을 하고 있다는 신호를 보낸다. 만약 당신이 거짓말 하는 누군가를 잡아본 적이 있다면, 대화의 뒷부분에서 만들어진 진술이 처음에 만들어진 진술과 모순된다거나 아마도 그나 그녀의 몸짓이 말하는 단어들과 모순되는 것처럼 보였다는 것을 알아차렸을지도 모른다. 그 사람은 조용하고 초연했지만, 동시에 자신의 발을 떨거나 버튼이나 보석을 만지면서 높은 음성으로 말하고 있었을지도 모른다. 법정에서의 증언에 대한 사람들의 인식에 대한 시험들은 틀에 박힌 사기성 행동이 반드시 의심을 불러일으키지는 않는다는 것을 보여 주지만 일관성 없는 비언어적 행동은 수행되는 특정 행동에 관계없이 종종 거짓이라고 해석된다. 연구는 사람의 전형적인 비언어적인 행동에 익숙해지면 속임수를 쉽게 발견할 수 있다고 밝혀 왔다. 특히 사람들은 상대방의 진실된 행동에 대한 이전의 경험이 있을 때 상대방이 진실을 말하고 있는지 거짓말하는지 더 잘 알 수 있다.

보기 ① 속임수를 드러내는 행동 패턴들
② 속임수로 이어지는 심리적 요인
③ 비언어적 메시지의 일반적인 특성
④ 속임수로부터 자유로운 강력한 관계 개발
⑤ 사람들의 진실 또는 속임수에 대한 부정확한 평가

26 어휘 periphery 주변부

해석 교육과 마찬가지로, 스포츠는 공통적으로 공유되는 핵심적 의미를 가지고 있으며, 추가적인 의미들의 주변은 문맥에 따라 크게 다르다. (①) 다른 말로, 우리 중 대부분은 스포츠가 무엇인지에 대해 공통적으로 이해하고 있지만, 여전히 다른 사람들에게 다른 것을 의미할 수 있다. (②) 일반적으로 우리는 축구는 스포츠라는 것을 인식하지만 볼룸 댄스는 그렇지 않다. 모터 레이싱은 스포츠다. 그러나 일하기 위한 운전은 그렇지 않다. 바다에서 보트를 항해하는 것은 스포츠이지만 유조선을 타고 항해하는 것은 아니다. (③) 그 단어가 사용될 때마다 스포츠가 의미하는 것을 정의할 필요는 없다. (④) 그러나, 같은 스포츠가 서로 다른 집단의 사람들에게서 다른 의미를 가질 수도 있다.) 이러한 서로 다른 의미의 예로서 테니스의 스포츠를 생각해 보자. 전문 테니스 선수에게 테니스는 직업이다. 동호회 선수에게, 아무리 경쟁적일지라도, 테니스는 근본적으로 오락이다; 윔블던 관중에게 테니스는 일시적인 기분 전환이나 모든 소비하는 대리 열정일지도 모른다.

27 어휘 altruism 이타주의 / sibling 형제자매

해석 플라밍고, 펭귄, 타조, 기린, 돌고래, 악어 등 많은 종들이 그들이 새끼를 잠시 다른 어른들에 보호 속에 남겨둔다. 이를 통해 부모는 가족을 부양하기 위한 가장 영양가 있는 음식을 찾아 볼 자유를 가질 수 있다. (①) 그 새끼를 돌보는 대리 부모들은 누구인가? (②) 그 보모는 무작위로 회전하는 부모일 수도 있고 부모와 알고지내는 비번식자 일수도 있다. (③) 이타주의처럼 보일 수도 있지만, 보모는 단지 자신이 돌보고 있는 어린 조카 또는 형제자매에게 묶여있는 자신의 유전자를 증진시키는 것일 뿐이다.(④) 그들의 목표가 그들의 유전자를 발전시키는 것이라면, 왜 자신의 새끼를 갖지 않는가? (⑤) 안전하고 완전히 차지된 서식지에서, 충분한 둥지가 부족하거나 임신한 동물들이 자신을 부양하기에 그 해에 이용 가능한 음식이 충분하지 않을지도 모른다.) 가장자리 둥지 부지로 억지로 쫓겨나기 보다는 1년을 연기할 수 있고, 그 사이에 더 나은 부모로 만들어줄 기술들을 배울 수도 있다.

28 어휘 consumption 소비

해석 일상생활에서 사람들은 소비의 여러 측면에 반복적으로 노출된다. 광고, 기차 여행, 식료품 쇼핑, 텔레비전 시청, 음악 청취, 인터넷 서핑, 쇼핑 의류, 책 읽는 것은 모두 사람들이 소비하는 것들의 사례들이다. 인간이 참여하는 거의 모든 행동은 직간접적으로 소비와 관련되어 있다. 크리스마스와 같은 전통적인 휴일조차도 주로 소비에 대한 것이다. 원래 종교적인 휴일이었던 것을 산타클로스가 선물을 전달하는 가장 전형적인 예를 사용하여 소비의 측면으로 바뀌었다. 기본적으로 소비는 인간의 일상생활의 일부라는 사실을 피할 방법이 없다. 그러므로 소비가 개인과 집단에 어떤 영향을 미치는지 연구하지 않고 우리가 인간을 이해한다고 진정으로 말할 수 없다.

29 어휘 complications arise[set in] 복잡한 문제가 생기다

해석 한 예술가가 자신의 문화적 경험에서 벗어난 이야기를 설명하려고 할 때 문제들이 발생한다. 만약 그 예술가가 특정 영역에 배경지식이 거의 없고 연구를 철저히 조사할 의지가 전혀 없거나 할 수 없는 경우, 특히 그 시도가 "원래의" 스타일들을 모방하도록 만들어진다면, 삽화들을 통해 이야기를 잘못 전달할 위험이 있다. 외부인이 자신들이 쓸 전반적인 상황을 이해하지 못하고 세부 사항을 효과적으로 추출하는 것은 매우 어렵다. 그것은 할 수 없다는 말은 아니다. 예를 들어, 에드 영(Ed Young)은 그가 다른 문화권의 전통 이야기를 위해 만든 작품에서 확실한 세부 사항에 주의를 기울이는 것으로 유명하다. 예를 들어 Kimiko Kajikawa's Tsunami에서, 영은 19세기 중반 일본의 의복, 헤어스타일 및 건축물 특성을 정확하게 묘사한다.

30 어휘 endorsement 지지, 보증

해석 스포츠 마케팅은 새로운 것이 아니다. 유료 입장을 요구했던 최초의 운동 경기는 관람객에게 50센트씩 청구한 1858년 뉴욕 롱 아일랜드(New York)의 야구 경기였다. 스포츠 주최자들은 곧 스포츠 경기 및 프로 운동선수의 재정적 잠재력을 깨달았다. 골퍼 진 사라센(Golfer Gene Sarazen)은 1923년 윌슨 스포츠 용품 (Wilson Sporting Goods)과 보증 계약을 체결했다. 최초 계약은 연간 6,000달러에 여행 경비를 합산한 액수였다. 1949년 Babe Didrikson Zaharias는 Wilson Sporting Goods와 함께 1년에 10만 달러로 첫 번째 중요한 여성 보증 계약에 서명했다. 코카콜라는 1928년 하계 올림픽과 제휴를 맺고 현재까지도 후원사로 남아있다. 최초의 유료 시청 체육 대회는 1975년 필리핀에서 조 프레이저(Joe Frazier)를 상대하는 무하마드 알리(Muhammad Ali)의 권투 시합인 "마닐라의 스릴라(Thrilla in Manila)"였다. 276개의 유선채널로 방송되었다. 스포츠의 인기를 바탕으로 ESPN은 1979년에 데뷔하여 광고주에게 목표 시장에 도달할 수 있는 새로운 방법을 제시했다. 오늘날 많은 고등학교와 대학에서는 스포츠 마케팅 프로그램을 제공한다.

보기 ① 스포츠 마케팅의 출현과 확장
② 스포츠 마케팅 활동을 위한 효과적인 예산 책정
③ 스포츠 마케팅에 영향을 미치는 사회적 변화
④ 스포츠 마케팅에 대한 오해
⑤ 스포츠 후원의 어두운 면

31 어휘 propaganda 선전

해석 세기 초에, 광고에 대한 관심이 커지면서 광고의 잠재력을 볼 수 있는 것은 제조업체들만은 아니었다. 정치인들 또한 "제품을 판매하는 방법"이 자신의 아이디어를 판매하는 데 적용될 수 있다는 것을 깨달았을 때 관심을 갖게 되었다. 이것은 제1차 세계 대전 중 선전 운동이 사람들이 계속 싸우도록 유도하는 도구로 사용되었을 때 특히 두드러졌다. 예를 들어 영국인과 미국인은 적군 병사들로 비누를 만드는 것과 같은 독일인의 소름끼치는 행동에 관한 소문을 퍼트렸다. 이것은 사람들로 하여금 그러한 끔찍한 국가가 전쟁에서 승리하도록 허용할 수 없으므로 싸우는 것을 계속할 가치가 있다고 생각할 수 있도록 하기 위해 행해졌다. 많은 소위 "극악 이야기"가 사용되었고 일부는 사실의 요소를 포함하고 있지만 많은 것은 영국과 미국 정부의 이익을 위해서만 날조되었다. 그럼에도 불구하고 이들은 정치적 의제를 국민에게 판매하는 데 효과적이었던 것으로 보인다.

보기 ① 다양한 문화에서 다른 광고 방법들
② 선전으로 야기된 정치적·사회적 갈등
③ 광고 선전의 영향력 증가
④ 광고와 선전의 차이점
⑤ 정치 문제에 대한 광고의 적용

32 어휘 doctorate 박사학위 / master's degree 석사학위

해설 ③ 박사학위가 아닌 석사학위를 취득했다.

해석 Romain Rolland는 1915년 그의 문학 작품의 고상한 이상주의에 대한 기여로 노벨 문학상을 수상한 프랑스 극작가, 소설가 및 미술 사학자였다. 그는 1866년 니예브 클레시(Cléecy)에서 태어났다. 우수한 학생인 그는 École Normale Supérieure에 입학하여 예술과 음악에 중력을 기울이기 전에 그곳에서 철학을 공부했다. 1889년 졸업 후 르네상스 이탈리아의 걸작을 연구하면서 이탈리아에서 수년을 보냈다. 프랑스로 돌아온 Rolland는 1895년 초 유럽 오페라 연구에서 박사학위를 받았다. 같은 해 <u>그는 16세기 이탈리아 유화에 관한 논문 석사학위를 취득했다.</u> 그는 1912년까지 대학에서 가르쳤다. 그는 자신의 지위를 사임하면서 글쓰기에 전념했다. 그의 가장 위대한 문학 작품은 연극 형태로 나왔다. 그는 연극이 육체적으로나 지적으로 대중들에게 환영을 받아야한다고 굳게 믿었다. 그는 관객들에게 프랑스의 혁명 역사를 연상시키는 연극을 선호했다.

33 해설 ④ 도표에 따르면 2013년 일본에서 판매된 차량의 수는 같은 해 중국에서 판매된 차량의 약 4분의 1이다.

해석 위의 그래프는 2009년과 2013년 사이 5대 경제 대국에서 판매된 차량 수를 나타낸다. ① 5년 동안 중국은 미국을 계속 앞서며 지속적으로 가장 큰 자동차 판매량을 보여주었다. ② 중국에서 판매된 차량 수는 2009년 1400만대, 2013년 2,100만대 이상으로 매년 꾸준히 증가했다. ③ 중국과 미국에서 판매된 차량 수의 격차는 2009년에는 300만대 이상, 2013년에는 500만대 이상이었다. ④ 매년 세 번째로 많은 차량이 일본에서 판매되지만, 2013년에 일본에서 판매된 차량의 수는 같은 해 중국에서 판매된 차량의 3분의 1이다. ⑤ 매년 4번째로 많은 차량이 독일에서 판매되었으나 5년 중에 어떤 해에도 400만대가 판매되지 못했고, 프랑스는 매년 최소 차량 판매량을 기록했다.

34 어휘 indication 말(암시/조짐) / perceptual constancy 지각 항등성

해석
> 너는 친구가 너를 향해 달려오고 있다는 것을 본다. 그가 다가올수록 그는 점점 커진다. 그러나 너는 그가 실제로 성장하는 것이 아니라, 너의 친구가 가까워지고 있다는 것을 알고 있다.

(B) 이것은 당신의 기억 속에 사람들의 크기에 대한 지식을 가지고 있고, 사람들이 그렇게 빠르기 크기를 바꿀 수 없다는 것을 알기 때문이다. 사실, 망막의 이미지는 확장하고 있으며, 그리고 그 확장의 속도는 너의 친구의 경우에서처럼 대상이 얼마나 빠르게 다가오고 있는가에 대한 지표이다.

(A) 마찬가지로, 자동차가 너를 지나가거나 거리를 두고 벗어날 때, 그것은 점점 작아진다. 그러나 사이즈의 인식이 망막의 이미지에서의 변화로부터 예측되는 것과 크게 다르지는 않다고 알려진다.

(C) 이러한 것들이 지각 항등성의 사례들이다. 기본적으로 우리는 자동차가 멀어지는 것을 경험하거나 한 사람이 가까이 다가오는 것을 본다. 우리는 크기가 변하는 우리 자신에 모습을 걱정하지 않는다. 우리는 깊이면에서 움직임을 주는 것으로써 정보를 해석한다.

35 어휘 continuously 계속해서

해석
> 사람들을 지도하는 것으로부터 가장 가치 있는 결과들 중에 하나는 당신이 감독하는 과정 속에서 당신 자신을 발전시킬 수 있다는 것이다. 우리가 우리 자신을 변화시키도록 밀어 넣는 다른 사람들을 기르는 것은 진정한 열정과 의도이다.

(C) 다른 사람들을 발전시키기 위해, 우리는 먼저 우리 자신을 발전시켜야 한다. 그리고 지속적으로 다른 사람을 변화시키기 위해서, 우리는 계속적으로 우리 자신을 변화시킬 수밖에 없다.

(B) 감독기간 동안에, 우리는 직접적인 경험을 얻고 코칭 기술을 연습한다. 감독 후에는, 우리는 대화 동안 무엇이 발생했고, 무엇이 잘 되었으며, 무엇이 그렇지 않았고, 어떻게 다음 번에 우리가 더 잘 할 수 있는지를 되돌아 본다.

(A) 이러한 학습의 순환은 전 감독 관계 속에서 계속해서 돌고 돈다. 우리가 더 많은 사람을 감독할수록, 우리의 전문적이고 개인적인 삶속의 많은 측면들에서 우리를 도와줄 감독에 있어서의 지식과 기술 그리고 능력들을 되풀이하여 가르친다.

36 어휘 durable 내구성이 있는 / fragile 부서지기 쉬운 / expire 만료되다 / prevail 만연하다 / attachment 애착 / aversion 혐오감

해석 과거에는 검소와 절약이 당시의 질서였다. 아무리 작은 가치를 지니고 있다고 하더라도 아무 것도 버려지지 않았다. 구입한 모든 제품은 중요했으며 모든 달러는 절약할 가치가 있었다. 오늘날 제품은 (A) 내구성이 떨어지며 이는 버려짐을 의미한다. 담배 라이터, 콘택트 렌즈, 시계 및 카메라조차도 버려지게 되었다. 유사하게도, 의류 및 액세서리는 일단 스타일이 촌스러워지면 유용성이 만료된다는 점에서 (B) 수명을 다한다. 새로운 쇼핑 트렌드와 관련하여 이것은 나이와 상관없이 소비자들이 사물들이 신속하고 쉽게 폐기되는 세상에서 생활하는 데 점점 더 익숙해진다는 것을 의미한다. 그리고 그것들은 새로운 것을 사기 위해 교체된다. 삶의 속도가 꾸준히 증가함에 따라 더 많은 버려지는 제품들의 수요가 증가하고 있다. 개인 제품에 대한 우리의 감정적인 (C) 애착은 시간이 지남에 따라 줄어들고 있으며, 이는 더 많은 제품에 대한 더 많은 요구가 있음을 의미한다.

37 어휘 abstract 추상적인 / postpone 연기하다 / exaggerate 과장하다

해석
> 심리학적 연구에서 연구자들은 두 그룹의 학생들에게 설문지를 작성하여 전자 메일로 응답하도록 요청했다. 모든 질문은 은행 계좌 개설과 같은 일상적인 업무와 관련이 있었다. 그러니 두 그룹은 질문에 대답하기 위한 다른 지시를 받았다. 첫 번째 그룹의 학생들은 어떤 개인이 은행 계좌를 가지고 있는지와 같은 개인적인 특성과 같은 일부 무형의 정보에 대해 활동이 암시한 바를 써야 했다. 두 번째 그룹은 과정의 특정 단계에 대해 간단하게 기록했다. 즉, 은행 출납원에게 말하고, 양식을 채우고, 초기 입금을 하는 등의 작업이었다. 두 그룹의 응답 시간 간에는 상당한 차이가 있음이 입증되었다. 첫 번째 그룹의 학생들은 연기하는 경향이 있었다. 실제로 일부는 전혀 완료하지 못했다. 대조적으로 두 번째 그룹의 학생들은 방법, 시기 및 장소에 초점을 맞추어 첫 번째 그룹보다 빨리 과제를 완료했다.

연구에서, 더 추상적인 관점으로 생각을 요구하는 임무를 받은 첫 번째 집단은 다른 집단의 학생들보다 더 높은 수준으로 그들의 대답을 연기한다고 드러났다.

✧ [38~39]

어휘 ecosystem 생태계 / Disease ecologists 질병 생태학자 / susceptible 민감한 / hypothermia 저체온증

해석 인간의 건강에 대한 생태학적 접근은 보다 넓은 생태계의 일부로서 인간을 고려한다. 질병 생태학자들은 인간과 그들이 살고 있는 환경 사이의 상호 작용에 초점을 맞추고 장소를 걸친 건강과 질병의 패턴을 기술하고 설명하는 것을 돕는다. 인간은 그들을 질병과 건강에 더 또는 덜 견뎌내도록 만드는 다양한 방식으로 그들의 환경과 상호작용한다. 예를 들어, 추운 날씨에 너무 오래 머무르는 것은 저체온, 위험할 정도로 낮은 체온의 상태를 야기할 수 있고, 또는 태양에 너무 많이 노출되면 피부암의 발병을 촉진시킬 수 있다. (A) 그러나, 모든 연결이 직접적인 것은 아니다. 질병 생태학이 질병 패턴을 설명하는데 유용하게 사용되는 주된 방법 중 하나는 환경의 어떤 특징들이 질병을 야기하는 유기체나 그것들을 옮기는 매개곤충이 살 수 있는 장소에 영향을 끼치는지를 고려함으로써이다. (B) 예를 들어, 많은 질병이 일년 내내 따뜻한 온도로 인해 모기와 같은 매개 곤충이 번성할 수 있는 열대 기후에 국한되어 있다. 온난한 기온은 또한 바이러스 및 박테리아와 같은 미생물뿐만 아니라 이들을 전달하는 무척추 동물의 번식률을 높여 인간 사이의 질병 전파를 더욱 빠르게 할 수 있다. 사람과 질병 전염의 주체들 사이의 관계를 분석하는 것은 질병 생태학자의 첫 번째 초점 중 하나였으며 오늘날에도 질병 생태학의 근본적인 부분으로 남아있다.

38 보기 ① 질병 예방을 위한 효과적인 위생 관행
② 과학 분야로서의 질병 생태의 기원
③ 전형적인 질병 유발 생물의 진화
④ 환경 변화가 질병의 확산에 미치는 영향
⑤ 질병 생태학자들의 우려 : 환경 및 인간 질병

38 해설 (A) 앞에서 나열한 예들이 모두 직접적인 연결은 아니라는 내용이 이어지므로 역접의 'However'가 적절하다.
(B) 앞에서 이야기한 내용에 대한 예가 이어지고 있으므로 'For example'이 적절하다.

[40~41]

어휘 purposeful 결단력 있는 / proximity 가까움 / tribe 부족

해석

> Machu Picchu는 요새 아래 2,000피트에 위치한 Urubamba강으로 둘러싸여 있다. 이 강은 자연이 그들에게 신성했기 때문일 뿐만 아니라 자연이 그들에게 가져다 주는 이점들 때문에 잉카 사람들에게 신성한 것으로 여겨졌다. 그것은 Machu Picchu가 있는 산 주위를 구부러지고 어떤 농경지는 강으로 길을 확장한다. Machu Picchu의 위치에서 강을 항해할 수는 없지만 보트를 타고 아마존 강과 대서양으로 이동하여 사람과 물자를 이동시킬 수 있다. 이것은 사람들이 Machu Picchu로 직접 이동하는 것을 피하기 위해 의도적이었지만 여전히 (A) 운송의 상대적으로 가까운 경로를 제공한다. 열대 우림과의 근접성은 분명히 Machu Picchu의 지형의 또 다른 이점이었다. 열대 우림은 다채로운 조류 깃털, 나비, 코카 잎, 이국적인 과일과 채소 및 치유 허브와 같은 잉카 문명의 희귀한 제품의 유일한 원천이었다. 잉카 사람들은 감자, 기니피그, 보석, 퀴노아, 금과 같이 그들에게 없는 것들을 위해 열대 우림의 부족들과 본인들의 물건들을 교환하였고 그것들을 종교적인 의식에서 사용하곤 했다. Machu Picchu를 건축할 때 잉카 사람들은 (B) (거래)무역경로로 열대 우림에 가까운 혜택을 고려했음에 틀림이 없다.

40 해설 ② Machu Picchu 건설에 있어, 잉카 사람들은 그들의 주변 지형을 고려했다.

41 해설 이 글은 Machu Picchu의 운송과 무역에 관한 글이다.

✦ [42~43]

어휘 national anthem 국가(國歌) / be called to task 나무람을 듣다 / subtly 미묘하게 / swallowed the bait 미끼를 삼키다, 덫에 걸리다 / intimidate 겁을 주다

해석

> 제2차 세계 대전 중, 작곡가 드미트리 쇼스타코비치(Dmitry Shostakovich)와 그의 동료 몇 명이 러시아의 통치자 조셉 스탈린(Joseph Stalin)과의 미팅에 요청받았고 그는 새로운 국가를 쓰라고 그들에게 의뢰했다. Shostakovich는 스탈린과의 만남들이 (A) 무서웠다는 것을 들었다 : 하나의 실수가 당신을 어두운 복도로 끌고 가버릴 수도 있었다. 그는 당신이 목구멍이 조여짐을 느낄 때까지 당신을 내려다보며 응시했고, 그리고 스탈린과의 만남이 종종 그러했듯이 이번 만남도 나쁜 방향으로 나아갔다 : 통치자는 형편없는 편곡을 이유로 작곡가 중 한 명을 비판하기 시작했다. 어리석게도 겁을 먹고, 그 남자는 형편없게 일하는 한 편곡자를 사용했다고 인정했다. 여기서 그는 몇 개의 무덤들을 파고 있었다 : 분명히 형편없는 편곡자도 책망을 받을 것이다. 그 작곡자는 형편없는 편곡자의 (B) 고용에 책임이 있었고, 그도 역시 실수를 책임져야 했다. 그러면 Shostakovich를 포함한 다른 작곡가들은? 스탈린은 일단 그가 두려움을 느끼면 잔인해질 수 있었다. Shostakovich는 충분히 들었다 : 그는 주로 명령을 따르는 편곡자를 비난하는 것은 어리석은 것이었다고 말했다. 그린 다음 그는 작곡가가 자신이 직접 관현악 작곡을 해야 할시의 다른 주제로 대화의 방향을 미묘하게 바꿨다. 이 문제에 대해 스탈린은 어떻게 생각했을까? 그는 항상 자신의 전문성을 증명하기를 열망하기에, 그는 미끼를 물었다. 위험한 순간이 지나갔다.
>
> 쇼스타코비치는 여러 면에서 침착성을 유지했다. 첫째, 스탈린이 그를 협박하게 만드는 대신에, 그는 자신을 그와 같은 짧고, 뚱뚱하고, 못생기고, 상상력이 없는 남자처럼 보이도록 만들었다. 따라서 독재자의 유명한 날카로운 시선은 그저 자신의 불안정을 나타내는 속임수였다. 둘째, 쇼스타코비치는 스탈린을 똑바로 쳐다보고 평범하게 그리고 직접적으로 이야기했다. 그의 행동과 목소리로, 그 작곡가는 자신이 협박당하지 않았음을 보여 주었다.

42 **어휘** fascinating 매력적인 / terrifying 무서운 / hire 고용 / dismissal 해고 / creativity 창조성 / insecurity 불안정

43 **해설** ④ Stalin은 자신이 전문적 지식을 지녔음을 입증하는 것을 원했다.

어휘 majestic 장엄한

해석

(A) Don이 25살 때 그는 동남아시아로 배낭여행을 갔다. 그 3주 동안, 그는 부키팅기(Bukittinggi)라고 불리는 아름다운 마을에 잠깐 들르는 것을 포함해서, 인도네시아 주변을 여행했다. 게스트하우스에서 그는 스웨덴에서 온 좋은 친구인 Stephen을 만났고 그는 (a) <u>그</u>가 오랫동안 쉬고 있는 화산 꼭대기 인근 호수를 탐험할 것을 권했다.

(D) (e) <u>그</u>의 조언에 따라, Don은 그를 데려갈 버스를 발견했다. 그렇게 가깝지 않았고 오히려 가파르고 바람 불고 다소 위험한 길을 올라가는 4시간짜리 여정이었다. 꼭대기의 경치가 장관이었기 때문에 그것은 가치가 있었다. 한때는 화산의 입이었던 산꼭대기에 엄청나게 장엄한 호수가 있었다. Stephen에 의하면, 그것은 걷는 데 약 2시간이 걸릴 아름다운 길에 둘러싸여 있었다.

(B) 호수로의 (b) <u>그</u>의 트레킹을 시작할 때, Don은 산을 내려가는 마지막 버스가 오후 5시에 떠난다는 사실을 알고 있었다, 그래서 그는 확실히 그 시간에 버스정류장으로 돌아와야 했다. 오후 한 시였을 때, 그는 그가 산 아래로 내려갈 마지막 버스로 제시간에 돌아가고 호수 주변의 길을 걸을 충분한 시간이 있다는 것을 알았다. 정말 멋진 하이킹이었다. 그러나, 오후 4시가 되었을 무렵, 그는 (c) <u>그</u>가 호수 주변 절반 도처 어딘가에 있다는 것을 깨달았다.

(C) 그는 그가 온 길을 되돌아 내려가기로 결심했다. 그는 버스 정류장에 가까이 갔을 때 마지막 버스가 (d) <u>그</u>를 두고 가버리는 것을 보았다. 숨차하며, 그는 산을 걸어 내려가는 것밖에 선택의 여지가 없었고, 다른 사람들이 그를 데리러 오기를 희망했다. 그는 심지어 어떤 차량이 오기 전에 몇 시간 동안 걸어야 했다. 다행히 결국 멋진 인도네시아 신사가 도움을 주려고 멈춰 섰다. 그는 그 상황을 매우 동정했고 Don을 그의 게스트하우스로 데려다 주었다. Don은 표현할 수 있는 것보다 더 감사해 했다.

44 **해설** 여정에 따라 순서를 나열하면 (A) – (D) – (B) – (C)이다.

45 **해설** (e)는 Stephen을, 나머지는 Don을 가리킨다.

2019학년도 정답 및 해설

01	02	03	04	05	06	07	08	09	10	11	12	13	14	15	16	17	18	19	20
⑤	②	②	④	①	②	③	②	①	①	④	①	②	④	⑤	③	④	⑤	④	③
21	22	23	24	25	26	27	28	29	30	31	32	33	34	35	36	37	38	39	40
④	②	⑤	⑤	③	①	①	③	①	⑤	③	⑤	②	④	③	④	②	②	③	③
41	42	43	44	45															
①	⑤	⑤	③	⑤															

01 해석 Ms. Smith : 자, 여러분, 이제 태양계를 다시 들여다 보겠습니다.

Sunny : 선생님, 또 봐야 하나요? 지난 주에 공부했었고, 너무 지겨워요, 행성들, 달 등등.

Ms. Smith : 음, Sunny, 그러면 아마 네가 몇 가지 질문에 답해볼 수 있겠네. 만약 네가 태양계에 대해 잘 알고 있다면 우린 네가 원하는 것을 공부할 거야. 괜찮지?

Sunny : 네, 멋지네요! 선생님, 정말 최고에요. 물어보세요.

Ms. Smith : 첫질문: 화성은 몇 개의 달이 있을까?

Sunny : 쉽네요. 하나죠.

Ms. Smith : 미안하지만 첫 번째 시도에서 틀렸구나, 두 개란다.

Sunny : 아, 제가 그걸 어떻게 알 수 있겠어요? 거기 가 본 적도 없는데!

보기 ① Smith 선생님은 학생들이 태양계에 대해 다시 공부해야 한다고 생각하지 않는다.

② Sunny는 행성과 달에 대해 굉장히 흥미가 있다.

③ Sunny는 그녀가 왜 Smith 선생님 질문에 대답해야 하는지 이해하지 못한다.

④ Sunny는 Smith 선생님의 첫 질문에 올바른 대답을 했다.

⑤ Smith 선생님은 sunny에게 화성은 두 개의 달이 있다고 말해 준다.

02 어휘 starving 몹시 굶주린 / transit pass 교통카드 / hop 뛰어오르다, 타다

해석 Julie : 배고파 죽을 것 같아. 강 근처에 괜찮은 치킨 파는 데가 많이 있어.

Rachel : 멋진데. 근데 여기서 꽤 멀지 않아? <u>어떻게 가는지 잘 모르겠어.</u>

Julie : 음, 지하철이 있잖아. 나 교통카드 있어. 넌 있니?

Rachel : 아니, 거기다 우리가 내내 돌아다녀서 내 발이 벌써 아파. 우리 지하철역까지 계속 걸어가야 하잖아.

Julie : <u>택시 타도 돼.</u> (지하철이) 더 싼 게 아니라면 그게 더 편하겠다.

Rachel : 아냐. 나 돈이 그렇게 많지 않아.

Julie : 그러면, 내 생각에 그냥 버스타야 할 것 같아. <u>바로 가는 버스 하나 있어.</u>

03 `해석` Dan : 저기 저것 봐! 너 저런 거 본 적 있어?

Paul : 어.. 물론 티비에서, 근데 저 식물은 눈으로 직접 보면 좀 무서워 보일거야. 마치 이빨이 있는 것 같아.

Dan : 맞아. 근데 저거는 이빨이 아니야. 그냥 특이한 잎들이지. 저건 여기서 가장 독특한 식물중 하나야.

Paul : 음, 그러면 더 가까이 가보자.

Dan : 좋아, 근데 있잖아. 이제 생각해 봤는데, 냄새가 너무 나면 나 갈거야. 아침을 많이 먹어서 다 뱉어내고 싶지 않아.

Paul : 철 좀 들어. 이건 자연이야. 어떤 꽃들은 냄새가 고약하기도 해.

Dan : 넌 알아서 해. 난 코를 막을 거야.

`보기` ① 유령의 집에서 ② 식물원에서 ③ 재활용센터에서 ④ 화장품 가게에서 ⑤ 아쿠아리움에서

04 `해석` Nick : 우리 어젯밤에 본 그 영화 정말 괜찮더라. 훌륭했어!

John : 그래? 내 기대에는 못 미치던데. 후속편은 절대 1편 만하지 못해.

Nick : 동의할 수 없어. 내 생각엔 영화 어벤저스 2는 1편만큼 괜찮았어.

John : 응, 네 말 인정해, 하지만 아이언맨은? 아이언맨 2는 별로였어.

Nick : 그렇긴 한데 다른 아이언맨 후속작 3편은 훌륭했잖아!

John : 맞아. 그건 일리가 있어.

Nick : 그리고 앤트맨 2! 그거 정말 1편만큼, 아니 훨씬 더 괜찮지 않았어?

John : 응, 니 말이 맞아. 내가 일반화하기 전에 좀 더 생각해야겠네.

`보기` ① 두 사람은 어젯밤 영화를 같이 봤다.

② Nick은 John의 후속편이 1편보다 별로라는 생각에 동의하지 않는다.

③ John은 어벤저스 2가 1편만큼 괜찮았다는 걸 인정한다.

④ 두 사람은 아이언맨 2가 훌륭했다라는 데 동의한다.

⑤ John은 앤트맨 2가 1편처럼 훌륭한 영화라는 Nick의 생각을 받아들인다.

05 `해석` 의사 : 어디가 문제인가요?

환자 : 제가 위장에 통증이 있어요. 오른쪽 아래 여기.

의사 : 여기 누워 보세요. 제가 여기에 이렇게 누르면 아픈가요?

환자 : 아야, 네 굉장히 아프네요. 다시 누르지 않으셨음 해요.

의사 : 체온을 재 봅시다. 음, 예상대로 꽤 높군요.

환자 : 예상대로요? 의사선생님, 뭐가 문제인지 벌써 알고 계신 건가요?

의사 : 문제가 뭔지 확실하네요. 제 생각엔 수술을 해야 할 것 같습니다. 하지만 확실한 건, 수술일정 전에 한 단계가 더 있습니다. <u>또 다른 검사를 해봐야겠어요.</u>

06 `해석` Lisa : 나 John과 레스토랑을 차릴 거야!

Suzy : 엄청나게 용감한데. 전체 레스토랑의 50%가 첫해에 실패한다고 들었어.

Lisa : 넌 믿음을 가져야 해. 우린 오랫동안 요리를 해왔고 그래서 멋진 식당을 차릴 수 있을거야.

Suzy : 어떤 요리를 제공할 생각이야?

Lisa : 멕시칸이나 베트남 요리로 좁혀 봤어.

Suzy : 와우, 그 두 개는 꽤 다른 스타일인데. 그 두 개를 특별히 생각한 이유가 뭐야?

Lisa : 멕시코 요리는 굉장히 유명하지만 경쟁을 많이 해야 하고, 베트남 요리는 다소 생소해서 좋은데 반면에 사람들이 그 요리에 별로 익숙하지 않아.

Suzy : 음, 너 대출받으러 은행가기 전에 결정을 내려야 할 거야.

① Suzy는 레스토랑을 새로 열 것이고 좋은 요리사를 찾으려 하고 있다.
② Lisa와 John은 레스토랑을 열 것이지만 요리에 대해선 최종결정을 내리지 못했다.
③ Lisa와 Suzy는 오늘 밤 레스토랑에서 어떤 음식 종류를 먹을지 결정하려고 한다.
④ Suzy는 Lisa가 레스토랑을 위한 대출을 받을 수 있도록 함께 은행에 갈 것이다.
⑤ Suzy는 Lisa의 새 레스토랑이 성공할 것을 확신하지만 Lisa는 그렇지 못하다.

07

어휘 at hand 가까이에, 곧, 바로 쓸 수 있는 / render 만들다. 주다 / intuition 직관 / regardless of ~와 상관없이 / gut feeling 직감

해석 모든 결정이 완벽한 자료로부터 만들어지는 것은 아니다. 비록 가장 가능성 있는 해결책을 주기 위해 준비된 자료를 모두 사용하는 것이 중요하겠지만, 때로는 당신은 여전히 정보를 놓치고 있고 그 해결책이 확실해 보이지 않기도 한다. 이런 경우에는 당신의 직관이 길잡이가 되어 주어야 한다. 이는 자료가 어떤 방향을 가리키고 있는가와 무관하게 스스로를 믿고 있고 당신이 믿는 것이 진실인가에 귀 기울이고 있다는 것을 의미한다. 당신이 결정을 내리는 과정을 겪고 있고 쓰레기정보를 제거해서 좋은 정보만을 수집하기 위해 그물망으로 휘젓고 있을 때, 당신이 모은 정보에 대해 어떻게 느끼는지 자문해 볼 것을 기억해 둬라. 이것은 매우 중요하다. 가장 훌륭한 결정들은 명료한 선택을 해주는 좋은 자료를 결합하고 "딩신은 올바른 신댁을 했다."라고 하는 느낌을 주는 것들이다.

08

어휘 adjust 조정하다. 순응하다 / affliction 고뇌 / trial 시련 / deprivation 박탈 / disguise 가장, 변장 / friction 마찰

해석 우리가 즉시, 또는 아마 결코 다룰 수 없는 어려움들이 있다. 바뀔 수 없는 것을 참아내는 인내심을 가질 것을 기억하는 것 뿐 아니라, 불가능해 보이는 상황에 순응하는 다른 방식들도 있다. 많은 정신적 스승들은 고뇌, 시련, 고통 그리고 박탈을 내적 정신력이 자극되고 정화되고 고상해지는 "위장한 축복"으로 여긴다. 공자는 "보석은 마찰 없이는 광이 날 수 없고 인간도 시련 없이 완벽해질 수 없다"라고 말했다. 반면 Helen Keller는 "나는 나의 신체장애에 대해 신에게 감사한다. 왜냐하면 장애를 통해 나 스스로를, 내 일을, 나의 신을 발견했기 때문이다."라고 글을 썼다. 만약 우리가 불리한 조건들을 올바르게 사용한다면, 인생에서 실패, 시험, 어려움들이 우리의 정신을 정화시키고 기질을 강화시키는 수단이 될 수 있다. ʻAbduʼl-Bahá의 인용은 이것을 특히 잘 보여준다: "우리는 모든 장애물을 진보하는 디딤돌로 만들도록 노력해야 한다."

보기 ① 교육을 받을수록 더욱더 문명화된다.
② 역경은 성취로 이어진다.
③ 남에게 대접받고 싶은 대로 남을 대하라.
④ 협동은 기적을 낳는다.
⑤ 잘 생각해 보고 행동하라. / 돌다리도 두드리고 건너라.

09

어휘 insist on ~ing 계속 ~하다 / deem 여기다

해석 웹사이트가 당신에게 "다시 보지 않기"라는 창에 체크하도록 물었을 때 많은 사람들은 기꺼이 그 창에 체크하게 된다. 만약 공무원이나 의사가 선택형 문제를 올려놓고 당신에게 같은 질문들이 있는 수많은 양식을 기입하도록 요청한다면, 당신은 엄청나게 좌절해서 적어도 그런 선택지 중 일부가 당신을 위해 만들어졌기를 바랄 것이다. 공공기관과 사설기관들이 기존의 서식채우기 요건을 극적으로 줄인다면 사람들에겐 상황이 더 나아진다. 그리고 택시운전사가 당신이 낯선 도시에서 어떤 길을 가길 원하는지 선택하도록 계속 요구한다면 당신은 그가 묻지 않고 그냥 최고라고 여기는 길을 선택하길 바랄 수도 있다. 당신이 친구와 점심이나 저녁을 먹을 때 친구에게 장소를 선택하라고 하기보다는 어떤 장소를 제안하는 게 가장 현명한 것이다.

10 　**어휘**　evaluate 평가하다 / associate 연관짓다 / awe 경외심을 일으키다 / aesthetically 미학적으로 / get across 이해되다, 이해시키다 / lessen 줄(이)다

　해석　기술이 모든 것이라고 생각하는 사람들이 있고 그들은 전적으로 관련된 기술의 양에 기반해서 예술작품을 평가한다. 그런 사람들은 현실적으로 대상을 그리는 것과 연관된 기술 때문에 회화에 있어서 사실주의에 더 흥미가 있다. 그들은 또한 공예품들에 주로 더 관심 있고 그것을 만드는 데 관련된 기술에 경외심을 느낀다. 확실히 우리는 예술작품을 만드는 데 들어가는 많은 요소들에 대해서 인정해야 한다. 하지만 그런 요소들과 미학적 요소 사이에 차이점은 있다. 우리는 노력, 기법, 기술, 재료, 규모 그리고 작품을 만드는데 걸리는 시간에 대해서 인정해 줄 수 있다. 예술의 가치는 그런 특성에 의해서 측정되어선 안 된다. 누군가가 예술작품을 만들기 위해 아무리 열심히 노력하더라도 그것은 여전히 심미적으로 실패할 수도 있다. 어떤 사람이 금으로 작품을 만들 수 있겠지만 그것 또한 심미적으로 실패할 수도 있다. 형편없는 예술작품에서 크고 형편없는 예술작품보다 더 나쁜 것은 없다. 결국에 성공적이지 않은 한 작품에 대해 수년 동안 작업해 온 것이 얼마나 아쉬운 일인가. 만약 기술이 예술작품의 미학적 요소를 이해시킬 만큼 충분히 잘 발전하지 않으면 작품의 가치는 줄어든다.

11 　**어휘**　bound to ~에 연관된 / irrelevant 부적절한, 무의미한 / discarded 버려진

　해설　지식전달이 많이 이루어져 왔으나 그것을 어렵게 하는 세 가지 요인에 대한 설명을 하고 있다.

　해석　지식전달은 그룹웨어와 네트워킹 도구들의 발달과 함께 최근에 엄청난 관심을 받아왔는데, 이 도구들은 그룹과 개인들 사이에 지식의 흐름이 가능하게끔 설계되어 있다. 그런 도구들의 목표는 궁극적으로는 공유된 기억과 이해이다. 사실, 이는 이루기가 힘든데 지식이라는 게 "까다롭고" 살아있고 또 풍부하기 때문이다. 지식은 의미를 제공해 주는 맥락과 굉장히 밀접하게 엮여있기 때문에 "까다로운" 것이다: 맥락이 없으면 지식은 그저 정보일 뿐이다. 지식은 끊임없이 변하고 성장하기 때문에 지속적으로 관리받아야 한다는 점에서 살아있는 것으로 여겨질 수 있다. 또한 사라지거나 구식이 되고 부적절해져서 버려져야 하기도 한다. 하지만 그것을 맡을 적임자는 누구인가? 마지막으로, 지식은 다차원성이 풍부한데, 엄청난 양의 내용, 문맥, 경험을 포함하고 있다. 이 세 가지 요인 모두가 지식을 전하는 것을 매우 어렵게 한다.

　보기　① 전통적 문화지식의 보호
② 지식과 맥락의 깊은 관련성
③ 지식의 원천으로써 경험의 중요성
④ 지식전달을 어렵게 하는 특성들
⑤ 정보기술로 더 용이한 지식분배

12 　**어휘**　occur 발생하다 / vulnerable 영향받기 쉬운, 취약한

　해설　항공화물은 고가의 물건인 경우가 많고, 운송하는 방법이 복잡하고 밤 시간대에 대부분 운송이 이루어지므로 도난에 취약하다고 설명하고 있다.

　해석　많은 특별한 보안문제들은 항공화물을 실어나르는 것과 관련이 있다. 항공화물은 다른 화물운송방법에 의해 수송되는 물건들보다 더 비싼 물건들인 경우가 많다: 그래서 분실의 가능성이 더 크다. 또한, 어디에서 분실이 발생하는가를 확인하는 것은 더 어렵다. 다른 운송방법에선 물건들을 단순히 들어올려 옮기고 선창에 배달한다. 항공화물의 이동은 훨씬 더 복잡하다. 화물은 우선 수송터미널에서 비행터미널로 이동되고 항상 도난의 가능성 때문에 싣기 직전에 화물기에 실린다. 화물이 여객기에 실릴 때 더 위험해지는데, 그것은 반드시 여객터미널로 옮겨져서 추가적인 취급자에게 다뤄지기 때문이다. 많은 공항에서 카트들은 불이 켜지지 않은 길을 따라 비행기에서 비행기로 오가면서 여전히 도난의 가능성이 발생한다. 게다가 항공화물의 90%는 밤에 실리는데 이때가 범죄가 가장 많이 발생하는 시간대이다.

　보기　① 항공화물을 도난에 더 취약하게 하는 요인들
② 비행기 승객 안전 심사의 문제점들
③ 항공화물운송의 장점과 단점
④ 항공화물운송서비스의 짧은 역사
⑤ 화물을 운송하는 다양한 방법들

13 어휘 paleolithic 구석기시대의 / ingenuity 창의력, 기발한 재주 / shed light on ~을 분명히 하다, ~에 실마리를 던지다

해설 인간이 언어를 사용함으로써 집단 안에서 정보공유를 하고 그 집단에서 합의, 협력을 통해 큰 변화를 일으켰다고 서술하고 있다.

해석 인류에 관한 흥미를 끄는 것은 바벨탑 이야기에서 잘 보여지는데, 단일 언어를 사용하는 인류가 천국에 너무나 가까워져서 신이 위협받는다고 스스로 느끼게 된다는 것이다. 같은 언어는 공동체 구성원들을 강력한 집단적 힘이 있는 정보공유하는 조직안으로 연결시킨다. 누구라도 번뜩이는 천재성, 행운의 사건들, 다른 누군가에 의해 누적된 시행착오에 의한 지혜로부터 혜택을 받을 수 있다. 그리고 사람들은 팀으로 일할 수 있고, 그들의 노력은 합의에 의해 조정된다. 그 결과 인류는 남조류나 지렁이같이 지구상에서 광범위한 변화를 이루어낸 종이 되었다. 고고학자들은 프랑스 절벽 바닥에서 만 마리의 야생마들의 뼈를 발견했는데 그것은 17,000년 전 구석기시대 사냥꾼 무리로 인해 절벽 꼭대기를 넘어 몰려다닌 야생마떼의 잔해였다. 이러한 오래된 협동과 공유된 창의력의 유산들은 왜 검치호랑이, 마스토돈, 거대한 털코뿔소 그리고 수많은 다른 거대한 포유류들이 현대인류가 그들의 서식지에 오게 된 시기에 멸종되었는가에 실마리를 던질 수도 있다. 명백하게, 우리의 조상들은 그 포유동물들을 전멸시켰다.

보기 ① 언어장벽 허물기 : 힘든 과제
② 언어 : 인류의 협농심의 토대
③ 고대에서 현대까지의 언어의 변화
④ 동물과의 의사소통, 동물언어의 이해
⑤ 어떻게 언어가 시작됐는가 : 인류진화에 있어서 몸동작과 언어

14 어휘 assess 평가하다 / emphasize 강조하다 / to a degree 상당히 / take ~ into account ~을 고려하다 / availability 유용성

해설 외국기업들이 교육의 양적인 측면과 수준을 고려해서 인력 채용, 직업훈련 등을 하고 있다.

해석 교육은 공식적이든 비공식적이든 문화를 물려 주고 공유하는 데 있어 큰 역할을 한다. 한 문화의 교육수준은 문맹률과 중등 또는 고등교육의 진학률, 즉 간접적인 자료출처로부터 입수가능한 정보를 이용해서 평가될 수 있다. 국제기업들은 교육의 양적 측면, 즉 특정한 기술에 대한 다양한 주안점, 그리고 제공된 교육의 전반적인 수준에 대해 알아야 한다. 예를 들어, 한국과 일본은 서구권 국가보다 과학, 특히 기술을 상당히 강조한다. 교육수준은 다양한 비즈니스 직무에 영향을 미칠 것이다. 생산설비를 위한 훈련프로그램들은 훈련받는 사람의 교육경력을 고려해야 할 것이다. 예를 들어, 문맹수준이 높으면 인쇄물보단 시청각 자료를 사용할 것을 제안할 것이다. 지역근무 판매직 채용은 잘 훈련된 직원의 유용성에 의해 영향받을 것이다. 어떤 경우에는 국제기업이 정기적으로 지역근무 인력 훈련을 위해 본사로 보내기도 한다.

보기 ① 사회적 이동 수단으로서의 교육
② 교육경력과 경제적 지위
③ 교육과 직업구조의 추세
④ 교육 : 외국기업을 대한 한 가지 중요한 고려할 점
⑤ 숙달된 노동력 : 경제성장을 위한 원동력

15 어휘 account for ~을 차지하다 / compared with ~와 비교할 때 / in contrast 대조적으로

해설 두 시기간의 무기구매율 격차가 가장 큰 곳은 사우디아라비아가 맞지만 격차가 가장 작은 곳은 터키가 아니라 알제리다.

해석 위 도표는 2007-2011년 과 2012-2016년 두 기간 동안 7개국의 전 세계 무기구매율을 보여준다. ① 2012-2016년 기간 동안, 인도가 전 세계 무기수입의 가장 큰 부분을 차지했고 다음으로 사우디아라비아, 아랍에미리트, 중국, 알제리, 터키 그리고 호주가 뒤를 이었다. ② 2007-2011년과 비교해서, 인도, 사우디아라비아, 아랍에미리트, 터키의 전 세계 무기수입률이 2012-2016년에 증가했다. ③ 반대로, 중국, 알제리, 호주의 무기수입률은

2012-2016년 사이에 떨어졌다. ④ 특히, 중국의 무기수입률은 5.5%에서 4.5%로 가장 많이 떨어졌다. ⑤ 2007-2011년과 2012-2016년 사이에 전 세계 무기구매율 격차가 사우디아라비아에서 가장 컸고, 터키에서 가장 작았다.

16 어휘 implication 영향, 의미, 연루 / investigate ~을 조사, 수사하다

해설 1차 세계대전 이전이 아니라 이후에 연극으로 성공을 거두었다.

해석 Bertolt Brecht은 20세기 연극에 중요한 영향력을 주었다. 그는 새로운 양식의 연극을 탐구했는데, 청중들이 자신의 연극이 주는 도덕적, 정치적 영향에 대해 생각하게끔 하려는 그의 목표를 이루기 위해 독특한 연출과 다른 연기방식을 사용했다. Brecht은 독일 아우크스부르크에서 태어나 뮌헨대학교와 베를린 대학교에서 의학과 철학을 공부했다. 제1차 세계대전에서 군복무를 마치고 자신의 연극 Drums in the Night로 성공을 거두었다. 1920년대와 1930년대 초 기간 동안 그는 더 많은 연극을 썼다. 히틀러가 집권한 후 1933년에 그의 아내와 함께 독일을 떠나야 했다. Brecht은 결국 미국으로 갔지만 거기서 공산주의 이념을 가진 이유로 조사받았다. 그는 미국을 떠나 1974년에 동베를린으로 돌아왔고, 그 곳에서 세계적으로 유명한 극단인 Berliner Ensemble을 세웠다.

17 어휘 acknowledge 인정하다, 확인하다 / dismiss 해임하다, 물러나게 하다

해설 ①, ②, ③, ⑤는 General Geroge McClellan을, ④는 President Lincoln을 가리킨다.

해석 미국 남북전쟁이 한창일 때 링컨대통령과 육군장관은 긴급업무 차 맥클렐란 장군의 임시처소를 방문했다. 그가 집에 없었기 때문에, 그들은 거실에서 기다렸다. 장군이 마침내 집으로 돌아왔을 때, 그는 방문객이 와 있는 걸 봤지만 그들이 누구인지 알아차리지 못했다. 대신에, 그는 곧장 방으로 가버렸다. 그가 곧 나올 거라고 가정하고 그들은 기다렸다. 한 시간 후, 그가 계속 나오지 않자 그들은 가정부를 보내 물어보게 했다. 잠시 후, 그녀가 돌아와서 "죄송하지만 장군님이 굉장히 피곤해서 잠자리에 들 거라고 말하라고 하셨다"라고 전했다. 국방부 장관은 놀라서 "대통령님, 이건 있을 수 없는 일입니다. 즉시 그를 장군직에서 해임시켜야 합니다."라고 말했다. 링컨은 잠시 생각하고 나서 이렇게 말했다. "나는 그를 해임시키지 않겠다. 그는 훌륭한 장군이네. 그는 전쟁에서 승리했어. 만약 그가 한 시간만이라도 이런 유혈사태를 줄일 수 있다면 내가 그의 말고삐를 잡고 장화에 묻은 흙을 씻어주겠다."

18 어휘 dominance 우세 / grasp 잡다, 이해하다 / transplant 이식 / undergo 겪다, 받다 / commonplace 흔한 / malfunction 고장 / remedy 치료하다

해설 ⑤ which → that

보어인 so familiar이 문두로 나가서 주어 these ways of thinking about the body와 동사 are가 도치되어 있다. 문장 전체는 '너무나 ~해서 …하다'라는 의미로 so ~ that 구문을 사용했다.

(= These ways of thinking about the body are so familiar that to some of us the ideas ~)

해석 서구문화에서 신체의 자연주의적 관점이 우세하다는 점을 감안할 때, 신체의 문화적 개념은 아마도 이해하기 어려운 것일 수 있다. 사고 피해자들, 이식환자, 그리고 성형수술을 받는 사람들의 신체는 말 그대로, 물리적으로 외과의사에 의해 매일 복원된다. 그런 흔한 복원행위로 인해 신체를 상대적으로 쉽게 기계로 인식한다. 기계처럼, 신체는 어느 정도까지는 분해되고 재결합될 수 있는 부위들이 있다. 신체의 작동은 다른 기계와 같은 물체들과 비슷한 방식으로 검사되고 오작동은 진단받고 치료될 수 있다. 사실상 프랑켄슈타인 박사에 의해 만들어진 Mary Shelley의 괴물은 기계로서의 신체 개념의 고전적 결과물이다. 이런 식으로 신체에 관해 생각하는 것이 너무나 익숙해서 누군가에게는 신체의 사회적 구조의 개념과 문화적 개념이 아마도 터무니없어 보일 수도 있다.

19 **어휘** rebellion 반항 / strive 분투하다 / strive when possible 가능하면 / decent 괜찮은, 품위있는

해설 ④ 주어는 the child로 아이가 부모에 의해서 반응되어야 하므로 수동태인 be responded 표현이 맞다.

해석 청소년기는 반항과 독립하기 위해 분투하는 시기이다: 결과적으로 아이들이 당신에게 동의하지 않거나 사물을 정확하게 당신이 보는 방식으로 보지 않을 수 있는 영역이 많아질 것이다. 기억할 것은, 아이들이 무엇을 말하는가는 그것을 어떻게 말하는가 만큼 중요하지 않다는 것이다. 만약 그들이 가족정책과 자신들이 대우받는 방식에 의견불일치를 이야기한다면, 그들의 말을 분명히 듣고 가능하면 긍정적으로 반응하도록 노력해라. 자기 부모에게 "제가 휴대전화에 좀 더 많은 시간을 많이 쓸 수 있다고 생각해요. 하루에 15분은 너무 짧아요. 저는 숙제를 다 하고 점수도 좋아요."라고 논리적으로 말하는 아이는 자신의 휴대전화 사용시간 부족에 대해 화가 나서 소리지르고 불평하면서 시작하는 아이와는 전혀 다른 방식으로 반응해야 한다. 10대가 자신의 엄마에게 월요일 밤에 간요리를 먹고 싶지 않다고 말하는 건 받아들여야 한다. 그러나 아이가 월요일 저녁에 주방으로 들어와 자신이 이런 "쓰레기"같은 음식은 먹지 않겠다거나 엄마가 "괜찮은" 음식을 요리하는 법을 배우라고 협박하기 시작하는 건 용납해선 안 된다.

20 **어휘** at hand 가까이에, 곧 / stand a chance of ~할 가능성이 있다 / mishap 작은 불행

해설 (A) 주어 the task가 '고되게 하는' 의미로 쓰여야 하므로 exhausting, (B) attract A into B 구조로 목적어 A에 해당하는 부분이 선행사를 포함하고 energy to와 focus on의 복적어 역할을 동시에 하는 관계대명사 what 문장이어야 하고, (C) 접속사 as 문장의 주어가 other laws이므로 복수동사 are가 맞다.

해석 만약 당신 삶에서 어떤 일이 일어나길 원한다면 거기에 집중해야 한다. 집중과 당신이 이루고자 하는 것에 믿음이 없다면, 가까운 시일 내에 그 일을 성취할 수 없게 된다. 이런 집중의 법칙은 그 일이 아무리 힘들어 보이더라도 당신에게 포기하지 않도록 상기시켜 준다. 계속 그것을 믿고 집중함으로써 분명히 바라던 결과를 이룰 가능성이 있다. 에너지와 끌어당김의 법칙을 통해, 당신은 에너지를 쏟고 집중한 대상을 당신 삶으로 끌어들이게 될 것이다. 태양에너지를 모으는 데 사용되는 돋보기는 불을 점화시킬 수 있다. 당신은 생각과 믿음에 집중한 에너지를 통해 원하는 것을 분명히 나타낼 수 있다. 인생의 기복의 법칙과 같은 다른 법칙들이 배경에서 작동하고 있기 때문에 당신은 도전, 투쟁, 불행과 계속 마주할 것이다. 당신은 집중하고 있는 무엇에라도 힘과 생명을 불어 넣는다. 집중을 통해 당신은 그 진동을 증가시켜서 원하는 것에 마법을 가져온다.

21 **어휘** nomadic 유목의 / shelter 서식처, 피난처 / flint-bladed 부싯돌 날의 / stand 임분 / be reluctant to V ~하기를 꺼려하다, 마지못해 ~하다

해설 (A) 의미상 동사 harvest를 꾸미기 때문에 부사 efficiently여야 하고, (B) a family를 설명해 주는 관계대명사 문장이 와야 하므로 that worked, (C) the most suitable time을 꾸며 주는 형용사용법의 to 부정사가 와야 한다.

해석 수렵인들은 예전엔 일시적이거나 계절별 주거지를 옮겨 다니면서 완전한 유목생활보다는 반정착하는 삶을 이어왔지만, 곡물을 저장하는 능력은 사람들이 한 곳에 정착하도록 이끌기 시작했다. 1960년대에 실시된 한 실험이 그 이유를 보여준다. 한 고고학자는 부싯돌 낫을 사용해서 선사시대 가족이 지금도 터키 일부지역에서 자라고 있는 야생곡물을 얼마나 효율적으로 수확할 수 있었는가를 알아보았다. 한 시간 안에 2파운드 이상의 곡물을 모았는데 이것은 3주 동안 날마다 8시간 일 한 가족이 일 년 동안 구성원들에게 하루에 1파운드의 곡물을 제공할 정도로 충분히 곡물을 모을 수 있었다는 것을 보여준다. 하지만 이는 가족이 곡물을 수확할 가장 적기를 놓치지 않는 것을 확실히 하기 위해 야생곡물 임분 근처에 머물렀다는 것을 의미했을 수도 있다. 어마한 양의 곡물을 모았기 때문에 그들은 그것(모아둔 곡식)을 그저 내버려 두려 하지 않았을 수도 있다.

22 **어휘** ground-breaking 획기적인 / controversial 물의를 일으키는 / empathize with ~에 공감하다 / advocate 지지자 / footage 장면 / document ~의 증거를 제공하다

해설 ② 문맥상 파견근무하는 기자들이 군대와 친밀해져서 공정성을 잃은 보도를 할까 우려된다는 내용이 이어져야 하므로 gaining을 losing으로 바꿔야 한다.

해석 기자들의 파견근무가 획기적이었을 수 있지만 논란의 여지가 있는 정책인 것으로 판명됐다. 일부 비판자들은 파견기자들은 부대나 임무수행을 위험에 빠뜨릴 수 있다고 주장했다. 다른 이들은 기자들이 취재하는 군에 너무 가까워지고, 같이 생활하고 보호해 주는 병사들과 더 직접적으로 자연스럽게 일체감을 가지고 그리하여 객관성을 잃게 되는 것을 우려했다. 이런 현상은 스톡홀름 신드롬에 비유됐는데, 인질이 자신의 인질범에 감정이 입하게 되는 것이다. 그럼에도 불구하고 파견정책 옹호자는 이것이 몇 가지 이점이 있다고 주장한다. 이는 바로 가까이에서 개인의 관점을 제공하고 기자들을 군이 실제로 하는 그대로 전쟁을 경험하게끔 해서, 그들이 전쟁을 하는 병사들의 전투를 잘 묘사할 수 있다는 것이다. 파견은 전쟁터와 전쟁상황이 아니라면 가능하지 않은 방식으로 전쟁 사건들에 직접적으로 접근하게 해 준다. 실황의 장면과 생방송 보도는 현실적인 역사의 첫 장면을 제공하고 실제 전쟁이 일어나는 그대로 증거로 보여준다.

23 **어휘** polar cap 극관 / scarce 드문, 희귀한

해설 지구를 제외한 다른 행성에 많은 물이 존재했을 거라고 추측했고 그 예로 화성과 금성의 경우를 설명하고 있고 마지막 문장은 그런 관점이 구체화됐다고 결론짓기 때문에 ⑤는 부족한 scarce가 아니라 plentiful로 바꿔야 한다.

해석 당신이 좋아하는 해변가에 서서 멀리 바라봐라. 당신은 우주가 주는 가장 특별한 경치 중 하나를 보고 있다: 어마한 양의 물. 지구의 바다를 특별한 현상으로 보는 이런 인식은 꽤 새롭다. 공상과학 소설을 읽는 사람들은 화성의 운하, 금성의 습지에 대한 생생한 기억을 갖고 있을 것이다. 지금으로부터 25년 전도 안 되어 우리의 이웃 행성들의 자연에 관한 가장 과학적인 상상은 엄청난 양의 물의 존재를 추측했다. 화성에서, 흰 극관이 나타낸 것은 기온이 너무 낮아서 물이 유동체가 될 수 없고, 그래서 빙하에 갇혀 버린 걸로 믿었다는 것이다. 금성에서는, 하늘을 덮은 구름이 우리가 그 표면을 보지 못하게 막았는데, 이는 우리가 금성을 아마존 우림지대가 지나치게 자라버린 형태로 상상하는 것을 막은 것이 아니었다. 두 경우에서, 이웃 행성들에 대한 관점이 지구상에 풍부한 물이 분명 태양계 다른 모든 곳에서도 풍부할 거라는 예상으로 구체화되었다.

24 **어휘** causality 인과관계 / attribute A to B A를 B의 결과로 보다 / straightforward 간단한, 쉬운

해설 (A) 자료를 정돈해서 다루게 되는 공간 개수를 줄인다고 해야 하므로 reduce, (B) 서술기법을 사용하는 목적이 연대순으로 묘사를 하고 결국 인과관계와 함께 같은 방향으로 간다는 말이므로 imposing (C) 일련의 사건을 다 기억하지 않고서도 인과관계로 재구성되었기 때문에 훨씬 간단해졌다 straightforward가 적절하다.

해석 아주 훌륭한 책 Black Swan의 저자인 Nassim Taleb에 따르면, 우리는 우릴 둘러싼 모든 자료를 이해하려고 노력하는데 왜냐하면 정보저장에 비용이 부가되기 때문이다. 그래서 우리가 그 정보를 더 정리할수록, 점점 더 우리 마음속에 저장하는 게 더 쉬워지고 비용이 덜 들게 된다. 이것은 우리는 자료가 더 정리되고 덜 무질서하기를 선호한다는 말이다. 우리에게는 처리하는 공간의 개수를 줄이는 드라이브가 있고 그래서 복잡한 자료를 그것을 잘 해낼 수 있는 방식으로써 훨씬 단순한 순서로 배열해 둔다. Taleb은 이것이 서술뿐만 아니라 인과관계의 용도이기도 하다고 생각한다. 우리는 복잡하고 무작위의 세상을 대하도록 두기 보다는 설명하고 이해할 수 있도록 인과관계를 사건들의 결과라고 보려고 노력할 것이다. 그리고 서술을 도입하는 목적은 그것이 연대순의 감각을 만들어낼 수 있다는 것이고, 그래서 둘 다 한 방향으로 움직이게 된다. 서술은 우리가 이야기에 잘 어울리고, 묘사가 영속시켜 온 인과관계의 필요조건들을 충족시키는 그런 사실들을 떠올리게 하는 경향이 있다는 것을 의미한다. 그리고 나서 우리는 정확한 일련의 사건들을 떠올리지 않지만 인과관계를 만드는 재구성된 하나의 사건이 예전보다 훨씬 더 간단해 보인다.

25
> **어휘** persist 지속되다 / sacrifice 희생 / in recognition of ~을 인정해서 / incidental 부수적인 / a consequence of ~의 결과

> **해설** (A) 군봉사자들이 영웅이라고 하고 but으로 연결되므로 '인정받지 못한' unrecognized, (B) 군인들이 나라를 위해 희생하기 때문에 표창을 받는 건 '당연히'로 표현해야하므로 rightly, (C) 군봉사자들이 사회에도 혜택을 준다고 했으므로 그 가치가 '어마한'인 enormous로 골라야 한다.

> **해석** 부상자, 병사, 봉사 구성원들과 참전용사들과 함께 그들을 돌보는 일반인들로 구성된 단체가 있는데 우리는 군 돌봄 봉사자라고 일컫는다. 군 돌봄 봉사자들은 그 자체로 영웅인데 그들의 노력은 종종 인정받지 못한다. 그들은 전쟁의 그늘에서 봉사하는데 그들의 보살핌 임무는 군사충돌이 끝나고 나서도 수개월, 수년 동안 지속된다. 자국을 위해 희생을 해온 남녀 군인들은 보통 봉사에 대한 공로인정으로 명예, 보상, 혜택을 받는다. 이것은 그들이 마땅히 받아야 할 표창과 기회이다. 하지만 그들의 돌봄 봉사자들은 신체장애가 있는 군인들을 걷고 먹게 도와 주고 상처치료를 돌봐 주거나 진찰받는 곳으로 데려다 주지만 명예와 보상을 받는 건 드물다. 이런 돌봄 봉사자들은 부가적인 인원인데 그들이 돌봐주는 사람(군인들)에 집중한 결과로서만 정책배려를 받아온 사람들이다. 그러나 그들의 가치는 이루 말할 수 없다. 군봉사자들은 그들의 사랑하는 사람뿐만 아니라 사회에도 혜택을 준다. 그들이 행하는 돌봄은 정보와 사회에 드는 의료보험비용을 줄이는 데 도움이 된다.

26
> **어휘** correspondent 특파원 / in particular 특히 / bureau 책상, 사무실, 부서 / reverse 뒤바꾸다, 역전하다 / by a wide margin 큰 차이로, 여유있게

> **해설** 미국의 방송망들이 해외부서를 폐쇄하고 국제뉴스 보도를 줄여 왔다고 말하므로 ① 해외특파원이 멸종위기, 즉 사라진다는 표현이 어울린다.

> **해석** 몇몇 역사학자들은 해외특파원-나라 밖 사건들을 다루는 기자-이 멸종위기에 있다고 분명히 말한다. 이런 표현은 특히 전통적인 언론매체 특파원들에게 해당된다. 1980년대 이후로, 미국 방송망은 대부분의 해외부서를 폐쇄해 왔고 국제뉴스 보도를 줄여 왔다. 2001년 9월 11일 테러와 이라크 전쟁 둘 다 이런 경향을 바꾸지 못했다. 예를 들어, 이라크 전쟁이 여유있게 그 해 기사였던 반면, 방송망의 해외부서는 2001년 이후로 업무량이 가장 가벼웠다는 사실이 2007년의 한 보고서 TV뉴스 방송망을 모니터하는 Tyndall Report에서 발견되었다. 경제적 압력, 세계 상호의존, 기술혁신-그리고 대중의 무관심에 대한 인식-이 해외뉴스가 보도되고 소비되는 방식을 바꾸었다.

27
> **어휘** counterpart 상대, 대응하는 것 / justifiable 정당한 / significant 중대한

> **해설** 개발도상국의 소비수준이 미국의 1/4이고 2차 세계대전 후 미국에서 증가한 인구수가 개발도상국 전체 인구보다 더 적음에도 불구하고 환경에 미치는 (나쁜) 영향은 비슷하므로 결국 환경문제에서 중요한 것은 소비수준라고 볼 수 있다.

> **해석** 만약 당신이 미국과 같은 나라에 산다면, 인구가 환경을 보호하는 데 주요 문제라고 쉽게 말할 수 있다. 하지만 이것을 좀 더 깊이 생각해 보면 당신은 소비와 우리가 사용하는 기술의 종류 또한 미래의 지구를 위한 장을 마련하는 데 매우 중요하다는 것을 곧바로 이해할 수 있다. 예를 들어 브라질이나 인도네시아 시골에 사는 사람들은 개발도상국에 사는 시골 사람들처럼 미국에 사는 사람들의 약 1/4 소비수준으로 산다. 만약 당신이 우리가 2차 세계 대전 종식 후로 미국 인구에 1억 3천 5백만 명이 더해졌다는 걸 고려한다면, 당신은 미국에서의 추가 인구가 지구에 미치는 영향-소비수준, 인구규모, 그 자체로 파괴적인 부적절한 기술의 사용과 관련해서-이 개발도상국의 전체 인구 42억 인구가 지구에 미치는 영향과 거의 똑같다는 것을 깨닫게 된다. 이는 인구가 유일한 요인이라고 말하기에는 타당하지 않다. 정말로 중요한 것은 지구를 대하는 우리의 방식이다.

> **보기** ① 지구를 대하는 우리의 방식
> ② 복지문제에 대한 우리의 관점
> ③ 개발도상국에 인도주의적 지원
> ④ 가난과 폭력을 끝내는 방법
> ⑤ 경제적 평등 정도를 측정하는 방법

28 어휘 define 정의하다 / attribute 특질 / dispositional 기질적인 / saturate 넘치게 하다 / matter 중요하다

해설 뒷 문장에서 사회심리학자들이 보여준 연구에서 우리는 다른 사람이 보이고 행동하는 것을 토대로 그 성격 특성을 추론해낸다고 했기 때문에 ③이 알맞다.

해석 성격적 특성은 우리 스스로를 어떻게 규정하는가 뿐만 아니라 어떻게 다른 사람을 인식하는지에 있어 중요하다. 사회심리학자들은 우리가 다른 사람의 인상을 형성할 때 그들의 성격의 특질에 대한 정보를 그들이 어떻게 보이고 행동하는가로부터 이끌어내려고 노력한다는 것을 보여왔다: 친절한지, 믿을만한지, 감정적인지, 권위적인지 등등. 인상을 형성하는 것은 다른 사람들의 성격에 대해 기질적 추론으로 알려진 것과 모두 관련된 것이다. 마찬가지로, 우리가 특정 사회집단에 대해 가지는 고정관념은 성격적 특질로 가득 채워져 있다. 정확하든 부정확하든 이런 편견은 집단구성원들의 성격묘사를 나타내는데, 가령 그들이 태평스러운지, 공격적인지, 사회성이 부족한지, 탐욕스러운지 등등. 또한 성격적 특성은 우리에게 사회적 인지자로서 중요한데 왜냐하면 그것들은 사람들에게 핵심적으로 중요한 측면이기 때문이다.

보기 ① 우리가 성격을 어떻게 형성하는가
② 잘못된 정보를 구분해내는 것
③ 우리가 다른 사람을 어떻게 인식하는가
④ 인과관계에 대한 추론하기
⑤ 성격에 맞는 직업을 찾는 것

29 어휘 controversial 논란이 되는 / involve 관련시키다, 연관시키다 / within the confines of ~의 범위 내에서 / incite ~을 조장하다 / patron 후원자

해설 글의 중반부터 19세기 이전에는 예술가들이 혼자서 작품활동하지 않았다는 내용이 나오고 이를 뒷받침하는 내용으로 조수들과 함께 한 작업장을 언급했고 심지어는 같은 예술인들과도 함께 작업했다는 내용이 와야 자연스럽다.

해석 르네상스 예술가들이 자신들의 직업을 자유로운 예술로 평가하려는 노력 때문에 서구사회는 지극히 사적인 어떤 것을 표현하기 위해 개인 단독으로 자신의 예술작품을 만들어내는 발상을 대중화해 왔다. 19세기와 20세기에는 예술가들이 자신의 작품의 등장과 내용을 개인적으로 결정하고 자기표현의 새로운 형태의 연구에서 종종 굉장히 논란이 된 예술을 만드는 것이 더 흔해졌다. 이것은 오늘날에도 사실이다. 하지만 이 전 수세기 동안에는 예술가들은 혼자서 작품활동을 하지 않았다. 심지어 창의적인 천재라는 개념을 장려한 르네상스 예술가들조차도 예술가들의 조수가 제공된 작업장을 운영했는데 조수들은 스승의 디자인을 예술작품으로 만드는 과정과 관련된 대부분의 노동을 수행했다. 심지어 오늘날은 Jeff Koons같은 일부 유명한 예술가들은 자신들의 아이디어를 실현하는 데 있어서 다른 예술가들을 고용하기도 한다.

보기 ① 자신들의 아이디어를 실현시키기 위해 다른 예술인들을 고용하다
② 한 틀의 범위 내에서 일하다
③ 그들의 작품이 논쟁을 일으키기를 원한다
④ 수많은 점진적인 해결책을 얻다
⑤ 재정지원을 위해 후원자에 의존한다

30

어휘 antiquity 고대 / range over ~을 아우르다, 다루다 / legacy 유산 / inhibit ~을 저해하다, 못하게 하다 / irreverence 불손, 무례함 / mount 시작하다 / appreciation 평가, 공감 / allow for ~을 참작하다

해석 고대 모든 사상가들 중에 아마도 아리스토텔레스가 가장 포괄적이었는데, 그의 업적은 물리학, 정치학, 윤리학 같은 전반적인 지식을 아우른다. 하지만 바로 그러한 아리스토텔레스 업적의 규모가 문제가 되는 유산을 남겼다. 아리스토텔레스같이 우리 인류를 위해 지나치게 똑똑한 작가들이 있다. 말을 너무 많이 해 온 그들은 결정적 발언을 했던 것처럼 보인다. 그들의 천재성은 계승자들의 창의적 작품활동에 필수적인 무례함(도전)을 억제시킨다. 역설적이게도, 아리스토텔레스는 자신을 가장 존경하는 사람들을 자신처럼 행동하지 못하게 한 것 같다. 그는 그 전에 이뤄져 왔던 많은 지식들을 의심함으로써 위대함을 발휘했는데, 이것은 플라톤이나 헤라클레이토스를 읽기를 거부하는 게 아니라 그들의 강점에 대한 공감을 기반으로 한 일부 약점에 중요한 비평을 시작하는 것이었다. 진정한 아리스토텔레스 철학의 정신으로 행동하는 것은 가장 업적이 뛰어난 권위자들로부터의 지성적 일탈을 고려해 보는 것을 의미할 수도 있다.

보기 ① 여러 지식분야에 걸쳐 함께 일할 기회
② 정치학, 윤리학, 문학과 같은 인류의 자랑거리
③ 철학자들에 의해 공유된 가치에 기반한 강한 유대
④ 개별사례의 특성에 대해 이루어신 일반화
⑤ 가장 업적이 뛰어난 권위자들로부터의 지성적 일탈

31 **어휘** perceive 인지하다, 여기다 / on one's own 단독으로, 혼자서 / doze 깜빡 잠이 들다

해석 부모와 일반대중에게는 학급 규모가 우수한 학교의 시금석이 될 수 있다. 소규모 학급의 학교들은 큰 규모의 학급이 있는 학교보다 더 나은 것으로 여겨진다. 여러 조사에서 부모들은 학교 안전을 제외하고 학급 규모를 그 어떤 것보다 더 신경쓴다는 것을 보여준다. (B) 요컨대, 교사 한 명이 한 교실에 15명 정도의 학생들을 담당하면 그 교사는 각 학생에게 개인적인 관심을 줄 가능성이 훨씬 높다. 아무도 크게 뒤떨어지지 않을 것이고, 그래서 아무도 혼자서 나아가야 하지 않을 것이다. (C) 반면, 학생이 30명 정도되는 반 규모의 교사들은 개별 학생에게 단순하게 가르칠 수가 없다. 이런 교사들은 해당 학년의 수많은 과제물들, 계산해야 하는 점수들, 결석한 학생들에게 보충수업, 부모와의 연락, 대답해야 할 이메일 등이 있다. (A) 게다가 훈육은 훨씬 더 어렵다: 예를 들어, 학생들이 수업 중에 졸 수 있는데 교사는 이를 알지 못한 상태고, 그래서 분명 교사가 학생이 공상에 빠져 있는 상황을 모두 바로 잡을 수 없다.

32 **어휘** resist 저항하다 / chronic 만성적인 / obvious 명백한 / frustration 좌절감

해석 먹는 것은 1살짜리에게는 여전히 즐거운 일이지만 그 아이의 인생에서 더 이상 주된 즐거움은 아니다. 아이들의 음식에 대한 욕구는 그들의 활동 수준과 키와 몸무게가 성장하는 속도에 의해 대부분 결정된다. (C) 이 속도는 인생의 두 번째 해에 크게 감소하기 때문에 많은 아이들이 8-10개월일 때보다 15-18개월 시기에 실제로 덜 먹고 있다. 예상한 대로 이것은 아이들이 덩치가 더 커지고 나이가 더 들수록 더욱더 많이 먹어야 한다는 게 확실하다고 생각하는 수많은 부모들을 걱정시킨다. (B) 그런 우려로 인해 종종 부모는 아이들을 더 먹도록 강요하게 된다. 부모는 강요하고 아이들은 저항할 때, 만성적인 다툼이 시작되는데 이 다툼은 우선 그 싸움을 시작하게 한 음식에 대한 문제보다 관련된 모든 사람들에게 더 중요해질 수도 있다. (A) 만약 이런 일이 일어나면, 부모와 자식 모두 다툼에서 패배한다. 부모는 아이들이 먹는 방식에 좌절감을 극복하지 못해서 패배한다. 아이들은 정말로 식성이 까다로운, 먹는 게 힘든 사람 아니면 만성적 과식하는 사람이 되기 때문에 패배한다.

33 어휘 discomfort 불편, 불쾌 / manufacture 제조하다 / repel ~을 쫓아내다

해설 주어진 문장의 주어 That은 앞문장 매일 입은 속옷이 박테리아 감염과 불쾌감의 원인이고 이것 때문에 화학물 퇴치 기술을 옷과 속옷에 적용했다고 연결되어야 한다.

해석 1991년 Gulf 전쟁에서 사막의 폭풍작전(Operation Desert Storm)에서 엄청난 사망자 수가 박테리아 감염 때문이었다는 걸 누가 알았겠는가? 전투에서 군인들은 언제나 깨끗한 속옷으로 갈아입을 수 있는 사치스러움이 없다. 갈아입을 깨끗한 속옷 한 벌이 있더라도, 그런 무더운 사막의 조건에서 매일 입은 속옷은 박테리아 감염과 불쾌감의 중요한 원인인 것으로 밝혀졌다. 이것은 군대가 군인들을 생물 무기에 저항하도록 개발한 화학물퇴치 기술을 도입해 티셔츠와 속옷에 적용하도록 했다. 이 속옷은 극초단파 에너지를 사용해서 미세한 나노입자를 속옷천에 섬유조직에 연결해서 제작된다. 그러면 기름, 물, 박테리아 그리고 다른 물질들을 쫓아내는 화학물질이 나노입자에 결합된다. 그 결과는 더러워지기가 매우 매우 힘든 속옷이 되고 사실상 아무것도 속옷에 달라붙지 않을 것이기 때문이다. 그리고 박테리아가 절대로 생길 수 없기 때문에 그 물질로 만들어진 속옷류는 세탁하지 않고 또 입는 사람의 건강에는 아무런 위험 없이 몇 주 동안 입을 수 있다.

34 어휘 property 재산, 부동산 / sacred 성스러운 / modify 수정하다 / betterment 개선, 향상 / for the betterment of ~을 위하여

해설 토지 소유주가 자신의 땅이고 마음대로 하겠다라고 주장하는 내용이 나오고 나서 이어지는 내용이 however로 역접관계의 내용인 사유재산권이 선성시되지 않는다는 주어진 문장이 들어가야 한다.

해석 조경수준의 복원은 거의 항상 공공재산(특히 물과 관련된 장소)과 관리기관 그리고 개인의 사유재산의 혼합을 포함한다. 결과적으로 조경 접근의 엄청난 장벽은 바로 환경보호와 재산권 사이의 불가피한 갈등이다. 작은 습지가 있는 사유지의 주인은 습지를 매우고 배수공사 또는 개조하는 게 불법이라는 말을 들을 때 아마 화가 날 것이다. 때로는 소유주가, 이 땅은 사유재산이고 "내 땅을 내 마음대로 할 것이다."라고 말한다. 하지만 사유재산권은 신성시되지 않는데, 심지어 이 문제에 대해 강경론을 가진 사회에서조차도 그러하다. 개인은 사유지에서 뿐만 아니라 다른 사람들과 공유된 더 큰 생태경관에서도 산다. 그래서, 핵심질문은 이렇다: 개인, 기관, 국가의 행태가 다른 사람들을 위해 그리고 또한 다른 종을 위해 어느 정도까지 바뀌어야 하는가?

35 어휘 mediocrity 평범함, 범인 / abuse 학대 / hypocrisy 위선 / flaw 결함 disillusioned 환멸 나는 / conform to ~에 순응하다

해설 재능 있는 아이들이 자신의 예민한 감수성과 분석력으로 현실세계의 부조리함을 잘 인식하지만 그것을 뛰어넘을 수 없는 현실의 벽에 좌절하고 낙오자가 되거나 회피하게 된다는 내용이다. ③은 사회규범에 순응한다는 것으로 전체 흐름과 반대되는 문장이다.

해석 재능 있는 아이들은 지나치게 감정적으로 예민하고 이상적인데 종종 가정에서, 학교에서, 공동체에서 그리고 더 넓은 세상에서 어떠한지와 자신들이 어떠해야 하는지 사이에 큰 차이를 목격한다. ① 그들의 예민한 마음과 날카로운 사고와 추론 능력 때문에 그들은 사회에서 평범성, 탐욕, 빈곤, 부패, 폭력, 학대, 오염, 위선 그리고 다른 결함들을 뚜렷하게 인지한다. ② 아무도 신경쓰지 않거나 이런 문제들이 절대 고쳐질 수 없어서 그들은 낙담하고 환멸을 느끼게 된다. ③ 그들은 또래집단의 사회규범 또는 행동규범에 따르면서 편안하게 느끼고 빠르게 행동할 수도 있다. ④ 이런 "핵심이 뭘까?"라는 태도의 결과로, 많은 지적인 재능 있는 아이들은 학교에서 능력보다 좋지 않은 성적을 내고, 또 일부는 고등학교, 대학을 중퇴하거나, 심지어는 사회에서 완전히 낙오되기도 한다. ⑤ 그들은 사회위선이나 그들을 불편하게 만드는 사회의 다른 측면들을 상대할 필요가 없는 곳에서 인생 또는 직업을 찾기도 한다.

36 여휘 squarely 정면으로, 정확하게 / predict 예언하다 / be convinced that ~을 확신하다 / rule out ~을 배제시키다 / fundamental 근본적인 / with 목적어 ~ing (목적어)가 ~인 채로

해설 동물도 인간처럼 그들의 문화가 있다는 과학적인 증거가 나오고 있지만 아직까지 논쟁이 계속되고 있다는 내용 중에 ④ 동물들의 법적인 지위를 논하고 있는 것은 자연스럽지 않다.

해석 일부 동물이 도구를 이용하고, 도덕률에 따라 살고, 복잡한 의사소통체계를 사용하고, 문화를 가진다는 과학적 증거가 증가하고 있다. ① 이런 발견들은 찰스 다윈의 진화론 내에서 정확히 맞아 떨어지는데, 이 진화론은 인간과 다른 동물들 사이에 차이점이 종류가 아니라 정도에 있다는 것을 예측한다. ② 하지만 자연의 본질과 동물들 간의 문화에 대한 충분한 증거에 관한 계속되는 논쟁이 있다. ③ 일부 학자들은 동물 행동에 대한 생태학적이고 유전적 설명이 모든 경우에서 배제되어 왔다는 것을 확신하지 않는 반면, 다른 학자들은 인간이 아닌 일반 동물들을 제외하는 방식으로 문화를 정의한다. ④ 동물들의 법적 자격을 이해하기 위해서 법체계가 어떻게 작동하는가에 대해 근본적인 것을 이해하는 게 필수적이다. ⑤ 해결되지 않은 논쟁은, 새로운 발견과 중요한 진전이 계속 생겨나면서, 이것을 활발하고 흥미로운 연구분야로 만든다.

37 여휘 embark on ~에 착수하다 / assess 평가하다, 가늠하다 / concret 구체적인 / specify 명시하다 / ambiguous 모호한 / abstract 추상적인

해설 마지막 부분에서 관리자가 직원들의 기획능력을 알아보려면 지시사항이 구체적이고 특정 표현을 사용하는 것보다 추상적인 게 더 좋은데 그 이유는 직원들의 생각과 계획하는 데 있어서 창의성을 발휘할 수 있기 때문이라고 설명하고 있다.

해석 새로 온 관리자가 자신의 직원들의 계획기술을 점검하길 원한다고 생각해 보자. 그녀는 직원들에게 특정 업무에 대한 문서로 된 계획을 진행시켜 보라고 요구할 수도 있다. 관리자는 그 과제를 설명하기 위해 매우 구체적이고 특정 언어를 사용할 수 있다: "난 여러분들이 이 제안된 기획에 대해 5쪽짜리 계획을 진행하길 원해요. 첫째, 기획의 개요를 도입부분에 포함시키는 걸 명심하세요. 두 번째, 나는 우리가 이 기획을 왜 시작하는가에 대한 여러분들의 분석을 강조하는 부분이 있길 원합니다. 세 번째, 보고서에 해결에 대한 영역이 있어야 합니다. 마지막으로, 여러분이 제안한 해결방안의 성공을 가늠하기 위한 기준과 기준점에 대한 설명이 있어야 합니다." 이런 요구는 매우 구체적이고 특정 언어를 사용하지만, 이것이 관리자의 요구를 충족시키는가? 기획 제안서의 길이와 구성방식을 설명함으로써, 관리자는 자신이 원하는 것을 분명하게 명시하고 그렇게 하면서 직원들의 기획능력을 가늠할 기회를 줄인다. 그녀는 자신의 요구를 더 모호하게 했을 수도 있다: "이 기획에 대한 제안서를 진행시키세요. 나는 여러분들에게 너무 많은 것을 말하고 싶지 않습니다. 이유는 여러분들의 창의성을 제한하고 싶지 않기 때문입니다." 비록 이런 표현이 더 추상적일지라도, 이것은 관리자에게 직원 각자가 어떻게 생각하고 계획하는가에 대한 더 나은 이해를 안겨줄 수도 있다.

요약
직원들의 계획기술을 가늠할 때, 관리자는 과제에 대한 지시사항에서 (B)추상적 개념의 수준을 조절함으로써 그들에게 (A)창의성을 보여줄 기회를 제공할 수 있다.

어휘 absurd 터무니없는 / come up with ~을 제안하다 / ridiculous 우스꽝스러운(=absurd) / distasteful 혐오스러운 / evacuation 대피 / infinite 무한한 / shoot down 비난하다 / prematurely 시기상조로

해석
> 소위 나쁜 생각이 언제 그 안에 위대함의 씨앗을 가지게 될 것인지 당신은 결코 알 수 없다. 우리는 작업하면서 이것을 수도 없이 봐왔다. 나쁜, 심지어 터무니없는 생각은 주어지고 몇 분 내로 그것은 혁신적인 생각의 훌륭한 본보기로 변형된다. 우리는 참여자들에게 상상할 수 있는 가장 최악의, 가장 터무니없는, 심지어 혐오스러운 생각을 제안해 내도록 하는 효과적인 생각 생성방법들을 사용한다. -그리고 나서 그 생각들을 멋진 것으로 바꾸거나 변형시킨다.
> "우리가 창문 밖으로 다 뛰어내리면 어떻게 될까?"라는 극단적인 예를 생각해 보자. 이 나쁜 생각으로부터 당신은 초고층 빌딩에서 일하는 사람들을 위한 획기적인 비상용 개인 낙하산 제품을 개발시킬 수 있다. 또는 화재가 났을 때 높은 층에서 대피하기 위한 개선된 과정을 상상해 보자. 새로운 팀 행글라이딩 극한 스포츠 이벤트. 한 구성원의 사람들이 신제품 음료를 마시고 나서 날 수 있다는 개념을 광고하는 어떤 돌파구. 무수히 많은 다른 가능성들이 방에 있는 모든 사람들이 창밖으로 뛰어야 하는 나쁜 생각으로부터 생겨날 수 있다. 즉, 생각이 너무 조급하게 미리 비난받지 않는다면 그 안에 훌륭한 생각은 활짝 필 수 있는 기회가 생긴다. 그래서 어떤 생각이 그것이 가지는 모든 것을 보여줄 공정한 기회를 가질 때까지 <u>판단을 보류해 둬라.</u>

38 **보기** ① 창의적인 광고는 당신에게 감명줄 것이다
② 나쁜 생각들이 큰 생각으로 이어질 수 있다
③ 왜 창조적 집단사고가 효과적이지 않은가?
④ 좋은 의도가 나쁜 결과를 가질 수 있다
⑤ 사람들은 혼자서 아니면 함께일 때 더 창의적인가?

39 **해설** 글쓴이의 주장에 의하면 나쁜 생각에서 수많은 좋은 생각이 생겨날 가능성이 많기 때문에 빈칸은 미리 판단하지 말라는 의미의 ③이 정답이다.
보기 ① 실수를 감지하라
② 전통을 따르라
③ 판단을 보류하라
④ 잘못을 벌하라
⑤ 몽상을 줄여라

어휘 discriminatory 차별적인 / offend 불쾌하게 하다 / substitution 대용 / ridicule 조롱하다 / satirize 풍자하다 / overcompensate 과잉보상하다 / foster 조장하다 / hoped-for 기대된

해석

우리의 주의를 지휘하는 언어능력의 한 예로, 'politically correct(정치적으로 정당한 : 차별적 언어사용, 행동을 피하는)', 즉 PC 언어라는 용어에 대해서 생각해 보자. 이것을 지지하는 사람들은 차별과 장애를 언급하는 방식에 의해 사람들을 불쾌하게 할 수 있는 어떤 단어나 구절을 우리가 사용하는 언어로부터 없애서 우리 마음에서 차별적인 사고를 제거할 수 있다고 주장한다. 캘리포니아의 로스앤젤레스 주는 문화적 민감성 때문에 컴퓨터장비에서 master(주인), slave(노예) 같은 용어들을, 비록 주 하드디스크와 2차 하드디스크 드라이브를 지칭하는 데 흔히 사용되는 용어라고 할지라도, 공급회사들에게 사용하는 일을 중지하라고 요구했다. policeman 대신 police officer를 쓰는 것 같은 다른 대용어들은 남자, 여자 둘 다 그 말에 위치에 있다는 것을 강조하기 위해 의도된 것이다.

(A) 하지만 PC 언어를 사용하고 PC가 되는 것은 부정적으로 여겨지고 심지어는 그것들이 다른 사람들의 민감도를 과잉보상하기 때문에 조롱당하고 풍자되어 왔다. PC 언어가 비웃기 쉬운 한 가지 이유는 그것의 정치직 의제가 광범위한 사회적 문화적 제도와 항상 언결되시는 않다는 것이다. (B) 예를 들어, 우리는 남녀 사이의 평등한 관계를 만들기 위한 노력으로 직장에서 성차별적 언어를 없애야 한다고 말하는 것이 그 한 가지다. 하지만 이런 지시는 남녀 임금평등과 진급과 승진의 동등한 기회를 조성하는 더 폭넓은 의제와 연결되지 않는다면, 단지 직장에서 성차별 언어를 제거하는 것만으로는 기대하는 효과를 낳을 수 없을지도 모른다.

40 **보기**
① 정치적 정당성을 지지하는 이유
② 사회발전이 언어변화에 미치는 영향
③ PC(정치적으로 정당한) 언어 사용의 찬반 양론
④ 남성과 여성의 언어 사용의 차이점
⑤ 확실한 표현으로 명확한 생각을 가질 필요성

41 **해설** 앞 문단은 PC 언어의 찬성에 관한 것이고 두 번째 문단은 부정적인 시각에 대한 내용이 나오므로 (A) however이고, (B) 앞 문장에 대한 예시로 남녀의 평등한 관계가 나오고 있으므로 For example이 맞다.

어휘 impostor 사기꾼

해석

> 한 소년이 가나 출신 부모에게서 영국에서 태어났다. 영국에서 태어났을 때 소년은 자연히 영국시민이었다. 청소년이 됐을 때, 그는 어머니, 두 여동생, 그리고 남동생 하나를 영국에 두고 아버지와 살기 위해 가나로 갔다. 몇 년 뒤에 어머니와 형제들과 살기 위해 다시 영국으로 돌아갔다. 이 지점에서 이야기가 복잡해진다. 출입국관리소는 소년이 사기꾼이라고 의심했고 그의 어머니의 혈연관계가 아닌 자식이거나 조카 중 하나라고 생각했다. 출입국 관리당국의 의심을 토대로 소년의 거주신청은 거부되었다. 소년의 가족은 고향에서 살 수 있도록 그의 신원을 규명하기 위해 싸웠다. 의료검사의 첫 단계로 장기기증자와 수혜자를 맞추는 데 주로 사용되는 유전자 표지뿐만 아니라 혈액형을 사용했다. 그 결과는 소년이 어머니라고 주장하는 여성과 가까운 친족관계인 것을 확정했으나, 검사는 그녀가 어머니인지 이모인지 말해 주지는 못했다.
>
> 그 가족은 도움을 구하기 위해 Leicester 대학의 과학자인 Alec Jeffreys에게 의지했다. 그들은 Jeffreys의 연구실에서 개발된 기법인 DNA 지문채취가 소년의 신원을 확인할 수 있었다. 하지만 이모들과 소년의 아버지 DNA는 검사에 사용되지 못했다. 이런 문제점에도 불구하고 Jeffrey는 그 사건을 맡기로 했다. 그는 소년과 형제라고 믿는 아이들, 그리고 어머니라고 주장하는 여성들의 혈액샘플을 채취했다. DNA 지문채취로 알려진 밴드의 형태가 소년의 신원을 결정하기 위해 분석되었다. 그 결과들은 소년이 형제들과 같은 아버지가 있다는 것을 보여줬는데 그들은 모두 아버지와 연관있는 DNA 단편을 공유했기 때문이다. 가장 중요한 질문은 소년과 어머니가 친족관계인가였다.
>
> Jeffreys는 그 여성 DNA의 25 단편들이 소년의 그것과 일치했다는 것을 발견했는데, 이는 그녀가 사실상 소년의 어머니라는 것을 보여줬다. 이 증거에 직면한 출입국관리소는 그 입장을 바꿔야 했다. 관리당국은 소년이 가족과 영국에서 살게 허가했다.

42 **해설** ⑤ Alec Jeffreys는 소년의 형제, 자매와 어머니의 혈액 샘플을 받았다.

43 **해설** 처음엔 출입국관리소가 소년이 사기꾼이라고 의심해서 영국거주를 허가해주지 않았으나 DNA 검사를 통해 영국에 있는 여성이 어머니라는 증거를 찾고 결국 영국에서 거주하는 것을 허락했기 때문에 ⑤ maintain을 반대 의미로 바꿔야 한다.

어휘 ridiculous 우스꽝스러운 / novice 초보자 / hunch 구부리다 / erase ~을 지우다 / crouch 구부리다 / absurd 우스꽝스러운, 터무니없는 / humiliating 굴욕적인 / be about 중요하다

해석

(A) 여름이었고 Mary는 14살이었다. 그녀의 가족 모두가 강에서 매주말을 수상수키와 수영을 하면서 그저 좋은 시간을 가지며 보냈다. 하지만 Mary는 그녀의 오빠와 언니들처럼 스키를 탈 수 없었다. 너무 부끄러워서 타 보려고 애쓰지 않았다. 그녀는 우스꽝스럽게 숙련되고 경험 많은 형제들 옆에서 초보자처럼 보인다는 생각에 겁에 질렸다. 어느 날 그녀는 엄마에게 이것에 대해 다 털어놓았다.

(C) Mary는 수상스키 초급자가 처음으로 물 밖으로 일어설 때, 하체를 내민 채 스키 위로 몸을 구부려져 앉아서 출발했는데 완전히 우스꽝스럽게 보였다고 설명했다. 그리고 화창한 주말에 강에 사람들이 많이 있었다. 그 중 일부는 소년들이었고 Mary가 굴욕적인 자세를 취했을 때 모두 보고 있었다. Mary는 엄마에게 자신이 기꺼이 이런 수치심을 무릅쓸 생각은 없었다고 말했다.

(D) 이 대화가 끝난 직후 어느 목요일에 Mary의 엄마는 점심 먹고 일하러 갔다가 집으로 돌아왔다. Mary는 엄마가 왜 집에 있는지 이해하지 못했으나 엄마가 그녀에게 보트트레일러를 차에 거는 것을 도와달라고 말했다. 엄마는 뭔가를 제안하고 있었고 Mary는 그 제안을 받아들여야 했다. 그녀가 무슨 일이 일어난지 알기도 전에, 그녀와 엄마는 보트에 있었고 고요한 물 위에서 따뜻한 햇살을 받으며 강으로 향했다. 어느 목요일이었고, 다른 누구도 중요하지 않았다. Mary가 우스꽝스러운 모습을 볼 사람은 아무도 없었다.

(B) 그날 Mary는 스키타는 법을 배웠다. 엄마는 인내심 있고 세심했다. 그것은 Mary가 생각했던 것 만큼 어렵지 않았다. 그리고 어떤 구경꾼도 없어서 그녀는 스키 위로 구부정해지는 것에 대해 불편해 하지 않았다. 오후가 지나고 나서, 스키 위로 점점 더 똑바로 서게 됐다. 다음 주말 강으로의 여행에서 Mary가 형제들과 함께 행복하게 스키타는 것을 볼 수 있고, 그녀의 쑥스러움은 엄마의 다정함으로 사라졌다.

44 **해설** Mary가 엄마에게 고민을 털어놓는 내용인 C, 엄마가 Mary의 고민 해결을 위해 제시한 D, Mary가 스키를 탈 수 있게 된 B 순이 적절하다.

45 **해설** (a)~(d)는 모두 Mary, (e)는 Mary의 엄마를 가리킨다.

2020학년도 정답 및 해설

01	02	03	04	05	06	07	08	09	10	11	12	13	14	15	16	17	18	19	20
④	①	①	②	⑤	③	⑤	①	①	③	②	①	①	⑤	⑤	④	③	④	②	③
21	22	23	24	25	26	27	28	29	30	31	32	33	34	35	36	37	38	39	40
②	④	③	③	②	②	①	②	③	②	⑤	③	④	④	③	④	⑤	①	④	②
41	42	43	44	45															
⑤	④	⑤	④	⑤															

01 해석 론 : 더 이상 못 갈 것 같아

댄 : 어서, 이 사람아! 밀어, 정상까지 1km 정도 더 남았어. 지금 그만두지 마!

론 : 그렇게 말하기는 쉽지! 너는 몸이 좋잖아, 그리고 네 자전거는 탄소 섬유야! 그것은 내 자전거보다 10킬로 그램이나 더 가벼울거야!

댄 : 멈추지 않고 성공한다면, 내가 끝난 후에 저녁 사줄게. 네가 원하는 어떤거라도.

론 : 난 심지어 먹을 생각도 못하겠어. 다리가 떨어져 나갈 것 같은 느낌이고, 목은 사막보다 더 마른 것 같아. 정말 그만하고 쉬어야겠어. 나는 들어가고 싶다. 좋은 몸매를 원하지만, 너무 피곤해. 이거 너무 어렵다.

댄 : 너 자신을 몰아붙여야 해. 너는 휴식을 취해서 그렇게 많은 지방을 빼지는 못할 거야. 도와달라고 한 건 너야.

론 : 알아. 네 말이 맞아.

보기 ① 론과 댄은 함께 간신히 정상에 올랐다.

② 론의 자전거는 댄의 자전거보다 가볍다.

③ 론은 (자전거를) 타고 난 후에 아무거나 먹을 수 있다고 말한다.

④ 론은 필사적으로 휴식을 취하고 싶어한다.

⑤ 론은 댄의 체중을 줄이는 것을 돕고 있다.

02 해석 판매원 : 음, 저는 이 SUV가 당신이 찾고 있는 바로 그 차라고 생각합니다.

밥 : 좋아보이지만, 내가 예상했던 것보다 훨씬 크네요.

판매원 : 그렇다면, 이 세단이 당신에게 더 맞을까요? 더 작고 가격도 합리적인데요.

밥 : 좋네요. 짙은 남색인가요?

판매원 : 여기 전시장에 남색 모델이 하나 있습니다. 정가는 7만 5천 달러 입니다. 시승해 보시겠습니까?

밥 : 아니, 지난 주에 다른 대리점에서 같은 차를 몰아봤어요. 그냥 가서 그 차를 살까봐요.

판매원 : 좋아요. 제가 서류 정리할테니 당신은 출발하세요.

① 좋아요. 제가 서류 정리할테니 당신은 출발하세요.
② 좋아요. 제가 당신의 동네의 다른 자동차 딜러를 소개해 줄 수 있습니다.
③ 문제없습니다. 시운전을 위해서 충분한 시간을 줄 수 있습니다.
④ 걱정 마세요. 두 차 모두 당신의 가격대 안에 들 것입니다.
⑤ 죄송합니다만, 저희는 짙은 남색 색상의 차가 없습니다.

03 해석 랜디 : 우리 저녁으로 뭐 먹을까?
마사 : 사실, 난 내가 정말 뭘 먹고 싶은지 모르겠어.
랜디 : 멕시코 음식은 어때? 근처에 엘 고르도라는 새로운 멕시코 식당이 오픈했는데.
마사 : 좋은 생각 같지 않은데. 저번에 멕시코 식당에서 매운 음식을 먹었는데, 이틀 동안 배가 아팠어.
랜디 : 그럼 Waffle Shack은 어때? 난 정말 거기 저녁메뉴가 먹고 싶어.
마사 : 나도 그래, 하지만 항상 기다리는 시간이 너무 길어.
랜디 : 네 말이 맞을지도 몰라. 피자는 어때?
마사 : 다시 못 먹겠어. 난 이미 이번주에 3번이나 먹었어.
랜디 : 음... 엘 고르도를 먹어보는 건 어때? 우리는 안 내온 음식을 고를 수 있거든.
마사 : 알았어. 네가 원한다면.

a. 좋은 생각 같지 않은데.
b. 난 정말 거기 저녁메뉴가 먹고 싶어.
c. 난 정말 배고파.
d. 난 이미 이번주에 3번이나 먹었어.

04 해석 M : 그래서 난 그게 바로 네가 구입하고 싶어 하는 거라고 생각해. 너는 어떻게 생각해?
W : 음, 솔직히, 난 그게 좋아. 그 동네는 환상적이고 내 예산 범위 안에 있어.
M : 그럼, 우리가 주인에게 제안을 해야 할까? 나는 그 집에 관심이 있는 사람들이 몇 명 더 있다는 걸 알아.
W : 그래, 하지만 난 한 가지 걱정이 있어. 옆집이 항상 그렇게 생겼니? 집이 비어 보이고 지저분해 보인다.
M : 사실, 거기엔 아무도 살지 않아. 그것은 수리가 필요하지만 주인은 그것을 할 마음이 없어.
W : 난 원하지 버려진 집 옆에 살고 싶지 않아. 나는 그 지역의 다른 장소를 보고 싶어.

① 경비원 – 방문자
② 부동산 중개업자 – 주택 구매자
③ 관광 가이드 – 관광객
④ 주택 소유자 – 세입자
⑤ 건축가 – 기자

05 해석 제프 : 나는 오늘 좋은 파도가 오기를 바랬어.
Paul : 그래, 하지만 (오늘은 파도가) 좋을 것 같지 않아. 넌 방금 그것을 놓쳤어. 어제는 환상적이었는데. 머리 위로 파도가 일었어.
제프 : 나는 항상 좋은 서핑을 놓치는 것 같아. 지난 달 바하 반도에서가 내가 멋진 서핑을 했던 마지막이었어.
Paul : 나도 이전에 그런 슬럼프를 겪어본 적이 있어. 때때로 서핑 신들은 우리에게 미소를 짓기도 하고, 때로는 그렇지 않기도 해!
제프 : 내일 기상은 어때?
Paul : 비는 오고 파도는 없지만, 모레는 맑은 하늘과 환상적인 파도가 있을 것 같아! 언제 떠날거니?
제프 : 내일 밤. 파도타기 신들은 나를 미워할 것임에 틀림없어.

① Paul은 어제 파도가 환상적이었다고 말한다.
② Jeff는 서핑을 할때 운이 아주 좋지 않다.

③ 제프는 지난달 바하 반도에서 멋진 파도타기를 했다.
④ 일기예보에 의하면 내일은 비가 올 것이라고 한다.
⑤ 제프는 서핑을 즐기고 모레 떠날 예정이다.

06 해석 톰 : 미안하지만, 그 모든 플라스틱 파이프는 뜯어내고 교체해야 해. 그리고 나서 우리는 거기에 새로운 샤워기를 설치해야 할 거야.
제인 : 오 안돼! 비싸겠다! 그것처럼 하면 비용이 얼마나 들까?
톰 : 글쎄, 견적서를 작성해야 할 것 같지만, 대충, 2천 달러 정도라고 생각해. 내가 작년에 이거와 비슷한 일을 했었어.
제인 : 오, 이런! 그건 너무 비싸. 나는 몇 백 달러만 예상했어. 나는 마지막 사람에게 500달러를 지불했다. 그 정도로 할 수 없겠니?
톰 : 내가 여기 온 이유는 네가 마지막 사람에게 500달러를 지불했기 때문이야. 그는 끔찍한 일을 형편없이 했어. 그래서 모든 파이프가 다 새고 네 샤워기가 교체되어야 해.
제인 : 글쎄, 난 그냥 잘 모르겠어. 난 선택의 여지가 없는 것 같아. 700달러면 어때?
톰 : 만약 내가 그 일을 700달러에 했다면, 나는 엄청난 돈을 잃을 거야. 그것은 적어도 1,800달러가 될 거야.

보기 ① 제인은 톰에게 샤워 시설이 어디에 있는지 물어보고 있다.
② 톰은 제인의 샤워기를 깨뜨렸고, 이제 그녀는 그가 샤워를 고쳐주길 원한다.
③ Tom과 Jane은 새 샤워기 수리에 대한 비용을 협상하고 있다.
④ Tom은 Jane에게 파이프 몇 개를 팔려고 하지만, 그녀는 그것을 사고 싶어하지 않는다.
⑤ Jane은 Tom이 수리하는 일을 부탁하는 만큼 기꺼이 돈을 지불한다.

07 어휘 addict (약물) 중독자 / definitive 최종적인, 확정적인 / pull 매력 / shut off 차단하다 / provoke 유발하다 / urge 충동 / give in to 굴복하다 / debate 생각(하다) / cue 단서 / ambiguity 모호함 / Internalize 내면화 하다

해설 글의 소재인 사고 중지(thought stopping)에서도 알수 있듯이 약물 충동에 대한 반응을 생각할 여지를 남겨두지 말라는 내용의 글이다. 따라서 필자가 주장하는 바는 ⑤번이다.

해석 마약 중독자를 회복시키는 일을 하는, UCLA의 리차드 로손(Richard Rawson)에 의해 만들어진 용어인 사고 중지는 보상의 매력에 반응하지 않기 위한 최종적인 결정이다 :(다시 말해서) 자극을 만나면, 그것이 유발하는 행동을 차단하라. "텔레비전처럼 그것을 생각해봐."라고 로손은 말한다. "채널을 바꿔." 생각을 끄는 것은 거의 즉각적이어야 한다. "당신은 이것에 속수무책인 것이 아니다 ; (오히려) 당신은 결정을 내릴 수 있지만, 빨리 결정을 내려야 한다."라고 로손은 말했다. 여러분이 충동에 직면하여 무엇을 해야 할지에 대해 생각하는 데 더 많은 시간을 보내면 보낼수록, 결국 그것에 굴복할 가능성이 더 커진다. 일단 "내가 해야 하나 말아야 하나?"를 생각하기 시작하면, 싸움에서 진 것이다. 신호를 경험하고, 관련된 생각을 끄세요. 애매모호한 것도 없고, 어떠한 망설임도 없다. 생각에 시간을 낭비하지 말고, 당신의 반응에 고군분투하지 마라. 그냥 기억에서 지워버려. 의심에 대한 어떠한 공간도 남겨놓지 않은 채 절대적이고 심지어 단단한 충동에 대한 반응을 내면화하십시오.

08 어휘 collective 집단적인 / accumulate 축적하다 / inherit 물려받다 / trial and error 시행착오 / counterproductive 역효과를 낳는 / strain 짜다, 물기를 빼다 / pound 치다 / sacred 성스러운

해설 시간이 지남에 따라 축적된 집단적인 지식은 어떤 한 개인의 지식(마음)보다 더 중요하다는 첫 번째 문장이 주제문이다. 따라서 옛 지혜로부터 배우라는 ①번이 정답이다.

해석 시간이 지남에 따라 축적된, 어떤 문화 집단의 집단적 정신은 전형적으로 어떤 개별적인 인간의 정신보다 더 똑똑하다. 그래서 문화 학습이 매우 중요하고, 또한 크라우드소싱과 같은 그런 기술이 매우 효과적이다. 초기 사상가인 쉰지는 그의 세대에 의해 계승된 유교적 길을 깊고 빠른 강이 아니라 얕은 강가를 가리키는 표기로 비유한다. 경험이 있는 사람들은 신중한 시행착오를 통해, 강을 건널 수 있는 가장 좋은 장소를 알아냈고, 우리가 강을 찾는데 도움을 줄 표기를 남겨두었다. 우리는 그들을 무시하고 그냥 날갯짓만 할 수도 있지만, 그것은

역효과적이고 심지어 위험할 수도 있다. 다른 말로 해서, 만약 지역 사회의 존경 받는 구성원이 뿌리채소를 두 시간 동안 끓이고 물을 빼고 나서, 당신이 이 성스러운 노래를 스무 번 부를 때까지, 성직자한테 축복받은 나무로 그것을 두드리라고 하면, 아마 당신은 그냥 입을 다물고 정확히 시키는 대로 그것을 해야 할 것이다.

보기 ① 옛 지혜로부터 배워라.
② 쉽게 버는 돈은, 쉽게 잃는다.
③ 실수하는 것은 자연스러운 것이다.
④ 교만하면 파멸한다.
⑤ 모험이 없으면, 얻는 것도 없다.

09 **어휘** turn out ~로 판명되다, 입증되다 / in the fullness of time 때가 무르익었을때 / commitment 약속, 전념 / zero-base 출발점으로 되돌아가 결정하다 / be involved in ~에 연루되다 / ongoing 계속되는 / aggravation 악화 / irritation 짜증

해설 시간이 흐르면서 과거에 내렸던 결정이 틀린 것으로 판명되기 때문에, 처음으로 돌아가서 다시 출발해야 한다는 내용을 담고 있는 글의 전반부가 주제문이다. 따라서 ①번이 정답이다.

해석 당신이 내리는 많은 결성들은 때가 무르익었을때 잘못된 것으로 판명될 것이다. 결정이나 약속을 했을 때, 당시의 상황에 근거해서, 아마 좋은 생각이었을 겁니다. 그러나 지금은 상황이 바뀌었을지도 모르며, 다시 출발점으로 되돌아가 결정할 때이다. 당신은 대개 그것이 야기하는 스트레스 때문에 당신이 제로 베이스 사고 상황에 있는지를 알 수 있다. 지금 여러분이 알고 있는 것을 알면서, 여러분이 다시 빠지지 않을 어떤 것에 관여할 때마다, 여러분은 계속되는 스트레스, 악화, 짜증, 그리고 분노를 경험하게 된다. 때때로 사람들은 사업이나 개인적인 관계를 성공시키려는 노력을 하는데 엄청난 시간을 보낸다. 그러나 이 관계를 제로베이스로 한다면, 올바른 해결책은 종종 그 관계에서 완전히 벗어나는 것이다. 유일한 진짜 문제는 자신이 틀렸다는 것을 인정하고 상황을 바로잡기 위해 필요한 조치를 취할 용기가 있느냐 하는 것이다.

10 **어휘** exclude 배제시키다 / narcissistic 자애적인 / irrational 비이성적인 / envious 시기하는 / grandiose 거창한 / aggressive 공격적인 / astray 길을 잃은 / delude 속이다, 착각하게 하다 / tendency 경향 / trait 특징 / motive 동기 / spot 발견하다 / humble 겸손한 / weigh down 짓누르다 / embrace 포용하다 / falsify 위조하다, 조작하다 / saint 성자 / relieve 안도하다 / hypocrisy 위선

해설 인간은 부정적인 측면을 스스로로부터 배제하려고 하지만, 인간의 부족함은 매우 자연스러운 것이기 때문에 이것을 빨리 인정할수록 부정적인 면을 극복할수 있는 힘을 더 키울 것이다라는 내용이다. 따라서 ③번이 정답이다.

해석 인간 본성의 더 어두운 자질에 대해 읽거나 듣는 것에 대한 우리의 자연스러운 반응은 우리 자신을 배제하는 것이다. 자기 도취적이고, 비이성적이고, 시기심이 많고, 거창하거나, 공격적인 사람은 언제나 (내가 아닌) 다른 사람이다. 우리는 거의 항상 우리 자신을 최선의 의도를 가지고 있다고 본다. 우리가 길을 잘못 든다면, 그것은 상황이나 사람들이 우리에게 부정적으로 반응하도록 강요하는 것이다. 한번 그리고 이 모든 자기 기만 과정 동안 멈춰 서라. 우리는 모두 같은 천에서 잘려나갔고, 우리 모두는 같은 경향을 공유한다. 이것을 빨리 깨달을수록, 당신의 힘은 당신 안의 잠재적인 부정적 특성을 극복하는 데 더 클 것이다. 그대는 자신의 동기를 조사하고 자신의 그림자를 보게 될 것이다. 이것은 다른 사람들에게서 그러한 특징들을 발견하는 것을 훨씬 더 쉽게 만들 것이다. 당신은 또한 당신이 상상했던 방식으로 다른 사람들보다 우월하지 않다는 것을 깨달으면서, 더 겸손해 질 것이다. 이것이 당신으로 하여금 죄책감을 들게 하거나 자기 인식에 짓눌리게 하는 것이 아니라 정반대가 되게 할 것이다. 당신은 선과 악 모두를 포용하고, 성자로서의 거짓된 자기 이미지를 떨어뜨리면서, 스스로를 완전한 개인으로 받아들일 것이다. 당신은 당신의 위선에 안도감을 느끼고 더 당신 다운 사람이 될 것이다. 사람들은 당신 안의 이런 자질에 끌릴 것이다.

11 **어휘** for all ~에도 불구하고 / grandeur 웅장함 / conquer 정복하다 / conquistador 정복자 / immunity 면역 / smallpox 천연두 / measles 홍역 / typhoid 장티푸스 / influenza 유행성 감기 / malaria 말라리아 / whooping cough 백일해 / indigenous 원산의, 토착의 / epidemic 전염병 / successor 계승자 / estimate 추정하다 / viral 바이러스의 / demoralize 사기를 꺾다 / contribute to ~에 기여하다 / conquest 정복

해설 구세계의 질병으로 인해 잉카 제국이 멸망했다는 내용이다. 따라서 ②번이 정답이다.

해석 그 규모와 웅장함에도 불구하고, 잉카 제국은 1532년부터 스페인인들에게 정복당하기 전까지 겨우 1세기 동안 지속되었다. 스페인 정복자들이 중남미에 도착하기 전부터 잉카인들은 유럽의 신세계 도착으로 고통을 받기 시작했다. 왜냐하면 유럽인들은 아메리카 대륙의 사람들이 면역력이 없는 질병을 가지고 왔기 때문이다. 유럽인들이 남아메리카에 상륙한 직후에, 천연두, 홍역, 장티푸스, 인플루엔자, 말라리아, 백일해와 다른 질병들은 아메리카 원주민들을 죽였다. 이러한 구세계 질병들은 1520년대에 잉카 제국으로 퍼졌다. 스페인 사람들이 안데스 산맥에 도착하기 직전에, 전염병은 그들의 황제와 그의 후계자를 포함한 많은 잉카 지도자들을 죽였다. 결국 잉카 제국의 전체 인구 중 3분의 1에서 2분의 1로 추정되는 사람들이 이 바이러스 살인자들로 인해 죽었다. 살아남은 사람들은 사기가 떨어졌고, 이것은 잉카의 비교적 쉬운 스페인 정복에 기여를 했다.

보기 ① 신대륙의 스페인 정복자들과 그들의 잔혹함
② 잉카제국의 붕괴의 원인으로서 유럽의 질병들
③ 구세계와 신대륙의 충돌이 유럽인들에게 미친 영향
④ 잉카 제국의 흥망성쇠를 추적하는 과학적 방법
⑤ 구세계에서 오는 질병을 치료하는 잉카의 자연요법

12 **어휘** forewarn 미리 경고하다 / in advance 미리 / persuade 설득하다

해설 만약 사람들이 공격이 온다는 것을 안다면, 그들은 스스로를 방어할 준비를 할 수 있다. 는 내용의 첫 번째 문장이 글의 주제이다. 따라서 정답은 ①번임을 알 수 있다.

해석 만약 사람들이 공격이 온다는 것을 안다면, 그들은 스스로를 방어할 준비를 할 수 있다. 연구에 참가한 고등학생들은 2분에서 10분 전에 "왜 10대들에게 운전하도록 허락되지 말아야 하는지"에 대한 연설을 듣게 될 것이라고 미리 경고받았다. 나머지 학생들은 같은 이야기를 들었지만 미리 경고를 받지 못했다. 그 결과는 어떠한 경고도 받지 않은 학생들이 가장 많이 설득되었고, 2분 전에 경고를 받은 학생들이 그 뒤를 이었으며, 10분 전에 경고를 받은 학생들이 그 뒤를 이었다. 사람들은 누군가가 자신을 설득하려 하고 있다고 믿을 때(그리고 선택의 자유를 빼앗는 것) 심리적 반발이라고 하는 불쾌한 감정적 반응을 경험하게 되는데, 이는 그들로 하여금 설득력 있는 시도를 저항하도록 동기부여한다. 종종 사람들은 그들이 하도록 설득되는 것과는 정반대의 행동을 할 것이다. 셰익스피어 희곡에서 로미오와 줄리엣의 부모는 로맨스를 끝내려는 그들의 노력이 어린 사랑새들을 더욱 가깝게 만들었을 때 이런 효과를 발견했다.

보기 ① 경고가 설득에 미치는 영향
② 설득력 있는 연설의 특징들
③ 대화형 프레젠테이션의 중요성
④ 미리 경고 사인을 주는 것의 필요성
⑤ 교육에 있어서 설득력 있는 의사소통의 기능들

13 **어휘** reconstitute 재구성하다 / assumption 가정 / reverse 반대 / brass 놋쇠 / symbiotic 공생의 / dissent 반대 / arrangement 준비, 배열 / appropriate 적절한 / institution 기관 / unnecessarily 불필요하게 / sharpen 날카롭게 하다 / knife-edge 칼날 / stifle 숨막히게 하다 / selfishness 이기주의 / accommodate 수용하다 / legitimate 합법화 하다 / sensitive 민감한 / charge 공격하다

해설 적절한 사회적 준비가 주어진다면, 다양성은 안전하고 안정된 문명을 만들 수 있다. 는 내용의 글이다 따라서 ①번이 정답이다.

해석 우리의 현재 비슷한 민주주의를 재구성하기 위해서, 우리는 증가된 다양성이 자동적으로 사회의 긴장과 갈등을 불러온다는 무섭지만 거짓된 가정에 도전할 필요가 있다. 사실, 그 반대가 사실일 수 있다. 사회의 갈등은 필요했을 뿐만 아니라, 한계 내에서 바람직하다. 그러나 백 명이 모두 같은 놋쇠 반지를 간절히 원하면, 그들은 놋쇠 반지를 위해 싸울 수밖에 없을지도 모른다. 반면 백 명의 사람들 각자가 서로 다른 목표를 갖고 있다면, 그들이 교역하고, 협력하며 공생관계를 형성하는 것이 훨씬 더 보람이 있다. 적절한 사회적 준비가 주어진다면, 다양성은 안전하고 안정된 문명을 만들 수 있다. 소수민족 간의 갈등을 불필요하게 폭력사태로 칼끝까지 날카롭게 만드는 것은 오늘날 적절한 정치기구의 부족이다. 이 문제에 대한 해답은 반대의견을 억누르거나 소수 민족을 이기주의로 공격하는 것이 아니다. 정답은 다양성을 수용하고 합법화 하기 위한 상상력 있는 새로운 준비들, 다시 말해서, 변화하고 늘어나는 소수의 급변하는 필요성에 민감한 새로운 제도들에 있다.

보기 ① 다양성이 민주주의를 해치는가?
② 민주주의의 약점은 내재되어 있는가?
③ 다양성의 상승은 민주주의에 대한 위협이다.
④ 다수결의 원칙: 민주주의의 기본 원칙
⑤ 민주주의는 전염된다: 발전하고 있는 민주화

14 **어휘** overhear 엿듣다 / inventory 재고 목록 / shipment 수송, 적화물 / file 발송하다 / ambiguity 모호함 / ambiguous 모호한 / weaken 약화시키다 / trustworthiness 믿을 수 있음 / misfile 서류를 잘못 철하다 / ensue 뒤따르다

해설 글의 후반부에 단순한 것으로 포장되어 있는 모호함은 정말 놀랍다라는 내용을 통해서 정답이 ⑤번이 정답임을 알 수 있다.

해석 당신이 레코드 가게에서 일하는 첫날, 당신의 매니저가 "우리의 레코드는 알파벳순으로 정리되어 있다"고 말한다고 상상해보라. 이런 방향 아래 첫 번째 앨범 꾸러미를 쉽게 정리한다. 나중에 동료가 "미안해, 지금 마이클 잭슨이 다 팔린 것 같아."라고 말하는 것을 우연히 듣게 된다. 당신의 매니저는 "J" 아래를 보고 재고를 확인하는데, 그것은 그 상점에 스릴러라는 앨범이 한 장 있어야 하는 것을 의미한다. 당신은 그것이 방금 당신이 발송했던 기록물 발송의 일부였다는 것을 기억한다. "J"가 아니라면, 그 기록을 어디에 둘 수 있었겠어? 어쩌면 "M" 아래일까? "이것을 알파벳화 하라"처럼 단순한 것으로 포장되어 있는 모호함은 정말 놀랍다. 우리는 하루 종일 지시를 하고 받는다. 모호한 지침은 우리의 구조와 신뢰도를 약화시킬 수 있다. 그 첫 번째 앨범이 잘못 처리되고 나서야 혼란이 뒤따른다.

보기 ① 알파벳 분류는 일을 쉽게 만든다
② 복잡성은 버리고, 단순함과 함께 하세요
③ 관리자: 동료냐 적이냐?
④ 오래된 앨범은 수집하기 어렵다.
⑤ 모호함은 단순성 속에 숨는다.

15 **어휘** occupational 직업적인 / active-duty 현역의 / concentrate 집중되다 / administrative 행정적인 / seamanship 선박 조종술 / distribution 분배

해설 통신분과에 있어서 남자와 여자의 비율은 같다. 따라서 어떠한 분야에서도 동일한 분배를 가지고 있지 않다는 ⑤번은 도표의 내용과 일치하지 않다.

해석 위의 그래프는 2010년 미군의 직업적 역할에서 남녀의 비율을 보여준다. 현역 여성은 현역 남성보다 행정적 역할에 훨씬 더 집중되어 있었다. 즉, 여성의 비율은 행정적 위치에 있는 남성의 두 배 이상이었다. 그리고 군인의 6%만이 의학적 역할을 하고 있는 반면, 여성의 15%는 이런 직업을 가지고 있었다. 전기 분야에서 남성의 비율은 여성의 비율보다 높았다: 즉, 22%의 남성이 전기 분야에서 일을 하고 있는 반면, 12%의 여성만이 그 분야에서 일하고 있었다. 보병, 총기 승무원, 선박 조종술에 있는 남성의 19%에 비해, 오직 3%의 여성만이 이런 역할에 있었다. 어떤 직업적 역할도 군대에서 남성과 여성의 분배를 똑같이 보여주지 않았다.

16 **어휘** spell 기간 / flee 도망가다 / the latter 후자 / relocate 이전하다 / resign 사임하다 / outspoken 노골적인 / stroke 뇌졸중

해설 글의 후반부에 매사추세츠주 브랜데이스 대학 교수가 되었다고 했다. 따라서 ④번은 글의 내용과 일치하지 않는다.

해석 1898년 베를린에서 태어난 헐버트 마르쿠세는 1922년 프리부르크 대학에서 문학 박사학위를 받기 전에, 제1차 세계대전에서 독일군과 함께 복무하였다. 베를린에서의 책 판매상으로서 짧은 기간후에, 그는 마틴 하이데거 밑에서 철학을 공부했다. 1932년 그는 사회연구원에 들어갔지만 프랑크푸르트에서는 일한 적이 없다. 1934년, 그는 미국으로 도망쳤고, 그곳에 남아 있게 되었다. 막스 호크하이머와 함께 뉴욕에 있는 동안, 후자는 컬럼비아 대학으로부터 연구소를 그곳으로 옮기자는 제안을 받았고 마르쿠세도 그와 합류했다. 1958년 마르쿠세는 매사추세츠주 브랜데이스 대학의 교수가 되었지만, 1965년 노골적인 마르크스주의자의 견해 때문에 사임할 수밖에 없었다. 그는 캘리포니아 대학교로 옮겨갔고, 1960년대에 사회 이론가, 철학자, 그리고 정치 활동가로 세계적으로 명성을 얻었다. 그는 81세의 뇌졸중으로 사망했다.

17 **어휘** spit 침 뱉다 / pucker 입술이 오므라지다 / spray 뿌리다 / saliva 침 / naughty 무례한 / fall on deaf ears 무시하다 / bet ~이 틀림없다 / shame 수치심 / as long as ~하는 한

해설 ①, ②, ④, ⑤번은 벳시의 부모를 ③은 벳시와 벳시 아빠의 친구를 가리킨다.

해석 네 살짜리 벳시는 침 뱉는 것을 좋아했다. 누군가 "안녕, 벳시"라고 말할 때마다, 그녀는 입을 오므리고 그 사람에게 침을 뿌릴 준비를 하곤 했다. 그녀의 부모는 당황했고 그녀가 어떻게 그런 '나쁜' 습관을 시작했는지 이해할 수 없었다. ①그들은 둘 다 매우 존경받는 사람들이었고 벳시가 어디서 그런 "무례하고 역겨운" 것을 배웠는지 이해하지 못했다. 벳시를 멈추게 하려는 ②그들의 모든 노력은 무시당했다. 어느 날 그들은 그 가족의 친구를 방문했고, 벳시가 침 뱉기 위해 입을 오므릴 때, 그 친구는 활짝 웃으며, "베시, 넌 침 뱉는 것을 좋아할 거야. 우리 둘 다 화장실에 가서 변기에 침을 뱉자. 그렇게 하는 것도 재미있을 것 같다."고 말했다. 벳시의 부모는 벳시가 친구의 손을 잡고 두 사람이 화장실로 사라지는 것을 수치심과 놀라움이 뒤섞인 눈으로 지켜보았다. 몇 분 후, ③그들은 돌아왔고 벳시는 침을 뱉는 것을 멈추었다. 벳시의 부모가 깨달은 것은 ④그들이 벳시의 행동을 통제하려고 노력함으로써 권력투쟁을 만들고 있었다는 것이다. 이제 ⑤그들은 선택권이 있었고 벳시에게 "네가 화장실에서 하는 한 침 뱉기는 괜찮아."라고 말할 수 있었다. 벳시가 자신의 '습관을 포기하는 데는 그리 오래 걸리지 않았다.

18 **해설** ④번은 주절의 주어 자리이다. 따라서 know를 주어가 될 수 있는 명사형태인 knowing 이나 to know로 바꾸어 줘야 한다.

보기 ① what은 주어를 이끄는 명사절로 쓰였으며, 주어가 없는 불완전 구조로서 적절하다.
② 앞에 있는 seem은 불완전 자동사로서 뒤에 형용사가 나와야 되며, ~처럼 보이다의 의미로 쓰이며, appear 와 바꾸어서 쓸 수 있다.
③ 부사절이 분사구문으로 바뀐 형태로서 seem은 자동사로서 Vpp형태가 될 수 없다.
⑤ 재귀대명사의 재귀용법으로서 주어와 목적어가 동일하기 때문에 재귀대명사가 쓰였다.

19 **해설** ②는 동사로서, 주어가 앞에 있는 a debate가 주어이다. 주어가 3인칭 단수 주어이기 때문에 3인칭 단수 주어이기 때문에 3인칭 단수 동사 leaves가 쓰여야 한다.

보기 ① 가정법 과거 완료 문장으로서 도치가 된 형태이다. 원래 문장은 Depression-era regulations had not been removed ~의 형태에서 if가 도치되면서 주어 동사가 도치된 형태이다.
③ 병렬구조로서 관계대명사의 목적격을 나타낸다.
④ them은 앞에 those를 의미한다. 복수로서 적절하고, 인칭대명사 목적격이 들어가는 것이 적절하다.
⑤ 앞의 want와 연결되는 병렬구조이다.

20 해설 (A)는 SV수일치를 묻는 문제로서 주어가 10 percent of those remaining을 의미한다. 복수명사(those)의 퍼센트(10 percent)는 복수를 의미하기 때문에 복수 동사인 are가 적절하다.

(B)는 정동사인지 준동사인지를 묻는 문제로서, when절의 동사가 없기 때문에 정동사의 자리이다.

(C)는 관계대명사 & 전치사 + 관계대명사 구조로서, 관계대명사 뒤의 구조는 불완전 구조여야 되고, 전치사 + 관계대명사 뒤의 구조는 완전구조여야 한다. 뒤의 구조는 S + V(완전 자동사)의 완전구조이기 때문에 at which가 적절하다.

21 해설 (A)는 형용사&부사를 묻는 문제로서 형용사는 명사를 수식하거나, 2형식과 5형식의 보어자리에 와야 하며, 부사는 문장전체, 동사, 형용사, 또다른 부사를 꾸며주는 곳에 와야 한다. 적절하게 반응한다로 해석이 되기 때문에 동사 respond를 꾸며주는 것으로 볼 수 있다. appropriately가 적절하다.

(B)앞에 등위 접속사 and가 있는 걸로 봐서 병렬을 묻는 문제이다. 문맥상 offering에 걸리기 때문에 asking이 적절하다.

(C)는 능/수동을 묻는 문제이다. 능/수동을 묻는 문제는 가장 먼저 뒤에 목적어의 유무를 확인해서 목적어가 있으면 ~ing, 없으면 ~pp로 고르면 된다. 본문에서는 더 많은 매력(more pull)이라는 목적어가 있기 때문에 능동인 ~ing인 exerting이 적절하다.

22 어휘 essence 본질 / capitalism 자본주의 / perpetual 영구적인 / insight 통찰력 / paranoid 편집증 (환자) / popularize 대중화 하다 / breakthrough 돌파구 획기적인 발전 / obsolete 더 이상 쓸모 없는 / free up 해방하다 / perish 멸망하다 / fall behind ~에 뒤지다

해석 Joseph Schumpeter는 자본주의의 본질은 오래되고 덜 효율적인 제품이나 서비스를 파괴하고 그것을 새롭고 더 효율적인 것으로 대체하는 영구적인 순환인 "창조적인 파괴"과정이라는 견해를 표현했다. 앤디 그로브는 "파라노이드만이 살아남는다"는 Schumpeter의 통찰력을 받아들여 많은 방식에 있어서 그것을 세계화 자본주의의 사업모델로 삼았다. Grove는 오늘날 극적이고, 산업을 바꾸는 혁신이 점점 더 빠르게 일어나고 있다는 견해를 대중화하는데 도움을 주었다. 이러한 기술적 발전 덕분에, 당신의 최신 발명품이 쓸모없게 될 수 있는 속도는 이제 번개처럼 빨라졌다. 따라서, 자신을 파괴할 새로운 것을 누가 만들어 내고 그리고 나서 그들 앞으로 한 발짝도 앞서 있는가를 어깨 너머로 끊임없이 바라보고 있는 사람들만이, 즉 편집증 환자들만이 살아남을 것이다. 돈이 풀리고 더 혁신적인 기업으로 향하게 하기 위해서 자본주의가 기꺼이 비효율적인 기업을 빨리 파괴하는 그러한 나라들은 세계화 시대에 멸망(→번성_thrive)할 것이다. 이러한 창조적 파괴로부터 그들을 보호하기 위해 그들의 정부에 의존하는 나라들은 이 시대에 뒤처질 것이다.

23 어휘 graduate 대학원생 / postdoctoral 박사과정 수료 후의 연구자 / by definition 정의상 / expiration date 만기일 / melting pot 용광로 / farewell 작별(인사) / resident 거주자 / turnover 회전률 / look to ~하기를 기대하다 / landlord 집 주인 / hand-me-down 만들어 놓은 / secondary 부차적인 / sociologist 사회학자 / relevance 관련(성) / embed 단단히 끼워넣다.

해석 보스턴과 캠브리지는 많은 사람들이 너무 오래 머물지 않는 도시다. 여기 있는 많은 사람들은 대학원생과 박사후 과정의 사람들인데, 이는 그들의 직위는 정의상 만기가 있다는 것을 의미한다. 보스턴과 캠브리지가 용광로이지만, 당신이 작별 파티에서 새로운 친구를 사귀는 도시들 이기도 하다. 높은 거주자 회전률과 교우관계의 조합은 케임브리지에서 가장 좋은 아파트가 결코 시장에 도달하지 못하는 상황을 만들어낸다. 누군가가 좋은 아파트에서 이사할 때, 항상 입주하려는 것을 기대하는 친구가 있고, 그것은 그들에게 새 세입자를 찾아야 하는 부담을 야기하기(→덜어주기_saves) 때문에, 보통 집주인들은 이 만들어 놓은 역학이 괜찮다. 그래서 교훈은 적어도 보스턴과 케임브리지의 경우, 아파트 부동산 시장은 소셜 네트워크에 비해 부차적이다는 것이다. 그의 생애 대부분을 사회 네트워크의 경제적 관련성을 연구해 온 사회학자인, 마크 그랜노베터에 따르면, 우리는 케임브리지에서 학생 아파트 시장이 사회적 상호 작용의 네트워크 속에 내재되어 있다고 말할 수 있다.

24 어휘 infinitely 무한히 / constrain 억제하다 / elegantly 우아하게 / analogy 비유 / take into account ~를 고려하다 / knot 매듭 / preexist 이전에 존재하다

해석 행동은 무한히 유연하지 않고, 어떤 방향으로든 쉽게 움직인다. 오히려, 유기체는 어떻게 학습이 일어나는지 그리고 훈련 절차에서 기대할지도 모르는 어떤 변화들을 (A) 제한하는 자연 행동 시스템과 경향을 가지고 태어난다. 이러한 한계들은 연구자에 의한 비유에 있어서 우아하게 묘사하였는데, 연구자는 학습을 나무로 된 조각상을 조각하는 것에 비유하였다. 조각가는 조각상과 거의 (B) 유사성이 없는 나무 조각으로 시작한다. 조각이 진행됨에 따라, 그 나무 조각은 점점 더 최종 제품과 비슷하게 보이게 된다. 그러나 조각가가 나무 곡물의 방향과 밀도, 그리고 나무가 가지고 있을 지도 모를 어떤 매듭도 고려해야 하기 때문에 그 과정에 제한이 없는 것은 아니다. 나무 조각은 이전에 존재했던 곡물과 나무의 매듭과 (C) 조화될 경우 가장 성공적이다. 비슷한 방법으로, 학습은 유기체의 이전에 존재하는 행동 구조를 고려한다면 가장 성공적이다.

25 어휘 chemist 화학자 / alchemist 연금술사 / evolve 진화하다 / biological warfare 생물전 / repel 격퇴하다, 쫓아버리다 / paralyze 마비시키다 / disorient 갈피를 못잡게 하다 / digestibility 소화가능성 / enhance 향상시키다 / endure 참다, 견디다 / lectin 렉틴(단백질의 한 종류) / dine 식사를 하다 / quantum 양자 / immune 면역성이 있는 / compound 화합물

해석 식물은 훌륭한 화학자와 연금술사들이다: 그들은 태양빛을 물질로 바꿀 수 있다! 그들은 포식자를 물리치기 위해-가량 독을 쏘거나, 마비시키거나, 그들에게 방향을 잃게 하는 것- 또는 그들의 종이 견딜 수 있을 가능성을 (A) 높이면서, 살아있는 상태를 유지하고 그들의 씨앗을 보호하기 위해서 그들 자신의 소화가능성을 줄이기 위해서, 생물전을 이용하도록 진화되었다. 이러한 물리적이고 화학적인 방어 전략은 둘 다 포식자를 멀리하고 심지어는 때때로 동물들이 그들이 원하는 것을 하도록 하는 데 현저하게 효과적이다. 그들의 초기 포식자는 곤충이었기 때문에, 식물들은 그들을 먹으려고 하는 불행한 벌레들을 마비시킬 수 있는 몇몇 렉틴(단백질의 일종)들을 개발했다. 분명히 곤충과 포유류 사이에는 양자 크기의 차이가 있지만, 두 가지 모두 같은 (B) 영향을 받는다. 분명히, 땅콩 한 개가 확실히 특정 사람들을 죽일 가능성이 있다고 할지라도, 여러분 대부분은 그것을 먹은 지 몇 분 안에 식물 화합물에 의해 마비되지는 않을 것이다. 그러나 우리는 특정 식물 화합물을 섭취하는 것의 장기적인 효과에 면역이 되지 않는다. 우리 포유류들이 가지고 있는 엄청난 수의 세포들 때문에, 우리는 수년 동안 그러한 화합물을 소비하는 (C) 해로운 결과를 볼 수 없을지도 모른다. 그리고 설사 이런 일이 당신에게 일어나고 있다고 해도, 당신은 아직 그것을 알지 못한다.

26 어휘 solely 오로지 / claw 발톱 / compassion 연민, 동정심 / trunk 코끼리 코 / tusk 엄니 / strenuously 열심히 / comrade 동료 / companion 동료

해설 죽어 누워있는 코끼리를 일으켜 세우는 것이라든지 총에 맞은 동료를 돕기 위해서라든지의 빈칸 문장 다음에 나오는 내용으로 봐서 동료들에게 동정심을 느끼고 보여준다는 것을 알 수 있다. 따라서 정답은 ②번이 적절하다.

해석 관찰자들은 야생의 동물들은 오직 "이빨과 발톱"만으로 사는 것이 아니라 정기적으로 동료들에게 동정심을 나타낸다는 것을 반복적으로 알아챘다. 한번은 늙은 수 코끼리가 죽어 누워 있을 때, 인간 관찰자들은 그의 온 가족이 그것이 다시 서도록 도와주기 위해서 모든 것을 시도했다는 것을 주목했다. 먼저, 그들은 그의 아래에서 그들의 코와 엄니를 다루려고 했다. 그리고 나서 그들은 그 늙은 코끼리를 잡아당기는 과정에서 어떤 코끼리는 너무 열심히 잡아당겨서 그 과정에서 엄니를 부러뜨렸다. 오랜 친구에 대한 그들의 걱정은 그들 자신에 대한 걱정보다 더 컸다. 코끼리는 충격을 두려워함에도 불구하고, 사냥꾼한테 총을 맞은 동지를 돕기 위해 오는 것이 목격되었다. 다른 코끼리들은 그들의 부상당한 동반자를 다시 걷도록 하기 위해 협력하여 일한다. 그들은 상처를 입은 코끼리의 양쪽을 누르고 걸으면서 이것을 한다, 그리고 친구를 그들의 거대한 몸 사이로 옮기려고 노력한다. 코끼리는 또한 코끼리를 먹이기 위해, 그리고 힘을 주기 위한 시도로 그들의 다친 친구의 입에 풀을 쑤셔 넣고 있는 것이 목격되었다.

① 부상에 대한 자가치료
② 그들의 동료들에 대한 동정심
③ 자식들을 위한 가족의 유대감
④ 포식자를 속이는 요령들
⑤ 야생에서 먹이를 찾기 위한 협업

27 어휘 withstand 견디다, 참다 / servicemen 현역군인 / theater of operations 전투지역 / enlisted 사병인 / reluctance 꺼림 / casualty rate / 사상자율 dreadful 끔찍한

해설 빈칸이 첫 문장에 나오면 그 문장은 주제문이다. 따라서 그 글의 대한 근거는 뒤에 나오는데, 보조석에 탄 사람보다, 운전자가 덜 불안하고, 일반 사병보다 조종사가 전쟁에 참여 하겠다고 하는 비율이 높은 걸로 봐서 ①번이 정답임을 알 수 있다.

해석 사람들이 두려움을 견딜 수 있도록 도와주는 요소가 통제되고 있다. 예를 들어, 차를 탄 앞좌석 승객은 보통 운전사보다 더 불안하다. 미군에 대한 연구에서 1944년 6월 유럽 전투지역에서 승무원이 "만약 당신이 그것을 다시 하고 있다면, 당신은 전투비행에 참가하기로 선택할 것이라고 생각하는가?"라는 질문을 받았을 때 이런 사실이 밝혀졌다. 조종사들은 항상 다른 사병보다(39~51%) '그렇다'(51~84%)고 대답할 가능성이 있었고, 전투기 조종사는 폭격기 조종사(51~74%)보다 혼자서 조종하겠다는 사람(84%)이 많았다. 중폭격기 승무원들은 그들이 더 많은 임무를 수행할수록 점점 더 주저함을 보였으며, 그 이유는 찾기 어렵지 않다. 사상자율(70퍼센트 이상이 6개월 후 전사 또는 실종되었고 17.5퍼센트가 전사 또는 부상)은 끔찍했다.

보기 ① 통제되고 있는
② 기다리면서 지켜보는
③ 좋은 사건들을 상기하는
④ 동반자와 함께 있는
⑤ 적절한 훈련 및 연습

28 어휘 contemporary 동시대의, 현대의 / ethical 윤리적인 / address 다루다 / emerging 최근 생겨난 / genetic engineering 유전공학 / prospect 전망 / humanity 인류, 인간성 / artifact 공예품 / relinquish 포기하다 / biotechnology 생명공학 / prohibit 금지하다 / genie 지니, 정령 / humility 겸손

해설 글의 전반부에서 "최근 생겨난 기술은 우리가 우리 아이들을 설계하고 인간성 자체를 일종의 공예품으로 변화시킬 수" 있는 내용으로 봐서 자연을 근본적인 방식으로 바꾼다는 내용의 ②번이 정답임을 알 수 있다.

해석 일부 현대 기술은 인류가 이전에는 결코 다루지 못했던 일종의 문제인, 새롭고 깊게 문제를 일으키는 윤리적 문제를 개방하는 것처럼 보인다. 예를 들어, 유전 공학의 최근 생겨난 기술은 우리가 우리 아이들을 설계하고 인간성 자체를 일종의 공예품으로 변화시킬 수 있는 전망을 만들어낸다. 일부 작가들은 이런 전망을 환영하는 듯하지만, 다른 작가들은 우리가 이렇게 용감한 새로운 세상을 만들 수 있도록 하는 지식을 습득할 기회를 포기하도록 요구하는 갈림길에 서 있다고 믿는다. 다른 이들은 생명공학과 유전공학에 사람이 사용되어질 때 어떤 경우에는 허락하고 또 어떤 경우에는 금지되어야 하는지 우리가 합리적인 제한을 할 수 있다고 믿고 있다. 식물과 몇몇 동물 종에 대한 유전 공학은 이미 널리 사용되고 있으며, 이 특별한 정령(지니)을 병에 다시 넣는 것은 이미 불가능할 수도 있다. 한스 조나스는 우리에게 능력을 주는 이런 기술들은 자연을 근본적인 방식으로 바꾸는 것이 '장기적인 책임감과 무엇보다도 겸손함을 가지는 마음으로 접근되어져야 한다고 믿는다.

보기 ① 과학을 미적으로 사용하는 것
② 자연을 근본적인 방법으로 변화시키는 것
③ 변형이 거의 없는 재료를 생산하는것
④ 복잡한 시스템에서 숨겨진 결함을 감지 및 찾는 것
⑤ 외부 및 내부 위험으로부터 유기체를 방어하는 것

29 **어휘** spoil 망치다 / grouch 불평대는 사람 / verbal 구두의 / identify 확인하다 / emotional 감정적인 / infectious 전염성의 / prolong 연장하다

해설 마지막 문장에서 "불과 몇 달 사이에 데이트 커플과 대학 룸메이트의 감정적 반응은 극적으로 비슷해진다"는 내용을 통해 사람간의 오랜 접촉을 통해 감정이 쉽게 전염될 수 있다는 것을 알 수 있다. 따라서 정답은 ③번이다.

해석 여러분은 거의 확실히 조용한 사람 주변에 있는 것이 여러분을 더 편안하게 느끼도록 해주고, 또는 이전에 명랑한 기분이 불평이 많은 사람과의 접촉으로 인해 상했을 때를 기억할 수 있다. 연구자들은 만약 이 과정이 빨리 일어나고 있다면, 많은 구두 의사소통이 필요하지 않다는 것을 증명했다. 한 연구에서 두 명의 자원봉사자가 그들의 기분을 알아내는 조사를 마쳤다. 그리고 그들은 2분 동안 서로 마주보며 조용히 앉아 연구원이 방으로 돌아오기를 기다렸다. 그 시간이 끝날 즈음, 그들은 또 다른 감정 조사를 마쳤다. 시간이 지남에 따라, 짧은 노출은 덜 표현을 하는 파트너의 기분이 더 표현을 하는 파트너의 기분을 닮게 하는 결과를 낳았다. 장기적인 접촉으로 감정이 더욱 전염되는 것을 이해하는 것은 쉽다. 불과 몇 달 사이에 데이트 커플과 대학 룸메이트의 감정적 반응은 극적으로 비슷해진다.

보기 ① 최적의 기능을 위해 가장 잘 관리할 수 있다
② 외부 자극과 무관하게 작동할 수 있다
③ 장기간의 접촉으로 훨씬 더 감염될 수 있다
④ 사회적, 문화적 규범에 의해 영향을 받는다
⑤ 전체적인 창조적 과정과 관련이 있다.

30 **어휘** facilitate 용이하게 하다 / spurt 분출 / apparatus 기구 / comparative 비교의 / profoundly 깊이

해설 글의 마지막 부분에서 "우리의 언어 사용이 단순히 의사소통을 가능하게 할 뿐만 아니라, 우리가 외부 세계를 인식하는 방식에도 크게 영향을 미친다는 것은 명백하다"는 내용을 통해서 빈칸은 ②번임을 알수 있다.

해석 언어의 사용이 우리가 사건을 훨씬 더 정확하게 기억할 수 있게 해준다는 많은 증거가 있다. 왜냐하면 언어의 사용과 관련된 자극은 두뇌발달의 더 많은 분출을 촉진시키기 때문이다. 침팬지들을 인간 가족 환경에서 키움으로서 그들에게 언어의 사용을 가르치려는 확대된 시도가 있어 왔다. 그들은 언어에 대한 성악기구를 가지고 있지 않기 때문에, 미국 수화를 사용하여 배웠다. 침팬지들이 생후 5년 동안 수백 개의 단어까지 배울 수 있다는 것이 증명되었는데, 이것은 인간의 아이들이 성취하는 것의 극히 일부분이다. 인간의 아이들과 침팬지의 비교 능력은 아이들의 언어가 발달하는 시점인, 그들의 첫 번째 두 번째 생일 사이 어딘가까지는 다소 비슷하다. 관련된 요점은 우리가 언어의 사용을 배우기 전에 그 시기에 대한 기억이 거의 없다는 것이다. 우리의 언어 사용이 단순히 의사소통을 가능하게 할 뿐만 아니라, 우리가 외부 세계를 인식하는 방식에도 크게 영향을 미친다는 것은 명백하다.

보기 ① 자연에 대한 우리의 호기심을 표현하도록
② 훨씬 더 정확하게 사건을 기억하도록
③ 우리의 지각적 경험을 다른 사람들과 공유하도록
④ 우리 주변의 동물들과 의사소통하도록
⑤ 창의적인 생각을 실천에 옮기도록

31 **어휘** profitable 수익성의 / analytical 분석적인 / encompass 포함하다 / empower 권한을 주다 / strategic 전략의 / capitalize 자본화 하다 / statistical 통계의 / analysis 분석 / visualization 시각화 / neural 중립의 / consequence 결과

해설 주어진 단락의 마지막에 데이터 마이닝에 관한 내용이 (C)의 데이터 마이닝에 관한 내용과 연결되고, 이어서 슈퍼마켓의 내용이 (B)의 슈퍼마켓의 내용으로 이어지며, (A)로 마무리가 되고 있다.

해석 오늘날, 많은 수익성 있는 기업들의 성공의 비결은 고급 분석 방법을 사용하여 데이터를 처리하는 능력에 있다. 정보 관리의 비즈니스는 단순히 데이터를 저장하는 것 이상을 포괄한다. 또한 새로운 형태의 비즈니스 인텔리전스를 이용하여 데이터를 처리함으로써 '데이터 마이닝' 또는 정보 획득을 다룬다.

(C) 따라서 소식은 데이터 마이닝 기법(통계분석, 시각화 및 신경망 지원)에 투자하여 숨겨진 패턴을 발굴하고 새로운 지식을 발견하며, 그 결과 현재의 비즈니스 상황에 대한 더 많은 통찰력을 얻을 필요가 있다. 예를 들어, 일반적인 보고서는 슈퍼마켓에서 가장 잘 팔리는 제품을 식별할 수 있다.

(B) 그러나, 데이터 마이닝이나 비즈니스 인텔리전스의 도움을 받은 보고서는 슈퍼마켓에서 가장 잘 팔리는 제품을 식별할 수 있을 뿐만 아니라, 왜 그 제품이 가장 잘 팔리는지도 설명할 수 있다.

(A) 그러므로 '왜'를 아는 이러한 능력은 조직이 필요한 전략적 변화를 할 수 있도록 힘을 실어줄 것이다. 예를 들어 조직은 고객과의 더 강한 일대일 관계를 구축함으로써 새롭게 발견된 지식을 활용해야 한다.

32 **어휘** negotiation 협상 / statement 언급 / manifest 나타내다 / entrust 맡기다 / tactic 전략 / diplomatic 외교의

해설 주어진 문장의 후반부에 나오는 "주의력 부족"이 (B)의 "주의력 부족"으로 이어지고, (C)에서 나오는 협상은 (B)의 후반부에 나오는 협상을 받고 있다. (A)의 이 조치는 (C)에서 캐나다가 협상 중에 퇴장을 한 조치를 말한다.

해석 캐나다–미국 자유 무역 협정의 사례가 보여주듯이, 캐나다가 협상에서 캐나다의 힘을 증가시키기 위해 미국의 정치적 지도자들의 관심을 받는 것이 중요했다. 강자의 관심 부족은 종종 상대방을 특별히 강력하거나 비중 있게 생각하지 않는다는 발언이다. (B) 이러한 관심 부족은 여러 가지 면에서 나타나겠지만, 거의 항상 협상의 권한을 제한하고 자국의 정치적 지도력에 집근할 수 있는 비교적 낮은 수준의 관리능에게 협상의 책임을 맡김으로써 증명된다. (C) 캐나다는 이번 협상에서 이 문제에 직면했다. 관심을 끌기 위한 전술에는 시간을 벌거나 협상에서 발을 빼는 것이 포함될 수 있다. 캐나다–미국 자유무역협정(FTA) 협상에서 캐나다는 미국이 협상을 심각하게 받아들이지 않고 있다는 생각이 들자 퇴장했다. (A) 이 조치는 오랜 동맹국인 두 나라 사이에 외교적 위기를 초래했고 미국의 관심을 얻는 데 성공했으며, 이로 인해 미국의 고위급 협상 참여가 이루어졌다. 캐나다는 역사적으로 강한 양국 관계를 이용하면서 세력을 키웠다.

33 **어휘** descriptive 기술하는 / thermodynamics 열역학 / predictable 예측할 수 있는 / inevitable 피할수 없는 / assertion 주장 / underlie ~의 기저를 이루다 / norm 규범 / distinctive 독특한

해설 주어진 문장에서 사회학자들은 앞에 나왔던 마르크스나 엥겔스를 가리킨다. 따라서 ④번에 들어가는 것이 적절하다.

해석 '법'이라는 용어는 매우 다양하게 사용되어 왔다. 우선 과학적 법칙이나 서술적 법칙이라고 하는 것이 있다. 이것들은 자연 또는 사회 생활에서 발견되는 규칙적이거나 필요한 행동 양식을 묘사한다. 가장 명백한 예는 자연 과학에서 찾아볼 수 있다. 예를 들어, 물리학자들에 의해 발전된 운동법칙과 열역학에서 찾을 수 있다. 그러나 이 법의 개념은 또한 예측 가능하고 심지어 피할 수 없는 사회 행동의 패턴을 강조하기 위한 시도로 사회 이론가들에 의해 채택되었다. 이는 마르크스가 역사적, 사회적 발전의 '법'을 밝혀냈다는 엥겔스의 주장과 경제 이론의 근간을 이루는 이른바 수요와 공급의 '법'에서 볼 수 있다. 그러나 대체 용도는 일반적으로 법을 사회 행동의 규범이나 기준을 시행하는 수단으로 다룬다. 따라서 사회학자들은 전통적인 사회에서 일반적으로 발견되는 비공식적인 절차에서부터 현대 사회의 전형적인 공식적인 법체계에 이르기까지 모든 조직화된 사회에서 법률의 형태를 보아왔다. 이와는 대조적으로, 정치 이론가들은 법을 다른 사회 규칙이나 규범과 분명히 분리되어 있고 현대 사회에서만 발견되는 독특한 사회 기관으로 보고, 법을 더 구체적으로 이해하는 경향이 있었다.

34 **어휘** antibiotics 항생제 / drastically 급격히 / life expectancy 기대수명 / fix 해결책 / side effect 부작용 / invasive 침입하는 / efficacy 효험 / render 주다 / in a matter of (시간적으로) ~내로 / staphylococci 포도상구균

해설 항생제의 또다른 부작용에 관한 내용이기 때문에, 항생제의 복용으로 신체의 유익한 박테리아도 죽게 만든다는 내용이 앞에 나오는 ④번이 가장 적절하다.

해석 처음에는 기적의 약으로 보여졌던 약인 항생제는, 일단 그것들이 널리 보급되자, 세균 감염뿐만 아니라 일반적인 감기부터 두통까지 모든 것에 사용되어졌다. 실제로 항생제는 20세기 동안 달성된 기대수명의 증가에 크게 기여하며 의학을 획기적으로 향상시키는 뜻밖의 선물이었다. 많은 기술적 해결책과 마찬가지로 항생제의 긍정적인 혜택도 부정적인 부작용을 가져왔다. 항생제는 침입성 박테리아와 함께 소화를 촉진하는 박테리아와 같이

인체에 많은 유익한 박테리아를 죽일 수 있다. 또 다른 예기지 못한 결과는 항생제의 메커니즘을 극복한 박테리아의 능력이다. 항생제를 쓸모없게 만들었다. 처음에 실험실에서 보여졌던 호기심인 항생제 내성은 항생제에 노출된 박테리아 개체군 사이에서 보편화되었다. 페니실린의 도입 이후 몇 년 만에 페니실린을 파괴하는 포도상구균(pastylocococci)이 나타났다.

35 어휘 far from 전혀 ~이 아닌 / inertly 활발하지 못하게 / surpass 능가하다 / sundew plant 끈끈이 주걱 / crawl 기다 / infallible 결코 틀리지 않는 / accuracy 정확성 / parasitical 기생의 / nectar 꿀 / stem 줄기 / enlist 요청하다 / herbivorous 초식성의

해설 이 글은 식물의 장점에 관한 글로서 보기 ③번은 식물의 단점에 관한 문장이다.

해석 기존의 불활성 상태와는 달리, 목초지의 주민들 또는 고대 헬레네스가 부르던 보탄이라고 불렸던 것은, 인간의 그것을 훨씬 더 뛰어넘는 정교함의 수준에서의 환경에서 일어나고 있는 일을 지각하고 반응할 수 있는 것으로 보인다. 끈끈이 주걱 식물은 먹이를 찾을 수 있는 곳을 향해 바로 올바른 방향으로 이동하면서 완벽한 정확도로 파리를 잡을 것이다. 일부 기생 식물들은 희생자의 냄새의 미세한 흔적을 인식할 수 있고, 그 방향으로 기어가는 모든 장애물을 극복할 것이다. 식물은 땅에 뿌리를 내리고 있기 때문에 어떤 것이 필요하거나 상황이 좋지 않을 때 움직일 수 없기 때문에 곤경에 처하게 된다. 식물들은 어떤 개미가 꿀을 훔칠지 알고 있는 듯하다. 이런 개미들이 주위에 있을 때는 문을 닫고, 오직 그들의 줄기에 개미들의 침입을 막을 수 있는 충분한 뜨거운 물방울이 있을때만 문을 연다. 더 정교한 아카시아는 실제로 확실한 개미들에게 보호를 요청한다. 다른 벌레들과 초식 포유동물을 막아주는 개미들의 보호를 아카시아는 꿀로 보상한다.

36 어휘 geography 지리학 / inherently 선천적으로 / facilitate 용이하게 하다 / considerable 상당한 / scope 범위 constrain 제한한다

해설 이 글은 "교통지리학은 경제지리로부터 진화한 지리학의 주제 분야다" 라는 내용으로서 빠른 개인들의 교통수단이 관광산업을 촉진시켰다는 내용의 ④번은 글의 흐름과 맞지 않는다.

해석 교통지리학은 경제지리로부터 진화한 지리학의 주제 분야다. 물론 관광과 마찬가지로 교통은 장소를 연결하고 상품과 사람들의 이동을 한 곳에서 다른 곳으로 용이하게 하기 때문에 본래 지리적이다. 교통지리학은 근본적으로 위치나 규모와 같은 지리적 개념에 의존한다. 예를 들어, 위치는 이동 패턴을 형성하는데, 움직임이 주어진 위치로부터 또는 주어진 위치로 이동이 가능한지를 포함한다. 교통망은 현지의 그리고 지역적 규모로 존재하며, 현대 세계에서 점점 더 글로벌 시스템으로 연결되고 있다. 훨씬 더 빠른 개인적이고 조직적인 교통수단으로, 오후 드라이브, 주간 여행, 야간 숙박과 주말은 관광산업뿐만 아니라 관광객들에게도 상당한 범위를 더했다. 또한, 장소의 지리적 요인은 물리적 요인과 사람 모두 교통을 허용하거나 제한한다.

37 어휘 dump 투기(하다) / sewage 오물 / septic system 정화 시스템 / disposal 처리 / bear 떠맡다 / internalize 내면화 하다 / assign 할당하다 / property rights 재산권 / externality 외부효과 / poach 밀렵하다

해설 개럿 하딘에 따르면, 지역이 (B) 개인적으로 유지 된다면, 호수 같은 접근이 개방된 지역에 대한 환경적 피해를 (A) 막을 수 있다고 한다.

해석 폐기물을 처리하고 보관하기 위해 정화 시스템을 구입하기 보다는 공공 호수에 하수를 버리는 가정을 생각해 보자. 이 "직선관" 처리 방법은 수상 스포츠와 식수 공급원에 대한 호수의 매력을 손상시킨다. 비록 오물을 투척하는 사회적인 비용이 정화 시스템 비용보다 더 크지만, 가구의 사적인 투기 비용은 가정이 전체 손상의 극히 일부만을 부담하기 때문에 정화 시스템 비용보다 크지 않다. 만약 호숫가가 하수를 버리는 가구에 속한다면, 그 가구는 투기의 사회적 비용을 모두 내부화하고 정화 시스템에 투자할 것이다. 만약 호수 지역이 다른 누군가의 소유라면, 그 사람은 투기를 금지하고 주의 깊게 감시할 동기를 얻을 것이다. 생물학자인 개럿 하딘은 토지, 물, 공기에 재산권을 할당함으로써 사회는 공장에서부터 시끄러운 음악까지 모든 것에 의해 야기되는 외부효과를 피할 수 있다고 느꼈다. 그의 논지의 증거로서, 재산권이 약한 나라에서 밀렵은 잘 정의되고 엄격하게 시행된 국가들보다 훨씬 더 큰 문제다.

어휘 divorce 분리하다 / intertwine 뒤얽히다 / inevitably 불가피하게 / dominant 지배적인 / proper 적절한 / ratio 비율 / appropriate 적절한 / metaphor 은유 / tremendous 엄청난 / subject ~의 권한 아래에 있는 / rein 고삐 / dominate 지배하다 / occasionally 때때로 / gallop 전력 질주하다 / boldness 대범함 / rationality 합리성

해석

> 우리는 감정과 사고를 분리할 수 없다. 그 두 개는 완전히 얽혀 있다. 그러나 필연적으로 지배적인 요소가 있는데, 어떤 사람들은 다른 사람들보다 더 명확하게 감정에 지배된다. 우리가 찾고 있는 것은 적절한 비율과 균형, 즉 가장 효과적인 행동으로 이어지는 것이다. 고대 그리스인들은 이에 대한 적절한 은유를 가지고 있었다: 기수와 말. 말은 우리의 감정적 본성이다. 이 말은 엄청난 에너지와 힘을 가지고 있지만, 기수가 없으면 안내될 수 없다; 야생적이고, 포식자의 지배를 받으며, 계속해서 곤경에 처한다. 기수는 우리의 사고 방식이다. 훈련과 연습을 통해 고삐를 잡고 말을 인도하여 이 강력한 동물 에너지를 생산적인 것으로 변형시킨다. 다른 하나가 없는 것은 쓸모가 없다. 기수가 없으면 지시된 움직임이나 목적도 없다. 말이 없으면 기운도 없고 힘도 없다. 대부분의 사람들에게 말은 군림하고, 기수는 약하다. 어떤 사람들은 기수가 너무 강하고, 고삐를 너무 꽉 잡고, 때때로 기꺼이(willing → unwilling) 그 동물이 질주하도록 내버려두려고 하지 않는다. 말과 기수는 함께 일해야 한다. 이것은 우리가 우리의 행동을 미리 고려한다는 것을 의미한다; 우리는 결정을 내리기 전에 가능한 한 많은 생각을 한다. 그러나 일단 어떻게 할 것인가를 결정하고 나면 고삐를 풀고 대담함과 모험심을 가지고 행동에 들어간다. 이 에너지의 노예가 되는 대신에, 우리는 그것을 퍼뜨린다. 그것이 합리성의 본질이다.

38 **해설** 글의 전반부에서 "우리가 찾고 있는 것은 적절한 비율과 균형, 즉 가장 효과적인 행동으로 이어지는 것이다." 라는 내용으로 봐서 1번이 정답임을 알 수 있다.

보기 ① 생각과 감정의 최적의 균형을 찾아야 하는 필요성
② 야생동물을 길들이고 이용하는 전통적인 기술
③ 감정적인 억압이 신체적 건강에 미치는 영향
④ 경마에서 이기기 위한 올바른 기술을 얻는 것의 어려움
⑤ 스포츠에서 철학의 중요성에 대한 고대 그리스 개념

39 **해설** (d) willing → unwilling, 따라서 4번이 정답이다.

❖ [40~41]

어휘 enhancement 증대 / prospect 전망 / quote 인용(하다) / prosthetic 보철의 / outperform 능가하다 / limb 팔 / executive 경영진 / norm 규범 / editorial 편집의 / equation 방정식 / diagnosis 진단 / ailment 질병 / trigger 초래하다 / dystopian 반 이상향의 / practitioner 의사, 변호사

해석

Yesterday's Observer는 9월 런던에서 열리는 퓨처페스트 축제를 앞두고 인간 증진에 관한 두 작품을 특집으로 다루고 있다. 이 기사에는 왼손 없이 태어난 스위스 남성 베르톨트 마이어가 최근 최첨단 생체공학(스마트폰으로 조종하는 것)을 장착했으며 닉 보스트롬, 앤디 미아 등 인간증강과 관련된 유명 작가들의 인용문도 포함돼 있다. 현재 메이어와 같은 보철기기는 부족한 사람들 사이에서 정상적인 인간의 기능을 회복하는 데 사용된다. 그러나 그러한 기기는 속도, 힘, 관리 제어 등의 측면에서 결국 "자연적인" 팔다리를 능가할 정도로 더욱 (A) 정교해짐에 따라 "이들 중 하나를 갖는 것이 표준이 될 것인가?"라고 마이어가 묻는다. 또한 옵저버 사설의 저자가 걱정하듯이, "이러한 기술과 기계들이 너무 똑똑해져서 인간이 그 균형에서 완전히 배제되면 어떻게 될까?" 예를 들어, 만약 우리가 적절한 치료 권고사항뿐만 아니라 우리의 질병에 대한 진단을 받기 위해 인간 의사보다는 스마트폰으로 간단히 돌릴 수 있다면 어떨까? 이러한 제안들은 인간이 직업 시장(경쟁력 있는 스포츠 포함)과 다른 맥락에서 경쟁력을 유지하려면 좋든 싫은 간에 "사이보그"가 되라는 압력을 받는 디스토피아에 대한 두려움을 (B) 촉발시킬 수 있으며, 보다 효과적인 기계에 의해 사람이 점점 더 쓸모 없게 되어가고 있다. 실생활의 인간 상호작용이 (슈퍼마켓 계산대에서 직원을 교체하는 기계들, 또한 일반 의사들 등) 줄어들고, 지금보다 접근성이 떨어지게 된다(인간의 의사를 보기 위해 상당한 프리미엄을 지불해야 한다는 것을 생각해보라).

40 **해설** 위의 글은 편해지려고 한 기술발달이 나중에 오히려 문제를 일으킬 수 있다는 내용의 글이다. 따라서 정답은 2번임을 알 수 있다.

보기 ① 기계가 인간을 대신할 수 있는 곳과 그들이 할 수 없는 곳
② 인간 향상 기술 : 축복이냐 저주냐?
③ 장애인과 동등한 치료권
④ 인공지능 : 과학 팩트 vs. 사이언스 픽션
⑤ 공상과학 소설은 미래 기술을 예언한다.

41 **해설** (A) Sophisticated(정교한) …… (B) trigger(촉발시키다), 따라서 5번이 정답이다.

어휘 barely 가까스로 / renovation 수선 / distract 산만하게 하다 / cognitive 인식의 / secure 한심하는 / profound 심오한

해석

마리오가 내게 치료를 받으러 왔을 때, 그는 모든 것이 걱정된다고 설명했다. 그는 새로 결혼해서 필요한 수리를 위한 돈만을 남겨둔 채, 평생 저축한 돈을 내야 할만큼 비싼 집을 구입하는 중에 있었다. "내가 제대로 된 사람과 결혼했나? 내가 미쳤나? 내가 제 정신이었나? 건망증이 심한 것 같다. 마이애미로 가는 비행기가 추락하면 어쩌지? 아버지가 파킨슨병을 할아버지처럼 키울까?" 걱정도 끝이 없었고, 마리오도 걱정하면 할수록 우울하다는 것을 알아차렸다. 고문 당한 마음을 달래기 위해 그는 식사를 함으로써 정신을 산만하게 하는 데 시간을 보냈다. 명상과 수용에 중점을 둔 인지 행동 요법의 과정을 거치면서 마리오는 공황에 대한 그의 감정에 당황하지 않는 법을 배우기 시작했다. 그는 최악의 경우에서 살게 될 자신의 마음 속에 간혀 있기보다는 정신적인 과정으로서 자신의 걱정을 의식할 수 있게 되었다. 그는 스스로에게 "이 걱정은 생산적인가 아니면 비생산적인가?" 라고 묻는 연습을 했다. 걱정이 생산적이라면 그는 실행 계획을 내놓았다. 그것이 비생산적이라면 몸과 마음의 감정과 생각을 알아차리고 현재의 순간으로 돌아가는 연습을 했다. 그는 긴장하면서 단 음식과 짠 음식을 먹고 싶은 충동을 느꼈을 때, 자신이 감정을 의미 있는 것으로 보고 내신 사신의 감정을 가지고 앉기로 했다. 무엇이 그의 걱정거리 뒤에 있었는가? 그는 부양자로서 봉사하고, 안전하고 사랑스런 가정을 세우고, 그의 아버지를 보호하는 것을 깊이 소중하게 여겼다. 그의 감정과의 관계가-너무 많은 것을 느끼고 그의 감정을 이해하지 못하는 것에 대한 깊은 두려움과 혼란 - 그의 감정으로 그의 기꺼이 받아들이고 배우고자 하는것을 방해 했음에도 불구하고, 그의 감정은 그에게 중요한 것을 부인(denied→reflected)했다. 마지막 세션에서 그는 "나는 일이 중요하기 때문에 느낀다. 나는 우리의 어려움에 대해 아내에게 말할 수 있고, 재정적인 문제를 해결하기 위한 조치를 취할 수 있으며, 내가 얼마나 신경을 쓰고 있는지를 아빠에게 보여줄 수 있다. 그것이 내 마음 속에서 달콤한 맛이 난다."고 말했다.

42 **해설** 글의 중 후반부에 "그는 긴장하면서 단 음식과 짠 음식을 먹고 싶은 충동을 느꼈을 때, 자신의 감정을 의미 있는 것으로 보고 대신 자신의 감정을 가지고 앉기로 했다."는 내용으로 봐서 ④번은 내용과 일치하지 않는다.

43 **해설** (e) denied(부인했다) → reflected(반영했다), 따라서 5번이 정답이다.

✥ [44~45]

어휘 blossom 꽃을 피우다 / beverage 음료 / cozily 아늑하게 / persistently 고집스레 / furiously 맹렬히 / chirp 짹짹 거리다 / unconscious 의식이 없는 / loyalty 충성 / determination 결단 / sacrifice 희생

해석

(A) 카나리아인 비브스는 옆집에 사는 조카딸이 있는 노부인과 함께 살았고, 그녀가 괜찮은지 확인하기 위해 매일 밤 그녀를 확인했다. 노파와 작은 새 사이에 따뜻하고 달콤한 우정이 꽃피었다. 아침마다 그들은 토스트를 나눠 먹었고 비브스는 여자가 마시는 음료수라면 무엇이든 홀짝이는 것을 좋아했다. 어느 비오는 날 밤, 이모집의 불이 켜져 있는 것을 보고 모든 것이 괜찮다고 가정하면서 조카딸은 이모의 집으로 점검하러 가기 보다는 남편과 함께 자리를 떴다.

(D) 두 사람은 불길에 아늑하게 쉬고 있을 때, 이상하게도 창문을 두드리는 소리에 깜짝 놀랐다. 처음에는 바람에 날리는 나뭇가지라고 짐작했지만, 두드리는 소리가 점점 커지며 끈질기게 이어졌고, 이어서 이상한 울음소리가 들려왔다. 마침내 조카딸은 창가로 가서 커튼을 젖히고 창문을 사납게 두들기며 지저귀던 비브스를 발견했다.

(B) 작고 노란 새는 이모의 집에서 탈출하여 폭풍우를 뚫고 옆집으로 날아갔다. 그곳에서 그것은 너무나 필사적인 분노로 창문을 쪼아댔기 때문에 기진맥진하여 쓰러져 그들의 눈앞에서 죽어 버렸다. 이제 완전히 놀란 조카딸과 그녀의 남편은 이모의 집으로 달려갔다.

(C) 그들은 그 할머니가 피를 흘리며 바닥에 쓰러져 있는 것을 발견했다. 그녀는 탁자 모서리에 머리를 부딪히며 미끄러져 넘어져 있었다. 그녀의 조카는 그녀를 급히 병원으로 데려갔다. 도움을 받으려는 작은 새의 충성심과 결단력 때문에, 자신의 목숨을 희생으로, 여자의 목숨을 건졌다.

44 **해설** (A)의 마지막 부분에서 조카와 조카남편이 나오고, 그걸 받는 (D)의 the couple, (D)의 마지막 부분에 Bibs를 받는 (B)의 The tiny yellow bird, (B)의 마지막 부분인 aunt를 받는 (C)의 old lady이다.
따라서 순서는 (D) – (B) – (C), 정답은 4번이다.

45 **해설** 조카딸 집의 창문은 Bibs가 쪼아댔기 때문에 소리가 난 것이다. 따라서 5번은 적절치 않다. 정답은 5번이다.

MEMO

MEMO

서원각이 취업을 찢었다!

봉투모의고사 **찐!5회** 횟수로 플렉스해 버렸지 뭐야 ~

국민건강보험공단 봉투모의고사(행정직/기술직)

국민건강보험공단 봉투모의고사(요양직)